Pranay Gupta and T. Mandy Tham
Fintech

Pranay Gupta and
T. Mandy Tham

Fintech

The New DNA of Financial Services

ISBN 978-1-5474-1708-7
e-ISBN (PDF) 978-1-5474-0090-4
e-ISBN (EPUB) 978-1-5474-0092-8

Library of Congress Control Number: 2018962040

Bibliographic information published by the Deutsche Nationalbibliothek
The Deutsche Nationalbibliothek lists this publication in the Deutsche Nationalbibliografie;
detailed bibliographic data are available on the Internet at http://dnb.dnb.de.

Published by Walter de Gruyter Inc., Boston/Berlin
Printing and binding: CPI books GmbH, Leck
Typesetting: MacPS, LLC, Carmel

www.degruyter.com

Dedicated to my wife Nupur and my daughter Aanya

— Pranay

Dedicated to my parents and loved ones including my mentors and students who have taught me great humility

— Mandy

About De|G PRESS

Five Stars as a Rule

De|G PRESS, the startup born out of one of the world's most venerable publishers, De Gruyter, promises to bring you an unbiased, valuable, and meticulously edited work on important topics in the fields of business, information technology, computing, engineering, and mathematics. By selecting the finest authors to present, without bias, information necessary for their chosen topic *for professionals*, in the depth you would hope for, we wish to satisfy your needs and earn our five-star ranking.

In keeping with these principles, the books you read from De|G PRESS will be practical, efficient and, if we have done our job right, yield many returns on their price.

We invite businesses to order our books in bulk in print or electronic form as a best solution to meeting the learning needs of your organization, or parts of your organization, in a most cost-effective manner.

There is no better way to learn about a subject in depth than from a book that is efficient, clear, well organized, and information rich. A great book can provide life-changing knowledge. We hope that with De|G PRESS books you will find that to be the case.

DOI 10.1515/9781547400904-203

Every revolutionary idea passes through three stages:
1. It's completely impossible.
2. It's possible, but it's not worth doing.
3. I said it was a good idea all along.

— Arthur C. Clarke

DOI 10.1515/9781547400904-204

Acknowledgments

We acknowledge the help and support of all companies and individuals who have partnered with us in this project to create a book which has wide applicability to many audiences. Despite the pressures of business, especially for start-up firms who have contributed to this book, these individuals have devoted their time, energy, and expertise in their individual fields to help create this text, which we hope will form the basis of many courses for investment professionals and students of any discipline to understand and appreciate the developing world of fintech.

We also specifically acknowledge Mr. Sopnendu Mohanty of the Monetary Authority of Singapore for his guidance and unwavering support for this project.

DOI 10.1515/9781547400904-205

About the Authors

Pranay Gupta CFA

Pranay has over 25 years of experience in Europe, UK, US and Asia in managing port-folios across all liquid asset class investments across global markets. His areas of experience and interest include multi-asset allocation solutions, risk management, and the deployment of data science and fintech in the financial services industry. He has advised several sovereign wealth funds and plan sponsors across the world on these subjects.

As head of multi-asset strategies at Fullerton Fund Management (a subsidiary of Temasek Holdings), Pranay was responsible for strategic and tactical allocation glob-ally for the liquid assets portfolio. Prior to that he was the chief investment officer at Lombard Odier and ING Investment Management Asia Pacific, where he led an investment team of over 300 investment professionals across 12 countries, to manage over US$85bn of institutional and retail assets. Previously, Pranay has held senior positions at Axial Investment Management in London, managing a US$55bn closed life insurance portfolio, at APG Investments in the Netherlands managing a US$25bn multi-asset multi-strategy fund, and Societe Generale in Hong Kong and JP Morgan Investment Management in New York. His recent book *Multi-Asset Investing: A Practi-tioner's Framework*, proposes that the basic structure of institutional and individuals' portfolios needs to evolve from asset class segmented active management, toward a multi-asset class multi-allocation framework.

As a mechanical engineer from IIT Delhi specializing in CAD/CAM, Pranay used robotic manipulator techniques for the design of automobile suspension systems for Suzuki Motor Co. Japan, fluid dynamic modelling techniques for the simulation of oil wells for Dowell Schlumberger and production planning control systems for missile manufacture. Using large-scale databases, Pranay has designed, developed and implemented advanced analysis and portfolio management systems for various orga-nizations. These state-of-the-art diagnostics platforms have been used to manage and monitor portfolios with assets of over US$400bn using quantitative analysis of big data, portfolio evaluation to re-engineer investment processes and in creating cus-tomized multi-asset client solutions for asset owners of all sizes and sophistication. Pranay has also used heuristic time series modelling, neural network and artificial

DOI 10.1515/9781547400904-206

intelligence techniques to manage over $1bn in pension assets. Pranay currently serves on the advisory board of StashAway, the first licensed retail robo-advisor in Singapore.

Pranay has served as an external curriculum director for the CFA Program, has authored CFA curriculum readings in portfolio management, and has been chairman of the Finance and Investment Committee at the CFA Institute Research Foundation. He currently serves as a research consultant at the Centre of Asset Management Research and Investments at the National University of Singapore and conducts the Reserve Management program for sovereign wealth funds, pensions, central banks and regulators from across the world at the Nanyang Technological University.

Dr. Mandy Tham

Mandy is currently an assistant professor of finance (education) at the Singapore Management University. She delivers years of experience as a curriculum developer designing and obtaining industry accreditation for wealth management courses customized to both institutions of higher learning and financial institutions. She teaches in both English and Mandarin, on both undergraduate and postgraduate programs in areas such as derivatives, investment and wealth advisory.

Her research interests span investments to behavioral finance and she has published in top journals such as the *Journal of Financial Economics*, *Management Science* and the *Journal of Financial and Quantitative Analysis*. Her research work has won awards such as the CFA Best Paper award and the TCW Best Paper award, and was published by *Harvard Business Review* and featured by Forbes. Besides academic research, she works closely with practitioners to write in-house cases and other literary works.

Her previous work experience includes being an independent Asian family business consultant in the greater China region, director (curriculum) at Wealth Management Institute Pte Ltd, and faculty member at the Nanyang Business School of Nanyang Technological University (NTU). She won the competitive college-wide NTU Business Teacher of the Year award in 2014 and the divisional Teaching Excellence Award in 2015. Besides her teaching role, Mandy also served stints as the school's assistant dean of alumni affairs where she spearheaded engagement activities with business alumni and as the CFA program director for NTU where she managed the school's partnership with the CFA Institute.

Mandy graduated with Ph.D (Finance) and M.A. (Applied Economics) degrees from the University of Michigan. She also holds Master and Bachelor of Electrical Engineering (first class honors) degrees from the National University of Singapore. She was trained in the areas of control and optimization engineering and previously worked as a software apprentice (robotics control) in Hong Kong and subsequently in Singapore as an engineer in the semiconductor industry specializing in testing and yield analysis. She continues to be interested in robotics and optimization technologies and works on independent projects related to digital skills.

An animal lover and a strong believer in education, she fosters and adopts rescue dogs, and volunteers in her free time for social and educational causes.

Contents

Preface

I spent the summer of 2017 in Silicon Valley bouncing from one meetup to another, while my daughter studied genetics at UC Berkeley at the age of 10! Having attended many of those meetings I firmly believed that the hype being created by the startup world was the ingredient of the next bubble, similar in structure to the dot com bubble of 2000, which I witnessed first-hand from Wall Street, as billions of dollars of capital was lay to waste. Returning to Singapore, I attended the 2017 Singapore Fintech Festival, which was the largest fintech festival in the world, and attended the innovation lab crawl of a number of companies. That same month saw the meteoric rise in the price of bitcoin and other cryptocurrencies, and it was practically impossible to look anywhere without being confronted by ads from every company trying to portray how smart they are as they spoke about artificial intelligence and took photographs with robots. Graphic images of brains everywhere and talk of robots taking over the world were pervasive. This was absurd—I worked on robotics as an engineer, managed billions of dollars in neural network algorithms and designed parallel processing systems myself. I wasn't convinced that a revolution was about to happen anytime soon. I was wrong.

Earlier that year, I had been approached by some founders to help them start a new robo-advisor. They were technically proficient, but wanted my advice on designing allocation methods. With my inherent disbelief in the success rate of startups I was happy to accommodate. In the 12 months that followed, I witnessed that company grow from a three-man startup to a 26-person company, licensed by the regulator, launch a product, raise funding, and expand. It opened my eyes to the scale of change that awaits the financial services industry as such startups become successful. This brought home the point that deployment of the technology toolkit available today to any part of the financial services industry is likely to have a dramatic impact on the industry in the next decade.

As an industry, financial services has facilitated the activities of individuals and businesses and the society at large for centuries. However, since the global financial crisis of 2007, it has come under severe criticism in many areas, such as the high compensation packages it offers to select employees funded by high charges to clients. Yet despite being a prominent and high cost ecosystem, it has largely managed to preserve its practices. All that is about to change.

Financial services can basically be thought of as an industry of middlemen. It doesn't manufacture anything and it doesn't produce anything. It simply provides a service for which it charges fees based on asymmetry of information, or the sourcing and use of capital. The most basic impact that technology has had, is to make information and access democratic and available to all. And that is a death knell for middlemen. Amazon did that to retailing, Uber did that to taxis and Airbnb is doing it to the hotel industry. The impact of fintech on financial services is going to be no different. The spread of fintech will change this business model of financial services

DOI 10.1515/9781547400904-208

dramatically over the next decade, it will change the cost structure for consumers, and it will change the skills that employees will need to survive within it. So, anyone who is still skeptical of the impact of the various facets of fintech, be it blockchain, cryptoassets or robo-advisory should be ready for a shock. Of course, there will be many failures along the way, and the ride will be as rocky as it was for dot com companies, while the new technologies create more efficient business models. There will indeed be many "copycat" companies and charlatans who pretend but don't actually do, but the fintech companies with real skill, and those that survive will change the face of financial services for ever. No one should doubt that.

Fintech requires knowledge in three areas—technology architecture/programming, mathematical econometrics and the domain knowledge of finance. People who are intimately familiar with all three aspects are rare, as each requires a lifetime of study and experience. Yet everyone in the finance or technology industry, or those aspiring to get into those industries, needs to know fintech to some degree, to be able to understand this new world. More importantly, almost every human and corporate entity across the planet has regular transactions of some kind with a financial services intermediary such as a bank or money agent, and each of us will be impacted with the advent of fintech. The common man needs to know fintech to some degree, no matter what discipline he is familiar with.

This book is specifically meant for an audience which does not know technology and programming yet is keen to understand the terminology and implications of fintech. While today it will find relevance for the existing finance practitioner, we believe that this content will progressively become required knowledge for students at the bachelor's degree level and subsequently even at high school, and finally to every person once fintech is the dominant process supporting financial organizations.

As each of the subtopics in fintech is a specialized field, we have partnered with leading companies in each field to write about their craft and toolkit, and we aim to cover the full landscape of fintech implementations as they spread across geographies and organizations.

This book is organized into four sections comprising a total of 26 chapters.

The first three chapters in Part 1 provide an overview of the disruption to financial services by fintech, discuss the ten enablers of the digital economy, and give an update on the current state of fintech including funding trends and developments, major players and investors, responses of traditional financial institutions to innovative and disruptive forces, and the near future trends.

In Part 2, we discuss the key enablers of a digital economy and their underpinning technologies. Topics include digital identity, data science and big data, blockchain and distributed ledger technology (DLT), implementation cases of blockchain, cryptoassets, digital payment, open banking, artificial intelligence and machine learning. Collectively, these topics ground us with a strong sense of how to build a trusted digital identity and trusted digital data hub, the architecture of customer consent rooted by principles of clear identification and authentication, security and privacy, and immutability, as well as the public infrastructure for the digital economy that ensures connectivity across sectors through open application programming interfaces (APIs).

Part 3 delves into the fintech innovations and disruptions to the asset services segment, capital markets and investment management. Besides chapters that inform on the disruptions, we examine innovations in the lending and crowdfunding space, the robo advisory front, wealth technology (WealthTech), regulatory technology (RegTech), and insurance technology (InsurTech). RegTech and InsurTech, while still relatively nascent, are both experiencing strong growth in order to improve efficiency, accuracy and experiences of customers in areas such as onboarding and fraud detection.

In Part 4 we examine the impact of technology on the fast and moving consumer goods (FMCG) sector, and discuss the legal implications of fintech and the talent and skill set development needs for a digital economy. Digital governance and risk management are the current focus of many central banks as key enablers of a digital economy as are data residency policies that govern proper, ethical and responsible use of this data.

Part 1: **An Overview of Fintech**

Chapter 1
Fintech and the Disruption of Financial Services

The financial services industry is comprised of multiple businesses, each of which is structured either as a division within a large financial firm or an independent stand-alone business unit. Regardless of how they are organized none of these business units produce real assets but rather they act as intermediaries or advisors to market participants. The financial services industry is basically an industry of middlemen.

Technology as a tool has had three principal impacts on business and industry:
- It has allowed the automation of processes, where manual work performed by humans is replaced by machines or algorithms.
- It has lowered the cost of information acquisition and hence made information more accessible to everyone. As a result, any business whose main reason for existence was information asymmetry has faced an existential threat. Examples of this include brokers and agents of any asset or product.
- It has made all manufacturing and distribution processes far more efficient. As a result, any middlemen in the chain between the producer to the consumer of a product or service may find that they are no longer required. An example of this is in the consumer retail industry, where automation has reduced the number of agents, wholesale distributors, and salespeople.

Arguably, given these facts, the financial services industry should have been deeply impacted a long time ago. However, in a structure where financial services are often deeply regulated and segregated by countries, a dramatic change has not happened until now. Since the global financial crisis in 2018, financial regulation across the world has become more uniform, the financial services industry has become dominated by global players rather than local players, and cross-border communication and transactions have been facilitated by the use of technology. The key implication of all these developments is that the industry today is at the stage where its business model and processes are about to undergo a profound change with the advent of *fintech*, or financial technology, as a discipline.

The Ecosystem of Financial Services Intermediaries

Figure 1.1 displays the principal external and internal activities in financial services, which happen due to customer requirements or services provided. One common characteristic of any of these activities is that it is either an exchange of information or an exchange of capital, and this sole objective enables the business for the finan-

DOI 10.1515/9781547400904-001

cial intermediary. With the deployment of technology in every part of this ecosystem, there are two possibilities, or combinations thereof:

– The institution adopts fintech as a technique that makes the existing process more efficient in every aspect, or

– The newcomer startups have a sufficiently improved business model and value proposition that they are able to disrupt the incumbents.

Although the jury is still out as to who is the business beneficiary of fintech (i.e. the incumbent or the newcomer), it is clear that the consumer stands to benefit from decreased cost or increased efficiency.

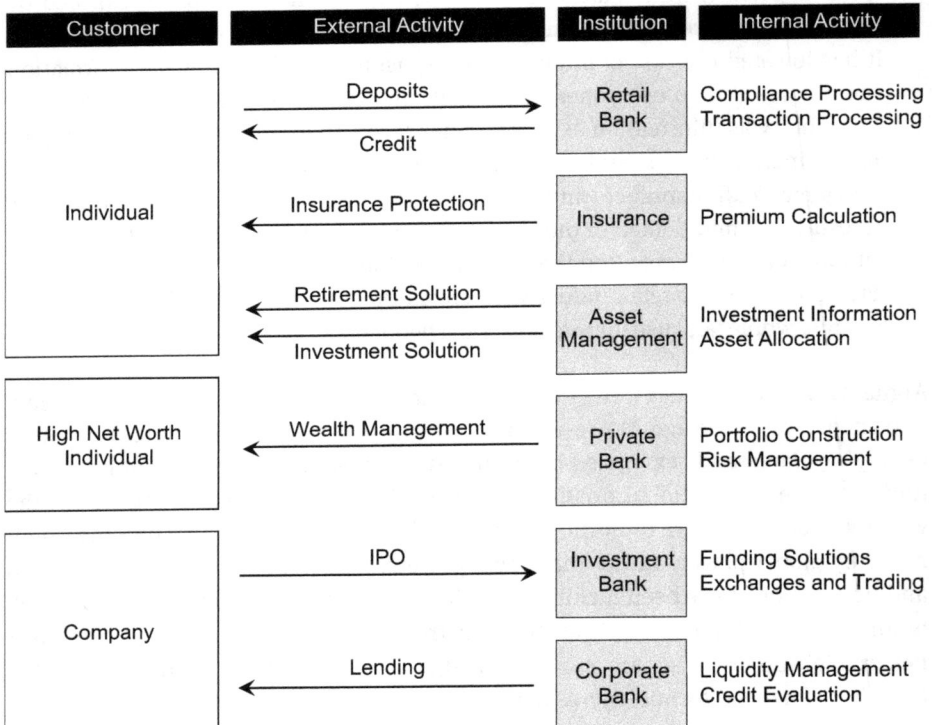

Figure 1.1: External and internal activities in financial services

Basic Skills of the Fintech Revolution

Fintech as a discipline relies on three basic concepts, no matter where it is deployed. These are

- Data capture: Processes to capture and store data and information about every individual person, company or activity, (who is or may in the future be a source of potential interaction of any kind, about their minute-by-minute activities in the physical or digital world
- Data analysis: Methodologies and tools to analyze these large and growing datasets to arrive at succinct information that can drive future decisions
- Intelligence and implementation: Use and implementation of this data-based knowledge to make existing services and activities more efficient or to create new services that do not exist today

These concepts, when applied to each of the preceding activities, result in new business models either within or outside the incumbent financial services institutions.

The Evolution of Financial Services Activities

Each of the activities in Figure 1.1 is being increasingly impacted by the use of financial technology. In this book, we describe how each of these activities is evolving and what may lie ahead as this revolution progresses.

Compliance Processes

Every financial institution in every country today is required by regulation to know various details about their clients and their sources of funds. This "know your client" process to prevent money laundering and the circulation of funds from illicit sources has largely been a client-by-client process that has been done manually. The advent of fintech provides a remarkable tool to make this process more efficient and has resulted in a branch of fintech called RegTech (or regulatory technologies). Whether used as an in-house tool within a financial institution or as an outsourced service provided by a specialized provider, it will make the compliance process far more effective than it is today.

Transaction Processing

Something common to financial services is the large number and variety of transactions that are performed by corporate and individual customers around the world and across borders. Although technology has been used for these processes for a long time, the invention of blockchain has the potential to completely change this landscape. The way simple financial transactions—such as payments at the point of purchase and money transfers between institutions or between customers and institutions—will likely change dramatically as and when these systems become widely implemented.

Insurance Calculations

Since its inception, the insurance business has relied upon estimates of risk based on long-term historical data. These are then used to calculate liabilities and thus insurance premiums. With the capture of data on every aspect of the insured, the risk calculations can be made much more accurately and transition the insurance business from a group-based average premium calculation to a customized calculation for the risk of an individual.

Investment and Risk Management Decisions

Collecting data on every aspect of any participant naturally leads to a wealth of information that can be used to forecast asset prices more accurately and at a higher frequency. This then enables investment and risk management decisions with a greater depth of knowledge.

Investment Solutions

Creating investment solutions for retail individuals, high net worth individuals and corporations has historically been done in a framework which is driven by distribution of standardized investment products and liability unaware. The ability to know the specific requirements of every customer will transition this framework to become liability aware and customized to the situation of every client. This encompasses investment solutions for all asset owners, as well as retirement solutions for individuals.

Financing Solutions

Every one of us and every company has the requirement of financing in the natural course of business. Individuals may take a loan or a mortgage, and companies may want credit or sell their equity through an IPO. This funding structure provided by the financial services industry relies on an estimation of the credit worthiness of the borrower and the ability to source capital through their network of institutions. Both of these aspects will be impacted by fintech. Assessments of creditworthiness can become more accurate simply by the collection of more data about the borrower, and the source of funding can expand beyond a bank's network to be more democratic across individuals, as well.

The Journey of Evolution for Financial Services Organizations

Companies and their management teams fall into four categories of progressive phases of evolution, when faced with a disruptive change such as fintech:

– The Naysayers: who deny any meaningful impact from a new technology or process and worse still gather facts to disprove its usefulness. This is why start-ups are difficult and why new technologies tend to be disruptive rather than augmentative.

– The Charlatans: who publicly say that their firm is using new technologies and techniques, because it's seems like a good marketing pitch, but in reality, are doing very little internally to actually incorporate its usefulness. This stage is present when a new technology has developed sufficiently to be noticeable but is still below critical mass or unproven.

– The Early-adopters: who have come to believe that utilizing the new technology is in their interest, have a business plan and have created internal teams to take advantage of the new paradigm to augment their existing business model.

– The Believers: If not the start-ups themselves, these are the firms who are convinced of the philosophy of a new technology and are prepared to reorient their companies for the future along with the implementation of a new structure.

This evolution is happening as we speak, and the different categories of fintech innovations are at different stages in this evolution. The journey to transform financial services is just beginning. It is not always easy to change incumbent processes that have been in existence for many years, and it is even more difficult to reskill people involved in those functions to adapt to the new world. Whether an institution can adapt will determine whether it survives in the new world with greater efficiency or gets disrupted. The same is true for an individual.

Pranay Gupta CFA has over 25 years of experience in managing portfolios across all liquid asset class investments across global markets. His areas of experience and interest include Multi-Asset Allocation Solutions, Risk Management, and the deployment of Data Science and Fintech in the Financial Services industry. Pranay was Chief Investment Officer for global asset managers where he led investment teams of over 300 investment professionals across 12 countries, to manage over US$85bn of institutional and retail assets. He has held senior positions at Axial Investment Management *in London, APG Investments in the Netherlands, Societe Generale in Hong Kong and JP Morgan Investment Management in New York. As a Mechanical Engineer from IIT Delhi specializing in CAD/CAM, Pranay used robotic manipulator techniques for the design of automobile suspension systems for Suzuki Motor Co. Japan, fluid dynamic modelling techniques for the simulation of oil wells for Dowell Schlumberger and the production planning control of missile systems. Pranay has designed, developed and implemented advanced analysis and portfolio management systems for various organizations, which are used to manage and monitor portfolios with assets of over US$400bn, and create customized client solutions. Pranay has served as External Curriculum Director for the CFA Program, and has been a member of the Board of Trustees of the CFA Institute Research Foundation as the Chairman of the Finance and Investment Committee.*

Chapter 2
Fintech in the Context of the Digital Economy

Individuals and businesses have operated in a physical world of commerce since time began. It was clear who was buying and who was selling, what they were buying and what they were using to pay. Authentication, transfer of goods and payments for services were conducted in the physical realm. Then came bank accounts, money transfers, credit cards and electronic payments, and suddenly the buyers and sellers had to interact with each other within a digital world where there was no direct physical contact. This laid the ground for the creation of a digital world, which is running alongside our physical world. With the advent of technology, especially in its application in financial services, the digital world will become more pervasive, including almost all human beings on our planet and covering an increasing list of activities which can be carried out digitally, which were once considered physical only. This then creates a digital economy for each country and a digital world for all of us, which is as important as the physical world.

Fintech Startups

Fintech is a word often used to describe almost any kind of startup that uses some level of technology to create a financial product or service. There are, however, two distinct kinds of fintech startup companies:
- Fintech startups that provide tech-enabled financial services in which the use of technology allows for greater efficiency, scale and speed in an existing industry product or process. They work with financial institutions (FIs) to replace existing processes and systems.
- Fintech startups that provide novel solutions for a specific financial service activity using technology. These tech-powered financial service offerings now dominate the fintech ecosystem.

Although both types of fintech companies have the ability to disrupt the existing ecosystem of financial services, tech-enabled financial services are likely to surround, replace, and eventually supplant processes and systems within incumbent organizations. These organizations would likely experience significant disruption if they fail to incorporate the new fintech systems and thereby limit their product or service offerings.

Tech-powered financial services, on the other hand, create new products and services that have the potential to disrupt the complete business models of specific organizations in the financial ecosystem.

The remainder of this chapter will describe the application of fintech in Singapore by the Monetary Authority of Singapore (MAS). This unique government

DOI 10.1515/9781547400904- 002

sponsored approach puts Singapore in a leading position in this fast-growing field, pulling together the necessary requirements to accomplish that goal, and can serve as a model example of how the regulatory body of any country can implement a fintech structure to enable innovation, while retaining stability and soundness of the financial ecosystem.

The 10 Stacks of a Digital Economy

The basis of fintech development is the transition of process-based organizations and systems into a digital economy. The digital economy can be driven by ten basic enablers, as depicted in Figure 2.1.

Source: Digital Economy Singapore, Presentation by Mohanty S., Monetary Authority of Singapore, 2018

Figure 2.1: The ten stacks of a digital economy

#1 Trusted Digital Identity

All transactions in the physical world between two participants are made possible because the identity of the participating individual or organization is confirmed physically and validated by documents that are made available for verification before the initiation of the transaction. A digital world, however, has participants that are "presence-less." Hence, the creation of a trusted digital identity both for individuals and entities is the starting point for validation and is the basis on which any player would participate in the digital economy and interact with other participants for the purpose of initiating a transaction. The role of a trusted national body that validates digital identity is critical to enable a digital economy.

In Singapore, for example, residents use SingPass, a national digital identity platform, for electronic services and transactions with government agencies. SingPass forms the basic digital ID for residents. A new national digital identity (NDI) system is under development to build on the SingPass platform for a more convenient and advanced authentication service. The NDI will provide residents with a single trusted digital identity to transact with both the government and private sector more securely and seamlessly. This trusted identity established in the digital realm transcends borders and will be able to underpin transactions with entities outside Singapore.

#2 Trusted Digital Data

In order to substantiate the digital identity of an individual or entity, data about the participant must be gathered, stored and confirmed. This is the basis for confirming the identity of the participant in a "presence-less" state. Hence, the role of a trusted digital data hub becomes critical.

Traditionally, physical documents are required for manual verification prior to establishing a business relationship or conducting any transaction. This method is prone to data errors, which lowers productivity and can result in a poor user experience. A trusted digital data hub can serve as a reliable and independent source for a collection of wide-ranging, verified attributes about an individual's identity. These attributes can facilitate customer digital on-boarding prior to establishing a business relationship, as well as support transactions in both the digital and physical world.

Singapore's MyInfo is an example of a personal digital data platform that contains government-verified personal details, such as national ID number, residential address, date of birth, and so forth. The platform enables residents to retrieve and provide their data via an independent secure channel for transactions with the government and the private sector. Following a successful pilot with a few banks, the MyInfo data platform is in the process of scaling up rapidly to cover other financial institutions and the rest of the private sector.

#3 Customer Consent Architecture

Even after the identity of a participant has been confirmed and supported with trusted digital data, initiating a transaction can occur only if this trusted data is shared with other entities with the participant's knowledge and agreement. For this sharing to happen, a consent architecture needs to be present that allows every participant to decide the parties with whom personal data can be shared. This ability to provide consent gives each citizen the power to control their own data in terms of what to share, when to share, and with whom to share or not to share. This consent process needs to be traceable, trackable and manageable for it to be governed properly and to prevent misuse or creation of fake data.

The MyInfo data platform in Singapore requires the resident to provide consent for the specific verified data attributes and fields registered with the government to be shared with a requesting entity for the purpose of rendering a service at any point in time, as well as to review and acknowledge the correctness of the data itself prior to sharing. Private sector entities and even foreign governments also can receive the verified personal data of the individuals who use their services or transact with them. Such data access, enabled through a trusted data platform (like MyInfo) with the proper digital identity and consent architecture, can unlock data sharing in the digital world.

#4 Public Infrastructure for the Digital Economy

In a physical economy, we consider the infrastructure of roads, hospitals, airports, and so on. Similarly, in a digital economy, we need to think about digital public infrastructure for the benefit of the economy. Digital infrastructure examples include shared utilities for regulatory validation of customers and efficient electronic payment systems. The objective of these public services is to facilitate seamless, simple and safe transactions. Figure 2.2 shows components of a digital infrastructure.

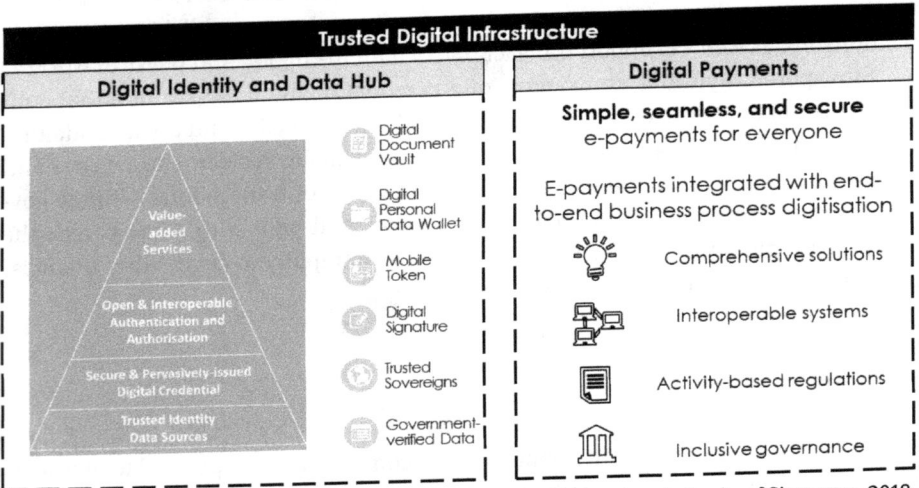

Source: Digital Economy Singapore, Presentation by Mohanty S., Monetary Authority of Singapore, 2018

Figure 2.2: Components of a trusted digital infrastructure

#5 Data Residency Policies

The heart of the digital economy is data. The policies that ensure the data is managed appropriately are the foundation of the digital economy. Data should be used in an open way, but with due consideration to privacy and ethical uses. Data residency policies therefore need to ensure the appropriate governance in the storage and use of data.

#6 Scaled Computing

When there is a mechanism by which data is created and stored, the speed and size of the data collection necessitates that a scalable architecture is available to process the data. This includes architectures from cloud computing (Chapter 5) to eventually, quantum computing. Policies are required to facilitate the transition from physical fixed capacity computing to scalable computing using the cloud to enable digital economy processes.

Recognizing that a secure cloud service infrastructure enables innovations, provides economies of scale, enhances operational efficiencies, and delivers potential cost savings, the MAS has set out specific guidelines in 2016 for the use of cloud services by financial institutions. Financial institutions are free to adopt private clouds, public clouds, or a combination of these to create hybrid clouds, as long as due diligence has been conducted and sound governance and risk management practices are applied to address potential vulnerabilities.

To further assist financial institutions in understanding approaches to due diligence, vendor management and key controls, the MAS and the Association of Banks in Singapore (ABS) have created an implementation guide on cloud services. This guide defines industry guidance that cloud service providers can use to deliver better cloud solutions that meet the security and control requirements of financial institutions.

#7 Open Architecture

When we have the ability to gather, store and analyze data, it needs to be used to create new products and services. This requires connectivity by using open application programming interfaces (APIs) and multi-sector APIs. APIs are one of the most important building blocks for innovation in the digital economy. They include sets of protocols that define how a system or application interacts with one another, usually from the perspective of enabling information exchange or transactions, without the need for human intervention.

MAS actively encourages financial institutions to adopt open architectures and develop APIs to offer to the broader community. In partnership with the financial industry, MAS and ABS have jointly published the "Finance-as-a-Service API

Playbook." The playbook provides guidance on common and useful open APIs that financial institutions in Singapore can make available, as well as standards for information security, data exchange and governance mechanisms to promote greater data sharing and interoperability. Figure 2.3 presents the benefits of using the APIs presented in this book.

Open architecture supports the creation of new products and services. Examples include the use of financial data by logistic merchants to create a better credit process and the use of purchase data by the healthcare sector to create better products.

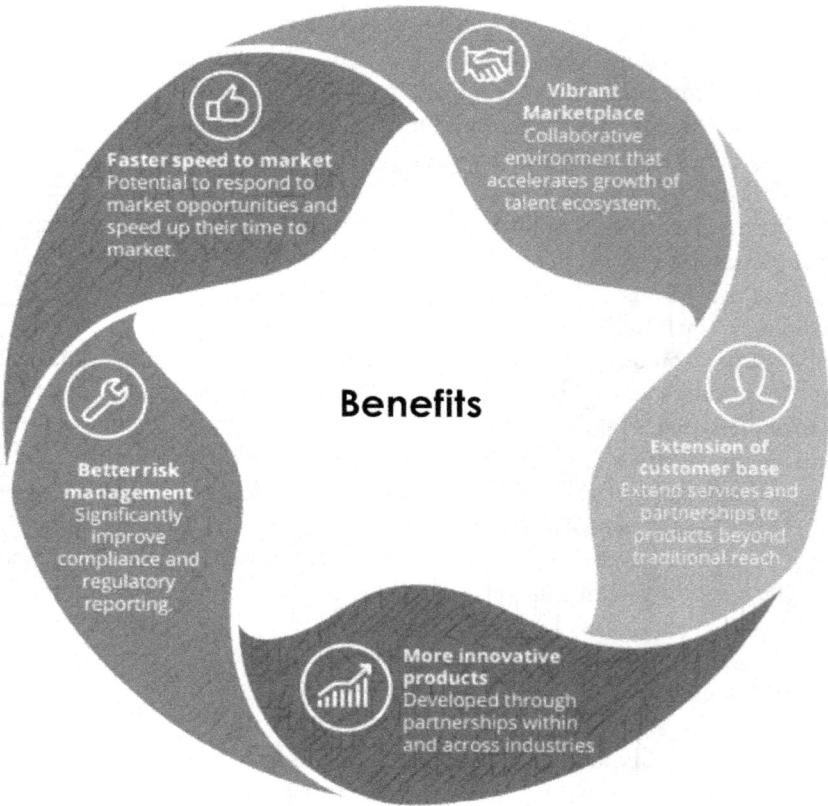

Source: Digital Economy Singapore, Presentation by Mohanty S., Monetary Authority of Singapore, 2018
Figure 2.3: Data, cloud and API-driven open architecture

#8 Digital Literacy, Talent and Entrepreneur Growth

In a digital economy, product creation requires talent and technology. Hence, it is important to provide policy support, such as grants and incentives, to develop these talent pools.

There are three parts to creating conditions conducive to developing talent:
- Creating platforms to educate citizens on how to operate within a digital economy
- Developing people who will work in organizations creating digital products and services
- Encouraging entrepreneurs to create new digital products and services

Singapore is building an entire system for talent to support the financial industry (see Figure 2.4). Talent is needed at every level of the industry, with varying digital skill requirements. To develop deep capabilities, Singapore aims to utilize the best international capabilities to create a local talent pool. The Capability Transfer Program supports attracting international talent with specialized expertise and facilitates knowledge transfer to local professionals. MAS also works with institutions of higher learning, in partnership with the industry, to build a local pipeline of specialized IT talent for the financial sector. To support the under-skilled and vulnerable segment of the existing workforce and to keep up with changes in the industry and stay relevant, the system supports upgrading skills or retraining affected workers and matching them to new jobs through the Professional Conversion Program.

Global Talent Hub

Attracting highly skilled global talent	Active pipeline of undergraduates
Attracting entrepreneurs and creating growth capital	Up-skilling of existing professionals
Capability transfer programmes (Global → Local)	Professional training programs for convertees to FinTech

Source: Digital Economy Singapore, Presentation by Mohanty S., Monetary Authority of Singapore, 2018

Figure 2.4: A hub for supporting digital literacy, talent and entrepreneur growth

#9 Policy Making by Experimentation and Empirical Data

In general, the speed of technology is often faster than the speed of policy change. Using sandboxes allows experimentation in a controlled environment, by creating empirical data to test, review and fine-tune policies at a faster pace. This allows polices to be in sync with the rapid development and use of technologies.

Fintech in Singapore is an excellent example of a fast-evolving landscape, with a proliferation of technological innovations and solutions. While MAS encourages financial institutions to test and introduce these innovations where they are relevant, they perform their own due diligence. In particular instances it is sometimes unclear if a new development complies with the existing regulatory requirements or poses unacceptable risks. This uncertainty can stifle promising innovation and result in missed opportunities.

MAS launched the FinTech Regulatory Sandbox in 2016 for financial institutions as well as fintech players to test their innovations (see Figure 2.5). The sandbox provides an environment in which experiments can fail safely and cheaply without widespread adverse consequences. Through the results and observations made from these experiments, MAS assesses and fine-tunes policies and regulations where appropriate to support innovation and new business models.

Similarly, MAS has partnered with the International Finance Corporation (IFC) and the ASEAN Bankers Association (ABA) to establish the ASEAN Financial Innovation Network (AFIN) industry sandbox (see Figure 2.5). The AFIN platform enables experimentation to help banks and fintech companies in ASEAN to collaborate, so as to broaden and deepen access to digital financial services across ASEAN. The AFIN platform also enables regulators to observe the experiments and benefit from the insights gleaned, and to spur discussions on cross-border policy harmonization throughout the region.

#10 Cyber-security

As more services are delivered online in the digital economy, the frequency, scale and complexity of cyberattacks are increasing. Hackers and cybercriminals are constantly probing IT systems for weaknesses they can exploit. The threat of cyberattacks is accentuated in the digital economy in two areas:
- The connectivity between entities means that a serious cyber breach in one entity can potentially escalate into a more systemic problem
- Repeated cyber breaches could diminish public confidence in online services and reduce customers' willingness to participate in the digital economy

Source: Digital Economy Singapore, Presentation by Mohanty S., Monetary Authority of Singapore, 2018
Figure 2.5: Policy making via experimentation and empirical data

To strengthen cyber resilience of the financial sector, MAS has adopted a four-pillar strategy (also see Figure 2.6):

- *Regulatory guidance*: MAS sets out principle-driven requirements and guidance for managing cyber risks in the Notice of Technology Risk Management (TRM) and Technology Risk Management Guidelines, as well as through periodic circulars and advisories
- *Supervision*: MAS inspects and supervises financial institutions to assess the quality of their cyber risk management
- *Surveillance and information sharing*: Through ongoing surveillance and research, MAS shares relevant cyberthreat intelligence with the industry so that financial institutions can take appropriate actions to address associated cyber risks
- *Competencies and capabilities development*: MAS works closely with peer regulators, government agencies, industry bodies and financial institutions to collaborate on industry projects to develop cybersecurity competencies and catalyze the adoption of sound cybersecurity and resilience practices

Source: Digital Economy Singapore, Presentation by Mohanty S., Monetary Authority of Singapore, 2018
Figure 2.6: Building cyber resilience

The Impact of Policymaking on the Journey of Fintech

The development of the fintech ecosystem creates the need for each country to develop policies which will then define the journey that each fintech player will have to go through to survive and incorporate the benefits of the new technologies. Each country has its own strengths and weaknesses, and policymakers need to balance the benefits that are possible with the deployment of fintech and the challenges to incumbent players as a result.

Singapore has focused on developing policies that encourage the enablement of large enterprise systems that can be unbundled into small subsystems and solutions. These subsystems can then be improved using fintech startups to create niche fintech solutions. When the niche offering is live, the connectivity will allow re-bundling as a comprehensive system in line with the digital economy.

Given the policy support and resulting lead that many fintech startups have in Singapore, it is likely that these startups will become regional in Asia and begin to offer their new products and services in many Asian countries. Given that fintech processes are generally very scalable, this also would facilitate a faster route to profitability for each of these startups. A roadmap for regional connectivity therefore is a critical step in creating a sustainable and profitable fintech ecosystem in Asia, especially as each Asian country may not be able to individually support a profitable fintech ecosystem. In other parts of the world, a similar situation may exist. In Europe for example, fintechs would need to be pan-EU to exploit the benefits of scale.

Challenges in the Fintech Journey

There are three categories of challenges in developing a fintech ecosystem, as discussed in this section.

Implementation of New Technology to Develop New Products and Services

Financial institutions are constantly evolving and innovating in response to fintech developments. Against the backdrop of new technologies being developed by major technology players and fintech startups, legacy systems often hamper the adoption of these new technologies by financial institutions. Legacy systems that are being used as a source of revenue today could become obstacles when confronted with the blistering pace of innovations that financial institutions need to adopt and implement to stay competitive and relevant. Financial institutions need to reengineer their legacy systems to an open architecture and embrace open APIs as an integral part of their business strategy. These APIs can enable the financial institution to absorb new technologies more efficiently, as well as collaborate with external parties more readily. Another factor can be the lack of staff with the skill set to implement and support new technology. Addressing this issue requires the establishment of a new system for talent, based on training local professionals and attracting international talent.

Deployment of New Products and Services within the Physical Ecosystem

An underdeveloped physical infrastructure such as telecommunication network coverage, payment systems, a trusted customer identity source and customer credit data can affect the provision and deployment of new products and services. Government, in partnership with the industry, needs to play a leading role to invest, develop and implement the relevant physical infrastructure that can enable the digital economy.

Speed of Adoption and Consumption of Fintech-based Products and Services

Although the use of fintech-based products and services is increasing among consumers, overall confidence and trust in fintechs can be improved. Traditional financial institutions have garnered public confidence by allaying security issues and maintaining the confidentiality and privacy of customer data over time. The adoption of fintech-based products and services requires an intricate balance between strengthening security and transparency of these platforms and maintaining a great customer experience and convenience.

Other factors that can affect the speed of adoption and consumption of fintech-based products and services include low levels of income as well as financial illiteracy. The ability of products and services to handle low transaction values and incur low fees, as well as the introduction of relevant consumer financial education and awareness programs, thus becomes an important element in tackling these issues.

Sopnendu Mohanty is Chief Fintech Officer at the Monetary Authority of Singapore (MAS) and is responsible for creating development strategies, public infrastructure and regulatory policies around technology innovation. Mr. Mohanty has spent over 20 years in various leadership roles globally in technology, finance and innovation. He has co-authored several patented works in the area of retail distribution of the financial sector. Mr. Mohanty extensively engages with ecosystems of various jurisdictions on innovation, policy making and tech-enabled financial services. He is on the Institutional Investor's list of influential fintech global dealmakers. Mr. Mohanty has been recognized internationally as a fintech thought leader, and he was recently named the Market Reformer of the Year by IFL, Euromoney.

Chapter 3
The Landscape of Fintech

Financial technology, or fintech, has caught the finance industry by surprise with their pace of innovation at improving and delivering banking products and services. The industry has seen an incredible growth since 2010 fueled by the developments in technology, strong funding support, favorable regulatory conditions, and, most crucially, a change in consumer behavior toward the adoption of technology. This chapter aims to demystify the world of fintechs by providing an understanding of the current state of the landscape through the lens of the BCG FinTech Control Tower. In this chapter, you will learn about the funding trends and evolution across major fintech segments, understand who the key players and investors are, how banks are responding to innovation and disruption, and finally conclude with a peek into the emerging themes in the near future.

Why Is the World Interested in Fintech Now?

Fintech is the term given to companies that leverage technology to provide financial services directly to the consumer, or provide solutions to the financial services. Based on the BCG FinTech Control Tower, there are close to 12,000 fintechs globally, attracting more than USD$130bn in equity funding as of December 2017 (see Figure 3.1). The industry can be broadly viewed through three main lenses:
- By *business line*, or the financial business line in which the solution operates:
    - Corporate banking, retail banking, SME banking, insurance, capital markets, cross-FI, including technology and support
- By *product cluster*, or the financial product(s) the solution offers:
    - Payments, lending and crowdfunding, trading and investments, insurance, retail accounts, technology and support
- By *business models*, or whether the solution is enabling or disruptive to a financial organization's revenue pool:
    - Enabler, disruptor

DOI 10.1515/9781547400904- 003

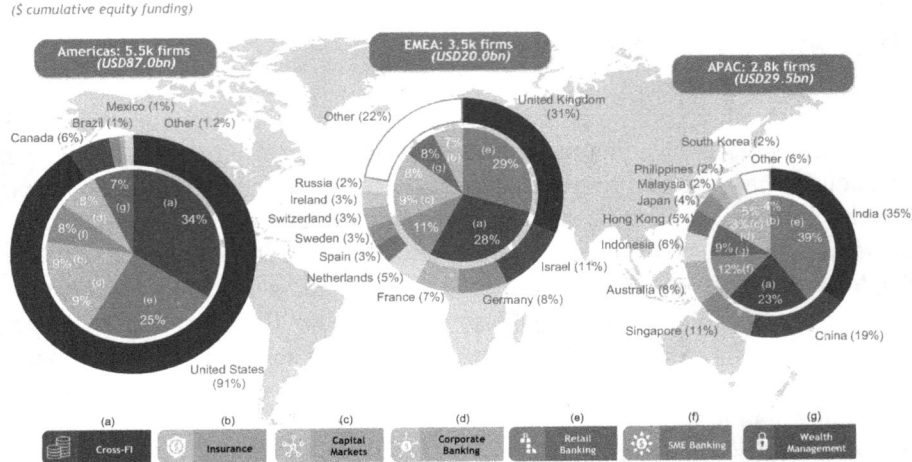

FinTechs by business segment
($ cumulative equity funding)

Note: *Cumulative equity funding from 2000 to 2017*

Figure 3.1: Global distribution of fintechs by count

The industry has witnessed an unprecedented growth since 2010, with global investments increasing 800% to a peak of USD$26bn in 2015. The fact is that fintechs and the technologies that enable them have existed for decades, so what is causing the buzz now? The catalyst to this pace of acceleration is *digitalization*, which has revolutionized the way consumers interact with their world. Financial services is no exception. Consumers today expect greater convenience, speed, reliability, and cost-savings from financial services; this translates into capabilities such as remote account opening, low-cost remittance, real-time money transfer, instantaneous loan approvals and disbursements, and so forth, all of which is made possible today through fintech innovation. In remote account opening, for example, the use of video and facial recognition technologies means that consumers can now open bank accounts without being physically present at branches.

Fintechs are here to stay. From start-ups to unicorns to TechFin (technology giants branching out into financial services), innovation is changing the face of finance as we know it. The continued modernization of societies, democratization of technologies, and push for greater financial inclusion from regulators will create more room for innovation and new business models in the future.

In this chapter, we will look into the state of fintech today through the lens of the BCG FinTech Control Tower, which will cover:
– Landscape, funding and investor trends
– How banks are responding
– A peek into the themes of the future

Landscape and Trends

Funding Trends

In this section, we consider current funding trends by geographical region, business model, and product cluster.

By Geography
The Americas, being the long-established innovation and technology powerhouse, is home to 46% of all fintechs and has attracted 64% of the total equity funding, with APAC and EMEA trailing behind at 22% and 14%, respectively (see Figure 3.2).

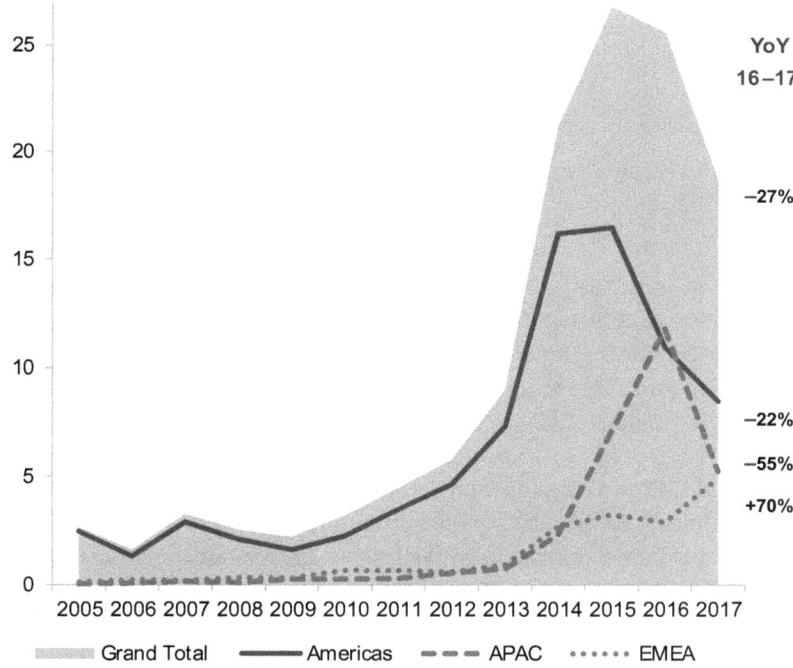

Figure 3.2: Equity funding by geography (USD$bn)

However, since 2014, funding has taken a sharp turn to the East as investors shifted their attention to the fintech hype across India and China. In 2010, APAC's share of the total cumulative equity funding was only 5% but by 2017, that number has more than quadrupled to 23% (see Figure 3.3).

In 2017, EMEA was the only region to receive an increase in funding, driven by renewed interest across insurance, lending, payments, and retail accounts clusters.

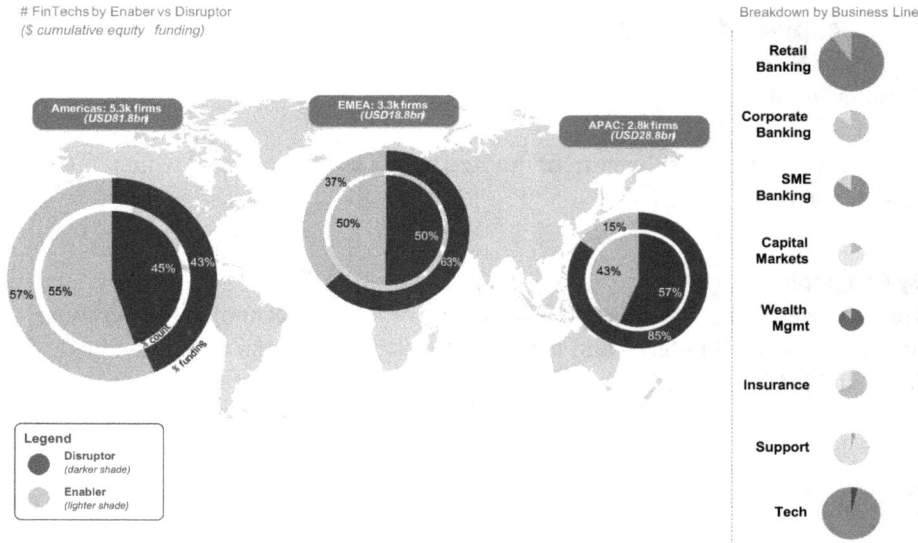

Note: Cumulative equity funding from 2000 to 2017

Figure 3.3: Equity funding by enabler vs disruptor

By Business Model

Across geographical regions, the profile of fintechs differ significantly. In the Americas, 55% of fintechs are enablers whose business models either complement that of incumbents or provide a direct service to the incumbents. In a similar vein, enablers in the Americas tend to attract more equity funding (see Figure 3.4).

In comparison, fintechs in APAC are primarily disruptors who disrupt banks by offering financial services directly to consumers. These fintechs generally operate in the retail banking and SME banking spaces, where the huge underbanked population in emerging markets across Southeast Asia offers a myriad of untapped opportunities for financial inclusion. More significantly as well, these fintechs are well funded by the investor community, taking up 85% of all funding raised in APAC.

By Product Cluster

Looking at the landscape from a product perspective, the payments and technology clusters have attracted the most funding to date. Table 3.1 describes each cluster in more detail and highlights their recent trends and developments

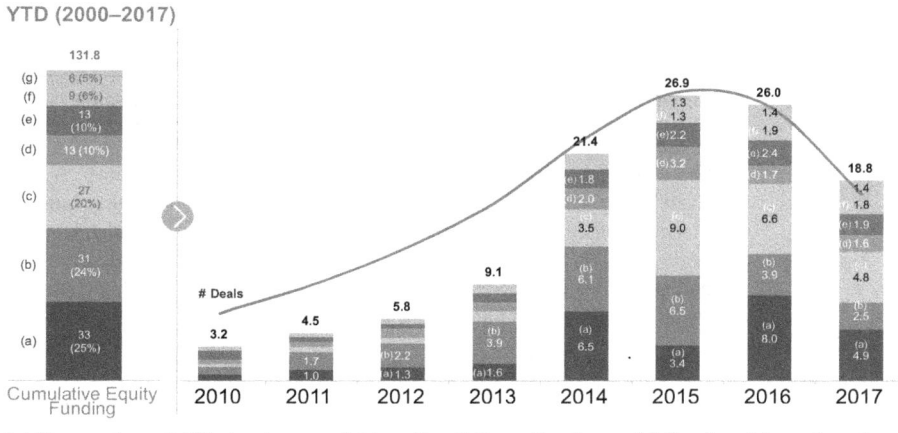

YTD (2000–2017)

(a) Payments (b) Technology (c) Lending & Crowdfunding (d) Trading & Investments
(e) Support (f) Insurance (g) Retail Accounts

Note: Cumulative equity funding from 2000 to 2017

Figure 3.4: Equity funding by product (USD$bn)

Table 3.1: Key highlights by product clusters

Cluster	Key Highlights	Example
Payments #: 24% $: 25%	Payments is the largest funded cluster to date, being the first fintech wave. Fintechs in this cluster include digital payments solutions, merchant acquiring solutions, and payment infrastructure providers. As the cluster matures, market consolidation makes it harder for new players to enter the market. Established players, however, are investor magnets with the ability to attract massive rounds, such as Ant Financial's record Series C round of USD$10bn in 2018.	**Square Ant Financial Payoneer Paytm TransferWise**
Technology #: 17% $: 24%	The technology cluster covers solutions across block-chain, data analytics, artificial intelligence (AI), digital identity, security, and infrastructure. Funding into the cluster has largely been driven by the explosion of data and the rise of big data analytics. Although funding has settled after the hypes of past years, the maturing of this cluster holds significant potential into the future, especially around the applications of AI, blockchain, and cybersecurity.	**r3 Palantir Ayasdi Sentient Cloudera**

Table 3.1: (continued)

Cluster	Key Highlights	Example
Lending #: 15% $: 20%	The lending cluster has received significant funding in the past three years, driven by strong demand for credit both in the retail and SME space. Funding has been focused on fintechs in the United States and China, collectively accounting for 80% of the total funding. However, emerging markets are seeing exponential growth, particularly as regulators push for greater financial inclusion.	**SoFi** **Dianrong.com** **Kabbage** **Lufax.com** **Funding Circle**
Support #: 9% $: 10%	The support cluster is primarily made up of B2B fintechs providing solutions across functions such as finance, compliance, risk management, human resources, and other business automation tools. Funding into the support cluster has generally been at a muted level across the years. However, within this cluster, regulatory technology (RegTech) is emerging as an area of growing interest from investors.	**DocuSign** **Avaloq** **AvidXchange** **Zenefits** **MetricStream**
Trading & Investments #: 17% $: 10%	The trading and investment cluster is made up of two main sub-clusters: solutions geared toward capital markets, such as core trading technology, high frequency trading (HFTs), eBrokerage, and market analytics; and solutions targeting wealth management such as digital wealth management (DWM), retail brokerage, and retail trading technology. Funding interest in this cluster is to a large extent led by VC money going into the disruptive B2C models across DWM and retail brokerage platforms.	**Kensho** **Digital Asset Holdings** **Betterment** **Symphony** **www.FUTU5.com** **Robinhood**
Insurance #: 7% $: 6%	The insurance industry was slow to catch on to the technology wave. However, InsurTech has gained momentum as a hot area of fintech investment today, with funding into life insurance and motor insurance growing 900% and 100%, respectively, year-on-year. The typical InsurTechs are disruptors offering insurance products not only across health, life, motor, property, and casualty (P&C), but also B2B solutions such as claims and benefits handling and distribution software. Overall, funding into InsurTechs has been small, as many are still at their early stages.	**Oscar** **Trōv** **ZhongAn Insurance** **Lemonade** **Decisely**
Retail Accounts #: 8% $: 5%	Retail accounts is the least funded cluster to date. Fintechs in this space include accounts and savings, financial planning, and SME accounting solutions. Funding into this cluster has grown substantially in the past year, driven especially by the favorable environment brought about by open banking regulation in the EU and the rise of digital banking platform players.	**Atom bank** **wacai.com** **Credit Karma** **Monzo**

Note: # refers to distribution by count of fintechs; $ refers to distribution by equity funding received

Investor Trends

Fintechs attract investments from a variety of investors who are attracted to the landscape for different reasons. The key investor profiles are venture capitalists (VCs), private equity firms (PEs), angels, accelerators/incubators, corporates, banks, insurers, and TechFins. Generally, VCs, PEs, angels, accelerators, incubators, and corporates invest with a goal of profiting from the success of the business while banks, insurers, and TechFins invest with a strategic vision of achieving synergy with their core business. In this section, we will further elaborate on some of the notable investor profiles.

VCs and PEs

VCs and PEs raise funds from other investors and invest with an aim of generating a profit. VCs and PEs are by far the most active investors, contributing to 65% of all deals raised since 2000. As the landscape matures, VC deal volumes have declined, particularly at the angel and seed rounds as investors shift their investment strategy from smaller ticket bets to placing larger strategic investments. Some of the most active VCs and PEs in fintech include Sequoia Capital and Accel Partners.

Accelerators and Incubators

Accelerators and incubators are entities focused on providing equity financing, mentorship, and other support to early stage fintechs. They typically run structured programs, taking on a cohort of start-ups for three–six months. The key difference between incubators and accelerators is in the business lifecycle of their cohort. Incubators are generally aimed at pre-seed to seed stage start-ups who are at the conceptualization phase of their idea while accelerators are aimed at early stage start-ups who already have a proven business model and are looking to scale the business. Specialized fintech accelerators have sprung up over the years, with notable ones being Y Combinator, 500 Startups, SuperCharger, and Techstars.

Banks

Banks have traditionally lagged behind VCs when it comes to fintech investments. Interest from bank investors has gathered momentum as the fintech landscape moves into the B2B space and more B2B models are proven successful at banks. Not to be left behind, specialized VC arms have been set up within banks for the strategic purpose of fintech investments. In 2017, we saw banks such as Goldman Sachs, Citi, and J.P. Morgan taking some of the top spots in terms of the number of fintech deals being made (see Figure 3.5).

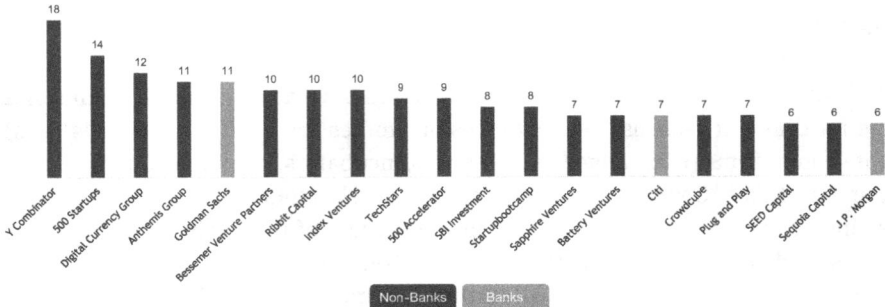

Figure 3.5: Number of fintech deals in 2017

Insurers

Insurers have been slow to join the fintech/InsurTech bandwagon and lag behind banks in terms of fintech investments. Interest has picked up particularly in the last three years, however, as we've seen insurers jumping into fintech mega rounds. Examples include Allianz X's recent USD$160m Series C investment into German challenger bank, N26, co-led by Tencent. In a similar fashion, Ping An Group, AXA, and Munich Re have also set up dedicated fintech venture arms.

TechFins

TechFins have ramped up their investments into the fintech landscape in the last three years, particularly as they move toward disrupting the financial services industry. Ant Financial and Tencent, for example, have been aggressively investing into fintechs especially in Asia as they look to replicate the success of their business models within China to geographies of similar demographics. Since 2015, Ant Financial has made a number of high-profile investments into players such as PayTM in India, Ascend Money in Thailand, Mynt in the Philippines, and KakaoPay in South Korea, which are among some of the most notable examples.

How Banks Are Responding

In the mid-90s, Bill Gates made a bold statement claiming that while *"banking is necessary, banks are not."* The statement has somewhat become a reality in the world we know today. Technology giants have started encroaching into various financial services' verticals. Amazon was said to be in talks with J.P. Morgan to offer current accounts; Facebook-owned social messaging platform, WhatsApp, has already beta-launched WhatsApp payments in India in March 2018 (though full deployment has been delayed by Facebook's recent data leakage scandal); Ant Financial, the subsidiary of ecommerce giant Alibaba, is now one of the largest banks in the world in terms of valuation after raising their record USD\$10bn Series C funding in 2018. In a different industry, Grab, the ride-sharing platform announced the launch of Grab financial in March 2018, which will focus on offering loans and insurance to the underbanked population in Southeast Asia, and the list goes on. Especially with the move toward open banking, anyone can now offer banking services—telcos, ecommerce, transport, automobile, and technology companies.

Banks have felt the heat as they increasingly fall behind competition in the ability to capture critical customer data points. In China, for example, a typical Alipay user can conduct most of their everyday duties without ever needing to leave the app. This includes chatting with friends, online shopping, booking a taxi, airline tickets, movie tickets, food delivery, bike sharing, paying for a ride on the metro, and investing in a money market fund—the functionalities keep growing. Alipay now processes more than 50% of all of China's mobile payment transactions and, according to the *Financial Times* in April 2017, Ant Financial's money market fund (Yu'e Bao) has overtaken J.P. Morgan's US government fund with assets under management of USD\$165.6bn. Faced with unrelenting competition, banks will need to innovate from within and through partnerships with the nimbler fintechs to catch up and keep up with the pace of innovation.

Banks Are Driving a "Technology-First" Agenda

The good news is that, in the face of disruption, banks are not standing still. From before, we have seen banks step up their fintech investment footprint, but that is only one of the many ways that banks have engaged the fintech ecosystem. From as early as 2010, banks ramped up resources dedicated to transforming their digital and innovation journeys (see Figure 3.6). Fintech investment funds and collaboration vehicles have been set up, giving rise to a variety of engagement models, described in Table 3.2.

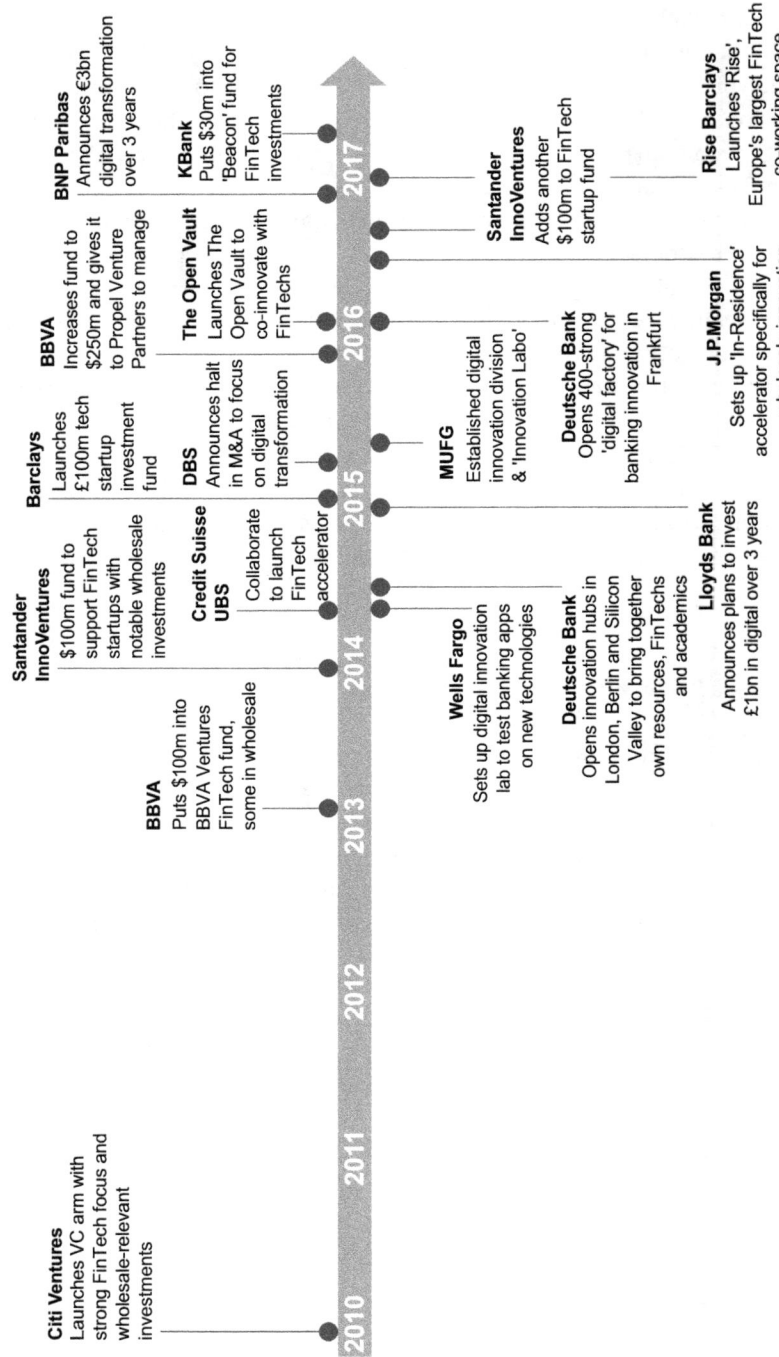

Figure 3.6: The bank fintech innovation journey

Table 3.2: Engagement models

Engagement Models	Benefits	Examples
Direct Clients	Develop new technology services	**Citi Ayasdi** Citi uses Ayasdi's big data software to discover patterns and critical variables in risk models
White Label	Reach new products and markets	**ADIB Fidor Bank** Abu Dhabi Islamic Bank (ADIB) developed a community site for personal finance using Fidor Bank's platform with a focus on attracting millennials
Partnership	Provide value-added services to existing customers; reach new customer segments	**Kantox Bpifrance** Bpifrance partners with kantox to offer real-time access to transparent foreign exchange (FX) rates to their customers and extends Bpifrance's FX risk products to kantox customers
Co-creation	Ability to shape and launch new products	**BBVA Kasisto** BBVA brings their knowledge of the banking industry to help co-create Kasisto's virtual assistant which offers a human-like digital interaction capability to the financial services industry
Incubation / Acceleration	Drives internal education, proof-of-concepts, and ideation	**Barclays Wave** Through Barclays Accelerator programme, powered by Techstars, Wave, and Barclays successfully executed a global trade finance deal on the blockchain
Capital Investment	Access to exclusivity, ability to shape development of product; upside from equity	**Santander PayKey** Santander InnoVentures invested in PayKey to enable peer-to-peer payments on major social messenger apps across Santander's markets
Industry Consortium	Creates a network impact as peers engage in common challenges	**r3** R3 leads a working consortium of over 80 members including some of the world's top banks to foster greater collaboration in the development of distributed ledger technology

The Move Toward Greater Digitalization and Ecosystem Platforms

The success of Alipay is precisely the result of an ecosystem around the customer's needs, and the ability to collect and harness user insights through these data channels. As financial services become more democratized, banks can more easily build their own digital platforms to access the ecosystem beyond banking. Today, this is done in three distinct ways: APIs, micro-services partnerships, and building new platforms.

Open Application Programming Interfaces (APIs)

Open banking is defined as the trend toward integration of banking platforms with third-party platforms to embed financial services within processes. This can go either by providing APIs to third parties or by utilizing APIs from third parties. Banks on this journey have released a range of open APIs to allow third parties such as other corporates, fintechs, and software developers to access a breadth of services offered by the bank.

For example, DBS claimed to have launched the largest bank API developer platform in November 2017, with 155 APIs across categories such as funds transfers, rewards, and peer-to-peer payment services. The platform allows DBS' strategic partners to incorporate DBS' capabilities directly on their platform. Corporates such as Grab and McDonald's can now call on the relevant API to give their customers the option to checkout using DBS PayLah!

Partnership with Micro-Services

A partnership approach primarily involves a one-to-one engagement with a fintech to offer micro-services through white labeling or by offering a third party product directly. In white labeling, the fintech solution is "rewrapped" to achieve a seamless look and feel consistent with the bank's. Both instances enable banks to integrate proven B2C use cases with relatively little technical effort.

For example, CBA partnered with Kounta to offer a complete point of sales (POS) experience, integrating a range of business, payments, and back-end processing on a single device. With Kounta, CBA's merchant clients can now accept payments, manage tables, take orders, split bills, and update their inventory levels on one device. On the back-end, the app also integrates with loyalty, accounting, inventory, rostering, and payroll applications, thereby empowering merchants to draw more insights from their businesses.

Building New Platforms

Banks have also taken the approach of building a completely new digital platform to bypass the challenges of having to integrate with legacy banking systems and infrastructure, allowing innovation to move in a quicker and more effective manner.

Yolt, for instance, is a mobile app created by ING in the UK, aimed at allowing users to aggregate their bank accounts. With Yolt, customers can gain better visibility of all their accounts, providing a one-stop shop for personal finance management. The platform is now integrated with 29 banks in the UK, including major banks and challenger banks such as Monzo and Starling Bank, with further rollout planned in France and Italy.

Conclusion

Fintechs have injected a new lease of life to the financial system, and their growth was very much fueled by the complacency of incumbents that allowed fintechs to find opportunities in white spaces and poor banking experiences. That said, the giants were awakened from their slumber and we can expect to see the banking sector change dramatically in the future ahead. As technology becomes more pervasive in our everyday lives, four emerging themes will shape the near future of digital strategy in financial services, as shown in Figure 3.7.

 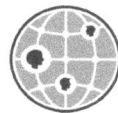  

Financial platforms	**Financial inclusion**	**Global regulation**	**Tech infrastructure**
Open Banking will see more FinTech services rebundled themselves around the most successful ecosystems	Technology, eCommerce, transport and telecom players increasingly entering the financial services space to serve the underbanked populations	Regulators are actively embracing and driving innovation, impact to the industry remains to be proven (e.g. PSD2 & GDPR in Europe)	Artificial Intelligence, Distributed Ledger Technology, Internet of Things and Biometrics will lead to a new generation of financial infrastructure

Figure 3.7: Emerging fintech themes

References
BCG/Expand analysis, Dealroom, TechInAsia

The FinTech Control Tower (FCT) *is a research framework developed jointly by BCG and Expand Research, identifying initiatives, technologies, and companies that matter most in today's fintech ecosystem and assessing their impact. The FCT has developed a proprietary platform that tracks fintechs globally providing insights into the landscape. We do this in a unique way by engaging directly with industry stakeholders and innovators to be at the forefront of research and trends. Our clients include the top global and regional financial institutions, regulators, investors, and technology giants, who chose us for the expertise to drive informed decisions around innovation management, ecosystem engagement, IT investments, and M&A activities. For more information, visit us at www.fintechcontroltower.bcg.com.*

Pauline Wray is Managing Director of Expand Consulting Pte Ltd, Head of Asia region operations and Global Co-Head of Distribution and Strategy for the BCG FinTech Control

Tower. Having worked in Expand offices in London and New York, she gained a very wide knowledge of major financial institutions, technology companies, and financial services regulators. Pauline has 15 years of experience in the financial services industry and 12 years at Expand, opening the professional benchmarking arm of BCG in New York and Asia. She is also a member of the Expand/BCG leadership and advisory board across all FI sectors.

Simin Liu *is Lead Analyst at BCG FinTech Control Tower and leads research and market intelligence for the BCG FinTech Control Tower across Asia Pacific, supporting clients in driving innovation through the use of technology in financial services. She brings an extensive understanding of working with both the financial services and the fintech industry with core expertise around innovation in RegTech, beyond banking, retail banking, and wealth management.*

Part 2: **Enablers of a Digital Economy**

Chapter 4
Digital Identity

Digital identity refers to a collection of information about any individual, company or organization that exists in any network. It refers to an electronically captured and gathered set of data points and characteristics that can identify an individual.[1]

A digital identity is created when individuals access the internet, make online purchases, buy travel tickets, make hotel reservations or through any other action for which they provide information about themselves to the network. Through these actions, individuals create virtual presences of themselves that mirror their actions, beliefs and thoughts.[2]

Often, individuals create their digital identities by providing to the network their personal information, and virtual profiles are created by the network based on the users' actions on the network. Digital identities are often seen as contextual as they are created based on selective data provided by the individuals to the network.

For example, when someone makes an online purchase on Lazada, they are asked to provide various pieces of information to Lazada, such as name, email address, date of birth, address, and bank card details and also to set a password. A user tends to scroll through Lazada's product suite to look at products that they are interested in buying. Based on the actions and data provided, Lazada is able to create a mirror digital identity of the individual. The next time the same individual logs on to Lazada or any e-commerce portal, they need to prove their digital identity. Many e-commerce companies and websites are also able to analyze user browsing, purchase and behavior patterns to better plan their advertising, product placement and product marketing strategies.

Some data streams that can help in creating a digital identity[3] are an identity number, date of birth, internet browsing patterns and social media activity (what we post, like, share and comment on), purchasing and transaction behavior, and repeated visits to a source that has collected their data on previous visits.

Why We Need Digital Identities

According to the World Bank in October 2017,[4] "More than 1.1 billion people in the world are unable to prove their identity and therefore lack access to vital services including healthcare, social protection, education and finance."

With many institutions and services adapting their products and services for online access, bringing these 1.1 billion people onto a digital identity platform will provide an immense benefit. The World Bank also highlights the benefits that digital identity has provided to such individuals in developing economies. If done right, digital identity can

DOI 10.1515/9781547400904-004

- Create unique identities
- Be made retrievable without a person providing personal documents or being physically present
- Be used across organizations to access various services
- Provide privacy and security

The World Economic Forum, in its August 2016 report titled "A Blueprint for Digital Identity," identifies the following as critical needs for digital identity.[5]
- Digital identity is becoming critical, and the number of digitally authenticated and processed transactions that depend on a digital identity for authentication purposes is growing.
- Digital transactions also are becoming more complex, involving newer entities and structures of transactions.
- Digitally active customers expect easy, seamless transactions and service flows.
- Global regulators are increasingly demanding higher levels of transactional transparency, which requires organizations to possess detailed and complete information about their clients and individuals for whom they are undertaking transactions.

Components of Digital Identity[6]

There are different layers of digital identity management, and each layer plays an important role in ensuring that the whole process is managed in a structured manner.

Application owners and service providers need to ensure that their users are rightfully granted access to applications by ensuring that there is a streamlined identity authentication process while also ensuring strict adherence to internal data security and privacy protocols.

Considering the importance of identity access management in protecting data and financial and business assets, the following five steps are considered important components of the IAM (identity access management) process:
1. *Authentication*: The process by which users who want to access their accounts or perform transactions prove to the network of the service provider (such as a bank or other financial services platform) that they are who they claim to be. Authentication structures must be easy to use with single sign-on or biometric authentication and additional higher layers of authentication for riskier or higher value transactions.
2. *Identity management*: The process of identifying users of a network or application and defining and controlling the amount of access to information or various resources that are present within these systems or applications. A good example of identity management is Apple Pay, which was introduced by Apple along with

the iPhone 6. Combining the touch ID (biometric authentication and identity Management) with NFC (near-field communications) technology to authenticate the user at the point of sale, Apple Pay has completely digitized the average person's wallet.

3. *Digital rights management*: An important component in ensuring copyright protection to software and applications.[7]
4. *Privileged account management*: The task of authorizing and monitoring privileged users of any systems. It allows one to flag suspicious account activities and monitor various accounts, rightly grant access to the correct users, provide timely access, revoke the same if required and create a history of account actions undertaken by the user. Password vaults and session managers are classic examples.[8]
5. *Compliance*: The implementation of sufficient systems and control mechanisms to provide data security and data privacy.

The Market for Personal Digital Identity Management

According to research done by SecureIDNews in July 2016, the personal identity market is currently valued at USD $8.7bn and is estimated to grow to USD $9.7bn by 2020. Considering the potential market size, many service providers, banks and other financial institutions are viewing this as a significant growth market. There are also many companies who offer digital identity solutions in combination with distributed ledger technology and machine learning.

Problems Solved by Digital Identity

Digital identity helps to solve two important problems: greater efficiency and security from the move from physical to digital authentication and enabling the complete digitalization needed to optimize its effectiveness.

Enhanced Efficiency and Reduced Risk

The current system of identity is predominantly based on the possession of physical documents, which is cumbersome to say the least. Possession of physical documents by an individual may not be able to establish a relationship between the user and the physical documents (may not be successful in authenticating the user). Also, physical documents can be forged, stolen or falsified. The possession of false documents by users creates issues in transaction security and authentication.

Currently, it takes a couple of weeks for a bank to sanction a loan to a client because it needs to create a risk profile of the client and consider other financial parameters by collecting physical financial documents of the client. Credit processing efficiency can be improved if technologies such as OCR (optical character readers) and cloud computing are employed to assist clients in upload the necessary loan documents. Banks could employ data-driven workflow systems in order to aggregate customer financial data and quicken the credit decisioning process. Some fintech companies have also able to design products that are able to predict risk profiles of clients based on their social media profiles or actions on the network. Such innovations will go a long way in ensuring ease in processing and disbursement of loans to customers.

Power Complete Digitization

Digital identity needs to be ubiquitous to be effective. It also has to be usable across different platforms and service providers, so a single identity must be created to operate across different services/platforms. Possessing a single digital identity that is interoperable across different services will lead to complete digitization of various process flows and will reduce time and enhance ease of service delivery.

The Chinese Government is currently developing a broad "Social Credit Scoring System" that aims to monitor the online and offline presence of its 1.3 billion citizens to score their trustworthiness. The system, which is being introduced to enhance and build a culture of sincerity and trust, is a prime example of creating digital identities and using such data to score the citizens.[9]

The Impact of Digital Identity on Business Models

How do financial institutions and other businesses change their business models to adapt to digital identity?[10]

- *Financial services*: Digital identity has led banks and financial institutions to focus on complete digitization of their platforms and services. Digital identities can be used to ensure process automation and better service delivery for a variety of functions, including opening new accounts, making mobile payments, providing investment solutions and approving loans.
- *Healthcare*: Many healthcare companies across the globe are launching digital portals and channels to ensure better customer engagement and allow customers to better manage their healthcare touchpoints. Healthcare companies have created online portals that facilitate digital onboarding and online communication with their doctors and nurses. Clients can also gain insights into their health data and execute a wide range of requests.
- Retailers: Many retailers are now replacing their expansion plans for physical stores with e-commerce portals. These e-commerce portals allow users to provide initial information to set up accounts for online transactions. Companies use big

data analytics to track the transaction patterns of their customers. Based on that data, they are able to predict purchase patterns and products that may be of more interest to a customer and provide relevant offers and discounts.

Issues Concerning Digital Identity Management[11]

As the amount of personal data that is collected to create and manage digital identities increases, questions on data security and data privacy tend to rise, too. Individuals today are concerned with identity theft and data leakages as they no longer control the data.

It is necessary for global digital identity programs to garner the trust of those enrolled by ensuring sufficient protection from data theft and data leakages:

- Standards need to be set to ensure that there is a clear consensus of the nature of data that is collected in order to prove a person's identity.
- Organizations must ensure that that data lifecycles are tracked. They must be able to control access and user privileges if the user leaves the organization or deletes his account.
- Companies must ensure better customer experience with the digital identity initiative.

A Digital Identity Application Use Case: Aadhaar[12]

The Aadhaar, which in Hindi means foundation, is a 12-digit unique identification number that is provided to all enrolled citizens of India. Various details about the individual such as demographic and biometric data are collected as part of this initiative. Aadhaar is the world's largest biometric digital identity creation initiative. This initiative is currently being carried out by UIDAI (Unique Identification Authority of India).

The current enrollment of Aadhaar is close to 1.2 billion Indian residents, which includes almost 99 percent of Indian adults. It was originally conceptualized to reduce fraud and ensure that the benefits of social programs reach the intended recipients. It also acts as a formalized system of identity for all Indians.

Why Was Aadhaar Conceived?[13]

In India, there is at present a large portion of the population that lacks formal identification and may possess only identification documents that are not nationally accepted. Considering the problem of common names and a lack of methods to authenticate and verify identification documents, government distribution agencies often provided government social security benefits to individuals who may not have qualified for the benefits. In 2005, the Government of India also estimated that close to 60 percent of food grains and close to 40 percent of kerosene that were provided at subsidized prices did not reach the intended beneficiaries. This resulted in enormous losses to the national treasury.

The Aadhaar initiative was launched in order to target India's Public Distribution System (PDS), which provides food grains to the poor of the country at subsidized prices. The PDS provides sustenance to close to 330 million families across the country through 50,000 outlets. The main issues with the Indian PDS are pilferage and fraud with respect to claiming food grains.

The Aadhaar aimed to minimize the inefficiency in the Indian PDS by setting up a streamlined and automated manner of tracking and distributing the food grains. It includes:
- Beneficiaries (Aadhaar Holders) are informed of availability of supplies through SMS from the PDS outlet.
- Beneficiaries also can view, through an app, the outlets nearest to them and the particular outlet's stock levels of various grains.
- Biometric authentication of beneficiaries at the point of sale ensures that the right individual gets access to subsidized food grains.
- Customers also can select the outlets where they would like to receive the benefits. All the outlets are monitored through a central agency that monitors the stock levels at different outlets and assigns orders based on customer requests.
- The diversion of food material was eliminated via real-time Aadhaar-based monitoring of physical weights at origination and destination points. If there was a difference between the initial weight and arrival weight at destination, there would be clear information on the details of the handler.
- Aadhaar-based, cashless payment options also are offered at the point of sale to ensure that no cash exchanges are made.
- Biometric authentication also ensures that users cannot claim benefits multiple times.

The Evolution of Aadhaar

From being a tool for the transfer of government social security benefits, the Aadhaar has now transformed into a multi-purpose utility that all Indian residents need to ensure that they can access basic services such as banking or healthcare. The following changes represent the evolution that this unique identity system has seen since its launch.

Financial Inclusion[14]

In 2014, the Indian Prime Minister Narendra Modi announced the launch of the Pradhan Mantri Jan Dhan Yojana (Prime Minister's People Wealth Scheme), setting a goal of opening close to 70 million bank accounts for those who did not have them. The goal also was to provide allied products and services such as debit cards, pensions and insurance schemes. An important step toward the success of this program was to ensure that the accounts opened under this scheme were linked with the Aadhaar numbers of the account holders.

Other key points:
- In 2013, the Reserve Bank of India (central bank) approved the inclusion of Aadhaar as an instrument of e-KYC wherein the biometric facility for instantaneous digital and online authentication and verification could be used to open accounts. This rapidly increased the pace at which accounts were opened.
- Banks saved close to USD $1.5bn by using the Aadhaar e-KYC initiative.
- After the Aadhaar was linked with all bank accounts, the government could ensure transfer of subsidies and social security payments to those accounts based on the Aadhaar numbers.
- The welfare payments for the five largest governmental welfare schemes, namely the social security net, scholarships for the poor, the PDS and the employment guarantee act were transferred to the accounts linked to recipients' Aadhaar numbers.
- The biometric recognition facility of the Aadhaar assisted in providing better reach for banking and financial services in rural areas. Rural consumers did not have to hold physical identification documents or remember passwords.
- As of July 2018, welfare scheme accounts had a closing balance of USD $11.6bn.[15]

Aadhar Pay[16]

Aadhar Pay is an online Aadhaar-based payment system that allows merchants to collect payments from customers through their biometric authentication. Merchants can download the Aadhaar payments app and link it to their bank accounts. They also need to purchase the fingerprint and iris scanners which cost USD $35. They can then upload invoices and opt for customers to pay via Aadhaar and biometric authentication. This increases the ease of collecting payments for the merchant. The Aadhar Pay facility is currently being offered only by a limited number of banks in the country

The Aadhaar-Based Biometric Attendance System[17]

As part of its "Digital India" initiative, the current Indian government decided to implement biometric attendance-monitoring systems for employees in all central government offices. It also was employed in various state government departments. Over 1000 biometric authentication devices have been installed in the central government, and over 83,000 government employees currently mark their attendance over biometric sensors. The shift to biometric attendance monitoring is expected to increase productivity of government employees.

Aadhaar-based Authentication[18]

The UIDAI, which is the Aadhaar repository and contains demographic data of the users, provides authentication services upon request. The UIDAI matches information received via dedicated channels against Aadhaar data in its database. If data that is received matches the data it possesses, then the nodal agency confirms the identity of the user. However, no further data is shared in order to protect the privacy of user data.

There are different levels of Aadhaar authentication:
–   Demographic authentication: This level matches information such as name, date of birth and address. Such data is disclosed by applicants when they apply for their unique identity numbers.
–   One-time password (OTP) authentication: When an attempt to authenticate a user has been made, the nodal agency sends a text message containing an OTP to the registered mobile number of the user which is valid for a short duration. The number has to be entered to successfully authenticate the user.
–   Biometric authentication: With this method of authentication, each user is identified by unique biological features such as fingerprints or iris patterns.
–   Multi-factor authentication: This form of authentication involves using more than one of the preceding modes of authentication. The choice of authentication mode may be made by the entity requesting authentication.

The Aadhaar e-KYC is currently one of the largest e-authentication modules employed by the UIDAI. It is an online, paperless and biometric authentication of one's identity through data present in the Aadhaar system. The current KYC norms involve collecting and storing attested copies of physical identity documents. However, e-KYC does away with the hassles of collection, attestation and storage of KYC information by replacing it with biometric authentication. The number of e-KYC transactions has risen rapidly, and the number of daily transactions is around 8.3 million to date.

The Aadhaar has also evolved into a complete digital identity program for all those who possess the 12-digit number. The Government of India, in many recent initiatives, has mandated that Aadhaar holders link various data points to the Aadhaar:
–   All permanent account numbers (tax IDs) must be linked to the Aadhaar. This was done to address the problem of one individual holding multiple tax IDs.

- All mobile numbers (both existing mobile numbers and newly issued numbers) are expected to be linked to Aadhaar. New mobile numbers are made available with biometric authentication through Aadhaar. This has helped to weed out mobile numbers being operated by unscrupulous individuals. It also helps solve the problem of SIM cards being owned and operated under fake names.
- New and existing bank accounts are to be linked to Aadhaar. This helps in ensuring effective transfers of social security payments and preventing money laundering.
- Mutual fund and insurance portfolios are to be linked to Aadhaar.
- Sales or purchases of property are linked to Aadhaar (although this is prevalent only in certain states).[19]

With so much information flowing into the Aadhaar system, we can see that an enormous amount of data is being collected, and the digital identity is created based on the transaction patterns and behavior of the individual. The Government of India has mandated that this data be used to prevent tax evasion, money laundering and other unscrupulous activities.

The Role of Technology in the Authentication Process

To understand the authentication process, let us look at an example of how it works with a UIDAI-registered device, such as the Samsung SM-T1161R. The Samsung India Identity SDK (software development kit) provides a set of application programming interfaces (APIs) are used to enable the capture, encryption, and authentication of iris data in accordance with UIDAI specifications. The authentication process works as follows:

1. The Samsung India Identity SDK provides a set of application programming interfaces that is capable of capturing user iris scan data and ensuring its encryption in accordance to UIDAI specifications. The iris data is captured by the registered device and is encrypted.
2. The encrypted iris data is then transferred to an AUA (Authentication User Agency) or ASA (Authentication Service Agency), which acts as an intermediary between the registered service provider and the UIDAI authentication server.
3. Upon receipt of this encrypted data, the UIDAI authentication server first validates the license of the ASA or AUA and then matches the biometric data provided against the data present in the UIDAI database.
4. Upon successful matching, the UIDAI authentication server relays a Yes/No message to the AUA or ASA, which then relays this message to the registered service provider.

The Issues and Concerns Regarding Aadhaar

Considering the enormous amount of data that the government has accumulated through this initiative, questions are being raised about data privacy and data security. Many experts argue that such profiling will turn India into a surveillance state. Many have also raised concerns regarding the security of the data considering the recent reports that surfaced about data leaks and hacking of the Aadhaar database. Recently, news surfaced that the Aadhaar data of close to 1.4 million residents had been leaked by a social security official. A major newspaper also went on to state that they were able to purchase Aadhaar data for a price. The newspaper also was able to procure software to print their own Aadhaar cards. The sources of this software were different private agencies contracted by the government to process new Aadhaar registrations. The government in response to such challenges has launched a process that enables every Aadhaar holder to generate and use a virtual ID, instead of providing the 12-digit number.

How Successful Has Aadhaar Been?[20]

Within a short timeframe, the Aadhaar enrollment has reached close to 1.2 billion Indian residents. It has given Indians a new super digital identity that encompasses other identification documents and access to various government services and social security benefits.

Close to 2.65 million transactions were processed in the month of January 2017 through the Aadhaar Pay app.

The implementation of Aadhaar has simplified various government services, and this is expected to enhance service delivery to citizens. Aadhaar also has helped to increase the efficiency of the Public Distribution System which has saved the government vast sums of money.

From a financial inclusion perspective, Aadhaar has helped ensure that most Indians today have a bank account. Through the Aadhaar e-KYC setup, opening an account has become hassle free and completely online. The Aadhaar-based Direct Benefit Transfer scheme also has assisted in raising the trust of citizens in the government by ensuring regular and timely transfers of subsidies and welfare payments.

Endnotes
1 Rouse, Margaret. "Digital Identity," TechTarget. August 2017. Accessed September 2018. https://whatis.techtarget.com/definition/digital-identity
2 Ibid.
3 Ibid.
4 The World Bank. "1.1 Billion 'Invisible' People without ID Are Priority for New High Level Advisory Council on Identification for Development." October 12, 2017. Accessed September 2018. http://www.

worldbank.org/en/news/press-release/2017/10/12/11-billion-invisible-people-without-id-are-priority-for-new-high-level-advisory-council-on-identification-for-development

5 World Economic Forum. "Platform for Good Digital Identity" 2018. Accessed July 2018. https://www.weforum.org/projects/digital-identity

6 Dr. Ina Nikolova. "What Are the 5 Key Components of IAM In the Digital Transformation Process?" Accessed July 2018. https://www.patecco.com/en/blog/what-are-the-5-key-components-of-iam-in-the-digital-transformation-process

7 Wallix. "Privileged Access Management for dummies: PAM Definition." June 2016. Accessed July 2018. http://blog.wallix.com/privileged-access-definition-pam-for-dummies

8 Mara Hvistendahl. "Inside China's vast new experiment in social ranking." December 2017. Accessed July 2018. https://www.wired.com/story/age-of-social-credit/

9 Andre Durand. "Customer identities are the common denominator in changing business models." March 2017. Accessed July 2018. https://www.pingidentity.com/en/company/blog/posts/2017/customer-identities-are-the-common-denominator-in-changing-business-models.html

10 IAM Insights. "Digital Identities—The Opportunities and Challenges." April 2016. Accessed July 2018. https://www.safewhere.com/digital-identity-the-potential-and-challenges/

11 https://en.wikipedia.org/wiki/Aadhaar

12 https://www.oecd.org/gov/innovative-government/India-case-study-UAE-report-2018.pdf

13 GSMA. "Aadhar: Inclusive by design. A look at India's national identity program and its role in the JAM trinity. March 2017. Accessed July 2018. https://www.gsma.com/mobilefordevelopment/wp-content/uploads/2017/03/gsma-aadhaar-report-270317.pdf

14 https://pmjdy.gov.in/

15 https://www.icicibank.com/Personal-Banking/payments/aadhaar-pay.page

16 Shweta Banerjee, Social Protection group, The World Bank Group. "Aadhar: Digital inclusion and public services in India." December 2015. Accessed July 2018. http://pubdocs.worldbank.org/en/655801461250682317/WDR16-BP-Aadhaar-Paper-Banerjee.pdf

17 http://www.e-mudhra.com/aadhaar-ekyc.html

18 https://uidai.gov.in/aadhaar_dashboard/ekyc_trend.php

19 https://economictimes.indiatimes.com/wealth/personal-finance-news/these-services-need-to-be-linked-with-aadhaar-and-here-are-the-deadlines/articleshow/62039634.cms

20 https://www.paisabazaar.com/aadhar-card/aadhaar-authentication/

Sriram Srinivasan *is a Private Banking Associate at Bank of Singapore. He holds a master's degree in Wealth Management from Singapore Management University. He was previously a commercial banker with Deutsche Bank in Bangalore. He also holds an MBA and undergraduate certification in Banking and Finance from prestigious universities in India. He is passionate about equity investing, fintech and politics.*

Chapter 5
The Importance of Cloud Computing

The *cloud* refers to software and computing services that run on a remote computer and are available over the internet using a web browser or applications on your computing device. The term *cloud* is new, but not the concept. Actually, it is a twist on an old practice. Remote computing is nothing new. Many organizations operate a data center that provides software and computing services throughout the organization over a *virtual private network* (VPN). Software resides on an application server—not on local computers throughout the organization. Data resides on a database server in the data center. All computing services are provided by the data center.

Cloud computing is provided by a vendor such as Amazon Cloud Drive, Microsoft OneDrive, Apple iCloud, Google Drive, Dropbox, Yahoo Mail, and Netflix. Many cloud computing services offer storage for data and applications. Some offer their own applications such as Microsoft Office and Google Docs, enabling collaboration on projects within and outside the organization. Data and applications are available 24/7 over the internet. The cloud vendor is responsible for maintaining the cloud environment—the data center, servers, network connections, power, and applications.

In theory, there is no end to the cloud. The organization can use as much or as little space as necessary—for a fee. The cloud vendor has computing resources ready to meet practically any demand for service. Cloud computing is any pay-per-use service in real-time over the internet that extends an organization's existing capabilities at a fraction of the cost of expanding a data center.

Rather than acquiring new servers, networks, and related applications within the organization's data center, the organization uses a cloud service. The cloud provider is an aggregator of computing services from other vendors, offering one-stop shopping for an organization. The benefits of the cloud are seen as a viable alternative to operating a data center. It is estimated that every piece of data—voice, data, and images—that is transmitted over a public network at some point is in the cloud.

It Can Rain Too

The cloud seems to be the utopia to all the organization's computing needs. However, there is a downside. Cloud-based applications and data require internet access. No internet connection means no access to applications and data. Furthermore, technical issues affecting the cloud vendor's data center become the organization's issues too, because when the cloud goes down, the organization no longer has access to applications and data. Compounding the problem is that the organization has no control over rectifying these issues. Unlike with the organization's data center where

DOI 10.1515/9781547400904- 005

the organization controls every facet of resolving technical issues, the cloud provider is responsible for fixing the problem.

Organizations that place their data and applications in the cloud are at risk of losing control. Data and applications that reside in the cloud vendor's data center are out of the organization's control. The organization must trust the cloud vendor to provide adequate security measures to protect the organization's data. Furthermore, the organization must determine if the organization itself can be sustained if the cloud vendor denies access to the data and applications.

Governmental Access

An organization's data is always at risk for being legally accessed by governmental agencies. The government typically gains access by serving legal notice to the organization that holds the data. The organization itself receives such notice if the data is held in the organization's data center. What happens if the data is held at the cloud vendor's data center? Must the cloud vendor hand over the data without notifying the organization? These are much-debated questions.

An organization can expect privacy unless data is disclosed to a third party. This is referred to as the *third-party doctrine*. A cloud vendor providing cloud computing services can be considered a third party; the government may search the organization's data with the proper legal papers and issue an indefinite gag order to the cloud vendor, preventing the cloud vendor from disclosing that the government searched the data.

Cloud vendors are taking steps to address privacy concerns. Microsoft relocated its cloud servers to data centers in Germany and transferred both physical and logical access to cloud data to a data trustee. This greatly reduces Microsoft's access to customer data. However, the privacy debate continues. Microsoft reported that within an 18-month period, the government made 5,600 legal demands of Microsoft to provide customer data stored on remote servers. Half required Microsoft not to inform the customer of the search indefinitely.

The Cloud and Data Science

Data science, commonly referred to as *big data*, focuses on making sense out of large amounts of data by finding data patterns that can be used to develop predictions. Data scientists were relatively stifled by technological limitations available to extract, store, process, and analyze huge data sets. The computing power available within an organization lacked the processing power, production environment, memory, and storage to effectively study sizable amounts of data.

Data scientists hit an electronic wall. The local computing environment was not scalable. Data grew on a magnitude scale monthly while the organization's computing technology remained stagnant, and resources for big data analysis competed head-to-head with mission-critical applications. They simply ran out of computing resources. Living within the allocated computing technology required big data analysis to be performed in steps—loading and unloading and loading data and applications resulted in reliability errors and performance degradation. Compounding the challenge was the heavily data processing requirements to clean the data for analysis and the need to test and retest fine-tuning data models using the massive amount of data.

The cloud radically changed data science by removing the electronic wall that held back the big data revolution that is driving machine-learning and other eye-opening knowledge. The cloud offers practically unlimited scalability, using the most powerful computing environments and technology that is available all at a cost that most organizations can afford. As large amounts of data compound monthly, the organization acquires additional cloud services to store and process the data at an incremental cost without the hassle of investing in new equipment, expanding the data center, and hiring staff.

There are cloud providers who have services especially designed to manage big data. They have the capability to acquire, clean, store, and share the data throughout the organization, and the resources to develop, test, and implement data models based on big data. The cloud enables data scientists to quickly build prototypes without worrying about computing assets. Once proven, the full version of the data model can be implemented in the cloud.

The Cloud Services

Cloud technology is the latest in the evolution that began with stand-alone computing. Late in the last century, computing devices were connected to servers using client/server architecture. The computing device, called a *client*, requested services from a remote server over a local area network, known today as an *intranet*. Services included applications, data, and processing. In client/server architecture, some processing is performed locally on the computing device while processing required by all clients is processed on one or more common remote servers.

Client/server architecture is referred to as *two-tier architecture*, with the client as one tier and the server as the second tier. Multiple-tier architectures are commonplace today. For example, a client accesses a remote application and the remote application accesses a database. This is three-tier architecture: client, application, and database. Client/server architecture has a major disadvantage (Figure 5.1). There are no economies of scale. Investments in new infrastructure and new software licenses are necessary to expand capacity.

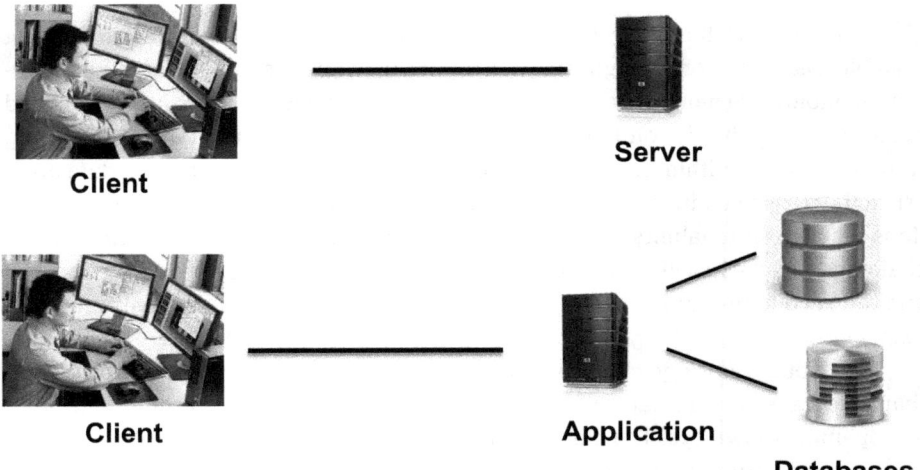

Figure 5.1: Client-server lacks economies of scale

There are three types of services offered by a cloud provider. These are:

1. *Software as a Service* (SaaS): With SaaS, the cloud provider offers access to applications hosted by the cloud provider using a web browser point of access. The cloud provider is responsible for deploying, managing, and maintaining applications. Examples are Google Apps, Dropbox, and Salesforce. Organizations subscribe to the service. The cost of ownership of applications is covered by the cloud provider.

2. *Platform as a Service* (PaaS): With PaaS, the cloud provider offers the platform that can be used to develop and deploy applications. The cloud provider offers the organization the operating system and related hardware and network infrastructures to develop and run the organization's own applications. The organization focuses on building the applications. The cloud provider offers the tools and scalability to enable the organization to quickly respond to changing markets by requesting access to additional resources from the cloud provider. Examples are: OpenShift, Heroku, and Google App Engine.

3. *Infrastructure as a Service* (IaaS): With IaaS, the cloud provider offers the basic infrastructure building blocks to the organization, enabling the organization to assemble computing resources on-demand. The cloud provider enables the organization to build a virtual data center. Components of the virtual data center can be accessed by the organization as if it were the organization's traditional data center. However, there is no need for the organization to invest in the data center. It simply pays for components as needed. The cloud provider is responsible for management and maintenance of the physical data center. IaaS gives the organization virtual control over servers, storage, and processing. Examples are:

Exoscale, Navisite, and SoftLayer. IaaS is sometimes referred to as *utility comput-ing* because it provides a utility-type service to organizations.

The Private Cloud

A *private cloud* is very similar to the traditional data center architecture in that ser-vices are provided only to entities within the organization. There are no commercial clients. An *entity* is a division of the organization, sometimes considered as inter-nal clients to the group that operates the private cloud. Internal clients don't have control over the cloud environment. Control resides with the group that operates the private cloud.

The private cloud operation creates a virtual environment for each internal client using a pool of computing resources. The group operating the private cloud recon-figures computing resources to respond to the needs of internal clients. The private cloud can be created in one of three ways. The organization can own and operate com-puting resources that create the cloud—the traditional data center environment. The organization can outsource the private cloud to a vendor where computing resources provided by the vendor are solely used by the organization and not shared with other organizations.

A hybrid is another option—referred to as *cloud bursting*—where primary computing resources are owned and operated by the organization and additional on-demand computing resources are provided by a cloud vendor. Non-sensitive computing assets are moved to the public cloud, freeing private cloud resources for sensitive computing assets.

Private clouds are ideal for organizations that require secured processing and storage because the organization is in total control of security. Communication with the private cloud is conducted over private-leased, secured lines with encryption. This offers greater security than is provided in the public cloud—all computing devices in the private cloud operate behind the organization's firewall and applications and personnel are under the organization's control. No resources are shared outside the organization.

Private clouds come at a cost because there is one client—the organization—who underwrites the entire operation. Economies of scale are limited to internal clients, compared to the many clients associated with a public cloud operation. The organiza-tion can allocate computing resources quickly since it controls cloud resources. Using a public cloud may delay allocation because an agreement to use those resources must be reached between the organization and the cloud vendor.

The Public Cloud

The *public cloud* offers computing resources to the public over the internet to individuals and organizations who do not require the security provided by a private cloud. The public cloud offers computing resources on demand for typically a monthly fee. Computing resources can include expensive sophisticated applications, processing devices, and storage devices that otherwise might be out of the financial reach of the client. Access is seamless from anywhere at any time. Clients pay for servers they need for as long as they need those services.

The public cloud offers economies of scale because expensive cloud infrastructure, computing devices, and applications are shared among many organizations. The public cloud vendor can provide state-of-the-art centralized operations with redundant architectures and environments because costs are leveraged among its client base. Redundancy enables the vendor to balance loads, which provides an expected level of services regardless of demand. Multiple computing devices and cloud operation centers located in multiple states and countries guarantee continuous availability of the cloud to all clients as long as the client has internet access.

The cloud vendor accepts the operational risks associated with the cloud. It ensures that services are available; applications and operating systems are updated; and computing resources are maintained to meet the client's and regulatory requirements. Furthermore, the cloud vendor incorporates sophisticated security measures that might be out-of-reach in a private cloud environment. The cloud vendor also has certified full-time staff with skill sets that that may not be economically available to organizations that operate a private cloud.

Hybrid Clouds

A *hybrid cloud* is a combination of a private cloud and a public cloud. The private cloud is used for sensitive processing and the public cloud is used for non-sensitive processing. Access to both clouds is seamless by using a browser. Users gain access through a browser-based portal that redirects requests to either the private or public cloud. A key benefit of a hybrid cloud is the private cloud can be used to satisfy regulatory requirements for secure processing and storage of data, while the public cloud provides the flexibility to meet growing demands.

There are a number of ways to implement a hybrid cloud. An organization can use two cloud vendors to supply the cloud—one for the private cloud and the other for the public cloud. Alternatively, a cloud vendor can provide a complete service where the private cloud computing resources are not shared and the public cloud computing resources are shared.

Still another option is for the organization to internally provide a private cloud and rely on a vendor to provide a public cloud. The drawback to implementing an internal private cloud is limited scalability. The organization would need to acquire more computing resources to expand. A cloud vendor needs only to reallocate existing resource to the private cloud (Figure 5.2).

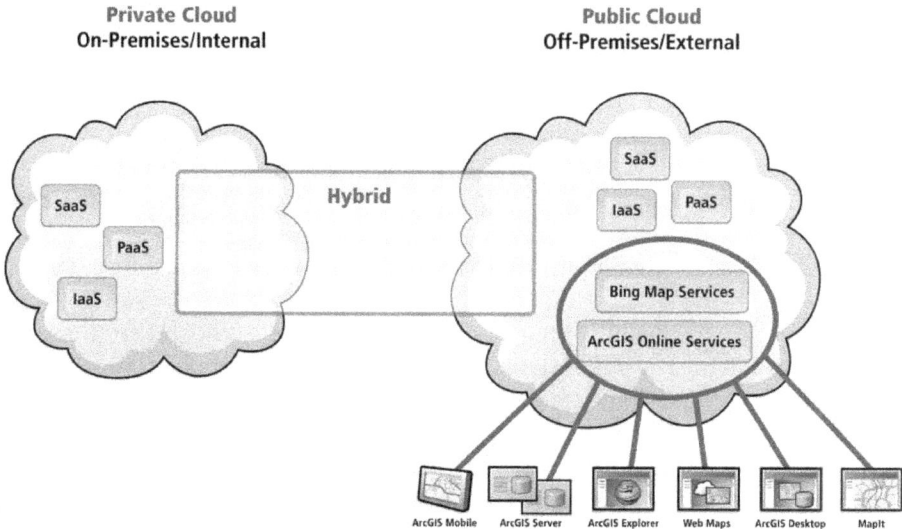

Figure 5.2: A cloud vendor offers flexibility

Why Implement a Cloud?

The cloud offers many advantages for an organization that is growing and whose computing resource requirements fluctuate. The cloud provides the operational agility to meet growing demands with a sound economic foundation.

- Easy to increase computing capacity.
- Scalability both up and down.
- A competitive advantage by increasing/decreasing computing capacity as needed without incurring long-term financial obligations.
- Taking advantage of the latest technology without the burden of acquiring scarce resources.
- Reduced time to market. Start-up time for a new initiative might require nine months to acquire computing resources. The cloud offers computing resources within days.
- Disaster recovery. The cloud provider has the computing resources and expertise to handle recovery in a disaster. A cloud provider typically has replicated cloud data centers throughout the United States and outside the country.

- Frees real estate. The cloud is off the organization's premises. Space used for computing resources can be reallocated for other purposes.
- No upfront investment in computing resources. The organization pays for computing resources using a subscription model.
- No maintenance. The cloud vendor takes care of software updates and security patches as part of their core business.
- No longer an information technology organization. Information technology has become a necessary part of the organization's operation, although information technology is not the organization's core business. The cloud shifts information technology to a cloud vendor whose core business is the cloud. The cloud vendor's investment in cloud technology is an investment in the cloud vendor's core business.
- Shared resources. The cloud enables the staff to collaborate in real-time, increasing productivity.
- Balanced work schedule. The cloud enables the staff to collaborate from anywhere in real time over the internet. Cloud vendors also offer cloud apps that can be used on mobile computing devices, giving staff access to the organization's computing resources while on the go.
- Reduces the carbon footprint. Rather than the organization maintaining computing resources that have a large carbon footprint, the organization shares those computing resources with other organizations in the cloud.
- Staff focuses on business. In many organizations, the information technology staff account for 25 percent of the employees. The organization frees up headcount by moving to the cloud. Fewer information technology staff are required.
- Hidden security. Staff can work with cloud-based applications that automatically save files to the cloud rather than on a local computing device. Files are never lost even if the local computing device crashes.

Why Not Use the Cloud?

The cloud is less than a perfect technological solution to computing. Here are common disadvantages:

- Connectivity. The cloud internally and externally depends on network operations. Internally, the cloud provision connects its data centers located around the world over a network—the same public network that is used to connected everyone else. The organization connects to the cloud over the same network. Any network issues are also a cloud issue.
- Traffic volume. The public network is a multi-lane highway that can handle very high volumes of traffic. An off-ramp is a narrower roadway to a cloud provider's site. A traffic jam occurs unless the cloud provider manages the load to its sites as

demand for its cloud services increase. Failure to do so results in slow response time, which is something an organization doesn't expect from the vendor.

- Software incompatibility. The presumption is that applications run on all computing devices, which is not necessarily the case. An organization may be using older applications and databases that are not compatible with computing resources offered by the cloud provider. The organization's custom applications and third-party applications are built using a framework such as Java, C++, MySQL, and Oracle that require frequent upgrades, both on computing devices accessing the application and computing devices running the application. Cloud vendors are noted for installing upgrades faster than the organizations that use their services. Some upgrades require upgrades to both computing devices. Failure to upgrade prevents access to the application. Likewise, some upgrades may not be compatible with an organization's applications, preventing the application from running in the cloud.
- Support. An advantage of using the cloud is to offload responsibility for most of the organization's computing responsibilities to the cloud vendor. The presumption is that it is economical for the cloud vendor to hire specialists since the expense can be allocated to other customers who also require those services. However, legacy applications that run an organization can become problematic since other organizations may not require the same specialist to maintain the application. The cloud vendor may refuse to accept the application or charge a premium to accept it.
- Security. Responsibility for providing cybersecurity moves from the organization to the cloud provider. The cloud provider has multiple data centers around the world, each connected to customers and to each other. If a security gap exists in any of the data centers or connections, then it is highly likely that the vendor's entire infrastructure is susceptible to the breach. An organization typically has one or a few data centers, decreasing points of failure compared with the cloud vendor.
- Dependency. By switching computing responsibility from the organization to the cloud vendor, the organization's sustainability is dependent on the sustainability of the cloud vendor. The organization cannot change cloud vendors quickly. If the relationship between the organization and the cloud vendor breaks down, the organization needs to have a contingency that enables the organization to move its cloud business to another cloud vendor with minimum interruptions. The breakdown in the relationship may not have anything to do with providing services. For example, the cloud vendor may be taken over by another cloud vendor, which might result in the organization sharing computing resources with competitors.

Mitigating Risk

Although computing risks seem to be offloaded to the cloud provider, the organization remains at risk. The organization remains exposed. However, steps can be taken to mitigate risk by carefully selecting a cloud provider. Here are steps that need to be taken (Figure 5.3).

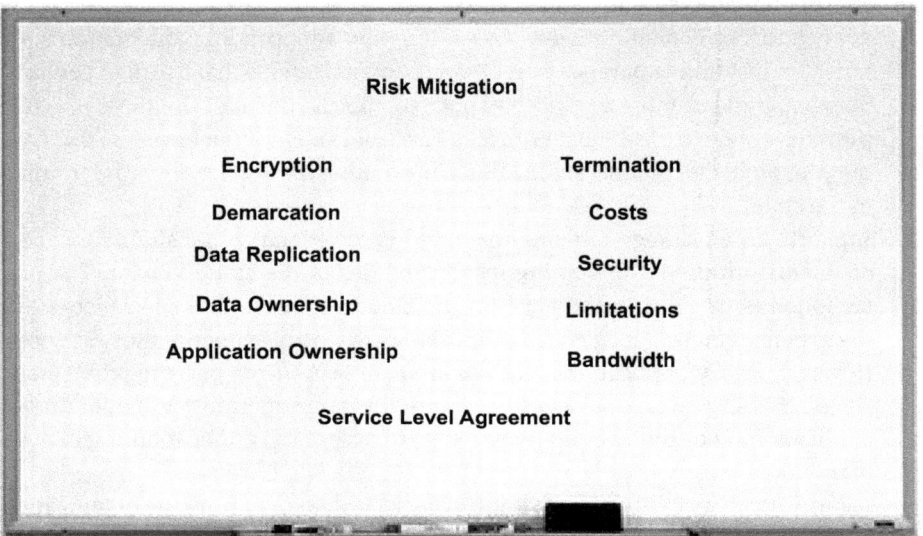

Figure 5.3: Cloud risks to mitigate in a SLA

Encryption. The organization's data must be encrypted at all times. AES-256 encryption is the most desirable because it has never been broken.

Demarcation. The cloud is a multi-tenant environment. All clients can share resources. Therefore, the cloud provider must demonstrate how the organization's applications and data are segregated from other customer's applications and data. There should be an electronic or physical wall between clients. The cloud provider may cage-in computing devices for each client and require a separate key to unlock the cage.

Data replication. The cloud provider must show the organization how data is replicated and restored as part of the organization's and cloud provider's data recovery plan, should the cloud provider's facilities experience a catastrophe.

Data ownership. Make sure it is clear to the cloud provider that the organization owns the data and the format of the data. The cloud provider is simply providing storage and applications to manipulate the data.

Application ownership. Make sure it is clear who owns the rights to the application. Let's say that the cloud provider licenses a SQL *database management system* (DBMS). Queries are used to interact with the DBMS. Who owns the queries? This is especially important if the cloud provider's staff writes queries for the organization. The sustainability of the organization may depend on those queries.

Termination. Negotiate terms of terminating the relationship prior to engaging the cloud provider. Termination terms clearly define who owns what and the process for moving the organization's owned resources to another cloud provider. Furthermore, the terms of termination should clearly explain how applications and data residing on the cloud provider's computing devices will be destroyed after they are moved to another cloud provider. Termination terms also identify the conditions under which the relationship can be terminated. If and when the time comes to move, simply execute terms of the termination agreement.

Costs. Identify all costs associated when engaging the cloud provider. There should be no surprises or hidden costs. Costs are initial setup costs; ongoing costs; maintenance costs; change costs; and termination costs. Initial setup costs involve expenses to transfer the organization's computing operations to the cloud provider. Ongoing costs are usually included in the monthly fee. Maintenance costs involve routine upgrades to applications and databases. Will the organization be charged a fee for moving data from the cloud to its own facility? Change costs involve non-routine enhancements to the cloud services, such as new applications, new databases, and services not covered in the original agreement. It is important to come to terms about these changes before they occur so there are no surprises at the time of the change. Termination costs are expenses associated with termination of the agreement, including transferring applications and data to another cloud vendor.

Security. Be sure that the cloud provider upgrades security to meet the organization's requirements. The organization should set minimum security requirements and not waiver from them.

Limitations. Ensure that the cloud provider has the computing resources and staff that they promise in their sales presentation. Trust but verify. The organization is buying experience and the cloud provider's organization should reflect that experience. Years of operation are not the only criteria to consider. The cloud provider's infrastructure must reflect current technology.

Bandwidth. The cloud provider must have sufficient bandwidth today to meet demand for the next five years. Think of bandwidth as highway lanes. There should be sufficient lanes on the electronic highway—both the off ramp from the internet and internal highways—to maintain an acceptable response time. Many cloud providers are in a Catch-22 situation. Do they invest in a super-speed infrastructure hoping to attract clients or build the super-speed infrastructure as they bring on clients? The organization should be looking for a cloud provider who has the financial resources to build a super-speed infrastructure first. How much bandwidth is needed? There are tools available such as the Microsoft Assessment and Planning Toolkit that help an organization assess its needs.

Service-level agreement. The service-level agreement defines the relationship between the organization and the cloud provider. It contains expectations, limitations, liabilities, responsibilities, termination, fees, and other understandings that govern the relationship between both parties.

The Cloud Life Cycle

The cloud offers many options from à la carte to full-service. The cloud life cycle process helps to decide which options to choose. There are eight steps in the cloud life cycle process.

1. Define the purpose. Decide the organization's requirements first. The cloud can meet a variety of needs once those needs are identified. An organization experiencing a surge can use the cloud to quickly expand its capabilities practically overnight. An organization that hasn't kept pace with technology can use the cloud to become current with technology to operate the organization. Still other organizations use the cloud to expand services to customers. For example, Adobe produces many creative applications, originally selling each product separately. The cloud is now used to provide customers access to all their creative applications online for one monthly subscription fee.

2. Define the hardware. The cloud vendor offers a variety of hardware to run an organization's applications, data, and computing operations.

3. Define storage service. Storage is the place in the cloud in which you house applications and data. Vendors offer different services that are optimized for backing up applications and data or archiving it.

4. Define the network. Decide on the requirements for communicating with the cloud. Factors to consider are security; amount of network traffic generated by the organization, such as data, voice, and video; and transfer speeds.

5. Define security. Security factors are authentication, authorization, encryption at rest, and encryption in transit.

6. Define management processes and tools. Management processes and tools are used to give the organization control over its cloud assets. These include monitoring activities and managing applications, data residing in the cloud, and developing and deploying applications to the cloud.

7. Define building and testing requirements. The cloud is more than a remote data center. The cloud can be the organization's computing environment within which developers build and test applications. Identifying the organization's needs to continue creating and maintaining applications in the cloud helps to select the best vendor and services to use for the organization.

8. Define analytics. Analytics are used to monitor operations and provide decision support information to assist management in making decisions. Vendors are able to provide an assortment of analytical tools that can provide instant results and can respond to any query for information. The organization must identify its analytical requirements when selecting a vendor.

Cloud Architecture

The cloud architecture is a service-oriented architecture where the focus is for the cloud vendor to provide a wealth of services to customers. Each customer picks services that augment its organization's operations. Customers pay only for services that they use. The vendor's objective is to identify needs and provide services to meet the needs of its customers. The vendor then leverages the costs of development, operations, and maintenance of each microservice across customers who subscribe to the microservice.

A key element of the cloud architecture is microservices used to develop an application (Figure 5.4). The microservices concept has been seen elsewhere in computing such as with the Unix operating system and web services. The basis of microservices is to create self-contained mini-applications called *services* that do something very well. Each performs a granular function that can be assembled with other microservices to form an application (Figure 5.4).

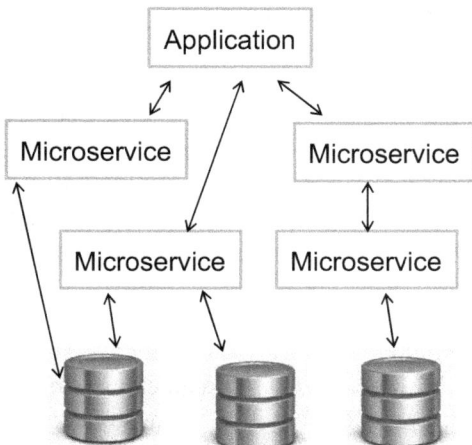

Figure 5.4: Microservices in a cloud architecture

Think of a microservice as an *event handler*. An event handler is a common structure in a Windows-like operating environment in which there are many events happening at the same time. An event handler is a self-contained function that responds to a specific event. For example, in a Windows-like operating environment there are multiple applications appearing on the screen. When the user resizes the window of an application, all other applications need to adjust their screen to accommodate the change. Each application has a function called an event handler that contains code that resizes its window. Microservices are like event handlers, except the microservice is outside the application and is called in response to events occurring within the application or with any application that uses the microservice.

Let's say an application needs to process credit card payments. Instead of embedding code that processes credit card payments into the application—and other applications that need to do the same—a microservice that processes credit card payments is created and is used by applications that need to perform this task. Developers need to call the microservice, provide it with necessary information, and process data returned by the microservice.

Each microservice is developed independently of other microservices to meet the needs of vendors in the cloud community. However, each has an *application program interface* (API) that is shared with developers. The API describes the microservice function; information that is needed to perform the function; any codes to turn on or off sub-features of the function; instructions on how to call the microservice; and instructions on how to interpret values returned by the microservice.

The microservice is maintained by a development team. Upgrades are made usually without the knowledge of developers who use the microservice unless the change affects the API. For example, a change in credit card processing is implemented immediately and brings all applications that use the microservice current. One change instantaneously occurs in many applications.

Furthermore, a microservice may be assembled from other microservices. For example, processing a credit card requires sub-processes such as authorizing access to perform the process; access secure information relating to the purchase from a database; and updating activity logs. Each of these might be a microservice that can be accessed by other applications aside from processing a credit card. The idea is that a microservice can be called from anywhere and from any application that is authorized to use the microservice.

There is a tendency to associate microservices with a vendor, but that's too narrow a scope to view microservices. Keep in mind that the cloud can be a private cloud, public cloud, or a hybrid of both public and private. An application can be configured to use microservices available on a private and public cloud—and clouds offered by different vendors.

Microservices must have a product owner who is responsible for maintaining the microservices and upgrade them based on feedback from developers. Microservices must be organized within a library management system, making it easy for developers to locate microservices that can be incorporated into their application.

Serverless Computing

Another element of the cloud architecture is serverless computing. When developing and deploying an application, the organization needs to consider the computing resources necessary to run the application. Computing resources include various hardware and software components. At times, developers are limited to building an application that can run on the existing computing resources. Other times, developers have to estimate computing resources needed to run the application, and then the organization needs to allocate the finances to acquire those resources. Furthermore, the organization has to allocate computing resources among applications.

The cloud practically eliminates the challenges of building an application to run in the organization's computing environment by giving developers the freedom to design an application without consideration of computing resources. In another words, developers and the organization are working with *serverless computing*, which is computing with a virtually endless availability of hardware and software to run an application. Yes, applications require computing resources, including servers. However, the cloud vendor has what appears to be all the computing power an organization would ever require. Therefore, it seems as if the cloud is serverless.

The cloud vendor offers computing resources on an as-needed basis. Let's say an application requires heavy data crunching, but only occasionally. The organization pays for the computing resources for those moments. There is no idling time. The organization no longer needs to acquire the computing power to crunch the data. Computing power is acquired just when it is required—and the acquisition is automatic once the application is configured for the cloud. The operation switches to the needed computing resources behind the scenes.

Developers and the organization focus on building the application using a blend of custom code and microservers without concern over limitations of computing resources. The cloud environment ensures that the necessary computing resources are available when required by the application. Configuration of the application for the cloud takes care of the fulfilling the computing requirements for the application.

DevOps

There are many scenarios that may be used inside or outside of a relationship with a cloud provider. The methods used may be the most important factor in your decision on a cloud vendor, multiple cloud vendors, or hybrids. How are you to run your sales organization, your backend services such as accounting and finance, your supply chain, your web presence and customer outreach, and your development needs on all of the above? Who provides these services?

Development operations (DevOps) is the process used in the cloud to eliminate barriers between applications' development and the operations that run the applications. DevOps replaces the traditional development and delivery methods that require many processes and staff who typically work in silos that impede the agility required for fast, economical responses to the organization's demands. This was commonly referred to as the *waterfall method*, in which one silo passed along the work to the next until the last silo deployed the application.

DevOps automate many of the processes required to move an application from development into production. Developers move applications into the cloud using DevOps tools directly. The cloud provider may then manage the process of functional and nonfunctional, unit and iterative testing (continuous testing); version control; configuration management; change management; and other functions necessary to deploy the application.

At each stage of implementation, the application is either returned to the previous stage if there are issues with the application or pushed forward in the deployment process. For example, the cloud returns the application to the developers if the application fails to pass a test. In doing so, DevOps refocuses the organization on developing the application while the cloud is focused on managing the process.

The DevOps process enables developers to build code and move it into building an application followed by automated testing, and then automatic deployment where the application is immediately used. The operations portion controls image management, rolling upgrades, security configuration, patch management, and environment configuration and deployment. The DevOps process brings a synergy of development staff and operations staff by forming a uniform process across silos, removing barriers that traditionally exist in the development and operational environments.

With the developer figuratively pressing the button in DevOps to test an application, testing then occurs that identifies policy issues, coding problems, quality problems, and issues regarding security. Test results are returned to the developer, who then modifies the code accordingly to address those problems. Results are returned by the DevOps process.

Before DevOps, the development team and operations team worked relatively independently, resulting in risky deployment of new applications because of a lack of collaboration and synchronization. This led to increased costs and challenges tracking changes to applications. DevOps enables both teams to work as one team, each looking to produce a quality application. There became a continual feedback cycle that uses automated DevOps processes to help the team monitor and share information about development. The entire process from development through operations becomes measurable, and any delays in the process clearly highlight the breakdown in the process, thereby making the delay actionable.

Key to DevOps is a lean methodology that automates hand-offs between development, operations, and customers. Prior to DevOps a "customer," internal or external, enters a ticket for a change to an application—perhaps through the help desk, which is part of operations. The operations team records and sends the request to the development team who works on the changes. The upgraded application is then sent to the testing team. The testing team needs operations to set up the testing environment. Testing also reviews security requirements, quality control, and compliance with the organization's policies. Results of testing are then sent to the development team. The application is then modified and returned to testing if changes are necessary. Otherwise, the application is turned over to operations to begin the deployment process. There are too many gaps and hand-offs where details can be overlooked. Furthermore, delays occur because each group knows about the application when it receives the application.

DevOps reduces the number of manual hand-offs by making all stakeholders aware of the status or the project beginning with the initial change request. Tools are used to automate the process where possible. In some situations the tool performs the process and in others the tool enables the team to efficiently perform its role. For example, DevOps typically produces real-time reports that help the teams improve the process. These include change fail rates that determine the rate at which changes fail to achieve the desired goal; mean time to recover (MTTR) that calculates the average time to recover from a failure; and lead time for change, which is the elapsed time from the time the request for change is received and the time the change is fully implemented.

DevOps uses selective automation to optimize the development and operations process. The goal is to automate the process of developing applications and getting the applications deployed so customers can use them. Each phase of the process is automatic to track the application and objectively measure the progress, giving feedback to both the development and operations teams who then improve the process. The DevOps process provides staff with tools needed to optimize their role in the development and operations process.

It is smart to begin adoption of DevOps with a pilot application that can be used as a proof of concept. This is often done in coordination with a cloud provider. The cloud vendor provides the tools and environment to implement the DevOps process. The pilot application uses a lean development and operations team of approximately ten staff compared with an estimate of thirty staff members for implementing a typical application. The goal is to demonstrate that the concept of DevOps is a viable option for the organization. Aspects of the DevOps process are proven and there is no need for the staff to reinvent it since they can leverage existing solutions. The pilot application also identifies training needs for the developers and the operations staff on how to use the DevOps tool to automate their processes.

Once the pilot application has successfully been developed and implemented using the DevOps process, the organization makes a conscious effort to break down silos and bring the entire staff onboard using the DevOps process. In its purest form, all applications going forward must use the DevOps process without exception. Applications should be designed around microservices. Rather than focusing on designing a complete application, developers should be focused on designing microservices that provide functionality that can be utilized by many applications.

The DevOps Maturity Model

Not all applications are suited for the cloud. The DevOps maturity model helps to identify applications that are appropriate for the cloud. The DevOps maturity model is used to categorize applications based on objective criteria that are organized into five levels. These are:

– Level One: Ad-Hoc Communication. There is no automation; no governance of the process; and no quality standards exist.
– Level Two: Controlled Communication and Collaboration. Automation is ad-hoc without a formal automation process. There are no governance standards and quality management is ad-hoc with no formal quality management plan in place.
– Level Three: Standard Communication Process. There is a standardized automation process in place and a standardized form of governance over the process. However, there are no quality standards in place.
– Level Four: Communication Metrics Exits for Improvement. Automation metrics are in place to measure progress in developing and deploying the application with application goals. There are also metrics to measure the effectiveness of governance over the process, and quality metrics are in place to measure improvement performance.
– Level Five: Constructive Communication Environment, Tools, and Processes. Optimization methods are in place to maximize throughput, govern the process, and provide continuous quality improvement.

Compliance

Depending on the business, organizations are governed by countless regulations. In the US, healthcare organizations must comply with the Health Insurance Portability and Accountability Act of 1996 (HIPAA) that requires the organization to protect health information. Public corporations must adhere to the Sarbanes–Oxley Act (SOX). Organizations that use information from European citizens must adhere to processes defined in the General Data Protection Regulation (GDPR). Failure to adhere to regulations exposes the organization to fines and possibly litigation.

The organization's data is in the cloud. It is critical that the cloud provider has the necessary measures in place to ensure that regulatory requirements are met. The organization needs to perform a detailed walkthrough of processes available in the cloud to provide the degree of compliance required by regulators. In addition to protecting data, the cloud provider must have tools in place for internal auditors and regulatory auditors to use to audit the organization's data to ensure regulatory compliance. The cloud provider and the organization must make sure data protection is compliant and both can prove it to regulators.

Cloud Security

The thought of placing the organization's mission-critical information and applications in an unseen, remote location called the cloud is frightening. All the confidential and innermost data required to run the organization seems to be somewhere in space—obviously not space, but in remote servers owned and operated by the cloud provider.

The reality is that the cloud is more secure than the organization's own facilities that house data and applications. The cloud provider has the resources and motivation to employ the latest security measures and to ensure that those measures are updated (at times, hourly). Many organizations see security as a necessary evil that is secondary to its business. This attitude usually exposes the organization to potential security faults.

"Trust, but verify" is the foundation of using any vendor. Trust that the cloud provider has the best security defenses in place, but also verify this fact before a cloud provider is engaged. Executives of the organization remain liable if a security breach occurs, even if it occurs in the cloud. Here are some data breaches:

- Denial of service. Denial of service occurs when services are cut off or in some way limited, often when a hacker floods the cloud's IP address with requests more than the cloud can process, resulting in decreased response time. The cloud provider must explain how it defends against such an attack.

- Encryption break-in. Breaking into an encrypted file is difficult—however, older encryption algorithms could be defeated. It is important to ensure that the cloud provider uses the latest encryption algorithms for files at rest and in-transit.

- Physical theft. By now you realize that data and applications don't reside in a cloud but on a server located in the cloud provider's data center. Visiting the data center provides the opportunity to assess the physical security policies and practices of the vendor.

- Ransomware. Ransomware is software that prevents access to applications and data (denial of service) by using encryption. Only the hacker has the ability to decipher it.

- Data theft. Employees from the organization and from the cloud provider have access to the organization's data. Assess what steps are employed by the cloud— and within the organization—to prevent such theft.

- Vulnerability exploitation. Operating systems, applications, and development tools are not perfect when it comes to security. Hackers are aware of this and exploit these vulnerabilities to gain access to information. The cloud provider— and the organization's applications—must be using the latest products that have removed these vulnerabilities. The old reliable sales management system, for example, may have known vulnerabilities that haven't been addressed. The cloud vendor may suggest that these be addressed or replace the system with new technology.

Levels of Security

A cloud provider typically has data center facilities in one or more regions, possibly in a region of the United States or in countries outside of the United States. The organization can select the region for its applications and data. Furthermore, the organization can have different regions used for specific applications and databases.

The organization can add a level of security by encrypting data on the client-side, where only the organization can decipher the data. This is in addition to encryption provided by the cloud vendor in-transit and at-rest in the vendor's facility. Even if data is intercepted, encryption makes the data useless to the hacker who gains access to this data.

Application-level security focuses on preventing unauthorized access to the application. The organization and the cloud provider should have logs that indicate when the application is accessed and the IDs and IP addresses that have access. Logs should also indicate all writing and reading of data with specific information to trace who had access or at least what computing device was used.

Another important security implementation is for the cloud provider to have *application programming interface* (API) logs. The cloud offers microservices that can be accessed from practically anywhere in the cloud. API logs record information about when the microservice was called and the application that called it. This enables the security staff to trace access back to the application if it was hacked.

Data import and export logs should also be in place by the cloud provider to record any large movement of data. Ideally, the cloud has an alert system that calls attention to unusual transfers of data. The security staff can immediately monitor and investigate the activity and possibly halt the transfer. Similar alerts should occur when there have been a set number of failed attempts to access the application or data. Alerts should also be sounded when access is attempted from an unexpected IP address. Alerts trigger a real-time response to a potential hack.

Object-level security is another area to focus on. Objects are a collection of data in a database. Security concerns are at the database level and at the data level. *Database-level security* centers on access of the database, while *data-level security* looks at access to specific types of data within the database. In addition to encryption, data can be limited by views of data. Based on authorization, the database management system can assemble virtual tables of data from tables in the database.

Platform-level security is a security process that prevents unauthorized access to the computing device such as computers, network services, application servers, and database servers. Without access, data and applications are secured. It is important to ensure that the cloud provider offers and implements all security levels to the product and the organization's applications and data.

Critical to successful security of the cloud is the organization's ability to manage security access. As employees are hired, terminated, and transferred into new roles, the organization must modify security access to the organization's computing resources. Some resources are internal and others are on the cloud. The cloud provider should offer a way for the organization to change security access settings for cloud resources quickly and in coordination with changes to internal security settings. Ideally, changes to the internal security settings should flow automatically to the cloud security settings.

An option to consider is acquiring security services from a third-party other than the cloud provider. Third-party vendors offer security services across cloud providers. This is a valuable service to consider, since organizations tend to use multiple cloud providers. These vendors have the knowledge to leverage the assets of each cloud provider to the advantage of the organization.

Jim Keogh is the author of over 85 books on networking, programming, project management, governance and other topics. He developed the electronic commerce track at Columbia University and was a team member who built one of the first Windows applications by a Wall Street firm that was featured by Bill Gates in 1986 on Windows on Wall Street. His book published in 2002, E-Mergers: Merging, Acquiring, and Partnering E-Commerce Businesses, *was ahead of its time.*

Chapter 6
Data Science and Big Data

Over the last decade, there has been a lot of hype about data science and big data. The hype has resulted in much excitement and has encouraged many students, researchers, academicians, and organizations to get interested in this subject. Organizations have become interested in using data science to reduce inefficiencies and generate growth. Students, researchers, and professionals have become interested in learning data science due to the exciting work in this subject. This also has created new career opportunities and new job titles such as "data scientists" and "data engineers." The Google Trends chart in Figure 6.1 indicates this hype. The trend clearly shows the increased interest in these search terms since 2014: data science, machine learning, artificial intelligence, deep learning and big data.[1] Furthermore, the trend has been rising recently and clearly, and search queries on "Machine Learning" have surpassed other terms and clearly show the increasing public interest. However, it would be unfair to say that all that the research in this domain has been carried out in last few years. Most of the research and algorithms in data science have resulted from decades of work by statisticians, mathematicians, and scientists.

The recent increase in the use of data science and machine learning algorithms is due to the availability of data and high computing power:
- Availability of data has increased usage of digital devices and services, and the rise in usage of sensors technology and connected objects has led to the generation of more and more data. Moreover, cheaper storage is available to collect and store the data.
- High computing power has become available at a low cost to process big datasets and use these complex algorithms.[2]

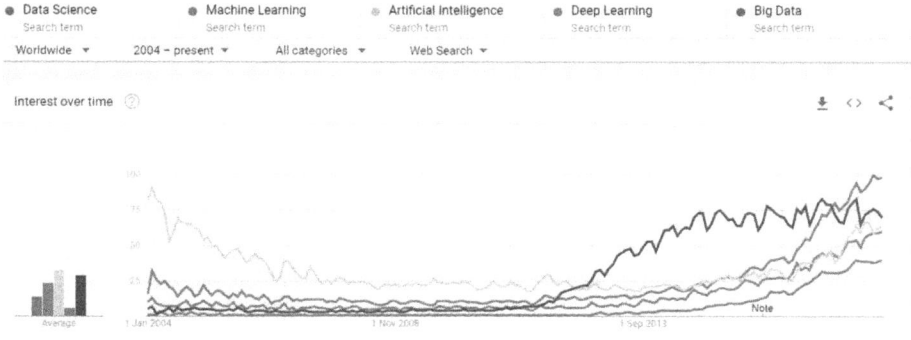

Figure 6.1: Google Trends, 2004–2018

DOI 10.1515/9781547400904- 006

In the midst of all this hype, there is a lot of confusion within this topic due to considerable noise in the literature. Many people get lost in the maze of terms like *data science*, *machine learning*, *deep learning*, and *big data* and do not know where to start. This chapter aims to clear up this confusion by providing a concise overview of data science and big data for business practitioners and discussing some commonly faced questions such as *What are data science, big data, AI, machine learning? What are the applications of data science used in industry? Moreover, what are the learnings and challenges of data science projects?* We introduce some basic data science concepts and big data tools, and discuss the typical data science project lifecycle in an organization.

Applications of Data Science and Big Data

Data science and big data are firmly embedded today in a lot of products and services that meet our daily needs. Some common examples of everyday applications of data science and big data include
- Biometrics, such as face and fingerprint recognition, for unlocking phones using our faces or finger
- Matching drivers and commuters to simplify booking rides using taxi or other ride apps
- Recommendations for watching videos and shopping on e-commerce websites
- Targeting, such as product advertisements based on search engine history

The exciting part is that most of these products have come into existence within the past one to two decades and have become a part of our daily routines. Such widespread use of data science has arguably led tech companies such as Google, Facebook, Amazon, Netflix, and others to proliferate and disrupt existing businesses, and to create new products and experiences for their customers.

Now, let us illustrate in more detail some industry use cases where data science and big data are used and have proven to be successful:
- Promotional emails and digital ads: On a typical day, people are contacted by several promotional email messages, SMS messages, or ads for things such as hotel discounts, airline vouchers, and shopping discounts. Sometimes, these promotional messages are targeted explicitly to specific customers. With the advent of the internet, companies have been gathering and storing extensive data related to their customers, such as customer demographics, past purchases, browsing patterns, and affluence level. They use this data to understand the characteristics of their customers and build machine learning models based on those characteristics to identify the likelihood of a customer responding to a particular ad at a given moment. Depending on this likelihood, customers are contacted with the right offers and in many cases even personalized offers. This

helps companies increase their sales by cross-selling and up-selling and also improve customer experience and engagement.

- Recommendation engines: Everyday, we come across various recommendation engines, such as for friends on Facebook, videos on YouTube, products on Amazon, and movies on Netflix. These systems show personalized offerings to people based on factors like their search histories and preferences. It is widely known that Amazon uses recommendation algorithms to personalize the shopping experience for each customer. Customers see recommended items that are based on their previous browsing behavior, product ratings, similar product purchases and other factors.[3] Along similar lines, Netflix recommends personalized content (movies and TV shows) based on a user's viewing history and ratings, the viewing history of similar users, and so forth. Furthermore, these recommendations are diverse, include new releases, and adapt with time in response to changing user preferences.[4]
- Risk management: Banks and credit card companies have used credit scores to evaluate loan or credit card applications for many years. Credit scores typically indicate the risk level of a customer, such as the likelihood of a customer to default. The model takes into consideration several parameters, such as payment history, length of credit history, inquiries, and income, to predict a customer's likelihood to default by comparing them to similar characteristics of other customers who have defaulted in the past.[5]
- Fraud detection: Fraud does not have a constant pattern. Fraud detection model is an evolving process, and by investigating and flagging more and more frequent cases, cases of fraud can be identified. In the case of credit card companies, investigating a large number of transactions one by one is not possible. Therefore, fraud detection models are used that can auto-approve legitimate transactions and raise alerts in case of any transactions that appear fraudulent. Events such as a sudden big purchase after many small purchases, purchases that do not fit the cardholder's profile, and unusual geographical locations can raise suspicion and block the transaction or card automatically.

What Is Data Science?

The term "data science" has been floating in various literature, journals and lecture notes for many years. In 1962, John Tukey, in his paper "The Future of Data Analysis," pointed to the existence of an unrecognized "science" that dealt with the subject of learning from the data.[6] Later in 2001, William S. Cleveland from Bell Labs proposed to expand the field of statistics to data analysis by emphasizing the importance of data preparation, computation, and presentation rather than statistical modeling.[7] However, the term "data science" gained widespread popularity more recently in 2012 through a *Harvard Business Review* article "Data Scientist: The Sexiest Job of the 21st Century."[8] In academia or industry, there is no single approved definition of data science because it is a broad term encompassing many domains, which leads to different views and ambiguity.

However, in simple terms, one can understand data science as an interdisciplinary field that uses the concepts of statistics, mathematics, computer science, and domain expertise to extract meaningful insights from data that can generate some business value. A data scientist is someone who is a specialist in these three domains and extracts meaning from the data by performing data and statistical analysis; building and applying machine learning models and algorithms; and visualizing, summarizing and communicating the results. Figure 6.2 describes a data scientist with skills from these three domains. In reality, it is hard to find someone who is a perfect data scientist—highly skilled in all three domains. Therefore, organizations build data science teams with people of complementary skillsets.

The terms, "business analytics" and "data analytics" have been used popularly over the years and are often confused with data science. Overall, there is a blurred difference between analytics and data science, and therefore these terms are sometimes used interchangeably. Our interpretation of this blurred difference is that the role of a business/data analyst involves using a lot of domain expertise and data analysis to generate insights from the data, whereas the role of a data scientist is slightly broader and includes machine learning modeling and programming. In many cases, the responsibilities of a data scientist also include data analysis, building models and developing those models into products or services.

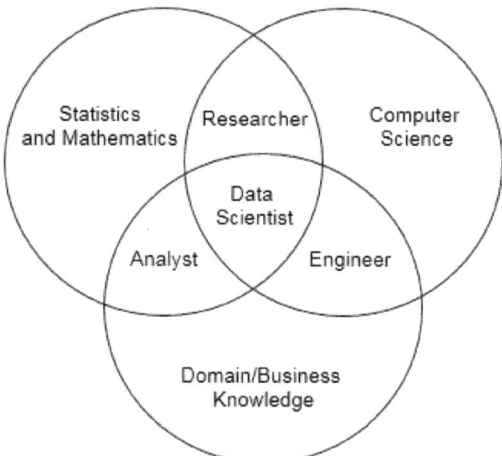

Source: Drew Conway's Data Science Venn Diagram. [Online]. Available: http://drewconway.com/zia/2013/3/26/the-data-science-venn-diagramce:

Figure 6.2: Data scientist Venn diagram

Machine Learning vs. Artificial Intelligence

Artificial intelligence (AI) is a field of computer science focused on making computers more intelligent so that they can imitate intelligent human behavior. AI is a medium to enable computers to learn and engage in human-like thought processes, such as learning, reasoning and self-correction. Traditionally, this involved hard-coding knowledge about the world in the form of computer programs, but success was limited because most human knowledge grows with experiences and is subjective, intuitive and challenging to articulate using a set of rules. The introduction of machine learning enabled computers to learn real-world knowledge by identifying patterns from the data, self-correction from this learning process to enable decision making [9]. However, machine learning algorithms also suffered from a trade-off as their performance was dependent on how data was presented to them. Deep learning algorithms solved this problem by extracting information by itself. Deep learning is a particular type of machine learning that makes the computer learning more powerful, flexible and abstract. The Venn diagram in Figure 6.3 illustrates how these concepts are interrelated.

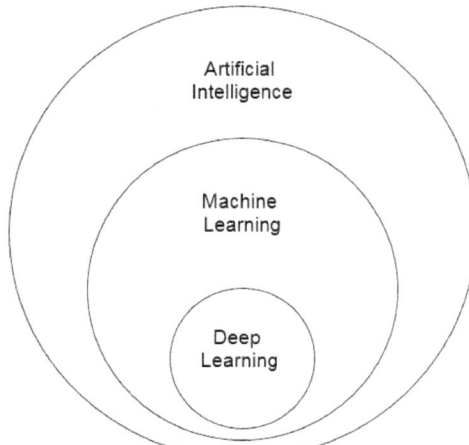

Source: Ian Goodfellow, Yoshua Bengio, Aaron Courville, *Deep Learning*, The MIT Press, 2016

Figure 6.3: AI, machine learning, and deep learning Venn diagram

What Data Science Is Not

AI, machine learning, and deep learning do not comprise a branch of data science. Rather, data science uses them to solve problems. Consider machine learning as a statistical toolkit that helps machines learn based on historical data and make predictions on the new data. On the other hand, data science is a broader term that includes the process for building this machine learning model, including data collection, data processing, data analysis, data visualization, modeling, making predictions, and so forth.

Big data also is not a branch of data science. Data science can be used to solve problems using various types and sizes of datasets.

What Is Big Data?

The origin of the term "big data" is still ambiguous, but one of the early and popular definitions is that big data is the amount of data that traditional database software tools cannot manage and analyze due to the complexity and size.[9] In simple terms, big data means *large data*, where large depends on the context and computational processing power. According to a report by IBM in 2013, about 2.5 quintillion bytes of data are created each day in the world.[10] The pace of creation is only accelerating with the growth of internet access, increase in mobile usage, and IoT (internet of things) devices around the world. Data points are created in our daily activities, such as:

- Social media activity (Twitter tweets and messages; Facebook likes, shares and messages)
- Search engine activity (Google searches, creating web pages)
- Video streaming (watching or uploading videos on YouTube or Netflix)
- Payments (using credit cards, internet banking)

To make any use of this data, it needs to be captured. In the past, data storage was quite expensive and inefficient, so storing big datasets was a challenge. Now, there are better and more economical data storage solutions that make it easier to store and process the data.

IBM defined big data in association with four Vs: volume (size of the data), velocity (speed at which the data is created, stored, analyzed and visualized), variety (different data sources for structured and unstructured data), and veracity (trustworthiness of the data for any analysis in terms of accuracy and ambiguity, for example).[11] Other researchers have defined big data as three Vs, six Vs and so on. Although there are several critiques of the V model, one thing is clear: there is a lot of data available that can be used for solving numerous business problems using data science.

Data Science and Big Data in Industry Practice

The key steps required in any data science project are shown in Figure 6.4. Regardless of the problem, any data science project can be deployed by following these steps. The multi-step lifecycle, from defining the problem to experimentation, is explained in this section. The big data technology stack used in this process, and also shown in Figure 6.4, is explained in the section "Big Data Technology Stack."

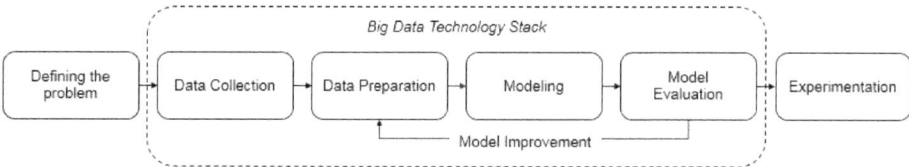

Figure 6.4: Data science project lifecycle

Step 1—Defining the Problem

Before starting to work on a data science task, the first step is to define the objective of the business problem clearly. This involves answering questions about different aspects of the problem, such as

- What is the business problem and how to translate it into a data science problem?
- What data is required for the problem and how to collect and to prepare it?
- What insights can be generated from the data and what machine learning/deep learning models can be useful for the problem?
- How to build and evaluate the model, define success (KPIs, metrics, and so on) for the solution of the problem?
- How to measure the impact of a machine learning model in the real world?

In practice, it is essential to simplify and structure the problem at this stage and precisely answer these questions. Depending on how the problem is structured at this step, the subsequent steps of data collection, data preparation modeling, model evaluation and experimentation can be different. This is illustrated using the following example over the course of the chapter:

Loan Delinquency Problem

A bank has disbursed personal loans to 800,000 existing savings/credit card customers over the last five years (2013–2018). This loan scheme was expected to help customers and also bring additional revenue to the bank; however an investigation revealed that the scheme resulted in losses to the bank. The loan is supposed to be repaid in the form of monthly installments—where the installment amount and number of installments depend on the loan amount, loan tenure and agreed interest rate. When the bank is unable to debit any monthly installments for a month from the bank account, the loan is considered to be "delinquent."

Since 2013, the delinquency rate is ~10 percent, or 1 out of 10 customers missed on their payment, but customers are charged with a hefty fee in case of any missed installment leading to dissatisfaction. The probability of missing payment is not yet considered in any risk management/account management decisions in the bank, which if considered can enhance the performance of savings/credit card portfolio as well. Given this information, bank management has requested that its data science team identify customers who are most likely to miss payment of the loan installment in next three months so that these customers receive a telephone reminder. Bank management believes that such preventive action can keep some customers from missing payment and wants to test out this hypothesis. After its success is established, management would like to make telephone reminders a regular practice. It is also known that the bank's call center's capacity is calling only 30,000 customers per month. Therefore, it is essential to identify the right customers to call at the right time.

Given this problem statement, what are different ways to structure this problem into a data science problem?
- Objective: The problem involves finding top 30,000 customers with the highest likelihood to miss payment of their loan installment in the next three months so that they can receive telephone reminders. A few ways to approach this problem are
    o Approach 1: Identify customers whose account balance falls below a certain amount, say, two to three times the amount of monthly loan installment. This approach might work well; however, it does not take into account the fluctuations in the account balance over the month. For example, some customers routinely pay their installments but have to wait for their pay to be deposited and might not need to be called. Can this be further improved?
    o Approach 2: Analyze the historical characteristics of customers who have missed payment of their loan installment in the past and understand the reasons behind it. For example, customers aged 30-40 years with income below $2500 per month are more likely to miss payment than other customers. Such insights can be used to generate rules to filter the right set of customers. Can these rules be further improved? Can these rules be made more robust?
    o Approach 3: Create a machine learning model using historical customer behavior and characteristics to predict a score for the likelihood to miss payment in the next three months. This score would be specific to each customer and can change with time.
- Data collection and preparation: To proceed with any of these approaches, having data about customers who have missed a payment vs not missed any payment since 2013 can be useful. This data can be used to study the characteristics, such as customer account balance history, demographics, and loan details that can help to understand underlying reasons for missing payments. The sections "Step

2—Data Collection" and "Step 3—Data Preparation" describe how to gather the right data for the problem and various methods to collect and prepare such data.

- Modeling: In the case of Approach 3, this step can be used to gauge which machine learning models would be useful for the given problem. The "Modeling" section describes the types of machine learning models suitable for different problems and steps needed to build any model.
- Model evaluation: After the machine learning model is built, it is useful to evaluate its performance. This step is needed to gauge the performance of the model (how correctly the model can predict customers with high likelihood to miss payments in the next three months) before starting to call those customers.
- Experimentation: Although a model can help identify such customers who are likely to miss payment in next three months, it is necessary to test whether the model works in the real world. Experiments can be carried out to check model accuracy and the impact of calling. For example, customers with a high likelihood to miss payment can be identified and either called or not called to answer these questions:
- Does calling customers with a high likelihood of delinquency actually prevent them from missing their payment?
- Do customers with a high likelihood of delinquency end up missing their payment when they are not called?
- Do customers with a high likelihood of delinquency end up missing their payment even after being called?

Answering such questions and analyzing the results can help to measure the success of the model in the real world. The "Step 5—Experimentation" section describes how such experiments can be designed.

Step 2—Data Collection

After precisely defining the problem, the next step is to gather relevant data for that problem. This is done by following a systematic approach to gather various data from the variety of sources to get a complete picture of the problem. The different types of data are discussed below.

Based on the source, data can be mainly categorized into: primary data and secondary data:

- Primary data is the data that is gathered from the first-hand experiences of a researcher for a specific project. Usually, collecting primary data involves a lot of time, effort, and cost. Examples of primary data include data collected using questionnaires, interviews, surveys, experiments, and so on.
- Secondary data is the data that was already collected and recorded in the past for a different problem. Usually, secondary data is readily available, so it is widely used in data science projects. Examples of secondary data include private datasets (for example, internal companies' records), datasets for sale (such as those available through data aggregator companies), scraping websites, and public datasets (like government publications, books, journal articles, and so forth).

Care should be taken to ensure that data is relevant for the business problem and captures sufficient events of interest. Both primary and secondary data can be used for a data science problem, but in most cases, secondary data is used. This is because secondary data is cheap and provides a longer history, which includes more data points that could give more insights even though it is less accurate when compared to primary data. For the loan delinquency problem, secondary data from internal bank systems can be used containing details such as:

- Customer demographics (age, gender, income, location)
- Bank account details (number of accounts, tenure of the bank account, account status—active, inactive, or other)
- Account transaction details (types of transactions, amounts spend on different transactions)
- Loan details (loan status—delinquency, defaults, paid-up, or other; principal loan amount; outstanding loan amount, the total number of paid installments, date of delinquency)
- Other data, such as customer interaction details and website usage

Types of Data

Raw data (including primary and secondary data) is not always of great quality. The quality of data mainly depends on how the data is captured, what tools are used to capture it and what measures are used to ensure the right type. There are mostly three types in which data is captured, namely structured datasets, semi-structured datasets and unstructured datasets. Their differences are shown in Table 6.1.

Table 6.1: Differences between Structured, Semi-Structured and Unstructured Data

Structured Data	Semi-structured Data	Unstructured Data	
Definition	Data that can be stored in relational databases (such as SQL tables) with rows and columns. They have a relational key and can be easily mapped into pre-designed fields.	Data that is not stored in relational databases but has some organizational properties that make it easier to analyze	All other data that has no organizational structure
Examples	Databases (tables with customer names, dates, addresses, and other data), CRM systems, ERP systems, and census records	Email messages, tweets, data contained on web pages within HTML tags, XML, JSON, and CSV	Audio, images, videos, text

Traditionally, models have worked well on structured and semi-structured data but not so well on unstructured data (audio, images, and patterns in the text). But recent machine learning and deep learning algorithms are significantly better at interpreting even unstructured data, which has led to many new exciting applications such as speech recognition, image recognition, and natural language processing on text. For the loan delinquency problem, all three types of data can be used depending on how the data is available in the bank systems. For example, both customer demographics recorded in structured databases and customer interactions recorded in the form of emails or voice recordings can be used.

Levels of Data
Structured data is captured at several levels. In this context, a "level" is the smallest unit of the data. For example, a transaction is the smallest level when money is transferred from one bank account to another. This transaction is captured as one row in the data. Similarly, a social security number uniquely represents a person, and one person will have consistent characteristics, such as gender and place of birth, associated with this social security number. Therefore, data can be captured at a person level using the social security number. On the other hand, for semi-structured and unstructured data, the levels may or may not be there. For example, unstructured text or images do have such levels. Table 6.2 illustrates different levels of data capture.

Table 6.2: Levels of Data

Level	Each Row Represents	Data gathered at each levels
Event	One event	Data for each event, like the time of a banking transaction
Entity	One user, product family, or other such entity	For example, age, gender, demographics, aggregation of event level data to user level—customer's month-end ledger balance
Segment	One segment	For example, a list of cities with average income more than $30,000

Data with more granularity captures more information. For example, a customer's daily banking transaction amounts provide more information about the customer's transaction behavior than the total transaction amount for the bank. Therefore, in the loan delinquency problem, event or user level data would be more useful than segment level.

Step 3—Data Preparation

After gathering data from various sources, the next step is to process and transform this data into a useable form for the analysis. Often data is collected from various sources, so it is untidy—has inconsistent data types, useful columns spread across multiple files, etc. Data preparation involves steps such as performing quality checks, filtering, and aggregating, joining, concatenating different datasets, creating features so that it can be used to generate some meaningful insights and further used for modeling tasks. The first step of data preparation is performing data quality checks. Data collected in the real world for practical purposes is usually of poor quality—data has incorrectly captured information, missing values, duplicate records, and so forth. Therefore, it is essential to perform quality checks (QCs) on the data and address issues before proceeding.

Data Quality Checks
The ideal method for performing data quality checks is to check every record against the source system. But if there is a large number of records across many files, such a method can be cumbersome. Therefore, some pragmatic means are needed to gauge the quality of the data. Some of the typical measures used to perform data quality checks include the following:[12]
- Completeness: Check whether all intended datasets and data items (fields, values) are captured. Compare the numbers of rows, columns, and fields; the size of the data at the source data; and the available data to ensure completeness.

-   Accuracy: Secondary data is not as accurate as primary data, but realistically, it should be checked to determine how well the data represents real-world observations and events. Therefore, check whether the data was captured accurately:
    -   By reconciling it with third-party source data that is trustworthy or confirming insights with the business teams.
    -   By checking for abnormal values in data, such as values that are too high or too low, or missing or incorrect values (numerical or categorical). If abnormal values account for too many of those in a column, then the result of data analysis can be biased. Thus, all abnormal values should be treated.
-   Uniqueness: Check whether all records are uniquely captured; that is, there is no duplicate information. Identify the unique keys of the data (for example, bank account number or customer ID) and check if the dataset is unique across these keys. For example—if same customer across one customer ID has duplicate records then de-duplicate the data by either removing duplicate rows or aggregating them to the customer ID level.
-   Consistency: Check whether the data is consistent with different representations of the same information across multiple datasets; that is, there is no difference between two representations of the same data. This can be done by analyzing patterns and verifying insights from the data fields. For example—dataset is inconsistent if number of registered bank customers is less than number of active bank customers.
-   Validity: Check whether data conforms to the standard data definitions, such as data types, size and format. This can be done by analyzing the data types of fields in the source data and available data.

Exploratory Data Analysis

After completing the quality checks on the data, the next step is to perform exploratory data analysis (EDA), or descriptive analysis. EDA is an approach to analyze the data by summarizing its main characteristics into summary statistics and graphical representations. For example, we might carry out a univariate analysis (such as frequency or central tendency—mean, median, and mode) on different variables, and perform a bivariate analysis, such as analyzing variables with each other and analyzing variables with the target variable. In the context of machine learning, the variable that is predicted is called the output variable or business outcome or target variable. In the loan delinquency problem, the target variable has two outcomes: delinquent (customers who miss payment of loan installment in the next three months) and non-delinquent (customers do not miss payment of loan installment in the next three months). This is illustrated in Figure 6.5.

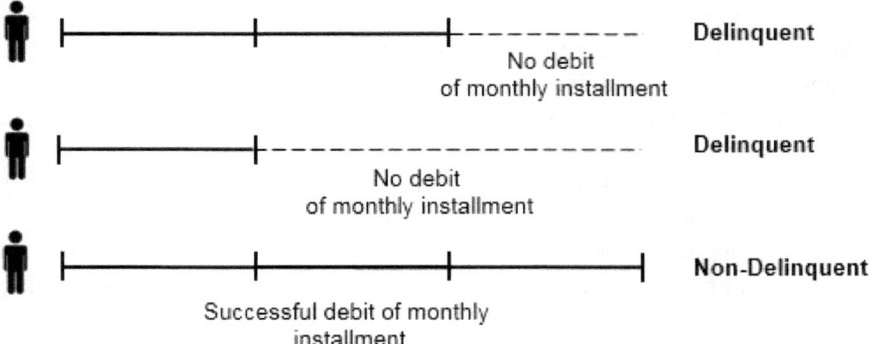

Figure 6.5: Target creation

At this step, it is also important to realize that dataset should be filtered for appro-priate customer cohort i.e. customers with that specific personal loan. EDA can help generate insights by analyzing different variables for the customers of interest. In this problem, variables such as the customer's month-end ledger balance, age, account tenure, and so on, can also be useful to look into. EDA could help us analyze account balance with respect to the target variable to tell whether there is any account balance pattern that suggests whether a customer is likely to miss payment. Overall, the objec-tive of EDA is to try and find these specific patterns from the data. For example, Table 6.3 suggests that customers with lower month-end ledger balances are more likely to miss on payments than other customers as delinquency rate increases with the decrease in balance. On the other hand, different age buckets do not indicate any significant difference in delinquency rates.

Table 6.3: Exploratory Data Analysis Using Tables

Month-end Ledger Balance ($)	Delinquency Rate
Less than 2500	15%
2500–5000	8%
5000–7500	9%
7500–10000	7%
Greater than 10000	5%

Age Buckets (Years)	Delinquency Rate
Under 25	10%
25–50	9.5%
50–75	9%
Over 75	11%

There are several approaches to performing an exploratory data analysis:
- Tables: Summarize the data in the form of tables (as in Table 6.3) and generate insights.
- Visualization: Visualize these variables (as in Figure 6.6) in graphical representations like histograms, pie-charts, or bar charts.
- Correlations: Find correlations of these variables with each other and with the target variable (in this case it's delinquent, Yes or No).

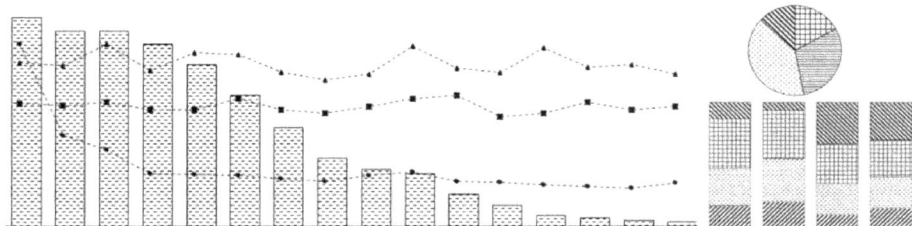

Figure 6.6: Exploratory data analysis

Feature Engineering

After completing an EDA, the next step is to represent raw data in a format that captures these insights in the form that can be fed to a machine learning model. Such transformation/engineering of variables into the formats suitable for the machine learning model is called *feature engineering*, and transformed variables are called *features*. Machine learning models take these features as input and learn from them to predict the output. Feature engineering is one of the crucial steps to build any machine learning model because good features improve model performance by producing high-quality output. In fact, a simple model with good features may outperform a complex model with bad features. The idea of feature engineering is to create more features using the data and present them in a simpler way, which can influence the output of your model. Often, feature engineering becomes a necessity as a machine learning model needs data to be presented in a certain way that it understands. Some models are more appropriate for the certain type of features; therefore, feature engineering involves creating the most appropriate features given the data, model, and problem.

In the loan delinquency problem, if the selected model only accepts numerical values, then any feature that is not numeric would need to be either dropped or transformed into a numeric. For example, in Table 6.4, a categorical feature "highest education level" with four categories—Ph.D., Bachelors, Masters, and High School—would need to be either dropped or transformed to a numeric field that captures the essence of these four categories. At the end, when all features are combined, the resulting feature table would be like Table 6.4.

Table 6.4: Feature Table

	Features						
Customer ID	Month-end Ledger Balance ($)	Age	Gender	...	...	Highest education level	Target
101	100	35	Male			Ph.D.	Delinquent
102	400	25	Female			Bachelors	Non-delinquent
103	500	34	Female			Masters	Delinquent
104	200	29	Male			High School	Non-delinquent

There is no right or wrong way to perform feature engineering, but Table 6.5 shows some basic techniques which can be used for structured data (example—tabular data) and unstructured data (example—text data). Note feature engineering for other unstructured data such as audios, videos and images are beyond the scope of this discussion:

Table 6.5: Feature Engineering Techniques

Type of Data	Technique	Description and Examples*
Structured data (for example, tabular data)	Quantization/ binning	Continuous numerical variables can be quantized into fixed categories (binary or multiple groups). For example, "age" can be quantized, corresponding to different life stages, into 0-25 years, 25-50 years, 50-75 years, and 75 years or older.
	Normalization/ scaling	Features with drastically different scales can be appropriately scaled before modeling. For example, if income ranges from $2,000 to $50,000 and age ranges from 15 years to 100 years, then income should be appropriately scaled to a hundredth scale as age or vice versa.
	New features	New features can be created from existing features to extract more information. This step should be done by using inputs of business stakeholders. For example, monthly income and expenses can be used to create a new feature "monthly savings" to identify customers who are not saving enough and may need a personal loan.

Table 6.5: (continued)

Type of Data	Technique	Description and Examples*
Unstructured data (for example, text data)	Cleaning text	Preprocessing and filtering can eliminate useless data that adds noise. For example, – Remove web page tags and attributes and special characters such as punctuations, alphanumeric characters, and symbols. – Convert words to a single case (lower or upper), remove stop words, frequent words and rare words, and remove prefixes and suffixes.
	Feature extraction	Numerical features are extracted from clean, processed/ text by using words as keys or features and different word frequencies as values. Popular feature extraction techniques include bag-of-words (BoW) and term frequency-inverse document frequency (TF-IDF).

Note: Zheng, A. and Casari, A. (2018) *Feature Engineering for Machine Learning*, California: O'Reilly.

Feature Matrix

After creating the features, the next step is to combine all the engineered features from structured and unstructured data and target column(s) into one table/matrix called feature matrix. A feature table from Table 6.4 would transform into a feature matrix as in Table 6.6 after feature engineering. Observe that a variable such as gender is converted into columns "Gender_Male" and "Gender_Female" with binary values (1 or 0); education" is converted as into 4 education level columns; unstructured text such as "car" is used to create Bag-of-words features like "BOW_car" and TF-IDF feature like "TF-IDF_car," etc. Now, this feature matrix can be easily fed into a machine learning model.

Table 6.6: Feature Matrix

Customer ID	Month-end Ledger Balance	Age	Gender	Education	Age_Bucket	Gender_Male	Gender_Female	Eud_PHD	Edu_Bachelors	Edu_Masters	Edu_HighSchool	Graduate	BOW_car	TFIDF_car	Delinquent
101	100	35	Male	PhD	25–50	1	0	1	0	0	0	1	1	0.21	1
102	900	24	Female	Bachelors	0–25	0	1	0	1	0	0	1	2	0.42	0
103	50	65	Female	Masters	50–75	0	1	0	0	1	0	1	0	0	1
0104	200	29	Male	High School	25–50	1	0	0	0	0	1	0	1	0.12	0

Note that this is just one illustration. Feature engineering steps largely depend on the type of problem, data and machine learning model one intends to use. For example, unsupervised learning problems do not have a target variable; therefore, the feature matrix would not have a target column. This is further described in the next section. Also, not all features in the feature matrix will be used in the model. Some categorical features, such as gender and education, which have already been converted into columns, can be dropped. Depending on preference, one can choose to merge features differently, but creating such a matrix makes it more efficient to experiment with feature selection in modeling.

Step 4—Modeling

After data collection and data preparation, the next step is to build the right model for the problem. This section provides a broad introduction to different machine learning algorithms with emphasis on how to build a model with the problem in mind. Broadly, machine learning models can be classified into two categories, *supervised* and *unsupervised* learning:

- Supervised learning involves building models to predict a target using different features. Often supervised machine learning tasks include building models to estimate future predictions using historical data, often called *predictive models*. Typical predictive model problems include *classification* and *regression*:
    - Classification is a problem in which the target variable is qualitative (two or more categories). The loan delinquency problem is an example of the binary classification problem where two prediction classes are "Delinquent" and "Non-delinquent." Other examples include predicting whether an email is spam and handwritten character recognition.
    - Regression is a problem in which the target variable is a quantitative value (numeric), such as predicting loan default amount for each customer. Typical examples include sales forecasting, price prediction, and loan default amount prediction.
- Unsupervised learning involves learning from the input data without any target. In this case, the algorithm tries to use an underlying structure of the data to find useful associations and patterns. Most of the raw data in the world does not have a well-defined target variable; therefore, unsupervised learning techniques are applicable to a lot of problems. Typical problems include *clustering* and *association*:
    - Clustering is a problem of dividing the data into similar homogenous groups. Typical examples of clustering include identifying similar customers based on purchase behavior (customer segmentation), similar documents, and clustering similar news articles.

o   Association is a problem of finding associations between different variables that can describe characteristics of the data. Popular examples include market basket analysis to find bundled products as they are mostly bought together—mobile phones with covers, milk and butter, beer and diaper.

Choice of Models

Several machine learning models have been developed that cater to different real-world problems. To apply a machine learning model, it is essential to identify the type of task: supervised learning (classification, regression) and unsupervised learning (clustering, association). Table 6.7 summarizes a few modeling algorithms.

Table 6.7: Supervised and Unsupervised Learning Models

Type of Learning	Models
Supervised learning	Naive Bayes
	Linear models, such as linear or logistic regression
	Decision tree
	K-nearest neighbors (k-NN)
	Bagging, such as random forest
	Boosting, such as generalized boosting machine
	Support vector machines (SVMs)
	Neural networks
Unsupervised learning	Clustering, such as k-means, hierarchical, or DBScan
	Associations, such as a priori

Each of these models has their uses, advantages, and disadvantages. One of the popular algorithms is linear regression or logistic regression when there is a linear association of features with the target, that is, target linearly increases or decreases with a change in features. In many industrial applications, linear models are adopted as they are simple and quite interpretable. However, these models can have limitations in terms of predictive power as real-world associations between features and target may be nonlinear. In such cases, nonlinear models, such as decision trees, bagging, boosting, neural networks, and support vector machines, should be used.

Model Building

A model is just a mathematical function that can be used to represent the relation between features in the data. Practically, there is no perfect model. One can only attempt to create good models that can meet business needs. Building a model can be an iterative process: one may try several models, a different combination of features, and different modeling techniques before finding one that satisfies the requirement.

There are several ways to build a supervised machine learning model, but typically, models include training, validation, and testing, as reflected in the following standard steps:

1. Split the data randomly into two sets, namely training data and validation data. A good starting point is a ratio of 80/20 (80 percent training data and 20 percent validation data).
2. Training data is used to train or teach the model to predict the target using the features. At this step, an appropriate model should be chosen based on the learning task.
3. Validation data is used to evaluate the performance of the model. At this step, errors in the model should be analyzed and used to make some adjustments to the models, such as tuning the model, selecting features, and making other decisions regarding the learning algorithm.
4. Lastly, the final model obtained after training and validation is applied to an entirely new dataset called the *test dataset* to which the model has not previously been exposed. The performance on the test set indicates the actual performance of the final model, or what performance to expect when using the model in the real world.

Please note that the preceding steps are not fixed and can vary depending on the problem, data, and approach. There are many different ways to split the data into training and validation data, create test sets, and perform additional steps to ensure model stability. Figure 6.7 summarizes the dataset splitting and modeling approach.

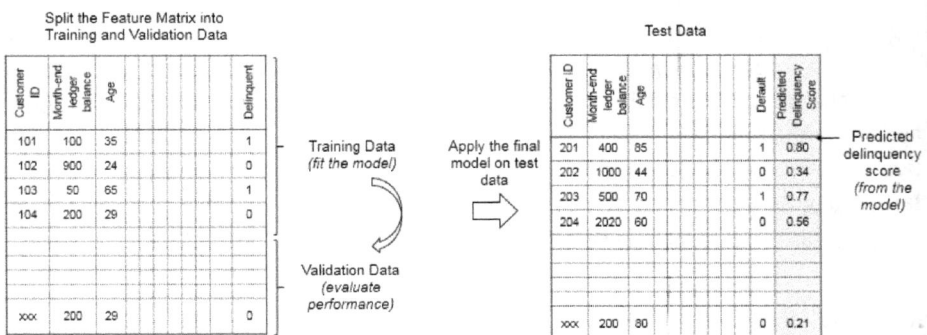

Figure 6.7: The modeling process

Building an unsupervised learning model is often more challenging than supervised learning model. Unsupervised learning models do not have a target; therefore, there is no way to check whether the model is performing well or poorly because there is no clear right answer. Often performance needs to be evaluated using past experience and domain knowledge. This makes model building quite a subjective process.

Model Evaluation

As described above, there is no perfect model. Every model suffers from some errors. The process to evaluate the prediction errors of a machine learning model is called *error analysis*. Ideally, each prediction output of a model should be checked to examine the error and understand its underlying cause. However, manually doing these checks is time-consuming, especially with large datasets. Therefore, evaluation metrics are needed to gauge the overall prediction performance of the model.

Machine learning offers a large choice of evaluation metrics depending on the task involved. For classification tasks, comparisons can be made between correct and wrong predictions of the true target by using a commonly used error matrix called a *confusion matrix*. For regression tasks, errors can be measured between the predicted target and true target. Table 6.8 shows some of the commonly used evaluation metrics for classification and regression tasks.

Table 6.8: Evaluation Metrics for Different Tasks

Task	Evaluation Metrics
Classification	Accuracy, recall, precision, F-measure, AUC ROC
Regression	Root mean squared error (RMSE), adjusted R-squared

Error Analysis

To evaluate the performance of any machine learning model, errors need to be measured and analyzed. There are primarily three sources of errors in any machine learning model, *irreducible errors*, *bias*, and *variance*.

An irreducible error (Bayes error or unavoidable bias) is an error that cannot be reduced regardless of the modeling algorithm. This type of error can be introduced by problem objective, noise and errors in the data capture; unknown variables that can influence each other and the target; and other factor. No model is perfect, so an expectation of 100-percent accuracy is simply unrealistic. Therefore, the objective of modeling is to create a model that comes as close as possible to the desired performance.[13]

Bias is another error which is introduced due to erroneous assumptions in the model while variance is an error due to variability in the model predictions. In simple terms, this concept is explained in the bulls-eye diagram in Figure 6.8.[14] The center of the concentric circle represents a perfect model which predicts all targets correctly, and each dot represents one model. Sometimes the model prediction is close to the ideal model prediction while sometimes it is far off.

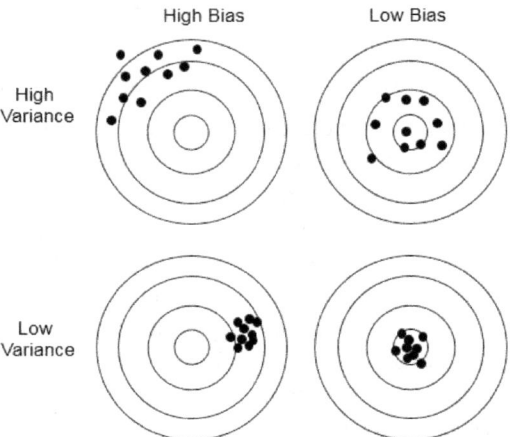

Source: Fortmann-Roe, Scott, Understanding the Bias-Variance Tradeoff, http://scott.fortmann-roe.com/docs/BiasVariance.html

Figure 6.8: Understanding bias and variance

Whereas bias measures how far off these model predictions are from the perfect model, variance measures how far off the model predictions are from each other. Typically, bias and variance have competing properties, and improving one usually compromises the other. That is, a low-bias model has high variance, and a high-bias model has low variance.[15] As seen in Figure 6.9, with the increase in model complexity model bias decreases but variance increases. The art is to find a model with the right level of complexity that has low bias and low variance.[16]

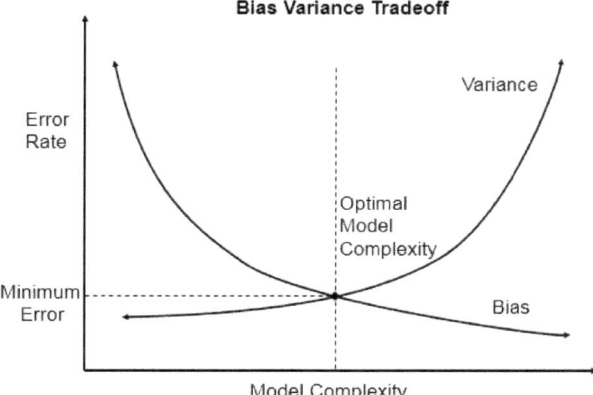

Bias Variance Tradeoff

Source: Fortmann-Roe, Scott, Understanding the Bias-Variance Tradeoff, http://scott.fortmann-roe.com/docs/BiasVariance.html

Figure 6.9: The bias vs variance tradeoff in a model

Suppose, after several modeling iterations on the loan delinquency problem, different error rates are calculated on training and validation data. Out of all the customers in the training dataset, the model is correctly able to predict 90 percent of customers if they would become delinquent or not. Then the error rate of the model is 10 percent, which includes irreducible errors, bias, and variances. After calculating errors on different iterations of the models, efforts should be made to reduce these errors as described in the following:

- A model with high bias is underfitting. That is, the model has barely learned on the training set to even perform well on validation and test sets. A good way to address this problem is by increasing the model complexity, such as by adding more features.
- A model with high variance is overfitting. That is, the model has tried to capture too much information from the training set and failed to generalize on new data. A good way to address this problem is by adding more training data.

Ideally, a model with low bias and low bias is a good model which should be finally selected.

Model Improvement
After evaluating the errors, the next step is to improve the performance of the model further to create a final model. Note that model improvement is also an iterative process and the modeling process goes through the steps of data collection, data preparation, modeling and evaluation again and again. There is no completely right

or wrong way to do this, but the following points should be kept in mind while experimenting with model improvement:

- Add external data, such as census data or credit scores, to create new features.
- Add more and more features but at the same time include features that influence the target.
- Have training, validation and test sets with sizes sufficient to have statistically significant data points to learn training and validation error rates.
- Use modeling technique suitable for the problem.
- Control for model complexity and generalization by reducing the number of features.

Step 5—Experimentation

Model evaluation techniques only help to evaluate the theoretical performance of the model on the validation and test sets. But theoretical performance does not guarantee the success of the model in real-world. For example, in the loan delinquency problem, customers identified as high likelihood to miss payment of loan installment would need some action such as reminder calls in order to prevent them missing their payment. A campaign can be designed to make preventive calls to all such customers. In practice, there can be lot of operational issues (e.g. capacity of call center, script designing and training to call center agents, IT issues in implementing the new process, data privacy/ information security especially in case of outsourced call center, etc.), in executing such a campaign. Therefore, it is essential to conduct such campaigns on small scale i.e. on small customer base, learn and address these issues before implementing such campaigns regularly for all customers. In addition to this, testing the model on a small base can also help in observing quantitative benefits from this exercise and qualitative feedback from customers.

Experiments should be designed in such campaigns in order to test out different hypothesis and quantify the actual impact of the models and know whether it meets the desired expectations. There are many different ways to design an experiment, but the following are important general steps:

1. Define a relevant success metric that meets the business objective. Examples of such metrics are conversion rate, customer retention rate, saving costs, or cross-sell rate.
2. Divide the population randomly into groups to measure the performance improvement of the model. One of the ways is to design an A/B test with two groups:
   a. A test group, on which the output of the model is tested
   b. A control group that does not use model output
3. Execute the experiment and measure the success metric for the test and control groups

In the loan delinquency problem, an A/B test can be designed to measure (a) the impact of then model (do the customers identified as having a high likelihood to miss payment actually end up missing payment) and (b) the impact of preventive reminder calls to customers using the call center (does call center calling prevent customers from missing payment).

Following the preceding steps, an experiment can be designed as follows (see Figure 6.10):

1. The success metric can be defined as the "delinquency rate": the percentage of customers who missed out their payment during the three months of campaign duration
2. Divide the population into test and control groups in equal proportions with enough samples to measure the performance between the groups:
    a. Test group: The customers identified by the model as having a high like-lihood to miss payment. Furthermore, divide the test group into two more groups: Group A, the customers who are called by the call center, and Group B, the customers who are not called.
    b. Control group: The customers who are randomly selected or selected using some existing rules (that is, without applying the model). Similarly, divide the control groups into two more groups: Group C, the customers who are called, and Group D, the customers who are not called.
3. An experiment can be conducted to measure the delinquency rate success metric over these four groups to quantify the real impact of the model based on the real impact of preventive calling. The call center can actively call customers under Group A and Group C, while customers under Group B and Group D can be left without calling.

	Test Group (Model)	Control Group (Random)
Calling	Group A	Group C
No Calling	Group B	Group D

Impact of model with calling	Delinquency rate in Group A / Group C
Impact of model without calling	Delinquency rate in Group B / Group D
Impact of calling customers from model	Delinquency rate in Group A / Group B
Impact of calling customers not from model	Delinquency rate in Group C / Group D

Figure 6.10: The A/B test design

After all the customers are successfully contacted, the delinquency rate of these groups should be measured over three months to observe whether the model and preventive calling helped. Ideally, if the model and preventive calling has a positive impact, the following should be true:

- The delinquency rate of Group B should be more than that of Group D. This would mean that the model is correctly able to identify customers who would miss payment: customers in Group B (who have a high likelihood to miss payment as per the model) end up missing payment more than the randomly selected customers in Group D.

– The delinquency rate of Group A should be less than that of Group B. This would mean that preventive calling leads to a lower delinquency rate in the customers identified by the model as having a high likelihood to miss payment. This is because customers in both Group A and Group B are identified from the model, but only Group A customers are called. Similarly, the delinquency rate of Group C should also be less than that of Group D.

– The delinquency rate of Group A also can be compared with the delinquency rate of Group C to measure the impact of the model on the customers who are called. Note that the impact of preventive calling can have different effects on customers from Group A (high likelihood to miss payment) and Group C (random customers). For example, preventive calling can remind customers and eventually reduce the delinquency rate, or it may have no impact at all as those customers might have already decided to miss payment.

These measurements can easily help quantify the success of the model and success of preventive calling. Additionally, these impacts also can be estimated in terms of dollar value to quantify the business impact. Once the success of the model and preventive calling is established from this experiment, bank management can implement such campaigns regularly. This can be done by preparing such list of customers with high likelihood to miss payment and conduct preventive calling every month.

Big Data Technology Stack

This section describes the big data technology stack, which forms a backbone for any data science project. As defined in the data science lifecycle (refer to Figure 6.3), different tools are needed for collecting the data, preparing and manipulating the data, building machine learning models and evaluating the performance of these models.

Figure 6.11 describes popular tools used for data ingestion and data storage (under data collection) and data preparation, modeling and evaluation (under data processing). Note that only open source software option licensed under Apache Software Foundation are described here because they are widely used across the industry and have good open source community support. But generally, companies use open source or commercial tools based on their needs.

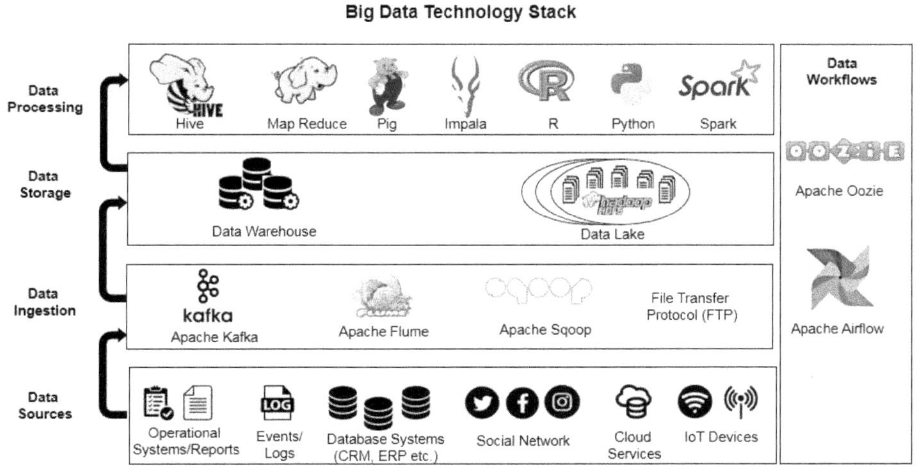

Big Data Technology Stack

Figure 6.11: The big data technology stack

Data Collection Toolkit

As explained in the preceding section, data collection involves ingesting data in different formats and from different sources. Depending on the volume, velocity, variety and veracity of data, different tools can be used. For example, a number of tweets about one topic on Twitter could be in the range of a few thousand per second, whereas the number of transactions on a stock exchange can be in the range of few hundred thousand per second or even more. Depending on the high volume and velocity of data from a stock, different tools may be required for ingesting and storing the data.

Broadly, data collection involves these two steps, *data ingestion* and *data storage*:

– Data ingestion: Data ingestion involves ingesting or importing the data from different sources. The ingestion can happen in batches or real time:

   o Batches: When data is ingested in batches, it is imported in discrete chunks at periodic intervals of time. The batch can run daily, weekly, or monthly depending on the requirement (for example, sales reporting or financial consolidation). The advantage of batch processing is that it allows for some high level of transformation on the data before storing.

   o Real time: When data is ingested in real time, it is imported from the source with a short execution time, providing near-instantaneous output. Real-time ingestion does not allow complex data transformation; therefore, it is mainly used in processes where data is needed quickly for real-time actions or decisions. Some examples where real-time ingestion is required include high-frequency trading, sentiment analysis on social media, and IoT (internet of things) data capture.

Data Ingestion Tools
There are many open source tools available for ingesting the data in real-time and batches. Some of these tools are the following:
Apache Kafka is a streaming platform used for handling real-time data feeds.
Apache Flume is used for efficiently collecting, aggregating, and moving bulk streaming data.
Apache Sqoop is used for efficiently transferring data from a relational database to Hadoop HDFS. (HDFS is a popular data storage system used by Hadoop architecture. It is just a type of distributed file system, or a system that stores a copy of files stored across multiple computers.)
Source: Apache Software Foundation. [Online]. Available: http://www.apache.org

In cases where only data transfer is needed, then FTP can be used. The transfer can be from the data source to the landing zone (temporary storage location) or from landing zone to a database, data warehouse or data lake (permanent storage location).

FTP (file transfer protocol) is a network protocol used to transfer files between a client and a server. It enables easy data transfer across the network. For more secure file access, transfer and management, SFTP (SSH file transfer protocol) is used.
Source: The TCP/IP Guide. [Online]. Available: http://tcpipguide.com/

– Data storage: Data storage involves storing all the data in a single storage place, which provides robustness, security, and flexibility. There are many data storage solutions over the cloud and on-premises that can be used according to need. Two popular ones are data warehouses and data lakes:

  o A data warehouse is a centralized repository that stores data from multiple sources and transforms it into a standard format for efficient storage, querying and analysis. In data warehouses, data is stored in RDBMSs (relational database management systems) in the form of tables, in which the table structure/schema is predefined. This ensures that the data organization is subject to database rules to ensure accuracy, credibility, and integrity. Due to the data warehouses rules, bad quality data is either rejected or treated according to special rules.

  o A data lake is a system that gives flexibility to store data in any format (relational, non-relational, and so on). The principle of data lake is "Store first, process later," or have single storage for all of the data that anyone in an organization might need to analyze. Data is kept in its raw form and transformed only when it is ready to be used. In contrast to a data warehouse, a data lake does not need a data table structure/schema before storage. These applications make data lakes an ideal choice to store all data of a company as it does not require any business specification before storage and saves a lot of time and effort.

Data Lakes with Apache Hadoop HDFS
Data lakes are commonly constructed with the Hadoop architecture because Hadoop provides a collection of open source software libraries that can efficiently store and process big datasets. Some advantages of using HDFS:

- HDFS is better than traditional distributed file systems as it is highly fault-tolerant. It can prevent data loss in case of system failure as a copy of files is stored across multiple computers.
- It can store massive datasets with easy access.
- It can break down data into separate pieces and do parallel processing.
- It has a low cost compared to a traditional data storage system.

Source: Apache Hadoop. [Online]. Available: http://www.apache.org

---

Data Processing Toolkit

After storing the data, the next step is to process and transform it into a useable form for modeling. The toolkit described in this section covers tools usually used for data preparation, modeling and evaluation. Often data is collected from various sources, so it is untidy. That is, it has inconsistent data types, useful columns spread across multiple files, and other unstructured characteristics. Data processing ensures that this data is organized so that is easy to retrieve whenever needed. This step is also called *data transformation* as it involves steps such as changing the data types, filtering, aggregating, joining or concatenating different datasets. The transformed datasets can then be used to generate some meaningful insights or business intelligence reports.

Traditionally, companies have followed an ETL (extract, transform and load) approach, which involves performing such transformations before loading data into the database. But many times, the entire transformation process can be cumbersome and significantly reduce the volume of the data that can be stored. With the availability of cheap and scalable data storage, such as data lakes, companies are gradually moving from ETL to an ELT (extract, load and transform) model where transformation can happen after storing the data. The advantage is that all the data can be stored first and transformed later according to need. However, in practice, companies are neither completely ETL (as they need to store more and more data) nor completely ELT (as storing entire raw data may consume a lot of disk space which can be unnecessary and add to the cost).

Data Processing Tools

Some of the data processing tools described here can be used for data preparation, building machine learning models and even perform model evaluations. Data processing for small datasets can be handled by commonly used spreadsheet tools, but processing of bigger datasets requires tools like R, Python, SQL, Hive, Impala, and Pig. The following are some of the commonly used data processing tools:

R and Python are open-source programming languages widely used in data science for data processing and modeling.

SQL is a programming language widely used for querying and managing data in relational databases.

Hadoop MapReduce is a programming model in Hadoop used for parallel processing of large datasets in a distributed manner.

Apache Hive is a data warehouse built on Hadoop for data processing, summarization, querying, and analysis using a SQL-like language called Hive QL (HQL).

Pig is a high-level scripting language for performing data analysis on top of Hadoop.
Impala is another query engine built on top of Hadoop in which querying is faster than Hive.
Apache Spark is a processing framework similar to but much faster than MapReduce. It supports various tools for different purposes, such as Spark SQL for structured datasets, Spark Streaming for data streaming, MLlib for machine learning, and Apache Storm for real-time computation.
Source: Apache Software Foundation. [Online]. Available: http://www.apache.org

Data Workflow Toolkit

Given the standard steps of data ingestion, data transfer, data storage and data processing, there are two ways these processes can be operationalized: either by manually executing these steps, or using data workflows that can carry out these processes automatically or semi-automatically. It is difficult to manually perform all of these tasks efficiently, accurately and quickly every time new data is received. Therefore, data workflows/pipelines are created to automate these processes.

Workflow Tools
Some of the popular open source data workflow tools include the following:
Apache Oozie is used to automate the entire data ingestion, transfer, storage, and processing process and schedule these processes as jobs. Apache Oozie is quite useful as it can fully integrate with the Apache Hadoop and supports Hadoop jobs for Apache MapReduce, Pig, Hive, and Sqoop. In addition to that, complex data transformations that need complex scheduling can be managed by creating sub-workflows.
Apache Airflow is another open source tool managing complex computational workflows and data processing pipelines. Overall, Airflow supports connectors to most of the cloud service providers, and it has a better UI, which can help you visualize your pipeline's dependencies and see how they progress.
Source: Apache Software Foundation. [Online]. Available: http://www.apache.org

In addition to the open source solutions for the big data technology stack, there is a mix of good commercial cloud platform solutions (standalone or built on top of these open source frameworks) offered by leading companies. A few such solutions are AWS (Amazon Web Services), Microsoft Azure, and Google Cloud Platform. The advantages of using these commercial solutions is that they can provide on-demand cloud computing solutions with software, databases, computing power and services on a paid subscription basis.

Challenges and Lessons from Data Science Projects

Data science is a rapidly evolving field with continuous research and development of new algorithms, big data and analytics tools, and products using machine learning. Yet, many organizations have started adopting data science only quite recently. Due to this limited experience, there are several challenges that companies face when they start working on data science. These challenges can be unique to the company, team, project or even the model, but broadly, most of the challenges are similar across the industry (based on the maturity of the data science practice). The following are the typical challenges faced while working on data science projects:

- Data platform (legacy systems): Many companies that are new to data science (but have been in existence for several decades) have legacy systems. It is difficult to connect these legacy systems seamlessly to data lakes, for example. It is complex to implement a new algorithm and way to feed data back to the legacy system for operations teams that need to use them in decision making.
- Data quality and data dictionaries: In most companies, raw data is dirty (missing, inaccurate, duplicate, misleading, and non-integrated), and data dictionaries are incomplete or absent. This poses a significant challenge to data scientists' productivity as they need to spend a lot of time in understanding the data and perform a lot of quality checks. And many times incorrect data can lead to erroneous results.
- Data privacy and lack of data access: In many projects, data is not available, or not available on time, due to data privacy issues. To resolve these issues, an upfront assessment of data privacy should be done at the scoping phase itself, and appropriate measures should be taken to address the issues. In some cases, a project may have to discontinue due to unresolved issues.
- Ethical Issues: Many times, data science projects involve working with sensitive data such as race, gender, religion, national origin, and medical history, and we should be careful to use only data that is allowed by rules and regulations. Some of the variables, even though allowed by the regulations, might introduce discrimination (or marginalize certain sections of the society). Organizations must take extra care to ensure that algorithms do not create discrimination and are used in ethical ways.
- Lack of project sponsorships: Many companies do not focus on investing appropriately in data science projects. This is due to a couple reasons:
  - First, data science projects usually have a high setup cost (cost of resources and big data tools). Also, management often does not fully understand the potential benefits of data science project.
  - Second, management usually underestimates the complexity associated with implementing a successful experiment in business operations. A lot of projects fail when implemented at scale in an organization even after success during experimentation. This is due to challenges associated with

integrating data science models with legacy systems, and due to the complexity associated with change management, as business processes need to be updated and teams have to accept new ways of working.

- Expectation management: It is difficult to manage expectations about the impact of data science projects with management. It can only provide you a limited boost in business or reduce inefficiencies. Remember that data science is not magic! The benefit of a data science project also may not immediately quantifiable when used to develop a data-driven approach for business, automatic processing, data-driven decision making for business transformation and change management, training existing employees with data science skills, and so forth, but can eliminate future problems and help create a data-driven culture. This should also be explained to management to set the right expectations.
- Focus on wrong problems: The lack of clear direction, unclear problem statements, and unclear execution plans can cause data science projects to fail. For example—building a cool product without any business utility is likely to fail, as in cases when the product or model was created by data geeks without involving business teams.

Conclusion

The field of data science and big data is very broad. The aim of this chapter was to provide a high-level overview of the data science and big data analytics field and explain some key concepts. To master this field and develop proficiency to apply these learnings in the real world, one must go through further readings and practice on real-world problems (under the supervision of an experienced data scientist) or on open data science competitions. Moreover, the field is rapidly evolving and therefore continuous learning is required to keep up to date about the developments.

In order to gain further knowledge about this subject, the following are some good resources:
- *An Introduction to Statistical Learning with Applications in R* by Gareth James, Daniela Witten, Trevor Hastie and Robert Tibshirani
- *Machine Learning: A Probabilistic Perspective* by Kevin Murphy
- *Machine Learning with R* by Brett Lantz
- *Doing Data Science* by Cathy O'Neil, Rachel Schutt
- *Deep Learning* by Aaron Courville, Ian Goodfellow, and Yoshua Bengio
- *Mining of Massive Datasets* by Jure Leskovec, Anand Rajaraman, Jeff Ullman
- *Coursera online course: Machine Learning* by Andrew Ng

Endnotes

1 Data source: Google Trends (https://www.google.com/trends).

2 Ng, Andrew (2018) Machine Learning Yearning—Technical Strategy for AI Engineers in the Era of Deep Learning, Unpublished book, www.mlyearning.org

3 Linden, Greg, Smith, Brent, York, Jeremy (2003) Amazon.com "Recommendations: Item-to-Item Collaborative Filtering, IEEE Internet Computing," v. 7, n. 1, pp. 76–80, January 2003. doi>10.1109/MIC.2003.1167344

4 Gomez-Uribe, Carlos A. and Hunt, Neil (2016) "The Netflix Recommender System: Algorithms, Business Value, and Innovation, ACM Transactions on Management Information Systems (TMIS)," v. 6, n. 4, pp. 1–19, January 2016.

5 Khandani, A. E., Kim, A. J., and Lo, A. W. (2010) "Consumer credit-risk models via machine learning algorithms." *Journal of Banking & Finance*, v 34, pp. 2767–2787.

6 Tukey, John W. (1962) "The Future of Data Analysis." *Ann. Math. Statist.* v. 33, n. 1, pp. 1–67. doi:10.1214/aoms/1177704711

7 Cleveland, William S. (2001) "Data Science: an action plan for expanding the technical areas of the field of statistics." *International Statistical Review*, v. 69, n. 1, pp. 21–26.

8 Davenport, Thomas & J Patil, D. (2012) "Data Scientist: The Sexiest Job of the 21st Century." *Harvard Business Review*. v. 90, pp. 70–76, 128.

9 Manyika, J., Chui, M., Brown, B., Bughin, J. et al. (2011) Big data: The next frontier for innovation, competition, and productivity, McKinsey Global Institute working paper. www.mckinsey.com

10 Jacobson, Ralph (2013) "2.5 quintillion bytes of data created every day. How does CPG & Retail manage it?" (IBM, April 24, 2013) [Online]. Available: https://www.ibm.com/blogs/insights-on-business/consumer-products/2-5-quintillion-bytes-of-datacreated-every-day-how-does-cpg-retail-manage-it/

11 IBM Corporation (2016), "The Four V's of Big Data," 2016. [Online]. Available: http://www.ibmbigdatahub.com/infographic/four-vs-bigdata

12 Pipino, L.L., Lee, Y.W., and Wang, R.Y. (2002) "Data quality assessment." *Communications of the ACM*, v. 45, n. 4, pp. 211–218.

13 Ng, *Machine Learning Yearning*, op.cit.

14 Fortmann-Roe, Scott Understanding the Bias-Variance Tradeoff http://scott.fortmann-roe.com/docs/BiasVariance.html

15 Ibid.

16 James, G., Witten, D., Hastie, T., Tibshirani, R. (2013) *An Introduction to Statistical Learning with Applications in R,* 2013, Springer Science and Business Media, New York.

We would like to thank AXA for providing an intellectual environment where we could devote time to write this chapter and receive feedback and guidance from colleagues. This chapter is written to provide a high-level introduction and motivation to readers on data science and big data. Most of what we discuss here has already been said in many books, research papers, blog posts, mailing lists, and so on. The further reading suggestions and references at the end of the chapter are great sources if you want to learn any specific area in more depth.

Ankur Agrawal is a seasoned actuarial, analytics professional heading AXA Data and Tech Innovation Asia lab. Objective of the lab is to drive AXA towards a tech-led company by leveraging data and emerging technologies at scale which have the potential to disrupt the current insurance business model and provide opportunities to shape future businesses. In his last role with AXA Business Services in India, he was a member of Exec team responsible for managing a team of over 200+ professionals supporting 20+ AXA entities across life, health and P&C actuarial, data science, and research areas spanning North America, Europe and Asia region. Prior to that, he has held various leadership positions in actuarial areas in direct companies as well as consulting firms across life, health and P&C actuarial, operational areas spanning North America, Europe and Asia region. Ankur is a qualified actuary from Institute and Faculty of Actuaries UK and Institute of Actuaries of India and also holds a Bachelor of Technology, Mechanical from Indian Institute of Technology, Delhi.

Siddhant Tiwari *is a data science professional working as a senior data scientist at AXA Data and Tech Innovation Asia lab. His role at lab involves executing high-impact data science projects for AXA entities and supporting them in their data transformation journey. He is experienced in leading data science projects involving opportunity assessments, customer acquisitions, cross-selling and up-selling, product recommendations, customer retention, risk management and fraud. Previously, at ZS Associates, he consulted various Fortune 500 pharmaceutical clients in devising sales and marketing strategies to improve brand positioning in the market using data analytics. He holds a BE Hons. in Electrical and Electronics from BITS Pilani, India and MSc. in Business Analytics from National University of Singapore.*

Chapter 7
Blockchain and Distributed Ledger Technology 2.0

Within the span of a few years, blockchain has evolved from a new innovative technology, experimented upon by sophisticated mathematicians and computer scientists, to a somewhat household name, widely expected to deliver pervasive benefits for the economy and business. Blockchain promises innumerable possibilities and, depending with whom one speaks, it appears that almost any industry that deals with some sort of transaction can benefit from or will be disrupted by this technology.

The term *blockchain* has caught on like a wildfire so much so that it is now compared in the same vein with the proliferation of the internet. In a like-for-like comparison between internet and blockchain, both are seen as revolutionary in terms of how information is shared directly from one user to another, removing the need for intermediaries and layers of channels.

To grasp the contribution of blockchain from a historical context, one should take a glance back at the 1960s. Then, semiconductors played an instrumental role in paving the way for the digital recording of data, replacing what is now seen as the more archaic physical recording of data. In the ensuing two decades, the proliferation of computing technology paved the way for automated teller machines and eventually took society into the realm of remote banking. Figure 7.1 captures the changes on a timeline.

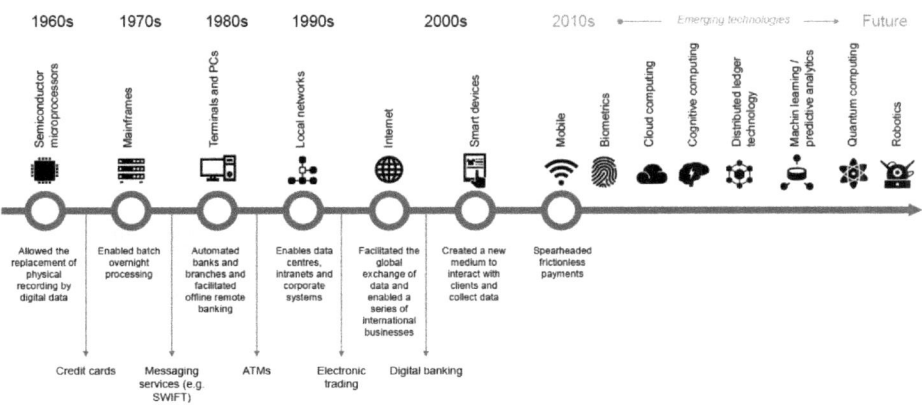

Figure 7.1: Technology and its rapid evolution

Blockchain technology has the potential to unleash a similar force because because in many ways, blockchain and the internet are similar.

Despite efforts to build a highly-efficient distributed network that date back to the early 1960s, it was only the formation of the Advanced Research Projects Agency

DOI 10.1515/9781547400904- 007

Network (ARPANET) in 1969 that laid the foundation for the first message that could be transmitted. This message was sent from one user to another in a rapid succession of transmissions through a network of computers. ARPANET was truly the ground-breaking packet switching network that became the technical foundation of the internet.

While the Transmission Control Protocol/Internet Protocol (TCP/IP) was developed in the early days following the emergence of the ARPANET, it was not until 1982 that it became widely accepted as a standard networking protocol. In the two decades following its birth, until around 1990, ARPANET was very much in the hands of the US military.

In 1990, the internet as we now know it started to grow firmer roots when the European Organization for Nuclear Research (CERN) British scientist Tim Berners-Lee developed the hypertext markup language (HTML). Now, it is widely regarded as a worldwide language of the internet because HTML paved the way for the world wide web (the web or WWW). The web was originally envisaged to meet the demand for quick information-sharing between scientists in universities and institutes around the globe.

In a series of quick successive moves, the first audio and video messages started moving via the internet, as the internet started touching millions of people. By the mid 1990s, the internet enabled everyday users to get onto a standard personal computer to "surf" the world wide web.

It took about 30 years before TCP/IP got a foothold, and over this period, it disrupted traditional business models and changed the dynamics of the world economy.

Today, from a historical perspective, blockchain is where the internet was at its conception. Both have somewhat mirror images:
- Both are similar in that a small group of passionate followers and supporters who were technically skilful and competent helped to conceptualize, fix, sustain and improve the technologies.
- Both blockchain and the internet TCP/IP protocol are by and -large open and continue to be maintained by volunteers and non-profit organizations.
- Both have been able to cut down the multitude of transactions by allowing people and organisations to easily communicate and share information, resulting in greater overall economic benefits to all.

Emerging from the Shadows of the Internet

Blockchain is conceptually designed very much like the way the internet was built, and it offers more. This is due to technological advances that can have far-reaching impact on the financial services sector and other industries in the economy.

Blockchain has a built-in robustness. By being able to absorb and store large chunks of information that are identical across its network, blockchain cannot be controlled by any single entity. In addition, because it has a large distributed computing network, it cannot fail in its entirety.

These attributes of blockchain drive many observers and participants to conclude that it is hot on the heels of the internet. They claim that a revolution is unfolding in our midst.

Going beyond this current rage, blockchain is, in essence, an ever-growing set of databases that are distributed across a network and not connected to any one processor. Each of these databases maintains a growing list of proper records, and within these data structures, there are *blocks*. Each block has a timestamp and a link to a previous block.

Cryptography, a method of storing and transmitting data in a form that only those for whom it is intended can read and process it, ensures that users can access only the segments of the blockchain that they own. They can do so only because they have a set of private keys that is instrumental to access the file. This is to ensure that everyone's copy of the distributed blockchain is kept in synchronization.

This was the notion introduced by Satoshi Nakamoto, a name that is widely accepted as a pseudonym, who applied software cryptography to digital currency. In essence, the underlying system was one of disguising and revealing information through complex mathematics. This breakthrough resulted in information that could be shared and viewed only by the intended recipients. Everyone else would be "blocked" out.

In a paper titled "Bitcoin: A Peer-to-Peer Electronic Cash System," Satoshi basically introduced blockchain in the form of a digital currency. This digital currency or software was designed such that it would be able to support a broad range of transactions. This implemented-solution enabled specialized codes and data fields from the very beginning through the use of a programming language. Figure 7.2 details key stages in blockchain development.

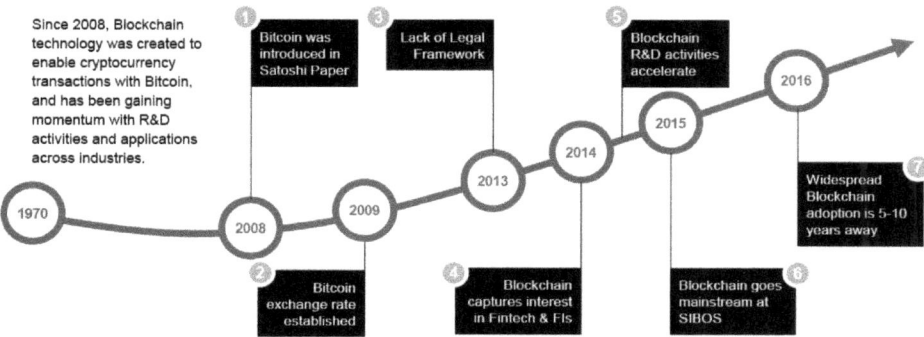

Figure 7.2: Blockchain genesis

By introducing and facilitating the use of blockchain, bitcoin was born from within this framework as the first digital currency that aimed to address the double spending problem. Unlike the currency commonly used in the real world, this currency can be owned, transferred or relied upon by everyone without the need for an intermediary such as a bank or a central authority like a reserve bank.

Blockchains have gradually become a means of ordering and verifying transactions in a distributed ledger, where a network of computers maintains and validates a record of consensus of those transactions with a cryptographic audit trail.

From the initial conceptualization, blockchain has been meant to be decentralized, and it paves the way for users to exchange information without the need for an external party. All exchanges and transactions are logged and made available in a public ledger, and this helps to ensure authenticity while preventing fraud.

Blockchain Technology Architecture

Broadly, a blockchain is a lattice network of computers linked not to a central server, but rather to each other (see Figure 7.3). Computers in this network define and agree on a shared state of data and adhere to certain constraints imposed upon this data. This shared state is simply a distributed state machine pioneered by an open-source, public blockchain-based distributed computing platform called Ethereum where each "block" can change the current state. (The section "How It Works" explains *blocks* in more detail.)

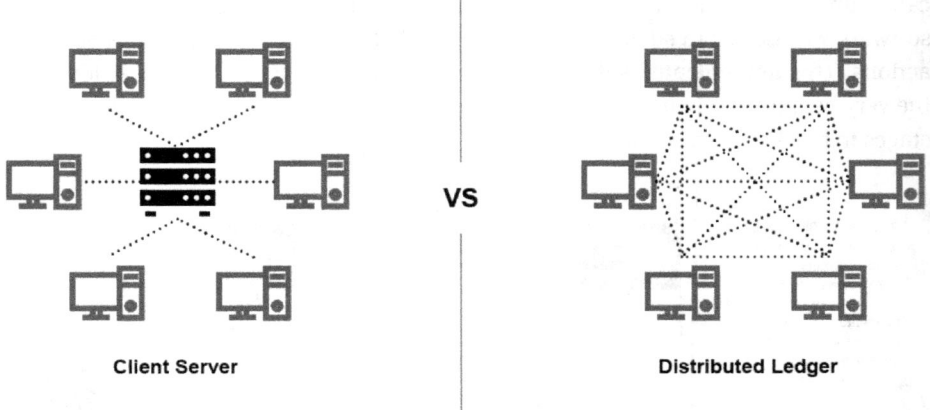

Client Server   VS   Distributed Ledger

Figure 7.3: Core characteristics of blockchains

This unique design of blockchain technology, while enjoying its limelight in terms of being compared with the internet, has its own attributes that make it very special.

Blockchain, by its very nature, was conceived to operate in a decentralized manner (see Figure 7.4). In this way, there is no one user who can claim ownership of the network, and all network participants have a full copy of the ledgers and of every block. In this way, the role of intermediaries and middlemen are removed.

This results in "trust" becoming a core attribute for the completion of transactions.

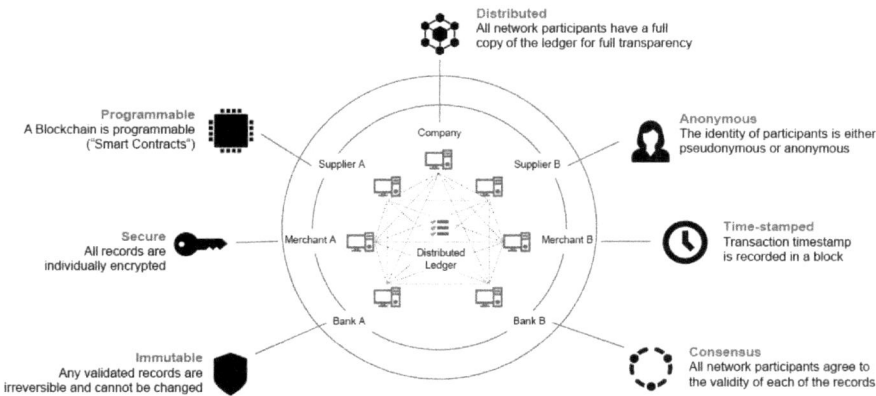

Figure 7.4: Attributes of a blockchain

Anonymity and privacy are additional traits that make blockchain technology very special. Privacy in blockchain can be maintained through encryption and cryptography. When the user publishes required data, the user is assured that the information will not be misused. For users wanting privacy for their transactions and identities, they can create private networks where access is limited and people can choose from a list of entities to be added onto that blockchain network.

Timestamping is *de rigeur* in the conventional business world, and blockchain mirrors this importance, which makes the technology useful. This is because blockchain technology keeps track of the creation and modification time of a document and records details of the specific date and time at which it happens. This allows the user in the system to know when the information was created by viewing its history. Upon the inclusion of any cryptographic digest file, blockchain can share details of what data existed at which point in time.

Hence, from the signing of important documents, like legal agreements to insurance contracts, to creating patents and even registering academic papers, there are endless opportunities to use blockchain because of this key feature of timestamping. Prior to the arrival of blockchain, this was a time-consuming and laborious process.

The term *immutable* is generally described as something absolute and irreversible. When this term is viewed in the context of a private blockchain, it implies that once the data is entered into the system, there should not be any discretion to change it. Within this context, each transaction is subjected to sufficient validation checks.

Subsequently, cryptography will ensure that the information is not altered or manipulated. With the private blockchain having this unique characteristic, it becomes easily acceptable for an organization to adopt such a technology given its advantages over conventional spreadsheets and databases.

A distinguishing feature that gives this particular blockchain a unique difference over other technologies and applications is its security feature. The use of *keys* to secure the blocks that exist in the ledger have created an enviable situation. There is no known case of any hacker who has successfully broken into a blockchain system because every block that has been created in the system has its unique cryptographic key created and stored in the next block. For a hacker to successfully make a change in a specific block, the user has to change the parent hash in the start block, and each and every subsequent bock until the latest block.

The unique programmability feature of private blockchains is one of the several reasons for its growing popularity among users. For any one blockchain, a user can create a "smart contract"—or set of computer-based software instructions meant to reside on a blockchain—to determine how the blockchain operates. Once this smart contract is created and shared in the blockchain network, any subsequent user or business can build new applications and incorporate them into the network because of the decentralized architecture.

These elements of programmable smart contracts, security, and anonymity, among others, make blockchain technology a magnet for business and governments. It is precisely these features that lead to the growing awareness, understanding and acceptance of blockchain technology.

Blockchain—How It Works

In its most basic form, a blockchain consists of a chain of blocks, each of which contains a set of information. In its raw form, this technique was developed in 1991 by a group of researchers who wanted to timestamp their documents in a digital manner without having to back-date them or giving other users the opportunity to tamper with them.

For the most part, after it was developed, it went unused and unnoticed until 2008 when Nakamoto revisited the technology. By then, blockchain developed an interesting proposition. When someone had recorded some information inside the blockchain, it became every difficult to alter it.

To understand the concept closer, it is good to look at a specific "block" of data. The typical block of metadata contains six core elements:
- Version, which states the latest version of the block.
- The previous block header hash, which is a reference to the block's *parent*.

- The Merkle root hash, a cryptographic hash of all the transactions included in the block. The existence of the hash is critical because the moment someone alters the data in the block, the hash changes.
- Time, which records when the block was created.
- nBits, which refers to the *difficulty* level that was used to create this block.
- Nonce ("number used once"), a random value that the creator of a block is allowed to manipulate however they so choose

These six fields constitute the block header. The rest of a block contains transactions that the miner can choose to include in the block that they create.

Basically, users create transactions and submit them to the network, where they sit in a pool waiting to be included in a block. Figure 7.5 illustrates the basic steps in a typical blockchain transaction.

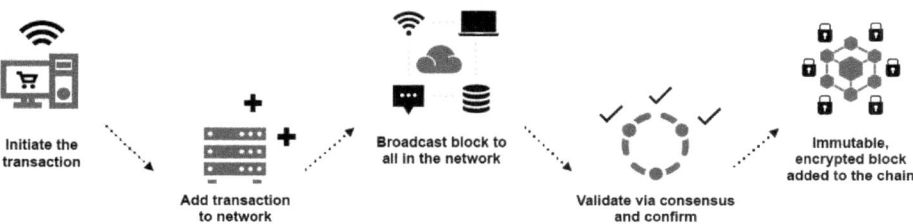

Initiate the transaction   Add transaction to network   Broadcast block to all in the network   Validate via consensus and confirm   Immutable, encrypted block added to the chain

Figure 7.5: A typical blockchain transaction

As the blockchain network grows bigger, and more nodes and miners participate in it, the overall consensus tends to become stronger on account of more participating players who tend to enforce their own rules (while other players also enforce theirs).

Miners play an instrumental role as they laboriously validate new transactions and record them on the global ledger, or blockchain. Specifically, their key purpose is to ensure that blocks remain secure and are not subjected to tampering. The role of miners is better understood when viewed within the context of public and private blockchains.

To recap, a public blockchain is virtually an open network where anyone can join and participate in it. It is a public network, and digital currencies, especially bitcoins, provide a prime example of how it exists today. Private blockchains, as the name implies, exist because the network has been commissioned privately and there are restrictions to participation.

Given this understanding of both public and private blockchains, there exists a protocol known as a *proof-of-work* (PoW). Broadly, PoW is an arduous effort that exists to ensure that external intrusions do not take place. Every time someone works on a block, there is a need for validation that the work took place, accompanied by a confirmation, and most of all, that it remains secure.

The existence of PoW makes it extremely difficult to alter any aspect of the blockchain. In this way, users and potential users are assured that the information they are sharing remains protected.

Hence, once a transaction has been issued, miners who operate in public blockchain compete vigorously with fellow miners to solve these complicated tasks. For solving these highly complex technical problems, miners are rewarded in the form of transaction fees.

Further, because of the volume of competition involved, PoW requires astronomical computing resources.

Equally important is that PoW should not be misunderstood with another concept called *proof-of-stake* (PoS). PoS is a type of algorithm in which the blockchain network aims to achieve distributed consensus. Here, the creator of the next block is chosen via various combinations, including random selection based on age and wealth (that is, the *stake*). Based on these criteria, the more stake that one has and the older the last validation was, the greater are one's chances of being selected.

In a private blockchain, PoW and PoS exist in a slightly different form. Given its nature as a private database operating as a deployment in its own right, there is less need to incentivize participants, and consensus protocols may vary from one private blockchain to another.

To put this discussion in perspective, blockchains have had the benefit of PoW to get mining going at the point in time when there was a fundamental need to get a certain volume of work done. With the passage of time, inefficiencies have emerged. PoS appeared to be the next logical answer because validators in the PoS system are selected by the algorithm, and it makes the overall validation faster and therefore more scalable.

PoS, where the stake has a money value, has now evolved into a new protocol called *proof-of-authority* (PoA), and here the validator's identity executes the role of stake. In this circumstance, identity refers to the exchanges between a validator's personal identification on the platform against what has been publicly certified for this same individual. This is to ensure that the two people are one and the same.

Private vs Public Blockchains—A Closer Look

Given the relative youth of blockchain technology, it has been an inevitable consequence that different strains of it have emerged, namely in the manner of public and private blockchains. Both have some core similarities:

- Both exist as decentralized peer-to-peer (P2P) networks, and their users replicate shared append-only ledgers of digitally signed transactions.

-   The consensus principle applies within permissible levels as this drives them to replicate the data so that it is synchronized within their respective networks.
-   The principles of immutability and anonymity are adhered to.

In a simple example shown in Figure 7.6, an individual wants to buy an asset from another. To get this done, he creates a transaction or a block to achieve his goal. Subsequently, the buyer's request in a public transaction is broadcast throughout the network. While the transaction flows in both public and private blockchains are broadly similar, consensus in a public blockchain is attained at the trust-less peering stage, allowing for the transaction to be completed.

Essentially, the buyer's purchase request in a public blockchain is completed because there are adequate mechanisms in place through which all parties in the public blockchain can reach a consensus on what the truth is. Trust and power are distributed (or shared) among the network's stakeholders, rather than concentrated in a single individual or entity.

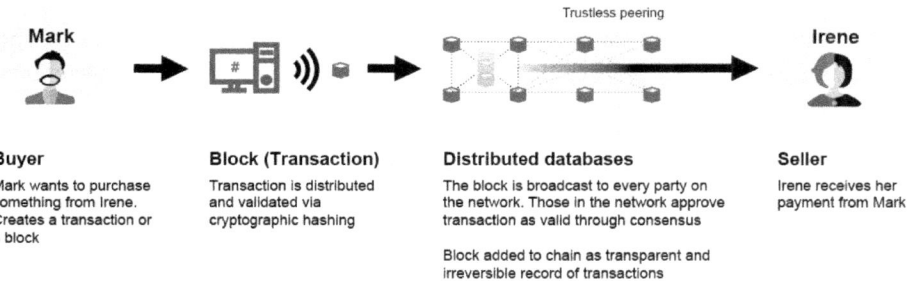

| Mark | | Block (Transaction) | Trustless peering | Irene |

Buyer

Mark wants to purchase something from Irene. Creates a transaction or a block

Block (Transaction)

Transaction is distributed and validated via cryptographic hashing

Distributed databases

The block is broadcast to every party on the network. Those in the network approve transaction as valid through consensus

Block added to chain as transparent and irreversible record of transactions

Seller

Irene receives her payment from Mark

Figure 7.6: Public blockchain—consensus prevails

One of the biggest challenges in a public blockchain is its need for large computing resources so that its users can maintain a distributed ledger at a large scale. Specifically, to achieve consensus, each node in a network must solve the previously mentioned PoW to ensure all are synchronized. This notion of PoW is specific and unique to bitcoins.

Another disadvantage of public blockchains lies in their openness, which suggests little to no privacy for transactions. In addition, it only supports a weak notion of security. Both of these are key deliberations for an organization in terms of how it wants to leverage the blockchain.

Public and private blockchains differ in terms of "who is allowed to participate in the network," "who is implementing the consensus protocol and managing the shared ledger" (see Table 7.1). A public blockchain network is mostly laissez faire. That is, within its ecosystem, it is completely open and anyone can join and participate in the network. The public blockchain typically has an incentivizing mechanism to encourage more participants to join the network.

Table 7.1: Comparison of Public and Private Blockchain

Blockchain Types	Public Blockchain	Private Blockchain
Ledger manager	Anyone	One or a small group
Incentivising user	"Cryptoeconomics"	Reputational risk
Data production	Anyone	Permissioned group of people (such as licensed banks)
Ledger access	Anyone	One or a small group
Ledger storage	Massively distributed	Permissioned entities' location

In contrast, private blockchains are not centralized under one organization. They are decentralized and are by invitation-only.

These chains also require an invitation and must be validated by either the user who started the network or by a set of rules put in place by the network starter. Restrictions are generally placed on who is allowed to participate in the network, and permission to access the blockchain is more tightly controlled in certain transactions.

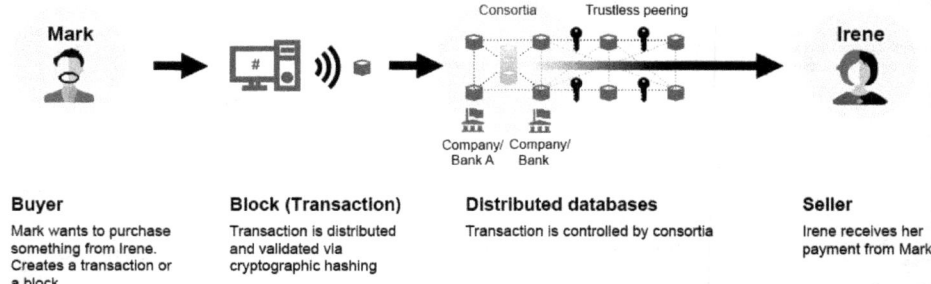

Buyer	Block (Transaction)	Distributed databases	Seller
Mark wants to purchase something from Irene. Creates a transaction or a block	Transaction is distributed and validated via cryptographic hashing	Transaction is controlled by consortia	Irene receives her payment from Mark

Figure 7.7: Private Ledger—Operates on Permissions and Approvals

Further, members of the network are selected before they are able to download the protocol and get onto the network. Only entities participating in a particular transaction will have knowledge and access to it, blocking out other entities who will have no access.

This type of blockchain, being a private network, helps with rights to modify or even read the blockchain state and are usually restricted to a few users. The access control mechanism could differ, depending on several factors: existing participants can decide on future entrants; a regulator could issue licenses for participation; or a consortium could be entrusted to make decisions. After an entity has joined the network, it will play a role in preserving the blockchain in a decentralized manner.

Taking the example of the same individual Mark, who wants to buy an asset from another, he still has to create a transaction or a block to achieve his goal within the confines of the private blockchain. See Figure 7.7. The transaction is still disseminated, but it has to be validated with cryptographic hashing before it reaches the controlling participants in the blockchain. Subsequently, only upon their approval will the block be readied for clearance and completion.

Table 7.2: Public and Private Blockchains—A Snapshot

Category	Public Blockchains	Private Blockchains
Participation	Participation is not restricted and is open to any participation.	Read/write permissions can be restricted.
Permissions,	Write: Anyone Read: Anyone	Write: Operators control who can submit transactions. Read: Public or restricted.
Transparency & Trust	Transactions are publicly recorded. Trust is established through node replication and consensus mechanisms.	Limited transparency (not all data is exposed). Trust is dependent on a central authority.
Valid Transactions	51% of participating nodes	Based on pre-defined validators
Mining & Consensus Process	Anyone can mine (validate), Proof -of-Work is the primary consensus mechanism	Only permitted nodes are allowed to validate, various consensus mechanisms can be deployed
Privacy	Transaction details are public. Transacting participants remain anonymous or pseudonymous. For example, ZK-Snarks allows one to verify transactions while protecting users' privacy.	Participants are known to the central authority/operator in the private blockchain. Privacy and security controls keep identities private. Transaction details are revealed only to transacting participants and remain confidential for non-transacting parties.
Cost	Relatively low transaction cost	May be lower than public blockchain because of lower computing power required
Control	Neutral and decentralized (cannot be influenced by a single authority)	Centralized

Table 7.2: (continued)

Category	Public Blockchains	Private Blockchains
Currency	Available cryptocurrency (such as bitcoin)	Proprietary crytocurrency
Performance	Generally slower. Dependent on the number of participating nodes and computational powers.	Generally faster because consensus can be limited to predefined validators.
Advantages	Open, greater chances for adoption, no single authority controls or governs	Greater degree of control, faster, greater degree of scalability (transaction volumes), privacy controls

Private Blockchain Technology—What Is Next?

Private blockchain has evolved rapidly, but it is still very much in the early stages of a transformative impact. Early indications suggest that private blockchains will increasingly make an impact on real estate transactions, medical records, supply chain, legal records, and financial reporting among other things.

The spirit in which blockchain has evolved remains the same: All data needs can be mitigated and recorded on the blockchain.

New types of private blockchain technology solutions are rapidly being developed and improved, and these are likely to be more suitable for use by enterprises and regulated sectors. These distributed ledger technologies or Blockchain 2.0 are more likely to gain traction as eventual replacements for many financial services' back-office systems. Some of these are capable of forming the backbone of emerging smart contract-based solutions and applications.

These blockchain-based networks make it possible for entities to collaborate, share data, and exchange assets even if they do not have complete trust in each other (not everybody knows everybody). The "entities" could also be machines or devices, which in the future, will increasingly be interacting autonomously. They will need even higher degrees of integrity assurance.

The Way Forward with Blockchains

Mathematical principles are a key element to supporting these new trust models, but they can provide value only within the context of a well-designed, well-implemented, and well-maintained governance model.

While the rate of innovation in the blockchain ecosystem remains high, there are tremendous amounts of work currently being undertaken to address key issues, such as the need for scale, permissioning, security and supporting confidentiality.

A key point is that the notion of addressing confidentiality is incompatible with the need for total transparency. Network participants will have to design governance models that provide appropriate and acceptable levels of assurance that the unobserved details are nevertheless valid.

Looking ahead, to really leverage the potential of blockchain-based networks, the following two conditions are needed:

- A new, potentially radically different, approach to how processes are run in both the public and private sector
- Leveraging technology that is scalable, secure, and usable, supported by laws and governance frameworks that are fit for the purpose

---

Leveraging Blockchain in Healthcare Insurance

Blockchain is essentially a permanent and immutable record of transactions within a network. At the root of the blockchain are digital ledgers that are distributed among all network participants to serve as a common source of truth. When a transaction is conducted, it is recorded in sequence in the digital ledger, and these blocks are then tied together into a blockchain. Because the system relies on references to other blocks that are cryptographically secure within the digital ledger, it is almost impossible to falsify. Most observers therefore believe the system to be immensely more trustworthy and transparent than traditional approaches to sharing data across a value chain or even within an enterprise.

Within this context, KPMG Digital Village embarked on a study to understand the information flow within a global insurance company with a view to ascertaining how private blockchain technology could be deployed. The ultimate goal is to help drive a wider transformation as part of the on-going data-driven "fourth industrial revolution."

The study worked on the premise that insurers view blockchain as a technology that can improve efficiency, lower the costs of transaction processing, enhance the customer experience, improve data quality, increase trust between parties and support auditability, among other benefits.

In the ensuing investigations, KPMG Digital Village recognized that insurers could potentially leverage private blockchain technology to deliver more efficient processes, improve the pricing and risk management of internal operations, and enhance the core principle of delivering trust through a better claims experience and the use of smart contract models. There was also the opportunity to reap the potential of distributed ledger technologies so that insurers could better serve clients through faster and more convenient and secure services.

In-depth investigations showed the potential of three significant results:

- Through the private blockchain solution, insurers would be able to manage multiple policies and all within a single private blockchain technology application. Within this context, their customers would be able to view their policies with the click of a few buttons on their smartphones.
- Customers and prospects would be able to browse and purchase products through their smartphones. Previously, this was not possible. Further, they would be able to purchase multiple policies with minimal disruptions and downtime.
- Perhaps most notably, customers could potentially submit claims and receive payouts faster,

delivering a significant improvement in total customer experience. Part of this involves claims data being shared simultaneously across all counterparties. At the same time, the identities and contract provisions can be immediately verified and payments automatically made.

As a result, an insurer will reap the benefits of less adjudication and negotiations, resulting in lower costs.

This is just one working example within the context of a health insurer. There are numerous applications of private blockchain within the insurance sector, and this is just a bird's eye view:
- Personal accident insurance: Creating a transparent and seamless claims journey that dramatically improves customer satisfaction
- Record keeping: Leveraging private blockchain to create, organize and maintain company records in a single, reliable and accessible repository
- Digital identities: Using blockchain data and digital ledgers to digitize and validate customer information and improve compliance
- Claims management: Automating the verification of coverage and streamlining claims settlements to improve operational efficiency and remove costs
- Peer-to-peer: Building a peer-to-peer network to establish smart contacts without the need for intermediary or administrator

In essence, private blockchain can accelerate the transformation in the insurance sector, resulting in a competitive, leading-edge advantage for the insurer.

Jan Reinmueller is founder and head of KPMG's Digital Village in Singapore. Jan brings international experience and knowledge of the US, Europe, India, and ASEAN markets. Jan helps organizations transform through innovation, building new business models or optimizing cost using emerging technologies.

At KPMG, true innovation begins with revolutionary ideas, but to deliver real business results, it needs to work hand-in-hand with business adoption and risk management.

At KPMG Digital Village, we bring corporates, start-ups, investors, and government bodies together in a collaborative ecosystem to drive the adoption and integration of innovative solutions. Like a living lab for innovation, we co-innovate to turn innovative ideas into robust, practical solutions.

Chapter 8
Use Cases of Blockchain Technology in Financial Services

After reading the previous chapter, it would be easy to imagine that blockchain and smart contract technologies have the potential to replace financial institutions entirely, by creating ledgers and workflow logic that can be executed between parties in a peer-to-peer manner, without the need for financial intermediaries.

The reality is that blockchain technology is still at an early stage. The first modern blockchain, Ethereum, was created in 2014. This is in contrast with the internet (TCP/IP was invented in the 70s) and artificial intelligence (IBM's Deep Blue beat Gary Kasparov in chess in 1997).

Granted, we are living in an age of ever-accelerating development and adoption of new technologies. Nevertheless, it is easy for industry participants and the media to be caught in a cycle of excitement and disappointment as they witness the transformative potential of blockchain technology, and then realize that its revolutionary promises have not yet been delivered.

In this chapter, we advocate strategic vision, pragmatism, and risk taking:
- *Strategic vision*, because the time has come to think deeply about the implications of blockchain technology and what they mean for the financial industry in the mid- to long-term.
- *Pragmatism*, because the technology is still in the process of being developed and optimized by hundreds of thousands of engineers around the world, feverishly addressing the issues of privacy, scalability, inter-operability, and user-experience.
- *Risk-taking*, because great technological changes tend to reward those who are prepared to invest ahead of the curve, rather than the ones who wait until new technologies are fully proven and accepted.

Also in this chapter we will consider the implications of this technology in fintech and look at a series of specific use cases that reflect the role and applications of blockchain.

What Is Currently at Stake?

Financial institutions around the world are engaged in a generational transition into the digital age. Physical channels are replaced by web, mobile, video, messaging interface. Human-assisted interactions are replaced by self-service machines, apps and bots. Decision-making is supported by scoring algorithms and artificial intelli-

DOI 10.1515/9781547400904- 008

gence. Risk detection and management is enhanced by access to proliferating data storage capacity and data analysis techniques.

The promise to all of us is an improvement in the richness and efficiency of customer interactions as well as internal processing activities by multiple orders of magnitude. However, a major impediment to this trend towards greater productivity is that financial institutions are less and less in control of their own business processes.

As a matter of fact, financial institutions are dealing with an ever-increasing number of stakeholders, resulting in growing fragmentation and complexity of their business processes. For instance, indirect distribution remains a cornerstone of the financial sector, despite expectations that white-shoe brokers and agents would quickly become a thing of the past. The advent of online information sources as the number one influencer of financial decisions has given rise to the emergence of price comparison portals and affiliate marketing arrangements. In a connected world, every shopping occasion is an opportunity to bundle financial products, be it auto financing, travel insurance, or extended warranties. High-net-worth clients and family offices require an increasing level of service customization that integrated banking channels struggle to deliver. One implication of complex distribution ecosystems is the cost of reconciling financial balances and databases between legal entities that do not trust each other.

Furthermore, economic globalization means that financial institutions are interacting with thousands of counterparties around the world in the context of payment services, financing activities, and exchange of financial assets. Each of these cross-border transactions requires complex contractual frameworks and multiple margins of safety in the form of risk premiums and collaterals, given the delays and costs of international legal action if something goes wrong. One implication of globalization is the cost of these risk premiums and working capital buffers, as well as the delays experienced by customers when they need to transfer financial assets across jurisdictions.

A final driver of complexity and friction is the web of regulatory and compliance requirements issued by dozens and sometimes hundreds of government agencies and regulatory bodies in multiple jurisdictions. Although the prevention of consumer abuse, systemic threats to the global financial system, money laundering and terrorism financing are all legitimate objectives, these risks are, more often than not, regulated by uncoordinated institutions that do not trust each other. Therefore, independent risk-management procedures and inspections are necessary. One implication of this phenomenon is the escalating cost of compliance and risk management for financial institutions, which is eventually passed on to customers in the form of increased margins or deteriorating financial inclusion for high-risk customers.

In this chapter, we will outline how blockchain technology offers the potential to help financial institutions to reduce the cost of dealing with this complexity and these frictions.

The stakes are significant. Each major financial institution spends dozens to hundreds of millions of dollars in administrative costs related to data vetting, data reconciliation, and manual compliance procedures. Global institutions have been fined billions of dollars for lapses in their internal vetting procedures.

But in the medium to long term, the stakes associated with blockchain technology are not merely driven by cost reduction. Blockchain technology also allows financial institutions to serve new markets and deploy new business models in several ways.

First, by reducing the cost of dealing with complex ecosystems, blockchain technology will allow institutions to serve low-margin and high-risk customer segments that they cannot properly address currently. This opportunity for greater financial inclusion can take many forms. It includes the potential to create and operate bank accounts for many more consumers and SMEs (small- and medium-sized enterprises) in emerging markets. By enabling cryptographically signed attestations of identity, property and credentials, blockchain technology also can enable many more consumers to access mortgage financing at lower risk premiums and SMEs to access working capital financing at higher loan-to-collateral ratios. Blockchain technology also makes it possible to offer more streamlined supply chain finance solutions to many SMEs that currently rely on open account trade arrangements.

Second, through a mechanism known as *tokenization* (the creation of digital equivalents to physical and financial assets), blockchain technology can create more efficient primary and secondary capital markets for assets that are currently exchanged through high-cost intermediaries, or not exchanged at all. The application of blockchain technology to post-trade settlement of listed securities has been widely discussed and is explained in this chapter. The technology also can be applied to non-listed securities such as real-estate assets, illiquid holdings of alternative and private equity funds, and commercial insurance of high-risk industrial assets.

Now, let's consider a variety of actual blockchain use cases.

Use Case: Payments

Problem Statement

At a high level, the payment industry is based on solving a simple problem: Party A wants to purchase something from party B. Party B does not want to lose the sale and therefore wishes to deliver the goods immediately in exchange for a proof of payment. Unless the payment is in cash, party B needs some kind of guarantee that the payment has been triggered and will eventually reach party B's bank account. Conversely, party A does is not keen to advance the cash unless it receives some kind of guarantee that it will eventually receive the goods.

This simple problem is a hard one to solve in the real world. How do we ensure that party A is not actually bankrupt when it promises the payment? Even if party

A has the money in its account, how do we ensure that it is not going to spend it on something else between the time of the promise and the time of delivery to party B's bank account?

The resolution of this problem has given rise to thousands of financial actors such as card issuers, card networks, merchant acquirers, international payment messaging networks, domestic payment utilities and others, all taking a fee because they offer some kind of guarantee to one or both parties as part of this exchange of goods and value.

Application of Blockchain Technology

When all ecosystem actors are connected to a common blockchain network, each possesses a synchronized version of the same database. This database can be queried at any time to find out the account balances of each actor, measured in a given digital token. The digital token can be bitcoin, ether, or any arbitrary token, such as a token that has a value pegged to the value of the US dollar, euro or the Singapore dollar.

Figure 8.1 describes how payments are initiated and recorded between parties. When actor A wants to make a payment, it generates a transaction request which is submitted to the blockchain network. As soon as the transaction is validated by the network, it is recorded in the shared ledger and the balances of each actor are simultaneously updated in each copy of the ledger.

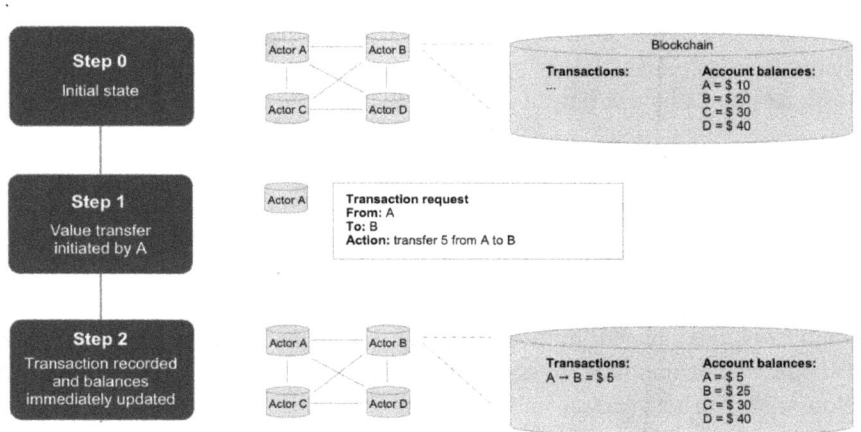

Figure 8.1: Transaction flow

This mechanism can be implemented in various ways. For example, it is possible to ensure the privacy of account balances by storing hashes of transactions in the shared ledger, rather than the transactions themselves. A *hash* is a type of digital signature that uniquely identifies the content of a transaction in a non-reversible and tamper-proof way. This allows all network actors to keep a record of transaction activity, without being able to read the content of individual transactions, which are only disclosed to the sender and the recipient of the transactions. Complex cryptographic techniques known as *zero-knowledge proofs* allow each network actor to verify that the confidential account balances and the public transaction hashes are synchronized at all times.

Implementation Examples

One of the best-known examplesof payment implementation using blockchain technology, is Project Ubin, spearheaded by the Monetary Authority of Singapore, involving ConsenSys as a pilot participant. As part of Project Ubin, 11 banks have implemented a real-time gross settlement system (RTGS) that allow them to settle large value transactions in a tokenized form of Singapore dollars with no single point of failure. Project details are publicly available online.

Other financial institutions, such as Banco Santander and the South African Reserve Bank, have recently announced successfully piloting similar implementations, following collaborations with ConsenSys.

Use Case: Workflow Tracking and Supply Chain Management

Problem Statement

A workflow is the visual representation of any business process that involves successive actions by various actors.

In today's world, most workflows are facilitated by application software, and the status and history of each workflow are stored in enterprise databases. For example, opening a bank account involves the collection of customer information, the selection of a particular account plan, the creation of the account, the creation of a payment card, the attribution of an online banking login device, and various attempts to cross-sell additional products to the customer. Customer service representatives execute this workflow by following a series of instructions displayed on their computer screens.

The electronic management and tracking of workflows become more complex when there are multiple organizations involved in the completion of a business process that trust each other enough to perform specific tasks as part of the business process, but do not trust each other enough to allow one single party to keep a centralized record of the complete information flow.

One example is the mortgage application process. Mortgage applicants are generally asked to provide information to the bank about their personal identity and income level, and the details and value of the property. However, applicant cannot be trusted to provide accurate information, and therefore they are asked to provide various paper certificates that allow the bank to corroborate their statements (birth certificates, payslips, bank statements, land titles). Often, third-party inspectors or information databases are asked to confirm the value of the property. In an ideal world, all these pieces of information would be stored in a single database operated by a trusted central party. In practice, no bank, employer, or government agency is quite ready to let a third party act as custodian of the entire information flow.

Another example is the claims process in the insurance industry. The claims workflow involves insured customers, third parties who have caused or suffered a damage, insurance brokers or agents, insurers, claims adjuster, and repair service providers. Each actor interacts with other actors as part of a complex, interdependent ecosystem. The transmission of one actor to the next often involves handwritten forms and original signatures.

Application of Blockchain Technology

When all ecosystem actors are connected to a common blockchain network, teach possesses a synchronized version of the same database. This database can be queried at any time to find out the status of each application or claim, and who has signed what attestation.

Figure 8.2 describes how workflows are implemented and recorded between parties using a blockchain network. When actor A has completed a process step, for example, the evaluation of an application with the record ID #2, it generates a transaction request that is submitted to the blockchain network. As soon as the transaction is validated by the network, it is recorded in the shared ledger and the workflow status is simultaneously updated in each copy of the ledger.

Using *smart contracts*, small software applications engraved in the blockchain, it is possible to trigger actions as soon as a process step has been completed. For example, the activation of a smart contract could trigger a disbursement in tokenized US dollars or Singapore dollars when an account-opening application has been accepted. This simple mechanism makes it possible to manage complex supply chain payments and financing products using blockchain-based platforms (such as invoice financing).

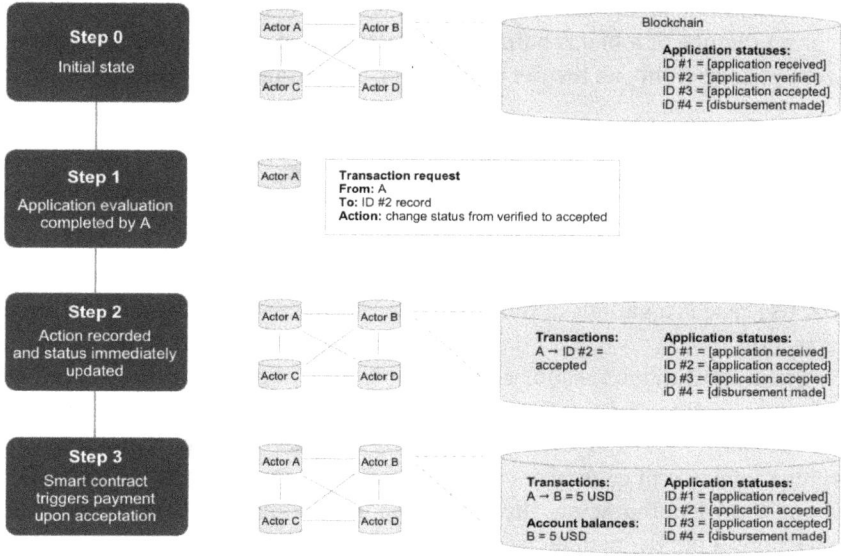

Figure 8.2: Workflow of an example blockchain transaction

Implementation Examples

The workflow-tracking use case is not specific to financial services. For example, BHP Billiton, the mining giant, collaborated with ConsenSys to develop a customized platform based on blockchain technology that will be used to track the status and movements of mining samples between the company and its numerous partners and third-party contractors. Similarly, Viant, a ConsenSys company, recently announced supply chain implementation pilots with GSK and the WWF for the tracking of pharmaceuticals and food supplies, respectively.

On the supply chain finance side, ConsenSys is currently supporting the development of a consortium platform in Europe that connects several commodity trading businesses and financial institutions.

In Hong Kong, a group of financial institutions is working with the Hong Kong Monetary Authority (HKMA) to deploy a blockchain-based platform to track the issuance and financing of invoices between customers and suppliers. Such a system makes it possible for banks to obtain real-time visibility on what invoices have been issued by which customer and to offer financing to mid-sized suppliers with no risk that a single invoice would be financed twice by two separate institutions.

In another implementation example, the French Federation of Insurers in France is exploring the use of a blockchain-based platform in order to track the transfer of insurance policies from one insurer to the other, as mandated by law.

Use Case: KYC (Know Your Customer) Process

Problem Statement

The KYC use case is a variant of the workflow tracking use case outlined in the preceding section.

Financial institutions are subject to ever-growing compliance requirements when it comes to collecting and verifying customer information prior to the opening of a financial account. This extensive data collection exercise is driven by multiple imperatives: the protection of consumers against misselling, the fight against money laundering and terrorism financing, the need to be absolutely certain about what kinds of transactions a family member or employee is authorized to perform and on which account(s), and so on.

This means that customers must provide the same extensive set of documents every time that they approach a new financial institution or even apply for a new financial product, resulting in painful customer experiences and, sometimes, frictions that act as barriers for innovative fintech companies to effectively compete with incumbent institutions.

The KYC process creates privacy concerns for consumers, who provide extensive personal data to brokers, online price comparison portals, and financial institutions, often with limited visibility into who has access to that data once it has been submitted. (This is a concern particularly when consumers do not end up opening an account with these parties.)

Even worse, financial institutions do not get it right every time, as is evident from the millions and billions of US dollars in fines that have been imposed on multinational and local financial institutions over the last 20 years.

Application of Blockchain Technology

When all ecosystem actors are connected to a common blockchain network, each possesses a synchronized version of the same database. This database can be queried at any time to find out the status of each application or document, who has verified what attestation, and who has accessed or deleted what document. The database can also serve as an immutable audit record that compliance officers and regulators can monitor in real time.

Figure 8.3 describes how many financial institutions, government agencies and regulators could cooperate and eliminate duplicative process steps in the KYC and account-opening process.

The customer (actor A) uploads and signs its personal information into a data vault (actor B) and then authorizes a first financial institution (actor Fi1) to access that information and verify that it is genuine, that is, by checking the original documents or arranging a site visit. Actor Fi1 and/or a local government agency (actor G) issues cryptographic signatures in order to confirm that each piece of information is genuine.

Subsequently, the customer (actor A) wishes to open an account at a separate financial institution (actor Fi2). Actor A is then able to authorize Fi2 to access the same information, along with the attestations already generated by Fi1 and the local government agency (actor G). In theory, this new process can speed up account-opening immeasurably.

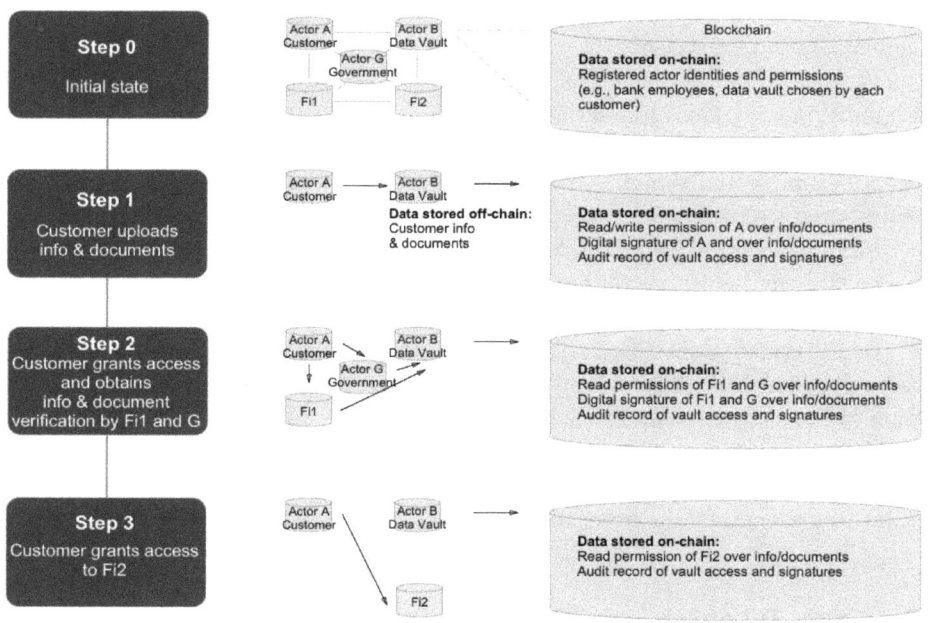

Figure 8.3: Account-opening workflow

Of course, a number of practical issues arise in this ideal process:
- First, generally, most regulators do not allow financial institutions to rely on verifications made by other institutions (though some exceptions exist, such as the

case of brokerage arrangements). Even if they did, the implications in terms of respective liabilities have not yet been explored (for example, what happens if an institution receives laundered money after relying on verifications performed by another institution). In a regulated world, we believe that these issues can be solved as soon as stakeholders realize that shared KYC will lead to more compliance, not less.

- o   Second, many financial institutions are not keen to allow their competitors to take advantage of verifications that they have completed and tap into their customer base. We believe that this issue can be solved via bilateral or multilateral arrangements, especially in situations where many small challengers are motivated to cooperate in order to compete with the top incumbents.
- o   Third, the KYC use case requires an ecosystem of third-party service providers, government agencies, and data vaults, all connected to the same regulated blockchain environment. This ecosystem does not exist yet.

Implementation Examples

A number of variations around the KYC use case are being researched and piloted by consortiums of financial institutions around the world.

For example, in Belgium, a consortium of four large banks is working on a blockchain-based KYC utility for corporate banking.

In Singapore, the Infocomm Media Development Authority of Singapore (IMDA) has collaborated with several major banks to deliver a proof-of-concept for a know your customer (KYC) blockchain.

On the crypto-asset side, Parity Technologies launched PICOPS (Parity ICO Passport Service) in 2017. The service offers a means to validate that the owner of an Ethereum wallet has passed an ID background check and is not part of a restricted set of users (for example, a US citizen or an individual on an official watchlist). The service was discontinued in May 2018 over concerns related to the compatibility of the service with GDPR (General Data Protection Regulation) in Europe.

Use Case: Tokenization of Investment, Consumption and Physical Assets

Problem Statement

To date, and particularly since the beginning of 2017, over USD $20bn in funding has been raised by technology companies via token launches. The explosive growth of funds raised via token launches has attracted the attention of investors, regulators, the media and society at large, even though the funds raised represent merely a single-digit percentage of the funds raised by venture capital-backed technology companies worldwide.

There are differing views as to whether token launches are solving an actual problem.

Some observers believe that token launches are primarily a way for companies to access the hundreds of billions of US dollars of liquidity currently held by consumers and investors in the form of digital assets such as Bitcoin and Ethereum. The existence of that liquidity and the enthusiasm of digital asset holders for blockchain-themed projects are undeniable. There is indeed a perception that some projects are more likely to collect funds by appealing to that enthusiasm, rather than relying on more traditional fundraising channels.

Other observers believe that we are at the cusp of a paradigm shift, allowing projects to be funded by their future customers rather than by purely financial investors and thereby enabling a greater alignment of interests between product developers and product users. According to this worldview, the enthusiasm around token launches is a reflection of the growing uneasiness of consumers regarding the business models of many technology companies that use investor funds to offer products and services well below their cost, acquire customers and their personal information, and subsequently monetize customer data once they have achieved enough scale.

Both worldviews coexist, leading many researchers and regulators to distinguish several types of tokens:
- *Payment tokens*, such as bitcoins or tokens pegged to fiat currencies (such as the US dollar or Singapore dollar), are mostly used as a store of value, allowing their holders to pay for products and services in a frictionless way.
- *Investment tokens* (sometimes called *tokenized securities*) are primarily the digital representation of a financial asset, such as a share in a company, a unit held in an investment fund, or a commodity asset such as gold, oil or wheat. They are purchased by holders with an expectation of profit.
- *Consumptive tokens* represent the prepaid right of a holder to consume goods, content and services on a digital platform. They are very similar in nature to software licenses, or service subscriptions.
- Finally, some tokens are issued with no financial consideration.

Application of Blockchain Technology

The technical implementation of a token launch is extremely simple. The blockchain database is used as a registry of record for the token balances held by each user address.

Most tokens take the form of a smart contract that contains a database of the token balances held by each holder address, and a series of functions that govern how tokens can be used and transferred by holders (such as lock-in periods, who can receive tokens, what tokens can be used for, and under what rules can new tokens be issued). Many tokens are currently issued according to a smart contract standard called ERC20.

Figure 8.4 describes how actor A (issuer) can simply transfer 10 tokens to actor B (holder) by calling a smart contract function, assuming that certain conditions are met, such as that actor B is authorized to purchase the token from a KYC and AML standpoint.

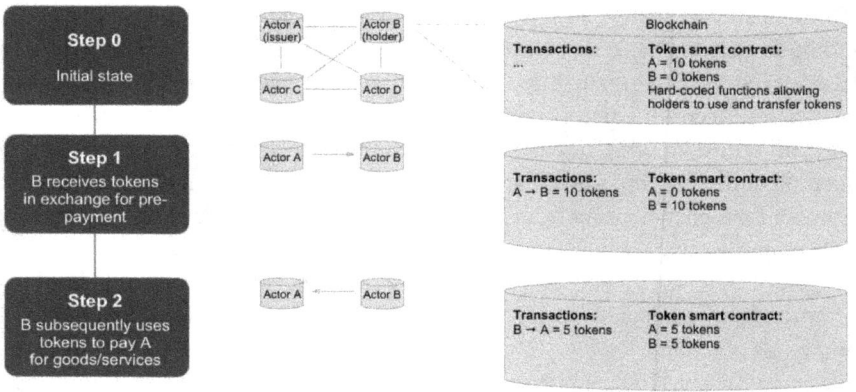

Figure 8.4: Smart contract function for a token transfer

Implementation Examples

To date, more than 1000 token launches have taken place, particularly in 2017 and 2018, including many investment tokens and consumptive tokens and a small number of payment tokens. Most of these tokens were issued on the Ethereum blockchain.

Far from being restricted to crypto-assets, the concept of tokenization is being applied to a broad range of traditional assets, as well.

For example, as part of Project Ubin, the Monetary Authority of Singapore used blockchain technology to tokenize Singapore dollars and to give them a digital existence on the blockchain. Several central banks and financial institutions (such as Banco Santander) are working on similar applications.

In another example, Medirio, a ConsenSys company, is using tokenization techniques to enable fractional ownership of real-estate assets, starting with a residential building in Brooklyn, NY, USA.

Use Case: Exchanges and Post-trade Settlement

Problem Statement

The global capital markets ecosystem involves thousands of intermediaries between investors, asset issuers, and regulators. These intermediaries play various critical roles currently. For example, brokers and exchanges help asset buyers and sellers find counterparties that are prepared to trade with them. Central securities depositories (CSD) hold securities in a central registry so that ownership can be easily transferred through a book entry rather than the transfer of physical certificates. Central counterparty clearing houses (CCPs) act as counterparties to the buyer and the seller and guarantee the terms of a trade, even if one party defaults on the agreement.

Although the global capital markets infrastructure is highly efficient when it comes to trading large volumes of frequently exchanged securities, it is often not adapted to low-volume assets that cannot carry the cost of these various intermediaries in every single trade. In fact, many assets are currently not traded on exchanges and rely on market makers, that is, financial institutions that set the price of these assets, create liquidity, and act as counterparties to buyers and sellers, sometimes taking a substantial profit in the process.

Many capital market participants around the world are currently exploring how blockchain technology can be used to streamline exchange and settlement processes for certain asset classes.

Application of Blockchain Technology

The application of blockchain technology to the capital markets infrastructure has generally revolved around three main questions:
- Can blockchains replace *asset registries*?
- Can blockchains and smart contracts allow investors to conduct their *trading activity* without relying on exchanges and brokers?
- Can blockchains streamline the *post-trade settlement* process?

Asset registries represent a fairly straightforward use case of blockchain technology, very similar to the tokenization use case described in the preceding section. In France, government agencies and legislative bodies are currently working together to allow asset issuers to rely on blockchains as registries of ownership of unlisted financial assets.

The application of blockchain technology to the trade activity itself is a hard problem. A key technical issue is that most blockchains involve validating nodes (sometimes called *miners*), which receive transactions from network users, put them together in blocks, and append these blocks to the shared blockchain ledger. The transmission of trade orders to these validating nodes would, in theory, allow these nodes to access and profit from advanced information regarding trading behaviors, unless these validating nodes are centralized and regulated as exchanges. Although many experiments are under way, they are at the research and development stage. The majority of so-called "decentralized" crypto-exchanges actually rely on centralized order books, or off-chain message boards where buy/sell orders are posted. (It is actually the post-trade settlement process that is decentralized.)

The post-trade settlement process, on the other hand, is a suitable application of blockchain technology, as the process is currently fraught with many delays and inefficiencies. After the asset registries are in place for both the financial assets and the means of payment (that is, when both financial assets and the means of payment are tokenized in digital registries), it is possible to use a smart contract to perform an atomic delivery of assets against payment. Here, the means of payment can be a crypto-asset or a tokenized fiat currency.

The mechanism is as follows:
1. First, a delivery-vs-payment smart contract is engraved in the blockchain. This smart contract is a simple program which, once written, cannot be manipulated by any party other than to execute exactly the functions for which it has been designed.
2. Prior to the trade, the smart contract receives in escrow both the tokenized financial assets from the seller and the tokenized payment from the buyer.
3. When the trade is agreed upon by the seller and the buyer, the smart contract receives independent confirmation of the trade by each party. It then sends the tokenized financial asset to the buyer and the tokenized payment to the seller.

If the smart contract receives conflicting information from the seller and the buyer, or no confirmation at all, after a certain due date, either party can call for the release of the tokens to their original owners: the tokenized asset to the seller and the tokenized payment to the buyer.

Thanks to the smart contract, the delivery-vs-payment can be conducted in an atomic manner, that is, with no risk that one party will lose its assets while the other party fails to deliver. Additionally, the delivery-vs-payment does not require any intermediary other than the financial institutions who are responsible for converting the financial assets and the means of payment into their tokenized forms.

Implementation Examples

In the realm of crypto-assets, several projects have implemented blockchain-based decentralized post-trade settlement. These include Airswap and Omega One, both ConsenSys companies, EtherDelta, RadarRelay, and various projects built on the 0x protocol.

In the realm of traditional financial assets, LiquidShare, a French consortium of nine financial institutions, is working on tokenizing shares of listed small and mid-sized companies and enabling blockchain-based post-trade settlement of these assets.

The Australian Stock Exchange (ASX) has also confirmed plans to use blockchain technology for the clearing and settlement of equity transactions.

Use Case: Parametric Insurance

Problem Statement

The processing of insurance claims, particularly in the property segment, can involve significant processing manpower and costs. As an example, in some countries, the processing cost of non-auto property insurance (such as home insurance, construction insurance, or company liability) can amount to 20 percent of the damages paid by the insurer.

Claims processing is observable and implemented in company systems as conditional logic: verify that conditions A, B, C, D are met, and trigger payment to claimant.

In some situations, the verification of a single condition can contribute to triggering many insurance policies. For example, a single flight delay can trigger the activation of travel insurance policies held by every single passenger; a single natural disaster can trigger the activation of many home and industrial insurance and reinsurance policies; and, in the case of complex commercial or industrial insurance syndication and reinsurance arrangements, a single damage can trigger the activation of multiple policies at multiple institutions.

Could a shared database of events and condition verifications allow insurers to process claims faster and at lower cost?

Application of Blockchain Technology

The concept of parametric insurance involves setting up automated rules-based logic in order to trigger the payment of insurance claims.

Using blockchain technology, the mechanism is as follows:

1. First, an insurer smart contract (or series of smart contracts) is created, and pre-loaded in tokenized assets (crypto-assets or tokenized fiat currency) with the maximum amount of damages to be paid. (Alternatively, the smart contract can be given the right to access an aggregated pool of tokenized assets representing the total amount put by the insurer in escrow.)
2. When a claim event occurs, the insurer smart contract receives digitally signed attestations from so-called "oracle" services, testifying that the various claim conditions have been met.
3. After all attestations have been verified, the insurer smart contract is able to release the funds to the claimant, based on a predefined logic engraved in the blockchain.

Implementation Examples

One of the best known applications of blockchain technology to consumer insurance is Fizzy, a parametric travel insurance product launched by AXA on the Ethereum blockchain.

Another example is a prototype developed by Zurich Insurance Group that uses a smart contract on Ethereum and an external weather data source API as the oracle to trigger the automatic payout of crop insurance in the event of drought or flooding.

However, the applications with the greatest economic potential are likely to be the least visible ones: where blockchain technology is used to streamline insurance arrangements between insurers and reinsurers, unbeknownst to customers. The Blockchain Insurance Industry Initiative (B3i), which includes Zurich and 14 other insurers and reinsurers, has been created to explore such use cases.

Looking Ahead

The year 2017 was largely dedicated to proof-of-concept experiments of many use cases of blockchain technology in the financial industry. Many financial institutions have already developed an initial understanding of ways by which blockchain technology can help them optimize their current business processes, serve new markets, and create new business models.

In 2018, we expect to see a few dozen production-scale deployments of blockchain technology by traditional financial institutions, escalating to several dozen deployments by the end of 2019. This is on top of the dozens of fintech startups currently working on new business and operational models based on blockchain technology.

Meanwhile, blockchain technology itself is undergoing profound transformation. Progress is being made almost on a daily basis to improve the scalability, privacy, interoperability, user-friendliness and compliance of both existing and new block-chain-based platforms.

Adoption of the technology is just starting and is likely to take place in business-to-business environments first, although there are several business-to-consumer applications where early technology adopters are clearly emerging (such as crypto-asset investors, videogame users, and software engineers).

Transformative technological changes tend to reward those who are prepared to invest ahead of the curve, rather than the ones who wait until new technologies are fully proven and accepted.

Ken Timsit is a Managing Director at ConsenSys (Paris), focusing Enterprise Solutions in France and continental Europe. As part of his role, Ken leads high-level relationships with large corporations and governments, executes application development and consulting projects, and identifies opportunities for new products and ventures externally and internally. He is a management committee member of the "EU Blockchain Observatory and Forum" (http://eublockchainforum.eu), a two-year long initiative launched by the European Commission. Ken graduated as an engineer from Ecole Polytechnique (Paris) and Mines Paristech. He started his career at The Boston Consulting Group (BCG) where he spent 15 years in Paris, New York and Singapore, and was a Partner and Managing Director in the Financial Services practice. He co-founded two e-commerce start-ups, GEMFIVE and POPLISTER, in Southeast Asia, and was an advisor to Fintech companies in Asia.

ConsenSys is a global formation of technologists and entrepreneurs building the infrastructure, applications, and business models that enable a decentralized world. Founded in 2014 in New York, USA, by Joseph Lubin, a co-founder of Ethereum, ConsenSys now operates in 40 countries with more than 1,100 team members. As a blockchain startup studio, it creates, incubates and scales up more than 50 venture projects that develop products and platforms on blockchain technology. As a provider of Enterprise and Government Solutions, it partners with public and private clients in order to make sense of the transformative power of blockchain and to jointly develop innovative digital ventures. Other activities include ConsenSys Academy, an education arm, ConsenSys Ventures, a venture capital fund, ConsenSys Diligence, a smart contract audit capability, ConsenSys Social Impact, and many other entrepreneurial teams focused on helping society realize the promise of blockchain technology.

Chapter 9
Cryptoassets

This chapter provides a comprehensive introduction to cryptoassets and presents the view that cryptoassets and blockchain technology will shape our future in a significant way—and in fact, has already begun to do so. We assume that readers have gained the fundamental knowledge on blockchain and distributed ledger from previous chapters and will proceed directly to describe cryptoassets. Frequent references will be made to the underlying blockchain technology driving the features of cryptoassets.

Introducing Cryptoassets

The upcoming section introduces the concept of cryptoassets to the reader by describing its key characteristics, explaining how it differs from traditional financial assets and defining the terminology that is crucial to understanding cryptoassets and crypto networks.

What Is a Cryptoasset?

Cryptoassets[1] (or "crypto" for short) emerged following the "Bitcoin" whitepaper by Satoshi Nakamoto in 2008.[i] Although "cryptocurrency" was first popularized, cryptoasset is increasingly preferred as it more accurately encapsulates the diverse characteristics and functions beyond that of a currency.

The three key characteristics of a cryptoasset are the use of
– Cryptography
– Blockchain technology
– A consensus mechanism

The "crypto" in cryptoassets is derived from the use of cryptographic primitives such as hash functions and digital signatures. A *hash function* is a mathematical function with the following properties: its input can be a string of any size, it produces a fixed size output called a *hash*, and it is also efficiently computable. In other words, you

---

i https://bitcoin.org/bitcoin.pdf

DOI 10.1515/9781547400904- 009

should be able to get the output of a hash function in a reasonable amount of time.[ii] A *digital signature* is like a digital version of a handwritten signature. They are similar in two key ways: you can create a unique signature (although anyone can verify it) and each instance of your signature is tied to a particular document or record.[iii]

A cryptoasset is the native asset of a blockchain (or more broadly, a distributed ledger), which is open, public and unpermissioned. Cryptoassets are native to their own blockchain in that they cannot cross over to another blockchain and can only work within the confines of their own blockchain. Conversely, a blockchain can exist without having a native token[2] or a corresponding cryptoasset. There are many examples of blockchains that do not have a native token, such as R3's Corda and IBM's Hyperledger Fabric. These are private, permissioned blockchains that are controlled by a single entity or a consortium. Refer to Chapter 7 for more discussion of public vs. private blockchains.

The last feature of cryptoassets is a *consensus mechanism*, which can be considered as more of an economic innovation than a technological one due to the application of game theory. A consensus mechanism is necessary in a decentralized network for an agreement to be reached and for the network to progress; it can be thought of as the shared rules by which the network participants agree to operate. Network participants who participate in validation include miners and nodes. For Bitcoin, the mechanism for reaching consensus is the Proof of Work (PoW) algorithm, previously discussed in Chapter 7 and explained in the following simplified example. The consensus rules are contained within the Bitcoin client which is an interface to the network. Consider the following example.[3]

Alice has a bitcoin. Alice wants to send her bitcoin to Bob. Alice adds Bob's address to the coin, signing it with her own private key (a special password known only to her). This transaction is transmitted throughout the Bitcoin network. Computers running the bitcoin software (nodes) compete to package these transactions into blocks. The computer that manages to solve a random mathematical puzzle correctly obtains the right to create the next block that will be added to the existing chain and, in so doing, obtain the block reward (transaction fees and newly minted bitcoins). The process creates blocks, also known as *mining*, and the computers are known as *miners*. The block is broadcast to the network together with the answer to the puzzle, and the other nodes or miners on the network check the answer to verify the authenticity of the block. As each node verifies the new block, it adds it to its own copy of the blockchain and broadcasts its agreement to the network. When the authenticity of the new block has been verified by enough nodes, consensus is reached and the

---

ii A. Narayanan et al., 2016, *Bitcoin and Cryptocurrency Technology: A Comprehensive Introduction.* Princeton University Press.
iii Ibid.

transaction is finalized. Bob now owns the bitcoin, and the race to find the next block continues.

This act of solving a random puzzle with computing power is part of the PoW algorithm. There are other mechanisms for reaching consensus, such as Proof-of-Stake, Proof-of-Authority, Practical Byzantine Fault Tolerance and many more, each with their own advantages and drawbacks.[4] The PoW algorithm relies on hardware, computation power and electricity, and is the most tried and tested. It has also spawned an entire mining industry, which we describe in this chapter.

Traditional Financial Assets vs. Cryptoassets

Parallels are easily drawn between traditional finance and crypto. From an outsider's point of view, both are assets that represent value and can be traded. However, there are distinct differences between traditional financial assets and cryptoassets due to the decentralized and open source nature of cryptoassets.

While crypto has evolved significantly from the days of the cypherpunk mailing list, where Satoshi Nakamoto first announced the "Bitcoin project," the culture of cryptoassets has still retained its roots as a technology project that started on the internet with open participation for anyone with an internet connection. This has contributed to how projects usually function in a decentralized and open source manner in the cryptoasset world, which is akin to many open source software projects such as Linux and Android. For instance, projects would typically have a GitHub page where their code is available for the community to view or even contribute, and communication takes place on sites such as reddit and public chat rooms where anyone can participate. This is in stark contrast to the heavily licensed and regulated financial services sector, where communications and interactions happen in a more formal, top-down manner, where access is restricted and information is not disclosed to the public.

Cryptoasset Terminology

There are many terms that are used in the cryptoasset space that may confuse newcomers. This section defines some of the unique concepts that are important for understanding cryptoassets:

Mining
The concept of mining arose because of the PoW mechanism in enabling consensus. There is often confusion due to the association with traditional gold miners. Bitcoin miners are not digging bitcoin out of the ground, but instead "running computer programs on very specialized hardware that automates the process of

securing the network."[iv] The mining process serves to validate all transactions with reference to bitcoin's consensus rules and creates a new bitcoin in each block.[v] This mining process applies to other cryptoassets that also employ a PoW mechanism for consensus, though certain parameters may vary.

The increase in value of bitcoin and other PoW-based cryptoassets led to the creation of a mining industry. In 2009, early bitcoin miners could use standard multi-core CPUs to mine bitcoin. In 2010, when the code for mining bitcoin with GPUs (graphics processing units) was released to the public,' mining difficulty rose and consequently so did the need for better hardware like GPUs. Once again, mining difficulty increased and field-programmable gate arrays (FPGAs) increased in popularity, which consumed less power but were as effective.[vi] FPGAs soon evolved into application-specific integrated circuit (ASIC) systems, essentially a microchip specifically designed to execute a hashing algorithm as quickly as possible, and bitcoin mining commenced on its path to industrialization.[vii]

Wallets

Like the misconceptions that arise with the use of the term "mining," cryptoasset "wallet" is a misnomer, too. The wallets that we keep in our pockets store physical currencies; however, cryptoasset wallets are software programs that store individuals' public and private keys and interface with the blockchain so that users can monitor their balance, send money and conduct other operations.[viii] When someone sends you a cryptoasset, they sign off ownership of the coins to your wallet's address. These coins can only be spent if the private key stored in your wallet matches the public address the coin was sent to. There is no exchange of real coins, and the transaction is recorded on the blockchain. Storing and spending cryptoassets is about storing and managing your private keys. Wallets can come in many forms and with different levels of security: desktop, online, mobile, hardware, paper and brain.[ix]

Note:
Did you know that a wallet is not absolutely secure? This is because there is a finite number of private keys that already exist. When you generate your private key, you are just discovering a key that already exists. It is possible for someone else to generate the same private key as you have! Thankfully, the chances of that occurring are 1 in 2^{160} for Bitcoin.

---

iv https://bitcoin.stackexchange.com/questions/148/what-exactly-is-mining
v https://github.com/bitcoinbook/bitcoinbook/blob/develop/ch02.asciidoc
vi https://thenextweb.com/hardfork/2018/02/02/a-brief-history-of-bitcoin-mining-hardware/
vii https://thenextweb.com/hardfork/2018/02/02/a-brief-history-of-bitcoin-mining-hardware/
viii https://blockgeeks.com/guides/cryptocurrency-wallet-guide/
ix https://blockgeeks.com/guides/cryptocurrency-wallet-guide/

Forks

A "fork" in software development happens when "developers take a copy of source code from one software package and start independent development on it, creating a distinct and separate piece of software."[x] For cryptoassets, a fork simply refers to a situation when the blockchain splits into two branches. This could be temporary and accidental or permanent and intentional. A temporary fork occurs when two or more miners find a block at the same time, this is typically resolved when the next block is found. One branch then becomes longer, resulting in the nodes switching over to the longest branch. A prominent example of an intentional fork would be the existence of Bitcoin Cash, due to disagreements on the block size for the Bitcoin network, a significant portion of the bitcoin community decided to fork to create Bitcoin Cash.

Airdrops

In an airdrop, tokens are allocated to existing holders of a particular chain. Instead of selling tokens through an Initial Coin Offering (ICO), tokens are given to holders of another cryptoasset for free.[xi] The value of an airdrop for a cryptoasset project lies in the increase in mindshare and engagement among token holders as a result of a wider token distribution. An example of an airdrop is the Ontology (ONT) airdrop. ONT was airdropped for all NEO token holders at a rate of 0.2 ONT for each NEO held.[xii]

Evolution of Cryptoassets

Following the publication of the "Bitcoin" whitepaper, the first use of bitcoin was for digital currency. Since then, cryptoassets have evolved rapidly. From functioning as digital cash by facilitating P2P (peer-to-peer) decentralized cash transactions to tackling use cases like supply chain tracking.

Blockchain 1.0

Blockchain 1.0 was the cryptocurrency era. The Bitcoin protocol allowed value to be transferred P2P, without an intermediary. As explained previously, this was enabled by PoW, which also solves the Byzantine Generals problem. The Byzantine Generals

---

x https://en.wikipedia.org/wiki/Fork_(software_development)#cite_note-1
xi https://www.forbes.com/sites/spencerbogart/2017/10/08/the-trend-that-is-increasing-the-urgency-of-owning-bitcoin-and-ethereum/#7ee18f07116b
xii https://medium.com/ontologynetwork/the-neo-council-airdrop-faq-4b1694928373

problem is a classic problem faced by any distributed computer network where each actor must agree on a planned strategy, but some of the actors are unreliable.[xiii] Simply put, this allows a network of unknown and untrusted actors to achieve common consensus and function as a cohesive whole.

Another distinguishing feature of cryptoassets during this period was that they had to be created through the process of mining. In the case of Bitcoin, the first 50 bitcoins were created when they were mined for the first block of the bitcoin blockchain on January 3, 2009. Bitcoins could only be gained by taking part in the mining process. Even the founder Satoshi Nakamoto was subject to the rules of the protocol. On the other hand, there were projects that had "premines." *Premining* refers to the process of creating cryptoassets before they are launched to the public. This typically involved project developers privately mining and allocating coins to themselves before announcing the launch to the public. Premined coins tended to have a negative connotation, as the practice had the potential to introduce centralization, and unfair distribution,[xiv] and a perceived deviation from the original ethos of decentralization pervasive in the community.[xv]

Cryptoassets launched in this period were designed to be a form of digital, decentralized money. Differentiating features cantered on equitable distribution of miners, scarcity, confirmation speed, incentive mechanism, tendency to be centralized and privacy. Examples of cryptoassets from this era include Bitcoin, Litecoin, Monero, Dash and Dogecoin.

Yet, there is still a debate on whether cryptocurrencies are a form of money.[xvi,xvii] Money has three functions, as a store of value, medium of exchange, and unit of account. On the basis of these measures, cryptocurrencies still fall short of meeting the same standards as traditional fiat or government-backed money, due to their extreme volatility. However, established cryptocurrencies like bitcoin can be considered a successful use case as a store of value, and perhaps that is why it is sometimes regarded as "digital gold."[5]

---

xiii Explained by Satoshi Nakamoto here: https://www.mail archive.com/cryptography@metzdowd.com/msg09997.html
xiv https://bitcointalk.org/index.php?topic=1506161.0
xv https://bitcointalk.org/index.php?topic=1506161.0
xvi https://www.bankofengland.co.uk/-/media/boe/files/speech/2018/the-future-of-money-speech-by-mark-carney.pdf?la=en&hash=A51E1C8E90BDD3D071A8D6B4F8C1566E7AC91418
xvii https://cointelegraph.com/news/is-cryptocurrency-real-money-brief-discussion-on-major-issues-surrounding-debate

Blockchain 2.0

Blockchain 2.0 commenced with the Ethereum white paper in late 2013 by Vitalik Buterin. Ethereum's innovation was the introduction of logic to the blockchain through programmable smart contracts. It aimed to be a "decentralized platform that runs smart contracts: applications that run exactly as programmed without any possibility of downtime, censorship, fraud or third-party interference. These apps run on a custom built blockchain, an enormously powerful shared global infrastructure that can move value around and represent the ownership of property."[xviii]

The advent of smart contracts increased the possible applications of blockchain. Smart contracts are "a set of promises, specified in digital form, including protocols within which the parties perform on these promises."[xix] A smart contract can be thought of as a vending machine. A vending machine takes in coins and dispenses the purchased product. Smart contracts embody similar properties to vending machines, going beyond to "embed contracts in all sorts of property that is valuable and controlled by digital means."[xx] This kick-started interest in blockchain in the mainstream industry, as it allowed for sectors beyond finance to get involved.

Yet, blockchains seen in this era are still constrained by their scalability, measured in transactions per second. Scalability is necessary for cryptoassets to meet industry needs: the current state of the bitcoin network, at 7 transactions per second (TPS)[xxi] and Ethereum,[xxii] with a TPS of 10–30, cannot support industry-wide applications. The Visa network is known to support more than 24,000 TPS.[xxiii] Scalability is not easily achieved; according to the *scalability trilemma*, a concept introduced by Buterin, blockchain systems can at most have two of the following three properties: decentralisation, scalability, and security.[xxiv] The challenge here lies in the block-size debate. While increasing the block size could potentially address scalability concerns, this comes at the cost of decentralization. Fewer nodes will be able to support the increased number of transactions due to the associated increase in costs. The increase in cost comes from the increase in the number of transactions, which require more powerful and more expensive hardware. Technological solutions such as Sharding, Raiden, Plasma and Casper have been proposed by the community to deal with the scaling problem on the Ethereum network but have yet to deliver impactful results.

---

xviii https://ethereum.org/
xix http://www.fon.hum.uva.nl/rob/Courses/InformationInSpeech/CDROM/Literature/LOTwinter-school2006/szabo.best.vwh.net/smart_contracts_2.html
xx Ibid.
xxi https://blockchain.info/unconfirmed-transactions, also this has increased to close to 30 tps with the adoption of segregated witness
xxii https://etherscan.io/chart/tx
xxiii https://usa.visa.com/run-your-business/small-business-tools/retail.html
xxiv https://github.com/ethereum/wiki/wiki/Sharding-FAQ

Ethereum also heralded in the era of Initial Coin Offerings (ICOs). In an ICO, a project creates a digital token and sells a portion of the total supply to the public, usually in exchange for other cryptocurrencies, such as bitcoin or ether. Although not the first project to do an ICO (Mastercoin was the first to conduct an ICO on the bitcoin blockchain), Ethereum made it convenient for other projects to carry out their own ICOs through the introduction of the ERC20 standard. As a result, the number of ICOs exploded, from 9 ICOs in 2015 to more than 1000 ICOs in 2017.[xxv] Through the use of smart contracts, people could simply send ether to an account and receive tokens belonging to the project in exchange. ICOs were essentially the same as a pre-mine, as it resulted in a pool of funds allocated to developers of the project before the launch of the token. Interestingly, the phenomenon of ICOs eventually became a norm, and a majority of the community did not question subsequent projects that allocated funds to the founding team. Aside from Ethereum, there are several other examples of blockchain 2.0, including NEO, Quotum, Lisk, NEM and Stellar.

Blockchain 3.0

Enter Blockchain 3.0. While this era has arguably not yet been defined by a particular feature, a strong contender for this title are *high-performance blockchains*. Such blockchains typically possess the features of both Blockchain 1.0 and 2.0, with scalability achieved either by sacrificing decentralization or by overcoming the scalability trilemma through technical innovations such as off-chain state channels. They are characterized by high throughput (measured in TPS) and low finality time (the amount of time needed to ensure that blocks do not change). The abundance of projects focused on attaining high TPS could be a response to the scalability issues faced by the Bitcoin and Ethereum networks. In December 2017, Cryptokitties, a DApp built on the Ethereum network where players spend ether to breed and trade digital cartoon kitties, caused the network to become congested and increased transaction fees due to the high volume of unprocessed transactions.[xxvi] Some high-performance chains also leverage a different technology that are technically not blockchains. For instance, Hashgraph is built on a Direct Acyclic Graph (DAG) structure. Examples of contenders for the title of Blockchain 3.0 are Zilliqa, Dfinity and Hashgraph.

---

xxv https://papers.ssrn.com/sol3/papers.cfm?abstract_id=3182169
xxvi https://qz.com/1145833/cryptokitties-is-causing-ethereum-network-congestion/

Real World Assets on the Blockchain

Besides creating cryptoassets that derive value from new virtual ecosystems online, teams have sought to create cryptoassets that represent existing assets in the real world too. Stablecoins and Investment tokens are key examples. Stablecoins exist to fulfil the role of a medium of exchange by maintaining a stable value. They can be fiat-collateralized, such as Tether (USDT) and True USD (TUSD), crypto-collateralized such as Dai or non-collateralized and reliant on algorithmic stabilization mechanisms such as Algorand. Investment tokens, covered in Chapter 8, represent real world financial assets. If cryptocurrencies are "programmable money" investment tokens can be compared to "programmable equity." These tokens potentially improve traditional financial products by reducing the need for middlemen, and thereby result in lower fees and increased access.

Initial Coin Offerings (ICO): A New Way of Fundraising?

As mentioned previously, ICOs have emerged as the preferred way to raise funds among blockchain companies, through the creation and sale of digital tokens.[xxvii] The borderless nature of ICOs has resulted in unprecedented access to participation in these projects from all corners of the globe.

There is a possibility that ICOs are becoming an alternate mode of fundraising for startups that do not want to obtain funding through the sale of equity. To investors, ICOs are more attractive than venture capital, as they offer access to startups at a venture stage but with liquidity. This phenomenon can be observed for blockchain startups, where 2017 saw "over 5x more capital deployed in ICOs than in equity financings to blockchain startups."[xxviii]

As a financing mechanism, ICOs allow for price discovery to take place at an early stage for the business. The ICO mechanism "allows entrepreneurs to generate buyer competition for the token, which, in turn, reveals consumer value without the entrepreneurs having to know, ex ante, consumer willingness to pay." However, this is also contingent on the main team behind the ICO committing to the original supply schedule and using the token as the only medium of exchange on the platform. There have been instances where accepting alternative modes of payment for the platform's service has resulted in protests from the community.[xxix]

---

xxvii https://www.coindesk.com/information/what-is-an-ico/
xxviii https://www.cbinsights.com/research/blockchain-vc-ico-funding/
xxix https://www.coindesk.com/quantstamp-fire-buyers-say-faith-shaken-65-million-token/

More importantly, ICOs have become the gateway for the creation of open networks. An ICO creates an opportunity to encourage adoption by incentivizing token holders. As Chris Dixon explains:

> Tokens are a breakthrough in open network design that enable: 1) the creation of open, decentralized networks that combine the best architectural properties of open and proprietary networks, and 2) new ways to incentivize open network participants, including users, developers, investors, and service providers. By enabling the development of new open networks, tokens could help reverse the centralization of the internet, thereby keeping it accessible, vibrant and fair, and resulting in greater innovation.[xxx]

ICOs are the starting point from which new business models based on open networks and incentivized ecosystems can be built. Accordingly, the term *token economy* has emerged, defined as an economic system, similar to a market economy, where decisions are influenced by the forces of supply and demand but facilitated with a token.[xxxi]

What Is a Reverse ICO?

In 2018, the market evolved to embrace a new type of ICO model. The reverse ICO phenomenon refers to the situation when an established business does an ICO. This allows the business both to raise funds and decentralize their business with a token, creating an opportunity for the business to be part of a token economy. Messenger app Kik with more than 300 million registered users,[xxxii] launched an ICO (for kin tokens) as a "first step to launching a decentralized ecosystem of digital services."[xxxiii] Close to USD $100 million from more than 10,000 individuals across 117 countries was raised with the sale of the kin tokens.[xxxiv] Doing a reverse ICO is typically more attractive to secondary and tertiary players in a market. These businesses have realized that the best way to compete with the dominant players is to decentralize their business model by employing the community to spread usage of the platform and get compensated for it, too.[xxxv]

---

xxx https://medium.com/@cdixon/crypto-tokens-a-breakthrough-in-open-network-design-e600975be2ef
xxxi https://medium.com/radarrelay/the-path-to-the-token-economy-6f7aad02cfe5
xxxii https://techcrunch.com/2016/05/11/kik-already-has-over-6000-bots-reaching-300-million-registered-users/
xxxiii https://kinecosystem.org/
xxxiv https://kinecosystem.org/
xxxv https://venturebeat.com/2017/08/16/the-reverse-ico-how-existing-businesses-will-start-tokenizing/

Drawbacks of Cryptoassets: "Blockchain, not Bitcoin"

Yet, there has been criticism from prominent figures in traditional finance regarding the necessity of a token.[xxxvi] Since 2015, there has been a "blockchain, not bitcoin" perspective. Proponents argue that blockchain technology has value, but not its native token. This belief has been pursued by large financial institutions, along with companies like R3 and IBM that integrate permissioned ledgers or centralized blockchain networks onto existing bank infrastructures.[xxxvii]

Implicit in the "blockchain, not bitcoin" narrative is the negative sentiment toward cryptoassets. Two key aspects contribute to this—their inherently decentralized nature and lack of stability.

The decentralized nature of cryptoassets makes centralized stores of cryptoassets such as exchanges like Binance and Coinbase an attractive target for hackers. Once the funds are stolen by hackers gaining access to a user's exchange account and sending funds out to their own wallet, there is no central entity to provide recourse. The many high-profile hacks of crypto exchanges did not help in building investor confidence in this asset class. A notable example is the 2014 hack of Mt Gox, a bitcoin exchange, that resulted in USD $460mn worth of bitcoin stolen by hackers.[xxxviii] Another potential hazard of decentralized cryptoassets is that they can be a means of laundering money due to their pseudonymous, and sometimes even anonymous nature.

Furthermore, cryptoassets and cryptoasset infrastructure have not reached a stable enough state where they can be trusted to support crucial applications. This is an especially pertinent concern as industry use cases often prize predictability and stability. For instance, a bug in the Parity Ethereum wallet resulted in some projects having a significant amount of their ICO funds frozen.[xxxix, xl] Besides the instability of the network, cryptoassets are also subject to extreme price volatility. This makes it inconvenient for users who may need price stability in order to use a cryptoasset as a medium of exchange.

---

xxxvi https://www.econotimes.com/ECB-officials-see-lot-of-potential-in-blockchain-technology-1077407
xxxvii https://www.newsbtc.com/2018/01/03/european-central-bank-latest-institution-use-blockchain-not-bitcoin-narrative/
xxxviii https://www.wired.com/2014/03/bitcoin-exchange/
xxxix https://paritytech.io/security-alert-2/
xl https://techcrunch.com/2017/11/07/a-major-vulnerability-has-frozen-hundreds-of-millions-of-dollars-of-ethereum/

Why Are Tokens Necessary?

The ICO mechanism brings benefits to the venture funding process for startups, and its open networks increase participation. However, this does not explain the necessity of a native token.

At the most basic level, tokens serve as the incentive/reward for supply-side participants to provide a service for the network that they belong to. Depending on the type of crypto network, tokens serve different purposes. In the case of the Bitcoin network, bitcoin (the native token) serves as an incentive for miners to secure the network and maintain consensus. For a distributed storage network such as Filecoin, Filecoins are paid to miners who provide storage to clients. Similar to Bitcoin, Filecoin miners compete to mine blocks with sizable rewards, but Filecoin mining power is proportional to active storage, which directly provides a useful service to clients.[xli] Rewarding Filecoin miners with bitcoin or USD instead of Filecoin would result in the loss of features and functionalities.[xlii]

The need for a native token is best exemplified in the founding story of Ethereum. Buterin, the founder of Ethereum, started out as a Bitcoin enthusiast, covering Bitcoin as a journalist on *Bitcoin Magazine* and even building on top of it. Buterin saw the potential in taking advantage of Bitcoin's trustless nature to expand the set of possible features. Buterin was involved in a project called "coloured coins." Coloured coins are bitcoins that "have special properties supported by either an issuing agent or by public agreement and have value independent of the face value of the underlying bitcoins. Such coloured bitcoins can be used for alternative currencies, commodity certificates, smart property, and other financial instruments such as stocks and bonds."[xliii] However, the bitcoin community enacted highly restrictive rules to prevent anyone embedding transactions on top of the Bitcoin protocol.[xliv] These difficulties among others, led Buterin to launch of Ethereum in 2014.

Therefore, tokens are necessary as they incentivize the continuity and growth of the crypto networks that they belong to and allow added functionality and features.

Possibilities of Tokenization

Another significant implication of ICOs and cryptoassets is the ability to create liquid markets for previously illiquid assets. This is known as *tokenization*, a process where

---

xli https://filecoin.io/filecoin.pdf

xlii https://filecoin.io/blog/why-is-decentralized-critical/

xliii https://docs.google.com/document/d/1AnkP_cVZTCMLIzw4DvsW6M8Q2JC0lIzrTLuoWu2z1BE/edit

xliv https://coinjournal.net/vitalik-buterin-early-versions-ethereum-supposed-launch-bitcoin/

rights to an asset are converted into a digital token on the blockchain.[xlv] Compared to the process of securitization that takes place in traditional finance, tokenization does the same for assets in a way that increases the functionality and access. Being hosted on an open ledger allows tokens to interact with multiple parties in a way that securities are unable to and removes the need for intermediaries that could increase costs and create barriers to access.

For example, the tokenization of energy allows the creation of peer-to-peer marketplaces for renewable energy. Instead of only being able to sell energy back to the grid, homeowners with energy generating units at home, like solar panels, will be able to sell excess energy to their neighbors at an affordable cost. In this case, the blockchain is used for matching energy buyers and sellers. Energy consumption data and energy transaction data also can be tokenized and sold to distribution and transmission network operators. With more accurate details of electricity requirements, these operators will be able to optimize electricity generation and storage. Additionally, this data could enable providers to segment customers according to appliance usage patterns and encourage energy usage behavior changes that support the grid-balancing requirements.[xlvi]

However, tokenization does not guarantee liquidity. Liquidity for tokens is highly dependent on the level of speculation and actual use of the token. ICO listings are somewhat unnatural as they force liquidity into spaces that typically do not have liquidity. Venture capital seed stage is one of the most illiquid asset classes, and ICO projects are similar if not at an even earlier stage. This means that critical or natural liquidity is often not there unlike for Initial Public Offerings (IPO) with established primary markets and much larger companies. While liquidity may not come easily, the increase in tokenization and creation of markets for every possible thing has also created new arbitrage opportunities.

The Cryptoasset Ecosystem

A thriving ecosystem has sprouted out of the original online communities that supported cryptoassets in its infancy. While this has shaped the culture of the ecosystem, activity has also spilled over into the offline world and traditional industries such as finance. This section explores the rapidly evolving cryptoasset ecosystem.

---

xlv https://bitcoinmagazine.com/articles/op-ed-how-tokenization-putting-real-world-assets-block-chains/
xlvi https://vlux.io/media/VLUX_Whitepaper.pdf

Cryptofinance

Started as just a technological innovation and application, cryptoassets have grown beyond a mere product to a network and more importantly, an ecosystem. Cryptoassets have even created a new type of financial market. Although there are some noticeable similarities between traditional finance and cryptofinance (IPOs vs. ICOs), the fundamental differences in the type of asset at hand (a digitally native, programmable asset) require a different type of financial organization.

Although traditional financial institutions have been slow to move into this space, newcomers are rapidly building a parallel financial system. Both centralized and decentralized entities have popped up to fill the void in this growing space. For instance, crypto funds like Mike Novogratz's Galaxy Digital Capital Management LP have emerged to cater to demand. At the same time, decentralized equivalents, such as ICONOMI's digital asset management platform, have allowed investors to participate in a novel, decentralized way. The same goes for crypto exchanges: Coinbase and Binance are well-known examples of centralized crypto exchanges, but decentralized exchanges (DEX) such as IDEX and Kyber Network are becoming viable alternatives to their centralized counterparts. In contrast to centralized exchanges, decentralized exchanges do not rely on a third party to hold customer's funds. Instead, trades occur peer-to-peer, directly through smart contracts and customers who hold their own private keys.

A whole crypto professional services industry has sprouted in response. Crypto trading, ICO advisory firms, smart contract auditing firms and community management agencies are some examples. Crypto trading firms, such as QCP Capital, facilitate Over-the-Counter (OTC) transactions and provide market-making and risk management services, whereas decentralized counterparts like Republic Protocol facilitate OTC trades through dark pools (liquidity pools that do not have a transparent order book). Custody also has proved to be a challenge for cryptoassets, with companies like Xapo and Bitgo approaching it with centralized solutions.

Case Study: QCP Capital and Trading Cryptoassets

To better illustrate the differences between a firm that handles traditional financial assets and one that handles cryptoassets, we will examine the business and operations of QCP Capital.

The differences in trading cryptoassets versus traditional financial assets can be attributed to two key factors: 1) the immaturity of crypto as an asset class and 2) the decentralized nature of cryptoassets.

As a frontier market that does not fit into traditional finance infrastructure or the existing regulatory regime, a main challenge in trading cryptoassets lies in the lack of infrastructure. Settlement and custody solutions are still lacking, which makes it problematic for institutions to participate and cryptoassets to scale up as an asset class. Due to the lack of regulation, extra attention must be devoted to managing counterparty risks. This is especially important when dealing with centralized exchanges.

The decentralized nature of the cryptoassets has also introduced an entire ecosystem of decentralized players for the trader to interact with. Decentralized exchanges are a key example. By allowing users to trade without a trusted third party, the responsibility for security and storage of private keys lies in the hands of the user. As a result, traders have to manage the interaction between private keys, wallets and exchanges, an experience unheard of in traditional financial services.

A feature (or bug) of decentralization is its irreversibility. The irreversibility of transactions makes it extremely risky when dealing with large amounts of a cryptoasset. Once you lose your private keys or make a wrong transaction, your crypto is lost forever, and there is no central entity to which you can prove your identity and claim your misplaced crypto. This is evident in the estimated 4 million bitcoins lost forever due to the loss of private keys.[xlvii]

All these challenges have proved to be significant barriers for infrastructure adoption, resulting in the liquidity profile and trading volume of cryptoassets being a far cry from traditional financial products. On the other hand, the inefficiencies of the cryptoasset markets present many opportunities for traders to exploit. QCP Capital conducts proprietary trading that takes advantage of arbitrage opportunities across trading pairs and exchanges. As a market maker, QCP also contributes to the crypto trading ecosystem by providing liquidity to decentralized cryptoassets like stablecoins.

Online Communities

A significant part of the cryptoasset ecosystem exists online. The online, borderless nature of cryptoassets has spawned swathes of online communities dedicated to following, participating and speculating on specific cryptoassets. These communities typically exist on platforms like reddit, Telegram, Slack and Twitter. For instance, community managers, who reply to questions on Telegram and other social media platforms, make up the new "investor relations" teams for crypto projects. In contrast to the walled and gated communities of traditional finance, anyone with an internet connection can join these communities and participate. This radical openness has led to unprecedented participation across the world.

---

xlvii http://fortune.com/2017/11/25/lost-bitcoins/

Emerging Blockchain Hubs

Although a large amount of crypto activity happens online, the ecosystem has developed offline, too, both organically and through countries with crypto-friendly regulation. Below outlines some of the activity happening in Asia.

In the Philippines, crypto companies are able to operate in the Cagayan Special Economic Zone.[xlviii] Japan's advent as a crypto haven dates to its Mt. Gox days, which introduced national lawmakers to the concept of cryptocurrencies at an early stage.[xlix] For instance, a government-backed study group in Japan has laid out guidelines for ICOs.[l] Singapore has emerged as a popular base for token sales,[li] and its status as a financial hub has formed the basis for its popularity, with a strong legal system, low taxes and business-friendly environment. For its part, China is the undisputed leader in mining, with its abundance of cheap electricity and dominance in hardware. Bitmain Technologies, the world's largest producer of bitcoin mining chips,[lii] is headquartered in Beijing. South Korea's fervor for crypto is evident both in trading volumes, with about one million registered daily traders in virtual currency, and in the involvement of some of its biggest corporations.[liii]

What's Next?

The cryptoasset space is one that is changing rapidly. We have attempted to capture the fundamental characteristics of cryptoassets and the ecosystem that has evolved around it, but this is not in any way conclusive. Previous chapters discussed blockchain as a technology; this chapter introduces cryptoassets as not only a technological innovation, but a social and economic one too.

Perhaps cryptoassets and blockchain technology are in the early stages of a technological revolution and following similar patterns of past technological revolutions. According to Carlota Perez, every technological revolution has two phases: the installation phase when the technology enters the market and the necessary infrastructure is built, and the deployment phase characterised by mass adoption of the technology by society.[liv] The inflection point between the two phases typically involves a financial crash

---

xlviii https://www.reuters.com/article/uk-crypto-currencies-philippines/philippines-to-allow-cryptocurrency-operators-in-economic-zone-idUSKBN1HW1KY
xlix https://www.bloomberg.com/news/articles/2018-04-10/while-the-world-cracks-down-japan-emerges-as-a-crypto-haven
l https://www.bloomberg.com/news/articles/2018-04-05/japan-plans-first-step-toward-legalizing-initial-coin-offerings
li https://www.techinasia.com/singapore-top-blockchain-hub-world
lii https://www.businessinsider.sg/bitmain-cryptocurrency-bitcoin-mining-jihan-wu-ipo-2018-6/?r=US&IR=T
liii https://www.technologyreview.com/s/609561/behind-south-koreas-cryptocurrency-boom/
liv *Technological Revolutions and Financial Capital: The Dynamics of Bubbles and Golden Ages* by Carlota Perez.

followed by a recovery. If so, we have an interesting question to ask ourselves: At which stage in this technological revolution are cryptoassets and blockchain technology now?

Endnotes

1 Coined by Chris Burniske in *Cryptoassets: The Innovative Investor's Guide to Bitcoin*. McGraw-Hill, 2017.

2 A native token is a token that is specific to a particular blockchain.

3 For a more detailed, technical explanation refer to *Mastering Bitcoin* (O'Reilly Media, 2017) by Andreas Antonopolous.

4 For an overview on different consensus mechanisms, refer to https://arxiv.org/pdf/1805.02707.pdf

5 *Digital Gold* (Harper, 2016) by Nathaniel Popper provides a good overview on the origins and history of Bitcoin.

Darius Sit is Co-Founder and Managing Partner at QCP Capital. Formerly a Macro Trader at Dymon Asia Capital, he spent years trading cross-asset derivatives before moving on to manage the Asia FX & Bonds book at BNP Paribas in New York. Darius has a particular passion for crypto-economics and is an advisor to a number of crypto projects, including Algorand and Terra, on trading structures and strategies.

Annabel Lim is an Analyst at QCP Capital who is interested in the future development of cryptoassets, its underlying infrastructure and its implications on society.

QCP Capital is Asia's leading digital asset trading firm headquartered in Singapore. The firm runs quantitatively-driven strategies with a focus on trading crypto derivatives. In addition, QCP runs a large over-the-counter trading desk and provides crypto-trading services such as risk management solutions and market-making operations. QCP has a strategic focus on Southeast Asia but also operates in the UK, Japan and Australia.

Chapter 10
Open Banking: Digital Payments Systems

Every industry is being disrupted by technology and changes in customer behavior, however it is regulatory changes for open banking that could drive the biggest change in banking. This chapter explores the challenges and opportunities for banks driven by open banking regulations, and looks at impact to the payments landscape.

A Changing Landscape

Banks and other traditional financial service providers, including insurers, brokerage firms and advisory firms, have dominated the financial services industry for decades. Until very recently banks faced minimal threat and competition, and so had no need to actively pursue the introduction of innovative services or to significantly improve the banking customer experience. Being able to manage customer acquisition, product development, sales, marketing, product management, customer experience, account information and data processing with ease, banks had clear control of what, where and how their financial services were consumed.

But in recent years, this value chain has experienced significant disruption, resulting in a far more competitive, innovative and transformative banking landscape. A variety of factors have contributed to this substantial shift, beginning with the now widespread consumption of digital banking services, particularly by technologically savvy customers less prone to bank loyalty. This willingness to switch banking provider and the lack of brand advocacy has caused growing dissatisfaction with the customer experience provided by banks. This began to pose genuine structural risk for banks in the longer term. While financial institutions (FIs) possess detailed data about their customer base, they struggle to use this data to offer exciting and accessible services that appeal to younger segments such as millennials.

Customer preferences and expectations have been heavily shaped by their experiences with technology giants outside the world of finance, including Facebook, Apple, Google, WeChat and Lazada (owned by Alibaba). These dominant technology players excel in offering compelling digital experiences through use of personalization, real-time services, speed-to-market and breadth of products and services. Many FIs are unable to offer experiences that are comparable to those offered outside of banking and struggle to keep pace with customer demands. For banks that are attempting to offer similar services, many are hindered by their outdated legacy infrastructure, bureaucratic processes and lack of agility.

The inability of many banks to successfully meet rising customer expectations has led to growing competition from consumer-oriented non-traditional players such as retailers, technology providers and fintech firms. Having mastered digital retail

DOI 10.1515/9781547400904- 010

experience, Amazon and Allibaba are extending into financial services for both consumers and merchants. Technology providers like Samsung and Apple have leveraged their handsets to enter the payments race and Fintechs have unbundled and reinvented almost every traditional banking product.

This dynamic industry shift is also prominent in payments services. With new initiatives and trends such as the introduction of real-time and instant payments, and the growth in payments channels and digital payments offerings from non-banks, traditional banks need to respond accordingly in order to remain competitive. Financial institutions need to be well positioned and equipped to react quickly to on-going changes. The twin drivers of digital innovation and customer behavior had an unprecedented impact on the banking and payments space as they expanded the variety and quality of services available (see Figure 10.1). Banking has shifted considerably from simple branch services facing minimal competition to customers now largely in control of the banking relationship, primarily due to technology that enables greater transparency and accessibility of financial products.

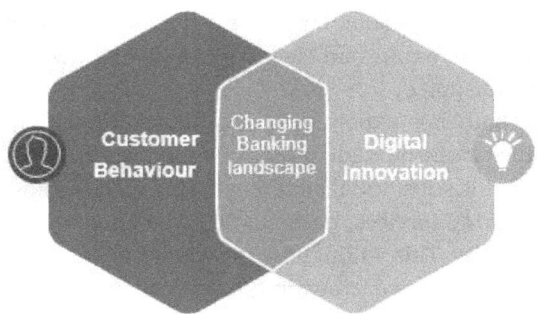

Figure 10.1: Drivers of change in banking

What Is Open Banking?

With the loss of their monopoly, banks must place customer needs and expectations at the forefront of their development of new services and experiences. By providing banking services that are innovative, in demand and easily accessed across channels, banks can offer unique experiences that enrich customers' lives and improve their perception of their bank.

Banks cannot achieve this ambitious goal on their own. Partnership and collaboration within the banking space is a viable means of improving the banking experience across the board, but fears over partnering with competitors, infrastructure and regulatory restrictions and the potential risks involved can deter collaboration. A proposed solution to this problem is *open banking*.

Open banking is the adoption of common standards for collaboration between banks and other players within the banking ecosystem, and arises from the global phenomenon of the disintermediation of the banking value chain. The intention of open banking initiatives is to develop common technology, security and data protection standards across the industry for open data. Open banking makes data, algorithms, transactions, business processes and functionalities available to other players in the banking ecosystem. These "other players" are known as third-party providers, or TPPs, and include fintech firms, technology and e-commerce players, payments processors, telcos and even retailers.

Open banking is a highly customer-focused movement intended to improve the banking experience for the end-customers from an increased collaboration of TPPs and Banks. This collaborative spirit encourages greater innovation and a wider variety of innovative banking services, while creating an opportunity for financial institutions to embrace change in a positive and proactive way. Providing the end-customer with greater control over which financial products and services they consume and from whom, is a fundamental tenet of open banking. With this customer-approved exchange of data between their bank and TPPs, customers can access an array of digital services and be offered a compelling experience, including account aggregation services, highly customizable budgeting apps and more precise and personalized price comparison options.

Open banking also offers notable benefits for both banks and the fintechs or other TPPs that they may opt to collaborate with. Banks are set to gain from the agility and scalability inherent to fintech services, which operate without the restrictions of cumbersome legacy systems and possess the ability to bring products to market very rapidly. Fintechs will find benefits in the long standing and trusted relationships in the broad customer base that banks possess, alongside the banks' expertise in areas such as regulation and fraud protection. There is more to gain from collaboration than competition between the two parties. Banks are best able to reach the common goal of enhancing every aspect of the customers' financial experience through collaborations with fintechs.

Open Banking Regulation and Adoption

The banking industry is often noted for its reluctance to changes, especially as dramatic as open banking. While the concerns and risks perceived by traditional banks to such changes are valid, the benefits of adopting these changes far outweigh the risk and costs. In order to encourage and increase adoption of new banking services and processes that have the potential to transform the industry, regulatory bodies across the globe may occasionally step in to ensure the desired level of progress is in place.

A firm regulatory approach, to which all banks that fit the criteria must comply with, is instrumental to accelerating the pace of open banking adoption. Open banking regulation began to have far-reaching ramifications with the introduction of the European-wide revised Payments Services Directive, known as PSD2. This important piece of legislation came into force in early 2016. Its intent is to increase competition and innovation within the European banking industry, so that banking experience can be improved for the end-customer. PSD2 removes the banks' monopoly on information relating to customers' accounts and allows TPPs such as aggregators of customer financial information across multiple institutions or payment providers access to this account information. Banks have until late 2019 to fully comply, though some banks have adopted a more proactive approach in order to gain a competitive edge and better serve their customers.

PSD2 is the catalyst causing a radical change in the industry's perception, understanding and willingness to embrace open banking. While it is a European directive, it has implications beyond Europe because of its stated intent to increase competition and innovation in the industry for the ultimate benefit of the end-customer.

While a number of nations have begun adopting similar legislated open banking directives (see "Compliance and Competitive Threats" in the following section), the global impact of PSD2 and the regulation it has inspired extends beyond mandatory adoption. Banks in countries that lack open banking regulation have taken the initiatives themselves to incorporate open banking into their services, having become aware of the opportunities for potential new revenue streams. For example, in the countries affiliated with the Association of Southeast Asian Nations (ASEAN), the market opportunity is clear: open banking is likely to appeal to the ASEAN millennial market, which comprises more than half of ASEAN's 630 million people,[1] while also presenting a chance to reach a portion of ASEAN's 264 million unbanked adults.[2]

Responding to the opportunity and growing global trend of open banking, Singapore's OCBC became the first bank in Southeast Asia to launch an open application programming interface (API) platform to enable open banking services. (See "Open APIs" in the following section.) Similarly, the Philippines' Union Bank has already implemented open APIs to facilitate open banking, and is expected to expand the program over time. Elsewhere in Asia, Japan's Mitsubishi UFJ Financial Group (MUFG) is planning to allow TPPs to access its data securely, while Mizuho Bank has also committed to connecting to fintech TPPs.

In the US, where open banking regulation is not imminent, banks like JP Morgan, Wells Fargo and Citi have recently launched open API platforms while technology giants like Apple, Amazon, Google and PayPal have been lobbying policymakers for greater empowerment to customers and small businesses in order to securely access their own accounts via whichever application or technology they choose. This dedication to open banking adoption across the globe, in nations both with and without regulatory mandates, highlights the important role that it is likely to play in the future of banking.

Essentials for Operating in the Open Banking Space

Whilst open banking presents new opportunities it also presents a number of challenges and threats to banks, these are discussed in this section. The section ends with what banks need to do to implement open banking.

Compliance and Competitive Threats

Open banking regulation, as addressed previously in the "Open Banking Regulation and Adoption" section, plays a crucial role in accelerating the interest and adoption of open banking across the globe (see Figure 10.2). For banks operating in areas that have established a regulatory requirement for open banking, it is imperative banks dutifully and thoughtfully consider the most appropriate method of compliance, and consider how directives such as PSD2 will significantly alter the banking landscape. The requirements of PSD2 and other similar pieces of legislation are fairly detailed and must be approached with care.

Under PSD2, banks will be obligated to provide account and payments information that have always been considered proprietary to banks, and to facilitate payments from third parties. *Account servicing payment service providers* (ASPSPs), such as banks and FIs, must provide account information to TPPs such as *payment initiation service providers* (PISPs) or *account information service providers* (AISPs) in a regulated and secure way. This information, which includes transaction data, account balance data, credit transfer initiation, identity verification and sufficient funds check, can only be used with the consent of the customer and only by the third party that has been given consent and only for the specific purpose consented. Though not part of the guidelines, industry consensus is that the information will likely be provided through open application programming interfaces (APIs), discussed later in this section.

Strong 2-factor authentication (through which a customer's identity is confirmed using two pieces of information) is required to be provided by the ASPSPs/banks and financial institutions. Third-parties too will face more regulation on data protection that will boost user confidence in the legitimacy and reliability of their services. For example, greater transparency is an important requirement as all PISPs must provide detailed information to the payer before the transaction on the terms and conditions of the proposed transaction. This is to ensure the customer is aware of the full cost of making the payment, such as exchange rate details and the expected execution time of the payment. Consumer protection is also expected to be improved, ensuring a payer's liability is limited when an unauthorized or incorrect transaction occurs.

Ultimately, the end goal of PSD2 is to drive competition and foster innovation by creating a level playing field for banks and new entrants alike, thereby enabling easy-to-use and secured digital payment services that benefit consumers. The positive implications and transformative outcomes of this goal have piqued interest in open banking for banks and regulatory bodies across the globe. Some nations are keeping a watchful eye on the developments in Europe, and may follow suit as European banks begin to demonstrate success from their open banking initiatives. Elsewhere, certain countries are adopting a more proactive approach to open banking and intend to remain competitive with the innovative services that open banking can facilitate.

In Australia, an open banking review, supported by the Reserve Bank of Australia, was commissioned in July 2017. It has since been completed and is intended to improve customer access and control of banking data. Australia's federal government has imposed a phased implementation of open banking by July 2019 for the big four banks—ANZ, NAB, CBA and Westpac. The Prudential Regulation Authority has also attempted to break the stranglehold of the Big Four by granting the first restricted retail banking license to a start-up, Volt. Responding to Australia's determination to embrace open banking, Macquarie Bank[3] launched its open banking portal in September 2017, allowing customers to securely move data to third parties.

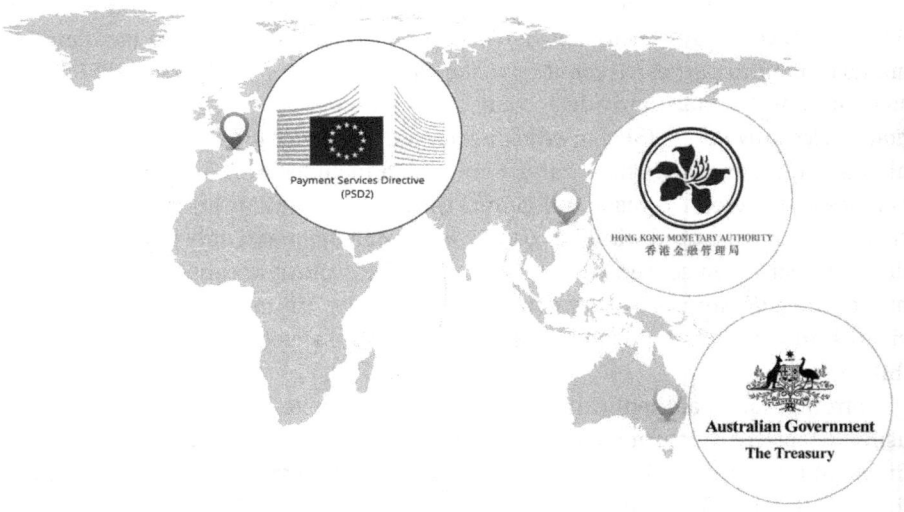

Figure 10.2: Open banking regulations around the globe

Other nations are beginning their journey towards open banking including Hong Kong. The Hong Kong Monetary Authority (HKMA) issued an industry consultation paper in January 2018 on an open banking framework. The framework has since been published, and sets out a selection of open API functions including product information, customer acquisition, account information and transactions. The HKMA has also announced that the implementation of the open API which started on July 23rd 2018 will be compete in mid-2019.

It is essential for banks to comply with their regional open banking and payments regulation, regardless of whether they wish to merely meet the minimum level of compliance or intend to take full advantage of the opportunity that open banking can offer to the innovation and transformation of their banking services. Banks and other traditional financial institutions around the world must face the open banking trend head on in response to legislation and market forces, and must act or risk facing disintermediation.

The risk of being left out of the banking value chain that banks are so accustomed to controlling should not be underestimated. It is widely believed that banks face the risk of being disintermediated by third parties under PSD2 and similar directives. 92% of respondents in a recent Market Force survey expected financial services portals (AISPs) to emerge by 2026, and that only 29% of these would be owned by banks. Similar findings can be seen from Accenture,[4] which predicts a 43% reduction in payments going through banks. Accenture also predicts 1 in 10 credit card and 1 in 3 debit card transactions will move to a PISP by 2025.

These predictions are supported by the growing popularity of bank competitors such as the fintechs. The "World Retail Banking Report 2016," from Capgemini and Efma,[5] found that fintech players are perceived among customers as "easy to use" (82%) and providing "a good user experience" (80%). This report also noted that 55% of respondents were likely to refer friends and family to their fintech provider, compared to just 38% who were likely to refer them to their bank. The growing dissatisfaction among customers with their banking providers is also supported by a 2016 EY survey,[6] which finds that 40% of bank customers expressed decreased dependence on their bank as their primary financial services provider and have used non-bank providers for financial services in the last year. Furthermore, some 20% of customers who have not yet used non-bank providers plan to do so in the near future. Combining this data with the threat that banks also face from new, challenger banks such as Varo or Monzo, and even from technology giants that are beginning to move into the finance industry, banks should not ignore the open banking opportunity if they wish to remain in a competitive position.

Fintech firms have continued to advance their services and differentiate from traditional banks, offering a variety of low-cost, customer-centric services from digital payments to money management assistance. With the opening of customer bank data through open banking to TPPs, fintechs will have more opportunities to reach new customers with greater ease. Fintechs are equipped to handle transaction volume and to respond to market needs rapidly and effectively. Historically, banks have struggled with responsiveness because of their outdated legacy infrastructure and a more cautious approach to changing services. However, it is not too late for banks to mitigate the risk of disintermediation by taking advantage of the opportunities in open banking and open data and leveraging TPPs to provide customers with more specialized, personalized services in order to improve customer experience. There are multiple options for banks to embrace the transformative potential of open banking, from forging strategic partnerships with reputable fintech firms to launching their own thoughtful platform-based approach to open banking, discussed in "Collaboration and Aggregation" later in this chapter.

The mandatory adoption of open banking through regulatory directives and the risks that banks face if they do not consider the impact of open banking forces banks to advance and improve. Regulation like PSD2 will impact banking services, customer habits and expectations. It is important that banks are mindful of the far-reaching impact of open banking, and prepare a thoughtful, measured approach to complying that gives them the best chance of survival in a changing landscape.

Open Banking Adoption Challenges

To operate successfully in the open banking landscape, banks cannot rush into providing open data without considering the risks and challenges that they face. Opening up access to customer data and facilitating third-party payment initiation poses significant technology challenges: four key technology concerns are summarized in Figure 10.3. The biggest concern is security, which the PSD2 regulatory technical standards (RTS) aim to address via the requirement for strong (2-factor) customer authentication and secure exchange of customer and financial data between organizations over the internet. Security concerns are a key area for other regulatory directives, too, with security standards comprising an important aspect of the Australian open banking regulation. Security threats and breaches can have a disastrous impact on a bank's reputation. Banks cannot afford to compromise their traditional role as custodians of customers' financial data. A multi-level security framework should be in place for banks engaging in open banking in order to pre-empt potential external cyber-attacks and unauthorized access. Even if one layer of security is breached, the bank's data must not be compromised.

To do so, API exposure must be limited to authorized entities only. For PSD2, mutual authentication is required between the bank and the third party, without the customer login credentials being shared with the third party. The customer must consent to share information with the third parties before banks can share customer data, and the customer can give this consent directly to the third party. When API requests are received by the bank, they must ensure that third parties are given access only to the specific information that they have been authorized for.

With the security of customer data at stake, banks must consider how they can deliver the quality of security required to operate in the open banking space. Banks need to evaluate the impact that open banking will have on data security and customer privacy, review their security and privacy processes and ensure that their customers understand that their bank is able to keep their data secure in the face of new open banking processes. Temenos, the leading provider of banking software, offers a well designed PSD2 solution for fulfil banking security needs. The consent control module within Temenos' "Core Banking" records and verifies whether the customer has given consent to the third party, what data can be shared and for what duration. This comprehensive and clear view of customer permissions for data sharing ensures that no unapproved data sharing will occur.

Open banking is also expected to significantly increase the volume of transactions for banks due to the proliferation of banking interactions through TPPs. This surge in transaction volume will require 24/7 fraud detection and security monitoring, and banks should ensure that they have the capability to do so. The combination of the anticipated rise in the volume of queries on the customer and transaction data that banks own, and the necessity of enhanced security and authentication methods, will place strain on incumbent banks running legacy-based IT architectures.

Figure 10.3: Key technology concerns of implementing APIs

The complexity of slow and outdated legacy systems creates difficulty in extracting the data required for open APIs and messaging, and the limitations of batch processing methods will significantly impair a bank's ability to support real-time, 24/7 access and payment execution for the end-customers of TPPs. Banks need to respond to third-party requests in acceptable timeframes in order to ensure a good experience for the end-customer but this could be a costly and complex exercise. Banks will also have to contend with the additional costs of vetting third parties and supporting and maintaining the open APIs that they publish.

As a number of banks are simply not equipped to contend with these changes due to their legacy systems, it is imperative that these banks consider the benefits of adopting a modern, API-based architecture instead. A 2017 study into open banking estimated that 80% of IT expenses within banks is spent on maintaining and improving existing applications and legacy systems,[7] indicating that this remains a costly problem for many banks. Software providers, including Temenos, are able to implement solutions to meet these challenges and overcome this barrier. The Temenos solution architecture will help banks to not only comply with regulation, but also to implement a strong API-based framework that will capitalize on the investment required to meet regulatory standards. This architecture fully corresponds to the commonly accepted industry definition of an API-based technology platform for open banking.

Considering an overhaul of traditional banking systems so that banks are in the best possible position to benefit from open banking is a strong strategy for banks to prepare for open banking. Responding to the open banking challenge in a thoughtful, measured way rather than rushing to meet regulatory minimums without considering the wider picture, is an important aspect of open banking strategy.

Banks must assess which elements of their value chain truly add value to the end customer and which do not, how much value is created, what are the associated risks and costs, and what are the opportunity costs of divestment. Accordingly, banks may decide to focus on certain processes themselves, may consider outsourcing and other innovative partnership models for sections of their value chain or may in-source certain business from other banks, leading to the rise of new banking models. Open banking creates an opportunity for banks to overhaul their business model and change their role in the banking landscape, though not all banks will wish to take such a proactive and transformative approach. For those that do, there are a number of options: banks could choose to become utilities servicing other customer facing institutions (manufacturers), digital marketplaces offering products to customers from multiple providers (distributors) or intermediaries connecting distributors to manufacturers (B2B platforms).

Open APIs

Regardless of how banks choose, or choose not, to transform their banking business model for the age of open banking, open APIs are a core component of open banking. Open APIs will impact every bank contending with open banking regulation, and banks intending to adopt open banking practices. APIs are not new in banking by any means. The banking industry has relied on shared services for years. An API is a set of protocols that allows software and applications to communicate with each other seamlessly in the background without users knowing. This is best exemplified by how a consumer app, such as a travel app, asks for authentication via a Google or Facebook login. Instead of having to sign up and enter new details to access the travel app, the app makes an API call to Google or Facebook to enable authentication.

There are three types of APIs: internal/private, partner, and public/open.

- *Internal or private APIs* are commonly used within a bank to allow communication between different internal applications.
- *Partner APIs* are only accessible to specific partners of the bank, similar to how many companies run portals or extranets for partner access.
- A *public or open API* is made available to anyone who wants to use it to connect to the bank's information store and provides a mechanism for applications or systems to collaborate with each other and operate together.

Open banking uses open API calls to allow banks to share their information securely with non-bank third-party financial providers (TPPs). The "From" part of Figure 10.4 shows a traditional banking model where the bank's technology is confined to its own specific channels, whereas the "To" part represents the open, more inclusive banking model. A key difference between the approaches today is that the open model grants access to customer data. This data can be public data such as a bank's products and services or it could be private data such as an account holder's transactional details. This, not surprisingly, is the most controversial part of the open model.

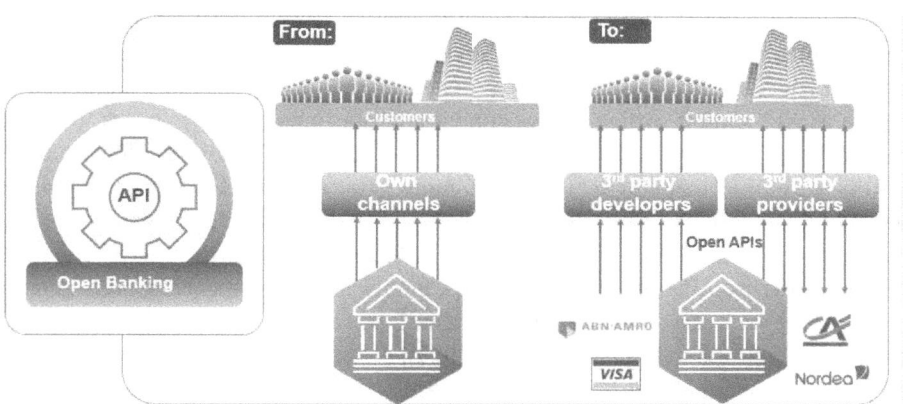

Figure 10.4: Shift of bank ony channels to bank and 3rd party providers

There is broad consensus in the industry that APIs are the de-facto standard to facilitate communication between the various parties in an open banking ecosystem as they are scalable, reusable and easy-to-use. APIs provide real-time access to open data and secured access to private data for third parties, and enable third-party developers to build applications and services around the bank. There is an increasing expectation in the industry that in the future banks will compete not only on the financial services that they provide, but also on the apps and app stores they bring to market. Banks are expected to open up their architecture through the use of APIs and become platforms for third-party innovation..

Banks are increasingly aware that APIs have far reaching potential and can be utilized to transform a bank's role in the open banking landscape. According to a 2016 survey of 174 respondents from banks, fintech firms, consultancies and payment providers by the Open Banking Project, banks are growing in API awareness and maturity with 39% of banks having introduced open API initiatives and 39% planning to do so in the twelve months after the survey was conducted.[8] The open API online journal ProgrammableWeb noted that in the five years spanning 2012 to 2017, there were between 216 and 425 APIs added annually, up from fewer than 20 before 2007.[9] It also noted that regulatory measures such as the PSD2 allowing TPPs to access account information or to initiate payment on behalf of customers in 2016 contributed to this surge.

Some banks are already seizing the open banking opportunity and incorporating it as a valuable element of their banking model and services. Credit Agricole was one of the first full-service banks to make use of open banking, launching their CA app store in 2012. This online marketplace crowd-sources new ideas for banking applications from customers and allows third-party developers to respond with new banking applications through the use of open APIs. Today, more than 50 third-party apps are available in the store. Examples include apps for gamification of savings goals, location of transactions on a map and healthcare expense management. Similarly, the Spanish bank BBVA now operates a well-established global API marketplace, known as API market, which allows companies, start-ups and developers to access these APIs and offer new products and services. BBVA's API market offers an array of APIs including customer account data, money transfer services and pre-approved loans, and has received a number of accolades for its success. Digital banks, such as European online bank Fidor, have also been enthusiastically forging ahead into open banking, offering APIs in areas including identity management, card management and loyalty points and fostering an active developer community. Banks that are dedicated to using APIs to improve their quality of service and create tangible value for the end customer are likely to see most success.

Leveraging the Open Banking/Digital Payments Opportunity

Aside from addressing regulations, have significant opportunities from Open banking. This section looks at what banks can do to take advantage of Open banking.

API Strategy

To flourish in the open banking space, banks should make full use of the potential of open APIs, offering APIs across various banking products with a clear API strategy in place. Banks must know which APIs they plan to open and why, develop plans on how they will engage fintechs and developers, and ensure that bank customers will be able to access the third-party offerings created. The combination of these three focused areas will allow banks to develop a lasting API capability that offer customers greater relevance and personalization, more transparency on pricing terms and conditions, greater choice and more convenience.

Figure 10.5 shows the three steps that banks need to take to implement an open API strategy: enablement, curation, and publication.

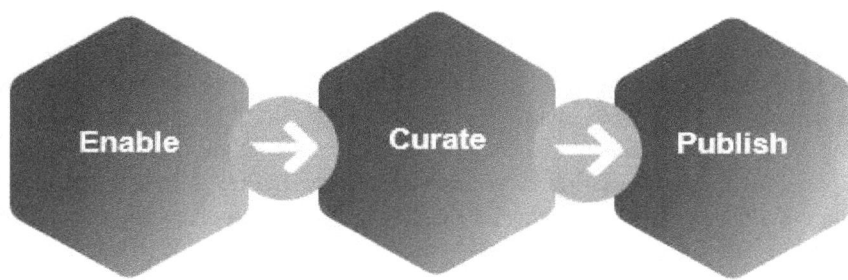

Figure 10.5: API strategy implementation steps

The first step of an API strategy is *enablement*; banks need to enable data and services to be shared through standard APIs and their own APIs. This is not as simple as rapidly opening a large number of APIs. Instead, banks must take a thoughtful, measured approach to opening APIs, and consider the opportunities, competition and risks that they may face. Banks need to have a clear understanding of what APIs and how many they intend to open, what developers and third parties that they would be attracting, what uses that these APIs could have for both developers and their customers, and how these APIs will impact and benefit their banking services. It is also important for banks to establish their method of API monetization, whether they intend for access to their APIs to be entirely free or seek to monetize the data that they possess. Monetization can be achieved using various pricing mechanisms, from fixed pricing and pay-per-use to freemium structures and tiered pay as you go. By being clear about the customer journeys that they want to own and treating APIs as a way of differentiating themselves, banks will have a detailed understanding of how they intend to operate in the open banking space and thus are more likely to succeed.

The next stage of a strong API strategy is *curation*—recruiting developers to use the API's to create new experiences that will add value to customers of the bank. For APIs to benefit banks and customers, APIs must be used by developers to create new solutions that improve customer journeys and experience. Therefore, banks need to be aware of the importance of proactively engaging developers and fintechs with enthusiasm for customer-centric services. Collaboration between banks and fintechs is a core feature of open banking and can be mutually beneficial. Reputable fintech firms have creativity, agility, technical expertise, a community-driven pulse of today's young and savvy consumers, and can provide new, tech-based solutions to put the customers at the center of banking. Banks have the resources, broad customer base, and regulatory expertise to advance open banking, and through collaboration, customers will benefit from the expertise of each party. To encourage and engage fintechs and developers with their banking APIs, banks must ensure they integrate a comprehensive and user-friendly developer portal. This portal provides an interface for developers to access APIs as well as helpful resources such as documentation about the APIs and community forums. The developer portal ensures that developers have the support necessary to encourage them to make best use of the APIs. Banks can also incite innovation outside of their API management systems, by hosting events that attract the attention of creative developers. Banks could tap on the brightest minds by organizing and participating in hackathons, giving an opportunity for new products and services to be "dreamt up" by the developer community. Barclays, Citi in partnership with IBM, and RBS have all experimented with such initiatives in the last two years. Overall, banks' developer curation strategy must focus on the recruitment, retaining and motivation of developers to result in the creation of high-quality products and solutions.

The third step of an API strategy is *publication*. It is important that bank customers can easily access the third-party offerings that are developed and published using the bank's APIs. Adding value to the customer's banking experience, increasing interaction with their bank through both banking and non-banking apps, and even attracting new customers are all valuable benefits of customer access to new and innovative apps and services. When Singapore's OCBC Bank began publishing open APIs in 2016, one of the clear benefits to OCBC customers was the ability to use a dining guide app to locate the OCBC ATM closest to the restaurant. Customers could also receive recommendations of which OCBC credit card would be best to use at the restaurant and get a rebate of up to 6% cash back on weekend dining. Customer benefits of the published third-party offerings are also seen through Citi's open API framework. An online concierge called honestbee was empowered to allow its customers to apply for a Citi Cash Back card on its website and mobile app, allowing a seamless card application process via Citi's merchant partners' sites.

Collaboration and Aggregation

Open banking facilitates aggregation and collaboration in a number of ways. One way is through the aggregation of the areas of expertise and market advantages of banks and third-party providers, through their collaborative efforts to provide customers with new third-party services and products using bank APIs.

With open APIs, banks can use the information derived to monitor customer spending patterns, reduce guesswork when doing promotions, deploy machine learning-based systems so that they can have a complete view of their customers' investments, advance know-your-customers efforts and the assessment of customers' risk profiles, or develop better cross-selling opportunities. This depth of customer information will allow banks to better understand and therefore service their customers, which if utilized effectively, could positively impact customer satisfaction and retention. Open banking will also improve on-boarding by reducing the costs and frictions through digital sign-ups. The costs of customer switching will decrease as automated porting of complete account history replaces manual uploads of select information. In addition, improved identity verification and authentication standards will enable better monitoring and detection services, thereby reducing fraud across the industry.

Open APIs enable aggregation of a wide array of services linked to a single bank Aggregation provides banks with the opportunity to cater more effectively to a much wider range of customer products and services, which are becoming increasingly individualized, with banking priorities varying significantly from person to person. For example, some customers are content to use the same insurance year in and year out regardless of cost efficiency, while others will actively seek out the best deal. Some do not see the need for an aggregated view of their finances, while others desire this so strongly that they resort to the non-standard practice of screen-scraping to gain this aggregated view. With third-party provider apps and services enabled by APIs, banks can effectively respond to this changing market by offering more personalized banking services that cater to the wide variety of expectations. An aggregation app providing a full single customer view of accounts across FIs can, for example, be brought to market without banks having to dedicate considerable time and money to its creation. There is also less risk involved if the TPP product does not perform as well as anticipated.

APIs can lead to the creation of a variety of valuable third-party services in areas including mobile money, payments, social trading, automated retail investment and personal lending. Through use of their APIs, banks can give customers the ability to make straight-through car insurance payments directly from the bank's portal, providing ex-ante recommendations of the best products to buy and providing better and cheaper access to credit because of the banks' access to third-party transactional data. Innovative services have already been developed using open APIs such as ABM Amro's Tikki, which allows customers to send payment requests via WhatsApp, and Starling Bank's integration with Money Dashboard, a personal finance management tool. Such partnerships create new value chains that increase customer loyalty by providing customers with the convenience of using a TPP within the banking service rather than having to create a separate relationship with them.

Banks are able to exploit these new, profitable opportunities in part due to the customer trust they possess. Despite the benefits that fintechs can offer to customers and the advantage that they have over banks in certain areas, such as their agility and scalability, customers still place greater trust in traditional financial institutions. According to Accenture's PSD2 UKI Banking Customer Survey, 70% of respondents would not trust a third party as much as a bank with their data. Through collaboration with TPPs using APIs, customers can receive the innovative and customer-centric new services and experiences that fintechs and other TPPs provide, with the comfort of knowing that their bank continues to play a role in the security of their data. Open APIs make it possible for banks to securely leverage new innovations from fintech firms without sacrificing or damaging their relationships with their customers.

Open banking collaboration also creates many opportunities to reach new revenue streams, from monetization of API access, as explained in the preceding section, to new platform-based banking models. For a traditional full-service bank, there are now three new banking models that they can adopt (see Figure 10.6). The first is the *manufacturer* model, where a bank provides its own products and services to other customer-facing third parties. Second is the *distributor B2C* model, where a bank sources products from TPPs to provide to their own customers, thereby retaining the customers and avoiding disintermediation. Third is the *platform B2B* model, where the bank acts as a market intermediary between manufacturers, distributors and customers. Platforms generate value by facilitating the exchange and delivery of financial products and services between multiple suppliers and consumers, leading to improved customer experience, innovation and growth. As open APIs are expected to expand the number of products and services that can be created and consumed, operating as a platform is a highly viable new business model for banks.

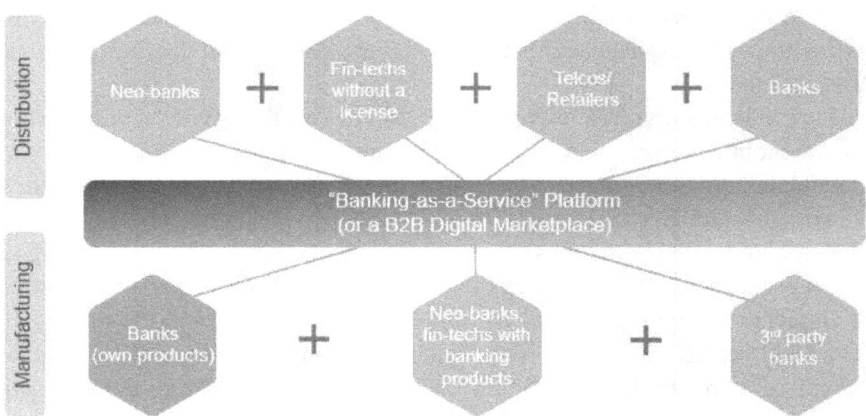

Figure 10.6: A banking platform for Fintechs and Banks

Open Banking Ecosystem

Open banking is a system built upon the concept of collaboration and data sharing, and in order for banks to excel in this new format, an open banking ecosystem should be curated. Banks have begun launching open API platforms, from traditional banks to challenger banks such as Fidor, Atom and Monzo, and inviting third-parties to build value-added services for their customers. Working in combination with an array of third-party providers, from fintech firms to players outside the finance industry, banks should endeavor to foster an ecosystem where the developers using their APIs feel valued, supported and have easy access to a well-designed developer-portal. A well-organized and maintained ecosystem will lead to better innovation (see Figure 10.7), as developers unhappy with the quality of an API developer portal and ecosystem are likely to be less interested in using the APIs it provides.

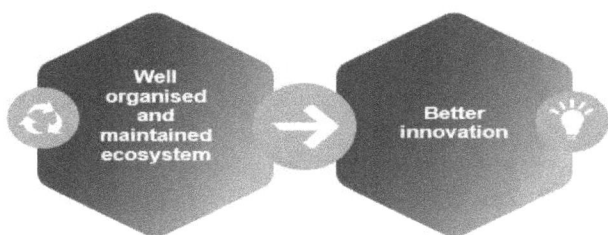

Figure 10.7: Benefits of an ecosystem

Creating and fostering an active ecosystem requires a long-term commitment and significant effort and planning. There will no doubt be fierce competition for developers' attention as more banks enter this space. Without a proactive approach, ecosystems can become stagnant, and many may fall by the wayside due to lack of investment or competitive strategy.

Without developers to use a bank's APIs to create new apps and services, there is no end-product for the customer and therefore, it is essential that developers are contented with the resources, support and quality of experience offered to them. To foster an ecosystem of quality, banks must ensure that they have a clear strategy to recruit, retain and motivate developers, as well as a plan to sustain growth of the ecosystem. To attract and retain developers, banks should offer a developer-portal that is easy to navigate and use and provides support such as documentation about the APIs and testing tools.

For example, the banking software company Temenos can provide the technology to build an API developer portal and the tools to target, assist and govern the community of developers who consume the open APIs. Full-lifecycle API management is also provided to aid the planning, design, implementation, publication, operation, consumption, maintenance and retirement of APIs. This includes the API developer portal as well as run-time management and analytics.

Another way to attract developers is by offering early access, a strategy that proved successful for Nordea. In February 2017, Nordea set up a site where third-party developers could register and request access to a soon-to-be-released sandbox environment for testing prior to live production. Within three days of going live, the site had registered more than 300 signup-requests from interested software companies and developers around the world. By generating interest and gaining press coverage, this strategy brought developers to an API platform that was not even available yet, showing that developers' contributions to the API lifecycle are respected and valued.

Strategies like early access are a successful means of motivating developers but to sustain this motivation, communication is another important element of cultivating the ecosystem. Banks should listen to the feedback from the developers, what they like and do not like, and take this on board to improve their experience. Offering forums where developers interact with and support each other can also foster a sense of community and provides another avenue for support within the ecosystem. When establishing the open banking ecosystem, planning to sustain growth of the ecosystem is also of significance, and the ability of the platform to support many developers and to scale in time is a key consideration. A developer portal that routinely crashes because it cannot handle heavy usage is likely to negatively impact satisfaction and the cultivation of a successful ecosystem.

Life Stage Management

With personalized, valuable services at the forefront of customer needs and expectations, using a life stage management approach is an innovative, targeted way to provide customers with a service that is relevant and meaningful to them, and will encourage consistent customer interaction with the bank.

In the current market, customers are increasingly more inclined towards saving time than finding the best deals. This trend is reflected by the numerous apps and services that prioritize customer experience and ease of use. A clear example of this is the rise in the popularity of contactless payments compared with the declining use of cash, due to the time and effort involved in both withdrawing and using cash. Customers want an easy, smooth experience, but the service itself must also be personally valuable to the customer in order to encourage regular use. Through life stage management, valuable services and guidance can be offered to customers and tailored to their specific life stage. By meeting customer needs as they progress and grow in life, customer loyalty can be retained and advocacy created.

Figure 10.8 shows a cycle of life stage management. The cycle begins with baby planning, where banks could provide a baby planner app to aid with the listing and purchasing of baby equipment and be able to provide product recommendations specific to the customer's needs and budget. A household budget function and monthly baby expenses could also be offered within the app. For children aged 6 to 18, a wide range of services that centered on social activities, pocket money or driving lessons can be included. For adolescents aged 18 to 24, products and apps could include college or first car financial planning and support. When considering young couples, banks could create apps focused on marriage and family planning, and for young families, products could focus on the process of buying a first home. As families mature, they could benefit from services focused on college expenses, retirement planning and healthcare finance. And finally, for retirees, healthcare plans, funeral planning and pension pot services could be beneficial.

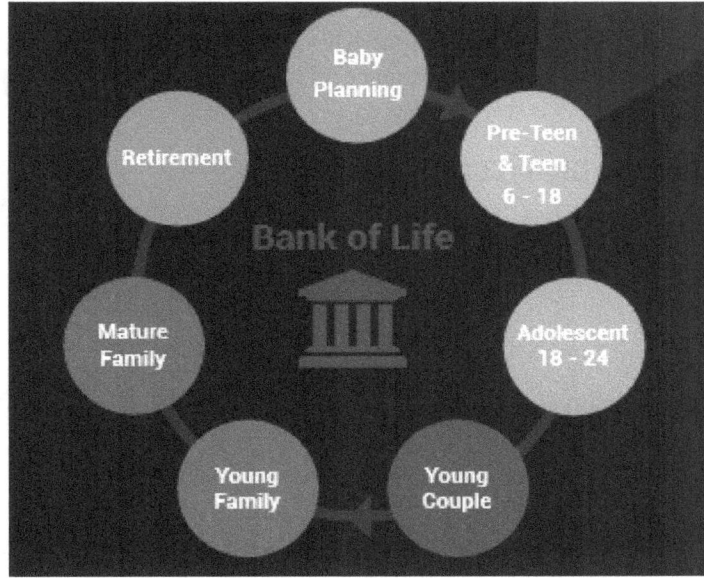

Figure 10.8: An example of a life stage management cycle

An example of the quality and level of personalization that life stage management can offer can be seen in the Pocket Money App under development at Temenos. This app is designed to engage young people between 6 and 18 years old. Its primary feature is the payment of allowance, on a weekly or monthly basis, with the adult having complete control over the amount and frequency. Children earn this money by completing tasks, which enables them to learn about the value of money while also offering additional engagement features such as negotiation (allowing children to counter a task reward with a different figure) and long-term and short-term goals ranging from becoming an astronaut to buying a newly released game. The app offers easy account management for the parent who is able to set up a regular allowance and quickly send extra "top-ups" to the child through the app. The app is also accompanied by a pre-paid debit card, which empowers children to make decisions on their spending at websites and stores pre-approved by the parent. The parent retains ultimate control of the card limit. Children can even use in-app augmented reality (AR) to locate ATMs.

Similar life stage management apps are currently available to customers from innovative, forward-thinking banks. For example, BBVA's Valora app is designed to support customers in the process of buying or renting a home, aiding customers in determining the value of a property and whether it is better to rent or buy it. Valora can provide published offers for similar homes nearby to the one that the customer is interested in, and analyses the area to present trends in estimated sale prices, as well as offer mortgage calculator services. These in-depth, engaging life cycle management services successfully meet customer needs while providing an exemplary customer experience. Such targeted, advisory services are likely to encourage regular use, and improve customer advocacy and dependence on the bank.

Digital Payments for the Digital Customer

One of the key areas of banking affected by Open banking and technology is payments. In this section we explore the key technolpogie ad changes affecting banks customers.

New Technologies Positively Impact Customers

The evolution of the banking landscape is not solely attributable to one change, and new technology in banking, from artificial intelligence to mobile wallets, has been positively impacting customers. The popularity of innovative digital banking services is expected to grow as they become more widespread and readily available. The global proliferation of mobile payments and digital wallets in particular is showing no signs of slowing down. Mobile payment revenue is expected to pass USD $1trillion by 2019,[10] as adoption of these easy-to-use, customer-centric services continues to increase across the world.

Technology giant Apple is experiencing year-on-year growth in adoption of its mobile wallet Apple Pay, with users estimated to have reached 127 million globally by the end of 2017. This is a significant increase from the prior year's 62 million users.[11] The success of Apple Pay is reflected in its continued international expansion, as the service regularly adds support for new banks and the recent launch in Norway, Brazil and Poland brings the number of countries where it is available to 23. Though Android smartphones comprise 64% of all smartphones in Poland,[12] Apple Pay is still able to establish itself, reaching around 200,000 users in its first ten days of operation. Pay-

Pal-owned Venmo is also proving to be a hugely popular mobile and P2P payments service that engages customers with its ease and speed of use and its social media elements, such as the ability to share payment activity with friends to like and comment on. Venmo processed over USD $12bn in payments in the first quarter of 2018[13] and is accepted as a payment method at over 2 million US merchants.

Interest in mobile wallets and payments expands far beyond the US. In India, the number of mobile payment users almost doubled from 32 million in 2016 to 56.2 million in 2017, with no signs of slowing down. This figure is expected to reach 77.8 million by the end of 2018, comprising a third of all smartphone users in India.[14] New mobile wallet services are also surfacing continuously in Southeast Asia, including the Go-Pay mobile wallet expected to launch in Indonesia in 2018 and the impending launch of Razer Pay in Singapore—a wallet app targeted at millennials and supported by United Overseas Bank.

The largest players in the mobile wallet space globally are the dominant Chinese wallets Alipay and WeChat Pay. The popularity of digital payments and mobile wallets in China results in heavy usage of these services, with WeChat Pay boasting 900 million monthly users and mobile payments totaling USD $13trillion in just the first 10 months of 2017.[15] This is due in part to the widespread acceptance of mobile wallet payments, with even buskers on the street accepting payment via a QR code.

Not all digital payments services are developed with the tech-savvy millennial in mind. Kenya's high mobile penetration posed an innovative opportunity to reach unbanked Kenyans using the digital wallet M-Pesa, which has now extended financial inclusion to almost 20 million Kenyans[16] and processed around 6 billion payments in 2016. The impact of targeting this previously inaccessible customer base has been invaluable for the Kenyan people, with access to M-Pesa leading to 194,000 Kenyan households being lifted out of poverty.[17]

The impact and adoption of digital payment and mobile wallet services is widespread and hugely accessible. It is able to improve financial experiences for a wide clientele whether they be digital natives with high expectations or unbanked populations gaining financial inclusion. Once again, personalization and understanding the customer is key to success. Innovations in areas such as international money transfer allow fintechs to service customers to greater satisfaction than banks because of their ability to charge lower fees due to their lower overheads and adept use of digital services.

International money transfer services from fintechs are garnering considerable success, with start-up TransferWise valued at over USD $1 billion and estimated to save customers USD $50 million in fees on the USD $2 billion of transfers processed through the platform each month.[18] TransferWise is heavily focused on the ease of the service and saving customers money, allowing customers to calculate currency conversion and providing transparent pricing of exchange rates and platform charges, as well as displaying how much money the customer will save by using TransferWise. The company continues to innovate, becoming the first service to offer international transfers through Facebook Messenger, and is launching a "borderless" account and debit card this year that is able to hold and convert 28 currencies. International transfer service Xoom, one of the few companies facilitating money transfer to inmates in US prisons, also proves popular and was recently acquired by payment giant PayPal. Mobile money transfer service Azimo, enabling migrants to send money home at up to 90% less than traditional services, continues to expand its service. It recently added 10 new countries to which customers in the Nordic region can transfer funds. By using new technology and having a clear focus on customer-centricity, fintechs and other innovative players are able to create engaging and beneficial digital experiences.

Changes to the Payments Landscape

With digital innovation now at the forefront of the payments industry, the payments landscape is likely to continue to change and evolve as the services improve and expand in response to changing customer expectations and preferences.

Non-traditional players, including social media platforms, are continuing to make an impact in the payments space, leveraging their advantage of a ready-made user base for any digital payments products that they may launch. The most successful example is the substantial impact of WeChat Pay in China, which we discussed in the preceding section. WeChat Pay is a mobile payment extension of China's most popular app, the social networking and messenger app WeChat, which has an active monthly user base of more than 1 billion people.[19] This high-frequency use aided the strong adoption of WeChat Pay after it launched in 2014. WeChat Pay now occupies the second spot for mobile payments market share. WeChat Pay claimed 40% of the market and caused rival Alipay's market share of 80% in 2014 to drop to 54% in 2017.[20] WeChat Pay is expanding into other territories, and is now available in Malaysia where the service aims to gain a solid customer base from the 20 million WeChat users in the country.

Other social media giants including Facebook are also attempting to position themselves in the payments market. In February 2017, international money transfer service TransferWise launched a bot allowing users to make international transfers through Facebook Messenger. Developed using a TransferWise API, the bot also features an exchange rate alert function, sending daily currency rate updates to the customer when enabled. Facebook's other successful chat app, WhatsApp, is preparing to offer payment services in India. WhatsApp is currently used by over 200 million Indians and provides a sizable user base for WhatsApp Pay. WhatsApp Pay is expected to threaten the market share of popular mobile wallets in India, Google Tez and Alibaba-supported Paytm, when launched and may contribute to greater financial inclusion.

The payments landscape is also undergoing change at the hands of shifting customer preferences, as cash use continues to decline in numerous nations across the world, with customers favoring cards and other digital alternatives instead. Contactless payment transactions across cards, mobile and wearable devices are expected to exceed USD $1 trillion in 2018,[21] as adoption and popularity continues to climb. Digital payments are particularly prevalent in China, where cards have largely been bypassed as customers jumped directly from cash to mobile. Mobile wallet services are far more user-friendly than registering for a credit card or engaging with China's state-owned banks, and payment acceptance is ubiquitous requiring as little as a QR code to send or receive payment. Ninety-two percent of the population in China's largest cities use mobile wallets such as WeChat Pay or Alipay as their primary payment method[22] and more than 90% of Chinese customers use mobile payments to make purchases offline.[23]

Mobile payments linked to credit cards are the most popular payment mode in Singapore, despite security concerns deterring some customers. In Australia, only one in five Australians prefer using cash to make purchases, according to research from the Australian Tax Office. The distinct popularity of cashless payments is attributed to convenience, faster transaction times and easier record keeping. Similar trends are witnessed in Canada, where 57% of payments are cashless,[24] and it is expected that by 2030, only 10% of purchases in Canada will be made using cash.[25]

Cashless transactions and preferences are also experienced in Europe, particularly in Sweden where 59% of payments are cashless[26] and cash is used in less than 20% of stores.[27] Only one in four people living in Sweden use cash at least once a week,[28] as card and mobile payments continue to rise in popularity and usage. However, 7 out of 10 Swedes would still like to be able to pay with cash in the future,[29] suggesting that much of the population do not wish to become an entirely cashless society. Cash payments are also falling in the UK, where the use of cash for payments is expected to drop to 21% of sales by 2026.[30] The global trend of the decline of cash use is expected to continue, and has a lasting impact on the payments services that customers prefer and expect to use.

Endnotes

1 http://asean.org/storage/2015/11/AECat-a-glance-2016_web_version2.pdf
2 http://blogs.worldbank.org/eastasiapacific/how-to-scale-up-financial-inclusion-in-asean-countries
3 https://www.afr.com/business/banking-and-finance/macquarie-trumps-big-four-with-new-open-banking-platform-20170914-gyhbxy
4 Accenture Payments: Consumers' initial reactions to the new services enabled by PSD2 2016.
5 https://thebankwatch.com/2016/04/19/world-retail-banking-report-2016-capgemini-and-efma/
6 https://www.ey.com/gl/en/industries/financial-services/banking---capital-markets/ey-global-consumer-banking-survey-2016
7 http://platformable.com/wp-content/uploads/dlm_uploads/2017/11/State-of-the-market-2017-1-1.pdf
8 https://static.openbankproject.com/bnpp/BANKING-APIS-2016.pdf
9 https://www.programmableweb.com/news/financial-apis-have-seen-two-growth-spikes/research/2017/08/09
10 https://www.forbes.com/sites/maggiemcgrath/2018/02/13/forbes-fintech-50-2018-the-future-of-payments/#411e08f43b4f

11 https://appleinsider.com/articles/18/02/22/apple-pay-used-by-estimated-127m-users-globally-but-analyst-claims-only-16-percent-of-iphones-used-for-payments
12 https://appleinsider.com/articles/18/07/01/ten-days-after-launching-in-poland-apple-pay-has-vastly-outpaced-google-pay-uptake
13 https://uk.reuters.com/article/us-paypal-hldg-venmo/paypal-launches-debit-card-for-its-mobile-app-venmo-idUKKBN1JL1WP
14 https://www.cmo.com/features/articles/2018/3/19/apac-buys-into-mobile-payments.html#gs.UIdpYgI
15 https://www.cmo.com/features/articles/2018/3/19/apac-buys-into-mobile-payments.html#gs.MawKFWU
16 M-Pesa and the Rise of the Global Money Market, Forbes, August 2015.
17 In Kenya, Phones Replace Bank Tellers, *The New York Times*, May 2017.
18 https://www.forbes.com/sites/maggiemcgrath/2018/02/13/forbes-fintech-50-2018-the-future-of-payments/#3f814e2a3b4f
19 http://uk.businessinsider.com/wechat-has-hit-1-billion-monthly-active-users-2018-3?r=US&IR=T
20 https://technode.com/2017/08/18/alipay-vs-wechat-challenges-and-strategies-of-two-payment-giants-going-global/
21 https://www.forbes.com/sites/maggiemcgrath/2018/02/13/forbes-fintech-50-2018-the-future-of-payments/#56763b5a3b4f
22 https://www.techinasia.com/wechat-cashless-china-data
23 http://www.visualcapitalist.com/china-digital-wallets-payments/
24 https://www.huffingtonpost.ca/2017/10/11/canada-at-1-in-ranking-of-worlds-most-cashless-societies_a_23240067/
25 https://www.moneris.com/en/about-moneris/news/canada-drop-in-cash-transactions-by-2030
26 https://www.moneris.com/en/about-moneris/news/canada-drop-in-cash-transactions-by-2030
27 https://www.bbc.co.uk/news/business-41095004
28 https://www.bbc.co.uk/news/business-43645676
29 https://www.bbc.co.uk/news/business-43645676
30 https://www.theguardian.com/money/2018/feb/19/peak-cash-over-uk-rise-of-debit-cards-unbanked-contactless-payments

Dharmesh Mistry is the Chief Digital Officer at Temenos, a market leading software provider for banking and finance. Servicing over 3,000 firms globally, including 41 of the top 50 banks. Dharmesh has over 30 years' experience in financial services organizations with technology and management expertise, supported by a proven record of accomplishments for innovation and vision. Prior to joining the company in 2013, he co-founded edge IPK, a market leading UXP and was CTO at Entranet where he pioneered the launch of many banks first internet banking solutions. Based in the UK, Dharmesh takes responsibility for defining and delivering Temenos's Digital strategy. His focus is on addressing the multiple challenges that are faced today by traditional banks, including how to create customer intimacy, achieve operational efficiency and drive innovation. Dharmesh has top-level expertise in banking, UX, channels technology, CRM, architecture and Data/Ai. He plays the role of a senior executive interfacing between business decision makers and digital innovation across the finance industry.

Chapter 11
Theories of Artificial Intelligence and Machine Learning

We have briefly described *artificial intelligence* and *machine learning* in the previous chapter. In this chapter, we will present a more in-depth discussion of these technologies. We shall review some AI/ML techniques and tools, followed by the prospects of AI/ML applications in financial services.

Artificial intelligence (AI) represents a computational approach to developing intelligent software and systems that can solve complex problems by adopting human intelligence and working in the ways of human mind. The history of AI dates back to 1956 when the terminology was first introduced at the conference on "Dartmouth Summer Research Project on Artificial Intelligence." The long-term goal of AI is to achieve *artificial general intelligence (AGI)*. AGI is a strong form of AI and can be aptly described as the idea that "the appropriately programmed computer with the right inputs and outputs would thereby have a mind in exactly the same sense human beings have minds."

With the technologies available today, humans can only perform tasks limited to specific areas—known as *weak AI*. The common method of distinguishing between strong AI and weak AI is to perform professional tests such as coffee testing (an intelligent machine is able to enter your home and figure out how to make coffee—find the coffee machine, find the coffee, add water, find a mug, and brew the coffee by pushing the proper buttons); Turing test (test if an evaluator can distinguish a human and a machine by the nature of conversations between them); and robot college test (a machine can pass the enrollment tests to a university, pass the required classes a normal student would, and obtain a degree).

With the emergence of computing power from the 1980s, researchers began to apply learning algorithms such as artificial neural networks[1] and used large amount of data to train machines through support vector machines.[2] Machine learning (ML) that emphasizes on learning algorithms became the core part of AI. The advent of the "big data" era in the past five years has helped researchers to develop a variety of learning algorithms that have enabled deep learning (DL) to flourish.

DOI 10.1515/9781547400904- 011

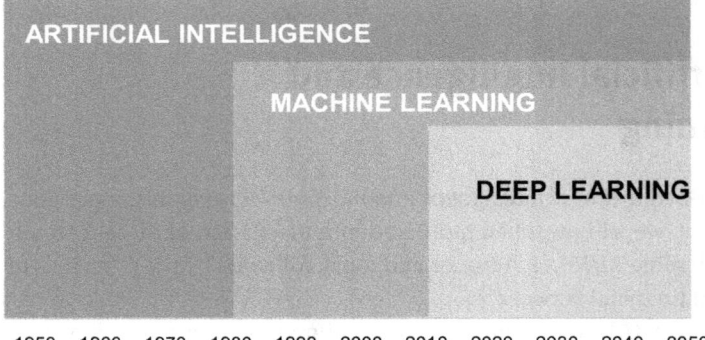

Figure 11.1: The evolution of AI/ML/DL

In recent years, AI/ML has received overwhelming attention from both academic researchers and industry practitioners. This is driven by the increasing use of *graphical processing units* (GPUs), which have become feasible with the exponential growth in computing speed and the prospects of incorporating AI in tangible innovations across industries and applications. For instance, AI is used in applications such as Siri, in self-driving motor vehicles, in facial recognition, and other biometric identification software. As illustrated in Figure 11.2, the number of AI papers published annually has grown more than 9 times since 1996, whereas the number of general computer science papers has increased by 6 times in the same period. The number of active US AI-related startups has grown 14 times since 2000. The annual VC investment funds into US AI startups have increased 6 times since 2000 (AIINDEX, 2017). There is no doubt that AI brings along time and cost efficiency for business processes, but it is also impacting human life, communities and society. In essence, AI adds value in solving complex problems more effectively, accurately, and innovatively.

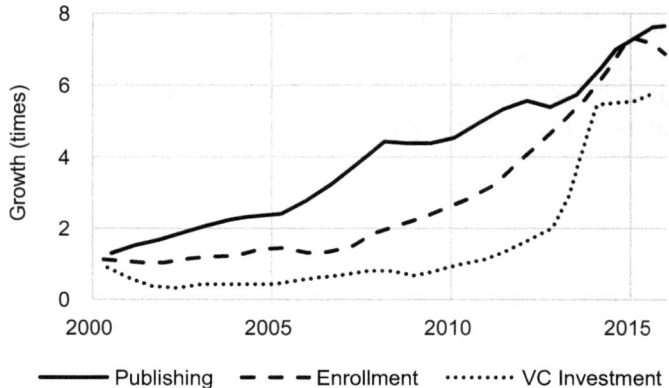

Figure 11.2: The growth of AI-activity

AI Techniques and Tools

An AI program should generally consist of three key features: knowledge base, navigational capability, and inferencing. *Knowledge base* is a repository of knowledge, data, facts and rules, and information from different sources. AI knowledge base should be in the form of explicit words and symbols that are readable, easily modifiable to correct errors, and useful in many situations even though it may be currently incomplete or inaccurate. In contrast with a computer database, a knowledge base can identify patterns rapidly and provide suggestions and informative solutions for designers to arrive at a higher level of expert decisions and thus can promote efficiency and productivity.

The navigational capability refers to a control strategy that determines the rule to apply, and perhaps some heuristics to apply. Inferencing is a process of searching through the knowledge base in order to derive new knowledge. AI is a very hot topic, though it is not a new science. The technology is rapidly advancing in response to a growing interest in human-to-machine communications and is supported by the availability of big data, computing power, and enhanced algorithms. In this section, we review some conventional and enhanced techniques, as well as the environment to which each technique is best applied. These techniques and tools include search algorithms, genetic algorithms, artificial neural networks, fuzzy logic systems, natural language processing methodologies, expert systems, robotics, reinforcement learning, and deep-learning methodologies.

Search Algorithms

Searching is a general problem-solving technique in AI. We will focus on more advanced conventional blind search techniques such as *depth-first search* (DFS), *depth-limited search* (DLS), *breadth-first search* (BFS), *iterative deepening search* (IDS), or *iterative deepening depth-first search* (IDDFS). We shall also introduce A* search subsequently, which is one of the advanced heuristic search methods. Last but not least, we will introduce another powerful search algorithm: genetic algorithm.

Throughout this subsection, we shall use a tree graph as an example of tree data structure to explain the above search techniques.

Depth-first Search (DFS)

The DFS exhaustively searches all nodes by moving at depth until there are no more nodes to be visited along the current path. It then moves backward on the same path to find nodes to traverse, after which the next path will be visited. The DFS will repeat this process until all nodes are visited. Figure 11.3 shows the basic idea of DFS for a simple tree data structure. It starts from a root (node 1, level 0), and goes for one of the level 1 neighbors (for example, node 2), and then further searches node 4 following the path. After this path, it goes backward to the adjacent path, i.e. node 5, and finally goes further backward to node 3. DFS is simple to understand and easy to implement. However, in DFS, no nodes can be visited more than once. It is necessary to differentiate the visited nodes from unvisited ones. In this example, the visited nodes are marked in gray, while the unvisited nodes are marked in dark black. No nodes can be visited more than once. If one node is visited twice, the algorithm may end up in an infinite loop, i.e. an endless search.

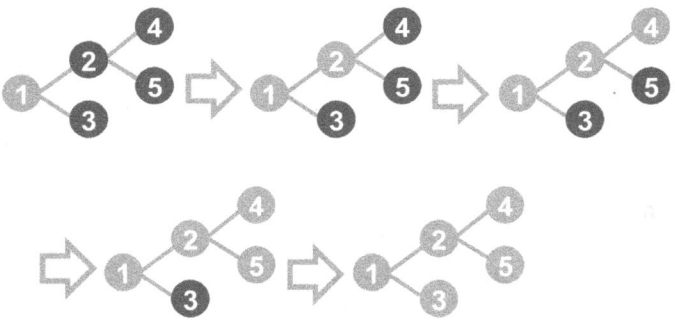

Figure 11.3: An example of DFS process for a tree data structure

DFS is a space-efficient searching method but it is less economical as it exhaustively searches all nodes. For instance, even if the optimal solution is next to the current node, DFS will continue to search through all nodes in the current path, go backward, and repeat the search process on a new path. In this sense, the path containing the optimal solution may only be achieved very late in the search process after repeated searches. Furthermore, DFS is not guaranteed to find the optimal solution. It may fall into an infinite loop if a node is revisited. DFS is hence an incomplete search.

Depth-limited Search (DLS)
DFS is not very efficient, as it searches all the nodes and may require a lot of computations. DLS is an improved search technique based on DFS, but a depth cut-off limit is imposed. The depth cut-off limit represents the point at which the search should be terminated. A specified depth is required to be set in DLS. An economical depth limit will find the optimal search while reducing computational time. The key issue then becomes "How to set the depth limit?"

Breadth-first Search (BFS)
BFS is a strategy that spans search area in each level, starting from a designated origin point. It explores the neighboring nodes first before moving to the next level neigh-

bors. Suppose the distance between two nodes is defined as the path of the shortest length between them. The path length is defined in terms of the number of edges. Figure 11.4 shows a tree with 5 vertices or nodes and 4 edges. The path length between node 1 and 2, 3, 4, 5 are 1, 1, 2, 2, respectively. The BFS can hence find the shortest path between two nodes in terms of the path length, and this is the key advantage of BFD over DFS. The path lengths of the nodes in layer 1 (nodes 2 and 3) are comparatively shorter than the nodes in layer 2 (nodes 4 and 5). Therefore, in BFS, it traverses all the nodes in layer 1 before moving to the nodes in layer 2, as shown in Figure 11.4. However, BFS needs more space.

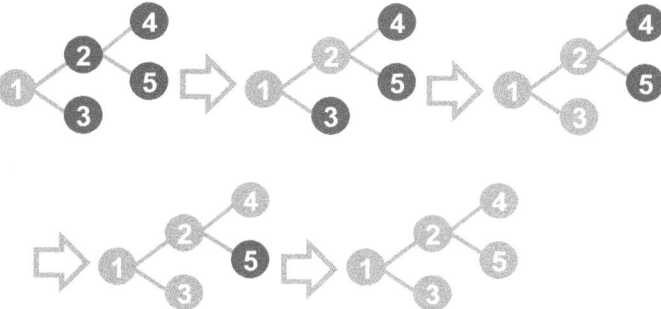

Figure 11.4: An example of BFS process for a tree data structure

A* Search

The above search methods are kind of like a blind search—that is, there is no right direction—and search algorithm can only recognize the solution once it is reached. However, if there is some coarse information of how good various states are, the search can be under the guidance of this information. Such a search method is called the *heuristic search*. The heuristic search can find solutions more efficiently than a blind search. Suppose the node G is the goal and the node N is the intermediate node to G. The idea is to solve an evaluation function to select a starting node A, which seems to be the best, and then moves toward the most desirable nodes in a decreasing order of desirability. Such an approach is called best-first search. A* algorithm is a special case of best-first search. It is one of the most important progresses in AI search algorithm.

Suppose is the lowest-cost path to N from the current node C, and is the estimated cost to G from N. The estimated total cost of the path from C to G (through N) is, then

$$f(N) = g(N) + h(N)$$

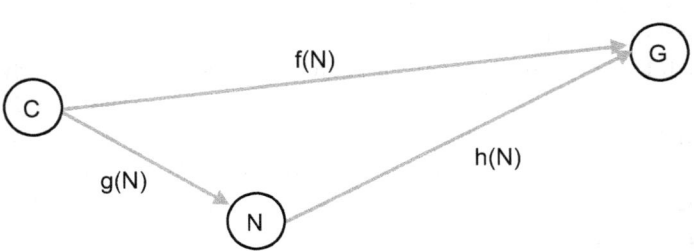

Figure 11.5: Illustration of the principle of A* search

The h(N) is a problem-specific heuristic. A* search is implemented using priority queue by minimizing. It can find a complete and optimistic solution.

There are some other local search algorithms such as the hill-climbing search, local beam search, and simulated annealing. A hill-climbing search starts with an arbitrary solution and iterates the search to find a better one by an incremental change until there are no further improvements. Local beam search is solving an optimization problem that maximizes an objective function. It will generate a number of solutions randomly at a given time and will stop once an optimal solution is found. Simulated annealing borrows the idea of modifying a metal's physical properties through the process of metal heating and cooling. Monte Carlo simulation is used to generate random states and the search is stopped when the criterion solution is found. Simulated annealing is widely used in travelling salesman problem (TSP), path planning, allocation problem and scheduling problem. These local algorithms only return local optimal solutions. They are neither complete, nor universally optimal.

Genetic Algorithm

Genetic algorithm is a special search algorithm inspired by Charles Darwin's natural evolution theory. It exploits natural selection principles of the "survival of the fittest" to solve complex optimization problems.

Natural selection was first proposed by John Holland in the 1970s (Holland, 1975). Suppose there is a population in a natural environment where the fitter ones survive and others are eliminated. Humans generate offspring who inherit the characteristics of their parents and some characteristics will pass on to the next generation. In some cases, some of the offspring's genes may be subjected to a mutation with a low random probability. If the parents are fitter, their offspring will be better than the parents and will more likely survive. By iterating such a selection process, the fittest individuals will be identified.

A genetic algorithm usually starts with a *search space*, which can be randomly generated or manually assigned and contains a number of individuals or solutions. Each individual who is also called a chromosome is a finite set of parameters or variables. The parameters or variables are represented as genes. A gene is usually coded as a binary alphabet 0 or 1. Hence, an individual or a chromosome is characterized by a set of binary alphabets. The relationship of gene, chromosome and population is depicted in Figure 11.6.

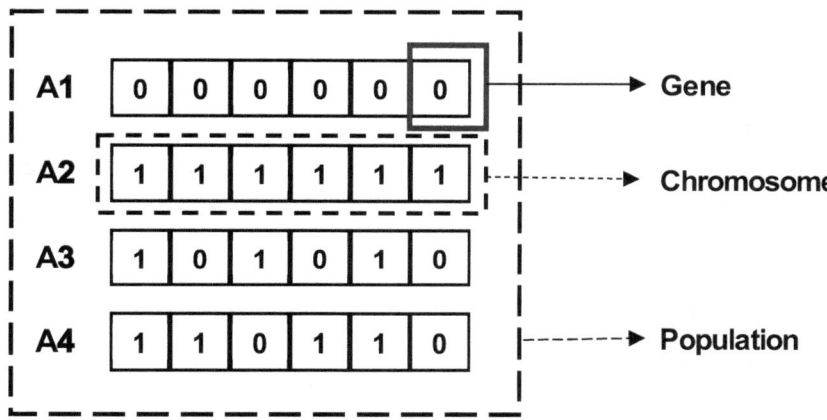

Figure 11.6: Gene, Chromosome, and Population

To find out a solution, three processes are required in a typical genetic algorithm: fitness selection, crossover, and mutation. The fitness selection is a process to determine the ability of an individual to compete with others using a fitness function, which can be an objective function or a subjective judgement. The individual with the highest fitness score will survive and be used in the next step—crossover. Crossover represents mating between individuals. For a pair of parents to be crossed over, their offspring are created by exchanging their genes until the chosen crosspoint is reached. The new offspring join in the population. An example of crossover is shown in Figure 11.7.

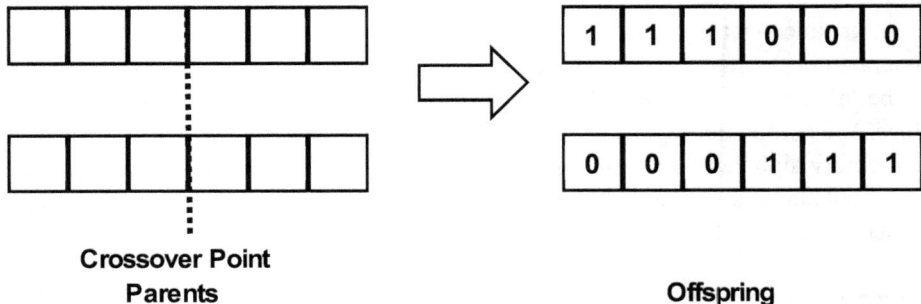

Crossover Point
Parents   **Offspring**

Figure 11.7: Crossover

Like biological life, the new offspring will share the genes from parents, but mutation occurs in some circumstances with a low random probability. This process is coded as flipping genes' binary values randomly, as shown in Figure 11.8.

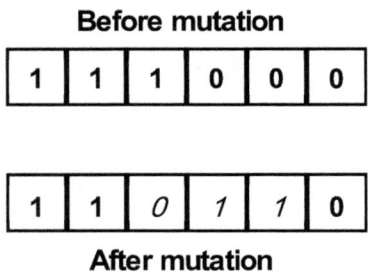

Figure 11.8: Mutation

The algorithm repeats the process of creating new offspring—fitness selection, crossover, and mutation—and ultimately results in the outcome that there are no offspring who are significantly different from the previous generations; the solution is found and the process is terminated. Genetic algorithms can also terminate when the minimum criteria are satisfied or a pre-defined condition is reached.

Genetic algorithms are common in quantitative financial applications. They can be used to calibrate the parameters for a trading rule. They can also help to build an *artificial neural networks* (ANN) model, which will be introduced in the subsequent section to illustrate the selection of stocks and identification of trades (Kanungo, 2004) (Lin, Cao, Wang, & Zhang, 2004).

However, there are two key limitations of genetic algorithms. First, genetic algorithms easily produce solutions after a large number of combinations. However, because of the lack of a consistent explanation on why the solution works, it may be overfitted and hence, not robust. Second, genetic algorithms may have a data-snoop-

ing bias problem—that is, found statistically significant but actually nonexistent relationships from data mining, if the mutation function is inappropriate.

Artificial Neural Networks (ANNs)

An *artificial neural network* is inspired by the structure of the human brain and is
intended to replicate human intelligence. It is one of the main machine learning tools
for AI.

A typical ANN consists of many connected nodes which represent artificial neurons
and connections. Some neurons are inputs—that is, sources of information. Some of
these are the outputs and others are intermediate neurons. The connection represents
the information flow from the input neurons to the output neurons potentially through
the intermediate hidden neurons. The receivers process the information and change
their internal states according to the input. This process is called *activation*. Then the
signal goes to the next neuron to produce output. Artificial neurons are generally organized in layers. The architecture of neural networks is shown in Figure 11.9.

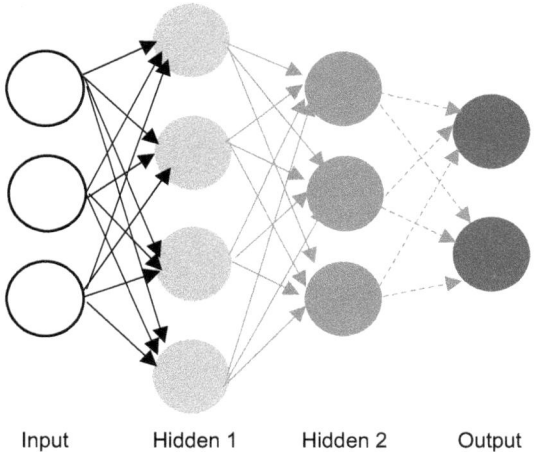

| Input | Hidden 1 | Hidden 2 | Output |

Figure 11.9: A conceptual example of ANN architecture

As a common practice, the information/signal at a connection between two neurons
is set as a real number, and the output is generally calculated by a non-linear function
of the sum of its inputs. In the learning process, weights and activation functions can
be adjusted to increase or decrease the strength of the signal as learning progresses.

An important advance in the ANN field is the backpropagation algorithm,
invented by Werbos (Werbos, 1974), in which it is possible to adjust the neurons in
the hidden layers by modifying the weights at each node when the outcome is unde-

sirable. Another important improvement is the technique of deep learning neural networks, which allows different layers of a multilayer network to extract different features until it can recognize the objective function. We shall review deep learning in a later subsection.

With the development of novel techniques, ANNs are used in a wide range of applications such as computer vision, machine translation, social network filtering, pattern recognition such as recognition based on human interpretable features, gaming, medical diagnosis, and even automatic trading systems.

Fuzzy Logic Systems (FLS)

Humans may rely on imprecise and inaccurate inputs in their decision-making process. For instance, instead of using a precise value as an input, the human may rely on a range of values or on vague qualitative responses such as "possibly yes/ no," "perhaps," and so on. Such human behaviors may arise from incomplete knowledge or psychological biases leading to a tendency to generalize, or to lean toward generality ambiguity, or vagueness. FLS can deal with these inputs and come out with an acceptable but definite solution. Fuzzy logic was proposed by Lotfi A. Zadeh (Kanungo, 2004).

FLS consists of four modules: fuzzifier, knowledge base, inference engine, and defuzzifier.

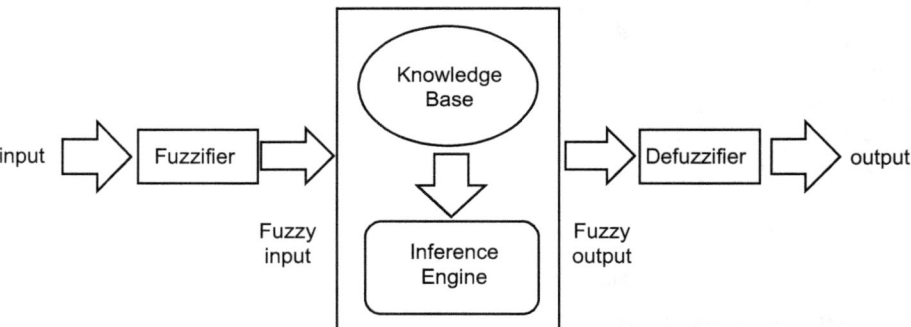

Figure 11.10: A conceptual example of FLS architecture

Fuzzifier is a module that converts the physical values as well as ambiguous input signals into a normalized fuzzy set. The normalized fuzzy set is defined as an interval that covers the range of input values with membership functions that describe the probability of state of the input variables. It generally splits the information/signal into five states: large positive (LP), medium positive (MP), small (S), median negative (MN), and large negative (LN).

Knowledge base stores the membership functions and the fuzzy rules. The fuzzy rules follow the principle of IF-THEN. The membership function quantifies the degree of membership between 0 and 1. In fact, many degrees of membership are allowed in a fuzzy set. A membership function generally maps all elements in the universe of discourse to the interval [0, 1]. For the sake of simplicity, fuzzy sets are often defined as triangle- or trapezoid-shaped curves. Figure 11.11 shows triangular membership functions for LP, MP, S, MN, and LN states.

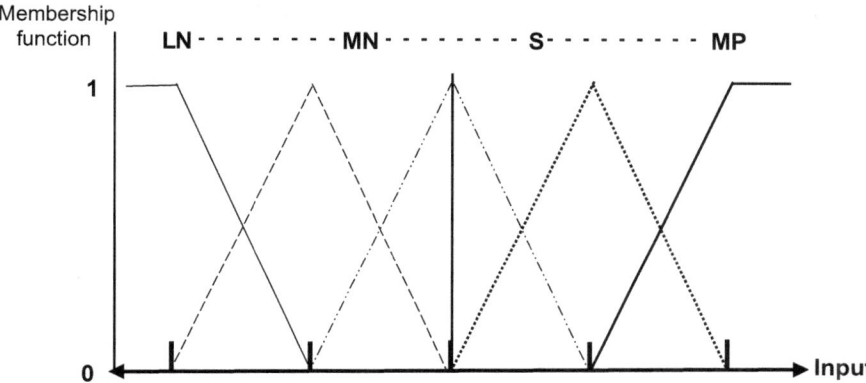

Figure 11.11: Triangle member functions for LP, MP, S, MN, and LN states

FLS can be applied to solve some complex human reasoning and decision-making problems when the input information is imprecise and even distorted or erroneous and when we do not need high-accuracy solutions. It is easy to implement and flexible to adjust the fuzzy rules. FLS is thus commonly used in various applications such as four-wheel steering and automatic gearboxes in automotive systems, home appliances such as microwave ovens, refrigerators, toasters, washing machines, televisions, and air conditioners. Other applications include photocopiers, Hi-Fi systems, and humidifiers.

Natural Language Processing (NLP)

NLP is an AI technique to build up a computational linguistics system using natural language data so that the computer can learn, analyze, and manipulate human language. An NLP system should be able to process both speech and written text.

Human-computer interaction has been a very difficult problem in computer science due to the ambiguity of human language at the lexical, syntactic, and referencing level. For example, the same words can be used in different contexts with different meanings, and computers without real life experience cannot guess the meaning. Today, we can have a relatively fruitful communication with the computer due to the advances in algorithm in NLP. NLP consists of two modules: *natural language understanding* (NLU) and *natural language generation* (NLG). NLU contains a database for speech tagging and word categorization. The task of NLU is to understand and recognize the human natural language received by the computer and interpret the different aspects of the language. The module maps the linguistic inputs into programming language and identifies words or text in their grammatical forms using a set of lexicon rules. This module is a typical machine learning process.

NLG is a process that converts the computer programming language into an audible or textual language for the user. It comprises three sub-processes: *text planning,* which retrieves the words or text from the knowledge base; *sentence planning,* which produces meaningful phrases and sets reasonable tone for the sentence; and *text realization, which* forms a well-structured sentence.

NLP is commonly used in the areas of automatic summarization, translation, speech recognition, automated question answering, sentiment analysis, social media analysis, entity extraction, and named-entity recognition. There are many common practices in our daily lives. Besides virtual assistant chatbots like Siri and Alexa, NLP is used to identify patterns and clues in emails or written reports to aid in detection and solving of crimes. Applications include chatbot, and robot investment consultant. It is also used to classify content into meaningful topics such as discovering trends that are generally hard to identify. Furthermore, it can track interest on a particular topic or event, and analyze the sentiment on a specific influential event from social media and trace the key influencer accounts.

Expert Systems (ES)

The first expert system (ES) was invented in the 1970s by Edward Feigenbaum (Feigenbaum, 1977) who was the founder of the Knowledge Systems Laboratory at Stanford University. It is an AI system that can serve as a "real" expert at the level of human intelligence in a particular domain. A qualified ES is characterized by high performance in expertise, reliability, stability, and promptness in response.

An ES incorporates three components: knowledge base, inference engine, and user interface. A successful ES relies on high-quality, complete, accurate, and precise knowledge of a specified domain. The knowledge base of an ES contains (i) factual knowledge—the information widely accepted by the scholars and knowledge engineers of the field, and (ii) heuristic knowledge, which is evaluation, accurate judgment, and guesses based on data, information, and past experiences. The knowledge is acquired from various experts such as scholars and knowledge engineers. The knowledge engineers generally obtain the information from recording, interviewing, or observations at work. The representation of knowledge is in the form of IF-THEN-ELSE statements.

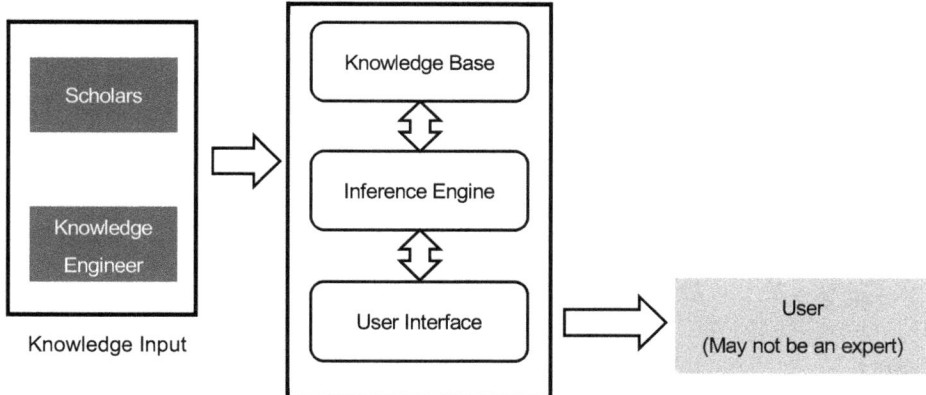

Figure 11.12: A conceptual example of an expert system

An *inference engine* is a set of rules for applying the knowledge base and deriving a solution to a specific problem. The inference engine applies the rules to the facts repeatedly, and adds new information coming from the rules and conclusions to the knowledge base until a solution is reached. The system can also resolve a conflict when multiple rules are applied to the same case. Forward-chaining and backward-chaining are the main strategies used in an inference engine. The forward-chaining strategy follows chain conditions and facts, and then deduces a solution by answering the question: What can happen next? It is hence a data-driven strategy. It is commonly used to solve more open-ended problems—for example, predictions on housing price as an effect of changes in interest rate. However, when the problem is to find out the cause or reason and the problem is well-defined, backward-chaining is preferred. The backward-chaining strategy is to find out which conditions could have happened in the past for the assumed result by answering the question: Why did this happen?

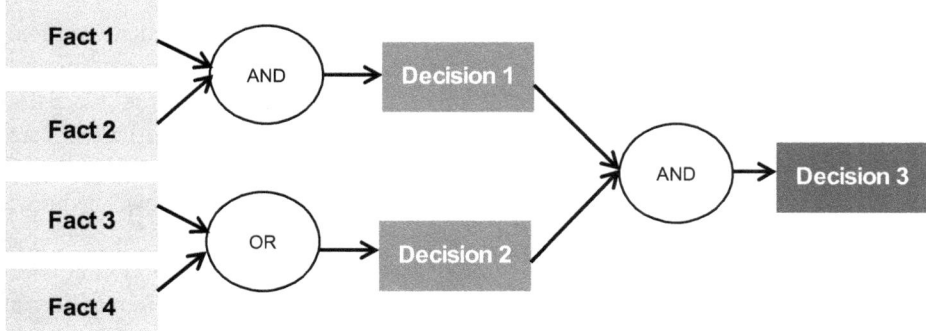

Figure 11.13: A conceptual example forward chaining strategy for an ES

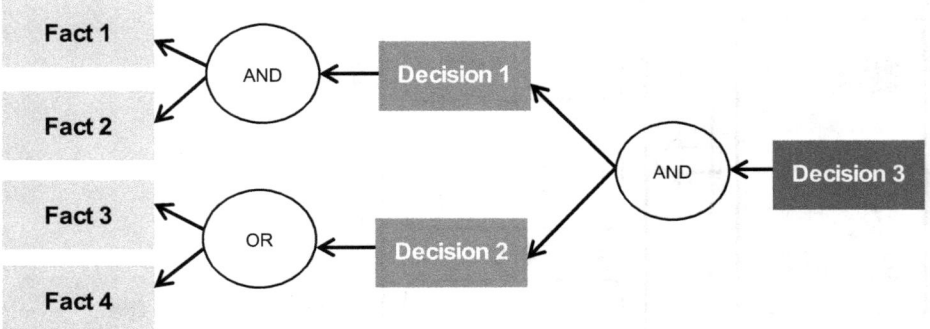

Figure 11.14: A conceptual example of backward chaining strategy for an ES

ES are widely used in healthcare. For example, the ES Dendral is used to identify organic molecules, and MYCIN helps to identify bacteria. ES can also be used in telecommunications, customer service, transportation, and financial services. In the financial field, it can be used for detection of fraud and suspicious transactions, in stock trading, and in investment advisory. ES can provide a competitive edge for an enterprise against competitors in a world that requires an ever more precise and prompt response.

Robotics

Robotics is to design, construct, and create robots that are artificial agents for specific purposes. For example, NASA used robots to explore space and other planets. Amazon's Kiva robotics system created mobile robots that could shuttle goods and pallets within complex distribution warehouses. In manufacturing industries, robotic arms play a large role in production assembly lines to free manpower from repeated tasks and hence, reduce manpower costs.

In contrast with other AI programs, robotics deals with a real physical problem instead of a computer-stimulated one. It involves the mechanical construction and design of a machine to fulfill a specific physical task that generally requires the machine to move in its environment. It needs special hardware and electrical sensors to control the machine and incorporates the detailed computational commands for the machine to do a particular task. The task typically includes the "how," "when," and "what" to do.

Most robots are composed of two important parts: locomotion and computer vision. A mobile robot needs locomotive mechanisms so that a robot can move from place to place. There are several types of locomotion such as legged, wheeled, combination of legged and wheeled, and tracked slip/skid locomotion. In legged locomotion, the robot's traveling capability depends on the number of legs. Legged locomotion requires more motors and consumes more power but show better stability, while wheeled locomotion requires fewer motors and is more power-efficient, but less stable. In tracked slip/skid locomotion, vehicles use tracks akin to a tank. A tracked vehicle is steered by moving the tracks at different speeds in the same or opposite direction. It is relatively stable because of a large contact area between the tracks and the surface. However, if the surface is hard, the vehicle is unable to slide.

With the rapid development of image processing, computer vision systems have become widely used in robots for purposes such as security surveillance and clearance, gaining of access, and in healthcare and entertainment. The digital image processing and analysis module is a critical part of the computer vision system. It converts scanned documents and images into editable text, facial detection, object recognition, and estimation of positioning.

Robotics application is evolving rapidly with the significant progress in AI technologies and revolutionary innovations in hardware. For example, humanoid robots can share learning and pool experiences with other humanoid robots through the data stored in cloud. Communications among robots may even become possible. Furthermore, the advances in reinforcement learning make it possible for robots to mimic and learn from human coworkers. The examples are humanoid robot Pepper and autonomous driving car Waymo.

Reinforcement Learning (RL)

Reinforcement learning (RL) is another important machine learning technique that allows learning through trial-and-error interactions between a learning agent and its environment or experiences. The critical assumption of RL is that the learning agent obtains delayed rewards after taking action. The rewards are associated with each state in the environment and depends on how good the action taken was. A typical RL process consists of three components: environment, reinforcement function, and value function. The RL environment follows a Markov decision process (MDP), which defines a finite state space, a finite action space, transition probabilities, value function, and reinforcement/reward function. The reinforcement function defines the goal of RL, which is the expected cumulative reinforcements and rewards. The value function calculates the maximum expected future reward that the agent will get at each state. The value of each state is the total amount of the reward an agent can expect to accumulate over time, starting from the current state.

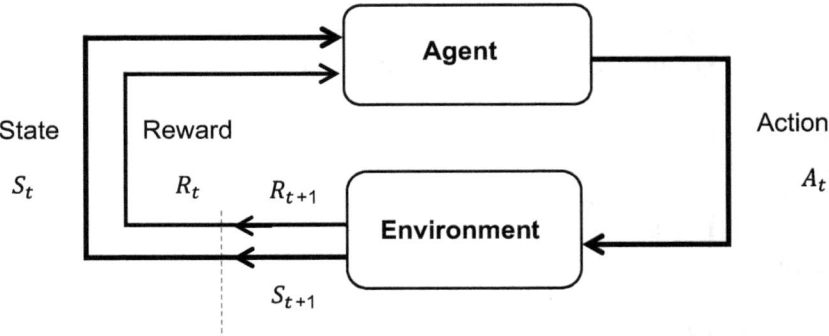

Figure 11.15: A conceptual example RL process

A *Markov decision process* (MDP) is a learning approach of reinforcement learning. Suppose a finite set of states S, a finite set of actions A, and a reward function R are defined. The set of actions define policy P and the rewards define value V. For a specific time, the agent takes action A_t to transition from the current state to the next state and obtains rewards R_t after the action. The reward could be positive when the action is better and could be negative when the action is worse. Iterate such a loop until the agent goes to the end state. The objective function of RL is to maximize $E(R_t|P,S_t)$, which is to maximize the expected rewards by choosing an optimal policy P for all possible values of S for a time t. The algorithm is described in the following steps.

Step 1: The agent starts with an arbitrary initial state S_0 from the environment E.
Step 2: Based on S_0, the agent takes an action A_0.
Step 3: E transits to a new state S_1 according to policy P and the agent gains a reward R_1. Check the objective function. If the expected cumulative rewards in the state S_1 are maximized, then stop. Otherwise, continue to loop through the steps until an optimal policy is found.

The algorithm creates a sequence of states, actions, and rewards. The solution is found when the expected cumulative reward is maximized. RL is typically used to solve sequential decision-making problems. Figure 11.15 describes a simple RL process. RL is commonly used in supply chain for inventory management to smooth the material flow and optimize utilization of warehouse space while fulfilling demands. It is useful in reducing response time as well as inventory costs. Another intensive use of RL area is in industrial automation. Google DeepMind employs RL technologies to its HVAC system in its own data center, which significantly reduces energy consumption annually. In the financial sector, Q-learning, one of RL algorithms, can be used to find an optimal trading strategy that maximizes portfolio value while balancing the market risk. Other applications include game theory and multi-agent interaction, robotics, computer networking, vehicular navigation, and in medical care.

Deep Learning (DL)

According to Andrew Ng who was a founder of Google Brain and led the productization of deep learning (DL) in a large number of Google services, DL is a system of large neural networks that can solve complicated problems with real-world, large-scale data. It is a revolutionary advancement of machine learning. DL, the use of GPUs in computing devices, and the availability of big data are driving forces behind the current boom of AI. The learning can be supervised, semi-supervised, or unsupervised.

In fact, DL is not solving a specific task. Instead, it is a class of algorithms and topologies based on learning data representation. The most important component of DL is hence the feature-extraction system or representation-learning system. The system captures spatio-temporal dependencies of data and represents it into a hierarchical artificial neural network by feature extraction. Such a process is called *feature learning*. Yann LeCun, another leader of DL and the director of Facebook Research, pointed out that DL is a learning hierarchical representation. Each level of network learns to transform its input data into a more informative and composite representation based on the data regularities. In conventional ML techniques, feature extraction is mainly done by humans, which is time-consuming and depends heavily on the knowledge base provided.

DL infrastructure is based on a large-scale, artificial neural network with multiple layers. There are various DL architectures proposed in the last decades. Among them, *recurrent neural networks* (RNNs), *convolutional neural networks* (CNNs), *deep belief networks* (DBNs), *deep stacking networks* (DSNs) and *gated recurrent unit* (GRU) are the most commonly used. These terms are introduced in the following sections.

Recurrent Neural Networks (RNNs)
Recurrent neural networks (RNNs) are one of the popular ANNs that use sequential information. In RNNs, output reached at time *t-1* is a source of input at time *t*. So RNNs have two sources of input, the present input and the output from the most recent past. It is often said that RNNs have "memory" which preserves sequential information in the hidden layer. In Figure 11.16, the circles represent the hidden layers and the sequence of the past decision serves as one of the inputs.

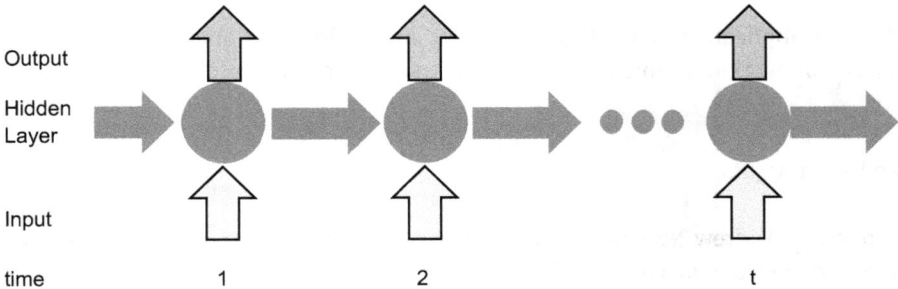

Figure 11.16: A conceptual example of RNNs

Note that the parameters are the same across all steps in a RNN. The computational tasks are the same, but with different inputs. The number of parameters to be learnt is significantly reduced. The feature of "memory" facilitates its successful application in NLP problems. However, the major drawback of standard RNNs is the vanishing gradient problem—the change of the training variables will not cause the change of the outputs, which produces inaccurate results. Moreover, in RNN, each module has the same structure and the same weights are used at each time step. This indicates that the prediction is based on only the most recent past units.

A more powerful and most commonly used type of RNNs is the long short-term memory (LSTM) units proposed by Hochreiter and Schmidhuber (Hochreiter & Schmidhuber, 1997), which have similar architecture with RNNs but overcome the shortcoming of standard RNNs such as the vanishing gradient problem by using different functions to compute the hidden states. A LSTM unit contains a cell, an input gate, an output gate, and a forget gate. The inputs include current inputs, current memory, and previous state. The cells decide what information to add or remove from the memory. The cells capture long-term dependencies and preserve the error that can be backpropagated through time and layers. The forget gate removes information that is irrelevant.

A more sophisticated extension of RNNs is gated recurrent units (GRUs) proposed by Kyunghyun Cho et al. (Cho et al., 2014) in 2014. A typical GRU is also regarded as a simpler variant of LSTMs and focuses on the gating mechanism and vanishing gradient problem. Indeed, GRUs have two gates: an update gate and reset gate. The update set combines the functions of the input gate and forget gate in LSTMs. Both are responsible for manipulating material information. The reset gate combines the new input with the previous memory and the update gate decides how much of the previous memory to be kept. GRUs have fewer parameters than LSTMs, and thus are more efficient. However, according to Chuang et al. (2014), GRUs achieve much better results for smaller datasets than LSTMs.

Convolutional Neural Networks (CNNs)

CNNs were first proposed by Yann LeCun (Yann, 1989), particularly for data with grid-like topology and had successfully trained many layers of hierarchical data in a robust manner, such as time-series financial market data, as well as images and videos. Take an image as an example (Figure 11.17): CNNs will first extract a part of the data parameters that is informative and train these parameters through forward propagation and backpropagation using a trainable filter. As a result, a small portion of the image is put into the lowest layer of the hierarchical network as inputs, which may contain information of "feature maps." This step is called *convolution*. The second step is *subsampling*, which further reduces the parameters and comes up with a smaller weighted "feature map" with robustness. The weights are adjusted during the training process through the use of gradient descent and backpropagation. This step is followed by forward propagation through activation function. The outputs form a new "feature map" as inputs. Repeat the process of convolution–subsampling–activation and then pass the final sequence to a conventional feed forward neural network, which outputs the final results.

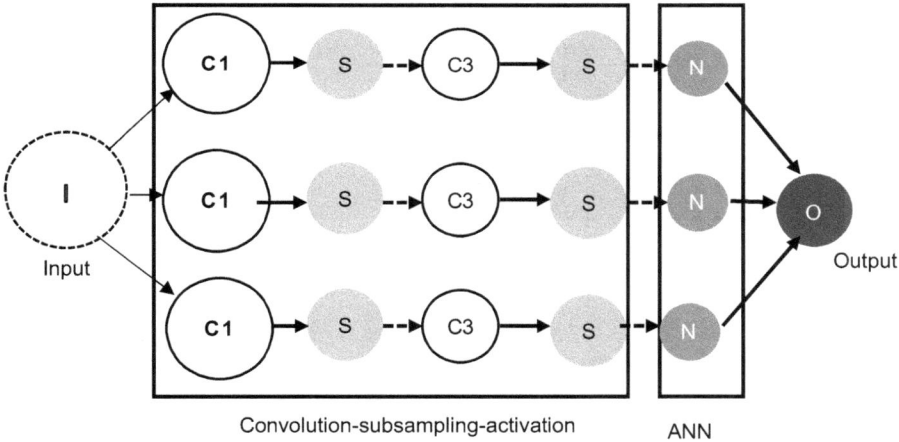

Figure 11.17: A conceptual example of CNNs architecture for DL

Deep Belief Networks (DBNs)

A *deep belief network* (DBNs) is a generative graphical model that provides a probability distribution over variables. The hidden variables are conditionally independent given the visible node. The model produces a *stochastic multilayer network with stochastic binary nodes and undirected edges between nodes*, which make the connectivity to exist only across layers, but the nodes within layers are unconnected. Each pair of connected layers is called a *restricted Boltzmann machine (RBM).* The system begins by training an RBM with the input data (see Figure 11.18). The second RBM is trained to model the distribution defined by sampling the hidden nodes of the first RBM. More RBMs can be added to generate as many layers as desired, with each RBM being modeled after the previous RBM. As a result, in a DBN, the connection at the top two layers are undirected, whereas all other layers are directed toward data (Figure 11.19). The output of the final layer of RBM is passed to a feed forward network to fine-tune and then the final results are generated. Such a structure makes learning easier and more efficient. The learning of RBM can be unsupervised, semi-supervised, and supervised.

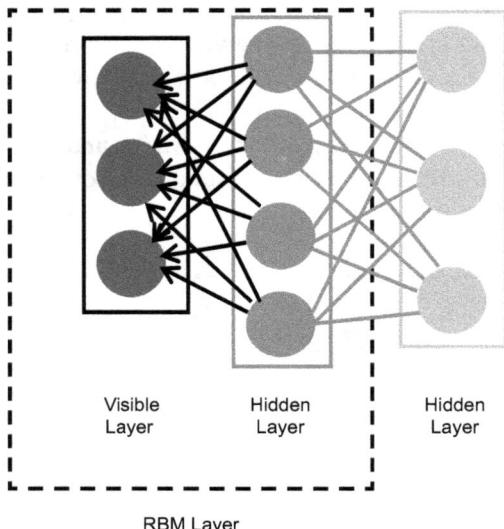

Figure 11.18: *An illustration of RBM*

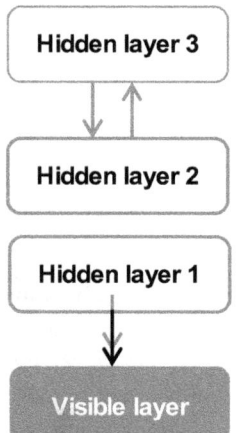

Figure 11.19: An illustration of DBN

Deep Stacking Networks (DSNs)

The *deep stacking network* (DSN) was first introduced by Deng and Yu (Deng & Yu, 2011). It is a new DL architecture of convex networks that focuses on discrimination with scalable and parallel learning. A DSN consists of many stacking modules (Figure 11.20). Each module trains the mean squared error (MSE) between the target value and the network prediction using convex optimization for learning perceptron weights. Compared with the stochastic gradient descent, MSE learning is much more simple and is easier to learn.

In each module of the DSN, the output layer is linear, whereas the hidden layer is sigmoidal nonlinear.[3] The linearity of the output and the closed-form estimation significantly reduces computation time. Furthermore, it allows weight training of full batch via parallel and distributed computing.

Efficiency and simplicity are the main benefits of DSN. It has been widely used in many applications, especially in large-scale image recognition, speech recognition, and speech understanding.

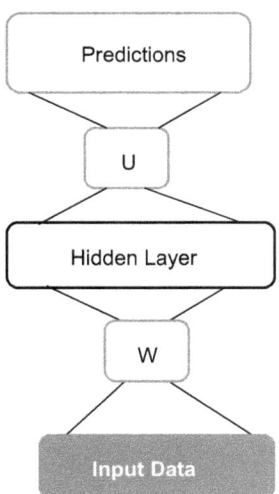

(W: the input weight matrix; U: the output weight matrix)

Figure 11.20: An illustration of DSN

AI in Financial Services: Present and Future Applications

AI-driven applications in financial institutions have become increasingly common. These applications go beyond mobile banking apps and chatbots to include loans/insurance underwriting, risk management, trade settlement, and quantitative investment. For example, an "intelligent" AI trading system can manipulate tremendous data concurrently and even big data from different sources, and hence it is able to achieve better trading decisions that could be unattainable previously. Robo-advisor and AI-driven trading platforms are now becoming common in the field of portfolio management. As the costs of hardware fall, we can expect a substantial increase in the future uses of AI by financial institutions which will then affect the ways that financial institutions operate and provide services.

AI has come to play an integral role in many phases of the financial ecosystem from managing assets to accessing risks. The present and future applications include AI algorithmic trading, robo-advisor, chatbots, fraud detection, and loan/insurance underwriting.

AI Algorithmic Trading

Algorithmic/quantitative trading has been used by hedge funds or other financial institutions since the 1970s. Today, AI has become the new emerging trend in the asset management landscape. Unlike traditional trading algorithms that were built to exploit specific market opportunities such as identifying the trend of price movement, AI has the power to truly act as an independent agent participating in market action.

Big data and various forms of artificial intelligence, such as ML and NLP, have changed the asset management industry. Using NLP tools, the machine can analyze the company's revenue calls to detect changes in management sentiment that may signal future performance and screen through the analyst report to indicate terms that are about to change its headline forecast. These tools can also be used to analyze a large number of unstructured data sources (such as news reports, blogs, and social media) to identify potential investment trends.

Advances in AI are being used to improve research and make informed investment decisions. In addition, big data and AI are also boosting automation and efficiencies across client servicing, data management, operational support, and compliance.

Robo-Advisors

Robo-advisors are online financial advisors that provide automated, algorithm-driven financial investment services. Robo-advisors are becoming an increasingly popular and convenient way for the individual to invest and manage portfolios. According to IDC Financial Insight (Araneta, Agrawal, & Kapoor, 2017), the hybrid model that combines traditional and robo-advisory will be the winner in the market. The total asset under management (AUM) by robo-advisors will reach US$500b by 2021 in APAC.

For those interested in robo-advisors, refer to Chapter 19.

Chatbots

A chatbot is a human-computer dialog system relying on auditory or textual methods. It has been widely used in our daily life. Many companies use the virtual chatbots built into social media platforms like WhatsApp, Facebook, or WeChat. WeChat's chatbot can, for example, call a taxi, check in for a flight, report traffic accidents, and make medical appointments. Most advanced chatbots use sophisticated NLP systems. Some simple chatbots scan for keywords within the input and then reply with the most matching keywords from a preset database.

Many banks and insurers leverage chatbots to respond to customer's inquiries. Chatbots not only significantly improve the service efficiency, but can also become a marketing channel to promote customer engagement as well as client acquisition. More importantly, chatbots collect user's information. Big data allows the company to know more about customer's preferences. Targeted marketing then becomes possible. Simpler chatbots are provided by social media platforms, and are cost-effective and easy to maintain.

Fraud Detection

The frequency of online financial fraud attempts has been increasing over time. Fraud detection is tricky, as fraud means change from time to time. One major challenge is to detect "Black Swan"–like fraud events, which are events that rarely happen but will bring about catastrophic losses if they happened. Fraud detection systems in the past were rule-based. The main defect of a rule-based system is that it cannot detect unidentified fraud means. As there is little data on such Black Swan–like fraud cases due to their low frequency of occurrences, detection using the old rule-based system is nearly impossible. Modern advanced fraud systems adopt sophisticated machine learning models to detect the potential fraud, which implies that fraud can be flagged before it happens. Rather than general machine learning black boxes, a fraud system is called "white boxing," which consists of a scoring system based on local linear approximation, a text mining system, graph generation, and a visualization system. It can thus detect emerging patterns by learning new data and generate a probability of potential fraud.

Loan/Insurance Underwriting

Traditional credit evaluation typically involves the applicant's FICO scores, debt to income ratio, and a number of inquiries into the financial status/employment state of the applicants. In recent years, as the AI ability to extract highly relevant information for a specific purpose from a massive amount of big data has greatly increased, online loan/insurance underwriting has become possible.

Many AI-enabled credit assessment systems have emerged and small loan underwriters tend to employ such an end-to-end AI credit system to assess borrower's credit using large amounts of data from social and ecommerce media, which has not been traditionally used for credit evaluation. The customers' behavioral traits from social media such as the contents of text messages, the patterns of call history, geolocation information, and mobile transaction, are valuable information. Such information provides insight into customers' identity, incomes, and expenses. The system adopts algorithms and machine learning to find useful patterns in the data and generates a default probability to gauge the suitability of the applicant for a loan. The whole underwriting process can be done using the mobile phone very quickly, even within 10 minutes. The granted loan can be transferred to the applicant's bank account or e-wallets within 15 minutes which enhances customer experience.

Similarly, insurance underwriting can also leverage on an AI system to extract and analyze data containing information on the applicant's hazard likelihood, historical claims, life attitude, and so on to generate an insurance quote quickly.

The AI underwriting system is superior as it can evaluate the borrowers without loan/insurance histories that are essential in traditional underwriting. Compared to traditional underwriting, banks and insurance companies will benefit from AI-based underwriting as it reduces employee costs and may also lead to a decrease in fraud cases as the social media data comes from the applicant's real life activities. The interested reader may refer to Chapter 23, a dedicated chapter on InsurTech.

Last but not least, AI will also assist compliance officers to ensure regulatory compliance. For example, AI-driven compliance system learns and complies with all applicable regulations such as know-your-client (KYC) and anti-money laundering (AML) regulations. It scans financial transactions to detect signs of money laundering or other illegal activities, which are not easy to be identified manually. The interested reader may refer to Chapter 21, a dedicated chapter on RegTech in this textbook.

In conclusion, AI technologies lead to a new era of efficiency and performance. We expect deep learning to be widely adopted within the next decade.

Endnotes

1 Artificial Neural Network is a system inspired by human brain neural activities. It simulates the way in which the human brain processes information. The system consists of a large number of nodes (or neurons) segregated into layers and gathers its knowledge by detecting the patterns and relationships in data and learning through the training experience.

2 Support vector machine (SVM) is a supervised machine-learning algorithm, which is based on the idea of finding a hyperplane that best divides a dataset into two classes. SVM can be used for both classification or regression challenges.

3 A sigmoid function is a mathematical function having an S-shaped curve (sigmoid curve), and is defined by the formula $S(t)=1/(1+e^{-t})$.

References

AIINDEX. (2017). Artificial Intelligence Index, 2017 Annual Report. AIINDEX.ORG.

Araneta, M., Agrawal, A., & Kapoor, S. (2017). *Robo-Advisory: Changing the Face of Wealth in Asia/ Pacific*. IDC Perspective.

Cho, K., Van Merrienboer, B., Caglar, G., Bahdanau, D., Bougares, F., Schwenk, H., & Bengio, Y. (2014). Learning phrase representations using RNN encoder-decoder for statistical machine translation. *arXiv:1406.1078*.

Deng, L., & Yu, D. (2011). Deep convex network: A scalable architecture for deep learning. INTERSPEECH (28). Florence, Italy: ISCA.

Feigenbaum E.A., 1977, The Art of Artificial Intelligence: Themes and Case Studies of Knowledge Engineering, International Joint Conference on Artificial Intelligence, pp 1014–1029.

Hochreiter, S., & Schmidhuber, J. (1997, 11 15). Long short-term memory. *Neural computation*, Vol. 9, Issue 8, pp. 1735–1780.

Holland, J. H. (1975). *Adaptation in natural and artificial systems: An introductory analysis with applications to biology, control, and artificial intelligence*. Ann Arbor: University of Michigan Press.

Kanungo, R. P. (2004, 4 26). Genetic algorithms: genesis of stock evaluation. *Economics WPA*, p. 17.

LeCun, Yann. (1989). Generalization and network design strategies. Technical Report CRG-TR-89-4, University of Toronto, 326–345.

Lin, L., Cao, L., Wang, J., & Zhang, C. (2004). *The applications of genetic algorithms in stock market data mining optimisation. Data Mining V, Data Mining, Text Mining and Their Business Application*, pp. 273–280. WIT Press.

Werbos, P. J. (1974). *Beyond regression: new tools for predicion and analysis in the behavioral sciences. PhD thesis*. Harvard University.

*Dr. **Bing Li** is the Managing Director at Yuanyin Asset Management and takes the Overall Management Oversight of the company. Before that, he was the president of Forwin Capital Management, a Hong Kong based multi-family office. Previously, he worked as an investment management professional at Lombard Odier, ING Investment Management, Pearl Insurance Group, ABP Investment, and TD Asset management, managed billions of dollars assets ranged from global equities, bonds, to fund of funds. Bing earned his Ph.D. in Chemistry from University of Western Ontario, and B.S. and M.S. degrees in Material Science and Engineering from Shanghai Jiaotong University. He is also a CFA charter holder.*

Dr. Min Cao is an Investment Manager at UCF Asset Management, focusing on global asset allocation and active equity strategies. Previously, Min worked as Investment Manager at Forwin Capital Management and Quantitative Analyst at Delta Asia Financial Group, with the research scope covers global asset allocation, high dividend Hong Kong stock hedging, and best stop loss strategy. Prior to that, she was a Senior Research Associate in the Department of Economics and Finance of the City University of Hong Kong, where she worked on macroeconomics and international finance. Min graduated from South China University of Technology, and obtained her master's degree in High Performance Computing from Trinity College Dublin, the University of Dublin, and Ph. D from the IMSE department at the University of Hong Kong.

Chapter 12
A Practical Approach to Machine Learning (ML) and Artificial Intelligence (AI)

In the previous chapter, the reader would have gained an understanding of the technologies underpinning machine learning (ML) and artificial intelligence (AI). This chapter aims to complement the previous chapters by providing a more practice-oriented approach to demystifying both technologies and to introduce the reader to the process of setting up a ML solution. We will succinctly recap some of the key concepts previously covered, but the readers should refer to the dedicated chapters on data science and big data for details.

Are AI and Machine Learning the Same Thing?

While it may seem that neural networks, deep learning, machine learning, and artificial intelligence are all the same concepts, each has its own history and origin, as well as hierarchy. The reason it might be hard to see this distinction is that all the research and media attention around the last decade of advances zoom in specifically on deep learning.

To aid in deciphering the many conflicting and overlapping terms used in this field, we will define an overall hierarchy to help break down the relationships within artificial intelligence.

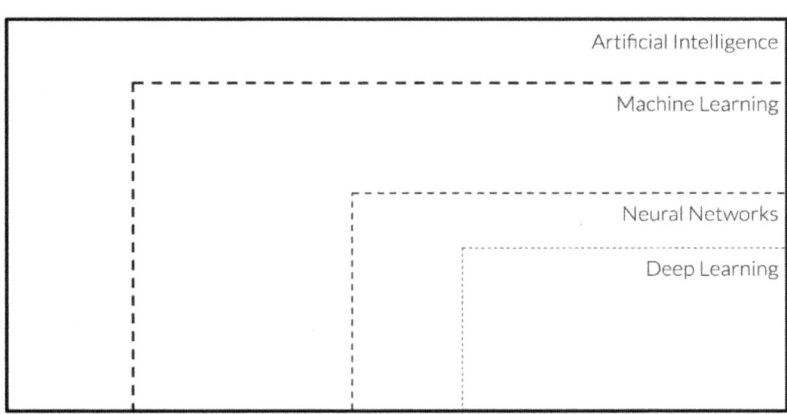

Figure 12.1: AI to ML to NN to DL

DOI 10.1515/9781547400904- 012

To put it simply, artificial intelligence is the capability of any system to exhibit intelligent behavior. Almost everything relevant today in AI relates to machine learning.

Machine Learning Covers a Lot

Let us succinctly recap machine learning, which as a term contains its own definition. Instead of the human telling the machine what decisions and rules to make, the human teaches it. A machine that learns. This leaves the methods of teaching and learning open-ended. What can you teach a machine, and what can it learn? We briefly summarize the primary machine learning methods in Figure 12.2 and in words below.

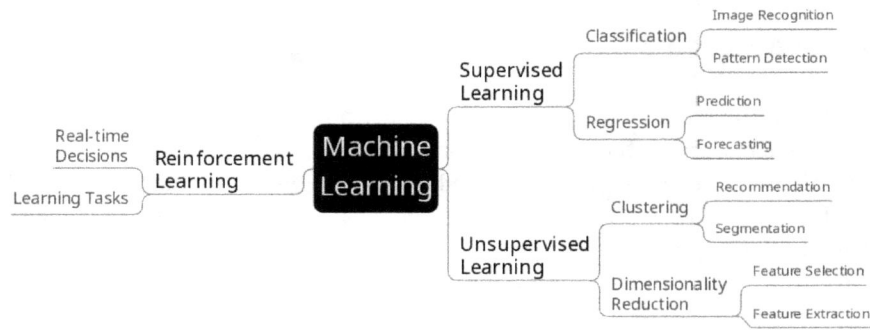

Figure 12.2: Primary machine-learning methods

-   **Classification** algorithms can be taught to split existing data into predefined groups, such as names of animals. When you feed the algorithm some new data it has not yet seen, it will predict which group the new data belongs to—for example, that this animal is a chicken.
-   **Regression** algorithms basically try to learn the function of a dataset, by predicting future data based on past data. If you have a series of data points that form a straight line, the algorithm will attempt to describe that line as a function. Of course, the line could be curved, a wave, a circle, or any kind of shape. While helpful to think of two-dimensional examples you can plot in your mind, these algorithms also work on any number of input dimensions.
-   **Unsupervised learning** can be used if you have lots of data with patterns, groups, or clusters that you wish to separate without explicitly defining them beforehand—that is, without human supervision. Perhaps you know that the dataset is comprised of different animals, and want to establish how many different kinds by clustering them using variables like weight and speed.

- **Reinforcement learning** has been widely popularized by the media attention on Deepmind's various game playing algorithms including the famed AlphaGo. These algorithms learn to choose actions through the use of rewards given based on the results of those actions in the game environment. Due to several break-through results such as AlphaGo, reinforcement methods have been an active area of research.

While the last two methods will continue to garner many headlines, the first two are more applicable to industries with a much lower learning curve. The rest of this chapter will mainly focus on classification and regression. There are many ways to implement both, and a neural network, which we have learned in the previous chapter, is just one approach. To ensure that the reader can follow the practical examples later, we will quickly revisit neural networks and recall how these fit under ML.

Neural Networks Are a Special Type of Machine Learning

Neural networks and the associated learning algorithms hold a special place within the machine learning community, largely due to the fact that their design is inspired by the brain. We know that neurons are connected in vast networks inside our brain, and that electrical signals go from neuron to neuron to produce all of our conscious experiences—seeing, hearing, thinking, and speaking—which involve all neural networks in action, as far as science can tell us today.[1]

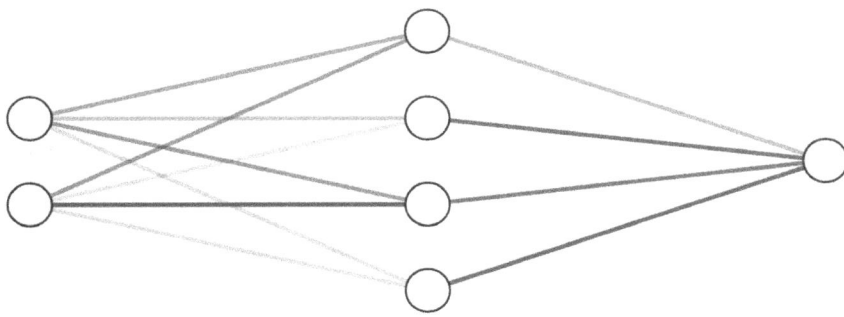

Figure 12.3: Simple neural network with weighted connections between layers

What is inside a neural network? Neurons organized into inputs (the left portion in Figure 12.3), hidden layers (the middle portion in Figure 12.3), and outputs (the right portion in Figure 12.3). Connections between these neurons have weights and biases.

The neurons, or nodes, themselves have activation functions, which act as filters on the input data. The primary function of all these elements is to introduce complex behaviors. Otherwise, you could only perform basic functions like adding numbers together. Combining these elements across hundreds or even thousands of neurons in several layers, these complex behaviors become very powerful indeed. This is called *deep learning*.

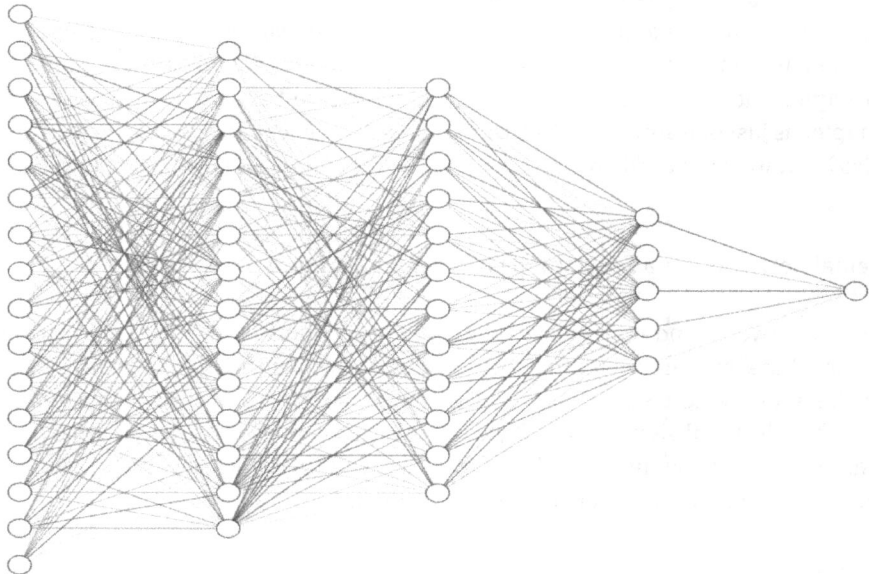

Figure 12.4: A neural network with a few more layers introduces increased complexity and is called a *deep neural network*

The types of neural networks used for relatively simple tasks like recognition of handwriting can contain hundreds of nodes in each layer, to a point where drawing the thousands of connections no longer helps. These specialized networks process parts of an image at the rate of a few pixels at a time to determine its contents.

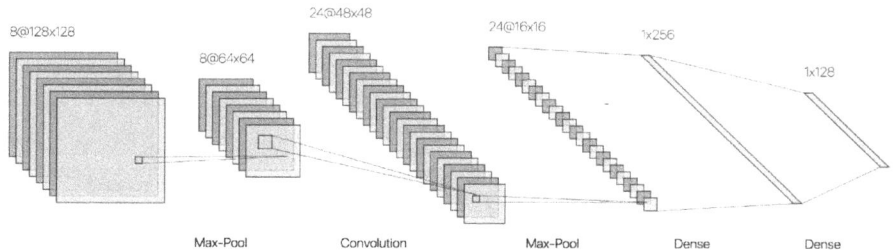

8@128x128   8@64x64   24@48x48   24@16x16   1x256   1x128

Max-Pool   Convolution   Max-Pool   Dense   Dense

Figure 12.5: Convolutional neural network used for image recognition

Still, even a large neural network can be represented visually in rather simple terms, yet the inner behavior becomes almost indecipherable. It can learn almost anything with a learning process called "backpropagation," which starts by comparing how far the prediction is from the intended outcome. Then it calculates a series of minute changes for the connection weights across that whole network to improve that prediction, and tries the prediction again to see if the result becomes better or worse. To achieve the desired prediction accuracy, this process will be repeated hundreds of times across large datasets of millions of inputs, creating the need for significant computing power and therefore computing costs.

What can you achieve with this powerful learning approach? Neural networks can read handwriting. They can generate language, too. They can recognize objects in pictures, or faces, and even play chess—all at human level or beyond. The complexity of the learning behavior also means that it is challenging to explain predictions or decisions for each case. You can change one input by a fraction, and the whole output changes. Why does the learning work? When does it work? How do we find the best and fastest way to train the network? While this spans an active area of research, there is no definitive answer today.

Should We Always Use Neural Networks?

In theory, the benefit of neural networks is their flexibility to tackle many forms of data. In practice, their lack of clear explanation and degree of specific configuration, or tuning, means that they are harder to work with. The following demonstration will illustrate the differences in behavior.

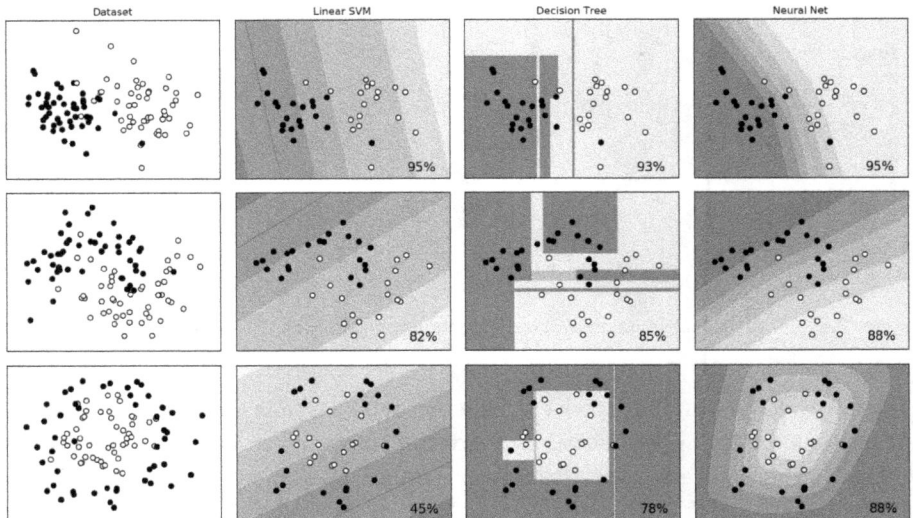

Figure 12.6: Comparing classifier behavior

On the left, you see three datasets with a white background. Going from left to right, each column represents a type of machine learning algorithm trying to separate the black dots from the white dots using only a part of the dataset called *test data*. Remember, we have informed each algorithm already which color each dot is. The algorithm is just trying to create a general rule to identify the area in which black dots appear, and the area where white dots appear. As evident, the approaches and results are quite diverse.

The bottom right corner of each square shows how accurately the algorithm has separated the two types of dots. Again, this score is based on a different group of dots than we used to train the algorithm. Why would we do this? If you tested the algorithm with the same data that it was trained on, you would expect great scores every time. What you really want is a robust algorithm that learns the nature of the dataset, and will be able to make accurate predictions for new data it has not yet seen.

You may notice that neural networks, specifically the one on the right, are doing something rather interesting. For each dataset, the behavior is different. How does that happen?

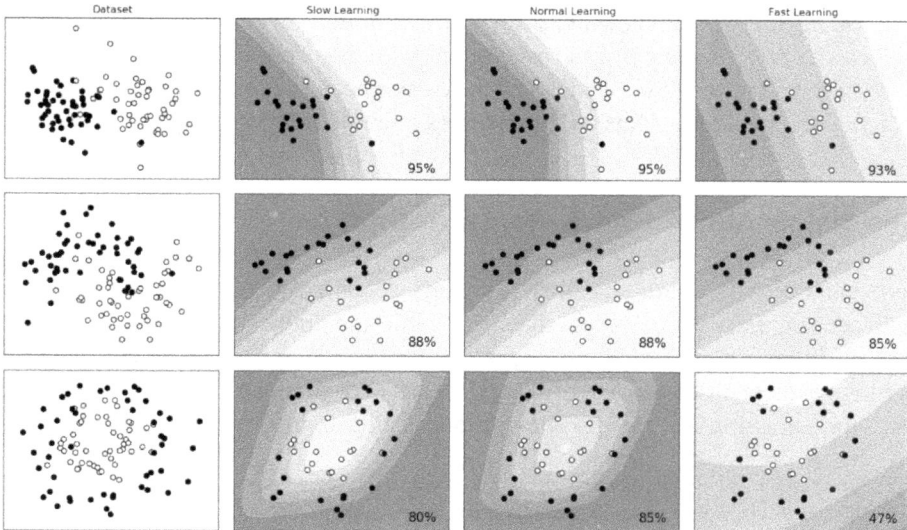

Figure 12.7: Hyperparameter tuning with neural networks

To really emphasize this point, the above picture is just one neural network with three different datasets. This time, the columns represent changing one configuration setting, called a hyperparameter of the network. The learning rate defines how significant the minor changes are that the backpropagation method makes during the learning process. Even with one hyperparameter changed, you can get wildly different outcomes. On the bottom dataset, a faster learning rate reduces the accuracy from good to awful.

Neural networks are therefore rather unpredictable by nature, which also makes them so powerful. Thus, the tradeoff is meaningful. However, there are reasons why you should not use neural networks every time.

Reasons Not to Use Neural Networks Every Time

1.   They are complex, and making informed decisions for their design still requires skills that most people have yet to possess.
2.   They are unpredictable, often requiring many attempts to produce any meaningful result, even if you know what you are doing.
3.   It is hard to ascertain if you have found a good configuration unless you try a lot of different configurations and compare the results.
4.   Even if there are many ways to measure how good your solution is, it can be difficult to understand how to address any problems.

5. Making up your mind about the above can require a lot of attempts, and each try can be time consuming and costly in line with the needs for large datasets.
6. According to the "No Free Lunch" theorem, one algorithm will never emerge as the best for all problems, and sometimes a simple solution can perform better.[2]

The Simple Alternatives to Neural Networks

As evident from the charts above, there are several alternatives to neural networks. We will focus on the two alternatives that give simple and predictable outcomes with two very different approaches. Why? Because they are simple and will often land a decent solution to most problems, and are generally fast to compute. Both alternatives can be used for regression and classification problems, depending on your dataset.

> "Anecdotal evidence from observing winning entries at data science competitions (like Kaggle) suggests that structured data is best analyzed by tools like XGBoost and random forests. Use of deep learning in winning entries is limited to analysis of images or text."
>
> — J.P. Morgan Global Quantitative & Derivatives Strategy

The difference between neural networks and all other machine learning methods is *how* they learn. neural networks are effectively making educated guesses on their way to a solution. The other methods actually calculate a solution, in most cases using an approximation method. That just means they consider the data you feed them, and use a large variety of mathematical optimization methods to find a best answer. Another benefit is these methods are fast to train as they lack the inner complexity of neural networks, and are therefore fast to execute.[3] These methods have less need for cloud computing or special hardware.

Linear Is Straightforward

The most logical and simple way to try to separate a dataset is to draw a straight line through it with a ruler. That is what a human would do instinctively, like cutting patterns from paper with a pair of scissors. That is also what support vector machines (SVM) do, despite the daunting name. The algorithm tries to find the best single straight line to separate your datasets, and then sets a buffer around that line to separate the datasets as far as possible. Refer to Figure 12.6 to see this in action under linear SVM. Many variations include non-linear solvers (not straight lines), but our focus is on the linear version for the sake of simplicity.

Trees Are Understandable

Decision trees choose which variables and values most predict the outcome based on your dataset. It tries to "cut" the number of your data points by separating variables at certain ranges within their values. Once it makes a cut, it moves to the remaining available variables and tries to do the same, while trying to do as few cuts as possible to keep things simple.[4] Again, you can see this in action in Figure 12.6 under Decision Tree.

The result is like fitting rectangular Tetris blocks on your data. This may sound rather crude compared to neural networks' true learning behavior, but because of this simple approach, decision trees have a huge benefit that sets them apart from all other algorithms of machine learning.

Decision trees can explain themselves. This is a key problem when dealing with neural networks, but in decision trees, the logic used for any given prediction can be traced backward step-by-step.

More so, there are tools that generate a visual representation of the resulting algorithm. You can actually confirm the decision path and be confident in the results. If the output of a given test sample is surprising, you can simply look at how it came about and adjust the learning dataset.

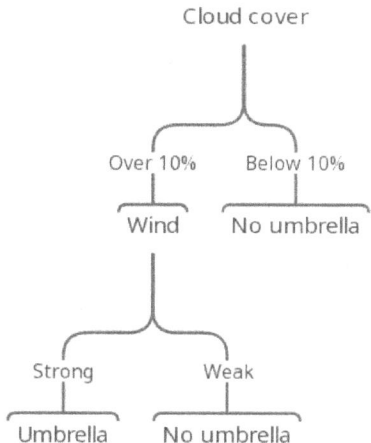

Cloud cover

Over 10%   Below 10%

Wind   No umbrella

Strong   Weak

Umbrella   No umbrella

Figure 12.8: Simple example of a decision tree

Putting It into Practice

How are applications created for machine learning? Is it programming? Is it mathematics? How do frameworks like TensorFlow fit in?

There are three parts to any machine learning application:

1. Dataset
The actual task that any machine learning application performs is learning to make predictions from a dataset. By construction, you must have some data to begin with. The better your data is, the easier the rest of the work is. Finding good data is often the main problem.

2. Trainer
Once you have data, you need to create a program that trains that data using some form of a machine learning algorithm. There are many developed frameworks to help you, but there is still some programming involved as of today. In the future, we will no doubt see drag-and-drop tools that allow us to skip the programming step.

3. Model
Once you have used your codes to train an algorithm on a dataset, you produce a model. This model is a program that has learned whatever patterns you were looking for in the dataset. The model is what you wanted all along. You give it some new data, and it will predict something for you. There are many ways to incorporate the model into your software applications.

Tools of the Trade

When it comes to creating your own machine learning algorithms, a few main communities have emerged around two programming languages. Academic research groups tend to favor programming in MATLAB and R, whereas most commercial teams work with Python. If you are starting from zero, the path of least resistance would currently be Python. There are abundant resources online, and all of the tools you will need are open-source and free to use.

Frameworks to Focus on Solutions

Besides some simple Python code to process your datasets, you will most likely want to use ready-made implementations of popular machine learning algorithms. There are almost too many out there, creating a difficulty in choosing the right approach.

This often is much more difficult a problem than using the algorithms, and will depend on the structure of the dataset you have.

The two most important frameworks to get familiar with are scikit-learn and Keras. Scikit gives you a large variety of tools that covers pretty much everything except neural networks. If you need a neural network, the most approachable framework is Keras. Keras itself is built on top of TensorFlow, but greatly simplifies the creation and training process for your neural network. Still, the challenge of choosing network architecture and tuning hyper-parameters can become overwhelming for beginners without solid theoretical knowledge. That makes scikit-learn a great place to start.

Creating Your First ML Solution

There are five steps to follow to create your own machine learning solution. The example code below is in Python. For basics and instructions on how to start using Python, refer to their website at Python.org.

Step 1: The Data

You need to have a problem to solve first. Do you need to figure out why your customers are leaving? Do you need to predict or forecast seasonal revenues? Do you need to identify squirrels from traffic cameras?

And you need data. Sometimes you can source datasets online, especially if you are working on images, audio, or text. In certain cases, you might have to create that data yourself. Perhaps you have a large set of images in which you want to identify an object. All you need to do is have a team of people manually label those images that contain that object. Sometimes you can start with whatever database of data you already have.

Reading data: The easiest way to get data into your Python program is the Pandas library. The obvious way to go is to read a CSV file, which can be generated from any spreadsheet or database system.

```
import pandas as pd
myData = pd.read_csv('example.csv')
```

Step 2: Data Exploration

The next step is to get a good understanding of the data. What is actually in the data? What are the types of data? How many types and how much of each type? What are the ranges of values? Are the values clustered together or almost random? Are there any interesting correlations to learn?

Analysis: There are a handful of tools in the Pandas library for Python that you can use each time you have a new dataset. These methods can be used on any dataset in Pandas DataFrame format.

Show the first few rows of data:

```
myData.head()
```

Show what columns and data types are in your dataframe.

```
myData.info()
```

Show various statistics from your dataframe.

```
myData.describe()
```

Explore value ranges for individual columns.

```
myData['someColumn'].min()
myData['someColumn'].max()
myData['someColumn'].unique()
```

Plotting: Humans work best with visual representations of data, so plotting libraries are useful. Seaborn's library contains plots like countplot, pairplot, jointplot, barplot, and heatmap.

Here is an example to plot correlations between columns of your dataframe:

```
import seaborn as se
se.heatmap(myData.corr())
```

Step 3: Feature Engineering
The most challenging part of this whole exercise is not the machine learning part. It is preparing the data so that the ready-made algorithms can do something useful with it.

Prep the dataset: For any learning task, you'll need two things: inputs and outputs. Both should already be in your dataset. Input columns are called *features*. Output columns are called *labels*. Based on your exploratory goals, you'll want to identify features with some correlation and therefore provide the predictive values for your labels.

Pandas again has several easy and useful tools to exclude what you do not need, and format what you want to be included.

You can create new columns from existing columns:

```
myData['NewFeature'] = myData['SomeColumn'] * myData['OtherColumn']
```

You can remove unnecessary columns (axis=1):

```
myData = myData.drop(['SomeColumn', 'OtherColumn'], axis=1)
```

Separate labels into a new dataset for the next step:

```
myLabels = myData['AnImportantColumn']
myData = myData.drop(['AnImportantColumn'], axis=1)
```

Encoding: This is often the hardest part to understand if you are relatively new to algorithms and statistics. Algorithms only work with learning numbers. They cannot differentiate a postal code from a telephone number, or names, or images. You have to feed it actual numbers. There are many ways to do this, and some get complicated quickly.

A trivial example might be to swap names with a placeholder number. If one of your features is a list of names like "Brad," "Chad," and "Sinbad" then you can replace them with numbers such as 1, 2, and 3. You can do more research on useful encoders from the scikit-learn framework like LabelEncoder and OneHotEncoder.

```
from sklearn.preprocessing import LabelEncoder
encoder = LabelEncoder()
myData['NamesColumn'] = encoder.fit_transform(myData['NamesColumn'].
astype('str'))
```

For training, split the data: To be able to run the training algorithm, you need two sets of data. Why? If you use all of your data to train the algorithm, there is no data left to test if the algorithm learned to predict or classify anything. So, you want to save some data to test if the learning actually worked. Fortunately, there are tools available to randomly pick these subsets for you. A typical choice is to split the data 75% training, and 25% testing data using your separated datasets for features and labels.

```
from sklearn.model_selection import train_test_split
X_train, x_test, y_train, y_test = train_test_split(myData, myLabels,
test_size=0.25)
```

Step 4: Training

Most people find it surprising how simple this step is. That is because decades of hard work have gone into standardizing and tuning these algorithms so that we can just use them.

Choose an algorithm: The choice of algorithm really depends on the problem to be solved. If you are predicting real-estate value or forecasting revenues, you are looking for regression algorithms that will give you a clear number as the output. If you are trying to make a decision, that would often fall under classification algorithms. Classification algorithms can give you the best answer or probabilities for all possible answers, depending on your objectives. There are dozens of flavors of each type, and some involve neural networks. Given the tuning challenges there, you are better off starting elsewhere though.

Often the best place to start is a simple linear algorithm, as it literally draws a straight line on top of your dataset. From there, you can optimize the result by exploring other methods such as decision trees or support vector machines.

Training: There are a few different ways to do learning besides the base case above of using all data at once, usually depending on how much data you have and how fast your computer is. Whether or not this is a one-time operation, you will need to add new training data in the future.

Basic Regression:

```
from sklearn.linear_model import LinearRegression
algo = LinearRegression()
algo.fit(X_train, y_train)
```

Basic Classification:

```
from sklearn.linear_model import SGDClassifier
algo = SGDClassifier()
algo.fit(X_train, y_train)
```

Prediction: To actually use the model you have just trained, you need to predict something. Again, if you are using regression it will be predicting a number as the output. For classification, you either get a label, or the probability for each label.

You can predict a single output for each row of inputs using:

```
algo.predict(x_test)
```

You can predict label probabilities for a classification problem, by manually entering inputs using:

```
algo.predict_proba([input1, input2, input3])
```

Step 5: Evaluation
At this point, it feels like you have completed the task. But you need to find out if the outputs are accurate, which just means that you want to know how many of the samples in your test dataset the algorithm predicted correctly.

Accuracy: To begin with, this is really the gold standard of measuring if your algorithm works. If it gets the right result often enough to solve your problem, you are good to go. There are a lot of exceptions to this. Foremost among them is how well your training data represents the real-life data that the algorithm will see in the future. Often this means training is not a one-and-done type of deal, but something you revisit if the accuracy with real data starts dropping dramatically.

You can measure accuracy on the testing set using:

```
y_pred = algo.predict(X_test)
print (metrics.accuracy_score(y_test, y_pred))
```

Here are a bunch of other metrics you'll have to read about to understand fully:

```
from sklearn.metrics import classification_report
y_pred = algo.predict(X_test)
print(classification_report(y_test, y_pred))
```

Repeat until Satisfied
At any step above, you may realize you have done something wrong and it just could not work. Most often, this involves the data itself. Having good, clean data to work with will make all other steps easier.

Automation of Automation

Given that it is now easier than ever to get started with machine learning, what will be the impact in the near future? Some of the early adopters of machine learning technologies have been industries such as ecommerce, financial services, logistics, and healthcare. In most cases, the algorithms are standalone solutions delivering a specific functionality.

The next phase of machine learning adoption will be the embedding of learning algorithms into all aspects of software.

How Software Is Currently Created

We now have some interesting new tools to apply to our business problems. If you mainly work with websites or mobile apps, you may think these methods are not applicable.

First, how is most software created today? Software is based on rules. This means that you define a set of rules on how things work, and then the software just continually repeats the same exact thing.

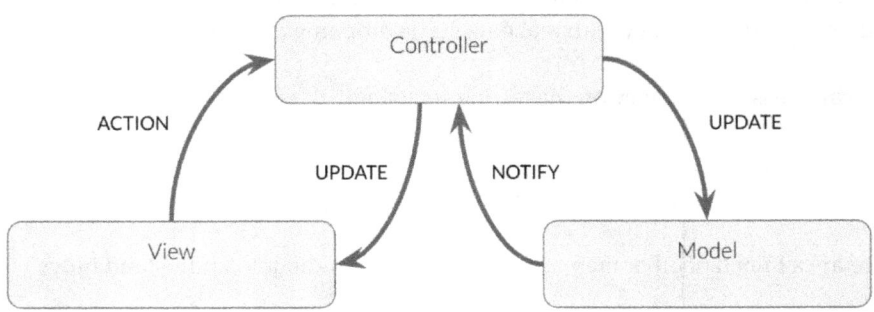

Figure 12.9: The widely adopted model-view-controller approach to writing software

This is a typical structure commonly used in modern software. You have three kinds of code. One that shows things (view), one that defines things (model), and one that decides what happens between the two (controller). In this kind of structure, there are two ways to impose explicit rules: the model itself, and the "business logic" of the controller. Business logic is a fancy way of saying "if this happens, then do that."

So what goes into the model box? A fixed model with fixed relationships. This is why software is slow and hard to create, because these relationships have to be modeled and implemented. The further along the process of creating a software solution, the harder it is to change anything. Innovation slows down over the iterations and versions, as the degrees of freedom are reduced to zero.

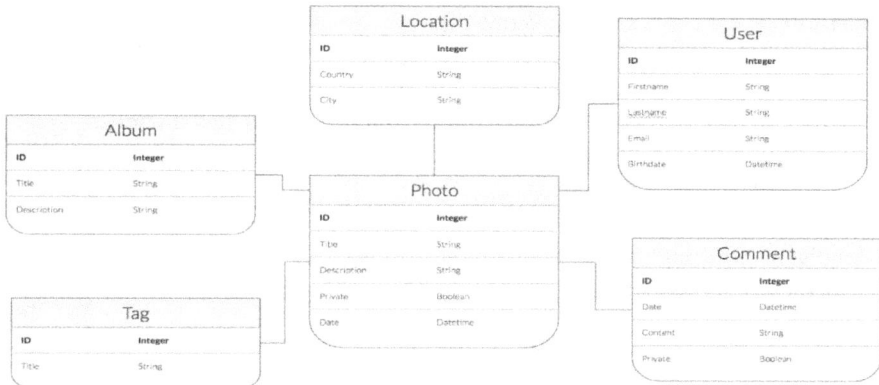

Figure 12.10: Traditional database structure underlying most applications

How (Simple) Machine Learning Can Help You Create Better Software

The terms *AI* and *ML* have become somewhat overused in certain industries, especially within the start-up community, to the extent that pitching a new solution without any of the terms seems odd. Ready-made models from providers like Amazon Web Services, Apple, and Google have already made it possible to claim such capabilities without any specific knowledge of their workings. Examples include facial recognition and processing of voice data. However, there are ways to create your own machine learning algorithms and add value to any software solution.

Teach Logic to Your Software

Rather than having to decide on how everything has to work at the beginning, what if you could just teach your software what to do? That way, if you had to change it later, you could just teach it again. This, in fact, is entirely possible with even rudimentary machine learning knowledge.

This is where we get back to classification, specifically. What is logic? What is decision making? It is connecting a number of inputs to a number of outputs. Also called *multiclass classification* in machine learning terms. What is a great algorithm for this purpose? Something that allows you to train on data rather than define the code, but is simple and explainable. The answer is a decision tree.

To train any classifier with scikit-learn, you need just two lines of code.

```
classifier = sklearn.tree.DecisionTreeClassifier()
```

```
classifier = clf.fit(inputs, outputs)
```

The best part is that it can replace complex logic and modeling work with one line of code. Yes, you read that right. Once you train a model, this is how it works:

```
output = model.predict(inputs)
```

Alternatively, you might want to get a probability distribution across all possible outputs for a set of inputs.

```
outputs = model.predict_proba(inputs)
```

This is quite elegant, as you can see. If you have new data or need to replace the model, you have to change one file: the model itself. No database migrations. No automated integration test suites.

Automation of Machine Learning Itself

While these learning methods are increasingly being adopted and applied, progress has been significantly limited by two key resources: programming skills and computing power. Even in the hands of the most skilled engineers, real-world deep learning algorithms can consume immense amounts of resources, even on the scale of cloud computing with thousands of individual processors harnessed to train the machine learning models.

This creates a long-term bottleneck for machine learning to become commonplace, as skilled resources are required and therefore expensive, and training on big datasets can be prohibitively costly.

One obvious solution to this bottleneck is to create a vast library of ready-made models, as mentioned earlier. In particular, large technology companies are incentivized to do so in order to attract developers to continuously adopt their frameworks. If your problem is complex yet common, like facial or speech recognition, it is unlikely that your own efforts are going to improve that of Google's or Amazon's capabilities, since these companies have already spent enormous resources to optimize every possible parameter.

There will still be need for custom algorithms to solve problems that are specific to your business or solution. To address this need, companies like Google and Nvidia are rolling out cloud services for training neural networks, running on custom chipsets and hardware optimized for that singular purpose.

On top of the decades of ongoing research into more cost-efficient computing, including specialized chips designed for neural networks, there is an increased focus on automating the hard skills required to design the algorithms. This branch is typically called "AutoML," or automated machine learning.[5] A simple form might be scripts to search the possible space of parameters to find the best combination, without much intelligence. Yet there are already algorithms that optimize for network architecture, a far more demanding task.

This path is likely to follow the path of business intelligence, which started as a specialist task, but is now reduced to the "drag-and-drop" style of online dashboards directly used by business leaders. This could take years, however, and meanwhile, knowledge of machine learning is rapidly shifting from competitive advantage to mandatory for many industries.

Endnotes

1 Kay, J.W. & Phillips, W.A. "Coherent Infomax as a Computational Goal for Neural Systems," *Bulletin of Mathematical Biophysics* (2011) 73: 344.
2 Wolpert, D.H. & Macready, W.G. (1997). "No Free Lunch Theorems for Optimization," *IEEE Transactions on Evolutionary Computation Archive*, Volume 1, Issue 1 (April): 67–82.
3 Lim, T.S., Loh, W.Y. & Shih, Y.S. (2000). "A Comparison of Prediction Accuracy, Complexity, and Training Time of Thirty-Three Old and New Classification Algorithms," *Machine Learning* 40: 203.
4 Quinlan, J.R. (1983), "Learning efficient classification procedures and their application to chess end games," in Michalski, R.S., Carbonell, J.G., Mitchell, T.M. (eds), *Machine Learning, Symbolic Computation*, Springer, Berlin, Heidelberg.
5 Thornton, C., Hutter, F., Hoos, H.H. & Leyton-Brown, K. (2013). "Combined Selection and Hyperparameter Optimization of Classification Algorithms." KDD13 Proceedings of the 19th ACM SIGKDD international conference on Knowledge discovery and data mining, 847–855, Chicago, Illinois.

References

Ho, T.K. (1995). "Random Decision Forests," ICDAR '95 Proceedings of the Third International Conference on Document Analysis and Recognition (Volume 1) – 278.
McCulloch, Warren & Pitts, Walter (1943). "A Logical Calculus of Ideas Immanent in Nervous Activity," 1943, *Bulletin of Mathematical Biophysics* 5:115–133.
Vapnik, Vladimir N. & Chervonenkis, Alexey Ya (1964). On a class of pattern-recognition learning algorithms. *Automation and Remote Control*, 25(6): 838–845.
Werbos, J (1974). Beyond Regression: New Tools for Prediction and Analysis in the Behavioral Sciences. PhD thesis, Harvard University, (103).

Aki Ranin is the founder of two AI startups in Singapore: Bambu in Fintech, and Healthzilla in Healthtech. The common thread in his companies and interests is intelligent automation through applied data. He holds a Masters degree in Computer Science from Aalto University in Finland. Aki also writes frequently on Medium about startups, philosophy, and technology.

Part 3: **Fintech Innovations and Disruptions**

Chapter 13
Disruption in Asset Servicing

A huge wave of technology disruption is heading toward the asset servicing industry. The processes in the asset servicing industry have changed as advances in computing have led to dramatic efficiencies in transaction processing and in other areas. These changes have expanded the market significantly and the traditional players performing these services have been able to grow with the increases in market size. However, today the changes in technology can actually replace services that slow transactions and take significant manpower giving rise to opportunities to technology-savvy organizations that are not burdened with the change management that will be required. Within a five-year timeframe, robotic process automation (RPA), blockchain and cognitive systems will drive dramatic changes and have a profound, lasting impact on service providers' operations. According to a survey by the CFA Institute, 54 percent of respondents viewed asset management as the industry most at risk from disruptive technologies.[1]

These disruptive technologies offer enormous potential for asset servicers in creating efficiency, reducing risk and improving quality of service to clients. It has been suggested that automation alone can reduce headcount in the asset servicing industry by 60 to 70 percent while also achieving a cost savings of approximately 30 to 40 percent.

The Asset Management Sector Is Ripe for Disruption

Why is asset servicing standing squarely in the path of disruption? The industry employs approximately 200,000 people[2] worldwide. Many providers are still constrained by the legacy of acquisitions, poor integration, multiple technology platforms, and a high level of customized manual activities. Some of the technology platforms still in widespread use date back twenty years or more and asset servicers still receive tens of millions of instructions by fax every year. It is argued that the industry employs such a large number of people due to inefficiencies that accumulated in its systems and processes over many decades. Many of the full-time employees (FTEs) in asset servicing perform manual, repetitive tasks that automated technology can now cost-effectively replace.

The challenge for asset servicers is considerable: since 2008, the regulatory environment has been the dominant consideration, thereby inhibiting the industry's development. The value of assets under management has been rising over the past two years, however expenses are on the rise as asset servicers have been unable to keep costs under control. It is generally felt that while technology has evolved, the industry has failed to keep abreast. With the market driving asset servicers to achieve

DOI 10.1515/9781547400904- 013

operational excellence, it is clear that some of these processes tied to legacy technology are the first in the firing line. Opportunities have emerged for new technologies to replace repetitive, manual, and cost-inefficient back- and middle-office processes, with improved process automation delivered on a continuous basis.

Disruptive Technologies

Disruptive technologies are technologies that do not develop in a linear way but evolve much faster and have a greater impact than traditional technologies, enabling change (see Figure 13.1).

In this section, we focus our attention on three particular technologies that respectively represent the greatest disruption posed in the short-term (*automation*), medium-term (*blockchain*), and long-term (*cognitive*). While all three technologies pose a potential disruption to the industry, what is important to note is the exponential impact of such developments.

Singularity University, in partnership with Deloitte, emphasizes the impact of exponentials, (technologies that enable exponential growth) on businesses as unprecedented opportunities as well as existential threats. The group warns leaders to understand that waiting for exponentials to manifest as mature technology trends before taking action may be waiting too long.[3]

Blockchain

The World Economic Forum has forecast that by 2025, at least 10 percent of global GDP will be stored on blockchain platforms.[4] As discussed in earlier chapters, blockchain is one of the most widely hyped technologies currently. A blockchain is one form of a distributed database for recording transactions where every participant on the network shares a copy of each transaction. Blockchain allows for decentralized processing, validation, and authentication of transactions. It also has several unique and valuable characteristics that over time could transform a wide range of industries.

Impact, Challenges and Risks
When applied to asset servicing, blockchain will result in a completely redesigned value chain. Blockchain may eventually go so far as to eliminate the requirement for multiple onerous reconciliations. If funds are selling directly to investors, and this is recorded on the blockchain, it may also remove the need for the transfer agent to monitor subscriptions and keep a share register of participants in the fund, further streamlining the whole process.

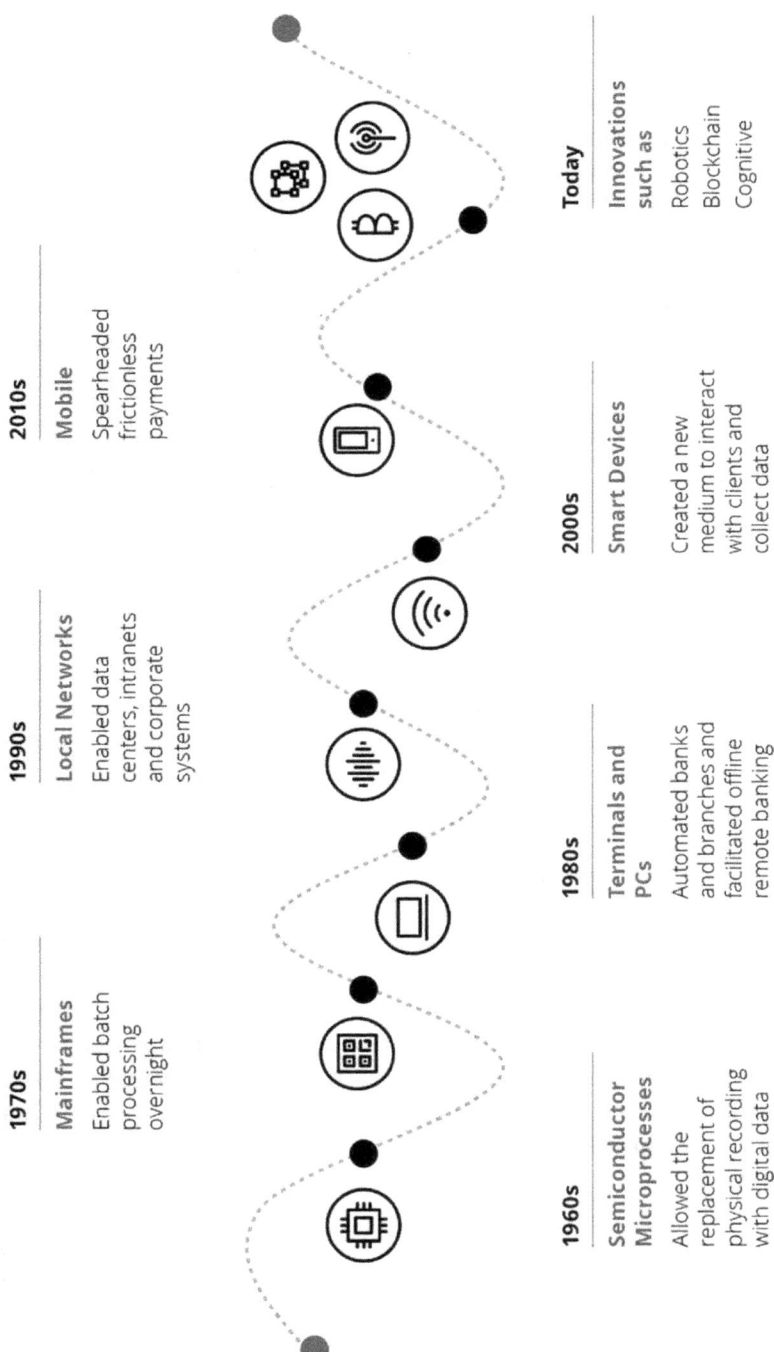

Figure 13.1: The evolution of technologies

Blockchain will also significantly reduce the volume of paperwork associated with asset servicing, and will lower the costs of processing information internally in the business, as well as lowering the cost to the client.

The function of a custodian is to safe-keep securities and ensure that they are properly assigned to an owner. Custodian banks are at risk of being replaced by a blockchain solution since transactions can be recorded in the blockchain and it is designed to be immutable.

A second group under threat is any risk management function that is working on trade activities. Trading securities today takes about three days to settle which requires a lot of people to manage potential risks such as exchange risk fluctuation. If same-day settlement occurs, the risk is greatly reduced, and as a consequence, so is the manpower needed.

In November 2016, the Monetary Authority of Singapore (MAS) announced that it was partnering with R3 (a blockchain-inspired technology company) and a consortium of the world's largest financial institutions on the production of a proof-of-concept (PoC) to conduct inter-bank payments facilitated by *distributed ledger technology* (DLT) including blockchain.[5] This endeavor, known as Project Ubin, is a digital cash-on-ledger project conducted in partnership between MAS and R3, with the participation of Bank of America Merrill Lynch, Credit Suisse, DBS Bank, The Hongkong and Shanghai Banking Corporation Limited (HSBC), J.P. Morgan, Mitsubishi UFJ Financial Group (MUFG), OCBC Bank, Singapore Exchange, United Overseas Bank, as well as BCS Information Systems as a technology provider. The aim of Project Ubin is to evaluate the implications of having a tokenized form of the Singapore dollar (SGD) on a distributed ledger (DL), and its potential benefits to Singapore's financial ecosystem. Project Ubin was also conceived as an opportunity for Singapore to take a leading role in the research on central bank currency on a DL and *central bank digital currencies* (CBDCs). The use of DLT offers the potential to improve domestic securities transactions as well as cross-border payments and securities transactions. Two key characteristics of DLT make this possible:

- Data on the DLT is immutable, and is thus resistant to double-spending, fraud, censorship, and hacking efforts, creating a more secure, transparent network.
- Data on the DLT is also secured by cryptography, a method for verifying digital identity with a high degree of confidence, enabled by the use of private and public keys. This allows for increased security and protection of data and identity in the system.

In order to achieve the hypothesized benefits, widespread adoption of DLT would be needed which would require advances in the existing technology. Nevertheless, the financial services industry requires answers to the perceived technical challenges of getting: interoperability between platforms, selective identification of relevant parties, appropriate levels of privacy, proven ability to scale and various systems upgrades over time. If these challenges can be solved as part of this project in the near future,

MAS can create "atomic" transactions for the first time for cross-border, fixed-income products with payments directly on central bank money. This would enable true delivery vs. payment where security and corresponding payment switches ownership simultaneously at the deepest technical level. This could remove the occurrence of late payments and payment failures. Certainty around delivery and near real-time, same-day delivery also becomes viable. These could make both domestic as well as cross-border transactions more attractive from both a technology and end-user experience standpoint. Furthermore, the reduction in counterparty risk may drive a reduction in collateral requirements in some circumstances.

Blockchain could also have ramifications for some of the key tasks that asset servicers carry out today — in particular, the reconciliation of transactions for institutional clients. In a "perfect world" virtual ledger scenario, if a financial institution can manage those functions on a costless basis, the price point and possibly the entire function of a physical ledger could potentially become obsolete because there is a free virtual ledger that allows these things to be executed.

Whereas RPA can be bolted onto existing technology platforms, blockchain represents a more fundamental, transformational change to asset servicers' IT infrastructure.

Debate rages over blockchain's readiness for the kind of wide-scale adoption that asset servicers need. Skeptics say the technology has yet to be proven at any other scale except laboratory scale: currently, it can handle around five or six transactions per second, which is not sufficiently fast to meet the needs of service providers. Performance and throughput issues will improve, but there are some more fundamental problems around anonymity and aggregation: blockchain potentially discloses sensitive information regarding nominee accounts, for example, which could lead to confidential information being leaked into the market.

Automation will streamline the older processing costs and cash settlement value chain, which will result in massive cost savings to the client. As a result, investors can expect to be the principal beneficiaries of savings resulting from blockchain, with a smaller amount going to the service providers.

Several use cases for blockchain within the asset servicing industry are aimed primarily at streamlining and improving back- and middle-office tasks such as *know your customer* (KYC) utility, risk reporting, securities settlement, and corporate actions. Kasikornbank (KBank) in Thailand has digitized their letter of guarantee process using blockchain.[6] The transparency provided by blockchain can help eliminate forgery and improve efficiency.

Blockchain will result in an industry that looks very different from a human resources perspective five years from now. The number of FTEs in the industry will decrease, as many manual tasks such as order processing and cash reconciliation will be encapsulated in a blockchain-like solution. However, although there will be significant job losses, there will be job creation in "satellites around the traditional asset servicers" in the form of positions required to create new businesses that formerly were not practical with existing technology, and to operate and run blockchain systems which do not exist in asset servicing today.

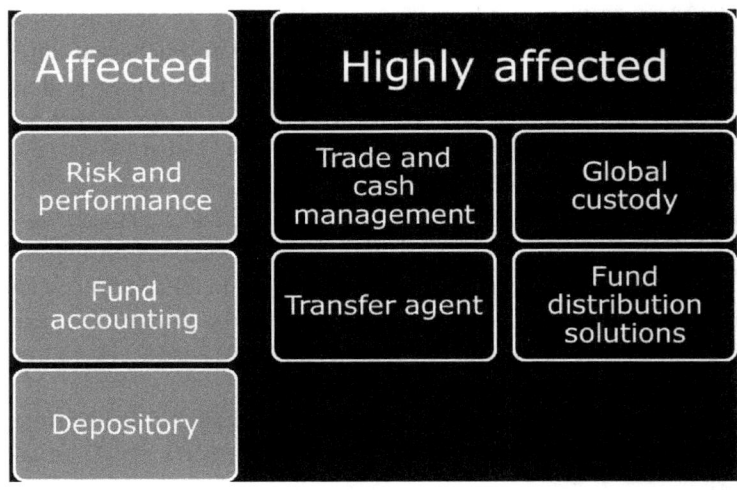

Figure 13.2: Impact of blockchain on the asset servicing industry

Robotic Process Automation (RPA)

RPA could replace much of the manual work involved in asset servicing to handle post-settlement tasks like trade processing, reconciliation, and reporting — both for clients and regulators. The technology has been maturing over the past decade to a point where it is now suitable for enterprise-scale deployment and can be implemented quickly and at low cost. A study of 10 financial services companies in Asia that are early adopters of RPA has found early success in cost savings and turnaround time. The study, undertaken by market intelligence firm IDC, revealed that financial services institutions could achieve costs savings of between 30 and 60 percent.[7] However, actual numbers would vary based on the cost base, the market, the business process itself, and the investments needed to support RPA. Early adopters also shared that the implementation time required is also short (ranging from as little as 6 to 12 weeks) and that technology buyers can recover their initial RPA investment between 10 to 24 months.[8]

A license for a software robot is likely to cost less than an onshore or offshore staff member, so the commercial attractiveness of this approach is self-evident. There are non-financial benefits too, as robot-based process performance is designed to be more predictable, consistent, and less prone to errors as compared to human processes. Moreover, a robotic workforce can typically be deployed in a matter of weeks. Once in place, new processes can be assigned to them within days, if not hours. A range of robotic tools can provide powerful skills to an integrated workforce as shown in Figure 13.3.

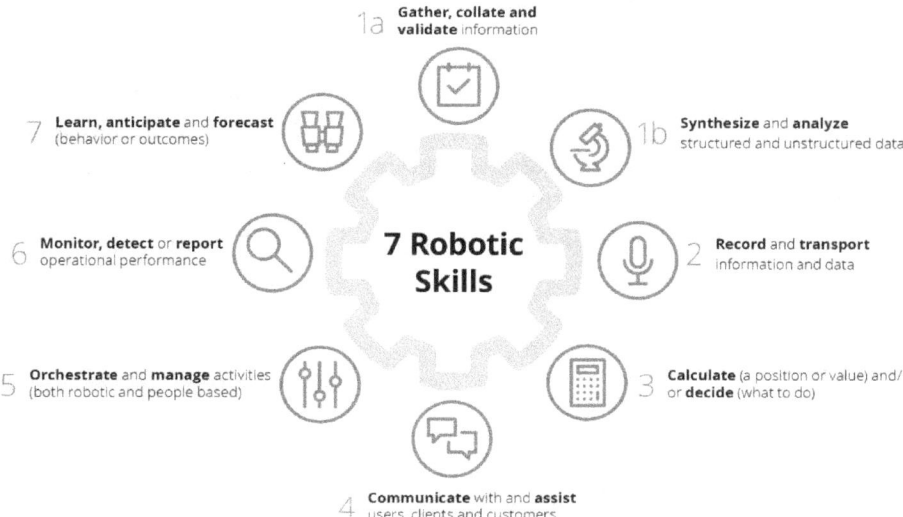

Figure 13.3: Seven robotic skills

Impact, Challenges, and Risks

RPA will be the first of the disruptive technologies to truly impact the asset servicing market. Simply using RPA tools to automate the processing of trade instructions has the potential to create significant value for any asset servicer. In addition, possible benefits also include identifying revenue leakage where invoicing processes were not aligned with price points for fund accounting and custody. India is and will be one of the locations most impacted by disruptive technology, as it is where many of the large global asset servicers—including Bank of America Merrill Lynch, Citi, HSBC and J.P. Morgan—have significant operations employing thousands of people as a result of the large-scale offshoring initiatives over a number of years.[9] The tasks and processes that have been offshored are "identified, documented, and transferred," making them ripe for rapid automation.

Some of the leading asset servicers have already started deploying RPA on a large scale to handle high-volume repetitive tasks, and India's banking and financial services sector is a popular location for these early-stage exercises.

Some proof-of-concept projects have identified the reconciliation function of asset servicing as a target for RPA. There is strong interest among asset servicers, who have a presence in India, to engage shared service centers or third-party outsourced partners in carrying out high-volume repetitive tasks.

The range of cost savings varies widely. Although automation will deliver much higher efficiency at a lower cost (see Figure 13.4), some error rates will remain, driving the need for additional checks. As a result, cost savings cannot be the sole measure of RPA success. In echoing this thought, it is important for organizations to be mindful of the limitations of RPA and not overestimate its capabilities. While RPA reduces the need for repetitive human effort, there are still distinct limitations in the types of work it can carry out.[10] Prior to deploying RPA, organizations need to spend time developing their automation strategy, beginning with the idea of a proof-of-concept or pilot implementation. Taking time to understand the critical success factors for RPA implementation, and building the business case around the same factors, can help avoid implementation disappointment.

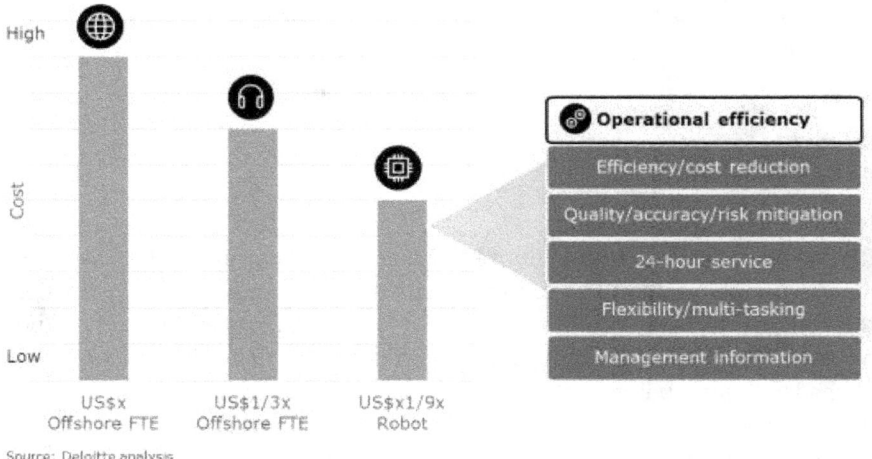

Figure 13.4: A comparison of cost

Cognitive Technology

Born out of research in artificial intelligence (AI), cognitive technology comprises several areas including natural language processing, computer vision, speech recognition, and robotics. These tools and technologies are also known as *intelligent automation*. More advanced than bots, which just perform process-based, repetitive tasks, cognitive technology mimics human judgement in its ability to recognize handwriting, identify images, and use natural language processing to interpret information. Machine-learning capability allows these tools to improve over time.

Though not yet as mature as RPA, we believe cognitive technology has even greater transformational potential. An important emerging trend is that enterprises are starting to employ RPA together with cognitive technologies such as speech recognition, chatbot, natural language processing, robo-advisors, and machine learning to automate perceptual and judgment-based tasks, which were traditionally performed by humans. Integrating RPA and cognitive technologies extends the automation potential to processes that require perception or judgement and unlocks new areas within the organization to deliver business outcomes such as greater customer satisfaction, increased revenues and increased efficiency. The decreasing costs of data storage and processing power are enabling rapid developments in the field of AI.

Today, wealth management firms use intelligent automation to review and analyze portfolio data, determine meaningful metrics, and generate natural-language reports for their customers on the performance of each of their funds. The uses of AI are potentially limitless, but the tools are also more expensive to deploy than RPA tools and they take months, rather than weeks, to implement.

Impact, Challenges, and Risks

Cognitive solutions will be more enterprise-wide, rather than be deployed to address specific areas in asset servicing. We have seen many case studies of organizations that have deployed automation and suggest that the majority of organizations are focused on increasing the efficiency and effectiveness of their workforce rather than eliminating it; the people relieved of routine tasks are refocused toward more valuable or rewarding activities. For example, OCBC Bank in Singapore has tapped AI and machine learning to combat financial crime.[11] The use of AI to monitor suspicious transactions will help cut down the time that typically takes several analysts a few days or even up to a week to process, depending on the complexity of the transaction, to just a couple of hours. Interestingly, with more advanced and complex automation comes not only increased efficiency, but also an increased dependency on the accuracy and skill of the human operators involved. Automation of tasks does not necessarily lead to loss of jobs. Instead, workforce augmentation, rather than replacement, may be a more likely outcome. By freeing up a person's time, employees can now focus on more advanced and engaging tasks, and over time, organizations could see lower turnover, higher morale, and increased internal innovation. Singapore's DBS Bank is investing S$20m to train its existing workforce in digital banking and emerging technologies, via an artificial intelligence-powered e-learning platform, curated curriculum, and module delivery.[12]

We expect to see further efficiency gains when RPA, blockchain and cognitive technologies converge, and service providers will face a choice of what savings to pass on to clients, and what to retain as profit. Lower FTE costs are the logical conclusion from introducing increased automation into a system, but there are also other initial benefits. The use of cognitive technologies such as bots has also resulted in increased efficiency and improved customer service. The use of bots in asset servicing can lead to improvements in processing quality and they enable 24/7 service. In December 2017, Schroders Singapore launched a beta version of Schroders GO, an online chatbot operating through Facebook Messenger. The chatbot allows clients to access information on any fund as well as market information without having to download an app. The bot is able to learn and answer three-dimensional questions, offering information about Schroders as well as similar funds for comparison.

As previously mentioned, when undertaking a proof-of-concept initiative, it is better to set multiple goals other than cost saving. Some initiatives were deemed failures simply because the sponsors did not define what success would look like. If it is regarded as a pure cost play and the cost does not reduce, then the project is considered a failure. Other useful goals to measure success of the initiative can include the ability to function with reduced headcount, to improve quality of process from 90 to 99 percent, or to reduce operational incidents by half.

Preparing for the Wave of Disruption

Five years from now, the asset servicing industry will look very different. The onward march of disruptive technology calls for a profound shift in thinking among asset servicing providers. Regulation was the driver for the past decade's activity; the next five years will see technology at the forefront of providers' strategic thinking. This means scaling investment in technology and the technological structure within their business. In the age of fintech, tomorrow's asset servicing organization will be a technology-enabled utility rather than today's service provider model. The alternative is obsolescence. Below are some actions that can help get an organization ready for these changes now:

Upskill senior management: Change the profile of your senior management team to include more technology-aware, technology-focused senior executives.

Shift hiring plans: Automation will replace functions, not jobs, and technology will augment, not replace, the role of humans. We foresee a hybrid workforce of autonomous FTEs and bots. Service providers should start thinking about the skills required around governance and managing this resource pool.

Recruit expertise: Hire an innovation leader who will be very close to the executive committee of the company and give real substance to the strategy business unit of asset servicing. In practice, this could mean moving power from the chief operating officer to the strategy and innovation function. Disruptive technologies have also given rise to new roles in management such as chief data officer and chief transformation officer. Under the leadership of a capable and experienced chief transformation officer, a company's chances of a successful transformation of its business operations relating to new disruptive technologies will significantly improve.

Move up the value chain: Asset servicers should focus more on how they provide more value-added services such as spending more time talking to the client, more time providing them with market and regulatory intelligence and becoming the trusted business partner of the asset manager instead of just being responsible for back-office administration.

Define success: Defining multiple project goals clearly and avoiding a focus solely on cost reduction will increase the likelihood of a project being determined a success. Experiments led from the bottom up rather than the top down work in most cases. Joint ownership between technology and operation also increase the chances of project success and avoids silos.

Get faster, fast: It is critical for asset servicers to form a point of view about the technology that threatens to disrupt their market. Many asset servicers rely on big, monolithic technology platforms. It is no longer acceptable to use 18-month IT deployment windows. You have to come to market faster, so you need to architect your IT to iterate faster.

Split divisions: Organizations should consider setting up a purely technology-focused operation with high levels of automation and no legacy systems and processes, possibly as a joint venture with a fintech player. This would run in parallel with the existing asset servicing business. It could even be independently branded. It could also be scaled up while winding down the legacy operations over a similar time period.

Possible Outcomes

Three outcomes have been identified as possible avenues that the asset servicing industry will take over the next three to five years. Scenarios A, B, and C, shown in Figure 13.5, discuss the potential impact that disruptive technology will have on the value chain of the asset servicing industry.

We believe scenario B to be the most likely outcome, whereby the value chain will be disrupted, but will not disintegrate entirely. However, in order to capitalize on the upward growth trend and increase profits, asset servicers will need to invest in new technology to meet the needs of their evolving client base.

RPA, cognitive systems and blockchain will create an asset servicing industry that looks very different from what we see today, but this disruption will happen in stages over the next three to five years. We anticipate a domino effect whereby asset servicers will begin implementing RPA to tackle low-level, repeatable, process-based tasks.

They will follow this with blockchain as this technology matures. As RPA becomes embedded, it will pave the way for introducing cognitive technology and AI that applies rules and human-like judgment to asset servicing roles.

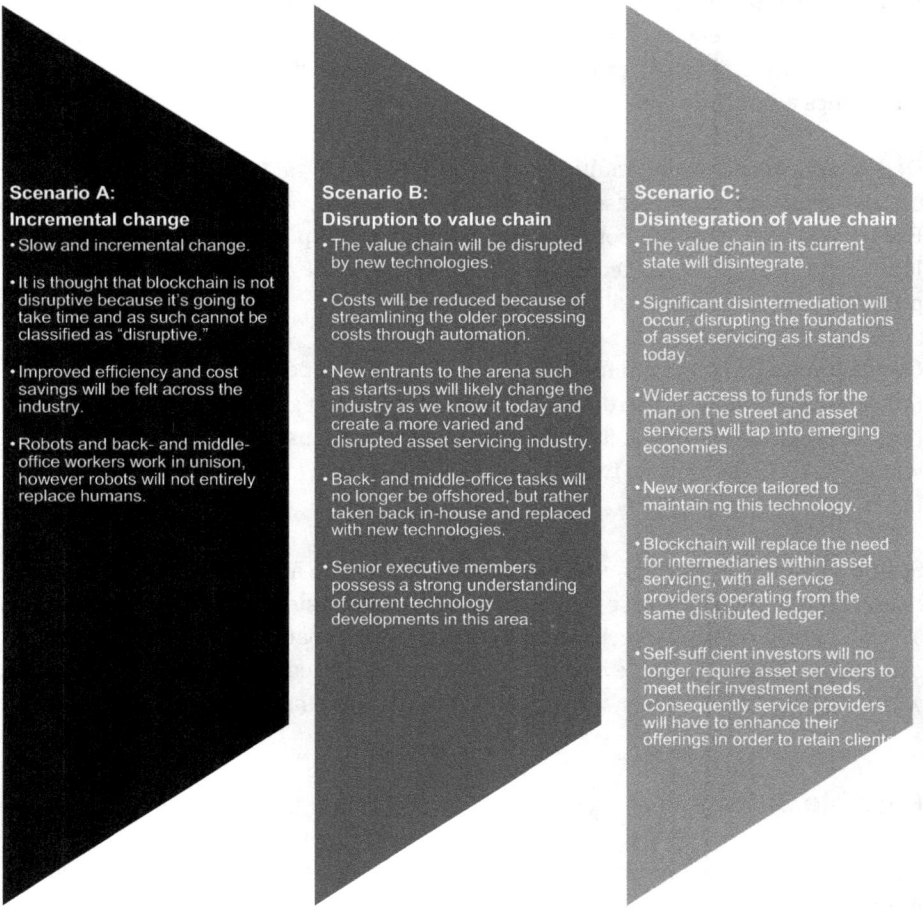

Scenario A:

Incremental change

• Slow and incremental change.

• It is thought that blockchain is not disruptive because it's going to take time and as such cannot be classified as "disruptive."

• Improved efficiency and cost savings will be felt across the industry.

• Robots and back- and middle-office workers work in unison, however robots will not entirely replace humans.

Scenario B:

Disruption to value chain

• The value chain will be disrupted by new technologies.

• Costs will be reduced because of streamlining the older processing costs through automation.

• New entrants to the arena such as starts-ups will likely change the industry as we know it today and create a more varied and disrupted asset servicing industry.

• Back- and middle-office tasks will no longer be offshored, but rather taken back in-house and replaced with new technologies.

• Senior executive members possess a strong understanding of current technology developments in this area.

Scenario C:

Disintegration of value chain

• The value chain in its current state will disintegrate.

• Significant disintermediation will occur, disrupting the foundations of asset servicing as it stands today.

• Wider access to funds for the man on the street and asset servicers will tap into emerging economies.

• New workforce tailored to maintaining this technology.

• Blockchain will replace the need for intermediaries within asset servicing, with all service providers operating from the same distributed ledger.

• Self-sufficient investors will no longer require asset servicers to meet their investment needs. Consequently service providers will have to enhance their offerings in order to retain clients.

Figure 13.5: Possible avenues that the asset servicing industry will take over the next few years

It is always better to be the disruptor than to be disrupted. Asset servicers who fail to embrace these technologies will likely cede important strategic advantage to competitors and new market entrants already riding the wave. Conversely, organizations that try to do too much too soon in pursuit of first mover advantage in the RPA, cognitive systems and blockchain space may also be at risk. The key is running a manageable set of pilot programs to test robotics and cognitive automation capabilities. This enables the insurer to align business outcomes with the expectations and facilitate a smoother implementation downstream.

Now is the time for asset servicers to start formulating tactical and strategic plans, in order to be ready when the technologies' tipping point arrives and the waves begin to crash down on the industry.

Endnotes

1 FinTech Survey Report. CFA Institute. April 2017. http://www.agefi.fr/sites/agefi.fr/files/fichiers/2016/04/survey.pdf

2 Deloitte Research, 2017.

3 Exponentials watch list: Science and technology innovations on the horizon, Tech Trends 2017, Deloitte. January 2017. https://dupress.deloitte.com/dup-us-en/focus/tech-trends/2017/exponential-technology-digital-innovation.html#my-take

4 Deep Shift Technology Tipping Points and Societal Impacts, World Economic Forum, 2015.

5 Project Ubin: Central Bank Digital Money using Distributed Ledger Technology. Monetary Authority of Singapore. November 2016. http://www.mas.gov.sg/Singapore-Financial-Centre/Smart-Financial-Centre/Project-Ubin.aspx

6 KBank and IBM Develop Blockchain-Based Letter of Guarantee Service. IBM Press Release. 8 August 2017. https://www-03.ibm.com/press/us/en/pressrelease/52961.wss

7 IDC Research Identifies Key Learnings from 10 Early Adopters of Robotic Process Automation (RPA) in the Asia/Pacific Financial Services. IDC Press Release. 19 April 2018. https://www.idc.com/getdoc.jsp?containerId=prAP43748018

8 Ibid.

9 Banks offshoring more than 80,000 tech jobs, efinancialcareers.com, 20 February 2013.http://news.efinancialcareers.com/ie-en/134803/banks-offshore-as-many-tech-jobs-as-apple-employs/

10 "The line between hype and reality for Robotic Process Automation," Genpact. 2014. http://www.genpact.com/docs/default-source/resource-/the-line-between-hype-and-reality-for-rpa

11 OCBC Bank is the First Singapore Bank to Tap Artificial Intelligence and Machine Learning to Combat Financial Crime. OCBC Bank Press Release. 7 November 2017. https://www.ocbc.com/group/media/release/2017/ocbc-bank-ai-and-machine-learning-to-combat-financial-crime.html

12 DBS to invest SGD20 million over five years to transform employees into digital workforce, in support of Singapore's aim to be smart financial centre. DBS Bank Press Release. 21 August 2017. https://www.dbs.com/newsroom/DBS_to_invest_SGD20_million_over_five_years_to_transform_employees_into_digital_workforce_in_support_of_Singapores_aim_to_be_smart_financial_centre "The future of asset servicing: Shaped by three disruptive technologies." Deloitte Consulting.

Deloitte provides audit, consulting, financial advisory, risk management, tax and related services to public and private clients spanning multiple industries. With a globally connected network of member firms in more than 150 countries and territories, Deloitte brings world-class capabilities and high-quality service to clients, delivering the insights they need to address their most complex business challenges. In Southeast Asia, Deloitte is uniquely placed to assist organizations across different industries to embed fintech technologies through innovation, collaboration, and integration. With the combination of our local industry knowledge and expertise of our global network, we have the right combination of experience and capability to deliver the value our clients require in today's disruptive business environment.

Chapter 14
Disruption in the Capital Markets

Whether you credit the start of electronic trading to the incorporation of the Institutions Network electronic crossing platform (now Instinet) in 1969 or the launch of the Nasdaq electronic stock exchange in the 1970s, it is fair to say that the pace and breadth of technology's influence on trading has increased exponentially in the past decades. Moreover, it is very likely to accelerate in the decades to come, further disrupting traditional business models and providing the benefits to end-investors and retail traders that had previously only been enjoyed by large, powerful global financial institutions.

As in other industries, the current wave of digital technology innovation is primarily an enabler and an accelerator in the trading space. By making trading and related processes faster, cheaper, and more efficient than before, technology is today enabling a wider range of service providers to compete and allowing a broader array of participants to trade and invest cost-effectively. To survive and thrive in this new paradigm, firms must combine expertise in financial service provision with mastery of technology. This has been a founding principle at Saxo Bank Group (who have authored this chapter), guiding both the development of our online brokerage services and our adoption of collaborative business models that leverage APIs and other fintech innovations. In the future, a grasp of technology's power and potential will be a pre-requisite.

As this chapter will describe, the recent fintech revolution is both a continuation of and a departure from the previous application of information and communication technology to trading processes. While significant and pioneering in their own right, many of the steps taken in past decades by innovators to improve the cost, transparency, and efficiency of trading have often been incremental. Moreover, they have typically benefited the wholesale and institutional markets more directly than the end-investor or the professional trader. Today, standing on the shoulders of those giants, a new generation of pioneers—both within incumbents and insurgents—are leveraging fintech to make more profound and transformational leaps forward.

Market by market—first in equities and listed futures, then in foreign exchange (FX) and fixed income markets—trading processes became cheaper, easier to access, and more commoditized over the 1990s and 2000s. Now, the building blocks of almost any trading business can be sourced, connected, and assembled at a lower cost and with more ease than ever before. Moreover, computer power and data processing capabilities are enabling firms to derive new levels of insight, customization, and functionality from multiple data flows. At the same time, regulation has been crucial in protecting investors and encouraging competition, particularly since the financial crisis of 2008.

DOI 10.1515/9781547400904- 014

The result has been an explosion of creativity that offers greater control over wealth for many, through their ability to make trading and investment decisions at their own convenience, based on their own individual priorities, with full transparency of the underlying costs, risks, and processes, and with full access to a wide range of market insights and instruments. Retail investors and small firms now have equal access to the markets and to the major players in a process of democratization of the market that has happened over the last twenty-five years.

In bringing trading power to the people, it may be considered an irony that trading professionals employed by global banking giants are less empowered now than half a century ago, often taking the role of machine-minders. However, it should be remembered that it is the role of the intermediary to serve the investor, and not the other way around.

How Did We Get Here?

When volatility in the financial markets pushes its way into the news headlines, the story is invariably illustrated by images of slightly panicked young men and women, signalling urgently to each other or shouting down a phone receiver, or both. But downtown trading floors have long since fallen silent, with pits surviving more for the benefit of tourists than traders. The real action, if you can call it that, mainly takes place in anonymous, high-tech, low-population, edge-of-town facilities, invisibly connected to similar centers across the world.

The exodus started in the 1980s and 1990s, as the financial markets' early waves of automation saw computer terminals replace fingers and blotters as primary data sources. Traders initially retreated from exchanges' trading floors to the giant trading rooms of global investment banks, surrounded by banks of screens and turrets (telephone consoles) that connected them to multiple counterparties and markets worldwide.

One way to understand the change in the trading landscape is to consider the changing fortunes of the bulge-bracket banks. The 1980s and 1990s also witnessed a period of large-scale consolidation, predominantly by M&A, which created a handful of "flow monsters," behemoths that bestrode the global financial markets. These "universal" banks typically combined wide-ranging corporate and investment banking business with wealth and retail franchises, the diversity of which enabled them to intermediate and offset the complementary financial flows of clients and leverage the information flows that accompanied them. This self-reinforcing business model generated huge revenues—which could be used to bankroll major technology infrastructure investments, while also masking significant process inefficiencies. It also generated huge conflicts of interest which sowed the seeds, at least in part, of the global financial crisis.

At the same time, exchanges were evolving, with changes to their ownership structures and business models driven by their need to invest in new technologies that enabled remote order exchanges. For much of their history, exchanges had served largely as user-owned utilities, owned and operated in the interests of brokers. But in the 1990s and 2000s, many went public to fund large expansions and investment plans, leading over time to conflicts between the revenue-maximizing interests of shareholders and demands of users.

From the early 2000s, the banks' trading rooms, like the exchanges' trading floors before them, also began to empty out as trade automation grew. First, high-volume exchange-traded markets such as equities and futures became more traded by machines than humans, as algorithms proved able to make more accurate and rational trading decisions, at scale and at speed. The financial markets followed the principle that automation first takes root where there are already the highest levels of volume, repetition, and standardization—companies typically issue one type of share, but many different bonds—representing the easiest opportunity to realize benefits in terms of greater efficiency, lower cost, and improved transparency.

Voice-based order taking and fulfillment on stock and futures exchanges gave way to various forms of electronic data transfer first on the sell-side (that is, banks and brokers that made up the exchange membership) and then extending into the buy-side (or the asset managers and other institutions acting on behalf of investors). Having previously offered a physical venue in which buyers and sellers could meet and interact, exchanges moved gradually to supplying exchange members with electronic notice boards or order books where the bids and offers of brokers could be posted and matched. Slightly behind the curve, the process by which stock orders were directed by the buy-side to the sell-side began to migrate from phone to electronic, boosted by the development of the FIX message protocol. Initially developed to enable efficient notification of orders by Fidelity equity dealers to Salomon Smith Barney in the early 1990s, the protocol became the standard format and mechanism for sending equity orders, initially just from asset managers to their broker-dealers.

Over time, FIX grew in sophistication—enabling more detailed information to be transmitted about orders, thus improving users' ability to specify and demonstrate outcomes—as well as scope, extending to a wider range of front-office processes and markets, notably FX in the mid-2000s. Once it became possible to send orders to an exchange electronically, members sought to explore the boundaries of the new medium, developing automated trading capabilities that buy and sell efficiently in different market conditions and with variable parameters with minimal human intervention. Initially, these algorithms were instructed to slice up orders and feed them into the market slowly to disguise order size and/or to execute orders in response to order book price movements within a certain range. Broker-dealers developed algorithms to reduce the cost of employing human traders and then, with some trepidation, furthered the principle of self-service by placing them directly in the hands of buy-side customers. Credit Suisse was a notable pioneer in the early 2000s, but on the eve of the Regulation National Market System (Reg NMS) and the Markets in Financial Instruments Directive (MiFID), the majority of bulge-bracket firms were competing for market share on the basis of the algorithms offered to help clients achieve best execution.

Less centralized markets with a more diverse range of buyers and sellers—such as foreign exchange (FX), fixed income, and derivatives—took slower and different routes to automation. But even in these more credit-intensive and over-the-counter markets, in which relationships remained highly significant factors, automation levels increased gradually, with regulation sometimes forcing the pace of change. Both in the highly liquid FX market and the liquid markets within the fixed income universe, inter-dealer activity moved to electronic platforms much more quickly than dealer-to-client volumes, with EBS and Reuters providing the two dominant venues for broker-dealers to trade FX in the 1990s, followed only later by other venues offering multiple liquidity options to institutional clients in the early 2000s. These combined API-based connectivity, FIX message standards, and Continuous Linked Settlement to level the playing field between buy- and sell-side FX market participants.

In each market, every step toward greater automation opened up the possibility for new business models to emerge, challenging dominant incumbent firms and offering opportunities for newcomers to leverage the transparency, choice, and efficiency enabled by technology change.

What's Happening Now?

Over the past decade, the authentic sound of the financial market has gradually become the hum of the data center, or perhaps the hushed tones of today's lean trading desks on which a handful of quants pore over data, pondering how to tweak algorithms and other automated routines to further enhance performance. Even these voices may fall silent soon as self-learning algorithms alter their own behavior to deliver optimal results without the need for human intervention.

Technology has reduced the noise of the financial markets, but it has also reduced the cost and the risk, thus lowering the barriers to entry and enabling competition, which drives further innovation, resulting in greater choice, service levels, and protection for the end-user. The reduced cost of financial market participation has opened the door to a much wider range of business models, as in other industries. This led, for example, to liquidity in financial market instruments being provided by a wider range of market-makers by 2010 than in the early 1990s, and traded on a wider range of trading platforms. As a result, more niche needs are being catered to than when there was less competition, albeit with mixed efficiency benefits. It also demonstrated that the components of a trading and investment business (including trade execution tools, market data, infrastructure, connectivity, compliance, and so forth) could be atomized, broken down, and disaggregated into their constituent elements. High-frequency traders (HFTs) were the first to recognize this, but many others followed, emboldened in their development of new business models as much by the banks' post-crisis travails as by the promise of digital technology.

In this section, we review the trading decade since 2008 to the present day on a market-by-market basis with reference to the significant shifts in regulatory frameworks and consumer expectations, as well as the cost reductions, process efficiencies, and execution speeds achieved via technology innovation.

Equities

By the time that the global financial crisis claimed first Bear Stearns and then Lehman Brothers in 2008, the equities markets had already embarked on a path of technology-enabled competition and transformation. Reg NMS in the US and MiFID in Europe recognized the increasing demand for off-exchange trading of liquid equities by market participants that wished to avoid the high costs and slow technology offered by incumbent exchanges. Since the mid-1990s, a growing volume of US equity trading has been conducted on electronic communication networks (ECNs), which match buyers and sellers more quickly and cheaply than the matching engines of the dozen or so authorized stock exchanges around the country.

Reg NMS legitimized these off-exchange mechanisms in 2007, while MiFID also introduced competition to Europe's national exchanges later in the same year, by rescinding concentration rules and promoting choice in clearing and settlement to further lower costs. The new generation of trading venues—typically regulated as multilateral trading facilities (MTFs) in Europe—were built on technology-enabled partnerships with multiple service providers. Unlike vertically integrated incumbent exchange groups, many MTF operators would supply the low-latency matching engine themselves, but outsource clearing and settlement facilities, market data capabilities, data centers, and other networking and infrastructure elements to existing providers, thus introducing greater competition to drive cost-efficiencies. Although it took several years after MiFID to gain regulatory approval in Europe for full interoperability between trading venues and clearing houses, the introduction of the principle of competition into the equity execution transaction chain demonstrated the cost and service benefits of technology-enabled connectivity between specialist service providers.

The new trading venues also needed to develop partnerships to guarantee supply of liquidity. Large bulge-bracket firms needed to protect their relationships with incumbent exchanges and so could only offer cautious encouragement and limited liquidity. As such, MTFs and ECNs (dubbed ATSs, or alternative trading systems, by Reg NMS) turned to the small but fast-growing group of electronic trading innovators that were already using algorithms to send equity orders to exchanges. These were the "flash boys" of Michael Lewis' 2014 book of the same name,[1] termed HFTs then and now largely known as electronic liquidity providers (ELPs).

Earlier pioneering efforts on trade standardization and automation in the late 1990s had laid the groundwork for the high-frequency technologies that employed significant additional firepower to trade at higher speeds than anyone previously considered necessary or possible. Partly driven by their desire to generate deeper levels of liquidity in competition with incumbent exchanges, alternative trading venues developed features and functionality that encouraged growth and innovation by HFT firms. For example, they supplied trading data with which to backtest new algorithms, introduced new order types and fee schedules that offered greater scope to develop innovative trading strategies, and offered low-latency connectivity and hosting facilities, which provided the fastest trading speeds to firms most willing and able to spend on trading technology and infrastructure.

But the collision between established and technology-enabled business models had mixed results for investment institutions and their end-users. Brokers and asset managers that tried to interact with HFT-supplied liquidity on MTFs and ATSs found themselves outwitted by faster, smarter market-making algorithms that would employ "bait and switch" tactics to give the appearance of further liquidity and lure liquidity seekers into paying slightly more than they had intended. As exchanges upped their game—employing similar tactics on price, order type, collocation—HFT firms deployed their well-honed technology to provide the lion's share of liquidity.

The fierce fight for equity market share between trading venues and liquidity providers should have been good news for those seeking to trade more efficiently in the world's more advanced stock markets. The reality was somewhat different, thanks in no small part to the difference in trading technology muscle. Trading costs rose, order sizes diminished and efforts to prove best execution (as required under MiFID) became highly complex and costly to achieve or demonstrate as liquidity fragmented across multiple venues. By 2012, over 40% of US equity trading volumes were conducted off exchange.

As complexity and fragmentation rose, so did systemic instability. The Flash Crash of 2010—when a rogue algorithm sparked a sudden 9% fall in the Dow Jones index—brought trading's frailties to a wider audience. But it was quickly followed by the collapse of US broker Knight Capital, caused by catastrophic losses by a malfunctioning market-making algorithm, and multiple glitches and outages as US and Europe upgraded their platforms in a bid to gain greater capacity and lower latency.

Disenchanted and frustrated by their experience on "lit" exchanges (that is, stock markets and other regulated venues required to provide pre-trade price transparency), market participants—especially buy-side firms seeking large-sized "block orders"—withdrew to other trading venues with more flexible rules. Some of these only allowed orders above a certain size threshold; most did not require pre-trade price transparency, thus offering a level of protection from more predatory players. Nevertheless, such dark pools proved controversial, partly because operators did not always admit to the full extent of HFT flow they permitted, but also due to the potential impact on price discovery. It is argued, often by exchange operators, that if too high a proportion of trading is conducted without contributing to the price formation process (and thus not subject to pre-trade price transparency rules), it is no longer clear what the best price is for a given stock. This weakens public confidence in the equity markets and diminishes end-investors' participation and savings appetite.

The perception that the equity markets no longer served the end-investor—nor the asset managers who in theory aggregate and represent their investment needs—is one that both regulators and the industry are trying to address, by new rules and new technology.

If the original MiFID aimed to reduce cost and improve outcomes by introducing greater competition, MiFID II takes a more direct approach to delivering a better deal for the end-investor. This includes restrictions on trades and venues that do not contribute to price formation, bans on commissions and inducements, and tougher standards on transparency, reporting, and best execution. With the regime still being rolled out, there is much discussion over whether MiFID II will reduce or increase trading costs, but like its predecessor the directive will rely on new, low-cost, technology-driven business models to deliver its promises to investors. ELPs have partnered with third parties to quickly establish new systematic internalizers (SIs) to deliver targeted liquidity in response to broker quotes; algorithms are being equipped with new artificial intelligence (AI) capabilities to self-monitor parameters, thus preventing risks to market stability; and trader and portfolio manager behavior is being monitored and informed by machine-learning tools in the interests of cost-effective and compliant trading.

In all cases, these tools and solutions are the result of collaboration between multiple service providers, with disparate components being brought together through digital technologies such as APIs, cloud, and AI. At the same time, similar approaches are resulting in new propositions in the retail trading investment space, with firms combining compelling app-based user experiences with global trading and risk management platforms to open up distant markets to new investors.

Foreign Exchange

As a high-volume, over-the-counter market with a diverse range of institutional, corporate, and retail participants, FX has adopted technology very quickly and successfully in some areas, but progress and benefits have been spread unevenly. FX market-making to institutional clients has long been automated, for example, with banks (and, subsequently, non-bank liquidity providers) supplying liquidity via automated price feeds, first on their own proprietary platforms then multi-dealer venues. Subsequently, retail / professional FX trading needs have been addressed successfully, with innovators supplying flexible, transparent, and low-cost FX services, increasingly via mobile apps. In the interim, the FX market has reformed itself in response to both industry-wide post-crisis regulatory change and the sector-specific rate-rigging scandals, with market participants committing to higher standards of transparency and integrity, via the FX Global Code. Technology has a crucial role to play in delivering on those commitments, as well as enabling further competition and innovation—for example, by shrinking the cost of providing customized FX services at scale to a wide range of participants.

The ten years since the financial crisis brought transformation to the global FX markets, with technology, regulation, and volatility all playing their part in shaping the priorities and business models of market participants. The decade was marked first by an increase in liquidity provision by non-traditional, tech-savvy non-bank liquidity providers competing with previously dominant global banks that were increasingly constrained by regulatory reforms as shocks in other financial markets boosted FX hedging activity.

As FX volumes were driven 35% higher to US$5.3tr between 2010 and 2013 (spot volumes rose 38%) by the increased hedging needs of pension funds and multinational corporates, non-bank liquidity providers gradually increased market share. According to the Bank for International Settlements triennial survey series, FX market turnover by large market-making banks was overtaken for the first time by other financial institutions in 2013, accounting for 53% of market share versus just 40% in 2007. Although this group of counterparties included a range of non-banks, institutional investors, and hedge funds, the growing activities of tech-enabled non-bank liquidity providers was a key factor. Technology not only helped to diversify liquidity provision away from banks, but it also fragmented liquidity across trading venues, which have grown from a handful in the early 2000s to more than seventy today.

To effect the shift in liquidity provision, ELPs utilized a combination of networking capabilities, data processing and computer muscle, and programming skills to develop low-latency market-making algorithms that could respond at unparalleled speed and scale to price movements on limit order books and price queries from a widening range of counterparties. Having started in the inter-dealer market, non-bank liquidity providers soon sent price interest directly and indirectly to banks and retail platforms and directly streamed them to other market participants. They had "significantly altered the FX market landscape"[2] by 2011. Inherent in the business models of the non-bank liquidity providers was access to credit and market infrastructure provided by prime brokering arms of banks, resulting in a complex relationship due to the impact of non-bank liquidity on those banks' FX spreads.

More recently, overall turnover has stagnated, with large banks' risk appetites still limited, accompanied by a degree of consolidation or withdrawal of market participants with volatility-based business models (such as some smaller non-bank liquidity providers and hedge funds). In the next three-year period captured by the BIS Triennial Survey, volumes reflected a post-crisis "new normal" in which banks and their institutional clients were using technology to help internalize flow. Between 2013 and 2016, the FX market fell 4% to US$5.1tr, with spot falling 19%, the first decline since 2001. As fewer trades hit the street, there was concern of an imbalance between a growing buy-side and a shrinking sell-side that may exacerbate liquidity challenges in a disorderly market. These concerns were reflected in the response of supervisory bodies, including the Bank of England to the market impact of the Swiss franc de-pegging in January 2015, which warned of over-reliance on a small number of highly interconnected counterparties.

A key challenge for the institutional FX market is to drive new efficiencies through application of technology innovation, learning the lessons not only of the non-bank liquidity providers' business models, but also the dynamism of the retail brokerage market, which is one of the few areas of FX volume growth. While total FX volumes plateaued between 2013 and 2016, retail activity increased, rising from 3.5% of total FX market turnover to 5.6% in three years, according to a Saxo analysis based on BIS and Bank of England figures. Indeed, other industry research suggests that this may underestimate retail growth.

Much of this growth is driven by the fierce competition between retail brokerages which are encouraging wider market participation by offering low costs, extensive market access, and rich functionality. They are able to do this largely through their adoption of business models that rely on access to a range of managed services and capabilities, streamlined and automated API-based interaction with counterparties and clients, and a focus on quality of user experience. Undeniably, the ability to offer high leverage due to a lack of uniform regulation is also a factor.

Across the decade, the common thread has been technology enabling new business models that challenge incumbents of the FX market, both brokers and trading platforms, resulting in a more fragmented market structure that is potentially more vulnerable to systemic risks, but which is also bringing new credit and liquidity services to the retail and professional market. Indeed, as the Swiss franc de-pegging amply highlighted, the question of counterparty credit continues to be one of the most important for FX market participants. Here too, technology has supported growth in the number of providers (prime of prime brokers) acting as credit intermediaries for smaller counterparties looking to access the market.

Fixed Income

The diversity of global fixed income markets has resulted in a wide range of trading tactics and channels used by buyers and sellers. Today, all markets use some form of automation, but the range of mechanisms and preferences is wider in fixed income, due partly to different levels of liquidity across instruments, but market structure issues and the needs of market participants also have significant influence. Highly liquid markets with global demand—such as US Treasuries—are as automated as any FX or equity market. But other large markets—such as interest-rate swaps—proved remained resolutely over-the-counter and bespoke and thus resistant to automation. It required a G-20 regulatory mandate issued in 2009 to force greater standardization and use of electronic trading platforms. Less liquid "buy-and-hold" markets with niche demand—such as US municipal bonds—can be traded partly by electronic means, but still retain strong elements of traditional structures.

A closer look at one of the best-known parts of the fixed-income universe—the corporate bond market—demonstrates how liquidity fragmentation and ingrained market practices can influence the often gradual and idiosyncratic application of technology. Until relatively recently, corporate bond trading has mainly resisted large-scale automation, using technology to support elements of the process, but with voice trading—discussion and negotiation with one or more sales traders at bank or broker counterparts—used for critical elements.

Liquidity fragmentation plays a major part in explaining trading processes for corporate bonds. Whereas four or five share types in a large corporate such as Volkswagen can be bought and sold on a handful of highly liquid exchanges, there are 136 different Volkswagen bonds to choose from, all with distinct characteristics in terms of tenor, yield, and other factors impacting attractiveness. Some of these issues will be frequently traded; others extremely rarely, but almost all are bought and sold over the counter—that is, a bilateral transaction typically between a broker and an investor, rather than via an exchange. Because they generally offer a predictable if low return for a long period, corporate bonds—especially those with a high credit rating—are held until maturity by relatively conservative investors. This means the portfolio manager interested in buying a bond that suits her precise needs has to cast a wide net, calling several brokers to find out whether they can track down owners in their client base that might be persuaded to sell.

Elements of this request for quote (RFQ) process can and have been automated, and the pace of innovation has increased recently in response to regulatory change. But historically the experience of most liquidity seekers in the corporate bond market has been one of opacity, inefficiency, and high costs in terms of commission, spread, and fees, which further serve to depress liquidity. In this context, only the largest corporate bond investors can expect to be able to access the bond issues they seek on a reliable basis, with smaller institutions having much more limited scope, let alone retail investors.

Automation of the RFQ process between dealers and clients started in the late 1990s, with single-dealer platforms soon giving way to multi-broker RFQ, where a request to buy a specific bond was sent electronically to a handful of relationship brokers simultaneously, delivering process efficiencies to both sides. During the 2000s, the adoption of electronic trading in corporate bonds grew gradually, albeit outstripped by the larger government bond markets—notably US Treasuries—where the dealer-to-dealer market in particular embraced technology. But it took regulatory-driven changes to the structure of the corporate bond market to accelerate migration to electronic trading. A key factor was the increasing costs of market-making and risk-warehousing under Basel III's regulatory restrictions after the 2008 recession, affecting capital, leverage, and balance sheets at banks, which have reduced sell-side holdings of bond inventory. This historic shift of bond holdings further toward investors and away from broker-dealers had a number of consequences for trading processes. Indeed, since 2008, the combined liquidity of tier-one dealer inventories in corporate bonds has slumped from 10% of total notional outstanding to approximately 1% today.

First, trading platforms launched new "all to all" trading protocols alongside existing RFQ-based trading services. These allow institutional investors to offer and take liquidity, in recognition of the decreasing likelihood that the required issue could be found via a broker acting in a principal capacity (that is, buying the bond from one client to sell to another). In this new paradigm for electronic bond trading, regional banks, brokers, pension funds, and asset managers all have the opportunity to offer price interest when a quote is requested—in essence, supplying event-driven liquidity on a virtual exchange.

Second, the stiffening liquidity challenge led to several initiatives that leveraged digital technology innovation to improve the quality and granularity of information available to liquidity seekers. Overall, these initiatives deployed AI and data analytics to leverage data across banks' internal systems to make it easier to identify liquidity holders in particular bond issues. Some proposed solutions went further toward a more comprehensive pooling and aggregation of supply and demand data.

According to Greenwich Associates,[3] 46% of fixed income investors now trade at least some of their volume by electronic means, up from around 35% a decade ago. Today, technology is also being used to broaden the multi-dealer RFQ process from large institutional investors to a wider range of smaller asset managers, family offices, and even retail investors. As in other classes, the latest wave of fintech innovation is bringing benefits previously only achieved by major institutions within the grasp of a larger population. New, fully straight-through-processing (STP) solutions are blending technology and connectivity in a way that rethinks the traditional value chain and enables any client type to access live RFQ multi-dealer competition, both in and out of standard trading hours. Using robotics to overcome traditional complexities of an over-the-counter market, such solutions widen market participation to a broader range of investors, thus helping to deliver price improvement and reduce overall transaction costs.

The pressure for change continues to mount. MiFID II extends best-execution requirements to trading in fixed income markets, demanding that investment firms demonstrate that they have taken all sufficient steps, rather than "all reasonable steps" as previously mandated. Other reporting and transparency requirements also demand a clearer audit trail for fixed-income trades. The combined impact not only encourages use of electronic trading protocols but also further automation of the overall process, from pre-trade analysis to post-trade reporting and compliance.

Open Banking

Although various markets, asset classes, and banking services had achieved distinctly varying levels of automation when the 2008 crisis hit, the large universal banks were impacted in similar ways by the regulatory response. Proprietary trading was limited or banned; risk-warehousing, liquidity-provision and other capital-intensive activities were heavily penalized; and compliance costs rocketed. Revenues, budgets, and return on equity all went in the same direction as interest rates in the era of quantitative easing, meaning the prior decade's process inefficiencies and 'build it and they will come' mindsets were a luxury few if any could now afford.

At the same time, the principles and practices that had already enabled technology-led start-ups to rip up existing business models in various consumer industries—e.g. entertainment, travel, and transport—were making their presence felt at the fringes of the bulge-bracket's retail franchises. Technology innovation had made it much easier than ever before for new entrants to put together a trading and/or investment business by buying the vast majority of the components off the shelf in support of a distinct value proposition. Critically, this wave of fintech innovation is driving greater choice, performance, and transparency in the retail space (for example, current accounts, wealth management, and micro-credit), whereas previous technology breakthroughs largely enabled advances and efficiencies in the wholesale or institutional space.

For large banks watching previously self-reinforcing business models unravel, fintech innovation may initially have been seen as a threat. But increasingly, it is appearing to be an enabler for incumbents willing to adjust to new market realities. Although challenger banks, peer-to-peer lenders, robo-advisors, and many others have been able to gain market share thanks in part to nimble, responsive business models and product development cycles, it is much harder to usurp existing service providers in tightly regulated, credit-driven, and highly complex wholesale markets.

As a result, start-ups and banks are increasingly working together to improve and transform internal processes and deliver superior, differentiated digital services to both retail and wholesale customers, based on complementary attributes. In addition to their grasp of new technologies and ecosystems, fintech start-ups bring a focus on customer experience, the understanding of heightened user expectations in the digital economy (in terms of service transparency, personalization, convenience, and speed), and the agile or "fail fast" approach to product development. In this model, solutions and services are developed and aggregated from a range of underlying components, often reliant on third-party capabilities, then quickly tested, rolled out to customers, and adjusted and refined in line with feedback streaming back from users' devices. Meanwhile, banks bring to the table a wide range of valuable capabilities, including deep customer relationships and assets; credit provision and risk absorption; compliance and regulatory expertise; domain and market knowledge; and robust operational infrastructure and controls.

But these nascent relationships are being bolstered by the fact that the infrastructure and resources for effective collaboration in solution development are fast-maturing. Having previously bought and operated their own data centers and networking capabilities to support market connectivity, risk management calculations, and algorithmic trading tools, even large banks are accepting the operational and financial benefits of sourcing managed solutions from third-party suppliers via public, private, and hybrid cloud solutions. This allows them to tap various infrastructure, platforms, and other tools and solutions "as a service," but also offers access to the computer power and related resources needed to fuel the AI/ML programs that will drive efficient service personalization, process improvement, and support regulatory compliance and anti-financial crime measures.

As well as cloud-based access, a critical enabler of these collaborative business models is the greater use of APIs in an open system to facilitate data flows between counterparties, partners, and clients (see also Chapter 10 on open APIs and banking). APIs are having a number of complementary impacts, tending to support the development of new services in some contexts, and more efficient processes in others, but facilitating new business models across the whole industry. In complex, highly-regulated wholesale markets, for example, where legacy systems can constrain functionality but are too ingrained to be replaced, APIs are helping to improve the quality and speed of data flows between departments and counterparties, and also to aggregate data from individual systems to allow AI-based analysis to improve process efficiency and client responsiveness. In retail markets, APIs are enabling separate services to be combined into the same seamless user experience, perhaps allowing payment services to be embedded in taxi apps, or transactions and balances from multiple accounts being viewed in a single window.

But in all financial markets, APIs are lowering costs of entry, enabling new connections, and increasing competition and service quality. In short, they are critical to the development of new service and business models. They are a fundamental building block of an evolving industry that is migrating to an open architecture, in which ownership of physical assets is much less important than the ability to aggregate and remold an evolving range of skills, processes, and resources in a way that keeps pace with client needs.

Newer service providers are developing and then scaling up their offerings by incorporating the capabilities of a range of third parties. These partners may be offering complementary services, access to customers in new markets, or infrastructure capabilities such as data centers or risk management tools, but they will almost certainly be doing so via APIs. Equally, incumbents can and are using APIs in an increasingly diverse range of scenarios, from developing collaborative relationships with fintechs and other service providers to enabling existing customers to interrogate their systems on a real-time basis, enabling access to the information they want, whenever and however they want it, rather than waiting for an end-of-day report trapped in a PDF.

The use of APIs by incumbent banks has been accelerated by regulatory mandates and government sponsored initiatives, specifically but not exclusively in the payments space. Both the European Union's second Payment Services Directive (PSD II) and the UK's Open Banking initiative require banks to free up access to customer data to authorized third parties, thus enabling them to supply new services to consumers. These started with account aggregation services that provide a consolidated view of a person's or small company's finances but also now use banking history to accelerate loan approvals and to generate more targeted, actionable information from price comparison websites. But regulators around the world are increasingly seeing APIs as a means of developing new solutions to tackle longstanding efficiencies and unlock new value for customers across the whole sector. For example, the Monetary Authority of Singapore identified 100 financial-sector challenges for fintechs to address in 2016, ranging from trade finance to portfolio management: 71 involved the use of APIs.

Adoption varies across markets, but in many areas API-centric business models are already maturing. In the markets serving retail and professional traders—notably but not exclusively FX brokerage—the technology, people and processes of leading brokers and market-makers are increasingly orientated toward APIs. This means not only that the business uses APIs to aggregate the required infrastructure and capabilities to operate in an efficient, flexible and scalable fashion in multiple markets, but APIs also become the main way in which the broker interacts with clients and counterparts to develop and test trading models and to source data and liquidity.

If one considers the characteristics of fintech services that are challenging incumbent providers—easily scalable, capital-efficient, highly personalized, user-centric, client-responsive, seamlessly multi-functional—it becomes clear that APIs, cloud, and AI are essential components of many if not all competitive service propositions in the trading space.

The Future

Already, it is possible to conceive of a virtual corporate and investment bank that could challenge and replace the conglomerates that were built from waves of consolidation in the 1980s and 1990s (and which may still run systems using code from even earlier decades). Building a digital bank from scratch will not be done primarily through M&A, but through the delivery of a unique value proposition via the aggregation of an easily interchangeable range of resources and capabilities, only the most quintessential of which will be developed in-house. Whether such a proposition will be brought to market by a tech-savvy bank or the banking arm of a tech giant is hard to say.

A quick look at any sub-sector of the trading and investment universe indicates the pace of fintech-driven change and the risks of making predictions. Fintech first made itself known in the wealth management space via robo-advisors, offering low-cost investments to the mass affluent, via menu-driven, AI-assisted platforms in competition with US financial advisors. But they soon became much more sophisticated and diverse, deployed to meet the precise demands of high-net worth individuals either directly as sophisticated apps or as relationship management tools for private banks. In either case, the key to value lies in the aggregation and integration of multiple front- and back-end capabilities, with enhancements, recommendations, and customizations informed by a data-driven feedback loop.

Across the spectrum, the opportunity is enormous. How far can fintech take automation of bond trading, for example? Over-the-counter markets may have been resistant to technology for a long time, but growing use of robotics suggests humans can be taken further out of the loop. And soon. By using robotics technology, bond investors and traders will soon be able to place an order and then leave the robot to navigate the all-to-all trading environment. If an offer or an RFQ pops up in the specific issue sought, the robot will respond, not only activating the order, but also countering RFQs with specific bids and sizes based on several parameters.

Further, cognitive functions (driven by machine learning and natural language processing) will enable trading robotics to move up the evolutionary ladder, learning from experience. If, for example, a bond market enters a panic sell-off mode, the robot will "remember" past similar occurrences and recall which venue has the highest probability of liquidity and also have a precise idea of the firm price levels to expect compared to indicative prices, the total slippage for a position unwinding, as well as expected maximum trading sizes available. The combined impact of new technology, new fintech participants, regulations, and a wish for efficiency and scalability have the potential power to transform the bond markets within the next three years.

One safe prediction is that APIs will continue to mature and diversify. Indeed, increasing efforts are being made on standardization to ensure continued interoperability of APIs even as they develop and specialize. One sign of API maturity in recent years is the evolution away from REST APIs, for which data is sent only in response to an incoming query. In contrast, streaming/push-based APIs are set up to transmit streams of data on a continuous basis—for example, sending out a message for every price movement of a particular instrument, when an order is filled, or when a certain threshold is broken or business process has been completed. Further, as APIs mature, they will become an inherent part of the product development processes for all financial service providers.

Whereas once the establishment of a global trading service to retail clients would have involved many months if not years of system investment, infrastructure integration, recruitment rounds, and regulatory approvals—all at a substantial cost—a new business idea can go global and grow market share in a matter of months. One implication is that no firm can ever afford to rest on its laurels; another is that any firm can grasp an opportunity quickly and decisively, without significant outlay of time or cost.

The traditional financial services conglomerate generated a complex technology stack that was fragmented by channel (branches, ATMs, call centers, telephone- and internet-based platforms, and sales teams), business silo (insurance, retail, wealth, corporate, and capital markets), and systems (disparate databases, applications, and CRM platforms). As such, it is little wonder that banks rarely had a complete view of the customer, or were unable to quantify their risk or optimize their opportunity across their service range.

In many other industries, the technologies that we have highlighted in this chapter have given rise to platform-based models, whereby firms derive revenues from bringing together third parties with common interests.

This model may have a future in finance too. Under a Banking-as-a-Service (BaaS) model, a service provider could put together the infrastructure, expertise, and processes needed to provide back-end banking and trading capabilities via open APIs to customer-facing service providers which can then focus their internal resources on providing a uniquely compelling user experience. Banks may not necessarily have to choose between being customer-focused (B2C) and being an infrastructure operator and supplier (B2B), but the technology-enabled ability to unbundle previously packaged components of trading and other banking services suggests a clear trend in this direction.

Service providers are already partnering with banks and brokers on a BaaS basis, providing integrated pre-trade, execution, and post-trade services serving self-directed, advisory, and discretionary clients, alongside integrated risk management, reporting, and compliance capabilities, on a fully integrated basis which supports rapid deployment of new apps. In this structure, open APIs facilitate partnerships with leading technology providers and communities, enable external provision of data, applications and solutions throughout the trade lifecycle, and drive operational efficiency and reduce cost through automation.

Case Study—Saxo

To survive and thrive in the new paradigm, firms must combine expertise in financial service provision with mastery of technology. This has been a founding principle at Saxo Bank Group, guiding both the development of our online brokerage services and our adoption of collaborative business models that leverage APIs and other fintech innovations. In the future, a grasp of technology's power and potential will be a prerequisite.

At Saxo, we already work under the assumption that any functionality we develop will at some point be shared with counterparties and or clients via an API. This very expectation will increase competition and service quality, forcing all service providers to make a conscious decision about where their strengths lie, and where they should rely on collaboration with third parties.

One template for future fintech collaborations could be Saxo's partnership with WeBull. WeBull was founded in 2016 by Anquan Wang, previously a driving force behind Alibaba Financial and Xiaomi Finance. The aim is to bring global capital markets' information and trading within easy reach of the average investor anywhere in the world via a state-of-the-art app, which to date has over eight million customers. Leveraging the integration with Saxo, WeBull is able to offer its customers immediate access to the entire trading value chain from wide-ranging market access through to execution, custody, and accounting flows.

Saxo's digital brokerage integration services include both onboarding information transfer and trading interface. This means that WeBull is able to gather and deliver all the necessary client information (such as identification documentation) directly into Saxo's systems, thus supporting a rapid and smooth client onboarding experience. Once the introduced client is approved, the client can immediately view real-time information of their Saxo trading account and place trades directly from WeBull's app. This seamless experience is made possible via a combination of APIs and order-handling technologies that are made available to Saxo's fintech partners. Hence, while Saxo handles all client account management, funding, connectivity, trade execution, and post-trade processes, similar to a traditional outsourcing partnership, fintech partners such as WeBull can focus on continuously improving the front-end user experience of their app.

The APIs also play a key role in ensuring that such apps are able to closely monitor the client's account activity and deliver highly personalized account representation to their customers. Saxo's API is able to persistently keep partner apps informed on any significant activities—such as a margin call or an order fill—so that clients can receive timely notifications via in-app push messages.

Even with such extensive capabilities, the speed of API integration can still be relatively quick, as was the case with the WeBull app

Endnotes

1 *Flash Boys*, W. W. Norton & Company, 2014.
2 "High-frequency trading in the FX market," Bank for International Settlements, September 2011. https://www.bis.org/publ/mktc05.pdf
3 Greenwich Associates 2008–2016 Global Fixed-Income Studies.

Saxo Bank Group *(Saxo) is a leading multi-asset trading and investment specialist, offering a complete set of trading and investment technologies, tools and strategies.*

For almost 25 years, Saxo's mission has been to enable individuals and institutions by facilitating their access to professional trading and investing through technology and expertise.

As a fully licensed and regulated bank, Saxo enables its private clients to trade multiple asset classes across global financial markets from one single margin account and across multiple devices. Additionally, Saxo provides institutional clients such as

banks and brokers with multi-asset execution, prime brokerage services and trading technology.

Founded in 1992 and headquartered in Copenhagen, Saxo employs more than 1500 people in financial centres around the world including London, Singapore, Paris, Zurich, Dubai and Tokyo.

Contributing experts: Adam Reynolds, CEO APAC; Aditya Laroia, Country Head of Origination, Singapore; Ashok Kalyanswamy, Chief Information Officer; Benny Boye Johansen, Head of Open API Chris Truce, Head of FinTech; Simon Fasdal, Head of Fixed Income and Tom Lee, FX Product Manager

Learn more: www.home.saxo/sg

Chapter 15
Disruption in Investment Management

Investment management as a business has faced disruption by many forces over the last few decades, especially as it has one of the highest ROEs of all industries and requires a relatively small amount of capital expenditure on an ongoing basis, implying relatively low barriers to entry.

The first wave of disruption to traditional active management, a fee-led disruption, started in the late 1970s, when John Bogle launched the first index fund, which provided a low-cost option to investors to gain exposure to equity markets. This philosophy of low-cost, no-load, passive investing gathered pace over the subsequent four decades to become a significant segment of the asset management marketspace. Augmented by the advent of enhanced indexing in the early 1990s, pioneered by the company later known as Barclays Global Investors (BGI), index and enhanced index products became a significant force in reducing the fee structure of active asset management products worldwide.

The second wave of disruption, a return-led disruption, gathered pace in the 1990s, with the proliferation of hedge funds, which promised to deliver pure *alpha*, or return uncorrelated to financial markets, which theoretically would be available in any market condition. While this promise has subsequently been challenged, at the time it created pressure on all asset managers to prove that their products also delivered alpha, and winnowed out the poor from the skilled manager.

The third wave of disruption, a distribution-led disruption, happened in the 2000s, after the bursting of the internet bubble. Financial services firms were forced to rethink the prevailing financial supermarket business model and question whether they were a distributor or manufacturer of asset management investment products. This led most banks and insurance companies to choose to become only a distributor with an open architecture platform for investment products made by multiple specialized asset management firms.

Since the global financial crisis in 2007, a new wave of disruption has begun in asset management, which is based on creating greater focus on the actual customized requirements of asset owners. This solutions-based disruption is gathering pace with the deployment of technology to the asset management investment model. In the previous waves of disruption, while the business model of the asset management business was impacted and forced to adapt, the investment model was largely untouched apart from progressive evolution. The large scale availability of extensive investment data and the greater use of technology and mathematical process to gain insights into that data will force a number of changes with the investment process itself. This disruption is likely to impact several fundamental principles of the incumbent investment model, some of which are detailed in this chapter.

DOI 10.1515/9781547400904- 015

The Transition Toward Outcome-Oriented Absolute Return Products

The asset owner investment problem can be articulated in a very simple manner—to maximize the probability of achieving a desired level of return, such that the assets are always sufficient to meet future expected liabilities, while at the same time minimizing the probability of having a shortfall of assets below liabilities. This is illustrated in Figure 15.1. No matter what the nature of the asset owner—sovereign wealth, pension, endowment, insurance, family office, high net-worth individual, or the retail individual—all articulate their investment problem as a target absolute return (calculated and expressed based on inflation, liabilities, or interest rates), subject to a threshold of risk tolerance.

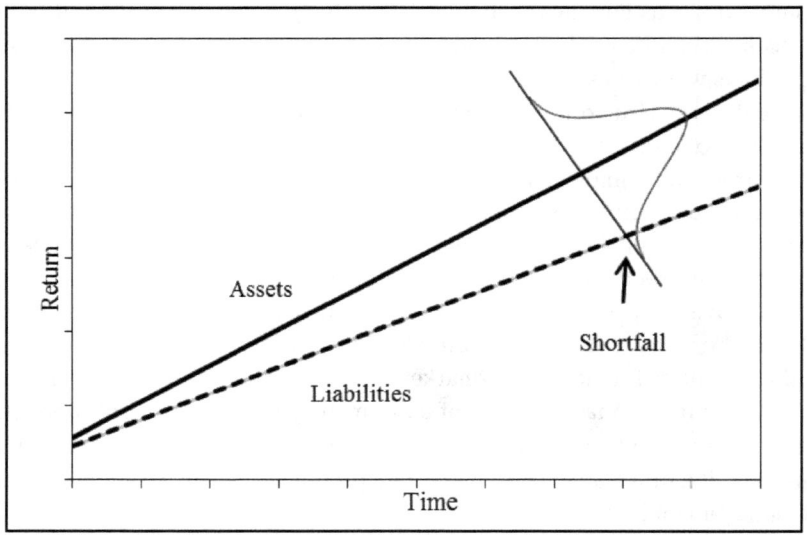

Source: Gupta P. et al., *Multi-Asset Investing: A Practitioner's Framework*, Wiley Finance.

Figure 15.1: The transition toward outcome-oriented absolute return investing

However, despite the knowledge that the asset owner only cares about total absolute return, the investment industry has chosen predominantly to create products which deliver return relative to market indices. This has resulted in a gap being created between the requirements of the asset owner and what is delivered by the asset manager. The basic asset owner investment problem remains largely unsolved by the asset management industry. Over the next decade, we believe that the presence of this gap will result in a shift toward outcome-oriented absolute return investment products and away from benchmark relative alpha products.

Transition Toward Allocation as the Central Investment Problem

In the traditional model of investing, it is believed that asset owners should follow two successive processes to construct their portfolio after having defined their requirement of risk and return—asset allocation, followed by manager or strategy selection. The former is labelled as *beta return*, or return to broad market indices, and the latter isclassified as *alpha*, or *portfolio return*, which is independent of market return and generated by skill-based strategies. In this context, it is well accepted that about 90% of the portfolio's risk comes from the asset allocation decision, and only the remaining 10% or so comes from the security selection decision. Yet the structure of the investment industry has resulted in exactly the opposite focus. Over 90% of the resources, investment skills, investment products, and fees generated are focused on the security/strategy/manager selection problem, which accounts for only 10–20% of the asset owner's portfolio; only the remaining fraction is time and effort spent on the allocation problem. And this is true for any kind of market participant, be it an asset manager, an investment bank, an investment consultant, or indeed the asset owner organization itself. This anomaly is illustrated in Figure 15.2.

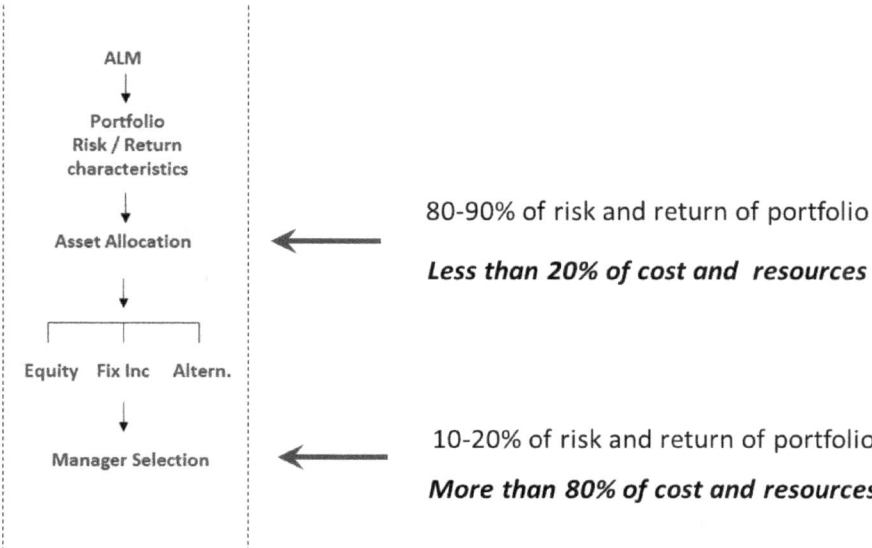

Source: Gupta P. et al., *Multi-Asset Investing: A Practitioner's Framework*, Wiley Finance.
Figure 15.2: Importance of the allocation process

We believe that this anomaly will rebalance over the next decade. The focus on the allocation process will increase while focus on the security and strategy selection deci-sion will decrease, as asset owners realise that allocation isthe central and paramount problem for all portfolios and in each segment of a portfolio. This will create the need for greater resources, greater skill, and more diverse products in the allocation space.

Implementation of Multiple Concurrent Allocation Investment Processes

The security selection problem has long been the focus of researchers, which has resulted in a rich and diverse set of strategies in the area. Indeed, portfolio managers and their institutions often go to great lengths to publicize the style of investing they adopt, in a bid to differentiate themselves and gain traction within a specific strategy category. It is frequently recommended that asset owners invest in a variety of such strategy categories concurrently in order to get the benefit of diversification.

However, the same logic has not permeated into allocation space. Even today, despite the knowledge that risk is concentrated in the allocation decision process, almost all asset owner portfolios follow a single allocation methodology that is created by a single investment process and done by a single team (internal or external consultant) at a single investment horizon.

As depicted in Figure 15.3, Gupta et al. demonstrate that the use of multiple allocation processes within a portfolio results in a more efficient portfolio. The ability to move across efficient frontiers by adding to the number of allocation methodologies facilitates the ability to generate the same return with a lower level of risk (Arrow A), a higher return for the same level of risk (Arrow B), or indeed follow the traditional approach of higher risk to higher return by moving along the efficient frontier (Arrow C).

With the realization that the majority of asset owner asset liability gaps are created with a sub-optimal allocation structure and are not the result of poor strategy selection, this facet will change. Every asset owner portfolio will progressively incorporate multiple absolute return allocation processes to garner diversification in the hitherto concentrated allocation space.

Diversity in Allocation Investment Processes

Just as there are multiple processes to select securities, there can be multiple approaches to construct an allocation. The traditional allocation process was confined to a long-term analysis of asset class risk premia, which created the basis for a strategic asset allocation for the complete portfolio. This, however, is one of the numerous approaches that can be followed within an allocation strategy and can be formulated at multiple horizons, similar to the security selection processes. Figure 15.4 categorizes a number of allocation approaches that are being used today, but this list can expand quite dramatically as more research in new allocation processes is done.

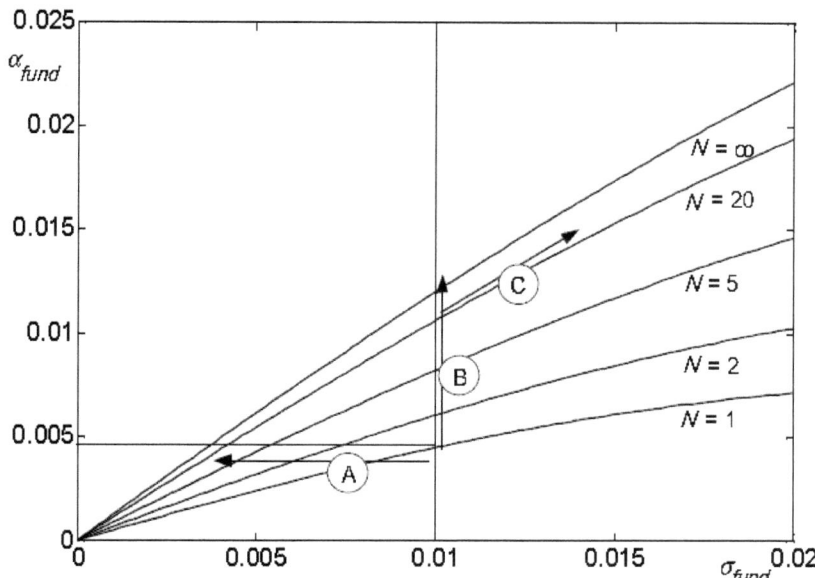

Source: Gupta P. et al., *Multi-Asset Investing: A Practitioner's Framework*, Wiley Finance.
Figure 15.3: The impact of using multiple allocation approaches in a portfolio

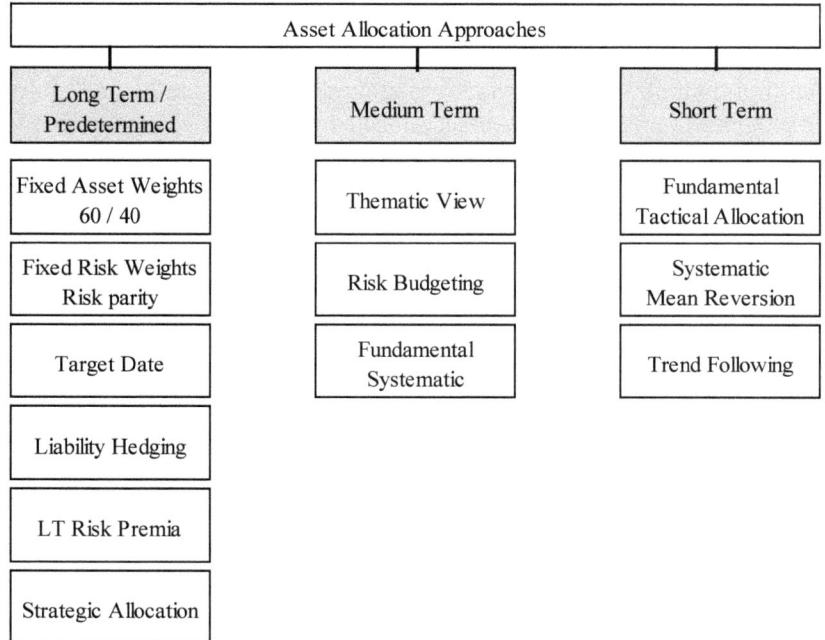

Source: Gupta P. et al., *Multi-Asset Investing: A Practitioner's Framework*, Wiley Finance.
Figure 15.4: Diversity in allocation approaches and their investment horizons

Asset management firms historically have felt compelled to choose only one style of investing across all the strategies managed by their firm. Hence at the organization level they were characterized as a value manager or a growth manager. This changed about a decade ago when it became apparent that all investment styles go through a performance cycle, and hence both from a business and client portfolio standpoint, it made sense to have strategies of different styles within the same firm.

In the allocation space, the same debate happens today with firms entrenching themselves as fundamental strategic allocators or quantitative risk parity allocators. In reality, just as in security selection styles, all styles of allocation investment processes are required both within an asset manager and within an asset owner's portfolio. As such, we believe that within the next decade, firms will begin to offer multiple styles of allocation products without the predisposition that they can only follow a single allocation style across their firm.

Change in the Asset Owner Portfolio Structure

While the rationale for the transition to multiple allocation processes is clear, the practical transition of asset owner portfolios to accommodate this fact will be gradual, as it is always difficult for any institution to discard a long-used philosophy and switch to unfamiliar territory.

Figure 15.5 shows that the first step toward the use of multiple allocation processes is being achieved today by the creation of a fourth silo of multi-asset absolute return in the traditional framework structured around equities, bonds, and alternatives. The progressive increase in the asset allocated to this box will result in the gradual decrease in concentration in the overall allocation decision toward the other three silos.

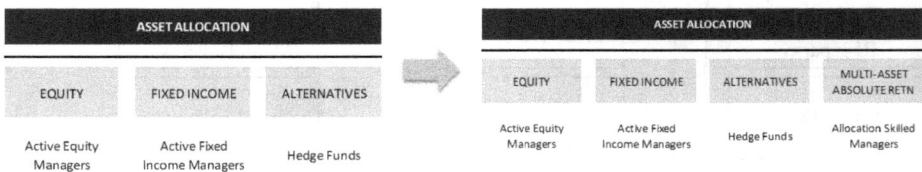

Figure 15.5: Transition of asset owner portfolios

The eventual state that should result, especially in progressive institutional investor portfolios, is one where multiple allocation methodologies are present, with each being allocated an appropriate amount of risk or capital.

Change in the Asset Owner Portfolio Process

The traditional investment process of most asset owners is based on allocation of assets by a single methodology into a neatly categorized asset class silos structure. However, as traditional asset classes have now been augmented by hybrid assets that span the spectrum of equity and fixed-income risk exposures, the neat categorization no longer provides an optimal allocation or analysis structure. To account for this instrument availability, the allocation structure of asset owners has to evolve from an asset class-based allocation to exposure-based allocation progress. However, rather than discard the old process at once, we believe there will be a stage wise migration to the new structure. Figure 15.6 shows the stages in this transition.

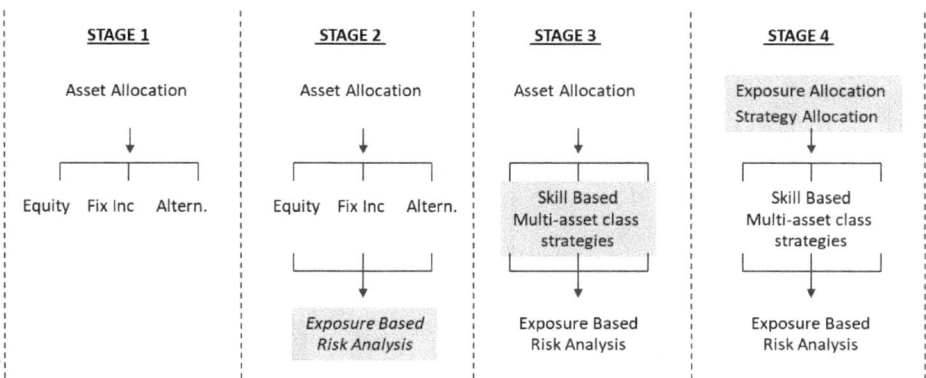

Source: Gupta P. et al., *Multi-Asset Investing: A Practitioner's Framework*, Wiley Finance.

Figure 15.6: Progressive stages in the transition of institutional portfolios

The conventional structure depicted in Stage 1 while allocated by asset classes, inherently is a composite of numerous exposures. Without changing the allocation framework, it is easily possible to analyze the composite portfolio by an exposure-based risk analysis system. This is Stage 2 in the evolution process. Once the actual exposures of the portfolio are known, the selection of additional strategies can be done not only with consideration of asset class allocation targets, but also including their impact of risk exposures in other dimensions. This Stage 3 thus expands the allocation process in numerous dimensions. Finally, as the organization becomes comfortable with an exposure-based analysis framework, the final Stage 4 would be to augment the allocation process with taking decisions on allocation along lines of strategy and exposure.

Redefinition of the Concept of Asset Class Risk Premium

The foundation of asset allocation was the belief in separate asset classes, which were historically thought to be synonymous with instrument categories—that is, equities and bonds. With the greater diversity in hybrid instruments spanning multiple exposures, this direct one-to-one relationship between asset classes and instruments is challenged. As a result, the concept of risk premium of an asset class is also subject to review.

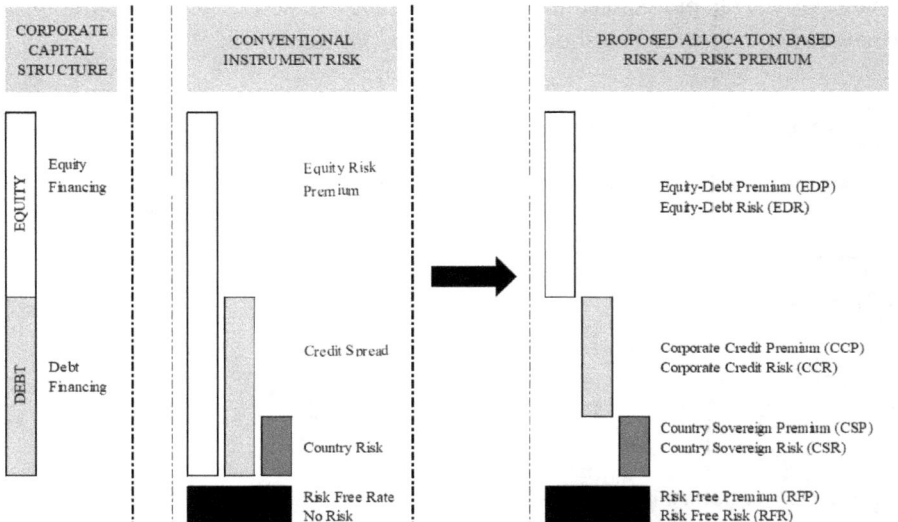

Source: Gupta P. et al., *Multi-Asset Investing: A Practitioner's Framework*, Wiley Finance.
Figure 15.7: Redefinition of asset class risk premium

We are of course aware that both basic asset classes are integrally related in the balance sheet of a company, in terms of capital structure and mode of financing for a company (first column in Figure 15.7). However, the classical academic definition of asset class premium (equity risk premium and credit risk premium) uses a common base of the risk free rate of return, and treats the risk premium of each asset class as independent. Any long-term return above this base rate for each asset class is labelled as its risk premium. This is depicted in the middle column in Figure 15.7.

Ironically, the very basis of allocation relies on the allocation silos being mutually exclusive and uncorrelated. An independent and overlapping structure of risk premium between equity and credit therefore defies logic from a practical allocation standpoint. This overlapping structure manifests itself in the frequent commentary in financial markets of the increased correlation between equities and bonds, especially in a crisis.

A redefinition of asset class risk premium to be mutually exclusive and laddered would improve the allocation framework. This is displayed in the right column in Figure 15.7. While this does not resolve the correlation problem completely, it does present a framework where the risk of an instrument is differentiated from the risk of an asset class, and there is logical alignment between the assumptions inherent in allocation and the framework used to make the allocation decision. This redefinition of risk premia to cater for the reality of investing in a multi-asset world allows for a more holistic approach to the asset owner investment problem.

The Transition to an Exposure-based Framework

A generalization of the laddering of risk premia leads us to a variation of the *arbitrage pricing theory model*, where the total return of an asset or portfolio is the result of the collective exposure taken in various dimensions of factor risk and the payoff as a result of those exposures. This is depicted in Figure 15.8, where r_p is the return of the portfolio above the risk-free rate; r0, bi are the risk factors; and λ is the payoff to the risk factor, all constructed in a time series of returns.

$$r_p(t) - r_0(t) \quad = \quad [\lambda_1(t)\, b_1(t) + \ldots + \lambda_p(t)\, b_p(t)] \quad + \quad [\lambda_{p+1}(t)\, b_{p+1}(t) + \ldots + \lambda_K(t)\, b_K(t)]$$

Commoditized beta	Non-commoditized beta
Traditional beta space	Traditional alpha space
beta = f(instrument availability)	alpha = f(non-commoditized beta)

Source: Gupta P. et al., *Multi-Asset Investing: A Practitioner's Framework*, Wiley Finance.

Figure 15.8: Alpha and beta return components in an exposure-based framework

There are many subtle implications of the transition to this framework:
- First and foremost, the concept of categorization of portfolio return into alpha and beta becomes obsolete. The return to any portfolio of assets is simply as a result of the composite risk exposures of those assets. Beta return is simply the return from the first risk factor: market exposure. More importantly, we should evaluate both alpha and beta using the same yardstick, which is not prevalent today.
- The discussion of active versus passive investing and which one is better also becomes obsolete. Each of those products is just a package of exposures, each with their own risk and return characteristics, and can be taken in any amount by any investor.
- This also provides a more rigorous framework for the evaluation of alpha, which is often represented as active management skill. If a manager generates alpha simply by taking a single static bet (for example to value, or to a size category),

then this is simply a "beta" return to a different risk factor. True skill would only be that component of the return of the portfolio which remains after all other factor bets have been accounted for.

– The alpha/beta divide thus also becomes a time-varying distinction. A risk factor that is not available today in a commoditized, liquid, cheap instrument would be categorized in alpha space. However, as and when such an instrument does become available, it would be a beta risk factor.

– There are multiple types of investment strategies that we believe exist today. Examples are fundamental and quantitative, top-down and bottom-up, macro and stock selection, high-frequency trading, and medium-term forecasting. However, in our factor framework, each of these strategies simply become a basket of risk factors that the portfolio manager has chosen to focus on, as he believes he has skill in forecasting those particular variables compared to the others. The strategy diversification concept becomes not a function of the skill of the strategy itself, but a function of the variables on which it is focusing.

Creation of Large Number of Indices as Passive Product Benchmarks

A further ramification of the exposure-based framework described above is the impact on benchmarks and their use in investing. The total market index constructed by many companies, such as MSCI and S&P, is simply a representation of the first risk factor, market exposure. Historically, the regular calculation of a market benchmark was cumbersome, due to technology processing and storage capability, and hence index creation became a business in itself, which was conveniently used by asset managers to create relative return products. However, with the ease and availability of security data, and the increase in computing storage and processing, it is easy for anyone to create an index of any kind. Nothing prevents an index being created, which is a representation of other or multiple risk exposures. Arguably, these are the benchmarks that are being constructed and followed in a passive style by enhanced index or smart beta managers.

An implication of the exposure framework is that that there will be a proliferation of benchmarks in all dimensions, which can be made by any firm. Hence passive investing as a philosophy will continue to grow, but the products will follow numerous benchmarks, apart from the currently available market index passive products.

The real investment problem of the amount of risk or assets to allocate to each investment product (index), is to generate the required portfolio return, which will dominate the portfolio problem.

Redefinition of Risk Measures to Include Intra-horizon Risk

Just as the process of allocation and analysis will evolve with the availability and use of technology and analysis methods, the risk process will evolve as well. Conventional risk measures such as volatility are easy to understand and use, but have serious short-comings particularly in terms of alignment with risk as articulated by an asset owner.

All conventional parameters used in risk analysis focus on risk at the end of the investment horizon, or the risk undertaken if the investor was to hold the asset for a specified duration. This, however, does not accommodate the path followed by the asset value. From a structural, regulatory, and behavioral perspective, all asset owners, individuals, or institutions are susceptible to the value of their portfolio at each point within the investment horizon. As such if two assets with exactly the same volatility were compared, traditional risk measures do not distinguish between them. However, one of those assets may undergo a substantially different intra-horizon drawdown than the other, despite overall end of period volatility being the same. The asset owner would inherently attribute more risk to the asset with a higher intra-horizon drawdown, and may even be forced to take investment decisions mid-stream as a result of this.

Figure 15.9 shows the path of two assets with the same volatility over a two-year period. While the asset with the light line is held for the total period to achieve the expected return, the asset with the dark line reaches the threshold of maximum loss of the asset owner, at which point he is forced to sell the asset and thus not realize the expected return.

Moreover, the real risk of these two assets is substantially different as the probability of the second asset breaching a loss threshold is higher than the first asset. We believe that the definitions and parameters used to measure risk will evolve to incorporate the intra-horizon risk of any asset.

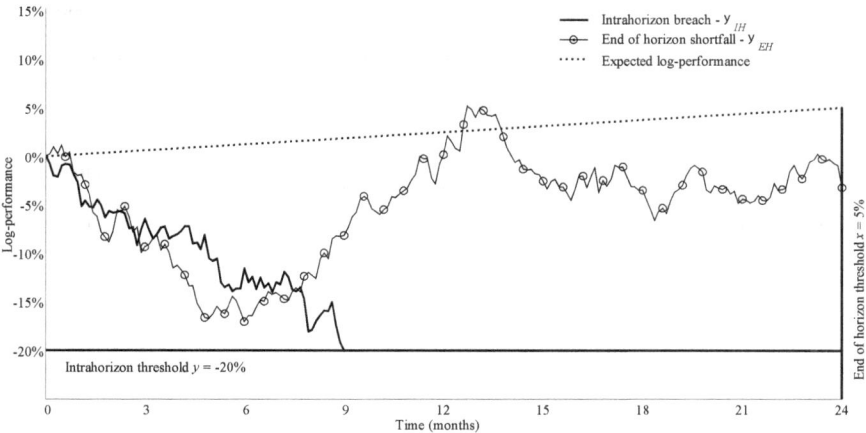

Source: Gupta P. et al., *Multi-Asset Investing: A Practitioner's Framework*, Wiley Finance.

Figure 15.9: Two assets with equal volatility, with one (dark) being liquidated when it reaches the threshold of maximum loss of the asset owner

Asset Management Distribution to Change from Product-centric to Client-centric

The traditional model of asset management has been based on the creation and distribution of standardized products which had a defined market index as a benchmark. This model operated largely in a structure where the asset manager was unaware of the actual constraints and liability structure of the asset owner. The same standard product was distributed to any asset owner, irrespective of their particular situation, and thus allowed the asset manager to have scale in products and to maximize profitability of the business.

In reality, however, each asset owner is faced with regulatory frameworks, governance frameworks, and different characteristics of liabilities that have a significant impact on the asset portfolio that is appropriate for them. This facet is not accommodated in the current asset management distribution structure. The availability of tools to have a grasp of asset owner liabilities, and the ability to use technology to create customized investment solutions at a low cost will change this situation. As a result, while portfolio managers can continue to focus on the investment problem of specific products that they manage, the distribution structure composed of sales and marketing and product specialists will need to evolve. This is depicted in Figure 15.10.

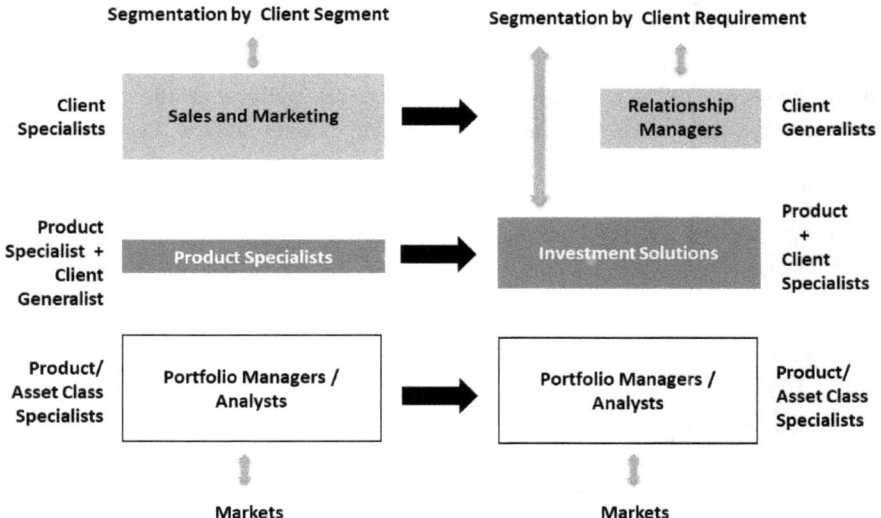

Figure 15.10: Evolution of the asset management distribution model with the advent of investment solutions

The current distribution structure is centered on sales and marketing staff being segmented by client areas and representing all products of the firm. They are supported in the representation process by product specialists who are focused on a single set of products. Neither is aware of client-specific requirements or has intimate knowledge of products across the firm, and so is not equipped to create a customized client solution.

The transition to a client-centric solutions model will imply that the relationship management function of sales and marketing staff will require fewer people. Concurrently, the product specialist function will likely need to expand to incorporate skills where they understand the liability structure of clients, become multi-asset skilled, and are able to use portfolio construction skills to create a customized client solution.

Incorporation of Technology in the Investment Model

The primary reason for all the preceding changes to happen in the coming years is the wider use of technology, data, and quantitative analysis methodologies in every aspect of the investment decision process. This incorporation will happen as each asset management firm develops an in-house analysis platform which can be customized to suit its product set and the clients it targets. Figure 15.11 depicts the variety of analysis and reports that are possible by implementing such a platform within an asset management business. Note that this is distinct and different from the existing middle-office, transaction, and trading systems that are present today. A quantitative analysis platform is used solely for the purpose of analysis. It is inexact in its data (unlike a performance system, which requires compliance-vetted data), extremely flexible in altering its methodologies, and managed and developed by the front office. Further, as the investment world evolves, it is natural for the analysis platform to also evolve in its methodologies.

A quantitative analysis platform can be built around a central database hub, with an integration of buy-and-build tools, such that it reflects the vision of an investment decision maker, rather than an off-the-shelf model of any kind.

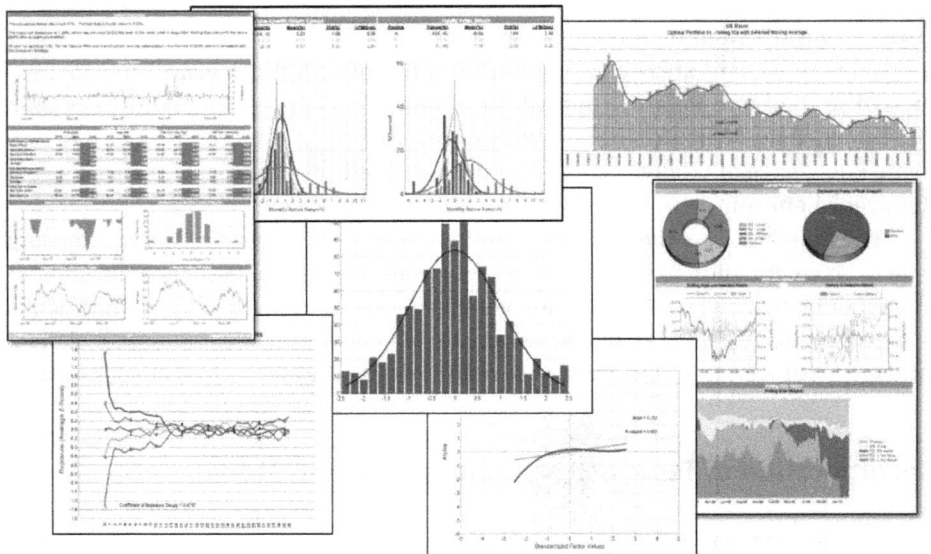

Source: Gupta P. et al., *Multi-Asset Investing: A Practitioner's Framework*, Wiley Finance.

Figure 15.11: An example of a sophisticated diagnostic analytical framework

A critical aspect of the implementation of a central quantitative analysis platform is its use in the true sense in investment decision making. Historically, quantitative systems have received lip service from traditional portfolio managers, and only have a presence as they present clients with a uniform way of calculating risk across asset management firms with different processes. Their use has therefore not made any meaningful impact in most asset management firms, despite their subscription to such services.

With the increasing availability of big data from various businesses in every aspect of consumption and production, it has become an information set that is too big to ignore, even for the most traditional of portfolio managers. In order to harness the insight from these diverse sources of big data, the implementation of a quantitative analysis system has almost become critical if the portfolio manager is to be able to continue to make a case for adding value with his decision process.

The availability of new data sources and their greater use across all asset management firms with in-house quantitative analysis systems is likely to bring quantitative and fundamental analysis skills much closer to a complete integration than ever before.

Implications of the New Investment Model

There will also be follow-up implications on the business model of asset management firms, as the new investment model proliferates. Robo-advisory, which is a business model based on large-scale customization of portfolios for all clients in a low-cost structure, will gain greater traction, as concurrently it also focuses on the allocation problem and not the security selection, nor does it have a high-cost fund structure. Wealth management will require greater investment skill from private banks, which have hitherto been driven by managing relationships instead of portfolios. The creation of customized retirement solutions for clients is likely to become a prominent business.

It is safe to say that fintech is likely to disrupt the investment model of asset management much more than any development in recent memory.

Pranay Gupta CFA has over 25 years of experience in managing portfolios across all liquid asset class investments across global markets. His areas of experience and interest include Multi-Asset Allocation Solutions, Risk Management, and the deployment of Data Science and Fintech in the Financial Services industry. Pranay was Chief Investment Officer for global asset managers where he led investment teams of over 300 investment professionals across 12 countries, to manage over US$85bn of institutional and retail assets. He has held senior positions at Axial Investment Management in London, APG Investments in the Netherlands, Societe Generale in Hong Kong and JP Morgan Investment Management in New York. As a Mechanical Engineer from IIT Delhi specializing in CAD/CAM, Pranay used robotic manipulator techniques for the design of automobile suspension systems for Suzuki Motor Co. Japan, fluid dynamic modelling techniques for the simulation of oil wells for Dowell Schlumberger and the production planning control of missile systems. Pranay has designed, developed and implemented advanced analysis and portfolio management systems for various organizations, which are used to manage and monitor portfolios with assets of over US$400bn, and create customized client solutions. Pranay has served as External Curriculum Director for the CFA Program, and has been a member of the Board of Trustees of the CFA Institute Research Foundation as the Chairman of the Finance and Investment Committee.

Chapter 16
Alternative Data in Portfolio Management

In this chapter we will investigate the significant impact of big data both in terms of its use in investment decision making and its potential to revolutionize the financial markets. This chapter starts from an overview of the historic background of quantitative investing and looks at its future. It also examines the analysis of alternative data in investment management.

Since the start of the first quantitative fund in 1978, in the past 30 years, systematic investing has gone through significant changes. As traditional value, momentum, and quality types of factors get more and more crowded, the efficacy of these signals has declined considerable. The next generation of alpha oriented strategies requires investors to embrace alternative data and advanced analytical tools.

In the first demonstration, we leverage satellite imagery data collected by RS Metrics and apply the consumer foot traffic data in sales forecasting. Using the Chipotle Mexican Grill as an example, we show that parking lot fill rate data is highly predictive of negative revenue surprise.

In the second case study, we study S&P Capital IQ's Call Transcript database. Rather than manually listening to management presentations or reading earnings call transcripts, we use our suite of NLP (Natural Language Processing) and machine learning algorithms to analyze the underlying textual data and drive investment insights. The signals derived from conference calls not only product strong investment performance, but also are uncorrelated with traditional models.

A Paradigm Shift in Active Investing

Traditionally, the focus for financial firms has been to have their employees assigned based on market segments for greater efficiency and specialty. As a result, investment managers are typically organized as:

- Active managers (who attempt to beat their benchmarks) and passive indexers (who try to replicate the benchmarks at a low cost)
- Discretionary (also called fundamental) and systematic (also known as quantitative) funds
- Top-down global macro and bottom-up securities selection

In addition, managers and research analysts are structured by countries, sectors, and styles. The current structure ensures efficiency, but is not optimized for information sharing.

Currently, fundamental managers rely on in-depth valuation analysis of subject companies (primarily based on financial statement data), interviewing company

DOI 10.1515/9781547400904- 016

management, and discussing with industry experts to form a view on the trend in the industry and in firms they want to invest. Similarly, quantitative managers build multi-factor models exploring market anomalies, taking advantage of the breadth and diversification benefit.

The big data revolution, however, has changed the playing field dramatically. We can now link the subject company with its customers, suppliers, competitors, joint ventures, and other partners. We can track and analyze key personnel (C-suite, board members and other insiders, sell-side analysts, and institutional shareholders and creditors) and connect them together. We can trace the products and services each company provides and then link to the changes in demographics and consumer spending patterns. Satellite imagery and mobile location tracking allow us to pinpoint the exact activities of a company, a shopping mall, an industrial site, an oil field, or a country. Even the traditional fundamental data now goes far beyond the main sets of financial statements—we can drill down to the specialized industries (e.g., banks, insurers, utilities companies) or countries (e.g., China, Japan). Unstructured data such as textual information (newspapers, websites, blogs, research reports, academic papers) and audio/video files are being presented to us in a way that was unimaginable even just a few years ago. How to analyze this mountain of data and form a consistent investment opinion poses a huge challenge to portfolio managers. We hope to shed some light on how to manage and utilize big data in this chapter.

Furthermore, artificial intelligence, machine learning, and computer algorithms have made enormous strides in fields like medical research, fraud detection, virtual reality, and driverless cars. AI has raised both hopes and fears among portfolio managers. Does technology provide us with extraordinary tools to identify market anomalies, or are computer algorithms replacing human analysts and traders? Big data and machine learning present new challenges and opportunities.

The History: 30 Years of Quantitative Investing

In this section, we briefly review the past 30-year history of quantitative investing.[1] We then discuss the challenges ahead of us. The availability of abundant data across a wide range of areas in vastly different structures provides us both opportunities and threats. Active managers face intense competition from not only other managers, but also passive and smart beta indices. The ability of machine learning algorithms gives us both aspiration and despair.

In the past 30 years, the systematic investing industry has gone through significant changes. We can roughly divide the history into three periods.

The Early Years in the 1980s and 1990s

Arguably, the first real quantitative investment fund was Wells Fargo's dividend tilt fund started in 1978. However, quantitative investing was on the sidelines until the early 2000s. The burst of the technology bubble caught many active investors off guard. The disappointment with traditional stock picking, the irrational, exuberant nature of human behavioral biases in investing, along with the availability of company fundamental databases and computing power triggered the start of the "Golden Years" of quantitative investing from early 2000 until the summer of 2007.

The Golden Years of 2000–2007

During the golden years, the performance of most quant funds was extremely strong, especially after adjusting for risk. The stellar performance attracted tremendous assets. With hindsight, the models used at the time were relatively simple—a mix of value and momentum, earnings revisions, and cash flow-based signals. More problematically, most quantitative managers had similar factors, models, portfolio construction techniques, and traded in similar fashions, which exposed the industry to potentially crowded trades.

Summer 2007 Quant Crisis and the Subsequent Risk-on/Risk-off Environment

Indeed, from August 1 to August 10, 2007, value and momentum[2] plunged by –7% and –4%, respectively, in less than two weeks (see Figure 16.1a). At the time, it was considered a fairly dramatic drawdown in such a short period of time. Ironically, both factors recouped the loss in the next two weeks. It is now generally accepted[3] that the considerable swing of quant factors in the summer of 2007 was caused by a sudden liquidation from a few multi-strategy funds and proprietary trading desks, possibly due to margin calls or risk reductions in other positions outside of their quant equity books. The initial liquidation triggered losses at many quant funds due to the similarity in their models, which exacerbated further sell-offs of stocks with the same characteristics.

While many quant investors were still struggling to comprehend the implications of the quant crisis and crowded trades, the subsequent 2008 financial crisis had changed the landscape once and for all. Quant funds initially benefited considerably from the onset of the 2008 global financial crisis, with the general nature of overweighting stocks with higher quality, lower risk, and cheaper valuation. The US equity market reached a bottom on March 9, 2009. Then, while the economy still struggled during the recession, the market sentiment turned the other way swiftly, as investors looked for a quick economic recovery. As a result, risky stocks rallied, while low-risk assets massively underperformed. Quant factors, in particular, momentum and low risk[4] factors plunged in the March–May 2009 risk rally (see Figure 16.1b). In less than three months from March 9, 2009 to June 1, 2009, the price momentum factor suffered a loss of over −45% and similarly, the low beta strategy suffered a loss over −50%. The loss was so severe that it completely overshadowed the summer 2007 quant crisis.

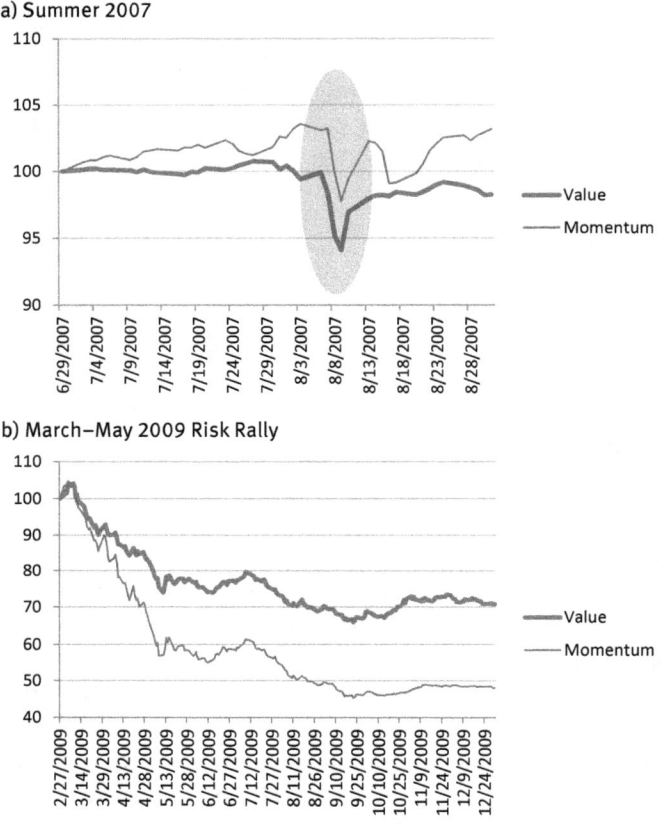

a) Summer 2007

b) March–May 2009 Risk Rally

Sources: Bloomberg Finance LLP, FTSE Russell, S&P Capital IQ, Thomson Reuters, Wolfe Research Luo's QES

Figure 16.1: Two episodes of quant crisis: a) summer 2007, and b) March–May 2009

Due to intense competition among active managers, changes in the underlying economic environment, and the periodic risk-on and risk-off in the US equity market, the performance of most common factors (see Figure 16.2a) clearly shows significant decay in the post 2008 period. Globally, in all major regions, factor performance has declined in recent years, especially in the US and Japan (see Figure 16.2b). As a reminder, factor return is computed based on a long/short portfolio, where we sort stocks based on a given factor. Active investment managers have to look for different ways to generate alpha in an increasingly challenging and competitive environment.

a) Average Factor Return in the US

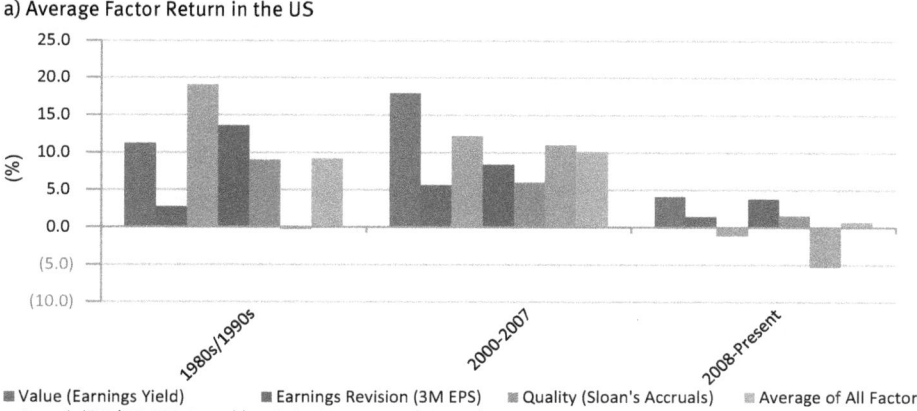

■ Value (Earnings Yield)   ■ Earnings Revision (3M EPS)   ■ Quality (Sloan's Accruals)   ■ Average of All Factors
■ Growth (FY1/FY0 EPS Growth) ■ Price Momentum (12M TR)   ■ Low Risk (Low Beta)

b) Average Factor Return Globally

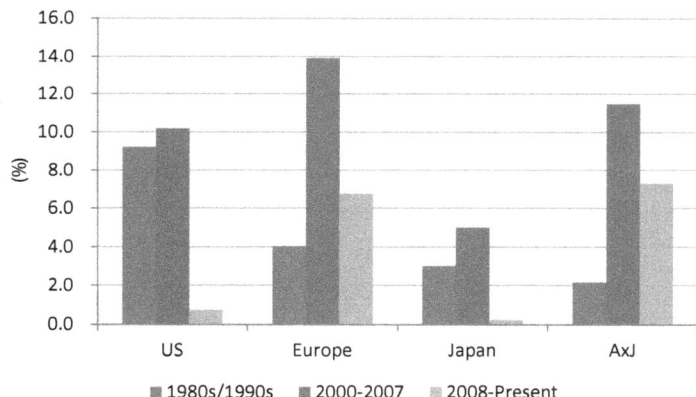

■ 1980s/1990s   ■ 2000-2007   ■ 2008-Present

Sources: Bloomberg Finance LLP, FTSE Russell, S&P Capital IQ, Thomson Reuters, Wolfe Research Luo's QES
Figure 16.2: The challenges ahead of us

Factor Payoff Patterns Are Becoming Increasingly Nonlinear

Many of the traditional market anomalies or stock-selection factors were discovered before 2007, as were the underlying academic papers. At the time, the relationship between factors and forward stock returns was primarily linear or at least monotonic. Not surprisingly, the predominant modeling techniques were also linear in nature, such as OLS (ordinary least squares) regression, mean-variance optimization, and so forth.

As the market evolves, possibly due to a combination of arbitrage by investors and changes in the underlying market regimes, the payoff patterns are becoming progressively nonlinear.

Figures 16.3a through 16.3d show the payoff patterns for one of the cornerstones of quantitative investing, price momentum, over four periods. We form five quintile portfolios, based on the month-end price momentum factor. Then we rebalance the portfolio monthly. The four graphs illustrate the average returns of the five momentum quintile portfolios over time. If the payoff pattern of the price momentum factor conforms to the Jegadeesh and Titman (1993) study, we should expect a linear monotonic upward trend. In the early years in the 1980s and 1990s (see Figure 16.3a), that was exactly what we would expect, albeit the Quintile 1 portfolio had a disproportionally low return possibly due to limit arbitrage.[5] In the golden years of 2000 to 2007, the pattern became much less linear, but low momentum stocks in Quintile 1 still massively underperformed; therefore, investors who had shorted poor momentum stocks would have generated outsized returns. In the third period from 2008 to 2015, the pattern resembled an inverted U-shape, where both poor momentum stocks in Quintile 1 and best momentum firms in Quintile 5 underperformed the middle three quintile portfolios. In 2016, the pattern completely reversed to a monotonic downward trend.

The Future of Active Investing—Big Data Evolution

The battle between active and passive investing will only intensify in the future. To succeed, managers need to either have access to better data that other investors do not have access to, or have better models and analytics that can extract predictive information in a more effective and efficient manner.

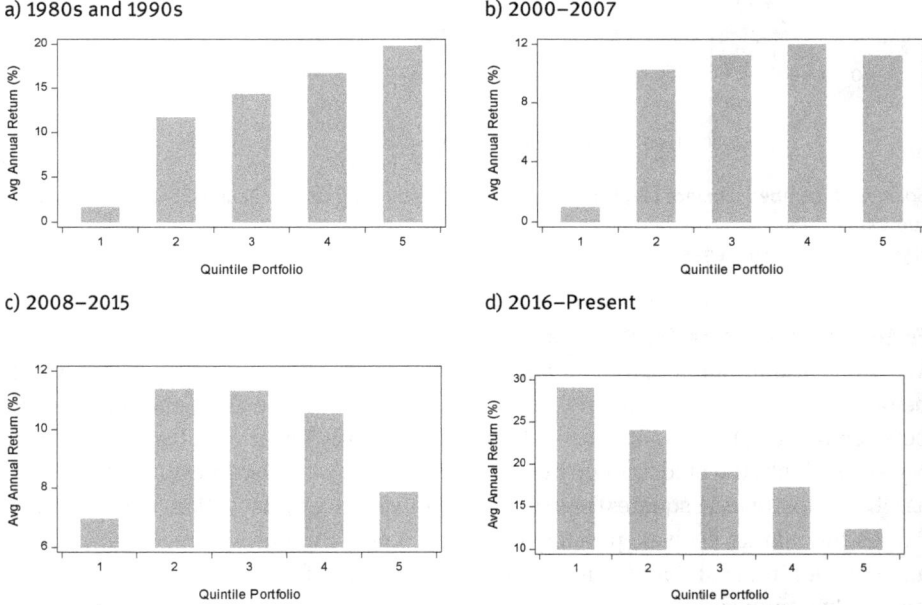

Sources: Bloomberg Finance LLP, FTSE Russell, S&P Capital IQ, Thomson Reuters, Wolfe Research Luo's QES

Figure 16.3: Price momentum factor in the US

- **New and uncorrelated data.** Many managers have discussed the idea of incorporating new and uncorrelated data and signals ever since the 2007 quant crisis. However, traditional factors still overrule the multifactor model world. The perception is that unconventional data tends to have short history, poor coverage, limited capacity, and is prone to data mining. However, a number of papers (e.g., Jussa et al. 2017a, Rohal et al. 2018, and Luo et al. 2018), have demonstrated how alternative data such as satellite imagery, manager presentation, and second-hand ship price can be used in stock return and commodities forecast. The scope of alternative has grown tremendously in the past few years. Nowadays, we need to have a separate database to track all available databases.[6]
- **Sophisticated modeling techniques.** OLS regression, linear multi-factor models, and mean-variance optimization were the main workhorses by quantitative managers prior to 2008. In recent years, nonlinear models and portfolio construction beyond mean-variance have received warm acceptance in the industry. Machine learning, despite its wide adoption in many other industries, is still in its infancy in institutional investing. As demonstrated in Luo, et al. (2017c) and Wang et al. (2018), we have found that machine learning algorithms can be more effective in stock return forecast and trading strategy development than traditional statistical techniques.

With our subject company in mind, we want to predict the return and risk of the target stock. A company is linked to its customers, suppliers, competitors, and other related entities. We can analyze a company along four dimensions:
- People (e.g., executive management, board members and other insiders, sell-side analysts covering the company, institutional shareholders and creditors)
- Products and services (that the company makes or provides, compliment and substitute products)
- Financials (GAAP, IFRS, and regulatory filings)
- Market data (including corporate events)

The vast array of data and related entities form an immensely complex and exciting web of data and opportunities (see Figure 16.4).

In the next two sections, we will use two concrete examples to demonstrate how alternative data and machine learning can be applied in active investing.

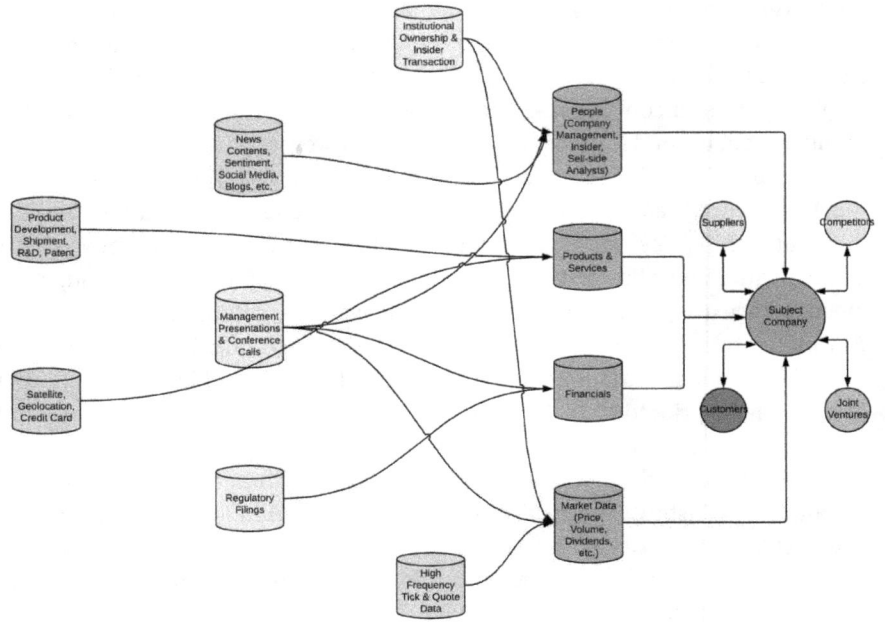

Sources: Wolfe Research Luo's QES

Figure 16.4: The complex web of big data

Using Satellite Imagery Data in Sales Forecasting

Satellite, geolocation, and credit card data has attractive significant attention among portfolio managers who invest in retail stocks. Obviously, retail companies release their financial statements on a quarterly basis, typically within a month after each quarter end. On the other hand, satellite imagery data, for example, is typically available on a daily basis in real time. Therefore, using satellite imagery data, we could potentially estimate each retailer's consumer foot traffic, which is highly correlated with revenue, a few weeks before a company's official earnings release. This section only provides a brief summary. More details can be found in Jussa et al. (2017a) and Wang et al. (2017).

A Brief Introduction

Traffic detection via satellites is a complicated process. Figure 16.5 provides an overview of the various stages involved in obtaining traffic data for retailers. Broadly speaking, geographic imagery is captured from global satellites, aerial/airplane photography, and drones. Images are processed and essentially digitized for feature extraction. Based on the imagery, various models as well as geolocation databases are used to isolate roadways and parking lots. Next, tools and software programs are used to detect vehicles within parking lots and roadways. Lastly, vehicle features such as size, color, and type (car, truck, passenger van) can be extracted.

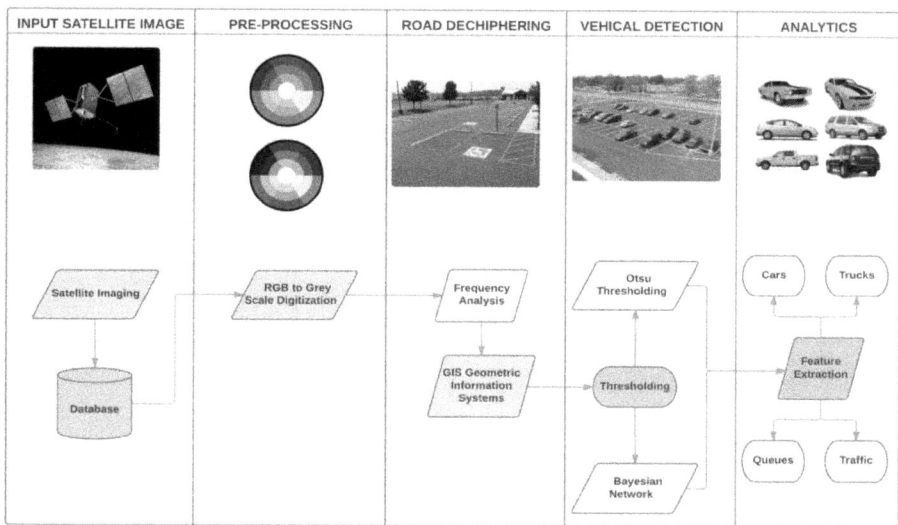

Sources: Wolfe Research Luo's QES

Figure 16.5: Satellite image processing flowchart

For this research, we utilize the RS Metrics data. RS Metrics works with a number of satellite providers to collect and process imagery data. More importantly, the firm maps each image to each major retailer in the US. Because of the earth's rotation and orbital time to circumnavigate, the satellites cannot image every single store. A good rule of thumb is that they are able to capture approximately 30% of the stores for each company, on average per month. The images tend to be taken at almost the same time every day, between 11AM and 1:30PM, when there is a sufficient amount of light. Figure 16.6 shows a map of the stores covered by each of the companies in the RS Metrics database.

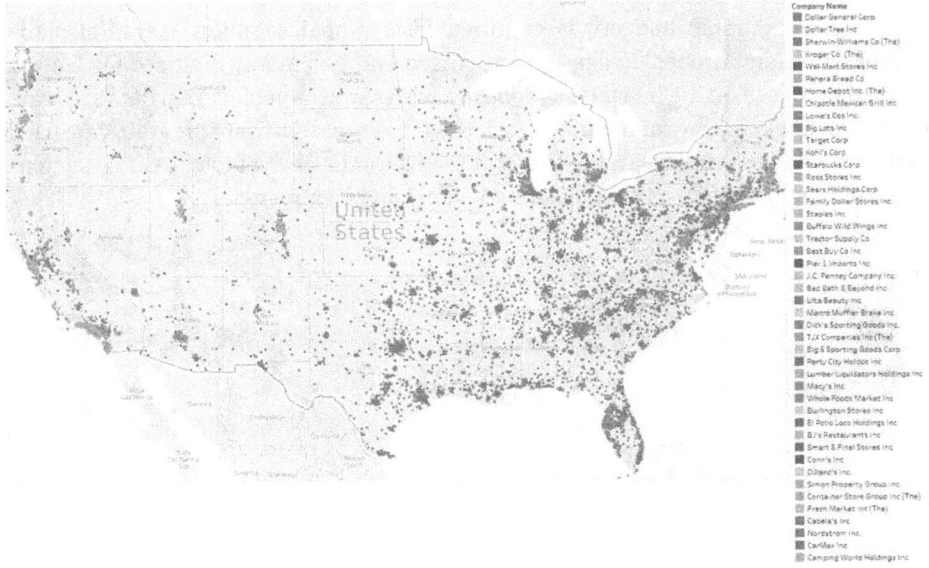

Sources: RS Metrics, Wolfe Research Luo's QES

Figure 16.6: Retail store coverage by RS Metrics

Fill Rate

Two of the most relevant metrics from RS Metrics are fill rate and the growth in fill rate. Fill rate essentially gauges parking lot traffic. Simply put, it is an estimate of the number of cars divided by available spaces for a particular company at a particular point in time. It is calculated as follows:

$$\text{Fill Rate} = \frac{\text{Estimated \# of cars parked at a company's parking lots}}{\text{Estimated \# of available car spaces among a company's parking lots}}$$

First, we estimate the number of cars in a particular parking lot for a company. Then, we estimate the number of available spaces. Obtaining the number of available spaces can be tricky. This is because multiple retailers can be situated in a single mall or strip center. In addition, malls, power centers, and outlets could have underground or covered parking, which invariably is somewhat difficult to capture by satellite imagery. As such, RS Metrics pre-assigns parking lot space for each company and each location. Figure 16.7 shows examples of parking space allocation for standalone retail venues.

a) Square Lot

b) Unconventional Lot

Cars: 151
Spaces: 400
Fill Rate:
37.8%

Sources: RS Metrics, Wolfe Research Luo's QES

Figure 16.7: Parking space allocation for standalone locations with a) square and b) unconventionally shaped lots

With strip centers and malls, the space allocation can get more complex. RS Metrics divides up available parking space based on the company's location within the mall and potentially its brand. Deterring the parking availability of anchor stores can also be tricky and tedious. Figure 16.8 shows examples of parking space allocation for multi-facility retail venues. RS Metrics typically revisits and updates its parking space allocation on a yearly basis.

a) Strip Center

b) Power Centers or Outlet Malls

Sources: RS Metrics, Wolfe Research Luo's QES

Figure 16.8: Parking space allocation for multi-facility locations

Association Analysis

Figure 16.9 shows a scatter plot of growth in fill-rate and the subsequent one-, three-, and six-month stock returns (forward returns). There is clearly a positive relationship between growth in fill-rate and future stock returns (especially with longer horizons).

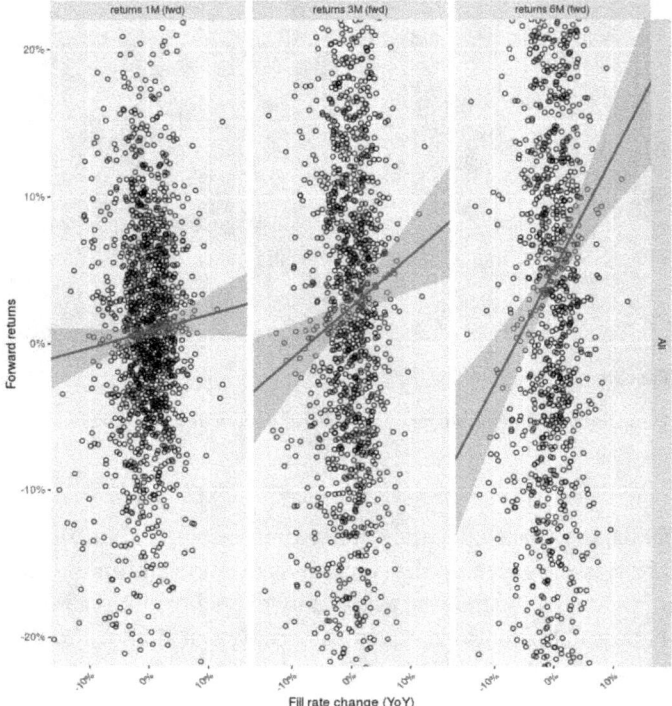

Sources: RS Metrics, Bloomberg Finance LLP, FTSE Russell, S&P Capital IQ, Thomson Reuters, Wolfe Research Luo's QES

Figure 16.9: Growth in fill-rate and future stock returns

An Example: Chipotle Mexican Grill, Inc. (CMG)

Satellite imagery-based consumer traffic data appears to add significant predictive power, above and beyond the consensus sell-side analyst estimates. For CMG, parking lot traffic growth has been a good predictor of *sales surprise*[7] (see Figure 16.10a). The relationship is stronger when parking lot traffic growth is negative—that is, when the satellite data suggests a decline in consumer traffic. In particular, we find that negative parking lot traffic growth predicts negative sales surprises 80% of the time (see Figure 16.10b).

Parking lot traffic growth was able to capture a series of negative sales surprises during the outbreak of E. coli, norovirus, and Salmonella in 2015 and 2016 at CMG restaurants. During this time, sell-side analysts underestimated the revenue impact resulting from the outbreak. Therefore, alternative data provides additional insights in sales forecast.

The data shows the relationship between sales surprise and parking lot traffic growth is stronger for restaurant businesses. This may be due to higher customer conversion rates for restaurants and the fact that satellites capture imagery around lunch time. Investors and analysts can use parking lot traffic growth as an incremental measure to fine-tune their sales estimates.

a) Traffic Growth and Sales Surprise   b) Success Rate

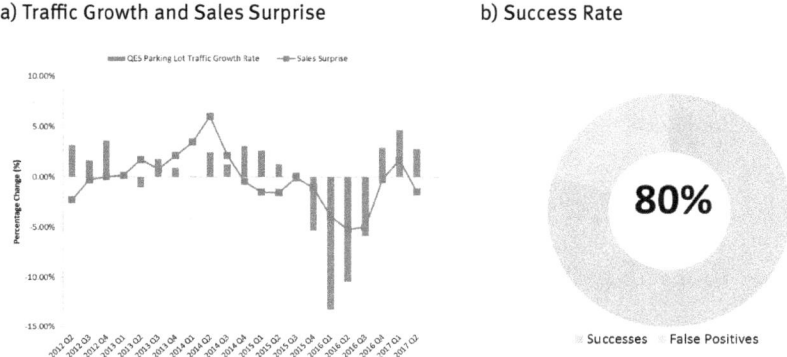

Sources: IBES, S&P Capital IQ, FTSE Russell, RS Metrics, Wolfe Research Luo's QES

Figure 16.10: a) Growth in parking lot traffic and sales surprise and b) success rate

Natural Language Processing and Management Presentation

In this section, we show an example of how alternative data and machine learning can be applied in active investing. In particular, we want to understand how we can use computer algorithms to read and process management presentations.

All public companies worldwide have to report their financial and operational performance, often via press releases and regulatory filings—both are heavily scrutinized by investors. Many companies also provide more detailed information via conference calls and investor conferences, where investors can hear the message from management directly and ask questions. Fundamental investors typically spend significant part of their time listening into these conference calls, attempting to understand the strength and weakness of each management team.

We source our raw data—management conference calls from S&P Capital IQ. Specifically, we use the call transcript database, which provides current and historical call transcript data covering approximately 7,000 public companies globally (see Figure 16.11a). Traditionally, investors either listen to the conference calls live or read the transcripts later, attempting to generate their own investment conclusions. The manual process is not only time-consuming, but also exposes potential behavioral bias. For example, as shown in Figure 16.11b, during the earnings season, there could be as many as 400 conference calls conducted on the same day. It is therefore impossible to actually participate in every management presentation.

a) Number of Earnings Calls by Region

b) Number of Daily Earnings Calls, 2016

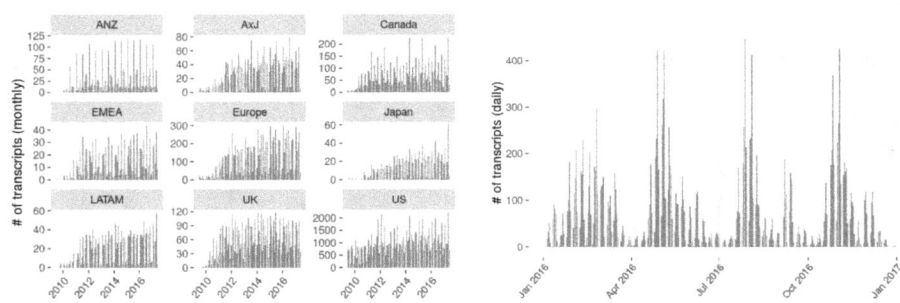

Sources: Bloomberg Finance LLP, FTSE Russell, S&P Capital IQ, Thomson Reuters, SEC, Wolfe Research Luo's QES

Figure 16.11: Call transcript data coverage

The transcript database provides textual translation of various types of calls: earnings, guidance/updates, shareholder/analyst, analyst/investor day, M&A, operating results, fixed income calls, and so on.

Each earnings call is typically split in two parts: the "presentation section" and "Q&A section." The presentation section usually includes a speech by company executives, such as the CEO and CFO. The Q&A section contains conversations between company management and buy-/sell-side research analysts, investors, or potentially, the media. Each sentence of the call is tagged to an executive or analyst. It also provides detailed metadata such as the speaker name, speaker type, and associated company for the speaker. Combined with two other closely related databases offered by S&P Capital IQ—the Professionals (background information on company executives, board members and investment professionals) and KDFE (Key Development and Future Events)—we can generate even greater insights.

Presentations in general are well-rehearsed and convey management's message to the investment community. While the Q&A section tends to be more spontaneous and at times unexpected, company management still maintains the control of information flow. We expect both sections to provide substantial and complementary information for the future business outlook of a company (financial and operational performance, stock return/volatility).

The text mining algorithms (that is, NLP or natural language processing) and the subsequent application of machine learning techniques to translate the information into investment insights are highly technical. In this chapter, we emphasize applications rather than technical details, which can be found in Rohal et al. (2018). There are many ways to analyze the call transcript data. For illustration purposes, we show two simple examples: readability and sentiment analysis.

Readability Index and Language Complexity

During earnings season, hundreds of companies around the world can all report on the same day. Most public companies conduct analyst conference calls in conjunction with their press releases. Fundamental analysts read press releases, supplementary documents, and the subsequent regulatory filings (with detailed financial statements, disclosures, and management discussion and analysis). Sell-side analysts, buy-side analysts/portfolio managers, and the media also participate in management calls in an attempt to gauge additional insights from the company presentation and Q&A sessions. As shown in Hirshleifer et al. (2009), investors' attention is limited. The human ability to process volumes of data and information is limited. We are also often biased by our prior views of a company and overconfidence can further shadow our judgment. Therefore, investors' ability to listen to hundreds of earnings calls, to read multiple call transcripts, and to derive their investment conclusions, all over a short period of time, is highly limited.

To measure the language complexity of each conference call, we can leverage a simple NLP technique called readability test. We can gauge the language complexity using readability indices. These indices generally output a number, which approximates the grade level of education needed to comprehend the underlying text. In other words, the higher the score, the higher the complexity.

Most of these indicators are based on two factors. One factor relates to the sentence structure, or the average number of words per sentence. The other factor relates to word structure or complexity and is usually based on either the proportion of easy words (defined by a lexicon/dictionary) or the average number of syllables per word.

One such an example is the *automated readability index* or ARI (1967). Like other popular readability formulas, the ARI formula outputs a number, which approximates the grade level needed to comprehend the text. Unlike the other indices, the ARI relies on the number of characters per word, instead of the usual syllables per word. The number of characters is more readily and accurately counted than syllables.

$$\text{Grade Level} = 4.71 \left(\frac{\text{characters}}{\text{words}} \right) + 0.5 \left(\frac{\text{words}}{\text{sentences}} \right) - 21.43$$

Where,

characters = number of letters and numbers,
words = number of words, and
sentences = number of sentences.

Presentations Are Getting Fogged with Complex Language

Figure 16.12a shows the median readability scores by each section/participant type. Larger scores correspond to higher education grades required to comprehend and hence lower readability. CEO presentation has become more complex over time, while the readability of analyst questions gets better in recent years. The average readability is better for the Q&A than the main presentation, as spontaneously spoken language tends to be simpler than heavily scripted presentations. We also observe a strong seasonal pattern in the readability index, which coincides with annual reporting season. Company management generally spends more time to deliver their annual results than quarterly/interim updates.

Now, we turn our attention to investigate whether readability indices predict future stock returns, using the *Spearman rank IC*.[8] As documented in previous research (see Rohal et al. [2017]), most factors derived from text mining tend to be weak but persistent. The forecasting power of readability scores is mostly negative, but weak (see Figure 16.12b). The negative relationship between readability and future stock returns is in line with expectations. Complex language is poorly understood by investors. Furthermore, many investors associate unnecessarily complicated words with management obscurity and uncertainty.

Interestingly, more complex questions by sell-side analysts lead to slightly positive future stock returns. Most analyst questions are simple ones, such as profit margin outlook or forthcoming product pipelines. More elaborated questions often mean analysts attempting to understand some contentious issues. Therefore, any sort of resolution is typically welcomed by the investment community.

a) Automated Readability Score

b) Correlation of ARI with Next Month's Stock Return

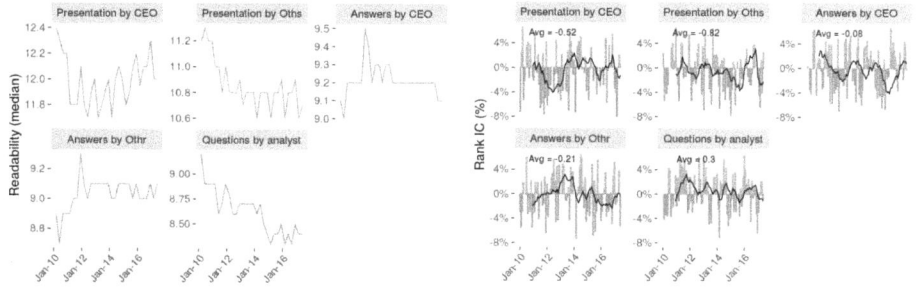

Sources: Bloomberg Finance LLP, FTSE Russell, S&P Capital IQ, Thomson Reuters, SEC, Wolfe Research Luo's QES

Figure 16.12: Readability score and stock return forecast

Sentiment or Tone Analysis Based on Lexicons

Next, we move to the most popular approach for NLP: sentiment or tone analysis. Sentiment analysis attempts to objectively characterize the message conveyed by the underlying textual document. A lexicon or dictionary is commonly used to calculate the tone of each individual word. There are two commonly used dictionaries—the Harvard IV-4 and an academic one by Loughran and McDonald. The tone is then aggregated for the complete text to arrive at an overall sentiment of the message. We have done significant work on sentiment analysis in previous publications (see Rohal et al. 2017).

Why would sentiment around earnings calls predict future stock returns? We have two hypotheses. First, it is related to the "limited attention" and under-reaction argument. Investors have limited time to listen, read, and analyze management conference calls, which causes delays in processing valuation information. As a result, investors often under-react the message in the management presentation, which leads to post-announcement drift (mostly likely in the same direction, i.e., positive tone in the call leads to higher subsequent returns and vice versa). Furthermore, we expect the tone of management to contain more useful information about the underlying fundamentals of the company (for example, profitability, solvency, and business prospects) than what is presented in the written materials (press releases, supplemental packages, regulatory filings, and financial statements). Our empirical results show evidences on both fronts.

The most common approach for sentiment analysis is to count the number of positive and negative words, using a pre-defined dictionary. The relative proportion of positive/negative words is used as the positive/negative tone measure for a document. The polarity score is defined as:

$$\text{Polarity} = \frac{(\text{Number of positive words} - \text{Number of negative words})}{\text{Total number of words}}$$

In this research, we use a generic (Harvard IV-4) and a finance-oriented (Loughran and McDonald) lexicon for our sentiment analysis.

Harvard IV-4 Dictionary

The Harvard IV-4 is one of the most extensively used dictionaries employing the well-known semantic text analysis program called the General Inquirer. Figure 16.13 shows the WordCloud (frequency count) of the words that appeared in the call transcript database, using the Harvard IV-4 dictionary, which categorizes each word into active (passive), strong (weak), overstated (understated), and positive (negative). We tag each individual word using two large valence categories labeled positive and negative from Harvard IV-4. This is then aggregated for the complete text to compute the overall polarity score. For example, the Harvard IV-4 dictionary classifies the following frequently appeared words as negative: expense, tax, low, cost, etc.

a) Presentation section

b) Q&A section

Sources: Bloomberg Finance LLP, FTSE Russell, S&P Capital IQ, Thomson Reuters, SEC, Wolfe Research Luo's QES

Figure 16.13: Harvard IV-4 dictionary words appeared in the call transcripts

CEOs Are Overwhelmingly Bullish in Their Tone

Figure 16.14 shows the percentage of positive/negative words in our call transcript data, based on the Harvard IV-4 dictionary. Overall, the use of positive words is much more prevalent than negative ones in management communication. Furthermore, the percentage of positive words has been rising, while the ratio of negative words has been declining in the past eight years.

We find that company executives (especially CEOs) tend to be selective in their choice of words, while analysts are more likely to be more critical. Analysts' questions are more cautious than management's answers. The management presentation section is more bullish than the Q&A section. Moreover, CEOs are more positive than other executives of the same company.

a) % Positive Words   **b) % Negative Words**

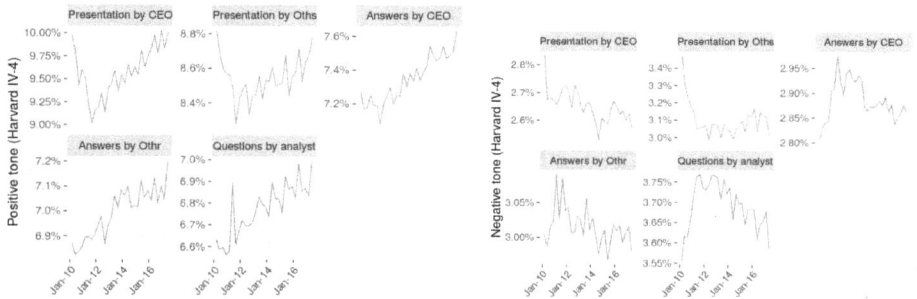

Sources: Bloomberg Finance LLP, FTSE Russell, S&P Capital IQ, Thomson Reuters, SEC, Wolfe Research Luo's QES

Figure 16.14: Positive/negative tone of call transcripts based on the Harvard IV-4 dictionary

The sentiment factors based on the Harvard dictionary show predictive ability of future stock returns, particularly for positive tone (see Figure 16.15). More interestingly, CEO speech, both from the presentation and Q&A sections, has much stronger performance than other executives/analysts. In the charts below, each bar represents the correlation between sentiment and future stock return. We can see that positive words typically lead to higher stock returns, and vice versa for negative tones.

a) Percentage of Positive Words   **b) Percentage of Negative Words**

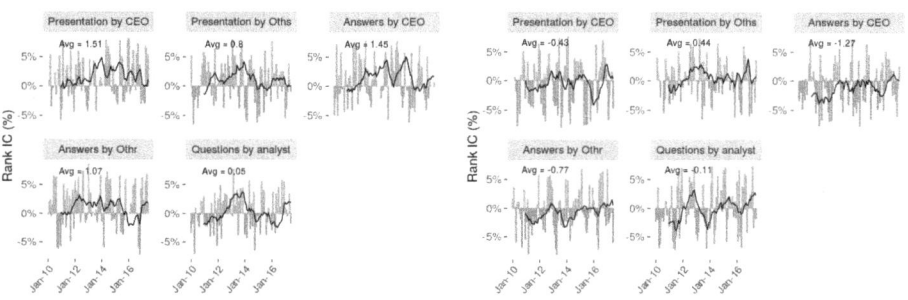

Sources: Bloomberg Finance LLP, FTSE Russell, S&P Capital IQ, Thomson Reuters, SEC, Wolfe Research Luo's QES

Figure 16.15: Correlation with next month's stock returns

Please note that readability and sentiment are only two simple ways of using NLP to analyze management presentations. In Rohal et al (2017, 2018), we have conducted extensive research on other NLP and machine learning algorithms, such as executive personalities, topic modeling, and deep learning. In summary, text mining offers interesting insights on management presentation that are different from human analysts' interpretations.

Conclusion

In conclusion, we are witnessing a paradigm shift in active investing. The big data evolution gives us the access to vast amount of unconventional information—connecting people (e.g., management, board members, and analysts), products, financials, market data, and global economy—via structured, textual, imagery, audio/video, and location data. The incredible success of machine learning algorithms in fields from the GO game, virtual reality, to driverless cars has also impacted investment managers. The next frontier of active investing is far beyond corporate access and value/momentum factors that we are accustomed to. It is about how to best integrate data and technology in the investment process. The investment manager who is best able to do so will ride the new waves of technology-enabled investing.

Endnotes

1 A more in-depth coverage can be found in Luo et al. (2017a).

2 We use trailing earnings yield (trailing 12-month EPS/price) and 12-month total return excluding the most recent month to represent value and momentum, respectively. Value and momentum factors are both constructed as simple long/short quintile portfolios, where we buy the top 20% of stocks with the cheapest valuation (or highest price momentum) and short the bottom 20% worst stocks, equally weighting stocks in both long and short baskets. Portfolios are rebalanced monthly and transaction costs are not included. More details on how to construct factor portfolios can be found in Luo et al. (2017b).

3 See Khandani and Lo (2007) for detailed discussion of the summer 2007 quant crisis. We have done extensive research on strategy crowding, using a wide range of metrics from short interest to trading patterns (see Cahan and Luo [2013] for one example).

4 The low risk factor invests in stocks with the lowest volatilities (or betas) and typically also shorts stocks with the highest risk at the same time.

5 Shorting was more difficult and costly in the 1980s and 1990s.

6 Service providers, such as Wolfe Research, have developed such database of databases. See Jussa et al. (2017) as an example.

7 Sales surprise is the percentage difference between expected and actual reported sales of a company.

8 As a reminder, we use Rank IC to measure the predictive power of a factor in selecting/ranking stocks. It is computed as the rank correlation between the current month's signal and the following month's return, among all stocks in our investment universe.

References

Cahan, R., and Luo, Y. (2013). "Standing Out from the Crowd: Measuring Crowding in Quantitative Strategies," *Journal of Portfolio Management*, Summer 2013.

Hirshleifer, D., Lim, S.S., and Teoh, S.H. (2009). "Driven to Distraction: Extraneous Events and Underreaction to Earnings News," *Journal of Finance*, 60, pp. 2289–2325.

Jegadeesh, N., and Titman, S. (1993). "Returns to buying winners and selling losers: implications for stock market efficiency," *Journal of Finance*, Vol. 28, No. 1, 63, March 1993.

Jussa, J., Luo, Y., and Wang, S. (2017a). "Space—The Next Alpha Frontier," Wolfe Research Luo's QES, May 17, 2017.

Jussa, J., Alvarez, M., Luo, Y., Wang, S., and Rohal, G. (2017b). "Introducing D2," Wolfe Research Luo's QES, November 2, 2017.

Khandani, A.E., and Lo, A.W. (2007). "What Happened to the Quants in August 2007," MIT Working Paper.

Luo, Y., Jussa, J., and Wang, S. (2017a). "The Big and The Small Sides of Big Data," Wolfe Research Luo's QES, February 8, 2017.

Luo, Y., Jussa, J., and Wang, S. (2017b). "Signal Research and Multifactor Models," Wolfe Research Luo's QES, February 16, 2017.

Luo, Y., Jussa, J., and Wang, S. (2017c). "Style Rotation, Machine Learning, and the Quantum LEAP," Wolfe Research Luo's QES, February 24, 2017.

Luo, Y., Alvarez, M., Jussa, J., Wang, S., and Rohal, G. (2018). "The Third Derivative in Forecasting Commodity Price," Wolfe Research Luo's QES, May 8, 2018

Rohal, G., Luo, Y., Jussa, J., and Wang, S. (2017). "Text Mining Unstructured Corporate Filing Data," Wolfe Research Luo's QES, April 20, 2017.

Rohal, G., Luo, Y., Alvarez, M., Jussa, J., and Wang, S. (2018). "Tone at the Top? Quantifying Management Presentation," Wolfe Research Luo's QES, January 23, 2018.

Wang, S., Jussa, J., Alvarez, M., Luo, Y., and Rohal, G. (2017). "Anticipating Negative Sales Surprise," Wolfe Research Luo's QES, October 24, 2017.

Wang, S., Luo, Y., Jussa, J., Alvarez, M., and Rohal, G. (2018). "Systematic Alpha from Risk Arbitrage (SARA)," Wolfe Research Luo's QES, May 15, 2018.

Yin Luo *is a Vice Chairman, Quantitative Research, Economics, and Portfolio Strategy (QES) at Wolfe Research, a premier boutique investment bank headquartered in New York. He joined Wolfe Research, LLC in September 2016. Prior to Wolfe Research, Yin was a Managing Director and Global Head of Quantitative Strategy at Deutsche Bank. Yin started at Deutsche Bank in New York in October 2009 and in seven years, he built a world class quantitative and macro research franchise. Before arriving at Deutsche Bank, he spent over 12 years in investment banking and at a management consulting firm with various roles in quantitative research, fundamental research, portfolio management, investment banking and consulting. Yin has been ranked #1 in Institutional Investor magazine's II-All America equity research survey in quantitative research in 2011–2016, 2018, and top ranked in Portfolio Strategy, Economics, and Accounting & Tax Policy sectors. At Deutsche Bank, Yin also led the team and achieved #1 ranking in II-Europe and II-Asia surveys. In 2016–2018, Yin was selected to the UPstanding's top 100 ethnic-minority executives in the US and Europe by the Financial Times. Yin holds a Bachelor of Economics degree from Renmin University of China, a MBA in Finance from University of Windsor, and a Master of Management and Professional Accounting from University of Toronto. He is a CFA charterholder, a U.S. CPA, a CGMA (Chartered Global Management Accountant), and a PStat (Professional Statistician). Mr. Luo is also an Adjunct Professor of Finance at Renmin University of China.*

Chapter 17
Online Marketplace Lending

Online marketplace lending refers to loans originated from Internet-based businesses rather than traditional banks. In this chapter, we will focus on online marketplace development in two major economies—the United States and China—and compare similarities and differences in online marketplaces between the two countries, including the drivers that caused the differences.

US

Online marketplace lending platforms, such as Prosper and LendingClub, emerged in the mid-2000s to provide an alternative source of loans for the underbanked in the United States. These early platforms matched individual borrowers and lenders on a Dutch auction model. The rise in online marketplace lending naturally led to scrutiny by the U.S. Securities and Exchange Commission (SEC), which resulted in the temporary closure of these online marketplace lending platforms, as they were labeled "sellers of investments" rather than merely lenders. However, operations at Prosper and LendingClub resumed in 2009 following registration with the SEC.

China

Similarly, China's first online marketplace lending platform, Pat Loan, emerged in 2007 to match individual lenders and borrowers. These marketplace lenders expanded rapidly in China as traditional banks focused on lending to large businesses or state-owned enterprises. Alongside the rapid growth of Chinese marketplace lenders, there was a general absence of standardization and security of products. As a result, Chinese regulations during the initial period allowed borrowers to bear a very low cost when they defaulted. This resulted in the loss of trust among lenders and investors, as they were not confident that borrowers could repay these loans.

This changed with the deployment of machine learning as borrower screening became a more effective process and supervised, deep learning algorithms could pick borrower features that would result in lower default rates and, equally important, better identify fraud. Coupled with more stringent regulations that were initiated in 2015, Chinese marketplace lending began a period of fast and sustained growth.

Today, these lending platforms have become recognized as part of the smaller borrower's lending options and any default on the platforms will be reported to the credit bureau and officially recorded.

DOI 10.1515/9781547400904- 017

Institutional Investors

As the online lending marketplace became more mature, it transformed from that of a cottage industry to one that has gained institutional recognition. Banks and institutional investors are funding loans as compared to wealthier individuals funding these loans in the past. Now, only 35% of the loan dollars are coming from fractional loans. In 2017, the other 65% of the more than US$3b loans on the Prosper and Lending-Club came from investors snatching up whole loans, which traditionally have almost always been made by institutional investors rather than individuals. Banks want to engage with these online marketplace lenders as they are drawn by the prospect of strong cash flows while avoiding the costs required to underwrite and service these loans. Furthermore, banks have started evaluating the loans that originated from marketplace lenders and have purchased these loans directly onto their balance sheets in ever-larger quantities.

As recognition from the institutional space grew, interest for this asset class followed suit. Institutions like the idea of trading liquidity in exchange for getting a short duration loan portfolio and a healthy credit spread. On top of that, rating agencies are currently looking at this space and have given the green light to these securities, acknowledging that a well-constructed loan product qualifies for investment grade rating. Thus, the combination of these forces allowed the securitization of these loans to occur and make it accessible to a much broader set of investors. Moreover, as most institutional investors can only invest in graded securities, this helps to expand the market and provide more liquidity as well as validation to the online marketplace lending ecosystem.

New Borrowers

As lenders profiles changed, so did that of borrowers. The average credit score for borrowers has increased year over year, which is a result of two factors. First, the type of borrowers coming to marketplace lenders has changed. Previously, the majority of borrowers that came to an online marketplace lender tended to be marginal borrowers who could not get a loan from a bank. Now, there are many individuals who can get a loan from a bank, but prefer the convenience and efficiency of going to a marketplace lender.

Second, marketplace lenders have expanded into new borrowers, including providing student loans and loans to SMEs. The learnings from risk profiling and fraud prevention have given marketplace lenders confidence to expand into these markets, as regulators have grown more comfortable with the business model and are willing to include new borrower types.

Requirements for Online Marketplace Lending

Establishing an online marketplace lending platform requires the usual business and technological investment of any internet-based business; however, there are four additional requirements for marketplace lenders: borrower data, historical default rates, the risk framework, and a machine learning platform.

The heart of the online marketplace lending business model is replacing human loan officers at physical bank branches with a centralized, programmatic approach to loan approval and rate setting. This requires the business operators to effectively combine consumer risk and advanced data analysis. The required components are both financial and technological expertise as well as the hardware and coding ability to operate the machine learning platform. The requirement discussions that follow assume a cold start, where vintage or processed data is not available.

Borrower Data

Borrow data is the raw material for analyzing loan quality and training a machine learning platform to select and grade potential loans.

Potential data sources include public, proprietary and third-party data. Public sources of borrower data typically include government or public research figures, such as unemployment figures for specific geographies or household debt-to-income ratios. Proprietary data could be drawn from companies that already have interactions with potential borrowers, such as payments providers, retailers, budgeting apps, etc. After a sufficient period of operation, borrower repayment history can also be another category of proprietary borrower data. Third-party data sources may include FICO scores, information verification databases, etc.

All borrower data, whether structured or unstructured, must be restructured into a homogenous taxonomy to ensure accurate processing by the machine learning platform. The taxonomy should be designed around the key features that the marketplace lender selects to use as the determining factors for creditworthiness. These features will be shaped by the risk framework as well as the available datasets. Data must also be pre-processed for correlation between features, such as credit score and age.

Historical Default Rates

To better evaluate borrower creditworthiness in an automated fashion, marketplace lenders must have access to historical loan default data. Ideally, this data would come from a dataset comprised of existing or former loans; however, this is not always possible. As a result, data on loan repayments and defaults must be acquired and, in the best possible way, be sequenced against the available borrower datasets to create a more detailed picture of binary repayments and defaults. When it is not possible to correlate the available borrower data to the available loan data, online marketplace lending operators may consider relying on their machine learning platform to explore potential correlations and patterns between seemingly disparate aspects of the data.

Risk Framework

Online marketplace lending employs supervised machine learning and classification, and the risk framework is the starting architecture for that classification. A critical task is to take the available borrower features, as determined by the available datasets, and assign default probability weightings to the features. The default probabilities are likely to be updated as the machine learning model learns and as the data science teams improve the model, but a base setting is required to begin this type of supervised computational exercise.

Machine Learning Platform

Running a machine learning platform that can productively analyze large volumes of correlated and uncorrelated data requires experienced individuals who can both program the algorithms and distinguish the features of the borrower. These data scientists may not need a financial background, but it may be beneficial. Backgrounds that are heavy in modeling and statistical analysis, such as meteorology, engineering, or mathematics, are needed.

In addition to the people who set up and run the machine learning system, a variety of technical architectures are possible for the type of high-performance computing that machine learning requires. Graphics processing units (GPUs) have been the standard for machine learning platforms, but new alternatives are emerging including tensor processing units (TPUs) and application-specific integrated circuits (ASICs). For data storage, solid state drives (SSDs) are the standard as they have faster load times. On the other hand, there are growing numbers of sophisticated cloud computing services that allow the user to rent computational power, but these may come with time limits.

Case Study: Applying Machine Learning to Online Marketplace Lending

Having assembled the required building blocks to run an online marketplace lending business, the company must develop a machine learning platform from the composite elements. This section provides a process-level overview of the establishment, training, and testing of a machine learning platform for online marketplace lending. The process consists of three steps:

1. Clarifying the business case and data model
2. Applying the algorithms to identify patterns in the data
3. Deploying the platform and ongoing iteration

We first discuss these steps and then explain a periodic model refit process.

Business Case and Data Model

The first step is to translate the business case into a data model. The majority of online marketplace lending businesses have similar business needs, which include the primary tasks of evaluating loan applications and selecting appropriate interest rates. For approval/rejection calculations, the answer is a discrete value, but the lending rate is a continuous value. In either case, most online marketplace lending operators use supervised learning at the start of the analysis because the end target is already known. Unsupervised learning can be used to identify patterns once the model has been active for a period of time.

To build the data model to analyze each business need, the borrower data drawn from the application must be structured into consistent features (such as credit score, gender, income, and so on) that are then overlaid with all third-party and proprietary data. Each feature is then placed in a separate line entry for each applicant profile. Taken together, the full table of features, often numbering in the hundreds, forms the training dataset.

Predetermined targets and definitions are then established for each process. Typical targets are *approved* or *rejected* for the application, and typical definitions include *paid off, default but now creditworthy, charged off,* and so forth.

Identifying Patterns

The next step is to apply the algorithm(s) to the training dataset to allow the machine learning platform to identify patterns among the features. Assuming that the marketplace lender is a new company, the process is known as a *cold start,* which means no prior analyzed data is available for comparison.

The algorithms typically fall into a few categories. One of these are simple binary rules—such as whether the credit score is below a certain threshold—the application is rejected. Another more complex algorithm would be a logistic regression, where the risk model is used to apply default probabilities for each of the features (for example, default_probability = 0.5*fico + 0.2*age + 0.1*balance, etc.).

Table 17.1: Example of application of a risk model to predict loan status

Loan Id	Amount	Age	Gender	FICO score	Bank balance	Loan status
00001	10,000	22	Female	530	$5,500	Paid off
00002	20,000	45	Male	710	$120,000	Overdue
00003	15,000	31	Male	600	$10,000	?

A third type of algorithm is a *word-to-vector analysis,* where the relationships between words are quantified based on observed patterns of usage. This can be especially useful for data that is not readily incorporated into the overarching data structure. In a word-to-vector analysis, relationships between words are plotted as vectors to reveal patterns. The classic example is [boy]−[girl] + [queen] = [king], which is one of the relationships illustrated in Figure 17.1.

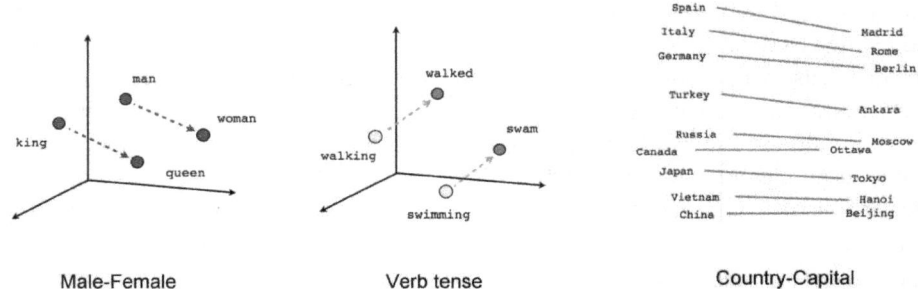

| Male-Female | Verb tense | Country-Capital |

Figure 17.1: Plotted vectors for several word relationship examples

Each of these algorithmic strategies can yield different results, but to combine all of them into a multi-layered analysis, a deep learning neural network is required. Simply put, a deep learning platform correlates the probabilities between the results of each algorithm in a matrix, which raises the overall accuracy of the model's predictive ability.

Deployment and Iteration

Having identified higher probability patterns in the data, the top-performing strategies are selected for live testing. The live application data received by the marketplace lender will be divided into traffic channels, sometimes as many as ten, to test the relative strength of each strategy against live data.

Many firms running big data analyses will commonly run what is known as a *champion challenge,* where each traffic channel competes against the others over a defined period of time. The lowest performing traffic channels are cycled out for refitting or retirement, and the firm can either increase the traffic allocation of the higher performing channels or introduce new channels for live testing.

While these are running, the marketplace lender must establish business intelligence monitoring systems to assess the quality of the decision-making as well as to identify any anomalies as quickly as possible. Hotfixes are performed in situations where the strategy might be working correctly, but where the physical architecture is not operating properly or where the different components of the platform (the data processing unit, data warehouse, algorithmic engine, and so on) are not interacting correctly.

Further iteration of the strategies that are currently used with live data is driven by model deterioration. Model deterioration comes from multiple sources, including changes in customer behavior, business processes, competitive landscape, regulations, products offered, or business expansion. In each of these cases, high-performing strategies are refit according to the changes without the model being taken offline.

While day-to-day iterations and hotfixes can be done while the model is still running, periodic reviews are still required for the data as well as the operation of the machine learning platform. For the data, the infrastructure of the data warehouse must be evaluated for performance and suitability, especially as the size of data grows. Checkpoints must be monitored at all the points where data is transferred from one component of the platform to another. Each step of the extraction, transformation, and loading of data into the data warehouse needs to be reviewed for any errors or issues with data handling and classification. From an operational perspective, the communication between components must be reviewed for deterioration, including examining the API calls between each of the interfaces.

Similarly, when introducing a new product, the first step of establishing the business case and data model must be reconstructed; however, the second and third steps of identifying patterns and iteration during deployment can be followed as laid out in the preceding discussion.

Comparison of US and Chinese Online Marketplace Lending

The US was the first market where online marketplace lending developed on a large scale; however, China quickly followed because of the high level of personal bank accounts and mobile-first online services. Both have developed into major industries, with billion-dollar champions leading in each country. However, significant differences have emerged in the way those leading players run an online marketplace lending business.

Many of the changes come from differences in regulatory regimes as well as customer behavior patterns. Major differences in the terms and interpretation of data privacy laws in the US and China significantly change the way online marketplace lenders gain information for acquiring and evaluating borrowers. US regulation largely held back the development of online marketplace lending for several years after its inception, while in China, it exploded before more stringent regulatory oversight was established. In addition, the US has multiple decades of personal credit history, while in China, although the People's Bank of China (PBOC) has established a reliable public credit bureau, historical data is limited and entirely unavailable for some new borrowers.

Drawing on primary research and interviews with platform operators in both countries, these primary differences can be categorized into four areas: customer segmentation, customer acquisition, charge-offs, and cost of funding.

Customer Segmentation

US

In the US, customer segmentation has matured from an early stage where marketplace lenders were mostly targeting borrowers who could not receive loans from established banks to now competing with banks for prime borrowers as well as boosting returns through selectively lending to sub-prime borrowers.

US marketplace lenders typically target a spread of prime and sub-prime borrowers, with the majority of the loan book coming from B- and C-grade borrowers. This approach increases yield for investors, while the platform uses risk mitigation strategies to reduce overall risk. The majority of the borrowers on the US online marketplace lending platforms come from marketing, referrals, and direct traffic. Unlike in China, making loans to constituents of a wholly-owned vertical is not very common.

China

Chinese marketplace lenders tend to target a more diverse set of customers. One of the major platforms focuses on younger borrowers with limited or no credit history. As a result, this platform has developed a proprietary credit-scoring system to supplant the limited public data available. Another platform targets borrowers with credit cards, relying on credit card issuer data as the basis of their credit-scoring system. A third model used by a leading marketplace lender segments their target customers based on their employment and assigns weightings to different industries to form a credit-scoring system. As a result, one of the leading platforms had more than 85% of its loan categorized as C- or D-grade borrowers, illustrating the Chinese platforms' willingness to take risks on new borrowers in an effort to gain market share.

Customer Acquisition

US

Given that US marketplace lenders target customer segments with more established credit history and demonstrated repayment ability, a commonly preferred and often the largest customer acquisition method is direct mailing because it allows the platform to directly reach their ideal borrowers. Email is often the second-largest channel for US marketplace lenders because they have been in operation for longer and have a larger pool of prior borrowers. In addition, email is a nearly free outreach channel. Referral partnerships are used selectively by US marketplace lenders to target new demographics through partnerships. Direct website traffic, either through organic visits or digital marketing, is a less preferred channel because of the higher cost of such campaigns.

As the sector is more mature in the US, most US platforms are willing to trade slower growth for sustainable customer acquisition costs. As the core competitors in the US are traditional banks, maintaining lower operating costs is a key competitive advantage that is rarely sacrificed in search of faster growth. As a result, marketing costs are often less than 4% of the total origination cost for US marketplace lenders.

China

While most Chinese borrowers have had bank accounts for some time, historically, many have not taken out loans from the traditional banks where they have their accounts. This is partly because banks have focused their loan portfolios on state-owned enterprises and large companies, but also because there are not many sophisticated retail-focused products available.

As a result, a large portion of customer acquisition happens online for many of the Chinese marketplace lenders. For some platforms, as much as 70% of borrowers come through online channels. In addition to customers acquired through digital marketing, many Chinese marketplace lenders use aggregation platforms and partner with lenders that have different target customer segments, to refer across to each other. Access to domestic champion platforms, such as WeChat or Alipay, gives marketplace lenders a large volume of target customers. However, the acquisition cost can vary depending on the rate negotiated with the platform.

Charge-offs

US

In the US, the maturity of the financial services regulation, combined with the extensive reach of legal recourse means the majority of charge-offs come from credit losses, which are triggered after four months of consecutive missed payments. Fraud is a small portion of charge-offs for US marketplace lenders, as they invest heavily in borrower verification, sometimes including manual verification. The predominant model is to pay for fraud upfront in the prevention process. US platforms outsource to the same collection agencies as the traditional banks. Unlike in China, debtors have protections, including cease-and-desist orders to bar communications, the use of a debt settlement company, and fixed hours during which they may be contacted about repayment.

China

Due to the imperfect Chinese credit system, the default cost of the borrower is very low and legal recourse is not always available. As such, marketplace lenders in China have had to work hard to obtain the trust of investors and grow the industry. While credit loss is still a factor in China, fraud far outweighs it, both in terms of notional value and overall volume.

Many have re-tasked their AI platforms, in combination with human investigation, to reduce fraudulent losses. The fraud recognition rate reported through the machine learning of one marketplace lender's anti-fraud model is around 60%. In addition to monitoring transactions and payments, Chinese marketplace lenders also have access to SIM card data, which allows them to map borrowers against known databases of fraudulent phone numbers and accounts to discover risk in real-time and raise a fraud alert. In addition, some Chinese marketplace lenders include a provision for fraud in their business model, while they take time to work out their fraud prevention strategies.

Cost of Funding

US

Marketplace lenders in the US typically maintain a low cost of capital, preferring sticky sources of capital that will buy loans through economic cycles. They often work with dedicated funds on long-term deals with caps limiting the funds' percentage of the marketplace lender's total volume. Between 25–30% of loans originated on US online marketplace lending platforms are typically held by banks. Retail investors are still part of the funding mix for the two older participants, Prosper and LendingClub, but retail investors typically contribute less than 25% of their total funding. Since the SEC changed the licensing regulations, it has become much harder for later participants to access retail investors. The two most common exit strategies for investors in US marketplace loans are securitization or hold and yield.

In addition to external investors, many of the US marketplace lenders operate a warehouse facility for loans they originate, which gives them a stake in the profits as well as emphasizing their investment to external investors.

China

In China, retail investors have retained an important part in the funding mix. For one major player, as much as 85% of outstanding loans are funded by individual investors, with the rest funded by institutional investors. Another leading Chinese marketplace lender recently reported that 100% of new investors in a calendar quarter were added through online channels, which is another way of saying that these are retail investors. While the larger marketplace lenders in China continue to receive institutional support in the form of direct investment capital and IPOs, both in China and the US, funding for loans continues to be dominated by retail Chinese investors.

Challenges and Areas for Further Development

The development of online marketplace lending has been driven by commercial factors at the borrower level, technological developments at the infrastructure level, and burgeoning investor interest at the funding level. These factors have and will continue to be guided, and occasionally restricted, by local regulatory bodies. As the industry develops, clear challenges and promising opportunities lie ahead.

One of the primary challenges that marketplace lenders will face in China, the US, and other markets is the limitation on data sources and usage. As many of these businesses are being built, online data is also growing in volume and depth. However, scandals about misused data have heightened awareness, among both the public and politicians, about the problems with data privacy and use of data. Regulations, such as the European Union's General Data Protection Regulation, which require higher levels of explicit consent for data collection and use, may limit the data available to marketplace lenders as they seek to build more accurate risk models for borrowers. Marketplace lenders in developing markets are less likely to encounter such regulations as quickly, but the pushback is likely to happen eventually.

Another significant challenge is the economic cycle. The last time the global economy experienced a significant contraction in 2008, only a handful of marketplace lenders were operating, and even those that existed had different operating models than the ones we see today. A risk model designed to capitalize on growth opportunities in a period of economic growth is likely to be ill-prepared for handling the fundamental changes to economic conditions associated with a major recession. The online marketplace lending industry will need to demonstrate a sustained capacity to manage credit risk, while still providing sufficient return to continue to attract investment.

Each of these challenges, if mishandled, are likely to draw unwanted attention from regulators. This may include punitive rules that push back on the amount and types of data available to be used in machine learning processes to such an extent that the models begin to lose the ability to make more accurate predictions than their competitors, including traditional banks. If significant losses result from an inability to react to increased risk, regulators may restrict the platforms' ability to loan to customers or create more onerous risk-provisioning requirements similar to the Basel Capital Adequacy Ratio rules that have forced traditional banks to divert significant portions of their free cash into reserve provisions.

While these issues will provide plenty of challenges for marketplace lenders, the opportunities on the horizon are also compelling.

As the industry grows, opportunities for scale will begin to attract competitors to form alliances or even merge. While operating costs are lower for many of these platforms, relative to traditional banks, scale will help merged marketplace lenders reach a larger pool of borrowers more efficiently. At the same time, larger loan origination volumes may strengthen the hand of larger marketplace lenders in the growing securitization market. Another key component of the maturing of the online marketplace lending industry may be the increasing standardization that often accompanies such mergers.

Another major opportunity for growth will be in new borrower categories, especially SME lending. US$600b in SME loans were originated as of 2015, and that figure is growing as the US economy continues to grow. Successfully applying the risk management principles as well as attracting businesses as borrowers will be a major opportunity for marketplace lenders to grow their transaction volume. On a related note, trade financing also holds considerable promise, especially for Chinese marketplace lenders, as they can look to fund the capital needs for suppliers throughout China's vast, layered network of supply chains.

FinEX Asia is the first fintech asset management firm connecting professional and institutional Asian investors with high-quality investments. The company maximizes return for qualified investors through technology, professionalism, expertise, and an extensive global network. Beginning with our flagship US consumer credit fund, FinEX Asia has leveraged its technology core to build new bond, hybrid, and leveraged funds and expand from asset management into private equity. Founded in Hong Kong, FinEX Asia now has offices in Taiwan and Singapore, with a dedicated technology team in China. FinEX Asia is licensed under the Hong Kong Securities and Futures Commission. For more information, please visit www.finexasia.com.

Dianrong is a leader in online marketplace lending in China. Founded in 2012 and headquartered in Shanghai, Dianrong offers small businesses and individuals a comprehensive, one-stop financial platform supported by industry-leading technology, compliance, and transparency. The company's sophisticated and adaptable infrastructure enables it to design and customize lending and borrowing products and services based on industry-specific data and insights, all supported by online risk-management and operation tools. Dianrong's specific offerings include marketplace lending-related services and fintech solutions. Dianrong was named in 2016 to the executive directorship of the National Internet Finance Association of China, led by the People's Bank of China. For more information, please visit www.dianrong.com/en.

Chapter 18
Lending and Crowdfunding

Crowdfunding is the practice of funding a project by raising small amounts of money from a large number of people, typically the public. As each crowdfunding campaign involves many contributors, it is usually only feasible when conducted through digital channels such as the internet, via desktop or mobile.

In this chapter, we will describe the three key methods of crowdfunding, how crowdfunding has developed to-date, its impact globally and in Southeast Asia, the technology, and the evolution in digital crowdfunding technology.

Crowdfunding and Its Entry into Lending

There are three key types of crowdfunding, namely rewards-, equity-, and debt-based crowdfunding. It is determined by the consideration that contributors receive for funding a project:

- In *rewards-based crowdfunding*, contributors receive the product and/ or service that the project aims to create.
- In *equity-based crowdfunding*, contributors obtain shares of the company imple-menting the project.
- In *debt-based crowdfunding*, contributors receive financial repayments from the company as lenders.

While crowdfunding platforms that first came into prominence such as Indiegogo (2007) and Kickstarter (2009) focus mainly on rewards, debt-based crowdfunding platforms such as Zopa (2005) and LendingClub (2007) took the limelight with their sheer volume of transactions. The massive adoption of debt-based crowdfunding globally came on the back of the global financial crisis in 2008, when banks stopped lending and the mistrust toward existing financial institutions hiked. Consumers and small-medium enterprises (SMEs) were looking for alternatives, a market gap that debt-based crowdfunding promptly filled. The repercussions of the financial crisis lingered for a prolonged period of time; consumer and SME access to bank lending continue to be limited, while debt-based crowdfunding platforms saw an explosive growth, with LendingClub crossing US$1b in loans issued in 2012.[1] This proved that debt-based crowdfunding was here to stay. It is now an integral part of the financial technology (fintech) industry globally.

At the heart of debt-based crowdfunding is capital allocation. As a two-sided mar-ketplace, it brings together borrowers looking for funding and loan investors looking for returns. To the borrowers, there are often no better alternative besides credit cards and (at times illegal) moneylenders. To the investors, these loans represent a unique

DOI 10.1515/9781547400904- 018

asset that is short-term and simple to invest with competitive yield. Initially, most borrowers and investors were individuals, resulting in the term *peer-to-peer lending* (P2P lending). Over time, both borrowers and investors have evolved to include institutions, giving it the name *marketplace lending*. The types of services offered to each customer segment differ, giving rise to new platforms. But the fundamental remains unchanged, which is to enable such lending to happen at scale enabled by technology, thereby providing better financial services.

Importance of Debt-based Crowdfunding

As an alternative to bank financing, debt-based crowdfunding is built on the premise that the current capital markets are inefficient. This is especially true for borrowers who may be creditworthy individuals and businesses but are unable to get loans due to two key reasons: the bank's inability to assess the creditworthiness of borrowers, and the prohibitive cost incurred by the bank to serve these clienteles.

Lower Cost to Serve

Some studies have shown that, through the use of technology, the operating cost of debt-based crowdfunding platforms is potentially up to 4% lower than that of banks for every dollar of loan outstanding.[2] It enables the platforms to serve consumers and businesses which banks may not profitably serve.

The World Economic Forum identified the cost of providing credit as the primary challenge to serving SMEs, giving rise to the global structural problem of the "Missing Middle,"[3] a term coined to describe the inability of SMEs to get the credit they need. Leading SME platforms such as Funding Circle in the UK and Funding Societies in Southeast Asia are increasingly lending to SMEs that are new to business loans.

Greater Accuracy and Access

The availability of alternative digital information and the emergence of new underwriting approaches enable debt-based crowdfunding platforms to assess the creditworthiness of individuals and SMEs with limited or no information, a phenomenon known as "thin file" or "no file," respectively. The higher accuracy in underwriting allows the platform to approve and provide loans to more individuals and SMEs (which otherwise would not have received a loan), at better terms and/or quantum, reducing the overall occurrence of *false negatives*. The use of technology to offer useful and affordable loans to under-served or unserved segments of society is a critical initiative to drive financial inclusion in both developed and developing markets.

Overall, debt-based crowdfunding platforms began to offer faster, better, and at times cheaper loans to borrowers. The actual application and value proposition differ by market. From the loan investors' perspective, consumer or SME loans are relatively efficient forms of investment. In addition to the promise of competitive returns, the low fees and lock-in period have attracted yield-seekers to try out this new asset class. The simple and transparent customer experience induces trust, which is particularly needed in the post-financial crisis period. Some see it as part of responsible investing to build an investment portfolio that is relatively counter-cyclical compared to other asset classes.

Impact across the Globe and in Southeast Asia

Since its advent in the UK and US, debt-based crowdfunding has speedily expanded globally, including China, India, and Australia. According to the Cambridge Centre for Alternative Finance, China is now the biggest debt-based crowdfunding market globally, lending about US$204b in 2016,[4] followed by the US and UK at about US$24b[5] and US$6b,[6] respectively.

The spread of debt-based crowdfunding reached the shores of Southeast Asia around 2015, starting with Singapore, Malaysia, and Indonesia as the first countries to introduce regulatory frameworks. In June 2016, the Monetary Authority of Singapore made regulatory clarifications to enable startups and SMEs to access debt-based crowdfunding. In November 2016, the Securities Commission Malaysia announced a regulatory framework and six recognized market operators. The Financial Services Authority of Indonesia soon joined the foray in January 2017. These regulatory frameworks provide much needed clarity in operational boundaries, investor safeguards, and legal legitimacy, which pave the way for rapid growth of the budding debt-based crowdfunding industry in these countries. In other parts of Southeast Asia, some platforms operate unregulated, while others are met with a sudden shutdown instruction from regulators.

While balancing between financial innovation and customer protection is not easy, governments have generally welcomed the entry of debt-based crowdfunding, as it is seen to drive financial inclusion, a key area of focus. Being a localized business, several homegrown debt-based crowdfunding platforms have also emerged in the region. Perhaps the most notable platform is Funding Societies | Modalku, for its regional coverage in the three regulated countries.

Based on a McKinsey report,[7] the growth in productivity of the "unbanked" population from tech-enabled financial inclusion (such as mobile money and consumer lending) could result in economic impact of US$17b to US$52b while the increased lending to SMEs due to big data underwriting and alternative lending platforms could bring about an economic impact of US$2b to US$6b in 2030 for Southeast Asia. For unserved and under-served consumers and SMEs, this represents a significant uplift.

However, the actual impact depends on the introduction of appropriate and timely regulation, market adoption of digital solutions, and performance of industry players. It is a long-run game, and still in its infancy, especially for SME financing and Southeast Asia.

Digital Crowdfunding Technology

The technology evolution of debt-based crowdfunding varies significantly from one platform to the other and is considered sensitive proprietary information. As such, we will be discussing a case study on digital crowdfunding technology in Southeast Asia.

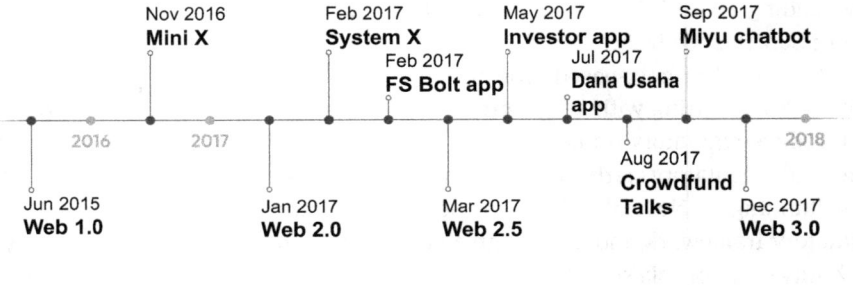

Tech behind Funding Societies & Modalku
Tech Milestones

Figure 18.1: Timeline of a product launch in Funding Societies | Modalku. System X and Mini-X represent internal tools. The rest are external application for users.

Successful startups have been built on almost every imaginable technology of their times. However, choosing a programming language, database, or framework because it is 'cool' can prove to be fatal to the outcome of an engineering team, and even to the firm's success. This section will cover technology and key considerations in digital crowdfunding firms, though many lessons may apply generally to startups, too.

Given the number of companies starting up in the digital crowdfunding sphere since 2006, several vendors emerged, offering backend functionalities in a platform-as-a-service (PaaS) model. Examples include Turnkey Lender (2014) and Mambu (2009). These firms are able to provide core banking engines and analytics services that enable companies to outsource the entire backend processes. Such solutions may be useful in accelerating the startup process and growth to some extent. However, one should be cognizant of evolving requirements, changing regulations, and other needs that may necessitate tweaks or improvements in the backend. Vendors should be screened early on pricing as loan volumes grow, on adaptability to new requirements, on building up new features well, and incident response procedures to avoid future adverse situations.

The Early Days

The key principle in selecting a technology (or stack), is usually to achieve leverage in growth. This requires different decisions at each stage of the company. Digital lending upstarts typically deploy a simple website and backend on the cloud with enough features to launch products in the market for maximal learning and to gauge initial market demand, commonly known as minimum viable product (MVP) in lean startup methodology.[8] In the case of crowdlending, features for lenders include sign-up, login, dashboards for ongoing, upcoming crowdfunding campaigns, investing in a loan, making deposits, withdrawals, or browsing through the website to learn more about the company and its operations.

The "other" side of this marketplace serves parties seeking funds, which are likewise typically enabled with features to sign up, login, submit their request for funds along with relevant documentation and be notified of the outcome via email, text message, or a phone call. On the backend, technology teams build a website serving internal users in onboarding lenders and borrowers as well as serving them through the loan lifecycle. Most of this functionality is provided through cloud services like Amazon Web Services, Google Cloud, Microsoft Azure, or a local provider.

At an early stage, decision criteria revolve around the expertise of engineers in the founding team. The technology stack is often based on what they are most familiar with. This could be Microsoft technology using a.NET backend with .aspx pages on the website or a full stack framework like Ruby on Rails, Django, or Python. As long as the website gets shipped and teams are able to learn from the market, the company is on a good track. Engineering for scale at this point does not make sense due to many factors such as low adoption rate, business requirements, team size, and low funding for tools and hiring developers. It would be wasteful to build for what is not needed, or in anticipation of future demand without clear data or evidence. Focus is paramount, especially in the early survival days of the firm.

Moving Past the Minimum Viable Product into Growth

As the firm grows, its technology stack has to evolve to incorporate new requirements imposed by businesses and users. The keyword "evolve" matters a lot. Intelligent foresight and meticulous planning are desirable to inform users of the design of technology. However, reality is a mix of such planning and needs which develop organically, resulting in messy codebases and hacks that were necessary to survive during spurts of growth in unexpected ways. As a result, building technology that is able to incorporate future requirements well and scale faster than the people needed to maintain it are prudent decision criteria for evolving the stack.

If building new features takes increasingly longer, rolling out products becomes a bug-ridden process, crowdfunding process is failing frequently due to load and so on, the time is right to revisit architectural decisions of the past. Firms experiencing growth have to decide when to transition from hackish solutions and re-architect for scale.

In the context of digital crowdfunding companies moving into a growth phase (typically post–Series A funding), the backend needs to evolve to serve the business in launching new products quickly, collecting information and documents about investors and borrowers, developing sophisticated features across the loan lifecycle for enhanced tracking, expedited automated underwriting, collection activities, etc. Firms also invest more to improve the user experience for investors and borrowers. As experienced by Funding Societies | Modalku in its journey from Web 1.0 to 3.0 (as shown previously in Figure 18.1), this may constitute a revamp of the website with fresh colors, consistency of look and feel across platforms, faster onboarding, more nuanced display of information in the loan portfolio and rewriting the backend.

Key Pieces of Technology in a Digital Crowdfunding Firm

Loan Lifecycle

A loan lifecycle is made up of five core aspects: origination, underwriting, funding, settlement, and collection. Digital crowdfunding companies build and/or buy technology for internal teams to service each vertical. For example, in origination, tracking borrower leads by sales team(s) can be done through external customer resource management (CRM) tools such as Salesforce; scorecards in underwriting can be leveraged from vendor Turnkey Lender depending on the needs of respective firms. Some may prefer to build each vertical in-house, preferring control over how tools are developed, to maintain greater degree of control as well as competitive advantages over peers in the market.

Auto-Invest Algorithm

For investors who are too busy in their day jobs to log in to a digital crowdfunding portal, study the available investment opportunities of the day, and click Invest in each loan, Funding Societies | Modalku has devised the auto-investment algorithm.

Via a slick user interface, investors can instruct Funding Societies | Modalku to automatically deploy their funds based on selecting loan parameters such as quantum, tenor, interest rates, and industries. Investors' choices are duly stored in Funding Societies | Modalku's systems and used by its algorithm for every crowdfunding effort in the future. From then on, investors can simply revise their criteria periodically, opt out of loans, or simply do nothing as a portion of their capital gets deployed to dozens of companies each month, earning interest over time.

Extensible, Scalable Backend System

As the firm grows, systems need to cater for multiple products, verticals, and markets. They should be able to accommodate surges in traffic, which get heavier as more investors seek to participate in crowdfunding campaigns. For example, an SGD 500,000 loan used to take five days to be fully crowdfunded in 2016, the early days of Funding Societies | Modalku. By 2018, the average time taken dropped to forty minutes. The capability of backend systems to process such influxes of requests to invest in a crowdfunding loan in a short span of time is crucial for a successful funding effort. This involves applying queues, scaling servers during a surge of traffic, and reconciliation across all relevant investor accounts. Developing an extensible and scalable backend system is required for operations of the digital crowdfunding company.

Data-driven Scorecards

A scorecard is a statistical method for evaluating the risk of a loan applicant. An overly stringent scorecard will result in significant rejections and false negatives—that is, a borrower who should have been approved for a loan gets rejected. Conversely, an overly relaxed scorecard will see high defaults, which can endanger the sustainability of a debt-based crowdfunding platform and even a bank.

As many borrowers who use debt-based crowdfunding platforms are underserved or unserved, there is limited data for a data-driven scorecard. Therefore, many debt-based crowdfunding platforms started by adopting an intuitive approach toward risk assessment. But as platforms like Funding Societies | Modalku mature, there is a major shift toward not only data-driven scorecards, but also advanced data analytics.

This is where piercing insights, from various data collection activities that feed into underwriting models, give startups leverage over incumbents and other players in the market. A key, known reason why banks under-serve SMEs is because of their credit teams' fixation on audited financial statements. Many SMEs in the market simply get disqualified because of this reason. Startups have proliferated touting use of alternate data to serve such SMEs. Some of these upstarts use data collected from mobile, social media (Facebook, LinkedIn, Google), bank statements, and psychometrics in arriving at a credit score. Quantum, tenor, and interest rates are determined based on a combination of these for a loan applicant.

In the US, the lending market has matured to an extent where credit scoring is applicable as a service by data analytics firms such as Fair Isaac Corporation (FICO).

Such services are lacking in Southeast Asia, thus competitive advantages reside in a firm's scorecards used in underwriting models.

Mobile Application for Investors and Borrowers

Serving both segments of users via mobile applications customized specifically for each is strategically paramount. This is because more than 90% of internet users in Southeast Asia use smartphones and spend an average of 3.6 hours daily on mobile internet. This is the highest usage rate globally, according to a joint report by Google and Temasek titled "e-Conomy SEA Spotlight 2017."[9]

In practice, a large segment of investors prefers to use Funding Societies | Modalku's smartphone application to invest in loans, due to the convenience of being able to do so from almost anywhere, on the go.

Dedicating a specific mobile application for borrowers is also a boon for collecting relevant data for underwriting, as shared in the preceding "Data-driven Scorecards" section, and to optimize for speed in loan application. Funding Societies | Modalku launched Bolt in 2017, a mobile app for SME borrowers, that enabled loan applications to be completed in two minutes, underwriting decisions to be available in two hours, and for funds to be disbursed into a successful applicant's company bank account within a day (see Figure 18.2). Such speed has been warmly welcomed in the borrower community, resulting in growth of Funding Societies | Modalku's loan book.

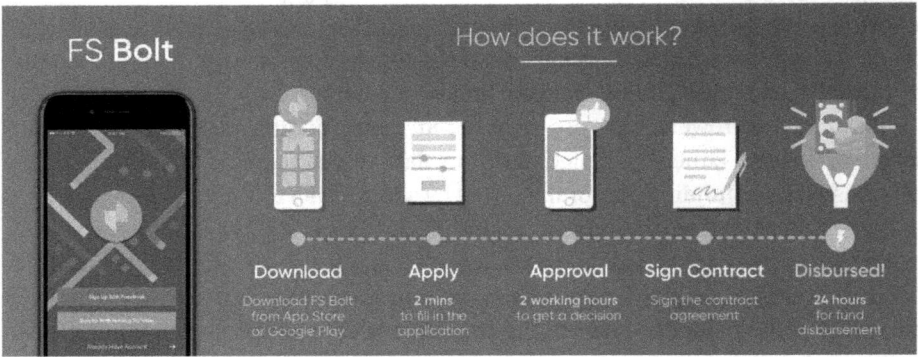

Figure 18.2: FS Bolt, mobile application for borrowers

Expedited Data Collection Activities

Lack of documentation is one of the primary reasons for incomplete loan applications. Borrowers may need to retrieve information from their bank, the Central Provident Fund (CPF), credit bureau accounts, and more. The more types of documents needed, the higher the rate of abandonment during loan application. This also contributes to lengthy processes as the teams need to wait or follow up on documents before being able to complete the underwriting stage. Thus, developing technology to automate the retrieval of such documents or parse them using optical character recognition (OCR) and/or screen-scraping can be highly beneficial to optimizing on drop-off rate as well as length of time needed to process a loan application.

Some of this requires innovation at the industry level by other players. For example, the Government Technology Agency of Singapore (GovTech) launched MyInfo, a portal for citizens to manage their personal information.[10] Firms, with consent of citizens, are able to verify the latter's identity and develop a financial picture using software (via application programming interfaces, or APIs). This directly reduces the need to upload one's identity documents and some financial information. More of such efforts are underway by industry players, as the concepts of API economy and open banking develop in Southeast Asia.

Limitations: Repayment Data

Regardless of the type and sophistication of technologies deployed at a digital crowd-funding firm, time is needed to collect repayment information, especially for debt-based products. This information is crucial for refining underwriting models and laying truth to the claims of alternate data being used in enabling underbanked, under-served SMEs to receive financing. As each loan can have a tenor ranging from 3 to 24 months, a few cohorts of loans have to be collected before useful iterations can occur in scorecards and models. Such an inherent limitation sets the timeline for innovation backwards by at least a few years.

Applications Developed at Funding Societies | Modalku

This section discusses three products of Funding Societies | Modalku. It portrays the journey of investors and borrowers via mobile applications dedicated to each segment. The same features are available to users via a website.

Investors can sign up, verify their email, onboard, make deposits, withdraw funds, invest, view their portfolio, adjust personal details, and sign up for auto-investment.

The most useful features for investors have been the Invest button and auto-invest algorithm. Both enable significant convenience and were warmly welcomed by users when rolled out.

FS Bolt was launched as a product for small businesses, designed to streamline the loan application process and enable quick disbursement of funds (see Figure 18.3). One of its key enablers is allowing users to upload documents via mobile. Also, users can be notified of more document requests and be able to follow up quickly, in comparison to emails or phone calls made by relationship managers.

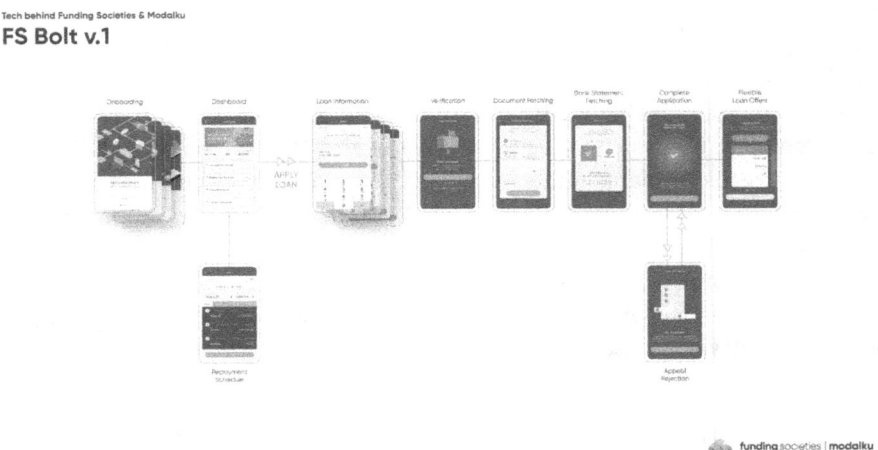

Tech behind Funding Societies & Modalku
FS Bolt v.1

Figure 18.3: Journey of a borrower during sign-up

In the early version of Bolt, Funding Societies | Modalku built features to automate fetching of documents. This feature, based on users' consent, sped up the loan application process. It was also controversial as the technology utilized screen-scraping, which is either banned or frowned upon by many firms. As a result, Funding Societies | Modalku improved on the feature to enable formal, consensual (from both end-user and institution) document fetching via APIs. For example, identity and some financial information is now retrieved via MyInfo from GovTech.

In addition, Bolt is Funding Societies | Modalku's first app to trial-run the use of unique features like flexible loan offers. Borrowers can choose from a combination of different interest rates, quantum, and tenor while backend systems learn their preferences as they evolve to automate the entire loan application process.

Unlike everyday products like Google or Facebook, users only think about financing when they need it. Likewise, investors are keen to log in only when investment opportunities arise. Having a strong, tightly-knit community of users is a strategy for staying at the top of many minds. As a result, CFTalks is a forum that was launched to develop a community of borrowers and investors who can unite on one platform to discuss anything among themselves or with Funding Societies | Modalku's staff (see Figure 18.5).

Tech behind Funding Societies & Modalku
Crowdfund Talks

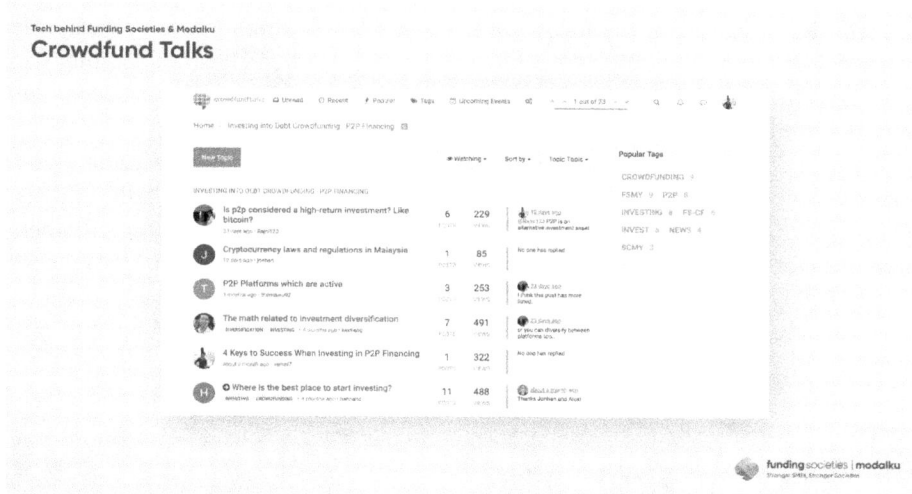

Figure 18.4: Crowdfund Talks community forum

Feedback and insights abound at CFTalks, which inform iterations in efforts and features by internal teams at Funding Societies | Modalku. When users are airing their views on CFTalks, staff at the firm are free to engage and address queries conclusively. Such rich interactions increase users' engagement, as well as retention on Funding Societies | Modalku.

Together, the offerings enable the user effective, state-of-the-art banking, a resource for information gathering and advice, and a site to get competitive rates on loans, offering services beyond what is expected of banking institutions.

A Competitive and Evolving Market

With regulations, Singapore, Indonesia, and Malaysia became the most active digital financing markets in Southeast Asia. The first debt-based crowdfunding platform in each of the countries was Moolah Sense (Nov. 2014), Modalku (Jan. 2015), and Funding Societies (Feb. 2017), respectively. Funding Societies and Modalku are the same company, also with presence in Singapore. By June 2018, Singapore and Indonesia FinTech Association each has about 50 companies registered for lending. They come in all shapes and sizes. The count continues to increase with numerous unregistered users.

While more choices are usually good for customers, the high number of platforms have prompted unhealthy competition, similar to that in China. Based on Citibank's research, interest rates of P2P loans in China had dropped from 20% p.a. in 2014 to 10% p.a. in 2016, as platforms competed for borrowers. It became adverse when the interest rates of P2P loans fell below their risk level, resulting in poor risk-adjusted returns for investors. With high defaults and low returns, the P2P lending industry in China has slowly acquired a bad reputation and started to lose investors. There are signs of a similar trend happening in Southeast Asia.

As the industry matures, there is a realization that debt-based crowdfunding platforms not only need to grow in transaction volume, but also manage defaults and disclose key statistics transparently. Hence, leading platforms are publishing numbers voluntarily for investors to make an educated decision and are undergoing audits for security and governance.

Figure 18.5: Funding Societies website

The industry will likely continue to see an influx of new entrants from startups, conglomerates, and adjacent players. As the speed of new entries outpaces the digital adoption by consumers and SMEs, the industry will likely soon reach a tipping point for consolidation, as observed in China, the US, and other mature crowdfunding markets. Other Southeast Asian countries will also likely open up to debt-based crowdfunding. It will become imperative for platforms to become regional, such as in the case of Funding Societies | Modalku, to remain competitive and achieve the necessary scale for sustainability.

Evolution in Digital Crowdfunding Technology

At the time of writing, exciting developments are occurring in the industry. We highlight two of these: open banking APIs and blockchain for credit bureaus.

Open Banking APIs

As discussed in Chapter 9, using APIs from financial institutions to enable third-party developers in building applications is a growing phenomenon in Europe and the United Kingdom. This was mandated by the European Parliament (2015) as well as the Competition and Markets Authority (CMA) (2016), respectively, with the view to encourage innovation in financial services and allow users to own their data, as compared to having it reside in silos within institutions.

Open banking APIs are meant to facilitate greater collaboration (and competition) between banks and fintech firms to create new revenue streams and more contextual services, centered around the customer.[10,11,12] For example, startups may build mobile applications where customers budget their finances, conduct investment, and receive financial advice in real-time using data obtained from bank accounts and infrastructure. Such efforts are already underway and can be viewed from both competitive and collaborative perspectives. Traditional banks are way behind in offering such services. Allowing startups to do so may cause users to be less sticky to the banks' services.

Without formal APIs, many startups use potentially insecure methods such as screen-scraping to get the data needed. Banks have to address this threat better through offerings provided by partnerships and also by building better products on their own. Such competition compels innovation in traditional banking and as bank executives strive for better services, they are partnering and/or acquiring startups in addition to launching digital products. The biggest beneficiary of such efforts is arguably the end-user, who can increasingly be banked online with cutting-edge solutions.

While adoption of open banking APIs appears relatively nascent in both the UK and Europe, the concept is growing in Southeast Asia. Major regional banks such as OCBC and DBS have launched API platforms in 2016[13] and 2017,[14] respectively, looking to plug into the developer ecosystems and benefit users by applications built from synergies between startups and the banks.

In addition to API access to citizen data, notions of entirely online banking experiences are becoming more realistic. Businesses are poised to benefit from reduced need for paper documents when submitting loan applications, from portability of their data across service providers and more.

Credit Bureau on the Blockchain

The advent of blockchain, starting from the bitcoin white paper in 2008, has spawned many use cases for a tamper-proof, decentralized, distributed ledger and its variants. Within the context of lending, blockchain's use case is being explored for use in credit bureaus.

In 2017, over 140 million accounts were hacked at Equifax Incorporation, one of the three largest credit reporting agencies in the US.[15] Such hacks have been growing in frequency and magnitude over the years. Many could have been avoided if users were in a position to prevent unauthorized retrieval to their data by having one of the private keys needed to access the repository of information. Currently, corporations store data of companies and citizens in centralized databases. Access to these can be obtained through social engineering, leading to the compromise of pre-authorized employees' documents or by penetrating systems' loopholes via open ports in databases. The blockchain, storing data in encrypted format and only allowing decryption based on one or more private keys by respective owners, is a promising technological solution to mitigate such hacks. While hacks may still occur, bad actors would need to compromise accounts one by one and would be stopped way before the count reached 140 million.

In addition, a more accurate picture of creditworthiness can be obtained by having a blockchain-based application store and record transactions of individuals or businesses, fed via a variety of sources. Traditional credit bureaus are limited by the variety, accuracy, and depth of identity, financial and non-financial information that is stored about people and companies. Blockchain applications offer opportunities to re-think this problem fundamentally.

Finally, cost is incurred each time a financial institution performs a credit search. This search may also negatively impact the creditworthiness of a loan applicant. Both of these can be improved if users own their data, are able to add to it from a variety of sources and share it at their own will. As a result, credit agencies stand to be dis-intermediated by blockchain-based applications. The latter promises to improve the accuracy and speed of underwriting. Some of the noteworthy startups trying to realize this include Bloom, Celsius Network, and Civic.

From Crowdfunding to Digital Financing Everywhere

As fintech companies mature, more traditional financial institutions are willing to lend to fintech players. This results in a new business model which some call "balance-sheet lending." Balance-sheet lending companies borrow from traditional financial institutions at lower interest rates and lend to consumers or SMEs at higher interest rates.

Balance-sheet lending differs from debt-based crowdfunding in two key ways. First, it does not involve retail investors. Second, such firms' earnings occur from the interest spread and consequently, they bear the default risk, while debt-based crowdfunding platforms only earn a service fee and face no default risk. There are pros and cons, but both seek to improve financing via digital means and are collectively known as digital financing.

However, digital financing is simply one of the numerous ways that the world is going digital. We are also seeing the rise of ecommerce, ride-sharing, and other marketplace platforms. Like digital financing, these marketplaces are powered through data and digital channels. As they grow, several of these marketplaces are exploring digital financing as a way to further serve their customers. Some consider balance-sheet lending, using the data that they gather from their customers for lending, especially for consumers. Others choose to collaborate with pure-play digital financing players like Funding Societies | Modalku.

As Southeast Asia gradually becomes digital, it also attracts interests of digital financing players across the world, especially from the UK and China. Having a head start in their home countries, they bring vast resources and often superior technology.

We believe while they may be seen as a threat to local players, these foreign players can make an excellent addition to the local fintech ecosystem if managed carefully.

Over time, we expect digital financing to be integrated with all forms of digital transactions, simplifying financing options everywhere. This is especially likely for consumer digital financing where the barriers to entry are much lower than SME digital financing. To stay competitive, pure-play consumer digital financing players will likely have to focus on a specific niche segment or even evolve into a credit scoring agency, helping traditional financial institutions and smaller ecommerce platforms to underwrite customers and provide credit. Some have even bet on global digital financing platforms that are powered by blockchain. This is still a story unfolding.

Conclusion

Crowdfunding was born from a spirit of sharing in reward-based crowdfunding, but grew out of necessity in debt-based crowdfunding. Since the global financial crisis, debt-based crowdfunding has gradually filled the gap left behind by traditional financial institutions. It offers unserved and under-served consumers as well as SMEs greater access to alternative financing with its lower cost to serve, enabled by technology.

Starting in the UK in 2005, debt-based crowdfunding is now a US$300b global phenomenon that may potentially be the solution to the "missing middle" and unbanked consumers in emerging markets, including Southeast Asia. Being the first to regulate, Singapore, Indonesia, and Malaysia became the pioneers in this fast-growing space. Many local, adjacent, and foreign players are rushing in, causing significant unhealthy competition which will prompt consolidation. For now, Funding Societies | Modalku seems to be leading player in the SME digital financing space in Southeast Asia.

Similar to the business model, the technology of debt-based crowdfunding platforms has also gradually moved from minimum viable product to growth phase, whereby platforms focus on more advanced features, scalability, data analytics, mobile access, and user experience. To build an integrated experience, platforms have also built additional data linkages with the rest of ecosystem, consistent with the move toward open banking. Blockchain will likely play a major role in the future too.

Like other themes of fintech, debt-based crowdfunding or digital financing as a whole will continue to evolve based on market dynamics and regulations.

Endnotes

1 https://www.lendingclub.com/info/statistics.action
2 https://www.p2p-banking.com/services/lendingclub-lending-club-cost-advantage-over-banks/
3 World Economic Forum, https://www.weforum.org/agenda/2015/10/5-steps-to-closing-the-2-trillion-credit-gap/

4 Cambridge - Asia numbers, https://www.jbs.cam.ac.uk/fileadmin/user_upload/research/centres/
alternative-finance/downloads/2017-09-cultivating-growth.pdf
5 Cambridge - US numbers, https://www.jbs.cam.ac.uk/fileadmin/user_upload/research/centres/
alternative-finance/downloads/2017-05-americas-alternative-finance-industry-report.pdf
6 Cambridge - UK numbers, https://www.businessinsider.sg/cambridge-report-uk-alternative-
finance-altfi-worth-46-billion-in-2016-2017-12/?r=UK&IR=T
7 McKinsey report, https://www.canback.com/files/2014_MK_MGI%20SE%20Asia_Executive%20
summary.pdf
8 The Lean Startup, http://theleanstartup.com/principles
9 e-Conomy SEA Spotlight, 2017 https://www.thinkwithgoogle.com/intl/en-apac/tools-research/
research-studies/e-conomy-sea-spotlight-2017-unprecedented-growth-southeast-asia-50-billion-
internet-economy/
10 MyInfo launched by Govtech, https://www.tech.gov.sg/Media-Room/Media-Releases/2017/11/
Businesses-can-tap-on-MyInfo-to-offer-faster-transactions-for-citizens
11 https://thefinancialbrand.com/65975/open-banking-api-fintech-partnerships/
12 https://wwwmulesoft.com/resources/ api/open-banking-apis-fintech-partnerships/
13 https://www.ocbc.com/assets/pdf/media/2016/may/media%20release%20-%20ocbc%20is%20
1st%20bank%20in%20southeast%20asia%20to%20launch%20open%20api%20platform.pdf
14 https://www.straitstimes.com/business/banking/dbs-launches-worlds-largest-banking-api-
developer-platform
15 https://techcrunch.com/2018/05/08/equifax-filing-reveals-hack-was-somehow-even-worse-than-
previous-estimates/

References

Blog post: The Gold Rush of 2015 https://fintechjunkie.com/2015/12/15/the-gold-rush-of-2015/
Article from Credit Suisse on Millennials, Responsible Investing https://www.credit-suisse.com/
corporate/en/articles/news-and-expertise/supertrends-millennials-want-to-invest-re-
sponsibly-201706.html
Crowdfunding: The Current State of Research https://www.researchgate.net/
publication/275657510_Crowdfunding_The_Current_State_Of_Research
How Big Will the Debt and Equity Crowdfunding Investment Market Be? Comparisons, Assumptions,
and Estimates https://funginstitute.berkeley.edu/wp-content/uploads/2013/01/Crowdfund_
Investment_Paper.pdf
Techcrunch article: The moment of the second-wave-of-online-lenders-is-gone https://techcrunch.
com/2016/05/22/the-moment-of-the-second-wave-of-online-lenders-is-gone/

Funding Societies | Modalku is the largest SME digital financing platform in Southeast Asia, backed by Sequoia Capital and Softbank Ventures. It offer loans to local small medium enterprises ("SMEs") for growth, crowdfunded by individual and institutional investors globally for returns. Licensed and operating in Singapore, Indonesia, and Malaysia, Funding Societies has been selected as a top 250 fintech firm globally by CB Insights, is winner of Global SME Excellence Award at the United Nation's ITU Telecom World and is a winner of the MAS FinTech Award. As the name suggests, Funding Societies | Modalku believes in financial inclusion for SMEs because "Stronger SMEs, Stronger Societies."

Kelvin Teo *is the co-founder of Funding Societies | Modalku. Recently selected as the Top 200 FinTech Influencers in Asia by Lattice80, Kelvin has spoken at major conferences such as LendIt Shanghai, Boao Hainan, and Money2020 Singapore. He has also been featured on Bloomberg, BBC and Business Times. Prior to this, Kelvin served as a consulting professional at KKR, McKinsey, and Accenture. Kelvin graduated from Harvard Business School and National University of Singapore (valedictorian) and is a certified Chartered Accountant. He started Funding Societies|Modalku because he believes in fairness and that everyone deserves a chance.*

Pramodh Rai *is chief product officer at Funding Societies | Modalku. Prior to this, he worked as a full-stack engineer – developing a bitcoin brokerage, payments and fraud mitigation at a travel firm (acquired by Homeaway, Expedia)—and also held roles as analyst, developer in technology teams at Barclays Investment Bank while working in London, Tokyo as well as Singapore. Pramodh has won two hackathons: the inaugural DBS Blockchain Hackathon and HackAway. He has also received the Young Social Entrepreneur Award from Singapore International Foundation and serves as its "citizen ambassador" currently. He graduated with dual degrees in computer science and business from Nanyang Technological University in Singapore, where he also served as president research scholar, publishing on trust in virtual communities.*

Chapter 19
Robo-Advisory and Multi-Asset Allocation

Robo-advisory services were established over the last five to eight years to provide better investing services to a very large segment of the population by leveraging digital technology. Robo-advisors aim at making investment advisory simple, personal, and cost-effective, thereby allowing individuals to invest intelligently. In Asia, this business model allows for the first time, investors with less than US$5m in investable assets to invest into portfolios built with sophisticated asset allocation frameworks. Additionally, investors can do so by only paying a fraction of the cost typically charged by distributors of simple, off-the-shelf products.

The success of the early entrants of robo-advisory in the US have pushed new entrepreneurs and traditional financial institutions to launch robo-advisory services around the globe. In the next few years, these services will most probably become the status quo for wealth management services for most clients in most geographies.

What Is Robo-Advisory About?

Rob-Advisors are tech-powered financial adviser that provide financial advice and investment management services online with moderate to minimal human intervention. They provide financial advice and manage investments using rule-based, algorithmic, automated systems of varying complexity and sophistication, and they strive to do so through simple-to-use, very cost-effective digital platforms.

It is May 2018, and Mark has US$500,000 deposited and managed in an account at a bank in Singapore.[1] Because of the significant account balance, Mark is granted "premium services," including a dedicated relationship manager, access to more products typically not available to customers with account balances less than US$150,000, and a dedicated website or mobile app.

While this sounds great, the devil is in the details: in reality, Mark is not receiving the level of service he needs to make the best out of his savings while paying significant fees for the premium services in the form of sales charges and management fees. One reason is that the relationship manager (RM) is typically not an investment specialist. Secondly, the RM may be conflicted as his key performance indicator is typically tied to the revenues that he can bring to the financial institution. The imperfect incentive alignment between what the client needs and what the RM is appraised upon may result in product pushing—that is, the client is sold certain products that may not be most suitable for the client's needs.

That is why Mark could be continuously pitched about buying either third-party products distributed by the bank with high retrocessions from the product issuer to the bank, or structured products offering high margins to the bank. Examples of some

DOI 10.1515/9781547400904- 019

third-party products are unit trusts[2] (or mutual funds) with up to a 5% initial sales charge and up to a 1.8% annual management fee, investment-linked insurance policies[3] (or ILPs) with complex fee structures amounting to 2–4% per annum when all expenses are included, and products with long lock-up periods that make it possible for the product issuer to earn high distribution charges. The RM is neither trained nor incentivized to provide financial advice to Mark and to help him understand how to manage his finances, how much risk to take for each part of his investable assets, and how to select the best products available to achieve his required risk exposure. Consequently, he will probably not be fully guided on asset allocation: what percentage of his portfolio should be exposed to equities, bonds, and commodities?

If Mark had less than US$150,000, the situation would be worse, as he would only be able to open a retail account at the bank, and would not have access to a dedicated RM. If Mark had more than US$1.5m,[4] the same bank would upgrade his account to "private" and Mark would have access to a wider array of products and, often, leverage for his investments. However, even as a private client, Mark could still not be getting unbiased advice and could be pushed products that may not be in his best interests. Nevertheless, as a private client, Mark may receive holistic advice on asset allocation and be charged lower percentage fees.

What are Mark's other options? Mark could open a brokerage account and build his own portfolio, potentially using exchange-traded funds (ETFs) as a good, cost-effective tool to build a diversified portfolio. However, he would need to do this autonomously, without leveraging the knowledge that a financial institution should have on asset allocation. He would also need to monitor and rebalance his investments. Mark, and many others like Mark, would prefer to have someone professionally trained to look after his retirement needs and his children's education funds, and he would like that person to be competent and unbiased. Here come robo-advisors to the rescue.

Pain Points Addressed by Robo-Advisory

Technology can be used to address most of the shortcomings of the current wealth management offering. Today, for the most part, wealth management services are basic and standardized, inconvenient and not particularly transparent, and incredibly expensive. Robo-advisors were born with the goal of addressing these three shortcomings and making investing simple, personal, and cost-effective so that each of us can invest intelligently. In fact, while they are called robo-advisors, their focus as of today is more on investing, and they may be more suitably called robo-investors or digital investment services.

The core non-financial value propositions of most robo-advisors are an easy-to-use platform, 100% digital onboarding and account management, and low and very transparent fee structure. On the financial side, all robo-advisors help customers invest in a diversified portfolio across asset classes, usually using low-cost ETFs as the instrument to get investment exposure. Some robo-advisors go one further step beyond a static, mean-variance asset allocation strategy to embed intelligent investment frameworks into their product offerings.

As of today, most robo-advisors have a stronger focus on the fund management part of the model than on the financial advisory part, with the "advice" usually being centered exclusively on risk-targeting and asset allocation.

Robo-advisory services typically target retail or mass-affluent/affluent customers, since most industry practitioners think that high-net-worth (HNW) individuals tend to prefer the human contact provided by traditional private banking models. Many banks see robo-advisory as a way to start offering wealth management services to retail clients, as such services are too expensive to be delivered via traditional models.

A Brief History of Robo-Advisory (including B2B vs B2C vs B2B2C)

Robo-advisors as defined today started to appear in the US shortly after the 2008 global financial crisis, as both New York–based Betterment and Palo Alto–based Wealthfront were founded in 2008 and started offering their services to customers in 2010. As of mid-2018, both companies manage in excess of US$10b and are considered the largest independent robo-advisors globally.

Given the success of these early players, the marketplace has evolved significantly, with a variety of new products being made available to customers across the globe. In the section "Competitive Landscape" later in this chapter, we will describe some of the more relevant players' business models and technologies.

Moreover, many of the industry's incumbents have decided to venture into robo-advisory: banks, brokerage firms, and asset managers alike have started to respond to the success of the first independent robo-advisors. Some incumbents have built or are building their own technological solution; some are purchasing a technological solution from a B2B robo-advisor; some have purchased B2C robo-advisors; and some have made minority investments in either B2B or B2C players. Some banks and financial advisory firms have adopted technological solutions that are advisor-facing instead of customer-facing, and these are sometimes also referred to as robo-advisory solutions.

For the purpose of this chapter, we will look at robo-advisors through the lenses of an end-customer, irrespective of whether the service is provided by an independent new B2C player, by a bank or brokerage that has built its own technology, by a bank or brokerage that has purchased the technology from a B2B player, or by a financial advisor using a platform provided by an asset manager. We will call any robo-advisory service (whether provided by an independent player or by an incumbent) a *robo-advisor*. We will not consider advisor-facing solutions, as while they might have similar back-end engines, the delivery mode is completely different and the customer experience is more similar to traditional models than self-service digital offerings.

Why Is Robo-Advisory Important?

Robo-advisory is important because it has the potential to significantly disrupt the traditional paradigm of investment in the financial industry and because it can dramatically improve the ways many people manage their savings and help them in their personal financial management.

Bringing Significant Changes to the Wealth Management Industry

Robo-advisory is the first recent attempt to use technology to improve the service of a gigantic industry called "wealth management": global private financial wealth in 2016 was US$166t, forecasted to grow to US$223t by 2021 at 6% CAGR (9.9% in APAC), according to the Boston Consulting Group (BCG).[5]

Recent technological impacts on this industry have been focused on narrower segments of the industry such as self-service online brokerages, and on back-end efficiency improvements for the incumbents. Robo-advisory has the potential to change the way many people make decisions about managing their savings and ultimately invest their money, and therefore completely change the competitive dynamics.

Helping People in Personal Financial Management

Robo-advisors can help individuals and families invest systematically, understand and implement asset allocation (which is the most important concept in investing), and increase net returns by reducing costs.

Investing Systematically

Investing is very important as savings will not be enough for retirement. A family saving $1,000/month for 30 years would have accumulated $360,000 if the savings were not invested, and $1,000,000 if the savings were invested and achieved 6%[6] net returns per annum. Many families are not aware of this and do not have access to the right advice to be guided to investing more; in fact, in many geographies, the percentage of cash in people's asset allocation is excessive. In Singapore, 36% of households' financial wealth is in bank deposits; this figure is 42% for Asia ex-Japan, compared to 14% for the US.[7]

Additionally, even people with the right knowledge may stop investing if the process is too complex and cumbersome. The best way to achieve medium-term returns while reducing risk is to invest systematically and dollar-cost averaging the entry into the various markets, for instance setting up monthly standing instructions that on every pay-day automatically wires a fixed amount of money to an investment account.

Robo-advisors have the potential to significantly change this, making it easy for everybody to invest and to do so regularly and systematically.

Understanding and Implementing Asset Allocation

Asset allocation accounts for the majority of returns variability among different investment strategies. In 1986, it was for the first time demonstrated that "investment policy (asset allocation) dominates investment strategy (market timing and security selection), and the former explained on average 95.6% percent of the variation in the total plan return."[8] This conclusion has been confirmed by several further studies, including one conducted in 2012 by Vanguard in which the study *reinforced the view that asset allocation explains the majority of a portfolio's return variability.*[9] Focusing on strategic asset allocation is the key investment principle of most robo-advisors: while the strategies and the sophistication may differ, all robo-advisors help their clients invest in portfolios that are diversified across asset classes.

Reducing the Cost of Investing

Reducing the cost of investing for customers can increase net returns significantly. A family investing $2,000/month for 30 years in a product with a 6% gross return (before fees) and being charged an average of 0.5% annually in fees will have US$1.8m after 30 years; if the fees were 1.5%, the total dollar net return would be US$1.5m; if the fees were 2.5%, the total dollar net return would be US$1.2m. Fees matter!

The effect of compound interest is shown in Figure 19.1, which illustrates how a monthly investment of $2,000 in two investments yielding 6% gross returns develops assuming that one option (solid line) charges 0.5% annual fees while the other (dotted line) charges 2.5% annual fees.

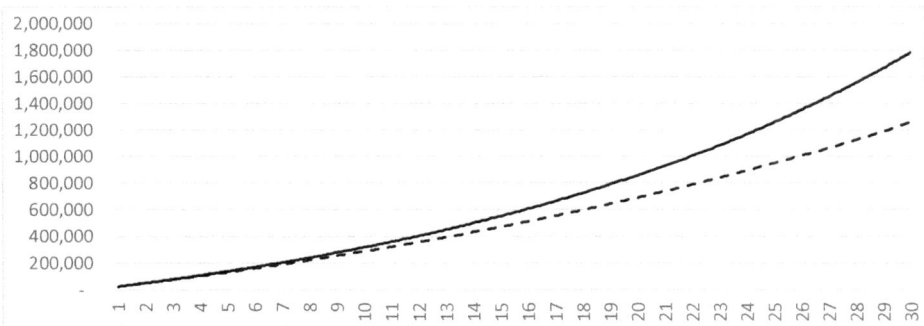

Figure 19.1: Change in growth in portfolio value of two equivalent investments with a 2.0% difference in annual management fees

Saving 2 percentage points in annual management fee can yield 50% more in capital ($1.8m vs $1.2m in the example above). One of the key value propositions of robo-advisors is the significant cost-reduction they offer to their customers. In most countries in Asia, the reduction is significantly larger than in the US, given the very high starting level of fees charged by incumbents in Asia.

How Does Robo-Advisory Work?

Robo-Advisory services rely on a set of different technologies that ultimately give to the end customer direct access to curated investment portfolios through a digital interface. The innovation relies more on the business model and on the merge of these technologies, rather than on any of these technologies by themselves.

Introduction to Robo-Advisors' Technology

Robo-advisors are client-facing digital platforms that advise individuals how to invest their savings, execute their investments, and manage them over time.

The technology required to fulfill these three functions include:
- A financial advisory algorithm
- An asset allocation model
- An order execution system
- A brokerage service or a connection to a third-party brokerage
- Connectivity to external banks and custodians
- A front-end platform that interfaces with the customer dynamically

The following two sections focus on financial advisory and fund management (asset allocation + order execution), as these are the areas where the largest design choices need to be made.

Digital Financial Advice

Financial advisory is a broad field and goes from short-term cash-flow planning to holistic goal-oriented planning; from tax planning to estate and charity planning, and can oftentimes include protection (i.e., health and term insurance). Some of these services have been and still are only available to the high-net-worth individuals.

Robo-advisors' financial advisory technology currently tackles goal-oriented planning and, in some countries, tax optimizations; everything else is sometimes provided by human advisors, without the use of technology. The objectives of the financial advisory functionality of most robo-advisors is to help the client understand the right risk level for his or her portfolio(s). Players have developed algorithms that can take into consideration a variety of inputs including the client's risk preference, financial situation, financial knowledge, investment horizon, and consider the client's entire investment portfolio when recommending an appropriate risk level for each specific portfolio. These algorithms also need to comply with the relevant regulations on client suitability, making sure that clients are only recommended products with a risk level that would be deemed suitable by the regulator. As the relationship of the client with the robo-advisor continues over time, the robo-advisor may collect information, including behavioral preferences of the client, that can be used to continuously improve and personalize these recommendations. Additionally, as the client's situation changes over time, the algorithm needs to take into consideration those changes and dynamically adjust its recommendations.

In countries where capital gains are taxed, some robo-advisors have introduced automated *tax-loss harvesting* services. In short, the algorithm would recommend the sale of an underperforming investment, thereupon realizing a loss, and replace it with a different equivalent investment so that the loss can be used to offset the taxable income generated by other positive investments.[10] In countries where the tax rate for long-term and short-term capital gains is different, the algorithm can take this into consideration as well, further improving after-tax returns.

A few robo-advisors attempt to help their customers save money using technology. For example, micro-investing robo-advisors have engines that automatically round up payments and invest the spare change: a $19.40 transaction becomes a $20 one, with $0.60 automatically invested.

Automated Fund Management

Once the risk-target level for a customer portfolio has been identified, robo-advisors have to match it with a target asset allocation plan and execute the buy orders required to build the portfolio. Most robo-advisors will automatically rebalance portfolios when one or more components have been over-weighted or underweighted due to asymmetric performance. In practice, if one security outperforms other securities, its representation in the overall portfolio will increase, making the portfolio diverge from its original target asset allocation: rebalancing brings the actual allocation back to target.

The first part of the fund management technology of a robo-advisor is the asset allocation model. In some cases, this can be very simple and actually not use any technology; in fact, it often is a simple static model using mean-variance mathematics that optimize expected returns relative to risk ratio in order to create *efficient portfolios*; the model uses historical average returns, average volatility, and a covariance matrix for the securities to be included in the portfolio as inputs to the optimization process. In other cases, this can be much more sophisticated, with dynamic components and with enough variables taken into consideration in the optimization to require artificial intelligence technology.

Once the target portfolio is identified, the back-end engine of the robo-advisor needs to generate the orders required to build the portfolio, usually aggregating them from thousands of customers in one single order per security. This process usually includes the rebalancing of unbalanced portfolios, triggering buy-orders for securities to which a given client is underexposed, and sell-orders for securities to which a given client is overexposed. This order management system connects to an internal or external brokerage platform that executes the orders, typically using an algorithm to improve trade execution prices.[11]

The ability to build an intelligent, automated asset allocation framework—coupled with an efficient, scalable, and sophisticated order management and trade execution system—will be of utmost importance for any player to achieve their desired levels of returns and control their trading costs. Success in the medium-term depends critically on whether the players are able to scale efficiently.

Limitations

Using the sophisticated service received by an ultra-high-net-worth individual as a benchmark and assuming that mass-affluent and affluent individuals could benefit from some of them, it is safe to say that as of today, robo-advisors are only able to serve a small part of these needs. For example, the automated advice provided by robo-advisors does not touch complex areas such as tax and estate planning, usually does not include protection as an area for advice, and is often very light in cash planning, as it focuses mostly on risk-assessment. A few players have made advances in these areas, starting from helping customers to understand their medium to long-term cash needs through a digital advisory process that enables customers to answer questions such as "How much do I need to save per month in order to accumulate enough to maintain my lifestyle during retirement?" Overall, the "advisory" part of robo-advisory services is still underdeveloped and has significant limitations. Open banking policies that are being adopted by regulators in a few geographies have the potential to fuel the development of better advisory systems, as more data and information will be digitally available without tedious data entry by the customer.

On the fund management side, robo-advisors tend to focus on giving exposure to liquid asset classes such as public equities, traded corporate and government bonds, and commodities. Illiquid assets such as untraded credit assets, private equity, venture capital, and real estate are not part of robo-advisors' offerings.

How Can Robo-Advisors Reduce Costs?

Robo-advisors can offer low fees to clients and therefore improve returns by focusing on keeping the cost of operations low. In particular, there are three main areas of potential savings relative to traditional wealth managers: customer acquisition, client management, and back-office processing:

– On *customer acquisition*, robo-advisors aim at reducing costs by offering a value proposition that is easy to understand with few barriers to entry, including lower minimum investment quantum below $10,000 and on-boarding processes that take less than 15 minutes.

– In terms of *client management*, the marginal cost of a digital interaction with a client is negligible, while the marginal cost of a meeting between an RM and a client is significant. This is an important area of cost savings for digital-first players.

– On *back-office processing*, automation is the name of the game. From on-boarding (KYC/AML) to risk management, from order management to clearing and settlement, from data management to cash processing, all these areas of operations can be run very efficiently by using technology and reducing human intervention wherever possible.

How Can Robo-Advisors Improve Quality?

Robo-advisors can significantly improve the quality of the financial advice and ultimately the investment products that are offered to customers compared to traditional players.

First, the improvement in the quality of advice can come naturally and immediately from the alignment of interests generated by a more transparent fee model: in countries where traditional wealth managers and advisors are still accepting retrocession, this change is sufficient to produce enormously better advice.

In addition, the current traditional model requiring an interaction between RMs and customers forces traditional players to significantly reduce the degree of complexity and the personalization that can be delivered to the end-customer. In order to have thousands of RMs and advisors distribute consistent advice, traditional players need to simplify: this is why there is very little personalization offered to banks' premium customers, and that the only asset allocation discussions that are possible are based on models with 4 to 6 options and can only be done at the overall portfolio level. By letting the client interact directly with the system, robo-advisors can offer truly personalized advice down to the individual goal level, and therefore achieve more sophisticated and better performing investment strategies.

Applications: The StashAway Case

StashAway is a Singapore-headquartered robo-advisor founded in September 2016 that started offering its services to customers in July 2017 with the goal of making it simple and cost-effective to invest intelligently: *empowering people to build wealth in the long term*. StashAway has developed a proprietary asset allocation framework, leveraging two decades of academic studies and institutional investors' experiences in using the relationship between economic data and medium-term market returns. The framework is called ERAA, for economic regime-based asset allocation, and uses a sophisticated three-pillar model to construct portfolios and dynamically manage them over time as the economy changes. For example, in good economic times, one customer might have significant equity exposure, particularly to emerging markets or consumer discretionary or technology; when the economy goes recessionary, the customer's portfolio would be adjusted to reduce equity exposure and to move into defensive sectors such as consumer staples and utilities—the portfolio would also have more exposure to fixed income as well as gold.

A customer can sign up through an internet platform or a mobile app in approximately 15 minutes, including goal setting and *know your customer* (KYC), the process of collecting enough data to verify the identity of the customer, the source of the funds, and the suitability of the investments. The customer can use the goal-setting process to understand in details the financial needs to reach a particular goal—for instance, the monthly investment required to be able to afford a certain type of retirement lifestyle at a certain age. Once the customer confirms one or more portfolios and starts depositing funds, the platform automatically invests the funds in the portfolios approved by the customer. Deposits can be made with the frequency and size selected by the customer: it can be a single lump sum, a monthly standing instruction, or a daily investment of any amount without any minimum or maximum limits. The customer may own fractional shares, as StashAway's technology makes it possible to own as little as 0.0001 units of a given security, allowing for very precise asset allocation even for small portfolios or small deposit amounts. The platform will check the status of the portfolio every day, and automatically execute a rebalancing whenever one or more asset classes are overweighted or underweighted relative to the targeted asset allocation by a certain threshold. Additionally, the platform offers an optional feature of automatic re-optimization of the portfolio, when a change in the economic cycle has been detected or when other optimization triggers have been activated. When the customer wants to withdraw part of or all of the funds, they can do so in the mobile app or on the web platform, and will receive the money in their preferred bank account at $T+1$, where T is the day of withdrawal instruction.

Competitive Landscape

Independent robo-advisors have been available for clients in the US since 2010, in Europe since 2012–2014, while in Asia and elsewhere, the first products appeared in 2016–2017. Likewise, the banks, brokerages and other incumbents have first launched robo-advisory offerings in the US in 2015–2017 and are now following in other geographies.

The following description of leaders in the space will aim at giving a sense of the current competitive landscape as of mid-2018. As the US is the most mature market by leaps and bounds, we will focus on analyzing the US market in more depth.

We do not look at B2B robo-advisors, or companies that provide technological solutions to financial players. Rather, we look at the financial players' final offerings, irrespective of whether the robo-advisory solution was built in-house or bought from a B2B player.

The US Landscape[12]

In the US, the three largest independent robo-advisors are recognized to be Betterment (US$13.5b assets under management), Wealthfront (US$10b), and Personal Capital (US$7b).[13] The three companies have all raised significant equity capital in the US$200m–300m range to build their businesses thus far, and have over time taken different approaches. On the one end, Wealthfront has taken a 100%-digital approach and its founder and CEO Andy Rachleff has been quoted as saying, "Our customers pay us not to meet us." Wealthfront does not offer the ability to talk or meet with a human financial advisor, and believes that software is the answer to provide better financial advice. At the opposite end of the spectrum, Personal Capital has always been offering a personal advisor to all of its customers, and for this reason charges higher fees and asks for a higher minimum (US$50k) than most other players. Betterment started with a purely digital approach, and in 2017 has launched a new "premium" offering which, for a US$100k minimum investment and higher fees, includes unlimited access to a financial advisor. More broadly, Betterment has launched an array of other products venturing into B2B2C distribution, including Betterment for Advisors, a platform for financial advisors, and Betterment for Business, its 401k offering to companies.

A few US companies have launched robo-advisory services with some twists in the value proposition.

For instance, Acorns is the largest *micro-investing* player, and allows its customers to save the spare change resulting from their credit card transactions automatically. Acorns was able to attract 1.3 million clients for US$0.5b assets under management (AUM), making it the largest robo-advisor by number of customers, but it manages only 4–5% of the assets managed by the leading independent robo-advisors.

Its average account size is US$420 vs US$39k for Betterment, US$51k for Wealthfront, and US$170k for Personal Capital.

In another example, Sallie Krawcheck, after being Citibank's CFO and running Smith Barney, Merrill Lynch Wealth Management, and Citi Private Bank, founded Ellevest, which is an investment firm aimed at helping women create wealth for themselves. She was able to raise US$44.6m to date to fund the business, and Ellevest recently reported US$91m in AUM with 7,600 clients.

As a third example, Motif Investing builds themed portfolios or "motifs" for its clients, so that the client can pick a trend that he or she believes in; these motifs typically follow specific investing themes or industries, such as biotech, cybersecurity, mining, retail, and more. Motif's parent company declares total AUM of US$361m.[14] Motif was founded in 2010 and has so far raised US$126.5m from investors including J.P. Morgan and Goldman Sachs.

Large financial institutions have launched their own products, and Vanguard, Charles Schwab, and TD Ameritrade are now considered the the largest robo-advisors with, respectively, US$101b, US$27b, and US$17b. It is important to note that these figures cannot be compared with the independent players: a substantial portion of these assets come from money that was already managed by these players. In the case of Vanguard, according to *Financial Planning* magazine,[15] 90% of its robo-advisor AUM are from clients who were already clients.

Both Fidelity and BlackRock were also early movers in this space. The former launched Fidelity Go in 2016 but does not disclose the AUM for the service; Black-Rock, the largest asset manager in the world, on the other hand, has been and continues to be very active as an investor in promising players. It first purchased independent robo-advisor FutureAdvisor for US$150m in 2015, and then, among other investments, participated in the latest fundraising rounds of European robo-advisor Scalable Capital (2017) and in micro-investing platform Acorns (2018).

Major banks have either recently launched or announced a pilot robo-advisor, including Wells Fargo, Morgan Stanley, JPMorgan Chase, Goldman Sachs, and others.

Some publications have argued that independent robo-advisors such as Betterment and Wealthfront have been struggling to grow since a few financial institutions have launched their own robo-advisory offering. As Figure 19.2 shows, the data does not seem to confirm this narrative.

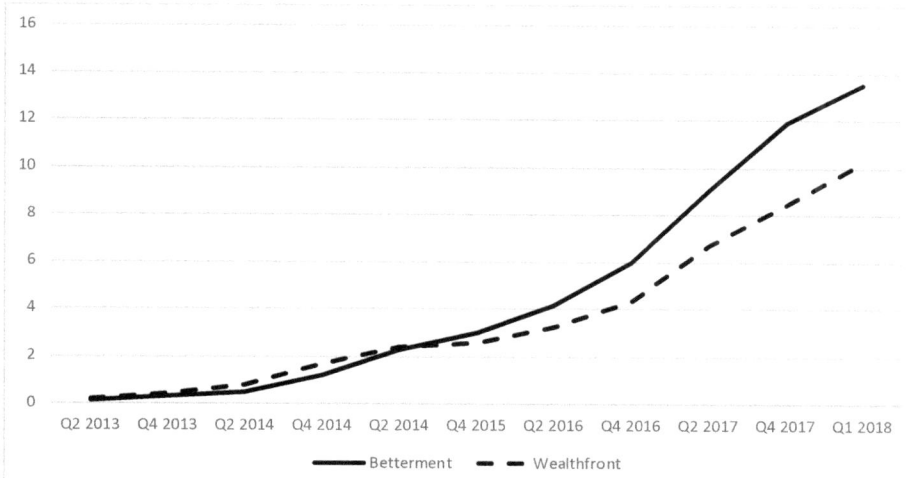

16

14

12

10

8

6

4

2

0

Q2 2013   Q4 2013   Q2 2014   Q4 2014   Q2 2014   Q4 2015   Q2 2016   Q4 2016   Q2 2017   Q4 2017   Q1 2018

—— Betterment   — — Wealthfront

Figure 19.2: Quarterly assets under management growth of Betterment and Wealthfront (USD billion)

The Rest of the World

The competitive landscape in the rest of the world is lagging the US by two to four years and it is very diverse. We will provide a quick update on the most developed global markets, and a macro-level view on Asia.

The most global player is Canada's largest player, Wealthsimple, founded in 2014 and now operating in Canada, the US, and the UK. It is the first player operating directly in two continents.[16] At the beginning of 2018, Wealthsimple is reported to manage AUM of US$1.5b and to have an 80% robo-advisory market share in Canada.

In Europe, there are a significant number of players, but only a few are reaching the required scale: Nutmeg, which operates in the UK, was a very early entrant as it was founded in 2011 and is now managing assets worth approximately US$1.0b–1.5b; Scalable Capital, operating in the UK and Germany, is seen as the up-and-coming player and has announced in May 2018 that they are managing US$1.3b only after 3.5 years since being founded in December 2014; Moneyfarm, which was also founded in 2011 and operates in the UK and in Italy, manages US$0.3b–0.5b. There are 50+ other independent players, but they are all very distant from these three players in terms of AUM.

In Asia, the situation is fragmented, with China accelerating and soon expected to become home to the largest global digital wealth managers; Japan and South Korea with a few players reaching scale and attracting significant investments; India with a multitude of new start-ups; and Southeast Asia in its very nascent stages.

In China, robo-advisory and other technology-powered investment models are merging, with the largest internet platforms starting to dominate the wealth management space. Notable players include both internet empires like Alibaba, through Ant Financial, and Tencent, as well as purer fintech players such as CreditEase and Lufax.

Across the globe, many large financial institutions are following the example set by BlackRock and are investing into or acquiring robo-advisors. A few examples include Allianz investing in Moneyfarm (UK and Italy), Schroder investing in Nutmeg (UK), Aviva investing in Wealthify (UK), Nomura investing in 8 Securities (operating in HK and Japan), and BlackRock's investment in Scalable Capital (UK and Germany). A few other asset managers are investing into B2B players, with examples in Singapore such as Franklin Templeton investing in Bambu, and Schroder investing in WeInvest.

How Is This Technology Likely to Evolve?

Robo-Advisory has only surfaced to the wider public and widespread globally in the last 2-3 years, and is therefore still in its infancy. With more and more new and traditional players looking at offering better financial advisory and investment management services through digital technology, both the Robo-Advisory business model and the technologies underpinning it will most probably evolve significantly in the next few years.

Is Robo-Advisory Here to Stay?

It is clear that the robo-advisory model is changing the way that wealth management services are provided in the US, and that this trend is quickly catching on in other geographies.

In April 2016, the CFA Institute ran a fintech survey report[17] asking questions to CFA members regarding fintech technologies. Robo-advisory was mentioned as the technology that will have the greatest impact on the financial services in the next five years by 40% of the respondents, ahead of blockchain (30%).

We are still seeing the beginning of this transformation, with robo-advisors in the US managing only approximately US$200b out of a US$55t+ industry, or merely 0.4%. In a June 2015 report, McKinsey estimated the potential value of personal financial assets that could be served by virtual advice stands at US$13.5t, assuming that 25% of affluent households and 10% of high-net-worth households are prime candidates for virtual advice.[18]

The start-ups have been joined in the race by incumbents including banks, brokerages, and asset managers that want to gain stronger control of their distribution channels. The entrance of large incumbents does not seem to have reduced the growth pattern of the larger independent players in the US, with both Betterment and Wealthfront combined adding approximately US$10b to their AUM in 2017, versus approximately US$5b in 2016, and with Q1 2018 showing even stronger growth at US$3b+, notwithstanding volatile markets.[19]

While there is little doubt that robo-advisory technologies and their evolutions will change the wealth management industry at an accelerated pace, the open question is whether new players will be able to benefit from this change or whether large financial institutions will be able to use their scale and financial resources to maintain their position and thrive in this new world. We believe that none of the extreme scenarios will play out. The incumbent financial institutions will not disappear, but some will face challenges; not all the independent players will be successful, but the ones truly improving customer experience will thrive, either independently or in partnership with one or more forward-looking financial institutions.

The winner in this race is definitely the end-customer, with quality of investment advice bound to increase and costs to decrease. 70% of the CFA members that responded to the above-mentioned survey believed that mass-affluent investors will benefit from automated financial advice tools.

How Will the Products and Technology Change?

If the consensus view is true, and wealth management becomes more digital, and robo-advisory models become the driving force of this change, we will definitely see significant changes in the way that these services are produced and marketed.

As a start, the current leading robo-advisors are more investing platforms than advising platforms. Some of them help with goal-planning and most guide the customer through understanding the appropriate risk to take, but very few have focused on the advisory part. With open banking becoming a reality in the US and Europe, and therefore greater availability of data, we will see more companies shifting their focus to the advisory part of the value proposition.

The investment products are also likely to evolve. First and foremost, most robo-advisors have very simplistic asset allocation models. These models will be put to test as soon as the equity markets go in bear territory. As we approach the end of this bull cycle, we can expect more robo-advisors to enhance their asset allocation models to incorporate strategies aimed at reducing downside risk in a bear market.

Additionally, most robo-advisors use exclusively ETFs to build their portfolios; while this brings along liquidity to the portfolio and introduces very cost-effective exposure to many asset classes, it excludes the portfolios from a number of asset classes that are not available through ETFs and that could provide further diversification benefits. We could see some robo-advisors add such asset classes to the offerings.

From a target-segment perspective, most robo-advisors are focused on either 30–45 year old, mass-affluent/affluent individuals, or 20–35 year old millennials. As the technology matures and wealth passes to new generations, we can expect services targeting high-net-worth individuals to become more prevalent, particularly in Asia, where wealth tends to be amassed by the younger ones than in the US or Europe.

Implications for Current Business Models and Processes

Robo-Advisors aim to disrupt the enormous wealth management industry globally with its many incumbent players. In this section, we look at how different existing models may get impacted, and what strategic options are available to each of them should they think that in fact robo-advisory is here to stay.

Impact on Existing Models

Traditional financial advisory businesses are built on a distribution model that is significantly more expensive than robo-advisory models. This means that traditional financial advisors are not able to compete either on price or on quality with robo-advisors, when looking at clients with less than US$500k–1m. For businesses serving wealthier clients, the impact will be less pronounced.

We'll briefly look at four different existing models: independent financial advisers (IFAs), retail and premium banks, brokerages and fund supermarkets, and private banks:

– In many parts of the world, and definitely in South East Asia, most *IFAs* tend to be distribution channels for unit trusts and ILPs, rather than actual advisory businesses. These are the businesses that are the most at risk, as their value-added proposition to the clients is very limited, and the cost of their model is large.
– *Retail and premium banks* will experience a mix of positive and negative impact from the growth of robo-advisory models. Banks that embrace robo-advisory will be able to offer wealth management products to retail clients that were previously uneconomical to offer, and therefore create an additional source of revenue and customer loyalty. For banks serving premium clients, the short-term effect might be negative with cannibalization of higher commission products; however, particularly in geographies with high cash penetration such as Singapore and Asia, the net result could be positive if the bank is able to increase significantly the offerings for the customer and to induce the customer to invest in a larger spectrum of products.
– *Brokerages and fund supermarket models* are already fully available online and are threatened by the emergence of robo-advisory as competitors, even if their value proposition is significantly different. Many brokerages see the robo-advisory model as a possible expansion of their current business, to a less commoditized model.

- *Private banks* are impacted more marginally by the emergence of robo-advisors for the time being, as some of the services offered and needed by clients are more difficult to provide digitally, although technology is likely to evolve over time and "invade" the private banks' areas of expertise, potentially utilizing machine learning and artificial intelligence.

Businesses targeting retail and mass-affluent customers will need to reinvent themselves and move to value-added, fee-only models that are more difficult to replicate digitally, such as holistic financial planning, tax planning, and estate planning.

Options Available for Incumbents

Broadly speaking, incumbents can decide to embrace the new technology and its value proposition, or focus more deeply on the parts of the value proposition of their current business model that serves a certain client segment well. For private banks, the latter means to focus on advice and relationship, on complex products, and on lending. For IFAs, the latter means to focus on advice, and develop the capabilities to deliver advice in areas such as holistic planning, tax planning, and estate planning, and moving to fee-based schemes.

For those players that decide to embrace robo-advisory, a few options are available.

From a strategic perspective, they can decide to move the entire organization toward a more digital setup, including robo-advisory, or start with smaller steps, such as building parallel models. The first case would likely require severe changes to their workforces, with large reduction in financial advisors and RMs, and large increases in engineers and product managers. From a technological perspective, either option to build the technology internally or to source the technology from a B2B player presents pros and cons that need to be carefully evaluated.

A few institutions have shown the desire to move faster and reduce the technological risk by partnering or purchasing companies. ING, the third largest retail bank in Germany, has partnered with Scalable Capital and its customers now have access to arguably the best robo-advisory service in the country and seem to appreciate it; Scalable Capital recently announced that ING customers have invested more than US$0.7b through Scalable Capital in the six months since they started operations. BlackRock, as mentioned above, has purchased a successful B2C player.

How to "Skills Future-proof" the Workforce

The wealth management industry of the future has a very different skilled workforce than the current one.

First, engineers will constitute a larger headcount in the company. Wealthfront's CEO likes to note that more than 50% of Wealthfront's payroll goes to technology; a traditional wealth manager probably spends less than 5–10% of its payroll on technology. This is a huge cultural change, as companies able to attract great engineers are very different from companies able to attract great financial advisors; some companies will realize that this is in fact too difficult of a cultural change, and that the best way to accomplish it is to partner with tech-first companies and to leverage on these partners.

In addition, cultural and skill changes will need to happen to the traditional parts of the business. As mentioned in the previous section, human-delivered advice will need to focus on value-added services that customers are willing to pay a fee for, such as holistic financial planning, estate planning, and tax planning. Institutions employing large numbers of financial advisors should train them to be able to deliver this kind of advice; the Certified Financial Planner program may become very important for advisors who want to stay relevant.

Conclusions

Robo-advisory firms have developed a value proposition that customers around the globe are increasingly appreciative of, fuelling the further development of these companies and calling for incumbent financial institutions to develop similar offerings. This business model, as well as the underlying technology, has the potential to significantly change the way wealth management products are created, bundled, and distributed.

We are still at the beginning of what is set to be a significant development that will change the ways millions of people invest their money. In emerging markets, Robo-Advisory will open up wealth management to a new class of investors.

In most of Asia, the wealth management industry largely looks like what it was 20 years ago. Until today, the customer experience offered by the wealth management industry has been only marginally affected by technology. Many observers think that customers and regulators' push for more accessibility, better transparency, lower pricing and more personalized products create a perfect set-up for Robo-Advisors to flourish in this region of the World, pushing the whole wealth management industry to innovate.

Endnotes

1 While the example is for Singapore, the situation is very similar in most Asian countries, and more pronounced in emerging markets.

2 Unit trusts are called mutual funds in a few countries and are funds investing in a set of securities including equities and bonds. According to Cerulli's "Asia Distribution Dynamics 2015," the sales charge for onshore equity unit trusts in Singapore ranges 2–5% and the median annual management fee is 1.5%. According to the same report, 100% of the sales charge and 42.3% of the annual management fee go to the distributor when it is a local bank, and 48.4% when it is a foreign bank. Any online link to the report?

3 Investment-linked insurance policies (ILPs) or investment-linked products are hybrid insurance policies that combine investment and protection into a single product.

4 Most banks differentiate between customers with US$1.5–5m and customers with more than US$5m in investable assets at the bank, with the former receiving services more similar to the "premium" customers (US$150k–1.5M), and the latter getting access to more sophisticated RMs, more products, and leverage.

5 BCG Global Wealth 2017 Report "Transforming the Client Experience." (https://www.bcg.com/publications/2017/asset-wealth-management-financial-institutions-global-wealth-2017-transforming-client-experience.aspx)

6 Note: The S&P 500 has generated average annual total returns above 7.5% for every 30-year period starting from 1926. For 30-year periods starting after 1967, average annual return has always been above 10%.

7 Sources: SingStats for Singapore's figure, Allianz Global Wealth Report 2017 for US and Asia Ex-Japan

8 Brinson, Hood, Beebower, Determinants of Portfolio Performance (CFA Institute Publications), https://www.cfapubs.org/doi/abs/10.2469/faj.v51.n1.1869

9 Wallick, Shanahan, Tasopoulos, Yoon, The Global Case for Strategic Asset Allocation (Vanguard), https://institutional.vanguard.com/iam/pdf/ICRGCAA.pdf?cbdForceDomain=true

10 For example, replacing S&P 500 exposure with Russell 1000 exposure. The S&P 500 is an equity index comprised of 500 of the biggest publicly traded companies in the US while the Russell 1000 includes the 1,000 largest publicly traded companies in the US.

11 The most common and simplest trading execution algorithms are VWAP (volume-weighted average price) and TWAP (time-weighted average price).

12 When not noted differently, figures are obtained from the First Quarter 2018 Robo Report, issued by Backend Benchmarking. (https://theroboreport.com/)

13 Personal Capital AuM figures as of March 2018, according to an email sent to clients.

14 SEC disclosure as of March 2018.

15 https://www.financial-planning.com/news/vanguard-digital-advice-platform-hits-100-billion

16 Acorns also operates in two continents (US and Australia) through a franchise model.

17 CFA Institute Magazine, September 2016.

18 Affluent defined as US$100k–1M in financial assets; HNW as US$1M–30M in financial assets.

19 StashAway's analysis based on Business Insider and SEC data.

StashAway is a data-driven digital wealth management platform that personalizes financial planning and portfolio management for the vast range of needs of retail and accredited investors alike. StashAway's proprietary investment strategy uses macroeconomic data to maintain each investor's personal risk preferences through any economic environment. To achieve this, it leverages technology that determines the appropriate asset allocations given the economic and market environment, and maximizes returns *for any level of risk. StashAway offers its services with no minimum balance, no lock-up period, flexible deposits and withdrawals, and annual management fees between 0.2% and 0.8%. StashAway was founded in 2016 in Singapore by Michele Ferrario (CEO), Freddy Lim (CIO), and Nino Ulsamer (CTO). StashAway has a Capital Market Services License for Retail Fund Management from the Monetary Authority of Singapore (MAS). More information is available at www.stashaway.com, on the iOS App Store and the Google Play Store.*

Chapter 20
WealthTech

WealthTech is the term for technology that is being adopted in the wealth management industry. This technology could be for internal use within institutions, for operational efficiency, or for product innovation reasons. It could be technology that is for the customer for efficiency reasons, or for the provision of a new service. WealthTech is a subset of fintech, with the broader term encompassing technology being used in finance.

Wealth management has always had technology innovation. The PR juggernaut that propels the fintech movement often forgets that financial technology has been implicit in the growth of "finance" since the industrial revolution. So does this make IBM, Oracle, and SAP, to name but a few, "fintech" companies? In a way, yes. However, the fragmentation of technology services and innovations into smaller parts since the global financial crisis of 2018 has been prolific, with the emergence of focused startup companies providing technology solutions to service a particular niche. Once upon a time, big financial institutions would not dare partner with a startup or growth technology vendor. Now, it is commonplace.

Banks are committing to huge spending in technology with the largest global institutions investing vast amounts to keep pace with market demands. Bank of America is spending US$3b on an overhaul; HSBC $2.3b on digital platforms, artificial intelligence (AI), and other new technology; and Bank of China is committing at least 1% of the bank's total income.

It is not just about banks though. B2C challengers are emerging, and some of the largest potential financial players are waiting in the wings, such as Google and Facebook. This is fostering a mood of competitiveness and anticipation that is driving unprecedented evolution in the sector and a new wave of wealth management customers who are disgruntled with the traditional model.

Asia and Greater China

And then there's Asia. Much is hyped and spoken about with regard to Asia. We will explore some of these myths and facts, and the impact they have, or will have, on the wealth management sector. Asia is often seen as the frontier of technology but, broadly speaking, technology innovation is not in the wealth management sector, as customers may not be tech-savvy, and institutions are playing catch-up relative to other consumer goods businesses. There is a significant variance in speed with which WealthTech is being embraced and adopted across the region, and that makes Asia a veritable melting pot. In many ways, it is a strong case study as an indicator on where WealthTech globally could head over the coming years.

DOI 10.1515/9781547400904- 020

Old business models are not working so well in the new era. We look at what is working and what is not, as well as which models are disrupting and which models are dysfunctioning. We will reference our home market "Greater China and ASEAN" as we explore how institutions will have to change over the next five years as the race to win Asia's coveted customer becomes a truly digital battle.

WealthTech versus Traditional Wealth Management

As pioneers in the WealthTech sector in Asia and Europe, the evolution that we see day to day at Privé Technologies is staggering. Strong forces are in play, pulling and pushing the wealth management industry to change.

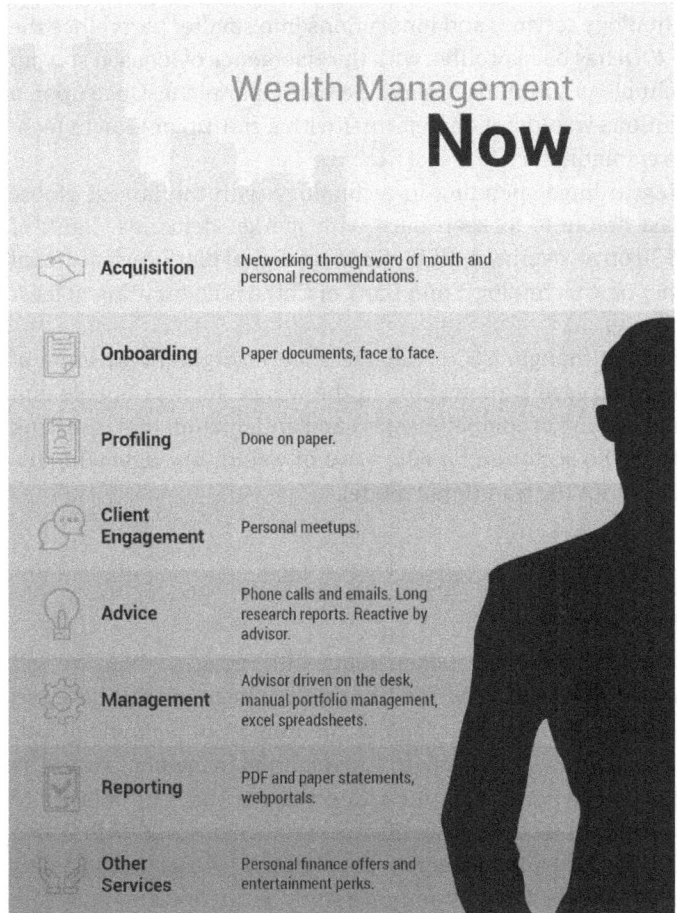

Figure 20.1: The current delivery of wealth management services

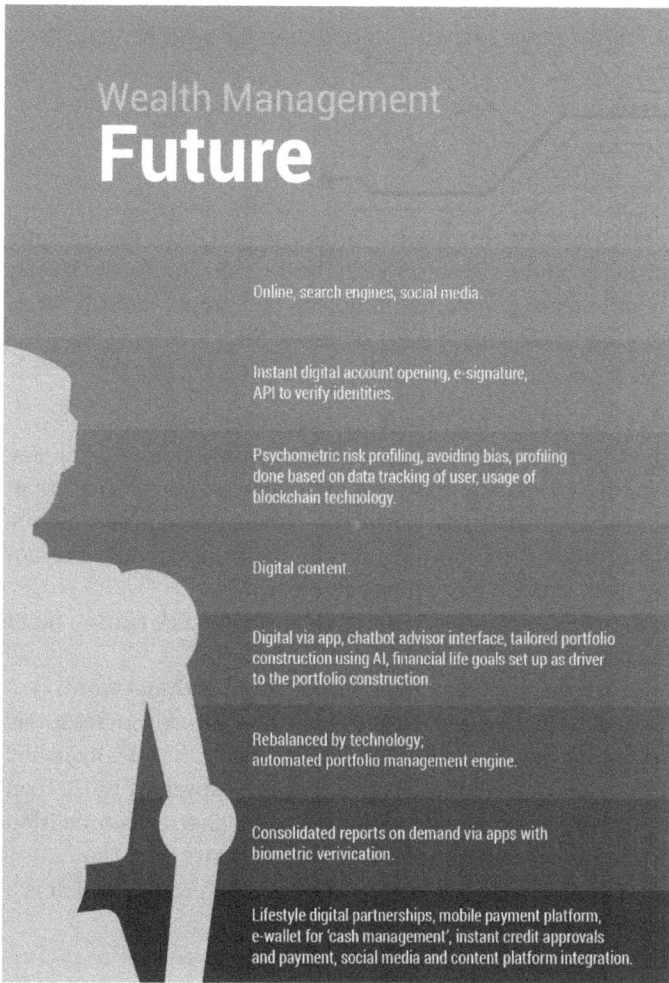

Figure 20.2: The future delivery of wealth management services

The Changes Taking Place in Asia

The way wealth managers have operated globally, and not differently in Asia, is by leveraging a model of opacity, secrecy, and tradition. None of these three factors sit well in the digital age, and four forces are starting to turn the tables on how business is conducted in the digital age:
- Customer demand
- Regulatory change
- New product evolution
- Operational efficiency

By understanding these four forces, we can truly start to plan for how the industry is going to change from today.

Customer Demand

When you consider the demographics, it is hardly surprising that customer demand is such a huge driver of business model evolution. Asia Pacific will witness the largest projected growth in the middle-class population, followed by Europe, in 2020, 2024, and 2030 relative to North America and other parts of the world.1

What Are the Opportunities Caused by This Rise in Customer Demand?

First, the demographics are very focused around millennial, lower-income customers. The customer is looking for digital touchpoints, and in many ways needs more than the traditional branch network of the industry. They have grown up in a purely mobile era. They do not like cash or bricks-and-mortar financial institutions. They are not familiar with "investment," nor are they particularly interested.

The challenge is how to engage and attract this customer to wealth management using a pure digital-driven offering.

Second, the acceleration of the number of mass-affluent and high-net-worth customers is the fastest in the world. But herein lies a dilemma: this group is increasingly disillusioned with the traditional way of service and the fees that are typically levied (often hidden). The emergence of some digital service offerings, especially those seen in the US and Europe, is driving customer acquisition costs higher as competition becomes fierce and attracting the customer becomes more expensive.

To add to the issues, the target customer is very often *not* tech-savvy, which is a stark contrast to the younger generation.

What Problems Can WealthTech Solve?

WealthTech plays an integral role of reframing the provision of wealth management services to the customer. Take robo-advisors as an example, which are effectively online investment portfolio managers that have made a significant impact on the global investment landscape.

It is not just about investment advice. It is also about acquiring and engaging the client. These are two areas in which traditional financial institutions are less adept. In the digital age, clients are being acquired through digital channels, most likely through partnerships with third-party networks that can send qualified leads to the business. The engagement aspect is also digital and best done through content. More detail on acquisition and engagement will be provided later in this chapter.

Greater China Analysis

The "China Private Wealth Report 2017," published by Bain & Company, said the China's high-net-worth individual (HNWI) population increased from 180,000 to 1.6 million in the past decade and total investable assets reached RMB165 trillion in 2016.

Nowhere have digital B2C robo-advisor tools made a larger impact than in China's consumer market.

Figure 20.3 illustrates the penetration of wealth platforms such as Yu'e Bao and Lufax as well as the explosive growth of fintech businesses like Alipay, which all point to an increasingly digital-savvy consumer.

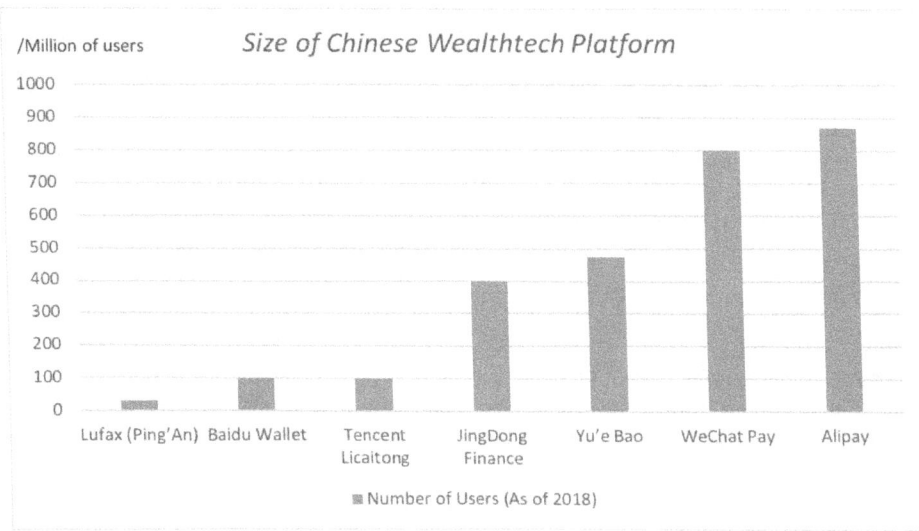

Figure 20.3: Size of Chinese Wealthtech Platform

Regulatory Change

Regulation is evolving fast, and in Asia the regulators are lagging behind the US and Europe in many respects. The offshore banking hubs in Hong Kong and Singapore are adjusting to an international environment of heightened anti-money laundering and anti-tax evasion, while the domestic centers such as Taiwan, China, Korea, and other Southeast Asian countries are investing heavily to boost their wealth management expertise in an attempt to challenge the offshore models.

It is the regulatory environment that is shaping a lot of WealthTech innovation and successful deployment.

What Are the Regulatory Issues?

We view regulatory changes not so much as issues as enforced drivers of change for the wealth management industry.

Regulators have heavily scrutinized client profiling and suitability, including account opening and KYC (know your client) procedures, which have resulted in an unprecedented scaling up of legal and compliance divisions within the financial institutions. This has caused significant margin compression as costs have increased.

What Problems Can WealthTech Solve?

Accelerating costs always lead to a technology adoption opportunity that can deliver enhanced efficiencies, and what is known as "RegTech"—technology that is focused on digitizing the regulatory side of the finance and wealth industry—and is a rapidly growing part of the WealthTech landscape.

WealthTech can digitize paper flows, automate KYC checks, store data in the cloud, and integrate this client data with third-party platforms such as portfolio management, for risk limit breakages or product suitability, as well as client relationship management (CRM), KYC checks, and digital account opening. This is particularly relevant when put in the context of new digital national identification programs because WealthTech can be leveraged to bring much faster and more accurate KYC.

Greater China Analysis

The impact of regulatory change can be a major impediment, although a morally justifiable one, to the explosive growth seen in wealth management in Asia. But this has not had a large effect in China. From 2012–2016, China's asset management industry enjoyed a compound annual growth rate (CAGR) close to 41%, with banks' financial wealth management being the core driver of growth with a CAGR of 75%. The growth is obviously not strictly comparable with growth elsewhere. Regulation between China and other regions is not comparable and in many ways, regulation in China is significantly more immature and of a lighter touch.

As a result, Chinese asset managers lagged behind on investment in overall asset management infrastructure, with the same cost-to-income ratio at only around 10%. Underinvestment in asset management infrastructure is particularly evident for banks' asset management departments, which have run the business under a model of regulatory arbitrage and implicit guarantee over the past decade. They simply haven't needed the huge capital investment that their regional and global competitors have had to make.

The new "Guidance Opinions Concerning Standardisation of Asset Management Operations by Financial Institutions" was launched on April 27, 2018,[2] and forbids implicit guarantees and enforces product and process standardization, which we believe will create industry challenges and yet great technology opportunities for

China's banking asset management business over the next two years to transition and return to the business roots of financial and asset management for customers.

New Product Evolution

Wealth management revolves around product. That has historically been more akin to a push of product on the client, be it a stock, or a particular security like a structured product. But that model is being forced to evolve as our four forces shape business models.

What Are the Issues with Product Evolution?

There are several issues specific to the Asian market:

–   Asian investors are very hands-on and advice-centric compared to the rest of the world, where investors are happier with arm's length portfolio management done by an expert.
–   The dominance of advisory investment management is an issue since it creates volatility and lack of visibility in revenue, and presents advisory risks that institutions are increasingly averse to taking.
–   At the same time, business models are being forced into a homogenized state, as regulation and cost pressure stifle innovation especially at the incumbents.

These challenges make product evolution more problematic. The Asian client does not look for portfolio management solutions as yet, and still wants to be offered ideas and opportunities on a product-by-product basis.

What Problems Can WealthTech Solve?

Technology is enabling big advances in the way that wealth managers are engaging clients in new products.

Most notably, customers can have tailored portfolios built in seconds by combining inputs from their risk profile, typically with efficient portfolio theory mapped to a risk-factored range of model portfolios. For the customer, it is fast, fresh, and a simple step to investing. For the institution, it is an innovative product that engages the user into taking action to build a portfolio.

Goal-based wealth planning is another trend sweeping the global wealth management industry, none more so than in Asia. This is an engaging process for customers who are not conversant with wealth management. It allows them to build and tag investment portfolios to their life financial goals such as savings for kids' education, retirement, and even the dream car.

Greater China Analysis

In China, the definition of "product" is interesting because it is reinventing the classic wealth management definition. Since the market is increasingly penetrated by non-financial brands like Alibaba and Tencent, product innovation now encompasses payments, crowdfunding, and credit functionalities—not to mention the innovation of delivery channels using social media and messaging.

Yu'e Bao, Alibaba's money market fund, illustrates how a simple wealth management product can captivate the retail audience so long as that audience is already acquired through a tangential business. This is a big threat to the traditional financial institutions. We discuss more on the ecosystems being built in China later in the chapter.

Although still in its infancy, the assets under management (AUM) of robo-advisors in China are expected to balloon to 6 trillion yuan (US$905b) by 2020, according to China Merchants Securities estimates, underscoring the potential for growth in an industry that was non-existent until recently.

Operational Efficiency

In an environment of increased regulation, competition, and costs to acquire and engage clients, margin compression is occurring. Technology is an enabler for streamlining and making processes more efficient, more scalable, and less costly.

What Are the Operational Issues?

Incumbent institutions have their inefficiencies to contend with—from a maze of legacy technologies that need to be stitched together to processes that must satisfy legal and compliance checks. New competitors do not have these burdens and bring newer technology builds which are more nimble and more scalable (let alone more cost-efficient).

Regulation is bringing to the forefront a lot of operational issues as changes to workflows and new processes are enforced by the regulators at a staggering rate. This in turn causes constant pressures internally to adopt smoother workflows and may lead to an over-focus on the servicing of business rather than on the business purpose itself.

What Problems Can WealthTech Solve?

Traditionally, the adoption of technology in wealth management has been driven by the need to drive more efficient workflows inside the institution. The benefits to this are improved human resource and financial efficiency, which are particularly important in the era of margin compression.

Looking at the Asian market highlights several speeds of evolution, from the extremely slow and cautious to the fast and dynamic. We see a full spectrum of appetite and dynamism when it comes to digital transformation.

In most Asian countries, workflows are extremely traditional and convoluted as a result of lack of investment in technology and a legacy of mergers and acquisitions. Much of the Privé platform is targeted at helping operational efficiencies through digitalization. In the frontier markets and SE Asia's so called "tiger" economies, digitization is only just starting, and outside of the top financial institutions, it is extremely backward and expensive as an investment.

The larger brands, often under increasing government and regulatory pressure, are cautiously entering large-scale digitization projects. From government-supported account opening (digital onboarding) and KYC (MyInfo—Singapore, MyKad—Malaysia), which help to shift away from paper storage and vastly harmonize client data systems, to portfolio management tools for the investment professionals in order to implement model portfolios and bulk rebalance and execute orders, the industry is now changing

Digital banking is also very much in the spotlight and, at the time of writing, Hong Kong is inviting applications for digital banking licenses. The concept behind digital banking, such as DBS's launch of digibank, is to build a digital bank with all processes powered by digital solutions. These are the banks of the future.

In sum, WealthTech is generating tangible benefits for the industry in a way that has not been fathomed before and the ecosystem now offers wide-ranging solutions (see Figure 20.4).

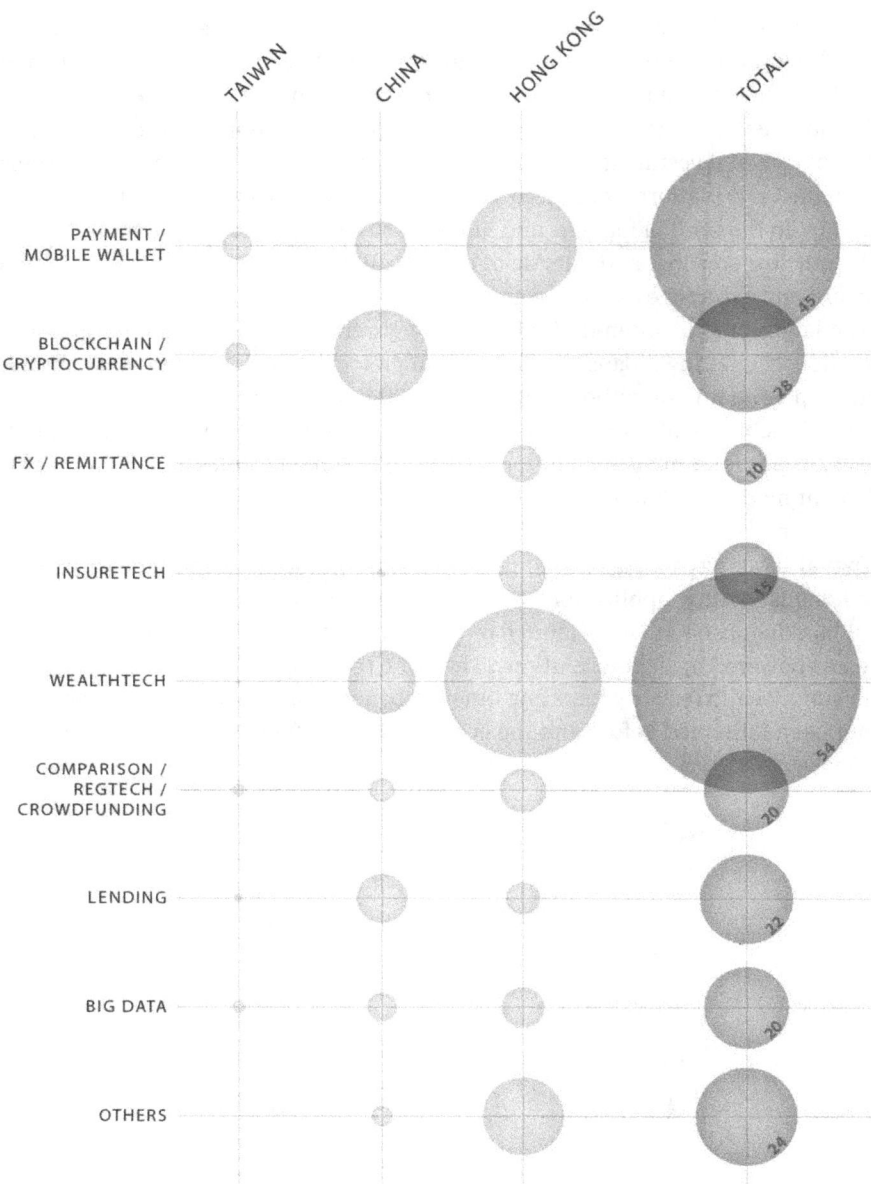

Figure 20.4: WealthTech ecosystem in Greater China

The Cutting Edge

Whenever there is talk of technology, there is typically also an overestimation of how quickly that technology will be adopted in the mainstream. We had flying cars in the 1960s, and the emergence of the robot taking over the world in the 1980s. Many generations later, technology is developing these two channels but in far more realistic ways. In other words, whether or not entrepreneurs challenge the status quo, there are strong barriers in place that will keep cars on the road rather than flying, and keep robots in the workplace rather than on the pavement.

But the evolution is most definitely in progress, and wealth management is no exception. In Figure 20.5., we highlight the growth of technology adoption in the various areas of Wealth Tech over the decade and in this section, we outline the four game-changers: AI, big data, blockchain, and cloud computing.

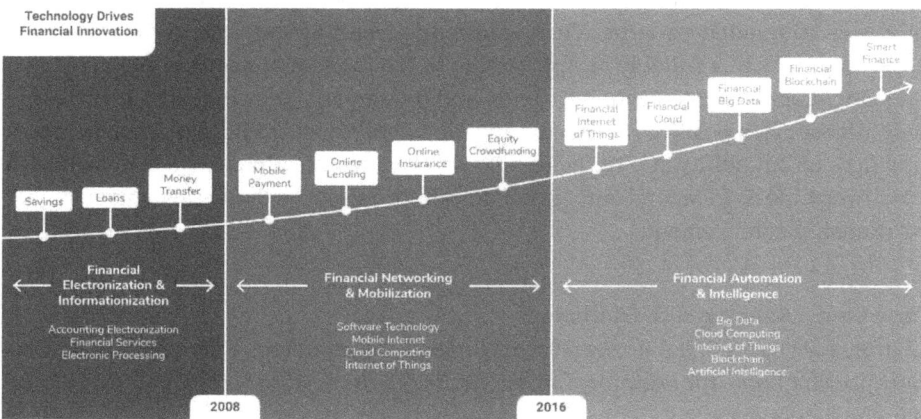

Figure 20.5: Technology adoption and evolution in Wealth Teach

Artificial Intelligence

As far as the current technological development is concerned, artificial intelligence (AI) uses machine learning (ML) and data mining as the two core technologies. Chapters 11 and 12 discuss these technologies in some detail. Here, we will focus on the use of AI and ML in WealthTech.

AI Uses in WealthTech

AI is going to be a key driver of innovation over the next five years in Asia and beyond.

Big data, or smart data, plays a major role for banks and is a key input to a functioning AI project. Data is the lifeblood for AI. The good news for wealth management is that banks and financial service providers have been collecting data for decades, and some have been storing that data in suitable databases and systems. The opportunity is to deploy AI-driven systems into the institutions that could finally use this data in a meaningful way.

AI at its purest may not be accepted by customers as readily as we might think. In fact, at Privé Technologies, we argue that the biggest opportunity in affluent segments of WealthTech over the next five years is the "bionic" approach. This means that the first step of evolution is augmented intelligence as opposed to artificial, whereby processes still have a human element attached to them, and are not purely dictated by a machine learned algorithm. Therefore a hybrid (we called it "bionic) model will be more applaudable

Behind the scenes, the positive impacts of machine learning affect the entire banking and financial technology industries. It helps to increase the accuracy and speed of a predictive analysis enormously, while minimizing risks and fraud. Possible applications are automated investment services, in which a self-learning algorithm produces stimulated patterns. Then it uses the resulting patterns to decide on the asset class which is suitable or appropriate to the individual needs of the customer. Showing clients targeted content, alerts, and investment ideas to match their profile and interests has positive revenue implications but it also will build regulatory best practices on suitability into the sales process. Other applications include detection of creditworthiness, PFM, and early fraud detection, as well as marketing and customer relationship management.

Case Study: Banking with Chatbots

Chatbots are becoming the new form of client engagement tool. Financial institutions now use chatbots—for example, CitiBot and DORI—to provide a personable customer banking experience.

Citi Singapore officially launched Citi Bot in March 2018 after piloting the bot with 600 customers and employees from September 2017. By connecting with clients on Facebook Messenger and leveraging natural language processing, the Citi chatbot offers customers an intuitive and convenient way to address everyday questions, including account-specific enquiries such as viewing of account balances and transactions, credit card bill summaries, rewards and points balances, and answering frequently asked questions.

Hang Seng Bank in Hong Kong rolled out HARO and DORI chatbots for retail banking services in January 2018. Using machine learning and natural language processing, the virtual assistants are equipped with the ability to simulate human-like contextual conversations to address customer enquiries and communicate in Chinese and English.

- HARO, which stands for "Helpful; Attentive; Responsive; Omni," handles general inquiries about the bank's mortgage, personal loan, credit card, medical insur-

ance, and travel insurance services. It can also assist customers with calculating repayment amounts for designated personal and mortgage loans.
– DORI, which stands for "Dining; Offers; Rewards; Interactive," can search and suggest credit card merchant discounts and online store offers and make reservations at selected restaurants. It is available through Facebook Messenger.

Chatbots look set to expand in popularity as a delivery mechanism for WealthTech innovations. At Privé Technologies, we have deployed text chatbots into institutions to provide client engagement on goal-based wealth planning and portfolio construction tools to customers in a simple form. Today's customer base is familiar with the interface style of a messaging app that is used by chatbots, so it has become an easy and effective approach to engage customers and simultaneously capture required data deemed onerous and boring. The next wave of innovation is the voice-powered chatbots. Asia is particularly suitable for this innovation given its popularity seen through WeChat voice messaging.

Chinas Endorsement of AI
China has the ambition to become the world's leading AI innovation center by 2030 with its "New Generation Artificial Intelligence Development Plan" published in July 2017 by State Council laying out the planning related to AI from the national level.3

For the financial service sector, the plan encourages the establishment of a financial big data system to improve the data processing and analytical capabilities, innovate smart financial products and services, and develop new financial industries. The financial industry is encouraged to apply technologies to provide intelligent customer service and surveillance, and develop intelligent risk warning, prevention, and control systems for financial risks.

Meanwhile, the establishment of the FinTech Committee within People's Bank of China in May 2017 marked the country's milestone of an institution that specializes in planning and coordinating financial technologies related works.

Big Data

In wealth management, much has been said about *big data* over the past five years, and many institutions rushed to adopt some technology in order to say they are using "Big Data." The challenge however is processing and using the data in a business positive way.

Although the financial industry has a huge amount of data, the receiving and processing of the extensive, true, and accurate financial data is critical. One of the major challenges in the application process, that is, if data is not used properly, data mining can lead to spurious results. This requires the service providers to understand the logic of data and finance in order to "dig deeper" into the true value from big data.

Meanwhile, in China, user data is highly concentrated in several companies such as the four largest internet giants in China: Baidu, Alibaba, Tencent, and JD.com (also referred to as BATJ), which tends to create data oligarchs and bring data monopolies, creating the so-called "data gap" problem which is not conducive to the industry development for wealth and asset managers to provide better personalized financial services.

Case Study: Tencent and WeChat

WeChat is Tencent's multi-purpose messaging, social media, and mobile payment app. It is now one of the largest standalone mobile apps with over 900 million daily active users.

Using WeChat and other social networks within Tencent group (QQ, QZone, CaiFutong, Tencent Weibo), Tencent collects large amount of information, such as payment frequency and shopping habits, which could be used for precision marketing by optimizing relevant advertisement content and engagement methods. Meanwhile such data can be derived from the users' credit scores, extending other financial services like lending and investments. Figure 20.6 illustrates the ecosystem of big data powered services offered by the Tencent/WeChat network.

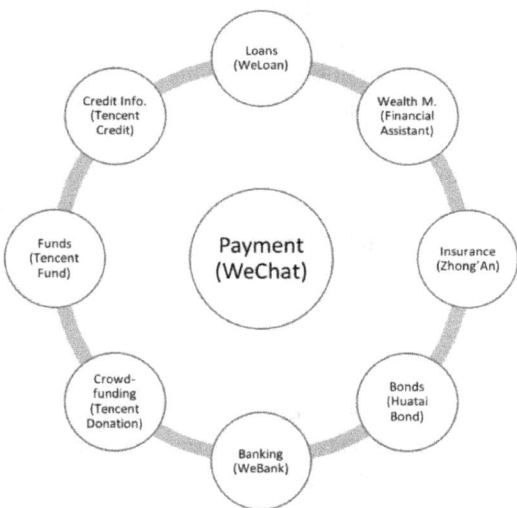

Figure 20.6: The eco-system of big data powered services offered by Tencent/WeChat network

Blockchain

This section outlines the main uses of blockchain being considered for WealthTech.

Client Onboarding

Banks are required to conduct lengthy know your client (KYC) and anti-money laundering (AML) checks on their new clients. Consequently, the time to onboard a new client can be weeks or even months. Clients must produce proof of ID, residency, marital status, business and political interests, and more before a bank can accept them as a client.

Automation of many of these examinations is now possible. Biometric scanning can compare a self-portrait with photographic ID. Optical character recognition can process the details of documents.

The recording of such verification outcomes on the blockchain means that client data becomes immutable and easily portable. Blockchain can therefore significantly reduce the time taken to onboard a new client. It also eliminates the role of intermediaries involved in collating all this information.

Conversely, this ease of onboarding may affect client loyalty—since data portability is possible now, the inconvenience to switch banks has been largely reduced.

Real-time Settlements

The current financial system is heavily reliant on intermediaries for the reconciliation and verification of trades. Using blockchain can reduce or eliminate the role of the intermediary, allowing the settlement of trades and transfers in real-time. As discussed earlier in the book, the Australian Stock Exchange has already announced a move to the blockchain, which will enable automated real-time settlements on a 24/7 basis, increase transaction speed, and bring multiple other benefits. Some of those benefits include making capital available quicker with a reduced transaction fee, ease of verification, and an overall cost reduction to clients. However, fees are also where wealth managers can generate income. It may be that banks have to look for other ways to create fee-generating value for their high-net-worth clients.

Automated Investment Vehicles

Smart contracts could manage the process of investment. For a client who wishes to keep a balanced portfolio of investments across asset classes, it could be a smart contract that takes over the role of portfolio manager. If a particular asset class in a portfolio increases in value above a certain threshold, the smart contract could automate the redistribution of funds into other asset classes to balance the portfolio.

Digital Asset Classes

Cryptocurrencies themselves offer an additional asset class for investors wishing to diversify their portfolio. Crypto index funds including Iconomi and Crypto20 provide an alternative to standard index funds. Banks wanting to set up a new index fund within the crypto class can now use blockchain tools like Blackmoon.

Security tokens are another exciting new development. They offer the chance to digitize any physical asset, providing investors with fractional ownership. Imagine owning your very own piece of a jet plane, or a superyacht. Wealth managers will need to ensure that they are kept apace of such events in blockchain wealth management (and other technologies) to ensure that they can appropriately advise their clients of opportunities and risks.

Cloud Computing

Cloud computing is an information technology (IT) paradigm that enables ubiquitous access to shared pools of configurable system resources and higher-level services that can be rapidly provisioned with minimal management effort, often over the internet and the opportunity to store data remotely and utilize those services.

The main enabling technology for cloud computing is *virtualization*. Virtualization software separates a physical computing device into one or more "virtual" devices, each of which can be easily used and managed to perform computing tasks. The goal of cloud computing is to allow users to take benefit from all of these technologies, without the need for deep knowledge about or expertise with each one of them.

Cloud Computing Uses in WealthTech

Cloud computing offers many benefits to organizations and users including safe backup of data, access to software as a service from your provider, security measures and many others. However, it does pose privacy concerns because the service provider can access the data that is in the cloud at anytime and anywhere. Also, if you are not connected to the cloud, you may not have access to data or an application that you need.

Cloud services have offered long-held promises of increased elasticity to adapt to the changing scale, and a way to balance costs and value. They help to achieve high processing reliability and other qualitative success factors such as more collaboration options and greater flexibility. With a high level of cloud maturity, wealth managers have the opportunity to deploy scalable, secure architecture with omni-channel capabilities and speed up innovation with agile solutions. The adoption of cloud technologies also allows wealth managers to use their resources more efficiently by means of better budget management and allocation. Last but not least, it can help the organization to obtain flexibility, optimize costs, and offer a great deal of flexibility in building an enabling IT infrastructure.

Around Asia, regulators have been slow to accept cloud storage of bank and client data. That is starting to change. At present, China's financial cloud market is at an initial stage of development with low market penetration, but is growing fast. Meanwhile, domestic policies encourage the financial sector to fully tap the financial cloud market, therefore big potential can be expected.

Despite the favorable policies, there are four major challenges for China's financial institutions' cloudification:
− Cloud migration and other capabilities are not enough in themselves
− High requirements of safety and risk control
− A low degree of automation
− No positive effect after cloudification

The cloud provider will offer software as a service, but if you have limitations there and they may well not be able to support in any way your home-grown software and even if they do, it will be at a premium. There are a large number of common modules that can be used directly for financial sectors, while some can be customized according to sub-sectors, such as retail platform, institutional platform, SME platform for banks, underwriting and claim systems for insurers, information and investment systems for trust companies, asset managers, and securities houses. These all would have to be carefully discussed with your cloud provider so that you know what to expect.

How Wealth Management Business Models Are Changing

The new WealthTech landscape, which is being shaped by our four forces, is already forcing change to traditional business models, and that looks set to accelerate in the future.

In our day-to-day conversations with wealth managers, we see three key trends in how WealthTech is changing wealth management business models: the rise of bionic advisory, client acquisition and engagement, and the provision of advice.

The Rise of Bionic Advisory

In markets outside of China, such as Taiwan, Hong Kong, and key Association of Southeast Asian Nations (ASEAN) markets, we strongly believe the customer offering provided by the wealth managers should focus on a *bionic* approach.

Why Bionic Is So Important for Asia

We believe the bionic approach, which synergises robotic process with human touch, addresses several key challenges in the Asia region

Talent Acquisition Is Difficult

The asset management business is a talent-driven business. We believe the hunt for experienced wealth/asset managers will become even more fierce and thus financial institutions should leverage WealthTech to empower advisors to serve more customers with high-quality, personalized products and services.

Talent is a valuable resource in Asia. In the bionic view, advisors control the technology. But where do these advisors come from?

Technology Is Not the Solution to All Challenges

Although, in theory, having digitized delivery of services and processes from front to back sounds perfect, the reality is very different and difficult to transform. First, there are legacy systems internally that have been cobbled together as institutions have merged and been brought together over the years. Then, there is the cost involved in digitizing large parts of the business—a cost that shareholders may deem undesirable at the current time compared to its short-term revenue and profitability impact.

Different Customers Want Different Kinds of Communication

The Asian high-net-worth (HNW) or ultra-high-net-worth (UHNW) individual still values a face-to-face approach to the relationship or at least for the last leg of the sales process. However, for the mass-affluent and retail segments, full self-service and customer-centric apps are becoming increasingly popular. The use of technology results in cost reductions with the elimination of manual relationship building, increasing the need for financial technological tools for the retail and affluent segments.

Despite its difficulty to hire talent for growth, full technology transformation is not conceivable. The middle ground is bionic-advisory with the provision of services backed by technology applications.

Case Study: Advisor-assisted, Goal-based Wealth Planning

Like so many banks with large advisor forces, one of Singapore's top three banks approached us with a common problem: How do they give their clients a more tailored, tech-driven and impressive investment service without disempowering their advisors?

We developed a new product and interface to enable an advisor to sit next to a client and create life goals and then see investment recommendations to match that goal at the click of a button. The "checkout" process then takes place during the meeting, or at the client's leisure.

The product not only gives the advisor much more power, but it also showcases great-looking technology with investment search and proposal generation at lightning speed that gives the client the feeling that the advisor has sophisticated tools and that investment recommendations are being made with a solid technical underpinning.

Client Acquisition and Engagement

Neglected in the last five years, but now coming back into focus for wealth managers, client acquisition is a crucial strategy to fighting new digital competition and the changing customer digital appetite.

Why Acquisition and Engagement Are Important
In the era of margin compression, the only way to grow is to acquire more clients and deepen your wallet share of existing clients.

Wealth management is not an easy product to sell to customers. Let's face it, the average customer, retail or affluent, tends to have more interesting things to do with their time than focus on choosing and monitoring a wealth manager.

In addition, there is the perception that they are all the same. To the industry outsider, their offerings are homogenized (a phenomenon that has accelerated in this new regulatory age), and the only difference is branding.

Client acquisition is one of the hardest but most important aspects of wealth management today. With the backdrop of soaring wealth and the number of wealthy individuals increasing across Asia and China in particular, this should be one of the key parts of a financial institution's strategy. Yet in recent years, financial institutions have all been playing defensively by focusing on containing costs, rather than growing income.

WealthTech is going to play a massive role in shifting focus toward acquisition and engagement.

How This Affects Business Models
Those who do not understand or invest in digital, will get left behind.

With the digital boom in Asia hitting online shopping and marketplace websites, an extension to this is finding a wealth manager online. Now with the boom in digital banking and robo-advisory, especially in the retail and affluent sectors in the US and Europe, this is going to sweep across Asia over the next five years (China excluded as it is already prevalent).

Today, it is critical to cater for potential users who do online searching. Google search is the prevailing search engine in most Asian countries, aside from Baidu in China. Not only do customers want to see a useful ranking that answers their search but they are less interested in a direct link. They want third party-validation. This is a pure internet phenomenon. Users are now so engrained to search via aggregator platforms—Expedia, Airbnb, Amazon, Alibaba, MoneyHero (Hong Kong)—every industry has one, apart from wealth management until we established wealthinasia.com.

Engagement is also key. Learning about clients by collecting their data and building personas is far easier done by tracking their online behaviors to their reading preferences and portfolio decision making than a question-and-answer session done with the advisor. Engaging clients of all wealth segments will increasingly happen over mobile apps and/or content and gamification of wealth management, the latest example being the new trend to give customers the chance to set their life goals and have the engine suggest a portfolio to allow them to best achieve the goals (goals-based wealth planning). Engaging clients better means more client interactions, more data-driven engagement (using big data and AI), better quality sales, and ultimately more sales revenue. It is a win-win for both the client and advisor.

Case Study: Wealthinasia.com

Today's consumer is searching for everything online—not just retail and travel, but also wealth related services, too. The issue in wealth is that the service providers are poorly represented online, their websites do not describe their services, and the industry does not have an independent aggregator.

In 2016, we founded a website to help Asia's investors, large and small, to find their best wealth services. By applying algorithmic matching technology akin to online dating, we are able to use a client's profile to find the best matching private banks, priority banks, independent financial advisors, external asset managers, and more.

For the client, this saves huge amounts of time and effort, often asking friends (which is inherently biased and unreliable) which providers they should approach. It puts the consumer into more of a competitive tendering situation for their business which drives down fees and fine-tunes service levels.

For the wealth manager, it is qualified lead generation. Advisors receive leads that match their service capabilities and want to be contacted. It is a more efficient digital marketing expenditure with the use of an aggregator to send qualified leads, rather than going head-to-head with other brands for unqualified ones.

Provision of Advice

Client demand is starting to shape new business models. As the robo-advisor revolution starts to penetrate the investor base, the larger financial institutions are being asked "Why can't you give me a service (or app) like that?"

Why This Is So Important

The larger institutions are under the threat from newer business models, perhaps not originating from the financial sector, and they need to make changes in order to keep up. First, that means identifying the models that they wish to pursue. For example, this might be baby steps to giving their advisors enhanced digital tools for added investment service functionality. Second, they need to make investments ready for digital application.

How This Will Affect Business Models

It means new investment, sometimes substantial, to digitize their processes. We expect to see the emergence of the digital bank in Asia, slowly but surely, as more and more players recognize the need to start building out a "new" bank from digital roots, sooner rather than later.

Cost-cutting remains in focus, with an emphasis on using third-party domain experts to build and manage the new technology rather than doing it in-house. This is already an interesting trend. Fewer and fewer banks want the overhead of in-house technology teams. More are adopting tech-light teams and using third-party domain experts to bring their new tech products to market far quicker than they can do themselves. The open-API architecture that is now available makes this even more appealing, whereby new tech products can be very fast and easy to plug in from a third party, making deployment fast and efficient.

Case Study: A Chatbot and Mobile-based Goal Setting in Malaysia

A traditional investment manager in Malaysia with a brand network and little online presence wants to digitize. One of their key business targets is to engage more youngsters into the wealth management, long-term savings and investment cycle. They also want to rotate current investors away from a traditional fund structure that is a legacy and very costly (for both the client and company) capital-protected style, to a market-norm mutual fund style.

We designed a self-serve interface via an app and web-portal that enabled new and old customers to set goals and assign their investments to those goals. By doing so, the legacy customers are incentivized to switch their older holding structure to a new one.

Looking to China: New Ecosystems

China has now established a complete financial and technology ecosystem covering payments, lending, and investments in a different business model from their counterparts in US, Europe and Japan. The main participants include the traditional financial sector and other businesses that have closed-loop ecosystems. But it is the internet/

technology magnates that are creating the biggest buzz, as the popularity of Alibaba and Tencent are gulping market shares in the financial service industry via their cashless mobile payment platforms. We believe these developments will have major industry impacts.

Key Impacts

First, these new platforms manage a huge capital chain and have exclusive advantages in payment and clearing management. Payment services are used as a carrier of fund flow services, and the speed and usability can also increase customer loyalty and retention.

The second major impact is the huge breadth and richness of customers' data and security information that is collected, which will provide a significant competitive advantage in offering personalized financial services to targeted users.

Case Study: Alipay (Yu'e Bao) and Tianhong Asset Management.

Alipay, owned by Alibaba's Ant Financial, is the largest Chinese mobile payment platform. Yu'e Bao combines e-wallet and money management services with the key features of being easy to use, easy access due to low minimums, and zero fees. Injecting money into the Yu'e Bao account means purchase of the money market funds while users can still use the payments service as and when it is required.

Tianhong Asset Management, one of five regulated money managers when it was founded, is a subsidiary of Ant Financial and is one of the largest public funds in China.

Before Ant Financial acquired a 51% stake in 2013, Tianhong was just a mid-size and loss-making asset manager. The net profit for Tianhong was RMB20.3 million in 2011 and RMB15.3 million in 2012. Tianhong finally had its turn around on June 13, 2013 when Yu'e Bao became linked to the money market fund managed by them. At the end of Q2, 2013, the assets under management at Tianhong was RMB13.647 billion. Just ten days after the launch of Yu'e Bao, Tianhong Asset Management successfully raised enough funds to return to profit, a remarkable reversal of its loss from the previous year.

In China, as WealthTech has risen over the last five years, artificial intelligence and big data technology have become the new production factors in the wealth and asset management industries, changing workflow processes and increasing productivity. But we have also seen two potential data challenges in China: data quality and data oligarchy.

User data is highly concentrated in several companies such as BATJ, which thereby creates data oligarchs and data monopolies, causing the so-called "data gap" problem which is not conducive to the industry development for wealth and asset managers to provide personalized financial services. This creates warnings for the Western economies; in China's centrally planned system, data control will be easier to manage than in a dispersed market-style economy. There will be a significant need for data regulation overhaul around the world to handle the potential dangers of working with this amount of personal information, such as the General Data Protection Regulation (GDPR) legislation that has been launched in 2018 in Europe.

Looking into the Digital Crystal Ball

Asia's digital opportunity is now powered by a customer who is vastly more internet plugged-in than ten years ago.

We believe the industry challenges which are going to lead to further development in WealthTech businesses will be centered on how to create "personalized" and "intelligent" products and services—the essential elements for the traditional advisor-driven industry, at the competitive cost.

We also see an air of collaboration rather than competition between most fintechs and financial institutions. But that depends on the institutions and whether the goliaths want to do it themselves, or at least most of it. At the time of writing, one of the largest Chinese insurers employs over 500 front-end developers and UX/UI designers. This unbelievable scale is hard to compete against.

We believe Asian wealth and asset managers need to speed up their deployment of technology through the combination of investment into new technologies via strategic cooperation with the fintech community and internal development of expertise. The areas of such investments can include but are not limited to: establishing or optimizing online portfolio distribution and advisory capabilities to service retail "long-tailed" customers; developing machine learning; natural language processing capability to process structured and unstructured data in investment research; supporting investment research; automatically generating investment ideas; and optimizing investment processes and decision-making mechanisms.

The application of AI in the wealth and asset management industry has a relatively short history and should not be considered as a "replacement" of human advisors. In our opinion, a "hybrid" or "bionic" model with omnibus channels to service clients is optimal for both customers and the financial service industry (at least in the next three to five years).

Here are our top five megatrend predictions for WealthTech:
1. IT will become the business driver at financial institutions, rather than serving in a support role.
2. The move from product pushing to providing portfolio advice will be difficult to provide at a reasonable cost and quality, unless the process is digitized. As a result, financial institutions and insurance companies are no longer asking "Can we do this ourselves?" but instead are asking what components they can buy

from third parties to get to the degree of digitization they require in order to scale faster and at a lower cost.

3. Regulatory pressure and margin compression will force internal process rationalization and digitization on an unprecedented scale.

4. Mega-financial brands will compete with mega non-financial brands (as we know them today) for wealth management business from consumers.

5. The adoption of augmented intelligence, evolving to artificial intelligence will enable a new form of investment solution provision across all the wealth segments.

We are only at the start of the WealthTech revolution. The case study of Asia and China illustrates just how challenging and varying this is across countries and markets. Whilst the region, and the world, may not be able to replicate the unique conditions that have fostered the frenetic WealthTech pace in China, one thing is for sure: the only way to evolve is to get onto the front foot with changing customer demand and external new entrant competitive forces leveraging technology, in particular, digitization across their internal and external workflows.

We believe that the digital evolution is what makes WealthTech in Greater China, and worldwide, one of the most exciting technology landscapes to be working in for the next five years and beyond.

Endnotes

1 https://www.brookings.edu/wp-content/uploads/2017/02/global_20170228_global-middle-class.pdf
2 http://www.pbc.gov.cn/goutongjiaoliu/113456/113469/3529600/index.html
3 http://www.gov.cn/zhengce/content/2017-07/20/content_5211996.htm

Privé Technologies is a leading innovator in the financial and wealth management industries. Recognized as the fastest growing technology company in Hong Kong by Deloitte in 2017 and ranked as the 14th fastest growing technology company in Asia in 2018 by the Financial Times' FT 1000 APAC rankings, Privé's three platforms—Managers, Avenir, and WEALTH—provide end-to-end solutions for banks, financial advisors, independent asset managers, and insurance companies. Our technology solutions help the financial institutions of today to streamline and transform, enabling them to operate more efficiently and effectively than ever before. Privé services over 60 financial institutional clients globally, including two of the world's largest banks by assets under management (AUM).

Steve Tsu-Wei Yang is a partner and board director at Privé Technologies overseeing operations and partnerships in Taiwan and China. Mr. Yang is also the responsible officer for Privé Financial Ltd., a SFC-licensed broker dealer, and currently the co-chair of WealthTech committee for FinTech Association Hong Kong. Steve brings over 20 years

*of working experience in the financial industry and has been involved in business devel-
opment, sales and trading, and financial product design and structuring. Prior to joining
Privé, he was former head of Greater China sales at Commerzbank AG. also held senior
and strategic positions at Citigroup, J.P. Morgan, and Deutsche Bank.Mr. Yang is a chartered financial analyst and an alumni of Haas School of Business, UC Berkeley.*

Chapter 21
RegTech: We are coming out of Fintech!

This chapter provides an analysis of the regulatory technology, or "RegTech" space; particularly in understanding how RegTechs use technology and through this, help to facilitate effective regulation or regulatory compliance. We begin with an examination of the critical problems that RegTech is able to resolve, in order to gain an understanding of its relevance and importance. Next, we describe the current RegTech landscape in terms of the distribution of firms, funding, and stakeholders involved — particularly the financial institutions (FIs), RegTech companies, RegTech associations and regulators. Thereafter, we examine how FIs can integrate RegTech into their operations with the use of examples and the potential challenges of adoption. Finally, the chapter concludes with insights into the future of RegTech, lending perspective to the tipping point of adoption through both industry-led and regulator-led initiatives.

Putting RegTech in Context

Following the financial crisis of 2007–2008, there has been a 37% increase (Figure 21.1) in regulatory changes as regulators acted on lessons learned. This presents challenges for FIs as they try to keep pace with increasingly complex and changing regulatory requirements in their efforts to avoid the rising penalties of non-compliance.

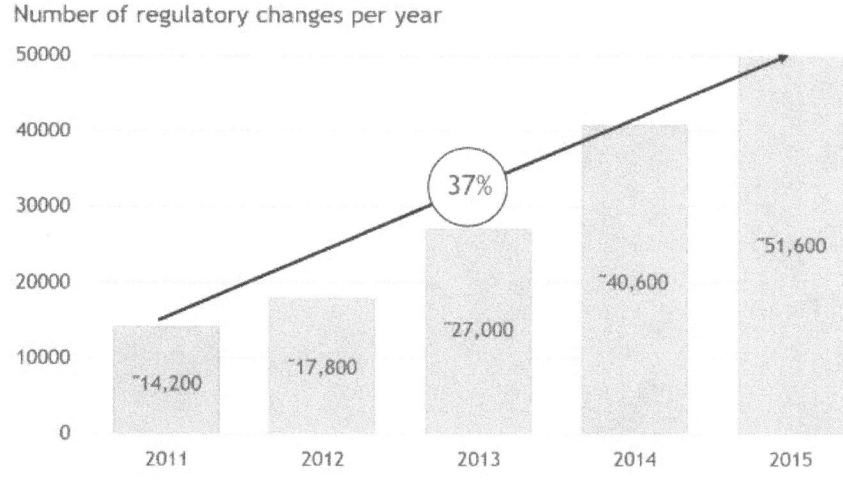

Figure 21.1: An increasingly complex regulatory landscape

DOI 10.1515/9781547400904- 021

From the financial crisis up to 2016, cumulative financial penalties worldwide totaled $321 billion.[1] In fact, the BCG report shows that banks paid US$42 billion in fines in 2016 alone, which is a 68% rise from the previous year.[2]

For example, in June 2018, the Commonwealth Bank of Australia (CBA) received a fine of AUD$700 million for its violations of anti-money laundering and counter-terrorism financing laws, and contraventions in risk procedures and due-diligence.[3] The repercussions of non-compliance go beyond monetary fines or reputational loss. In some instances, regulators have even revoked banking licenses. This occurred in 2016 when the Monetary Authority of Singapore (MAS) withdrew the merchant bank statuses of the Swiss bank BSI and Falcon Bank in Singapore for serious breaches of anti-money laundering (AML) requirements and management misconduct. These compliance failures were revealed during MAS' investigations into the scandal involving 1Malaysia Development Berhad (1MDB), where several institutions acted as conduits for fund transfers from 1MDB.

RegTechs to the Rescue

The BCG FinTech Control Tower (FCT) defines RegTechs as solution providers that leverage innovative technology to facilitate effective regulation or regulatory compliance and help FIs navigate through the headwind that may come with constant and complex regulatory changes. There are more than 400 RegTechs globally which can be broadly classified into seven key clusters (Figure 21.2): verification, reporting, data capture & integration, monitoring, risk analysis, regulatory analysis & training and general compliance. These clusters can be further broken down into 15 sub-categories.[4]

Cluster	Details	Sub-Categories
Verification	Enhancing the process of gathering and verifying information in due diligence, Know Your Customer (KYC) and Anti-Money Laundering (AML)	i) Data Sources ii) Automation iii) New Techniques
Reporting	Consolidating and computing data to generate reports for the purpose of regulatory or management reporting	i) Regulatory Reporting ii) Management Information
Data Capture & Integration	Capturing new data or breaking down data silos across the organisation for the purpose of enabling enhanced analytics	i) Data Capture ii) Data Integration
Monitoring	Monitoring transactions for AML, market abuse or surveillance of employee behaviour for suspicious activities	i) Transaction ii) Behaviour
Risk Analysis	Identifying impact on risk thresholds at real-time or managing risks through scenario analysis and forecasting	i) Limits & Thresholds Tracking ii) Modelling and Stress Testing
Regulatory Analysis & Training	Track, identify and interpret regulations as they apply to the firms' operating model; includes educating staff on compliance obligations	i) Identification and interpretation ii) Training and awareness
General Compliance	Enterprise-grade solutions and other process optimization tools such as document, case management, automated notifications etc.	i) Other process optimization ii) Enterprise solution

Figure 21.2: Overview of RegTech Industry

In fact, as a whole, the sector has grown a significant 292% since 2007 from just 134 RegTechs (Figure 21.3) in response to the increased regulatory pressure faced by financial institutions.

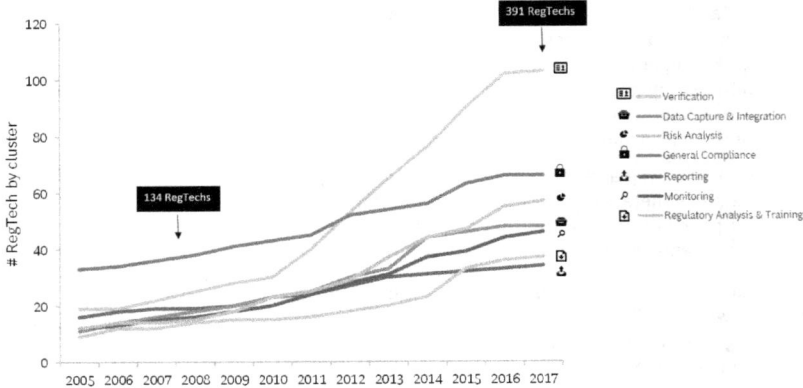

Figure 21.3: Growth in RegTechs

Ecosystem and Trends

Landscape of RegTechs

The Europe, the Middle East and Africa (EMEA) region comprises the greatest number of RegTechs with 195 firms followed by the Americas with 126 firms and the Asia Pacific (APAC) region with 70 firms. The United States has the highest number of RegTechs (120 firms) in the Americas while in EMEA, United Kingdom (82 firms) has the most firms followed by Switzerland (27 firms). In APAC, Australia has the most firms (27 firms) followed closely by Singapore (26 firms).

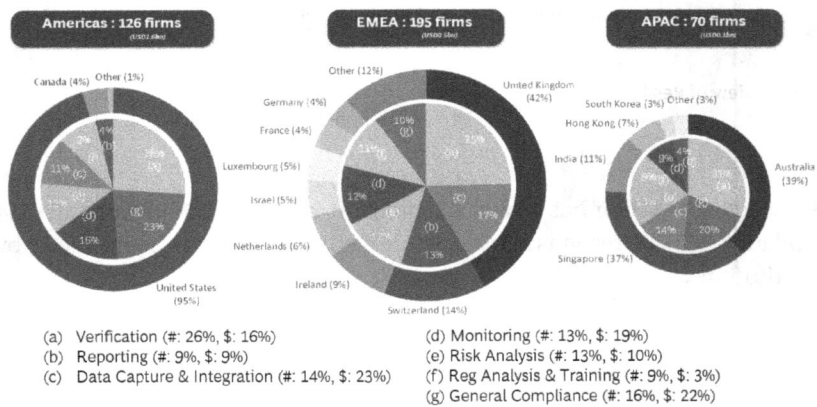

(a) Verification (#: 26%, $: 16%)
(b) Reporting (#: 9%, $: 9%)
(c) Data Capture & Integration (#: 14%, $: 23%)
(d) Monitoring (#: 13%, $: 19%)
(e) Risk Analysis (#: 13%, $: 10%)
(f) Reg Analysis & Training (#: 9%, $: 3%)
(g) General Compliance (#: 16%, $: 22%)

Source: The distribution of RegTechs shown is in terms of headquartered country. Data shown includes firms that have been acquired. Data source: BCG/Expand analysis, Dealroom, TechInAsia

Figure 21.4: Geographical distribution of RegTechs

Funding

Funding for RegTechs has increased significantly from 2010 to 2017, and though there was a dip in 2016, it recovered in 2017 with investments primarily in the mature rounds of funding such as the Series B, C and D rounds. *General compliance, monitoring, and data capture & integration clusters* received the most funding while *verification* is emerging as an investment hotspot (Figure 21.5). This can be attributed to the fact that verification is the largest and fastest growing cluster driven by the demand for automation of heavily manual onboarding processes; and that 75% of FIs identify it to be an area with the greatest need for innovation.

RegTechs are generally less funded compared to fintechs, receiving only 2% of the overall fintech funding despite constituting 4% of the total number of fintech companies. This can be attributed to three key reasons:

1. The founders of RegTechs tend to be veteran domain practioners, who tend to self-fund the business in the initial years.
2. RegTechs are geared toward being a service provider which means that they generate revenue in an earlier lifecycle stage than other fintech startups whose focus is on customer acquisition.
3. RegTechs, who are generally micro-services, lend themselves to early exits as they are often acquired by larger, more established firms which look to expand their services to provide a more comprehensive suite of solutions.

Investments

Venture Capital (VC) investors continue to be the more active investors of RegTechs by number count. VC investors have consistently contributed to more than 60% of the funding between the years 2011 and 2017, and also took part in the largest proportion of investment rounds within the same period (Figure 21.6). However, FIs' growing interest in the industry is apparent as we see larger investments made by FIs over the years. Funding contribution in terms of amount invested from FIs has increased from 10% in 2011 to 32% in 2017 (Figure 21.6) with the most active banks being Goldman Sachs, Santander and Barclays.

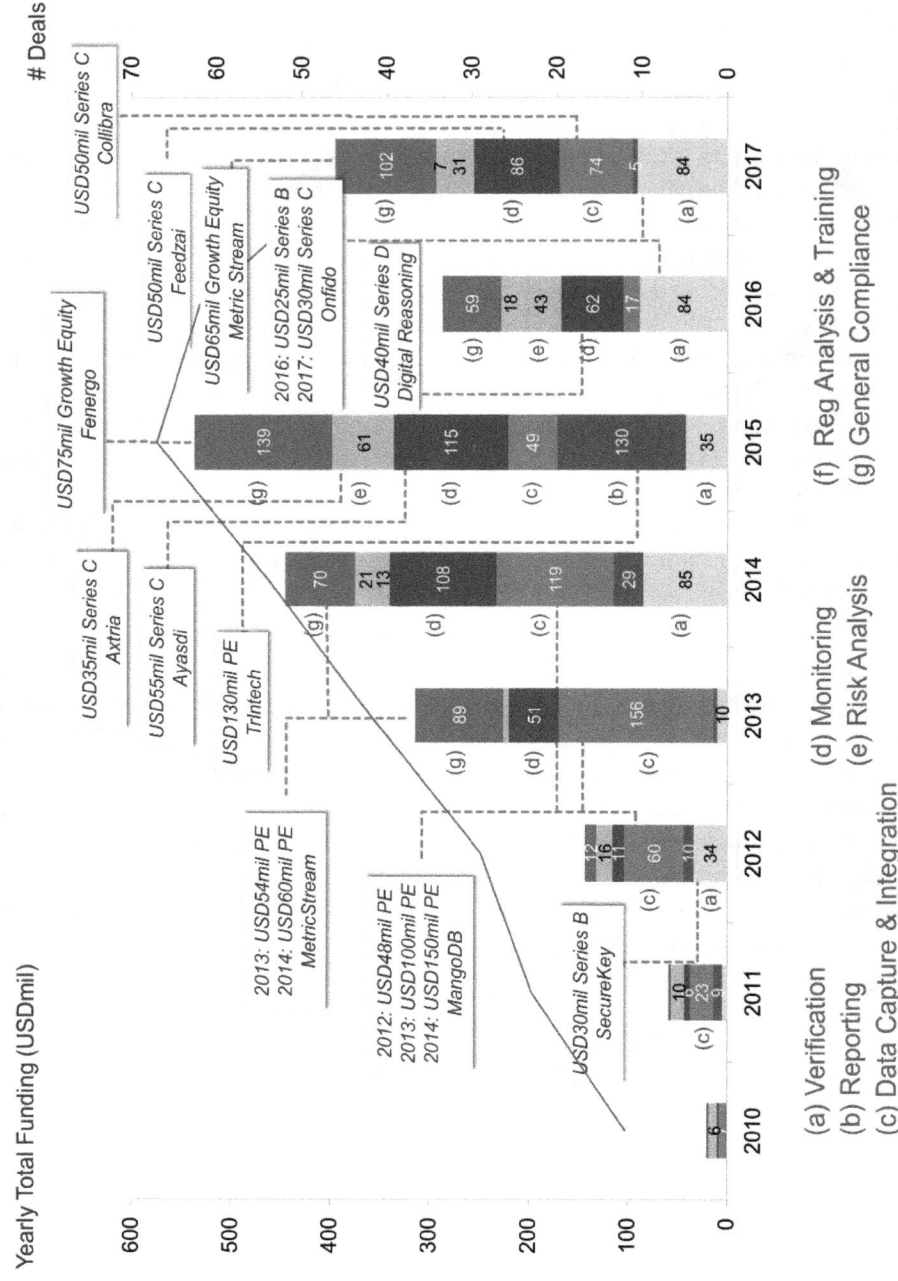

Figure 21.5: Funding growth of RegTechs

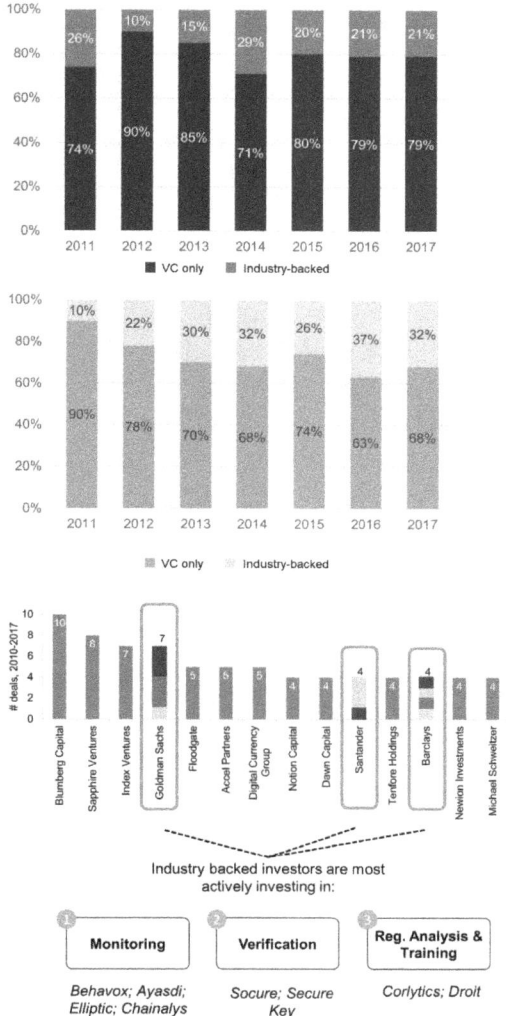

Figure 21.6: Investor Types

Exits

RegTech acquisitions have increased steadily since 2010 and saw a record year in 2017, particularly in the monitoring cluster. Acquirers of RegTechs are primarily technology providers themselves. In fact, acquisitions by technology providers amount to almost 59% of acquisitions between 2005 to 2017 (Figure 21.7). RegTechs may choose to be acquired by technology providers with the aim of supplementing or integrating with their exisiting suite of capabilities and FIs tend to prefer enterprise solutions with greater reputability and credibility which usually comes with being an established firm.

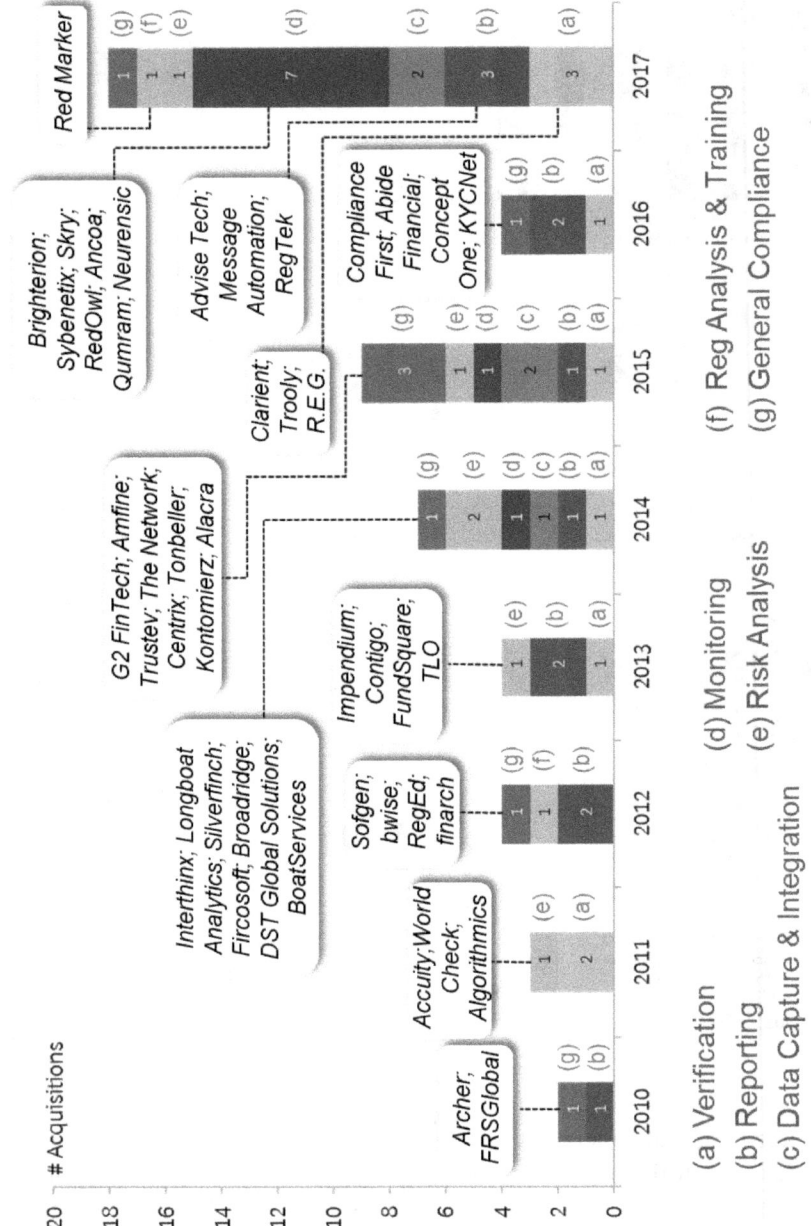

Figure 21.7: Acqusition of RegTechs

Ecosystem: Who Are the Stakeholders and Why?

Besides the RegTech companies themselves, the RegTech ecosystem is comprised of three key stakeholders: the regulators, banks and RegTech associations (Figure 21.8). We describe their roles in Table 21.1.

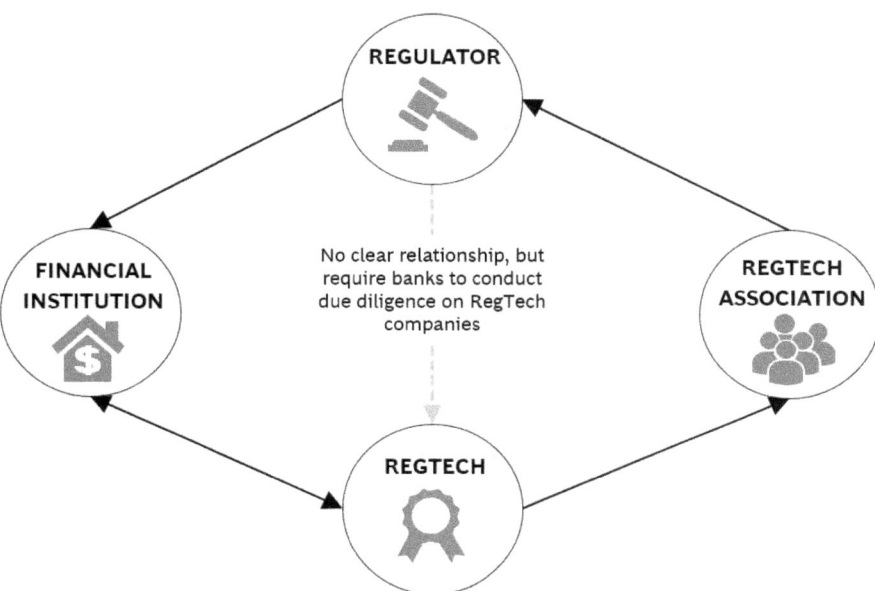

Figure 21.8: The RegTech Ecosystem

Table 21.1: Key stakeholders in the RegTech ecosystem

Banks

- Banks, or financial institutions in general, are the users of RegTech. They can on-board RegTech solutions to target the critical "pain-points" they face in meeting regulatory expectations; as it proves to be a cost-efficient means for banks to ease their compliance processes.
- RegTech solutions can be used during the verification of customer identities such as Know-Your-Client, which is done as part of the anti-money laundering (AML) procedure. With this, a bank can enjoy the benefits of an automated compliance process in terms of reduced processing time which may vary across the applications of different RegTechs.
- To give an example, Simple KYC's[1] automated customer on-boarding process management solution has helped Amex Australia to reduce their customer on-boarding time by 50% since adoption.
- In addition, the adept use of these technologies in compliance can help FIs to meet the various regulatory requirements, such as Chapter 186 of the MAS Act which stipulates regulations on the control and resolution of financial institutions.

Table 21.1: (continued)

Regulators

- Regulators are the supervisory body that inform FIs of their regulatory obligations and test effective compliance. They communicate their expectations via a combination of rule-making, requests for transparency of information and decision-making, consultation, inspection, enforcement actions and penalties.
- It is instructive to note that while there exists a distinct relationship between regulators and FIs, there is however no clear relationship that exists between the regulators and RegTechs themselves. Instead, the regulators require the banks to conduct due diligence on RegTech companies.

Association

- RegTech associations are emerging globally with a focus on helping RegTechs to circumvent the challenges to adoption and growth.
- Associations act as a lobbyist for RegTech, working to influence, support policies and initiatives vis-à-vis the RegTech industry. They provide thought-leadership representations of the industry on regulators' RegTech policies and collaborate with regulators to help raise visibility of RegTechs.
- Essentially, RegTechs are starting to "unionize" themselves to expand their reach as a group.
- These RegTech associations are typically formed in the local community, with the Australian RegTech association being one of the most active groups. In fact, there are four such organizations launched in 2017 encompassing more than 150 RegTechs. As the movement is nascent, the mandate and scope of activities are still being defined.

Note: Simple KYC is a business process management solution automating commercial customer onboarding process, enabling financial institutions to on-board new customers much faster, reduce the labor cost of processing, and improve compliance by reducing manual mistakes and creating an audit trail.

Broadly, there are three types of such RegTech associations as described in Table 21.2.

Table 21.2: The three types of RegTech associations

Natural association of like-minded RegTech companies

Here, RegTech companies, regulated entities, regulators and professional services firms come together to share knowledge, warm leads and advocate for action on common challenges. The focus is on working with policy-makers to shape development initiatives targeted at the industry. Currently, activities are concentrated in the Asia Pac region with members drawn from the UK, Singapore, New Zealand and Australia. Australia, the home base of The RegTech Association, is the most active hub. At the global level, the International RegTech Association (IRTA) has emerged as a representative body by forming alliances with several other associations operating at a local or regional basis. The IRTA has also indicated plans to monetize its operations by turning their RegTech network into a marketplace.

Table 21.2: (continued)

Entrepreneurs seeking to monetize the opportunity of early Ecosystem building	
	These entrepreneurs essentially act as service providers to the RegTech community, leveraging their international network and expertise to facilitate early stage RegTech companies to enter foreign markets, co-create solutions, provide branding and advisory services and develop a marketplace of RegTech offerings. Typically, in the early stages of building platform membership, they would also engage in traditional association type activities similar to the first category of RegTech groups.
Led by an incumbent	
	These associations are led by established RegTech players who are seeking to position themselves as market leaders driving and shaping conversations. They are sponsoring and launching RegTech committees that facilitate dialogue between regulators, standards bodies and other RegTechs. This level of activity is comparatively low and likely to see limited growth as other forms of groups gain traction.

FI Applications & Adoption

A survey of 15 global and regional banks showed that the top drivers for RegTech adoption is to improve (a) the efficiency and (b) the effectiveness of current regulatory compliance processes, with 40% and 35% of banks citing these reasons as their top drivers respectively (Figure 21.9).

Improving efficiency encompasses the idea of automating manual efforts, simplifying and standardizing compliance processes to reduce errors. Along a similar vein, increasing effectiveness helps to better satisfy stakeholders, allow for pro-active identification and a better management of risks.

In fact, increasing effectiveness, together with having a competitive advantage is an increasingly powerful driver and this combination stands as having the greatest perceived value-add in RegTech. This could be attributed to the use of RegTech which, when employed in an organization, can create cost-efficiency gains and also optimize and enhance a client's on-boarding experience which hones a competitive advantage for that organization.

In contrast, the bid to reduce operational costs is not ranked high as a reason for banks wanting to adopt RegTech, owing to just 13% of banks as shown in Figure 21.9.

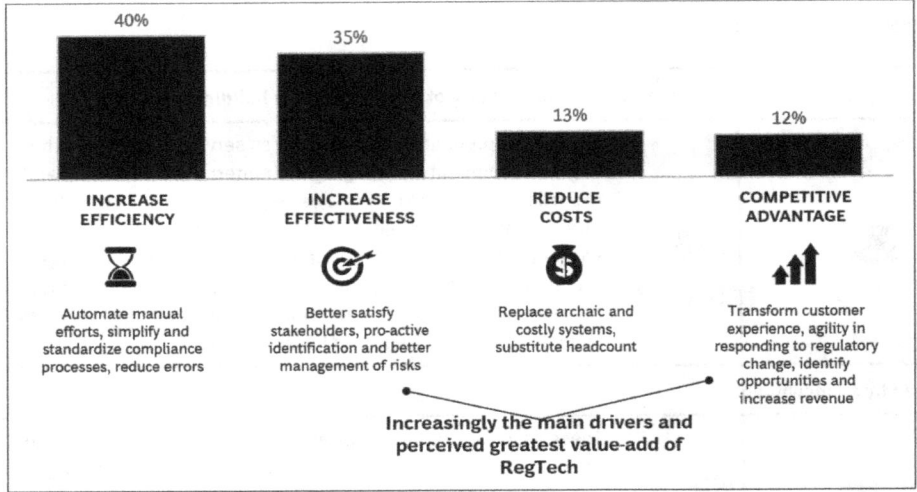

Figure 21.9: Benefits of RegTech

Case Example: Silent Eight

The application of new technologies by RegTechs can bring significant benefits to banks.

For example, a risk-based approach to customer screening, payments screening and transaction monitoring obligations in financial services result in an exponential growth in the volume of alerts, most of them being false positives. The investigative work in banks today is a very manual process leading to an unsustainable increase in compliance headcount. Here is where RegTechs come in to resolve such issues as seen in Figure 21.10 featuring Silent Eight's "verification-cluster" RegTech.

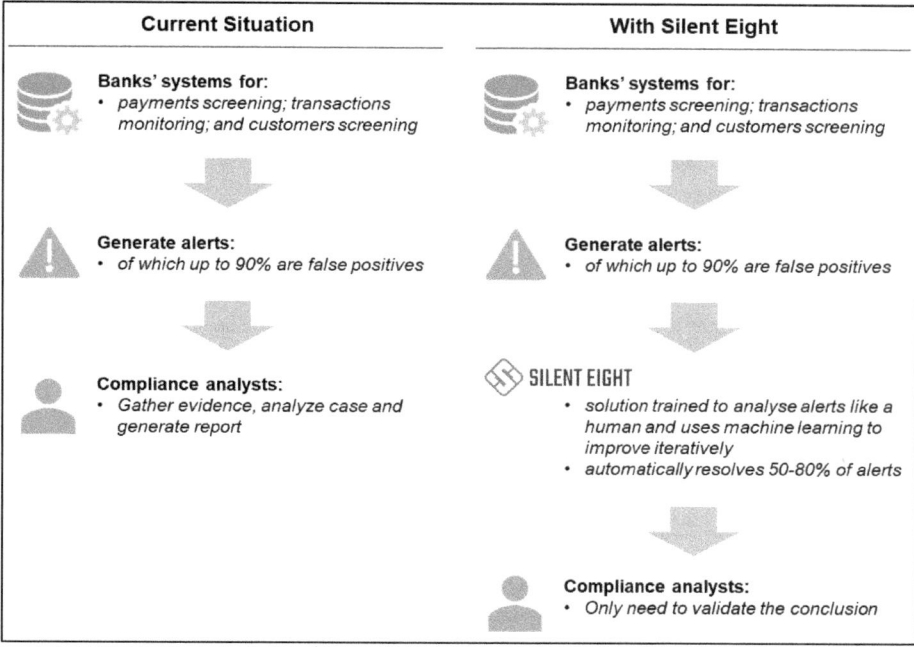

Figure 21.10: Silent Eight's Verification Cluster RegTech

Adoption

Banks recognize that innovation is needed across all clusters. However, when asked where innovation is most needed versus where pilot or adoption has taken place, it was observed that the level of adoption lags behind across all clusters aside from regulatory analysis (see Figure 21.11).

	INNOVATION NEED*	PILOT / ADOPTION**	KEY DRIVERS	DESCRIPTION
Verification	75%	33%		• Extract and validate KYC information • Ascertain identity remotely • Identify hidden relationships
Monitoring	63%	40%		• Identify suspicious behaviours • Reduce false positives
Reporting	50%	10%		• Convert, enrich and submit reports • Identify over, under-reporting and duplicates
Risk Analysis	50%	8%		• Identify patterns in large data sets • Create better risk models • Improve accuracy of stress testing
Data Capture & Integration	40%	33%		• Ensure data capture and record keeping • Interpretation of unstructured data
Regulatory Analysis	38%	47%		• Enable assessment of regulations • Adapt compliance workflows quickly
General Compliance	13%	13%		• Increase collaboration, transparency among business units and compliance functions

Cost   Efficiency   Effectiveness   Revenue

*Proportion of total interviewed financial institutions identified the area as a "pain-point" in 2017 or where they have most interest for RegTech application
**Proportion of total selected financial institutions (15) across APAC(30%), EMEA(40%) and AMERICAS(30%) with pilots or deployment of RegTech between 2015-2017. Source: Fintech Control Tower
Figure 21.11: Adoption Statistics

Challenges to Adoption

Challenges to broader RegTech adoption come from the perspectives of both the RegTechs (acting as the provider) and the banks (acting as the consumer).

RegTechs can face long sales cycles (as long as two years) and tedious procurement processes of up to two years when engaging FIs. This is largely because the procurement process has to go through multiple pain decision points in FIs and this can be costly for start-ups. For example, it takes a substantial amount of time to finalize the requirements involved for penetration testing. Another challenge is that FIs continue to have stronger preferences for large established providers as they remain unconvinced about the scalability of RegTechs. Banks adopt a more conservative attitude in the area of compliance, and particularly so with the use of innovative technologies. However, the biggest challenge being cited is the fear of rejection by regulators.

The industry is in a Catch-22 situation—FIs are hesitant to deploy new AI-enabled solutions as the lack of expertise in new technologies makes it difficult for compliance staff to explain the technology to regulators; regulators do not know what they need to regulate as FIs have not deployed and scaled these solutions. This is significant in the field of RegTech as 67% of them leverage newly enabled technologies across robotics process automation (RPA), machine learning, natural language processing (NLP), computer vision/biometrics and distributed ledger technology (DLT).

One of the main concerns of a bank when deciding to on-board a new technology is to ensure it is sufficiently secure to protect against security lapses such as potential data leakage.

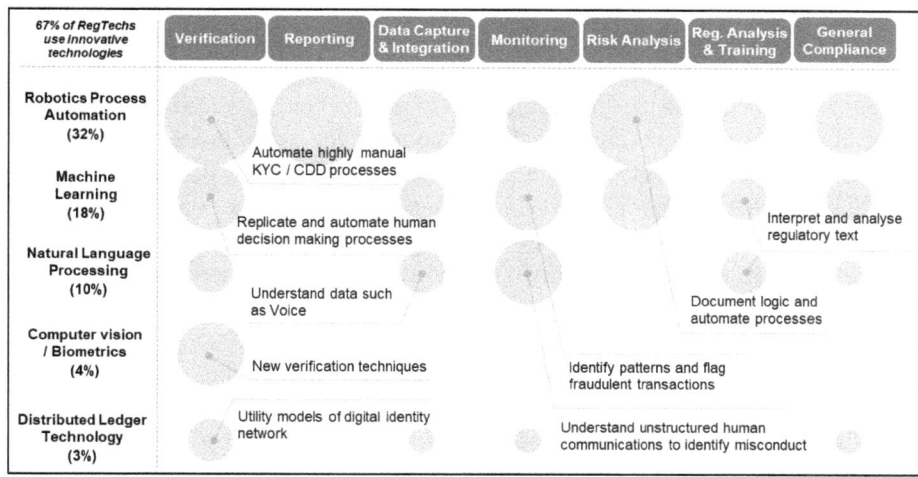

Figure 21.12: Technologies in RegTechs

The industry has come up with interesting solutions, led by both FIs and regulators, to address this challenge. This leads us to believe that the adoption of RegTechs by FIs is at a tipping point.

The Future: At the Tipping Point of Adoption

FIs are collaborating as an industry to test RegTech solutions by engaging the regulator at an early stage.

An example is the collaboration between The International Netherlands Group (ING) and Commonwealth Bank of Australia (CBA) to run a proof-of-concept (POC) with Ascent Technologies.

> In this example with Ascent Technologies, NLP and AI were used to interpret and convert 1.5 million paragraphs of regulation into streamlined tasks that made it easier for banks to act on. This helped ING and CBA save a substantial amount of time from manually processing the information and therefore to be able to quickly identify aspects of the regulation that needed action. In this process, the UK Financial Conduct Authority (FCA) was invited to take on the role of an observer. The FIs, regulators, legal firms and RegTechs collaborate to validate questions at one go so POCs are tested faster and decisions can move faster.

Regulator-led Initiatives

Regulators themselves are taking active steps toward acquiring a better understanding of emerging technologies and are also considering issuing guidelines on their adoption.

For example, the Monetary Authority of Singapore (MAS) has launched a $27million AI & Data Analytics grant to support the adoption and integration of such new technologies in FIs. They do so by engaging academics in AI and ML to help build a framework around the use and evaluation of a Blackbox.[5] The MAS will also help financial services professionals up-skill and adapt to the use of these new technologies to boost their familiarity and competence with them. Finally, the MAS also plans to work with other regulators to create a Supervisory Tech (SupTech[6]) alliance and explore how countries can collaborate to review exisiting regulations.

The Financial Conduct Authority (FCA), is also engaging closely with industry to keep up-to-date with advancements in the market. They currently run a monthly demo day, attend conferences and forums, and engage with industry POCs as an observer. They also work with an academic advisory board with experts from universities, and procure expertise from mature tech firms. In fact, they plan to release a publication on FCA's expectations for banks to adopt technology in the near future and will list examples of the use of specific technologies in specific activities.

The Australian Securities & Investment Commission (ASIC) is committed to running internal technology trials for supervisory and enforcement work. Following that, they will update the market and share their knowledge and experiences to encourage the wider adoption of technologies.

As more regulators become avid participants in the RegTech space, they will develop a heightened understanding of the opportunities and challenges that may come with the interaction of RegTechs and FIs and be in a better position to support the industry.

In fact, both FIs and RegTechs believe that regulators can further expand their respective scope of activities to champion RegTech adoption. Banks would like to see regulators show leadership by approving RegTechs and also take on an advisory cum supervisory approach. On a similar note, RegTechs would want for regulators to show a sense of "soft" endorsement towards RegTech and also encourage FIs to try out such technologies.

Currently, besides the initiatives of the three aforementioned regulators, the regulator's activities are centered around building a conducive ecosystem, and adjusting rules and standards for RegTechs to thrive.

To a smaller extent, regulators are adopting RegTechs themselves to aid in their supervisory duties and to demonstrate the feasibility of these technologies to the industry.

As seen in Figure 21.13, the hotspots in the regulatory activity scene point to aspects that constitute either building an ecosystem or adjusting rules. More specificially, holding roadshows, hackathons and tech-sprints provide a means to showcase RegTech solutions as ways to improve or even redefine the approach to regulatory compliance procedures across a spectrum. Additionally, digitizing legislation by making regulations machine-readable and executable makes it easy for information to be accessed and updated, promoting seamless and smooth collaboration across the parties involved. Table 21.3 gives examples of regulatory initiatives across the Globe in 2017.

Table 21.3: Examples of Regulatory Initiatives Across The Globe in 2017

Regulator	Initiative 1	Initiative 2	Initiative 3
FCA United Kingdom	Exploring the possbility of a banking industry global IT risk and controls framework to resolve challenges in leveraging new technology	Exploring the potential for mode-driven machine-readable regulations together with the Bank of England	Pilot with R3 and global banks on using DLT for regulatory reporting
CFTC United States	Began a series of innovative prize competitions to stimulate application of RegTech		
MAS Singapore	Established a data analytics group to promote capabilties and foster innovations		
ASIC Australia	Organized a RegTech showcase event to prompt the industry to develop solutions to identified problems	Implemented an informal assistance program for eligible RegTech businesses	
ASIC & JFSA Australia & Japan	Established co-operation framework enabling the sharing of information and support the entry of innovative businesses into each other's markets		

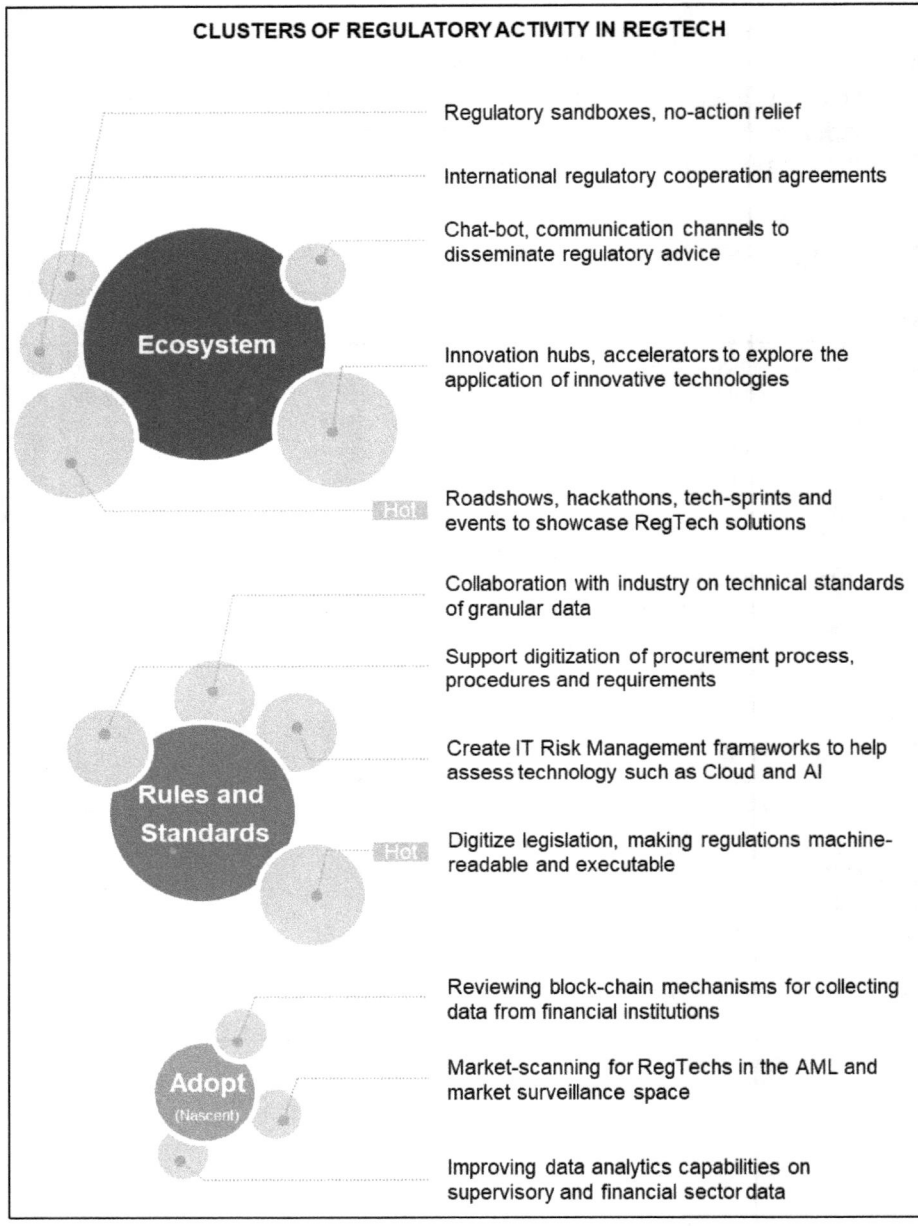

Figure 21.13: Regulatory Activities in RegTech

RegTech Association-led Initiatives

One type of Association-led initative can be described using the Design-box Concept suggested by The RegTech Association, Australia,[7] as shown in Figure 21.14, which focuses on four key design concepts—(1) what it is about, (2) how it is done, (3) how does it value-add, and (4) how can we trial run in the trial phase. It is beyond the scope of this section to delve in depth on the design concepts and interested readers are encouraged to refer to the report.

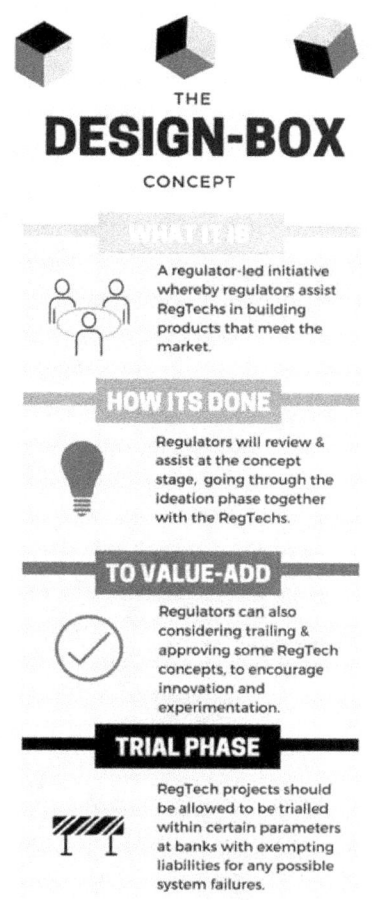

Figure 21.14: The Design Box Concept

RegTech Associations

RegTechs themselves are very clear about the challenges they face in adoption, being the very people that interact with the FIs and hear first hand the issues—which are often regulator-related. It is difficult for individual RegTechs to alter this state of mind in FIs or get regulators to help them fight the battle—as there is no clear direct relationship between regulators and Regtechs. Hence, RegTechs are beginning to join up as a community, where the effort of multiple RegTechs to alter the status quo is considered more effective and less costly compared to an individual effort. We can think of the key purpose of RegTech associations as trying to produce "public good" for all RegTechs, by influencing policy makers and changing misconceptions in the FIs.

Essentially, their focus is centered on helping RegTechs to circumvent the challenges to adoption and growth. Regtech associations are focused on promotional activities, advocating initiatives that could support the development and adoption of RegTechs. The benefits of being in a RegTech association can be summarized in three key points: to build membership, provide consultation feedback and opportunities to collaborate with other organizations (Figure 21.15).

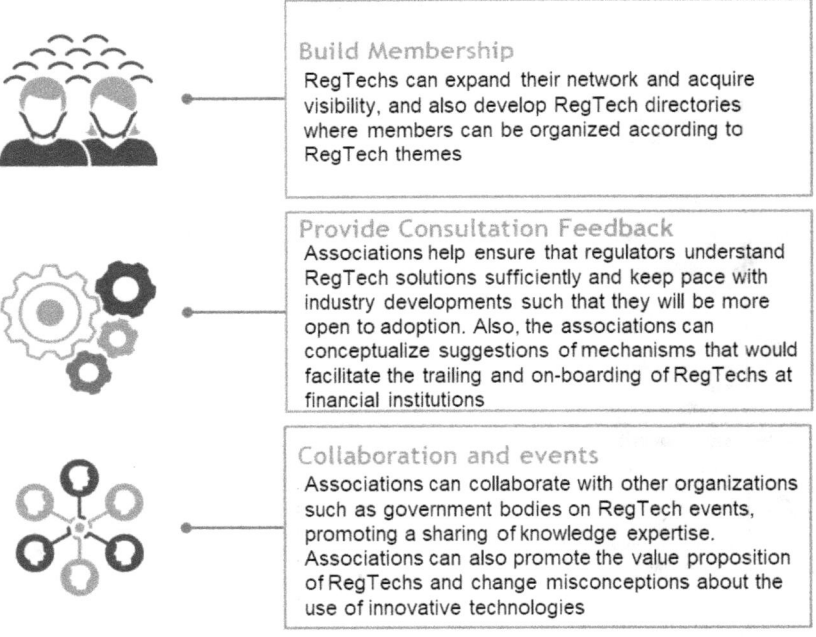

Build Membership
RegTechs can expand their network and acquire visibility, and also develop RegTech directories where members can be organized according to RegTech themes

Provide Consultation Feedback
Associations help ensure that regulators understand RegTech solutions sufficiently and keep pace with industry developments such that they will be more open to adoption. Also, the associations can conceptualize suggestions of mechanisms that would facilitate the trailing and on-boarding of RegTechs at financial institutions

Collaboration and events
Associations can collaborate with other organizations such as government bodies on RegTech events, promoting a sharing of knowledge expertise. Associations can also promote the value proposition of RegTechs and change misconceptions about the use of innovative technologies

Figure 21.15: Benefits of a RegTech Association

Conclusion

RegTechs can be credited with playing a pivotal role in driving innovation in compliance by providing FIs with the technological agility to navigate through the ongoing regulatory complexity and by doing so, it increases efficiency and effectiveness, reduces cost and gives a competitive advantage to its adopters.

The growing interest from investors, the multiple numbers of acquisitions, players coming into the market, and a growing sector priority among regulators globally leads us to believe that we are entering RegTech 2.0 and with it, an industry is likely to be at the tipping point of adoption.

Endnotes

1 Image source: http://image-src.bcg.com/BCG_COM/BCG-Staying-the-Course-in-Banking-Mar-2017_ tcm9-146794.pdf Statistic source: https://www.bcg.com/publications/2017/financial-institutions-risk-management-transforming-bank-compliance-smart-technologies.aspx
2 News source: https://www.straitstimes.com/business/global-banks-have-paid-453b-in-fines
3 Statistic source: https://www.bloomberg.com/news/articles/2018-06-03/commonwealth-bank-to-pay-a-700-million-to-settle-laundering-suit
4 Note that this refers to RegTechs in financial services only and excludes the cybersecurity sector.
5 A Blackbox test is a software testing method whereby the internal structure of the object being tested is unknown, therefore it can only be assessed based on the inputs and outputs.
6 Supervisory Technology is the use of innovative technology by supervisory agencies to support supervision. See FSI Insights on policy implementation No 9, Innovative technology in financial supervision (SupTech)—the experience of early users. SupTech solutions assist in automating and improving the data collection methods employed by supervisory agencies by reducing the time taken to retrieve and analyze the data, as well as and digitizing elements of the processes involved.
7 Refer to The Regtech Association Response to Asic Report 523.

The FinTech Control Tower (FCT) is a research framework developed jointly by BCG and Expand Research, identifying initiatives, technologies, and companies that matter most in today's fintech ecosystem and assessing their impact. The FCT has developed a proprietary platform that tracks fintechs globally providing insights into the landscape. Our clients include the top global and regional financial institutions, regulators, investors, and technology giants, who chose us for the expertise to drive informed decisions around innovation management, ecosystem engagement, IT investments, and M&A activities. For more information, visit us at www.fintechcontroltower.bcg.com.

Pauline Wray is Managing Director of Expand Consulting Pte Ltd, Head of Asia region operations and Global Co-Head of Distribution and Strategy for the BCG FinTech Control Tower. Having worked in Expand offices in London and New York, she gained a very wide knowledge of major financial institutions, technology companies, and financial services regulators. Pauline has 15 years of experience in the financial services industry and 12 years at Expand, opening the professional benchmarking arm of BCG in New York and Asia. She is also a member of the Expand/BCG leadership and advisory board across all FI sectors.

Simin Liu *is Lead Analyst at BCG FinTech Control Tower and leads research and market intelligence for the BCG FinTech Control Tower across Asia Pacific, supporting clients in driving innovation through the use of technology in financial services. She brings an extensive understanding of working with both the financial services and the fintech industry with core expertise around innovation in RegTech, beyond banking, retail banking, and wealth management.*

Nicole Rajoo *is an intern at the FinTech Control Tower, engaging with fintechs to understand their product offering and business model.*

Ian Loh *heads research for Expand Consulting across the Asia Pacific, supporting financial institutions in comparative benchmarking and industry research.*

Chapter 22
Digitalizing the Client Lifecycle and KYC/AML with RegTech

Beginning in 2009 and until a few years ago, many banks were mired in the depths of the financial crisis, trying to contend with regulation after regulation coming toward them at lightning speed. A recent statistic claims that the volume of regulatory change increased by a staggering 492% from 2008 to 2015. The last ten years have been characterized by a lot of uncertainty, instability, and downright hardship, with unprecedented fines being levied against household names in the banking community, seriously eroding reputational and business share value. The communal industry response to this was to arbitrarily cut costs by downsizing, forcing banks to do more (to ensure compliance and protect reputation) with less (resources, budgets, technologies).

Fast forward a decade or so and the industry dynamic has completely changed.

Today, banks are still concerned with compliance and the rate of regulatory change, and they're still challenged by operational costs, as they always will be. The difference is that banks have now moved beyond mere survival mode and are actively thriving once again. Where once the agenda was solely focused on the cost of compliance, the conversation has transitioned to one of client-centricity, while bank ambition has turned to innovative, digital business transformation programs that deliver exceptional client value.

This is where regulatory technology really comes into its own.

While regulatory compliance will remain at the forefront of banking operations, RegTech has enabled financial institutions to manage this *and* lead the charge toward a better, more efficient, and client-centric way of doing business.

And it is not just a small number of banks that are leading this charge. Every financial institution in the world is undertaking some level of business and digital transformation program. Some are more ambitious than others. Others are more global. Notably, this marks a stark departure from the days when digital transformation was considered the realm of retail banking alone. Now corporate, commercial, business, and investment banking clients are seeking—or rather demanding—a faster, more convenient, digitally led client experience.

If we consider that, by 2020, an entire generation will have grown up in a primarily digital world, then it's probably not too strong a statement to claim that whichever banks achieve and deliver a truly client-focused, value-added, digital client lifecycle management process will capture the hearts, minds, and wallets of this market.

In this chapter, we explore the increasing digitalization of Client Lifecycle Management and the benefits it delivers to onboarding, data management, and KYC/AML (anti-money laundering/know-your-customer) and regulatory processes.

DOI 10.1515/9781547400904- 022

What's Wrong with Client Lifecycle Management Today?

The area of Client Lifecycle Management (CLM) has grown by leaps and bounds over the last number of years. However, we are still in the very early stages of this journey. To really understand how we can transform Client Lifecycle Management into a highly optimized, efficient, and client-centric straight-through process, we need to take stock of where we are today with CLM and KYC/AML regulatory compliance management. Here's a snapshot of the reality of what banks face in the industry today.

Client Onboarding Still Takes Too Long

Data collection and regulatory compliance are the bottlenecks of onboarding a client. In some partly-automated CLM processes, it can still take commercial, institutional, and business banks up to 38 weeks to onboard a new client whose profile is of medium complexity.[1] Compliance and the evidencing of compliance (i.e., the collection of data and documentation to support the compliance decision process) consumes the vast majority of this time, with between 5 and 100 documents needing to be collected as part of the new client onboarding and refresh processes.[2] Client data collection is a nightmare of every bank almost without exception, with clients being asked to submit (and resubmit) data and documentation repeatedly by the bank (sometimes by the same product line or business unit). As a result, the client journey and overall experience is patchy, uncoordinated, and lacks transparency.

Rising Regulatory Requirements

The areas of AML and KYC compliance continue to be a challenge even for the more mature regulatory banks across the world. It is estimated that over 300 million pages of regulatory documents will be published by 2020 and over 600 legislative changes need to be cataloged by banks.[3]

Even in many of the more mature regulatory markets around the world, existing AML and KYC regulatory frameworks continue to undergo enhancements. In 2018, we've seen the passing of the European Union's Fifth Anti-Money Laundering Directive (5AMLD) (which is expected to enter into force in 2020) and FinCEN Final Rule CDD in the US. We are also seeing the continued global rollout of the Common Reporting Standard (CRS) and the introduction of increasing data privacy rules such as the General Data Protection Regulation (GDPR), which came into force on 25 May 2018.

In light of recent scandals such as the Panama Papers, Bahama Leaks, and Paradise Papers, current KYC/AML focus is increasingly centered on the creation of national beneficial ownership registers. This effort has spawned a huge global effort in information sharing and transparency so that criminals, money launderers, and terrorists cannot hide behind a veil of obscure shell companies.

On top of all this, global OTC derivatives reform continues apace and enforcement actions, while now on the decline, have risen to record levels. In APAC (the Asia Pacific region), home to 40+ regulators and one of the most complex jurisdictions in terms of regulatory compliance, we've seen fines in the last ten years of US$68+ million. In fact, in Singapore alone, the Monetary Authority of Singapore (MAS) announced in 2016 that it would redouble its KYC/AMLKYC-related enforcement efforts, and subsequently imposed seven fines, totalling US$12 million on banks that year.

To cope with the unrelenting pace of regulatory change, banks have been forced to prioritize efforts on meeting compliance deadlines over customer experience or risk incurring substantial penalties from financial regulators. A recent survey suggested that banks are spending up to $60 million on KYC procedures each year.[4] Most of this money is spent on repetitive processes—collecting data and documentation (repeatedly) from clients. If up to 100 pieces of data and documentation is required to evidence compliance during new client onboarding, imagine these 100 pieces of information multiplied by 1,000 clients and all data needs to be captured, processed, stored, tracked, reviewed, and updated regularly. This is where it becomes problematic.

Fragmented Systems Creating Data Silos

Over the last 30 years, the back to middle office, in particular, has suffered chronic underinvestment, with more focus being devoted to front office applications, particularly in the retail banking setting. This reduces banks' abilities to onboard clients quickly and compliantly.

Without the ability to connect and integrate these systems, banks find themselves asking clients to submit paperwork and information that they have probably submitted numerous times already to the same part of the bank. Now multiply this effect by three for a client who banks in the retail, business, and wealth segments of the same bank. The client must be wondering why their information cannot be shared (if they consent to it) among the other business units.

Costs Are Rapidly Going North … Manual Activities Are a Key Cause

Underinvestment in back-end technology is really hitting the banks in the form of higher regulatory costs, operational costs, and the opportunity cost associated with losing clients through a complicated and lengthy onboarding process. Manual processes are costly due to error-prone data rekeying, reworking, and the lack of traceability they elicit throughout the process. There are also high and ongoing costs involved in maintaining existing infrastructure that are not interconnected to provide the 360-degree view required for a robust regulatory and Client Lifecycle Management process.

Complex Customers Require More Expert Processes

Banks need to collect copious and extensive information and documents from different sources about individuals and entities that make up the collective legal entity "customer," integrate these data points with existing data held, and be capable of capturing changes in circumstances that may trigger an overall risk alert on continued suitability of the customer to the bank.

Figure 22.1 is a snapshot illustrating the difference between high-volume, simple clients (e.g., retail clients) compared to low-volume, complex clients (e.g., a CIB [corporate and institutional] banking client).

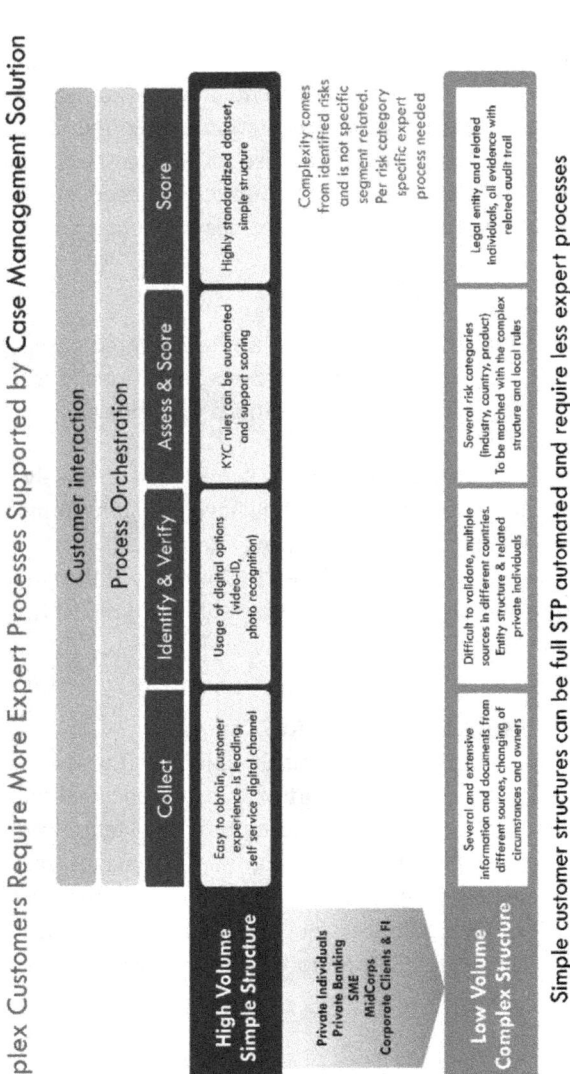

Figure 22.1: Differences between high volume simple clients and low volume complex clients

Client Outreach Is a Logistical Nightmare

Client outreach experience can be improved in most banks. Since the global financial crisis, the banking industry has undergone significant regulatory reform and change management. Each new financial regulation has necessitated the collection of additional client data and documentation to support the compliance process. Over the last few years specifically, we've seen the introduction of Dodd-Frank (US), EMIR (EU), MiFID II (EU), CRS (global), FATCA (US with global implications), GDPR (EU specific, but with extraterritoriality), FinCEN Final Rule ... and the list goes on. To comply with these rules, banks need to contact customers in an effort to explain the rules, solicit the new information from them, and process this information so that they can prove to the regulator that their clients comply with the new obligations. However, in the cold light of reality, this is an operational and logistical nightmare, often involving highly manual processes such as letters, phone calls, and emails, all of which process information differently and none of which is automatically centralized. This means that information needs to be picked up manually and re-entered into various systems to track compliance.

Client Offboarding Is Significant, Costly, and Problematic

There are many reasons why a client needs to be offboarded:
- The client has requested the cessation of a relationship with the bank
- The client is no longer attractive to do business with either from a risk rating point of view or from a profitability perspective
- The client's accounts remain inactive or dormant

It costs on average GBP £3k per year to maintain a client's record, even if they are inactive or dormant, as they must still undergo periodic regulatory reviews (AML/KYC) as well as creditworthiness checks.

It is not that banks like to incur this expense, rather it's that the disconnect in technologies and systems makes this an arduous task to complete efficiently. Like the client onboarding process, client offboarding is equally data- and document-heavy (due to the need to evidence all regulatory compliance obligations). Given that most financial institutions are quite siloed in nature (using numerous complex IT systems across various functional, business lines and jurisdictional divides, and storing client and counterparty data across a raft of data repositories with little or no interconnectivity), this adds a further level of complexity when attempting to off-board a client/account.

The Future of CLM Is Digitalization

The global financial services industry is on the edge of a massive technological disruption. The emergence of fintech (financial technology) and RegTech (regulatory technology) vendors has created a technology race for banks, helping to fast-track the innovation path for many of them. Conversely, it has also highlighted the laggards, who are weighed down by legacy systems and investments, leaving them to struggle to keep up with the competition.

What Does Digitalization Actually Mean?

The term digitalization is the latest buzzword but it means different things to different people across the banking industry. Digitalization has always been here in some form of automation or another. The term tends to evoke images of complexity, but it doesn't have to be complex. It just needs to reduce or eliminate the manual processes that have dominated back and middle office operations through the use of clever tools and technology.

At the recent Fenergo Global Client Council held in Ireland in June 2018, one client perfectly described the how and why they are digitalizing the client lifecycle process: "In our bank, we repeat processes 50,000 times a year. We're trying to automate basic processes so that we can save time in this area, and focus time and resources on higher-risk and higher-value areas that can add value or help us comply better. We're not trying to be too visionary—it's more about making sure we have solid foundations upon which to build. That is what digitalization means to us."

So Where Are We in Tech Evolution?

The last 10 years have focused on automating as much of the Client Lifecycle Management process as possible (including compliance (initial and reviews), data management, new client and product onboarding). This has involved investment in business process management (BPM), system integration, and rules engine technologies, and the effort has added a level of sophistication and efficiency to the process.

The industry has now moved onto the second tier of automation, which involves the increasing use of robotics, intelligent document management, and bots during the client lifecycle process.

The next stage of evolution will involve the application of myriad new, disruptive technologies to the areas of CLM and KYC/AML. These will include technologies such as natural language processing (NLP), big data analytics, artificial intelligence (AI), machine learning (ML), robotics process automation (RPA), large-scale processing, and other adaptive technologies.

It's important to understand that it's not one model or technology over another. No one technology will ever deliver what a bank requires to create a truly customer-centric, efficient, compliant client onboarding and lifecycle process. Instead, it will involve a unique blend of technologies that are prioritized based on the key objectives of the bank—efficiency, client experience, risk management, and so on. Therefore, the process may look like Figure 22.2 in terms of priority levels required to achieve a truly optimized and digitalized Client Lifecycle Management process.

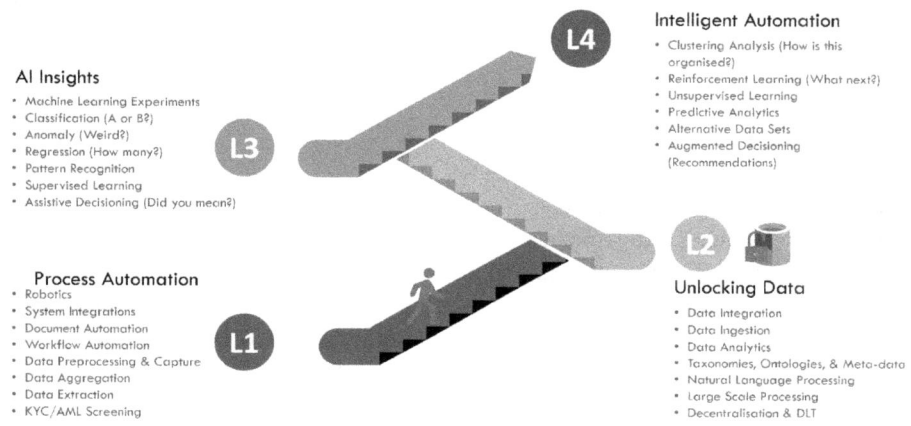

Figure 22.2: Priority Levels of technologies to achieve digitalized client lifecycle management

Pivot versus Disruptive

In terms of digitalizing Client Lifecycle Management and KYC/AML processes, there is huge room for improvement. There are two ways to look at digitalization or automation of CLM.

A *pivot* approach to digitalizing involves "rotating to the new" to unlock greater benefits than previous or traditional approaches. In other words, it's a deliberate approach to change. A pivot strategy involves using technology that is already available and has a large number of proven use cases. It involves blending the old and the new, innovating by design and being investment ready.[5]

Here are a few pivot innovations that are currently available in the market to facilitate the transformation of CLM, data management, and compliance processes: These include the increasing use of intelligent regulatory rules engines, eKYC utilities, centralized and integrated data processes, and cloud technologies and the extension of these cloud technologies to customers in the form of secure digital channels. These are not hugely disruptive innovations but can have a big transformative impact on front, middle, and back office processes when deployed properly. Most importantly, they can be immediately implemented to make a difference.

A *disruptive* approach, on the other hand, involves a radical shakeup of existing systems, processes, and approaches to managing the client lifecycle and generally includes the use of newer, more cutting-edge type of technologies. These are generally quite immature in their application within the areas of CLM and compliance. However, they are fast capturing the banking imagination in terms of being able to achieve what was once thought to be tri-opposing objectives of improved efficiency, greater compliance, and a better client experience. These innovations include artificial intelligence (AI), robotics process automation (RPA), and blockchain.

Pivot Innovation

Regulatory Compliance by Design

Banks are now moving away from a reactionary approach to managing compliance to one that involves designing compliance from end-to-end including a future-proofed approach to managing new compliance requirements. This involves unlocking regulatory value through digitalization. Here are a number of areas of transformation that KYC/AML and regulatory compliance is currently undergoing:

Regulatory Rules Engine

Regulatory compliance teams in banks are beginning to move toward a model of automating the interpretation of regulatory rules. This involves underpinning the compliance process with a regulatory rules engine which, when fed with specific information about a client (e.g., client type, client role, products, client location, etc.), can accurately determine all regulations that the client must be compliant with, all the data and documentation required to support the compliance process, the KYC questions that must be asked and the risk scoring that must be performed. This rules engine also enables banks to support the compliance process throughout the client lifecycle. For example, if a client moved from a low-risk jurisdiction to a higher-risk one, it would be automatically flagged through event-driven review processes, triggering the recalculation of risk score on the client based on the new information. If the change is materially significant, this may trigger a new compliance review process to ensure that the client remains compliant with existing regulations and to identify any new in-scope regulations due to the change in circumstance. Automating this process is critical to ensuring true and accurate compliance throughout the client's lifetime with the bank.

The Path to a Global Internal eKYC Framework
A few years ago, the industry tried to come up with a collaborative solution by creating KYC utilities that could consolidate client data and documentation among several banks, making this information available for other banks to draw upon when onboarding or reviewing compliance processes for different clients. Despite the industry desiring and needing a solution like this, it failed to get adopted. However, it did spawn the idea of banks creating internal KYC utilities, where client data and documentation can be captured, stored, cleansed, remediated, and centralized, available for any part of the bank to use at any time.

The idea of a single, centralized internal utility is very appealing, however, different data privacy laws prevent this from being a reality. This is where some banks have become innovative by creating a hub-and-spoke operational model to get around data privacy restrictions. Underpinned by Fenergo CLM technology, this involves establishing a small number of core KYC compliance units to serve multiple business units across different jurisdictions.

In the case of this particular bank, core KYC teams were established across three regions (compared to a previous 18), including APAC, North America, and Europe. Not only are KYC processes centralized to these three hubs, but all client data and documentation are centralized across the three regions, providing an almost perfect 360-degree view of any client. This has helped to accurately measure the size of risk posed by particular clients and to clearly identify and manage beneficial ownership compliance requirements.

There are a number of advantages of this federated shared services approach to Know Your Customer compliance:
- It helps to overcome data privacy laws, particularly across APAC, where data cannot be accessed from outside the jurisdiction nor be transferred out of the country in some cases. The aim of this operational restructuring is to ensure, first and foremost, that the banking group as a whole is fully compliant with all local and global regulations.
- The advantage of having a small number of jurisdictional functional units dedicated to the KYC compliance effort for the entire institution is that they can benefit from operations in multiple time-zones, thereby delivering a more localized KYC service to the local region.
- Banks can ensure a consistent KYC service for all clients and have the ability to re-use client data and documentation for multiple purposes (e.g., KYC reviews, onboarding of new products (upsell/cross-sell), or to comply with new regulations). This greatly speeds up the time it takes to onboard new clients and provides greater controls over the banking groups' KYC compliance programs.
- The ability to roll-up all regulatory and client data into an aggregated form efficiently positions these clients to comply with new data aggregation regulations such as BCBS 239, and the like.

–   Depending on the risk classification of the client, banks are obliged to perform regular KYC client reviews to measure and monitor the level of risk the client poses to the institution throughout their lifecycle. Having a central team of KYC specialists takes this non-demand generative activity away from the onboarding teams, leaving them to concentrate on new or add-on business. The availability and re-usability of client and counterparty data and documentation to the central team also holds client experience benefits in terms of not being contacted multiple times by different trading desks requesting data and documentation that was already submitted.

The future of KYC certainly revolves around the idea of a shared industry utility. It makes perfect sense. Now we just need a find a way to make it a reality. Whether that involves using blockchain technology or finding a way to do it the traditional way, one message is clear—the industry wants and needs it.

Data Centralization, Integration and Digital Channels
There is one thing that banks do not suffer a lack of—data!
However, data and document management is a mess in most banks as a result of disconnected and disparate technologies and systems, which create silos of data stacks that can not be easily located or re-used. As a result, compliance and client outreach teams are forced to put in numerous requests to clients to submit data and documentation that they probably have already submitted to some parts of the bank already. This has a serious impact on client experience.
However, there are so many solutions available today to address this issue:

Centralize for Re-Use

By centralizing client and counterparty data and documentation using a master data system that spans functions, business lines, and jurisdictions (data privacy laws prevailing), banks can re-use up to 75% of existing information for new product onboarding or regulatory purposes. This significantly reduces the need to reach out to clients to provide the information, leaving only a small delta of outstanding documentation to collect.

When new data or documentation is collected, it is attached to the client record in the CLM system and used to feed the integrated master data solution to ensure that all divisions have access to the latest up-to-date source of information. This data and documentation is then processed and risk-scored accordingly to provide a current client risk rating and profile.

Integration and the Client Ecosystem

In addition to using multiple internal and external data repositories (e.g., CRM systems), most banks use multiple data providers to validate client and counterparty data for regulatory compliance purposes. However, in a manual or part-automated process, most of this data is delivered to the front door of the bank where it is manually collated, processed, and routed (as best as can be managed) throughout the bank.

According to Chartis Research, the biggest area of risk technology spending for Tier 1 banks is focused on risk, governance, and integration technologies, especially data integration.[6] In any transformation project, banks dedicate about 80% of total project lifecycle costs on getting data ready, with only 20% of the budget spent on analytics and reporting.[7] Banks are now increasingly seeking intelligent API (application programming interface) integration tools that will allow them to integrate their CLM system to a host of providers across the entity and AML data landscape. This list also includes external KYC utilities. This integration process streamlines and automates the data capture of client and counterparty data, providing a space for the data/compliance teams to compare the data with what is currently held and challenge the data if doubt exists on its veracity.

The creation of a client ecosystem program in banks is very much a digital transformation program that provides a bridge between legacy systems and new technologies that can unlock additional value from existing systems. Therefore, building the client ecosystem is about leveraging an optimal mix of technologies to tackle specific opportunities and challenges that banks face while protecting existing technology investment. By creating an efficient ecosystem, banks can boost efficiency and profit, and improve client service and experience. It also involves breaking down historic silos, whether that's technology, data, or organizational silos to deliver a more client-centric experience.

Figure 22.3 is a snapshot of a fully integrated, end-to-end industry CLM ecosystem.

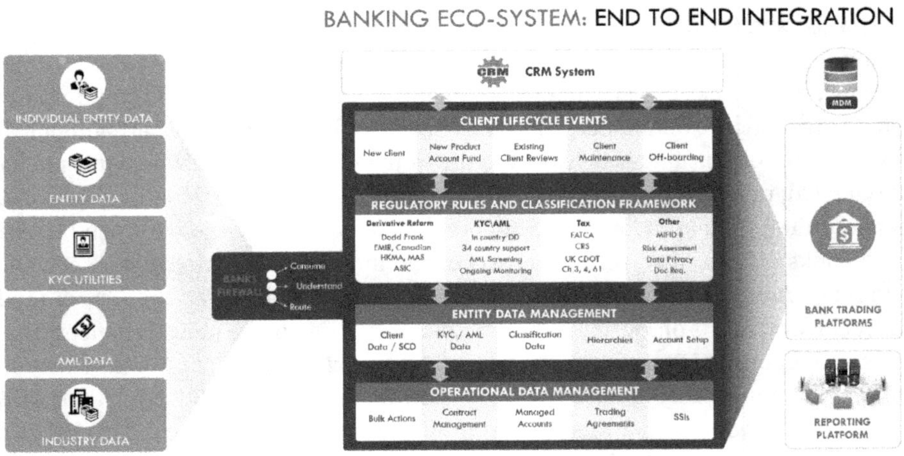

BANKING ECO-SYSTEM: **END TO END INTEGRATION**

Figure 22.3: Fully Integrated, end-to-end industry CLM ecosystem

The Cloud—Reaching an Inflection Point in Banking

In the past, traditional enterprise organizations that operate in heavily regulated industries and handle sensitive data have veered toward on-premise technologies in an effort to keep their data locked safely away in their own data centers and behind their own firewalls.

Even as late as a few years ago, any suggestion of putting this sensitive data in the cloud was generally not well received, mostly due to security concerns. This is especially true for the financial services industry, which has actively avoided entrusting data to the cloud, fearing the searing heat of regulatory scrutiny should that data become compromised in a breach.

The areas of Client Lifecycle Management (which includes client and legal entity data management, KYC, AML and regulatory compliance, and client onboarding) were particularly sensitive to cloud security, given the amount of client data and compliance rigor that needs to be protected.

However, in October 2016, something happened that would propel the use of cloud solutions for core banking services.

Rob Alexander, CIO of CapitalOne, the eighth largest commercial bank in the US, became the first bank CIO to loudly and proudly proclaim that his was a cloud-first bank, being a heavy user of AWS (Amazon Web Services). Having started deploying applications in the cloud in early 2015, Alexander said at the AWS RE-Invent Developer Show, "The ability to provision infrastructure on the fly is huge for our productivity and speed to market."[8]

CapitalOne is not alone.

Michael Araneta, associate VP, IDC Asia/Pacific, is quoted as saying, "With growing regulatory support for cloud and the intensifying competitive pressures forcing APAC banks to look at what cloud can offer in terms of cost take-out and quicker go-to-market, cloud adoption will increasingly scale up."

In an interview with McKinsey & Company last year, Don Duet, the former co-head of Goldman Sachs Group, Inc.'s technology division, claimed that 85% of the bank's distributed workloads run in the cloud.[9]

Singapore's DBS Bank uses AWS to create a hybrid cloud environment optimized for rapid changes of capacity and functionality to complement the banks' traditional use of data centers.[10]

Likewise, Commonwealth Bank of Australia used the cloud to reduce the time and cost of starting up a new server from eight weeks and several thousand dollars to eight minutes and 25 cents, making the bank much more responsive to changing customer demands.[11]

And it is not just the banks that are using the cloud.

Other players within the financial services industry are also getting in on the act.

The Financial Industry Regulatory Authority (FINRA), the brokerage industry watchdog, now runs 90% of its critical applications, including market surveillance, on Amazon's cloud, saving approximately $20 million annually. So are organizations such as Nasdaq and DTCC (the Depository Trust & Clearing Corporation) leveraging cloud technology to deliver benefits that on-premise solutions can't match.[12]

This goes to show that the use of cloud technology is far more prevalent in financial services than previously thought.

CLM in the Cloud Today

Today, the financial services industry is addressing many of its cloud concerns and correcting the myths that have grown exponentially around cloud infrastructure. Cloud innovation is fast becoming a fundamental driver in global digital disruption and is gaining more prominence and traction with banks.

The area of Client Lifecycle Management is ripe for cloud transformation, with many areas of Client Lifecycle Management potentially benefitting from the transformative fruits of cloud innovation. The cloud has the capability to help banks break away from legacy systems that confound their ability to meet future regulatory and data-specific obligations and demand high investment for the cost.

In the regulatory space, more and more banks are now rapidly embracing deploying their regulatory applications on the cloud to take advantage of scalability, lower capital costs, ease of operations, and resilience offered by cloud solutions. Due to the differing requirements on data residency from jurisdiction to jurisdiction, banks need to choose solutions that allow them to have exacting control over transient and permanent data flows. Solutions that are flexible enough to be deployed in a hybrid mode (i.e., on a public cloud infrastructure as well as private infrastructure) are key to providing banks the flexibility of leveraging existing investments, as well as the ability to meet these strict regulatory requirements.

The cloud also has the potential to open up a world of data for banks, enabling them to achieve the much coveted 360-degree view of their customers that will feed directly into their client risk profile. Of course, a lot of this is dependent on regulatory guidance and increased confidence in the environment.

Digital Channels for Client Self-Service

In the era of hybrid cloud solutions and higher client expectations, client self-service is now becoming normal practice with banks extending digital channels to their clients to submit and update client data and documentation that feeds directly into their risk profile, making the client outreach process more simplified, streamlined, and convenient.

While client self-service is fairly common in retail banking, this is becoming more and more prevalent in the world of corporate/institutional banking, commercial/business banking, and wealth management.

These digital channels move past the veneer of mobile apps or mere online banking. Instead they offer a secure solution designed to digitalize the collection of client data and documentation to support Know Your Customer (KYC) and client onboarding processes.

These solutions offer banks a powerful medium to connect and communicate with their business, commercial, and corporate customers to support customer requests and the end-to-end KYC process from regulatory outreach, periodic refreshes, and event-driven reviews. They allow banking customers to remain in control of their data in a Know Your Identity way (in a GDPR world, this is critical).

By extending digital channels to clients, banks can manage the following processes shown in Figure 22.4:

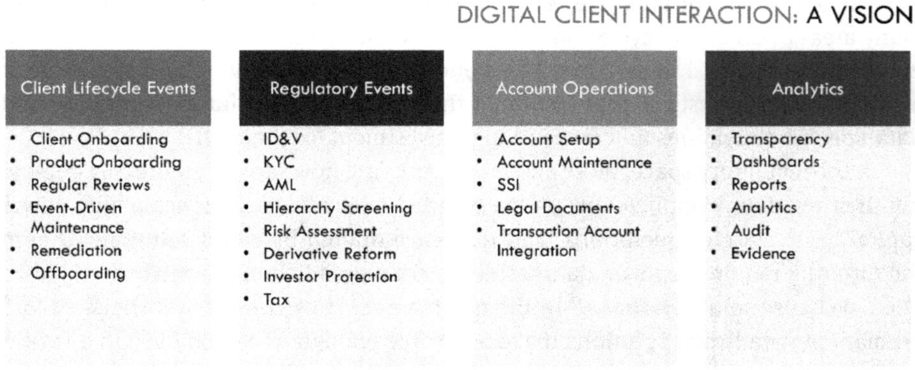

DIGITAL CLIENT INTERACTION: **A VISION**

Client Lifecycle Events	Regulatory Events	Account Operations	Analytics
• Client Onboarding	• ID&V	• Account Setup	• Transparency
• Product Onboarding	• KYC	• Account Maintenance	• Dashboards
• Regular Reviews	• AML	• SSI	• Reports
• Event-Driven Maintenance	• Hierarchy Screening	• Legal Documents	• Analytics
• Remediation	• Risk Assessment	• Transaction Account Integration	• Audit
• Offboarding	• Derivative Reform		• Evidence
	• Investor Protection		
	• Tax		

Figure 22.4: Extension of Digital channels to clients

Embracing Disruptive Technologies

We are reaching an inflection point where the possibilities for disruptive technologies are closer than ever. This is being driven by the following:
- The cloud has transformed computing power into a commodity (cheaper, faster, safer)
- The abundance of data available to banks enables intelligent learning
- Accessibility of machine learning algorithms and other technologies are making this a reality.

The pace of innovation and disruption is so fast these days that it's almost impossible to predict what Client Lifecycle Management will look like in five years. We can merely hypothesize. Four key challenges that banks have faced for decades are as relevant as ever. These include:
- Doing more with less
- Improving client experience
- Reducing risk
- Increasing operational efficiencies

The technology trends are clear: automation, artificial intelligence, robotics, and integration technologies will reshape the way we look at knowledge-based work. The technology that is empowering this new reality is related to: automating tasks, unlocking data, gathering insights for assistive decision-making to eventual full decision-making, and generally making it simpler to do business with a bank. All of this is geared toward delivering benefits to both banks and clients such as greater efficiencies, improved client experience, reduced risk, and decreased onboarding times.

And while the general prediction is that disruptive technologies will replace workers, the trend within the CLM space is less about replacing people and more about tapping into the expertise of bank employees to compliment the benefits that the newer technologies can bring. For example, in a maker-checker scenario, the bots become the makers and the human becomes the checker through the supervised learning of users' actions (via machine learning) instead of a static rules engine.

How AI and RPA Are Transforming CLM

Financial institutions all across the world are now actively exploring new technologies, such as artificial intelligence (AI) and robotic process automation (RPA) to further automate routine AML and KYC processes in an effort to increase efficiencies, improve return on investment and deliver a better client experience.

AI and RPA technologies have the potential to transform Client Lifecycle Management from an essential core competency to one that offers a distinct competitive advantage through:
- The ability to offer differentiated service levels to clients enabled by machine learning
- The automation of repetitive, non-value adding, and data-intensive tasks

All of this enables banking employees to claw back time spent on these repetitive tasks and refocusing them on higher-value, client-centric activities.

Intelligent Automation (via automated data pre-processing, decisioning, process augmentation, and automation through supervised learning) enables differentiated service levels and efficiency capabilities that can drive exponential service design and experience opportunities.

CUSTOMER DATA CAPTURE

Bots, DQ, & FDIM collect LE and organisation structure information, documents & conduct verification. Users can perform final review

AML SCREENING & CLASSIFICATION

Let the bots fetch the data when required. ML & Rules Engine will automatically assign categories to customer data (jurisdiction they belong to, customer type, connections to other customers)

WORKFORCE MANAGEMENT

Ability to capture statistics for workforce management and determine areas for desktop automation, process automation as well as build a ML knowledge base

AML RULES ENGINE & RISK RATING

ML & Rules Engine can make an initial risk assessment and make decisions around the AML alert types, PEPs, sanctions

REGULATIONS

Rules engine make a decision and apply reg with bots automating the data and docs (final review by users)

DOCUMENT PROCESSING

Bots and ML will scan documents and make best guess attempts to categorise them and index information. Users can do the final review.

Figure 22.5: A snapshot of how AI and RPA can improve CLM and KYC/AML compliance

Five Ways to Apply Disruptive Technology to AML/KYC

Computing power, data abundance, and accessibility to machine learning are driving the banking industry to a tipping point. AI has gone from science fiction to science fact. However, finding real-world examples in the CLM space is still difficult. There are many more real-life examples available when it comes to structured scenarios, for example, calculating ROI from repetitive tasks such as account closures, improved processing times, sharing structured data like ISDA information, or extracting data from legal documents, and the like. The harder problems, which require human knowledge, tend to involve proprietary Proofs of Concept (PoCs) or trials like AML checking and management of alerts.

However, in an KYC/AML context, AI has the ability to completely transform how banks perform compliance efficiently and effectively. AI is particularly valuable when performing repetitive tasks, saving valuable time, effort, and resources that can be refocused on higher client-value tasks. Here are five key ways that AI can help improve the KYC/AML and onboarding processes:

1. **Accurate Client Risk Profile and Enhanced Due Diligence**
   The real power of AI lies in its ability to intelligently extract risk-relevant facts from a huge volume of data, but then to also synthesize and deduplicate that information so that it is both meaningful *and* concise. This allows unstructured data from different sources and formats to be classified automatically for the KYC profile. Once data collection has been automated, it becomes much easier to generate better risk insights, leading to more accurate risk calculations. This means that AI can automate the creation and updating of the client risk profile and match this against the classification process (i.e., high, medium, or low risk) to ensure continued compliance throughout the client lifecycle. Furthermore, AI can make the process of identifying high-risk clients even easier for enhanced due diligence processes.

   The solution is flexible too. Models like AI and ML learn as external factors change (e.g., a jurisdiction becoming a high-risk country due to adverse news) and can override user actions. Machine learning can further identify candidates for automation by observing trends in user behavior. Once a client profile emerges, it becomes possible to predict or model future customer actions. By utilizing AI-powered solutions to delve deeper into customer relationships, financial institutions can prepare for a more regulated future.

2. **Ultimate Beneficial Ownership**
   AI's ability to "read" vast amounts of data (including unstructured text) and derive meaning from this can help in producing comprehensive, accurate and auditable risk profiles on companies and individuals in a matter of minutes. This can add huge advantages to compliance teams who are tasked with weaving through complex webs of data on shareholders, beneficial owners, directors, and

associates and will improve their ability to draw accurate conclusions for a risk-based approach to compliance.

This will gain even more significance over the coming years given the enhanced global focus on the identification and ability to perform customer due diligence on ultimate beneficial owners in the wake of the Panama Papers scandal and the establishment of national registers to improve transparency in this area.

3. **AML Screening and Investigation**

In today's world of increased regulatory scrutiny, financial institutions are under significant pressure to comply with a rising number of regulations, while striving to keep operational expenses and headcount to a minimum. However, the reality is that most financial institutions find it a constant struggle to balance costs versus compliance. In an un-automated world, the first response to ensuring compliance throughout the client lifecycle very often involves applying brute force to the problem (i.e., adding more headcount to screen, conduct reviews, and perform compliance checks). However, this just succeeds in further driving up the cost of compliance, with little or no leverage afforded to increase efficiencies dramatically.

The current state of KYC and AML requires manual investigation, especially at the alert investigation phase, which is costly, time-consuming, and prone to error. Today we take a blanket approach, where every alerted transaction requires human interaction. A recent Dow Jones-sponsored ACAMS (Association of Certified Anti-Money Laundering Specialists) survey reveals that the area of false positives is one of the most challenging for bank compliance teams.[13]

Underpinning the alert generation process with AI can result in fewer false positives, for example, by deploying linguistic techniques to undertake watch list management (e.g., OFAC (Office of Foreign Assets Control) lists) that can vary languages and scripts (spellings) and can listen to news feeds to identify people not currently on industry watchlists.

While they are a significant part of the AML compliance process, alerts are not enough to support an effective and thorough investigation process. What is required is the linking of high quality data to the alert (via interpretation and link analysis) to produce an accurate, graphical representation of the legal entity structure. AI can help leverage previously performed steps in the alert investigation process to formulate a recommended next steps approach.

4. **Improved Client Onboarding and Document Management Automation**

The banking industry would dearly love to move away from being so document-centric, however, this won't materialize for a while yet. Instead, we need to switch our thinking to how we can add and extract value from documentation. In today's banking world, much client documentation involves scanned documents, which means a best-guess approach needs to be deployed to categorize them appropriately.

Documents, in themselves, have a full lifecycle which includes incoming and outgoing documentation, as well as reviewing and refreshing documentation. There are many types of documents that are sent to clients and received from clients, and many different technologies that are useful to provide additional efficiencies around data capture, extraction, and processing of data held within documents.

When applied to workflow automation, AI has the ability to transform the generation of documents, reports, audit trails, and alerts/notifications. AI's natural language processing (NLP), which allows it to 'read' vast amounts of information in any language, can enhance the KYC process for new client onboarding applications through intelligent document scanning and its ability to sift through a vast array of external data sources. This can significantly improve the overall client onboarding experience.

Technologies, such as optical character recognition (OCR) and intelligent document recognition (IDR), can help to extract data from documents that can be transformed into useful, digitalized data that can be attached to the client record and used as part of the client intelligence process.

The main reason why banks need to produce and issue so much outgoing client documentation boils down to the lack of classification performed on existing documentation. By classifying documents, banks can eliminate the need to ask for the same document to be submitted again. To get around this process, banks are currently using document categorization technologies such as OCR, Tesseract, and machine learning (ML) to learn how to auto-classify documents. Furthermore, for evidentiary documentation (e.g. passports, utility bills, etc.), application programming interfaces (APIs) and pattern recognition technologies can be applied to verify the authenticity of the document and classify it.

Ultimately, banks will need to move away from paper/scan-based documentation and completely digitalize the data capture process. In ten years' time, we predict the end of documentation as we currently know it.

5. **Managing Regulatory Change and Compliance**

AI's ability to detect patterns in a vast amount of text (even unstructured text) enables it to form an understanding of the ever-changing regulatory environment. The panacea is auto-monitoring and interpretation. In other words, to automate the monitoring of regulations, transform them into a structured language, and create an ontology that allows the codification of rules with full traceability. In doing so, it has the ability to track changes in regulations around the world, identify gaps in customer information stored by the bank, and provide KYC alerts to perform a regulatory outreach to clients to collect the outstanding information.

Furthermore, NLP can analyze and classify documents and extract useful information such as client identities, products, and processes that can be impacted by regulatory change, thereby keeping the bank and the client up-to-date with regulatory changes.

Robotics Process Automation (RPA)

Robotics process automation (RPA) enables financial institutions to automate repetitive, non-value-adding, and data-intensive tasks. It is an ideal technology for a field like compliance that is predominantly rules-based and constantly evolving.

Implementing RPA can streamline KYC decision-making through more effective client data capture and regulatory client classification and evidencing. With the addition of bots, RPA automates the client data entry process and conducts initial verification, passing relevant client records to Client Services if data gaps prevail. In addition, RPA solutions can automatically consume information (data and documents) from multiple vendors and utilities. This improves overall data quality and speeds up the time it takes for account set-up and client/product onboarding.

RPA can be used to perform validation of existing customer information (structured/unstructured) by accessing databases, extracting data from documents, merging data from different places, and filling in forms. Much of the time, this information exists and is stored within several systems, such as CRM, or in repositories in other parts of the bank.

To unlock this data, banks are moving toward API-led integration, which connect formerly disparate repositories, systems, and technologies to create a straight-through process. However, a word of caution: The creation of APIs or any system-to-system integration can be slow to deliver, especially for legacy systems that are "API-less." Bots can reduce the friction of delivering API-led integration by taking a user-interface-to-user-interface (UI-to-UI) approach, providing the banking technology team with space and time to deliver longer-term API-based integration in the interim.

It goes without saying that if banks can unlock this client data and understand it better, then their interactions with their clients become more sophisticated and clever. For example, instead of a one-size-fits-all KYC questionnaire/checklist, banks can utilize a dynamic list based on advanced interpretation of KYC needs.

Blockchain—Hype or Hope for CLM?
Blockchain or Distributed Ledger Technology (DLT) is the current technology in vogue. And while there are many stories making headlines regarding banks' use of blockchain, it is still very much an immature, cutting-edge type of technology. In Fenergo, we say that blockchain is a technology solution that's still looking for a problem to solve.

Blockchain is based on three central tenets:
– It's distributed, i.e., no central owner
– It is dependent on consensus commitment
– It involves a list of immutable transactions of any type

There is no doubt that the decentralized aspects of blockchain can deliver efficiencies; but for it to work, there must exist a system of trust, as the technology puts trust back into transactions through mutual consensus.

The question is, does this level of trust exist in global financial services? After all, it was a distinct lack of honesty in the Lehman Brothers' balance sheet of assets that led to its bankruptcy, triggering the global financial crash. In other words, it was a lack of trust in the underlying transactions that led to the liquidity squeeze.

If trust is required for this to work, then the industry needs to create a new way of structuring economic organizations that will encourage trust between industry players.

At the moment, blockchain and its role in client lifecycle management is more hype than hope. However, with the current rate of innovation in the industry, this could drastically change in the next few years.

The three main areas that blockchain can help facilitate CLM revolve around:
- Clients sharing information with multiple financial institutions through a know your identity (KYI) approach
- Financial institutions sharing data with each other as a peer-to-peer network
- Creating an immutable audit trail to prove data changes in system records have not been tampered with

The know your identity (KYI) example (see below) is one of the most promising potential applications of blockchain technology.

Know Your Identity (KYI)
In the era of GDPR (General Data Protection Regulation), businesses and people want to own their own data. They want to know what data the bank currently has on them, who else has access to their data and they want the flexibility of sharing this data with other providers. In essence, they want full access and control over their own data.

Overall, a 2014 survey found that 91% of Americans "agree" or "strongly agree" that people have lost control over how personal information is collected and used by all kinds of entities. Some 80% of social media users said they were concerned about advertisers and businesses accessing the data they share on social media platforms, and 64% said the government should do more to regulate advertisers.

Another survey last year found that just 9% of social media users were "very confident" that social media companies would protect their data. About half of users were not at all or not too confident their data were in safe hands.

Moreover, people struggle to understand the nature and scope of the data collected about them. Just 9% believe they have "a lot of control" over the information that is collected about them, even as the vast majority (74%) say it is very important to them to be in control of who can get information about them.

Six-in-ten Americans (61%) have said they would like to do more to protect their privacy. Additionally, two-thirds have said current laws are not good enough in protecting people's privacy, and 64% support more regulation of advertisers.

The introduction of digital channels for client self-service is the first step in this process. Step two involves housing identities, data, and documentation in a secure way that is easily transferrable across different banking and corporate providers.

Blockchain has the potential to deliver KYI in a decentralized manner rather going through a centralized authority. We're already seeing the start of this journey with the introduction of the Payment Services Directive 2 (PSD 2) in the EU.

In the client-owned data model, the client supplies, maintains, and permissions data and documentation, while authorities are given access to validate the data and documentation. The information is made available to permissioned users on the blockchain network to banks.

This self-sovereign model involves the removal of the central authority (utility model), allowing corporate customers to create and manage their own identities (and relevant documentation) and to grant/revoke permission to multiple participants to access this data.

This is a very nascent application of blockchain technology, but one that can deliver great benefits to banks and clients alike.

Key Success Factors for Digitalizing Client Lifecycle Management

Before embarking on a new journey toward a fully digitalized Client Lifecycle Management process, there are a few lessons and caveats that need to be kept in mind. These include the following:

1. **Take a Back-to-Front Approach to Creating a Superior Client Experience**
   Digitalization requires a long-term, end-to-end strategy that sets new trends and weathers digital disruption. Most banks will see huge opportunities to digitalize the middle and back office, given the amount of investment neglect it has suffered in the last 30 years. They will also see more opportunities arising from the automation of the back and middle office that will have a direct and substantial positive impact on customer experience.

2. **Prioritize the Roadmap of Digitalization**
   While the end-to-end piece is important, it is even more essential to understand the starting point. After all, not all aspects of CLM should (or need to) be treated equally. Firms should focus on the areas or processes that can benefit most from digitalizing (or digitizing in terms of data and documentation). Aim to start small, implement, measure, tweak, and adopt further.

3. **Map the Right Processes to the Right Technologies**
   As mentioned previously, digitalization efforts will increasingly involve the integration of a growing number of technologies and vendors into the bank-client

ecosystem to create the optimized, efficient, and client-centric process that every bank wants to achieve. However, mapping the right combination of technologies to this ecosystem is no mean feat. In many financial organizations, there now exists a business case to create a new role that manages the end-to-end client ecosystem.

4. **Build with the Community for Industry Standard Processes**

Ten years ago, the banking industry was quite a closed industry, with little or no collaborative efforts between banking organizations. A lot has changed since then. These days, banks realize that there is a distinction to be made in terms of the operations and processes that are competitive compared to those that are not. This mentality encourages banks to learn from, collaborate with, and share more with peers in other banks to determine the best models and approaches required to achieve the vision of an efficient, digitalized, client-centric banking organization.

5. **Don't Ignore the Cultural Aspects of Transformation**

As the old saying goes, "Culture eats strategy for breakfast." Cultural change is a fundamental obstacle to any transformative project. After all, the key to digital transformation involves re-envisioning and driving change in how banks operate. It is very much a people challenge as much as a technology challenge. The digitalization of Client Lifecycle Management has the power to transform client and user experience. Therefore, it requires bringing together technologies, processes, content, and people to envision what might be and to unlock greater value. To bring people along this journey, change leaders really need to find a way to tell the story that describes the vision, repeating and adding new details and color on a continuous basis.

Conclusion

There is no doubt that the financial world is undergoing radical transformation, aided by the plethora of newer and more disruptive technologies. In fact, it's safe to say that financial services will be virtually unrecognizable ten years from now. However, some things remain the same. Banks will always have client, regulatory, operational, and data challenges that need to be solved.

While the technologies and approaches may change to help managed these challenges, one thing is clear: banks need to transform today to reap the benefits tomorrow. They will be given a menu of three options from which to choose: automate, integrate, or disrupt.

In a world of increasingly sophisticated digital customer experiences, banks are now no longer competing against other banks—they are competing against every service experience in the world. Therefore, the stakes are much higher than they have ever been. This will fuel rising demand from banks for new, disruptive, and pivotal technologies that will help deliver the Holy Grail of banking—happy, compliant, revenue-generating customers.

Endnotes

1 Le Claire, C. (2015). The Total Economic Impact™ of Fenergo's Regulatory Onboarding and Client Lifecycle Management Solutions. Forrester Research.

2 Ibid.

3 Groenfeldt, T. (2018). Financial Regulations Will Surpass 300 Million Pages by 2020 Says JWG. *Tech and Finance*. [online] Available at: https://techandfinance.com/2016/04/20/financial-regulations-will-surpass-300-million-pages-by-2020-says-jwg/

4 Consult Hyperion (2017). AMLD4/AMLD5 KYCC. Know Your Compliance Costs.

5 Three preconditions to pivoting wisely. (2018). [Blog] Available at: https://www.accenture.com/us-en/insights/consulting/wise-pivot-prepare-pivot [Accessed 4 Jul. 2018].

6 Chartis Research (2016). Global Risk IT Expenditure in Financial Services, 2017 Update.

7 Capgemini Consulting (2013). Backing up the Digital Front, Digitalizing the Banking Back Office.

8 Irrera, A. (2017). U.S. Financial Firms Embrace Cloud, "Fat Fingers" Notwithstanding. Reuters. [online] Available at: http://www.reuters.com/article/us-usa-finance-cloud-analysis/u-s-financial-firms-embrace-cloudfat-fingers-notwithstanding-idUSKBN16O0FO [Accessed 4 Jul. 2018].

9 Kaplan, J., Ishaan, S. (2016). Banking on the Cloud. McKinsey & Co.

10 Peyton, A. (2016). DBS Heads To Cloud With Amazon Web Services, Banking Technology. [online] Available at http://www.bankingtech.com/543352/dbs-heads-to-cloud-with-amazon-web-services/

11 Groenfeldt, T. (2014). Some Banks are Heading to the Cloud—More Are Planning To. *Forbes*. [online] Available at: https://www.forbes.com/sites/tomgroenfeldt/2014/06/26/some-banks-are-heading-to-the-cloudmore-are-planning-to/#2b2c21ee58c9

12 Irrera 2017, op. cit.

13 Dow Jones & ACAMS. (2016). Global Anti-Money Laundering Survey Results.

Niall Twomey is the Chief Technology Officer for Fenergo, with responsibility for technical strategy, design, and architecture. Niall has spent his entire career working with leading IT and consulting houses in financial services product development and in system integration roles with Barclays Capital, Fidelity Investments and Accenture. Niall is a regular speaker and has authored several papers on the topics of innovation and deployment of new technologies in financial services. Niall holds an honors MBA from UCD, Smurfit Business School of Business Dublin, and an honors degree in Business Information Systems from University College Cork.

Fenergo is the leading provider of Client Lifecycle Management software solutions for financial institutions and buy-side firms. Its solutions help banks to efficiently manage the end-to-end regulatory onboarding and entity data management processes. The intelligent rules-driven solution ensures compliance with multiple regulatory frameworks and supports the collection, centralization, and sharing of client and counterparty data and documentation across the institution. By expediting compliance and improving operational efficiencies, Fenergo's solutions can onboard clients faster, improve time to revenue, and enhance the overall client experience. Fenergo's recent accolades include:

Best Provider for KYC Software for Client Onboarding (RegTech Awards 2018), Chartis RiskTech100™ (fourth consecutive year, rising 25 places in 2017); Top Performer in RegTech Performance (Banking Technology/MarketFintech, 2017 and 2016); Best Compliance Product (Sell-Side Technology Awards 2016) and FinTech Forward Company to Watch (American Banker, 2015).

Chapter 23
InsurTech: Using China as an Example

Introduction

Technology is bringing about social and economic changes to society at a pace that is accelerating. The business of insurance and its value chain are also impacted as social, technological, and environmental factors force a rethink and transformation of insurance. InsurTech is the use of new or innovative technology in insurance—in the form of digital insurance, digitalization of propositions or processes, and technology-enabled new business models.

This chapter explores the trends and challenges of the insurance industry—how the technologies of digitalization, artificial intelligence, blockchain, mobile, and IoT are being used to innovate and transform insurance, and the current and future state of InsurTech. The examples are from China but as you will see, they could have been implemented anywhere.

What Is InsureTech?

Insurance is a transfer of risk in an event of loss, from the policy holder or the insured party, to the insurer. Insurers underwrite the coverage of risks through the prediction of losses on a group basis to determine the premiums for individuals within each group and, to do that, they require data. Insurance is essentially driven by data. It is about what the insurer understands of historical data, on a group and individual basis. That understanding determines the premium or the price required to protect the insured party and it has a huge effect on the insurer's bottom line and on customer satisfaction.

Insurance generally has not changed much over the years and it is still bogged down by fairly outdated practices. Historically, insurance products were designed as legal instruments that simply transferred risk from one party to another. Insurance businesses have focused more on complying with regulations rather than to satisfy their customers. Moreover, the way insurers underwrite a policy is fundamentally unchanged from decades ago and most policies are incomprehensible to the majority of customers. On the other hand, insurers are struggling to find ways to deliver tailored products at low cost.

Technology is seen as a key enabler to transform insurance, as it is in many other industries. An Accenture research paper in 2017 found that 93% of Chief Strategy Officers working in insurance companies agree that they will be reconstructed within five years; but only 20% feel highly prepared to deal with that. While insurers are slow to react to such opportunities and possibilities, startups and technology giants

DOI 10.1515/9781547400904- 023

are tapping into the greenfield of InsurTech by leveraging technology to develop new business models and to improve the customer experience.

Broadly, the term InsurTech refers to the use of new or innovative technology in insurance. InsurTech can be categorized into three segments as described in Table 23.1.

Table 23.1: InsurTech segments

Digital/Direct Insurance	Selling existing insurance products digitally or online
Technology innovation	Upgrading existing insurance products and processes through new technologies
Business model innovation	Creating new innovative products through technology enablers

Digital/Direct Insurance

Insurers are increasingly offering existing insurance products directly online, particularly those for property & casualty and personal accident. This is typically conducted through own-branded digital channels or with partner channels. For instance, travel insurance is typically sold at the point of purchasing an air ticket.

A number of comparison websites have also emerged providing means for consumers to research and compare offerings among insurers. However, these are more lead-generating channels for insurers instead of a completely online purchase of insurance.

Technology Innovation

With the advancement and consumerization of technology such as mobile phones, tablets, wearables, cloud computing, and internet of things, insurers are leveraging these technological enablers to improve the products and processes across the value chain. For instance, life insurance agents are now equipped with digital tools on their tablets and mobile phones to digitally assist them with customer sales and onboarding processes. In China, tapping into the popularity of WeChat and "micro-stores,"agents are enabled with their own "micro-store" to assist them with engagement on social media and giving them the ability to cross-sell.

However, not all the changes are at the front-line or at the customer interface; technology is also being leveraged to improve underwriting and claims management. Claim interfaces are increasingly online, and some insurers leverage technology to automatically process and settle claims.

Business Model Innovation

Technology is enabling the creation of new business models in insurance. Insurance is the socialization of risk, where an insurer underwrites the coverage of risks through the prediction of losses on a group basis and thus determining the premiums for individuals within each group. With technology, digital platforms or social networks could become pooling mechanisms for groups of people to self-insure.

Technology is also enabling the identification of risk of each single person, which in turn is enabling the ability to price policies individually. This differs from the approach of traditional insurance, which relies on aggregated historical data to price risk, and is potentially opening up new business model opportunities. In auto insurance, for example, there is already "pay as you drive" type of coverage where the individual and current driving behavior are analyzed to price the risk.

Trends and Challenges

There is a confluence of factors, primarily social, technological, and environmental, that is bringing about many challenges and opportunities to the insurance industry. There are six big macro trends that have a profound impact across the insurance value chain:

- Product development
- Product distribution
- Customer engagement
- Underwriting and loss prevention
- Claims management and fraud detection
- Operations

Changing Customer Landscapes

Emerging markets are contributing a significant proportion of global GDP growth, where the working age population outnumbers the dependent population. This is generating a growing middle class that is becoming aware of the need for wealth creation and risk protection, and this group is fueling increased consumption which leads to creation of many new businesses. This means that there will be increased demand for insurance in emerging markets for a demographic group that is new to insurance.

The growth of the internet, eCommerce, and shared-services economies is also creating new and improved protection requirements; for instance, coverage for deliveries, shared rides, and credit protection for peer-to-peer lending.

Changing Customer Expectations

The rise of the digital economy and the shift to mobile usage, or, in the case of emerging markets, skipped-generation adoption of mobile instead of desktop PCs, are creating a generation of consumers who expect simplicity, transparency, and speed in their interactions and transactions with businesses including insurers.

What this means is that:
- Increasingly, insurance will be bought and sold with online discovery fueling the selection and purchase of insurance products, instead of the traditional method of an agent selling the insurance to the consumer.
- Expectations revolve around simplicity, clarity, and transparency of insurance pricing and terms and conditions instead of pages of fine print and "hidden" clauses.
- Personalization of insurance with coverage and service tailored to the specific individual needs of the consumer.
- Customers expect of speed and mobility in terms of customer service and transactional capabilities.

The Impact of Emerging Technologies

In line with other industries, insurance is impacted by emerging technologies bringing about opportunities to improve efficiencies, increase revenues, and enhance the customer experience.

This means that:
- Customers have 24/7 access to the internet because of the proliferation of mobile phones and other computer devices coupled with cloud computing.
- There is massive generation of data and information through mobile phones and connected devices.
- Businesses have the potential to analyze big data with the advancement of computing power, artificial intelligence and data science.
- There will be disruption of business models, as technology enablers help transform propositions and processes.

Technology Enablers and Applications

Technology now not only has the potential to address the challenges and pain points in the insurance industry but to transform the value chain of insurance. Similar to many other industries, technology enablers are bringing changes and transformations at a much quicker pace than ever before. The key technologies include:
- Digital
- Artificial intelligence and big data
- Blockchain
- Mobile and internet-of-things (IoT)

While we look at the application of each technology enabler individually, the reality is that multiple technologies are used to enable a new proposition or service for insurance.

Digital

Direct/Mobile Purchasing Experience
With digital technology, insurers are now able to offer direct purchasing experiences for many insurance products. Approaches include:
- Own-branded websites or mobile applications
- Partner websites or mobile applications
- Embedded insurance offering as part of online purchase process, e.g., purchase protection insurance on an eCommerce website
- Online marketplaces
- Online comparison websites

The majority of these approaches offer a full direct purchasing experience, providing convenience and a better experience for customers in line with the shift to digitalization.

Direct Claim Interfaces
With other technology enablers, insurers increasingly are providing direct claim interfaces and improving on the claim settlement experience. Through use of third-party information and services, insurers can validate loss events automatically without the need for the customer to provide evidence through paper claims for further handling and investigation by the insurer. For example, with insurance for flight cancellations or delays—upon the online submission of the claim by the customer, the loss event could be validated against the flight information provided by aviation authorities on the internet.

On-Demand Insurance
With digital interfaces and platforms to meet the demands of the internet generation, on-demand insurance is being provided. It gives consumers the option to select insurance only for when they need protection instead of full coverage over a pre-agreed time period. For example, in property & casualty, consumers have the option to protect a specific item such as a drone. The customer could choose to protect their drone by providing their personal information and the model and serial number of the drone; thereafter, the customer will be given a real-time quote to complete the purchase. The protection of the drone could be turned on or off depending on the customer's requirements.

Artificial Intelligence and Big Data

The ubiquity of sensors and connected devices has meant that more and more data is generated and collected each day, data that is granular and increasingly real-time. Data on interactions between businesses and individuals, personal interactions, and social interactions are all being captured. Over 2.5M terabytes of data are created each day. This big data coupled with the progress of artificial intelligence has meant that it is now possible to understand the droves of data in real-time and to use it for decision making.

Artificial intelligence here refers to use of machine learning and should not be confused with rules-based programming or data science. The former relies on training of input and output data to determine what rules to apply, while the latter relies on specific rules that are written beforehand to determine the output based on the input.

The reader is encouraged to refer to the chapters on Artificial Intelligence and Machine learning but we will provide a brief recap here. There are three common ways a machine learns, or is trained to perform a specific task:
- Supervised learning
- Unsupervised learning
- Reinforcement learning

These are illustrated in Table 23.2.

Table 23.2: Common machine learning methods

Supervised learning	Machine learning algorithms are trained on labeled data that is prepared to help it understand the task at hand. For example, to identify cats in photos, a human expert first labels thousands of images of cats and its associated features. The algorithm is then trained on it. Supervised learning is the most common method for training machine learning algorithms.
Unsupervised learning	Machine learning algorithms are trained on unlabeled data where the algorithm identifies concepts, patterns, and common features to derive a conclusion on its own. For example, in learning to identifying cats, the algorithm will cluster common features based on the unlabeled data without first knowing what a cat looks like.
Reinforcement learning	Machine learning algorithms are trained on unlabeled data where the output and outcomes are assessed by human experts and that result is provided back to the algorithm to learn what is right or wrong. Over time, the machine learns through reinforcement and becomes very accurate in performing the specific task.

Typically, algorithms are created for one of these three areas:
- Cognition: the understanding of the input, e.g., voice recognition
- Prediction: the forecast of what will happen based on various inputs, e.g., disease forecasting
- Prescription: the recommendation or action required to achieve a specific outcome or objective, e.g., recommendation engines

Algorithms are also combined into systems to solve more complex tasks. For example, intelligent assistants like Amazon's Alexa contain speech/voice recognition, natural language processing, natural language generation, and recommendation algorithms.

Table 23.3: An intelligent assistant

	Speech recognition	To listen and understand the spoken language
	Voiceprint recognition	To identify the speaker's identity
Intelligent assistant	Natural language understanding	To understand the context and intent of the speech
	Relationship graphs	To link and find relationships between different pieces of information
	Recommendations	To analyze and determine the relevant response and action
	Natural language generation	To respond back to the speaker naturally

Automated Purchasing Experience

Artificial intelligence is being leveraged by insurers to aid the *discovery process*, which is the process of collecting information about consumers and specific situations, and to provide a seamless and automated buying experience.

Through geographic, social, and online behavioral data, machine learning is used to understand customer intentions and needs, derive relationships between distinct data points and to recommend relevant products. For example, the consumer's prior purchasing history on an eCommerce platform is used to understand when and which purchase would require shipping insurance. In the event of a similar purchase, the platform can trigger an automated recommendation of shipping insurance, thus simplifying the overall purchasing experience.

Behavioral Pricing

With the advancement of technology, the ubiquity of sensors, and internet of things (IoT) devices, there are tons of data that pricing engines can analyze to enable *behavioral pricing* for auto insurance where, for example, safer drivers pay less.

Through onboard devices that read the data from the vehicle's computer system to the accelerometer on a mobile phone, insurers are using machine learning algorithms for pattern recognition. Insurers can then understand driving behavior, such as speeding, braking, or cornering. Further algorithms can also be applied to predict aggressive driving behavior, helping insurers to price auto insurance accordingly. For example, at Swiss Re, a leading global reinsurer, their telematics team is taking this to the next level by developing algorithms that can detect specific dangerous maneuvers. In this case, machine learning is not only able to detect maneuver segments, such as cornering, lane changes, and maneuvering at obstacles or intersections, but it can also rate the maneuvers with respect to their risk qualities.

Better Underwriting

For underwriting, artificial intelligence can be leveraged to automate the entire process, scanning unstructured data to gather the required information and to identify patterns and trends. For example, Lemonade Insurance Company in the US uses big data and machine learning to underwrite personal insurance automatically and in minutes.

Another interesting use case is in property insurance, where providers like Cape Analytics and Orbital Insights combine machine learning with computer vision to analyze geospatial imagery to understand rooftop conditions, flood damage, crop yield, or vehicle inventory, and provide these data to insurers to improve the underwriting process by increasing quote speed and refining quote accuracy.

In life and health insurance, insurers are working with startups in the field of facial recognition and analysis to understand age and lifestyle behaviors such as smoking and other strong predictors of lifespan. This is possible through artificial intelligence algorithms for computer vision which detects your facial features, skin tone, and signs of aging.

Lapetus Solutions, using computer vision for facial analysis, partnered with Legal & General America to launch "Selfiequote." The tool enables consumers to get a life insurance quote by just taking a selfie—the artificial intelligence engine instantaneously estimates the age, gender, and body mass index (BMI).

Automated Claims Assessments

The claims management focus was initially on fraud detection but artificial intelligence is increasingly being leveraged to make it more efficient to assess, settle, and pay claims following a loss event.

In China, for example, auto insurer Ping An leverages computer vision algorithms to assess vehicle damage in an accident and settle a claim remotely. Photos of the damaged vehicle are taken through various angles and are uploaded through an app. First, the car model and registration numbers are identified through the images and verified against the customer database. The damage is then analyzed and a repairs report is generated, such as whether the fender needs replacing or paintwork on the door is required.

Artificial intelligence can also be used to further validate the loss event. The incident report can be cross-referenced with weather information, location data, time, social media posts, and video recordings from public monitoring cameras to assess the authenticity of the loss event. Suspicious cases are then escalated to human investigators to review the claim.

Intelligent Assistants and Advisors

Intelligent assistants and chatbots are increasingly being used by insurers to provide a better first-interaction experience and to improve efficiency. With speech recognition and natural language processing algorithms, intelligent assistants can handle more than 80% of standard enquiries, provide consistent and standard service quality, and have the ability to operate round the clock.

Robo advisory technology using artificial intelligence, prevalent in wealth and asset management, is now also being applied in insurance. This technology is used to understand a customer's life goals, life expectations, and total asset holdings, and then recommend relevant life annuity and protection insurance. In health insurance, insurers are also testing robo advisors to ask qualifying questions related to health, and then to understand the health quotient of the customer to propose an appropriate coverage. Oscar, for example, uses claims data to understand which doctor performs which procedure at what frequency, enabling them to discover narrow specialty areas and to refer patients to the right specialist.

Blockchain

Despite the advent of digital technology, many insurance policies are still transacted over the phone and other traditional means. Policies themselves are still paper contracts, or even if electronically contracted, the physical contract is still printed out for further processing—which means claims and payments are still human-intensive and prone to errors. The number of parties involved in the insurance value chain means more potential points of failure, where policies are misinterpreted and information miscommunicated, thereby adversely impacting the settlement times and the overall customer experience.

Blockchain technology, which is essentially a distributed ledger or book of records that is secured by cryptographic means, could potentially address the many pain points of insurance and transform the insurance value chain. However, for blockchain technology to be useful, it would require industry-wide participation or its use managed across national markets. The reader is encouraged to refer to the chapters on Blockchain and Distributed Ledger Technology for more detail.

Personal Data Management

Since blockchain technology is a ledger of tamper-proof transactional data that is distributed across multiple nodes, it is an ideal repository for personal data—one that could potentially be more secure than centralized data repositories. For example, with blockchain, networks can securely obtain and share individual behavior accessing a website or mobile app without compromising the private and confidential information that can only be shared with the individual's permission. The blockchain is able to do this with the use of private keys, where owners of the data can choose to authorize select networks to obtain the information.

By putting personal health data on a private blockchain, for example, the patient has full control over the records in terms of who can access or make changes. Patients could monitor edits from checkups and diagnoses made or even limit access to sensitive information such as mental health or sexually-transmitted disease tests.

Claims Management

Insurance is essentially a contract that states the premium that the consumer has to pay and the conditions in which the insurer is liable for damages. Upon a claim for damages or loss, the insurer needs to assess and verify that the conditions of each policy are met.

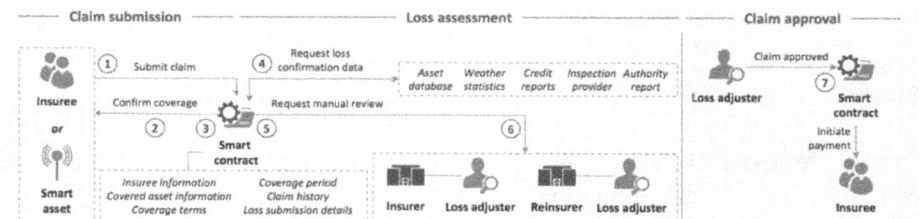

Credit: World Economic Forum

Figure 23.1: An insurance claim process on the blockchain.

Blockchain technology and the use of smart contracts could bring about efficiency and automation to the claims process (Figure 23.1). Smart contracts are digital contracts with code that is programmed into it to perform a specific action upon an event occurrence. A paper contract is enforceable by law while a smart contract is an agreement between two or more parties that is permanently recorded on the blockchain and is enforceable by the programming code. This allows for the insurance information to be recorded and encrypted as a contract on the blockchain. The benefits are three-fold: (1) it enables insurers to program the business rules, (2) to automate claims processing, and (3) provides a permanent audit trail.

In travel insurance, for example, insurers are already working with transportation authorities and airlines to introduce parameterized flight delay insurance that is recorded on the blockchain. Consumers can insure for a flight delay with flight details and delay compensation captured and recorded as a smart contract on the distributed ledger. This is then verified against the air traffic control database, and automated compensation is made when there is a flight delay or cancellation.

This is particularly beneficial to property & casualty (P&C) insurance, which can transform the way physical assets are managed, tracked, and insured—digitally. In auto insurance, for example, in the event of an accident involving multiple parties, insurers can access the policy information on the blockchain to speed up the claims and settlement process.

Fraud Management

The complexity of insurance processes, and the sharing of information among multiple parties across the value chain—typically in the form of paper—makes insurance susceptible to fraud. This comes in the form of multiple claims being made on a single loss event, policies being purchased for nonexistent assets, or claims being made for nonexistent events. Insurance fraud is a bane not just to insurers but also to consumers, as it results in increased premiums and poorer coverage.

Blockchain technology is seen as potential enabler to reduce and limit fraud in insurance by creating an audit trail. With the distributed ledger, policies issued can be recorded permanently on the blockchain, with information accessible according to the role of each party to the transaction. This ensures the security and confidentiality of the data. Similarly, claims made can be recorded on the distributed ledger giving insurers access and visibility to validate and track claims. Fraudulent claims can also be recorded on the distributed ledger, providing the industry access to identify and monitor suspicious behavior. This could reduce multiple claims being made on a single loss event.

Reinsurance

Reinsurance is the business of providing insurance to primary insurers to cover risks over a set period. It is mandated by regulation in some cases; but in others to cover specific large-scale loss events such as major catastrophes from natural disasters or man-made destruction. Such coverage is done on a case-by-case basis and is still primarily executed on a paper contract.

Reinsurance is currently a complicated and cumbersome process where each risk in a contract is written individually, at times taking up to two to three months to agree on the terms before signing. For very large risks, there will be multiple reinsurers involved requiring further exchange of information among multiple parties.

The exchange of information among multiple parties in the event of a claim can become more efficient on the distributed ledger by using blockchain technology. The need for reconciliation among different systems of each party involved in the contract can be reduced or eliminated, since the information relating to the coverage and claims will exist on each party's system.

Mobile & IoT

The prevalence of mobile phones and the increasing sophistication of the sensors on them mean an increasing amount of data is being captured in real-time about users. With just the standard accelerometer on the mobile phone, we can measure:

- Physical activity: walking, running, jumping, number of steps
- Driving behavior: speeding, braking, cornering
- Health condition: heartbeat, pulse, respiratory rate
- Daily routines: sleeping, eating, working (by inference)

Similarly, the rise of connected devices or internet of things (IoT) enables an ever-increasing amount of data to be captured on individuals and the environment. By 2020, experts at Cisco predict that there will be 50 billion connected devices around us generating over 300,000TB of data each day. Already, smart refrigerators can tell us what food and how much is being consumed, ambient light sensors can tell how much time is spent awake, and wireless sensors can detect presence and activity in a room.

All of this data and wealth of information offer insurers opportunities to underwrite differently and to provide new and personalized insurance for consumers.

Real-time Monitoring

Technology companies and insurers have been researching and developing means to monitor and track your health condition in real time. With data sensors on the mobile phone, fitness trackers and other wearables, coupled with machine learning algorithms for perception and prediction, real-time health monitoring that is non-intrusive has become possible.

The heart rate sensor on the Apple Watch, for example, is proven to be more than adequate to measure heart rate compared to dedicated heart rate monitors. It can even detect irregular heart rhythms which are early indicators of serious heart complications, including strokes. With the accelerometer and AI algorithms, there are applications that also measure the heart rate and respiratory rate by just holding the mobile phone on the palm next to the chest.

Usage-based Insurance

As shared in the previous section, behavioral pricing is already gaining traction for auto insurance. An extension of that is *usage-based insurance* (UBI), which is also known as "pay as you drive" insurance, where the auto insurance premium is based on the type of vehicle used, measured against time, distance, behavior, and place. For example, a driver who drives long distance at high speed with late braking will be charged a higher rate than a driver who drives shorter distances at slower speed.

The pricing mechanism for UBI differs from traditional auto insurance. The latter relies on aggregated data and statistics based on past trends and events, while the former relies on individual and current driving behavior, allowing for the premium pricing to be individualized. In markets where this is applied, it has proven to improve affordability for low-risk drivers and promote safe driving behavior.

Market Landscape

The digital transformation of insurance varies country to country, with both incumbents and disruptors operating at various stages of maturity. Incumbents are increasingly digitalizing their propositions and processes as they seek to adapt to the trends of markets they operate in. Many InsurTech startups have also emerged to enable customers to buy insurance digitally and provide insurers with technology to enhance their processes across the insurance value chain. Venture Scanner data (Figure 23.2) highlights 1503 InsurTech startups obtaining $22bn USD in funding. Big tech companies are also looking to technology that can transform high margin/low efficiency businesses. For example, Amazon recently led an investment round in Acko, a digital insurance startup in India.

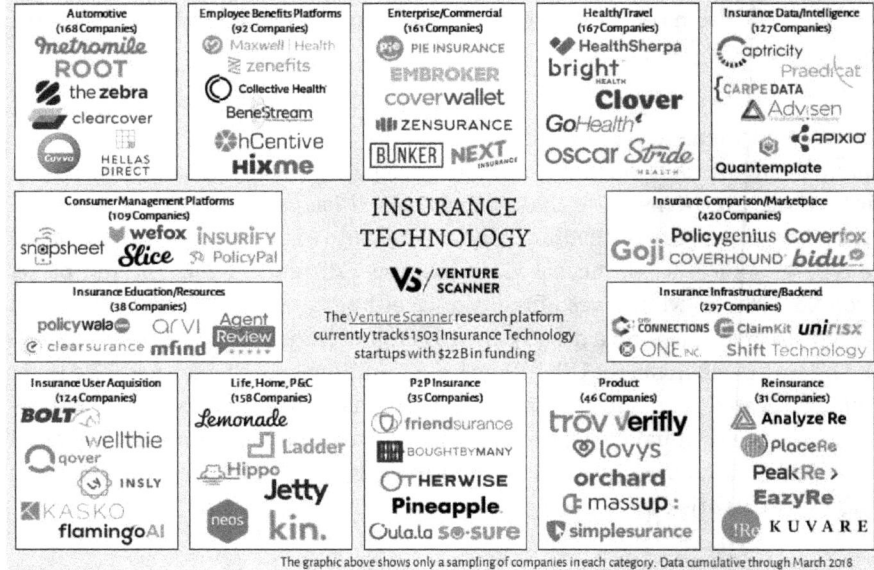

Credit: Venture Scanner
All logos exemplify the brand of the corresponding companies.
Figure 23.2: Some of the InsurTech startups

InsurTech Trends

Key trends observed in InsurTech are:

- Online marketplaces and comparison sites continue to be sources of digital-led acquisition for insurers
- Digital enablement of pooled or grouped insurance, where customers are grouped together and claims made against a common pool of premiums
- Provision of micro-insurance policies that have low premium value and higher transactional frequency; for example, insurance for eCommerce shipping
- Provision of pay-as-you-go insurance where premiums are paid on a usage basis; for example, auto insurance
- Focus on business-to-business-to-consumer (B2B2C) models where technology is used to enable the cross-selling of insurance products on B2C platforms; for example, eCommerce sites
- Increased investments by incumbents in early stage InsurTech companies through corporate venture funds, partner VCs, and accelerators

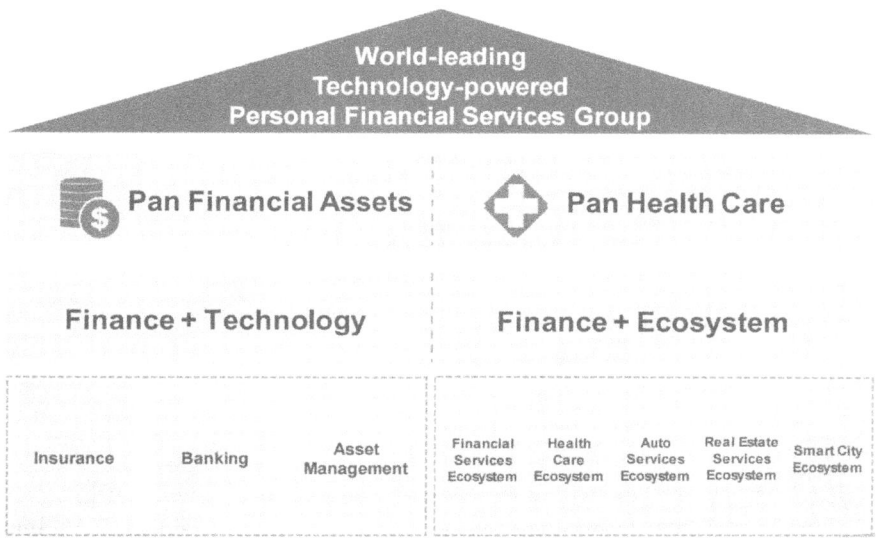

Case Study: Ping An Delivering Nontraditional Customer Service

Figure 23.3: Case study: Ping An

Ping An is a diversified ownership, integrated financial services provider in China and is one of the largest insurers globally by market capitalization and revenue. Cognizant of the digital shift that was happening in China, it embarked on a strategy that focused on the key life decisions of consumers, and built ecosystems around the verticals of finance, health, auto, property, and smart cities. Leveraging technology, the ecosystems offered access to services that serve the primary needs of consumers for each vertical, e.g., telemedicine for consumers who require medical advice, auto information portal for car owners. Figure 23.4 is a schematic showing how and ecosystem can utilize third parties to provide services to the customer for the benefit of all. The strategy required a shift in mindset for an incumbent financial institution—which typically focuses on acquiring customers for a specific financial product and then cross-selling other financial products over the customer lifetime—to one that is focused on acquiring users with primary needs and then converting them into a customer with financial needs over the user lifetime. The number of users across the ecosystems now exceed 436 million, and of that, over 166 million customers have purchased a financial or insurance product.

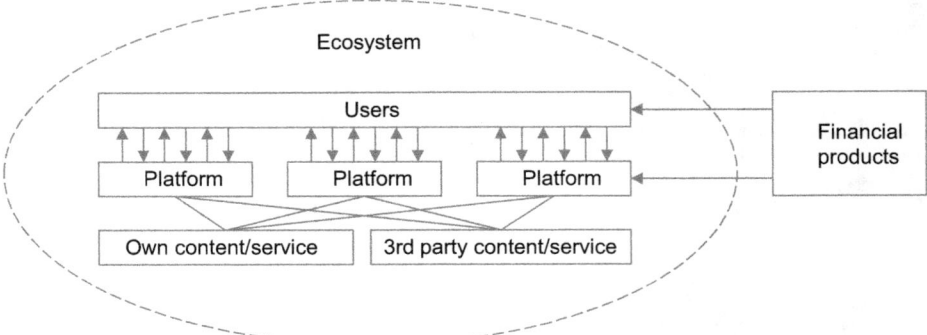

Figure 23.4: An ecosystem approach leveraging platforms aggregating content and services for end users

Technology is a key enabler—with a focus on applying artificial intelligence, blockchain, cloud, and digital technologies in use cases across the business, including insurance, to improve service offerings, customer experience, and productivity. In auto insurance, artificial intelligence is already being applied to improve the claims management process. In addition to the use of computer vision to determine vehicle damage from an accident and the repairs required, machine learning is also used for on-site accident assessment where geography, accident probability, and traffic data are analyzed to determine the ideal location of the physical assessors. This is based on the objective of the assessors' ability to reach an accident site within 10 minutes of the accident report.

With 436 million users and 166 million customers, engagements are critical with close to a million calls received each day. Here, artificial intelligence through voiceprint recognition, natural language processing, and emotion detection, is leveraged to intelligently understand customer inquiries without the need for Interactive Voice Response (IVR) type responses, and to assist agents to respond effectively and efficiently.

While the insurance business model at Ping An is still traditional, it has proven that technology can transform individual processes across the value chain and create a better experience for its customers while maintaining profitability.

Case Study: Lemonade

Lemonade Insurance Company is based in United States and it offers renters and homeowners' insurance for consumers. It is positioned as a technology company that is doing insurance, and not the other way around. Its business model is unique and is gaining traction particularly with younger, digital-savvy consumers who have different expectations on insurance.

Lemonade pools customers into groups (Figure 23.5), where premiums are paid into a joint pot. The company takes a fixed management fee, and claims are paid from that pot. The remaining balance is given to a charity chosen by the customer. The transparency, common charitable cause, and alignment of interests between the company and customers are all traits that the digital generation expects from businesses.

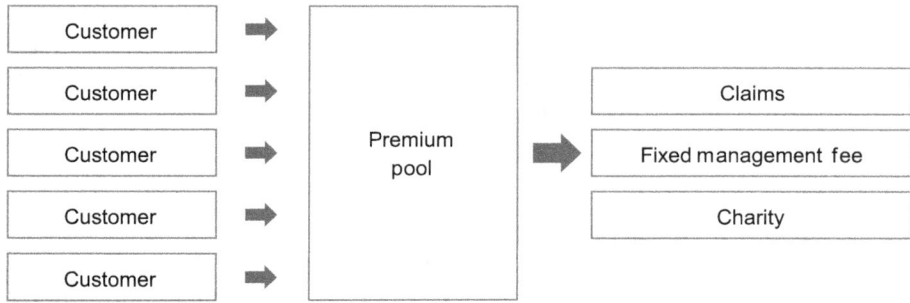

Figure 23.5: Lemonade's insurance pool model

The transparency is aided by technology so that the entire process from buying an insurance policy to making a claim can be completed via the app and it takes as little as 90 seconds to get insured and just three minutes to get paid, making the whole experience very simple and convenient. Claims are in-app with no paperwork required and are processed with no human intervention. Artificial intelligence is a key enabler, with a claims bot processing the claim, using a series of algorithms to review and check the claim before making the payment.

Future of InsurTech

InsurTech will continue to evolve as new demands for risk protection are created and new technologies emerge with mainstream adoption; and, with that, new business model innovations.

New Risks

An increasingly digital world also reveals a whole set of risks and potential catastrophic loss events in the cyber domain. Breaches in personal data and hacking of cryptocurrency exchanges in the past few years highlight the need for individual consumer protection from exposure of personal data, digital identity fraud, and financial losses from cybercrime. Digital businesses also face the risk associated with breaches and service failures. The challenge for insurers and underwriters is how to price such risks, and how likely it may be to require alternative approaches and the data to do that effectively.

Risks will also evolve; for example, in auto insurance, with the ride-sharing economy becoming the mainstream in many markets and autonomous driving likely to gain traction in the next 5-10 years. Accidents could be reduced significantly while car ownership will shift from individually-owned to fleet-owned. This will impact the auto insurance business and require different types of coverage. New risks will also emerge as digitally-connected vehicles could become susceptible to hacking or misuse. Already, researchers in Berkeley are highlighting means where computer vision systems could be tricked into interpreting road signs wrongly and thereby causing road disturbances and accidents.

New Technology

While we are already seeing the impact of emerging technologies like artificial intelligence and blockchain in insurance; it is still in the early days. The application of such technology will continue to transform the value chain of insurance, with deeper and richer use cases. The intersection of artificial intelligence and blockchain will likely give rise to more innovative approaches to insurance, as the benefits of machine learning, distributed data, and data privacy are melded together. For instance, one could imagine an insurance proposition where the machine leveraging artificial intelligence assesses your risk in real-time and adapts the coverage that is stored and updated on the blockchain as a smart contract. Upon a loss event, which is detected autonomously without input from the customer, the loss is validated against the smart contract and the claim is settled automatically.

Mixed reality technology, combining augmented reality and virtual reality, will also bring innovative interactions and experiences to insurance. It could mean better approaches to interact with the physical world remotely, potentially transforming customer engagement and claims management of insurance. For instance, one could imagine the ability to see through your eyes in real-time the assessed value of physical assets and, from a loss perspective, the assessed damage.

Quantum computing offers the potential to crunch and process huge datasets and models, that would have previously taken months or years, in days and weeks. Quantum computing, when mainstream, could boost computing power tremendously for artificial intelligence or potentially break many current encryption standards. The latter would mean more insurance demand, while the former means that insurers could have the ability to process massive amounts of information to calculate risks of any nature in real-time; for instance, the instantaneous modeling of the impact of a typhoon approaching China.

Technology will continue to evolve and advance, and will bring both opportunities and threats to insurance in general. It is critical that decision-makers and participants in the insurance industry continue to keep abreast of trends in InsurTech and technology, in order to understand where and when disruptions might occur, and the impact to business lines.

Jon-Tzen Ng *is the Chief Strategy & Innovation Officer at Ping An Technology where he focuses on corporate strategy, technology business incubation, and open innovation. He is also responsible for the strategy consulting practice and the Experience Design Centre, and supports the group's technology innovation and R&D agenda. Previously, Jon was Executive Director and Head of Digital & Innovation at Standard Chartered Bank where he led fintech strategic development and engagement with the ecosystem of startups and partners. He was instrumental to the setup and launch of the first home-grown fintech accelerator in Hong Kong, and was a founding member of the Advisory Board for the SuperCharger Fintech accelerator program. He is also a mentor at the Ping An Fintech Accelerator and PwC AI Accelerator.*

Part 4: **The Impact of Fintech**

Chapter 24
Technology and the Dislocation of the Fast Moving Consumer Goods Industry

There are significant forces of dislocation underway in the fast-moving consumer goods (FMCG) industry which will change the face of this industry forever. The word "dislocation" is used purposefully here since it is more accurate than another oft-quoted word "disruption" and is best explained by Craig Mundies (Former Chief of Strategy and Research at Microsoft): "Disruption is when someone does something clever that makes you and your company look obsolete. Dislocation is when the whole environment is being altered so quickly that everyone starts to feel they can't keep it up."[1] Not everyone working in the industry will survive this dislocation since the skill-sets and mindsets needed to operate in the new FMCG industry will be radically different. To understand this better, let us examine how the FMCG industry has evolved over the past 75 years. From a supply side, everything moved towards scale and this became a source of competitive advantage for consumer goods companies.

-   The growth of television in the 1950s gave marketers the ability to communicate their product features at scale. The move from black and white to color TVs, from national broadcasting to cable TV, and the growth of print and outdoor served to make this an even richer landscape.
-   The growth of big-box retailers in the 1960s and 1970s like Carrefour, Tesco, and Walmart gave FMCG companies unparalleled access to millions of consumers in fewer locations. There was now more shelf-space to bring in new products and to educate consumers on their benefits.
-   The expansion of companies into the developing and emerging markets post-World War II gave rise to global brands (think the golden arches of McDonalds in every country in the world).

These forces also had an effect on the demand side. As incomes grew and as more women entered the workforce, a new wave of consumerism swept the world and expanded the consumption of FMCG products in both developed and developing countries. Global brands were considered aspirational versus local brands and home-made solutions and were reflective of modern lifestyles. Hence, consumers were willing to pay premium prices (examples being Starbucks, Dove, Pantene, Colgate, and Maggi). The expanded shelf-space meant more consumer choices across categories (imagine the enormous range that exists today on the yoghurt shelf, the cheese shelf, or the dressings shelf in a typical Walmart or TESCO).

During this time (and until the start of the 21st century), the focus was for marketers to bring more effectiveness and efficiency to this scale; "360-degree communication" was a buzzword and the focus was on finding innovative ways to reach the consumer beyond TV given that it was becoming an expensive medium with high clutter.

DOI 10.1515/9781547400904-024

For young Brand Managers, it remained a dream to imagine a world where it would be possible to target consumers individually and send them messages that made sense to their unique, individual context. As John Wanamaker, the US department store magnate said: "Half the money I spend on advertising is wasted; the trouble is I don't know which half!!"

Around mid-2005, forces of disruption started to emerge (remember the definition from above) on the fringes of the industry. These started small and gradually snowballed into bigger forces of change around 2010 and 2011. From a demand side, the key drivers of change were the entry of millennials into the consuming class. As children born in the 1980s became consumers, their choices were driven by a different set of values than their parents. Nowhere was this witnessed more than in China where there was active rejection by the millennial generation of the brands from their parent's generation. Essentially, these consumers:

- Rejected mass brands and sought brands that connected with their aspirations
- Preferred to shop in non-mass channels
- Were influenced by referrals and feedback not generated by the brands themselves
- Were willing to pay more to make healthier choices (especially felt in the food industry)
- Were willing to pay more to make a sustainable choice (lower environmental impact of products)

According to Boston Consulting Group (BCG), half of US Millennials aged 18 to 24 and 38% of those aged 25 to 34 agreed that brands "say something about who I am, my values, and where I fit in."[2] While we are all familiar with the big brands that have become the favorites of millennials in tech, media, and entertainment (like Apple, Tesla, and Nike), who had ever heard, at the start of the new millennium, of brands like Pukka in Tea, Synder's Lance in snacks, The Honest Company in personal care, Schmidt's Naturals in deodorants, Seventh Generation in detergents, or The Ordinary & Glossier in skincare/cosmetics. Yet, these brands have, within a very short period of time, achieved such stature that they could challenge the big incumbent global brands in their respective categories and become sought after by the same global multi-national corporations that they disrupted.

From a supply side, there were new technologies with the potential to dramatically alter the landscape previously dominant in the FMCG industry. These technologies typically started in sectors like travel, entertainment, and media and soon found use-cases in the FMCG industry.

- **The Ability to Reach Consumers Individually Based on Different Needs or Contexts**
  The exponential growth of smart phones coupled with the explosion of social networks like Facebook, Twitter, Snapchat, and Instagram meant that it was now

possible to connect with consumers in a more meaningful manner. The holy grail of FMCG mass marketing had finally been broken, i.e., it was now possible for marketers to reach smaller/more distinct consumer segments more efficiently (i.e., without having to incur significant costs by using mass channels like TV). This can be termed as the move from Mass Marketing to Mass Customization and some companies have hugely benefited from this change.

Life-stage: Historically, there have been limits to the reach of targeted marketing. Johnson & Johnson built a multi-billion-dollar business targeted at babies and new mothers since it was possible to reach them via the hospitals where the babies were born. But the vast majority of other mass FMCG brands had to contend with more broadly defined audiences and hence less precision in their marketing. Even though we know that a 15-year-old, 18-year-old, 24-year-old and a 30-year-old have different preferences driven by their life stages, it was not possible for brands to target each with accuracy. That has now changed completely.

As examples: Gillette targeting students on their 18th birthday to sample their shaving products;[3] Rexona connecting with job-seekers to sell products that will make them smell fresh and be confident for that critical job interview;[4] Omo targeting first-time washing machine users for their premium liquid detergents.[5] These were made possible with the use of data-led communication through social media channels to target these groups more precisely.

Context: Technologies like geo-location targeting (the practice of delivering different content or advertisements to a website user based on a person's geographic location) has allowed FMCG marketers to be more precise in their marketing campaigns and to minimize the cost of marketing budgets. This gave rise to the concept of *Contextual Marketing*. Contextual marketing is a marketing strategy that delivers the right advertising message at the right moment to consumers.

As examples: Some brands of wipes use local market data to better target their ads in areas with higher incidence of flu; ice-cream and salad dressings brands can use weather forecasts to serve advertising linked to warm sunny days; super-markets and food service brands send advertisements, promotions, and new launches to consumers who are within a certain radius of their stores; hygiene brands use weather forecasts for rainfall and storms to advertise their sanitation and hygiene protection benefits.

Motivation: FMCG marketers always knew that there were consumers with different preferences in the broader population. While some were experience-seeking, others were protective of maintaining the status quo; while some were looking to stand out in a group and seek attention, others were looking to conform and protect their group. Addressing these disparate preferences gave rise to different segmentation models (Heylen's map, Censydiam, and the like) but the cookie crumbled when marketers wanted to convert these conceptual models into operating plans to drive mental and physical adoption of their products and services by these different groups. Now, with the rise of new technologies, this becomes easily possible.

As examples: Ben and Jerry in the US addressed the growing preference for Vegan products with the launch of a range of non-dairy 100% vegan pints, backed by communication programs that were more specifically targeted to consumers with a preference for such products (hosting vegan ice cream parties across the US, saying "we want to show our non-dairy fans that we love them as much as they love us").[6]

– **The Ability to Create Network Effects**
  Spread by word-of-mouth: This used to be an esoteric and invisible factor at play in FMCG marketing while being much more visible in white goods and electronics goods marketing. It has always been known that there was a product adoption curve in play for innovations—typically a smaller cohort of people, approximately 10% of the total population, known as innovators and early adopters would be the first users of new products and they would then drive the product by word-of-mouth to the rest of the population. However, as a marketer, it was impossible then to identify these effects let alone drive it actively. This has now changed with the advent and scaling-up of social networks, giving rise to the phenomenon of *Influencer Marketing*. In influencer marketing, the advertising campaign reaches out to the targeted audience via a brand ambassador. The brand ambassador is an individual who has potential influence over the targeted consumers.

  As examples: M&Ms for the first time in its 75-year history decided to let the fans decide on its new candy flavor.[7] They appointed an Emmy award-winning actor (Tony Hale) as official Campaign Manager for the Flavor Vote and partnered with nine social influencers (called Campaign Managers) to help spread the message and rally support for the new flavors. A further 20+ influencers created visual content to encourage people to try each flavor and vote. M&M considered these people to be campaign staffers and it became a big success.

  Connect on a real-time basis with communities: Marketers always understood the power of connecting with cohorts of people who were united in their interests, needs, and passions (think Nespresso, Weight Watchers, or Harley Davidson) and created big businesses based on the power of communities of coffee-lovers, people looking to lose weight, people in love with the real motorcycle experience, for examples). But now with technologies like artificial intelligence, virtual reality and augmented reality, chat-bots, and virtual assistants, the experience was taken to a whole new level—always available 24/7 and yet customized to each individual's needs.

As examples: A beauty company ushered in a new era of beauty with an app that allowed consumers to try out make-up virtually. This mobile innovation provided a realistic representation of what the product choice would look like and then allowed consumers to be able to purchase it with just a few quick taps on their phones.[8]

- **The Ability to Transact Online**
  The massive global expansion of companies like Amazon and Alibaba; the rise of payment apps like Paytm in India, Alipay in China, and ApplePay; and the creation of mega logistics operations (Alibaba spearheaded the establishment of Cainiao Network, a logistics data platform company comprising China's top logistics firms; Amazon Fulfillment Services signed a deal with Air Transport Services Group, the world's largest owner and operator of converted Boeing 767 freighter aircraft) meant that consumers could shop from wherever they were without having to visit a physical store. Millions of consumers without access to the formal banking system and a credit card could also participate in the massive online e-Commerce opportunity. This meant a big change in FMCG industry dynamics since brands no longer needed to be dependent on expensive retailer contracts (Walmart, Tesco, and the like) but could easily bypass the retailer and connect directly with the consumer. This was typically a huge entry barrier in favor of large FMCG companies and the direct access to consumers meant that many brands could start small, bypass the entire retail chain and build a business with direct access to the consumer.

  As examples: Dollar Shave Club delivered a successful brand using an online direct-to-consumer business model which has now reached scale (16% unit share of the US razor cartridge market, making it the Number Two player in the market).[9]

  Social commerce is also an emerging space and Sephora is an example where a unique consumer experience is created via the "Fragrance IQ" quiz.[10] The quiz covers a brief series of questions to help determine the ideal perfumes/ colognes for the quiz taker. Products are then recommended based on the results of the quiz.

  Another example is from the foods brand Knorr which has an AI-based platform called "Chef Wendy"[11] that develops recipes for consumers based on ingredients that they readily have at home.

- **The Ability to Create Content at Scale and in Real-time**
  In the older era of FMCG marketing, a brand manager would create one television advertisement, three or four print advertisements, and a few outdoor billboards in a year. Now, in the new era, there has been an exponential increase (sometimes 100x or 1000x) in the amount of content needed to support a typical campaign.

  Consumer journeys are now more complex with the explosion of touchpoints. A typical consumer journey in the past would be linear, i.e., a consumer would see an advertisement for a product on TV or in a magazine, would probably talk about it with her friends and then check out the product in the store during the next shopping trip. Today, consumer journeys are more complex with significant interaction between the online and offline world (think Google search, Amazon search, blog reviews, Facebook ads, and so on) before, during and after the purchase and consumption of the product.

It is now possible to target consumers more precisely at different life stages and in different consumption contexts. This has resulted in a need for more relevant content (for example, a campaign for a large drinks brand would need content that was adapted for time of day, weather, age groups, and different activities).

To manage the complexity of the media landscape and to lower costs, we saw the rise of a phenomenon called programmatic advertising.[12] This typically refers to the use of software to purchase digital advertising as opposed to the traditional process that involved proposals, human negotiations, and manual insertion options. It is all about using machines to buy ads in real-time. And this meant that there was a need for creative content to be generated real-time which has now become possible with the use of artificial intelligence to generate programmatic creatives. Programmatic creative is an advertising approach that algorithmically changes, adapts and customizes the contents of the advertisement to the audience receiving it.

Therefore, it is now possible to deconstruct a digital banner advertisement with different options for the headline, the key visual, the product usage shot, the lead character in the ad, and the end-line to suit different audiences. Algorithms can then combine these different units to serve up a customized advertisement that best addresses the specific consumer to whom it is served. And all of this is being done real-time in seconds by machines as the ads are being bought!

To feed into this development, there has also been a growth of more efficient raw content generation options: user-generated content, crowd-sourced content, curated content, and in-house studios. This has impacted and disrupted the traditional advertising agency industry.

Celtra Creative Management Platform is an example of a cloud-based, self-service platform that can be used to manage the entire creative lifecycle of digital advertising.[13] A great use case is the recent award-winning campaign run for Juan Valdez coffee using this tool. The campaign used two interactive mobile ad units combined with weather-relevant creatives, allowing the ads to feature hot coffee drinks to consumers in rainy or cold weather conditions, and cold drinks to those enjoying sunny and warm weather. Using Celtra's programmatic creative features, four separate options for messaging and images based on time of day and location were used. This included content that would be appealing for breakfast, lunch afternoon snack and a nighttime treat; all would show the respective ads at the corresponding times. Celtra's "Nearby" feature was also used to show the distance between the user and the nearest Juan Valdez Coffee location to increase foot traffic.

– **The Ability to Manufacture Smaller Volumes Efficiently and Innovate Fast**
Historical FMCG supply chains prioritized big volumes and massive plants to generate highly efficient manufacturing systems. However, it is now possible for smaller companies to gain access to world-class manufacturing facilities without having the scale of the big FMCG corporations via access to third party contract manufacturers who have advanced and digitized manufacturing systems. This removes another entry barrier and makes the economic viability of operations easier for smaller, better-targeted brands. At the same time, digital modelling technologies and technologies like 3D printing allow for much faster innovation cycle times since it is now possible to make changes in bottle shapes, adapt for-mulations to different factories with different machines, combine different ingre-dients/fragrances/flavors without having to do extensive and time-consuming repetitive trials for stability and quality.

The combined effect of all these forces has resulted in the first wave of dislocation of the FMCG industry after several decades of stability and predictability. The impact has been game-changing: scale is no longer the sole driver of competitive advantage in FMCG. Rather, the ability to intimately understand the consumer and create a user experience that is hyper-personalized is what determines success now.

Another signal reiterating the need for high quality brand experiences is seen in the dramatic rise of ad-blocker installation on devices (in the US alone, studies show that 30% of Americans connected to the internet will subscribe to some forms of ad-blocking service and this is growing faster every year).[14] These consumers are frustrated with irrelevant advertisements interrupting their online experience. It is unsurprising that we are witnessing the global decline of big brands and the growth of hundreds of smaller brands that are typically very local with a strong connection with local consumers and who are able to penetrate the popular culture and side-step all these barriers.

The next wave of dislocation is already underway and just like the previous round, the driving force is the arrival of the next generation into the consuming class: Gen Z (those born after the year 2000) have arrived to succeed the millennials and these consumers are most likely to have held a smart device in their hands before their first birthday. From a demand side, this will unleash some forces that will create even more disruption.

– A more dramatic move away from ownership to shared assets. We already see this with the rise of such services as Uber and Airbnb in some industries, but imagine this happening with more everyday items like clothing!

A great example is Gyynnie Bee, which is an online dress rental company based in the US. To quote from their own website: "Gyynnie Bee is a service that offers unlimited styles for women. Raid our closet as often as you want—anytime, anywhere—and never wear the same outfit twice! Shop better, wear smarter and rediscover the fun of fashion."[15] Such models will have dramatic implications for the big categories in FMCG since there will be a change in traditional consumptions patterns. Business models will need to adapt in order to service professional and institutional demand away from single user consumer demand.

– Even lower levels of trust with established institutions. This generation has seen the impact of the 2008 Recession on their families and homes, the impact of controversies and scandals related to established names like Facebook (Cambridge Analytica scandal), Volkswagen (diesel emission scandal), and Chipotle (quality issue). These consumers will pay a premium for brands that are 100% transparent about the ethics they display in their supply chains, the impact of these products on the environment, the internal equity in executive remuneration, and more.

– More demands on data privacy. This is a side-effect of lower trust but will also be enhanced with the changing regulatory framework. We already have GDPR in place in Europe (the General Data Protection Regulation, a law on data protection and privacy for all individuals within the European Union) but in fact, this has global implications for European head-quartered multi-nationals. Pre-consent from consumers will be needed to secure access to their data and this will happen only when brands provide a meaningful value exchange with the consumers for their data. Johnson & Johnson's Baby Center is a good example of a content platform that is rich and inspiring enough for consumers to want to share their data to have a meaningful relationship with a brand.

From a supply side point of view, we see the following technology developments that will feed into this chaos.

– *The advent of Industry 4.0:* Defined as the next phase in the digitalization of the manufacturing sector, this is driven by four underlying trends. (1) The huge increase in data volumes, computational power, and connectivity, especially new low-power wide-area networks; (2) the emergence of analytics and business-intelligence capabilities; (3) new forms of human-machine interaction such as touch interfaces and augmented-reality systems; and (4) improvements in transferring digital instructions to the physical world, such as advanced robotics and 3-D printing. However, the four trends are not the reason for the "4.0." Rather, this is the fourth major upheaval in modern manufacturing, following the lean revolution of the 1970s, the outsourcing phenomenon of the 1990s, and the automation trend that took off in the 2000s.

– *Blockchain, cryptocurrency* and *smart contracts*: This will allow consumers to engage directly with brands and other consumers without having to go through existing institutions like banks, credit card companies and media channels. In fact, in the near future, it will be possible to monetize "likes" and "shares" that consumers do on social media, thus giving them a shared financial stake in the success of brands they love. More power will go to the consumers!

- *Connected and smart homes*: The growing popularity of devices like Google Home and Amazon Alexa will have a deep impact on FMCG marketing. In the near future, marketers will have to learn how to market to devices rather than to humans. For example, smart washing machines will be able to automatically order detergent when it is used up without needing any human intervention. Smart refrigerators can automatically order food and grocery items when stocks are finished. This will require a whole new capability combining artificial intelligence (AI), internet of things (IoT), and new business models.
- *Growth of voice*: Consumers will engage more with their devices via voice and this will again dramatically have an impact on consumer marketing. Product names will need to be dramatically changed and simplified for easy voice ordering. At the same time, consumers are more likely to order products using the simplest category names and this will create a wave of commoditization for premium brands online. "Alexa, buy me batteries" is already a well-documented case where market leading brands like Duracell and Energizer are losing market share on Amazon to its own private label batteries as a result of more voice-led searches.

Finally, aspiring future FMCG marketers will need to have a different set of skills and competencies to thrive in this environment. While they will all be digital natives, they will still need to be:
- Knowledgeable about coding
- Able to design new business and revenue models
- Strong in managing Big Data
- Comfortable with constant change and being in perpetual Beta mode
- Able to collaborate with multiple external partners
- Driven by a strong sense of personal passion and purpose regarding their brand, allowing for impactful and meaningful dialogue with consumers.

It has never been a more exciting time to work in marketing in the FMCG industry!

Endnotes

1 Quote from Craig Mundie that was featured in Thomas Friedman's book, *Thank You for Being Late: An Optimist's Guide to Thriving in the Age of Accelerations* (First Edition), 2016, New York, Farrar, Straus and Giroux
2 "How Millenials are Changing the Face of Marketing Forever," January 2014, Christine Barton, Lara Koslow and Christine Beauchamp.
3 Gillette has been accidentally sending "Welcome to Manhood" packages to women, Dennis Green, July 17, 2017, Business Insider.
4 Egypt Innovate: Nafham and Digital Republic Partner with Unilever to Enhance Online Education Services.
5 www.campaignbrief.com: Lowe Vietnam teaches women how to use washing machines with The

Omo Matic Big Sale, Sept 2, 2015.
6 https://vegnews.com/2018/5/ben-andamp-jerrys-hosts-vegan-ice-cream-parties-across-us
7 Influencer Marketing Hub, 12 Influencer Marketing Examples that Prove Influencer Marketing is Digital Marketing's Next Big Thing, Now," #7.
8 www.Mccann.com/work/makeup-genius
9 Medium, Seven Reasons Why Unilever Bought Dollar Shave Club, April 16, 2017.
10 www.sephora.com/skincare-iq
11 Optima Blog, Chef wendy, April 12, 2016. www.optimagroupinc.com/chef-wendy
12 Digiday, WTF is programmatic advertising, February 20, 2014 by Jack Marshall.
13 www.celtra.com
14 www.statista.com/statistics/804008/ad-blocking-reach-usage-us
15 https://closet.gwynniebee.com/pages/about-us

References

www.muminthemadhouse.com
www.facebook.com/anthonybourdain
www.amodelrecommends.com
www.blog.feedspot.com/whiskey_blogs/ Top 60 Whiskey Blogs & Websites for Whiskey Drinkers
www.madamefromageblog.com
www.chocablog.com

Deepak Subramanian is currently Vice-President for Unilever's Homecare division in South-East Asia, Australia & New Zealand. In a career spanning 23 years with Unilever, he has worked across sales & marketing and more recently in board level general business management roles, bearing full P&L responsibility and revenue growth accountability. During this time, he has built significant strategic business and consumer insight by leading multi-million growth, turnaround and start-up business verticals, both in operational roles in local markets driving brilliant everyday execution and in regional/ global roles driving strategy and innovation. He has lived and worked in India, Asia and Europe and his international experience has helped him gain a strong perspective on how consumer goods companies and business executives must evolve to thrive in these volatile times.

The opinions expressed here are the personal views of Deepak Subramanian based on his career experience and this chapter is in no way commissioned by Unilever.

Chapter 25
Legal Implications of Fintech

From personal finance applications to cryptocurrencies to robo-advisors to peer-to-peer lending platforms, fintech and its yet undetermined consequences on the financial industry has generated a unanimous question for regulators across the world: what is it and how best to harness its opportunities while adequately managing its risks?

Our objective in this chapter is to focus, primarily, on the impact of fintech on the customer, exploring what we have termed the "Digital Customer Journey." To many on-the-ground industry participants, from business teams to legal and compliance officers, the world of fintech bears tantalizing opportunities but also significant challenges. By walking through each step of the Digital Customer Journey, from the conception of the product or service idea through to onboarding customers and beyond to the ongoing customer relationship, we will demonstrate that the challenges of fintech are not insurmountable and, in general, simply require a fresh application of existing knowledge and skills. Nevertheless, there exist certain areas of the fintech landscape (such as cryptocurrencies) which will require new thinking to produce innovative solutions.

The Challenge: How and Why to Regulate Fintech

The regulation of fintech is subject to a balancing act: How to promote and foster genuinely innovative solutions, while providing a sufficient level of protection for investors and the general public. Rolling out new digital services is about competitiveness and efficient delivery of services, but regulating such services is predominantly about ensuring consumer protection, the sound operation of manufacturers and distributors, and the reliability of the digital services industry and mitigation of new risks that arise from "digital."

The answer to this question and how to achieve the optimal balance will vary, depending on who you ask and in which jurisdiction. Some proponents of fintech solutions might, for example, try to convince you that fintech should be allowed to develop freely and remain unregulated. However, we think that the answer to the question of whether fintech should be regulated at all will be answered consistently by any financial regulator in a major jurisdiction (and that answer will be "yes!"). Nevertheless, divergence between regulators' approaches tend to quickly emerge when the details are explored.

Take for example the Monetary Authority of Singapore (the "MAS"). The MAS has a mantra in this area, first publicly espoused by Ravi Menon at the inaugural Singapore fintech Festival in November 2016 and oft-repeated since: *"regulation must not*

DOI 10.1515/9781547400904- 025

front-run innovation."[1] We will explore later in this chapter how the MAS approach compares to other jurisdictions around the world; but for now, it suffices to say that this quote exemplifies the MAS approach to fintech regulation. In Singapore, we have already seen some existing laws being applied to new financial services (e.g., securities laws being applied to initial coin offerings, where appropriate) while others are being developed to address specific fintech risks (e.g., the regulation of payments and digital advisory services; regulation of customer-facing robo-advisory services).

The Digital Customer Journey

Digital customer journey.

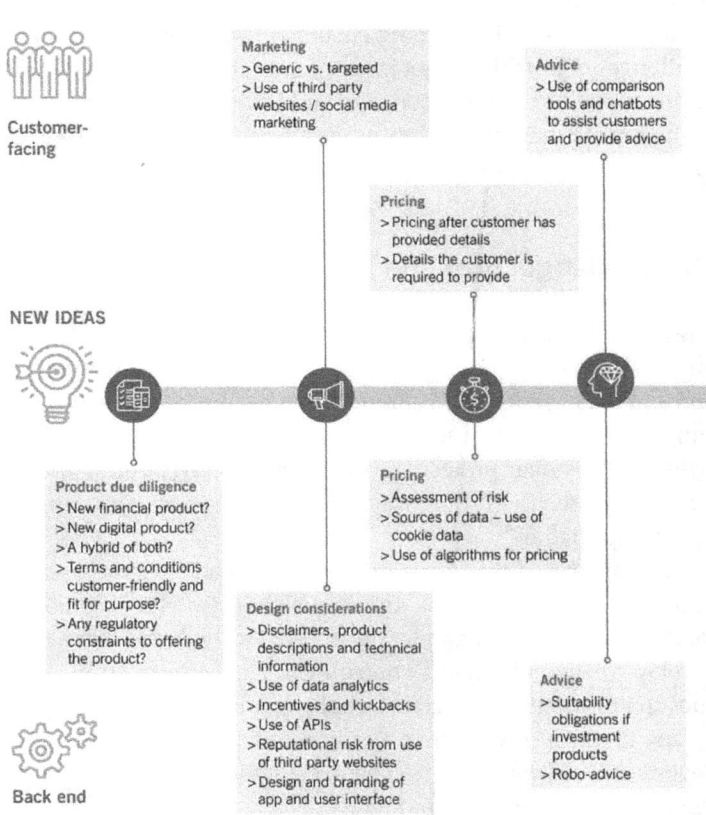

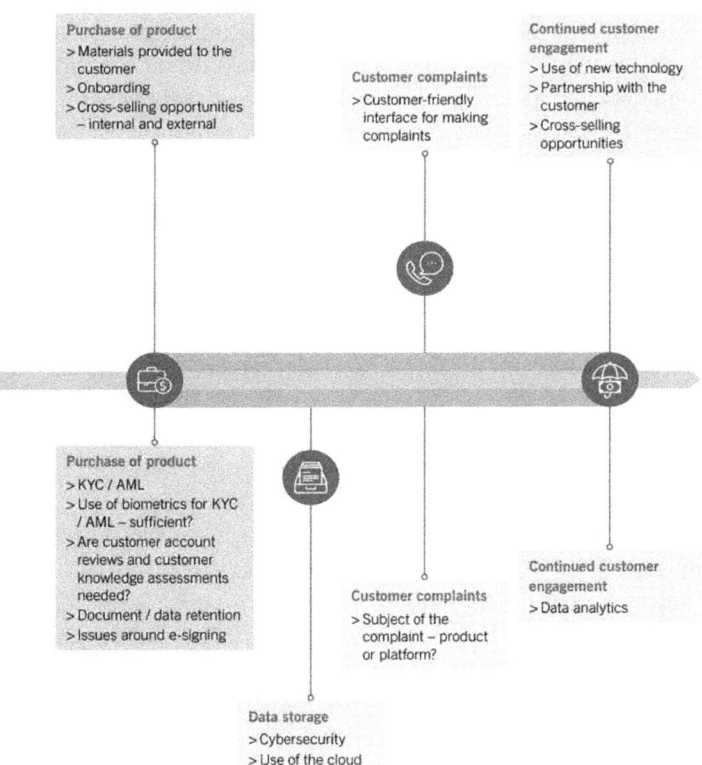

Purchase of product
> Materials provided to the customer
> Onboarding
> Cross-selling opportunities – internal and external

Customer complaints
> Customer-friendly interface for making complaints

Continued customer engagement
> Use of new technology
> Partnership with the customer
> Cross-selling opportunities

Purchase of product
> KYC / AML
> Use of biometrics for KYC / AML – sufficient?
> Are customer account reviews and customer knowledge assessments needed?
> Document / data retention
> Issues around e-signing

Customer complaints
> Subject of the complaint – product or platform?

Continued customer engagement
> Data analytics

Data storage
> Cybersecurity
> Use of the cloud

Due Diligence

The Digital Customer Journey begins before the customer knows about it—with due diligence of the new product or service. Much as with any new product/service launch, it is crucial to establish what the new product or service is. We break this down into three potential buckets:

- New financial products or services; for example, a completely new structured note or type of bank account
- Newly digitalized products or services; such as an existing structured note or bank account (or even an entire business) that will transition into an "online-only" offering
- Hybrids; that tweak the features of an existing structured note or bank account and change the distribution model to online-only

We focus on the considerations that must be considered when an existing product, service, or business line is digitalized, or has an element of digitalization introduced. Various other considerations would apply when launching a new financial product or service which apply equally in an analog world; we do not consider them here.

The key to this stage is establishing whether, as an institution, you are able to digitalize the product or service (and, if not, how digitalization can be enabled). For instance:

- Are the terms and conditions of the particular product or service adequate? It would not be unusual for terms and conditions to explicitly envisage an online offering, but other tangential issues should be considered; for example, as more customer data can be obtained through online channels, do the terms and conditions allow sufficient flexibility for dealing with customer data?
- Can a complex product or service be adequately explained through an online channel? This consideration becomes particularly acute when dealing with retail customers who may not be able to understand standalone materials with respect to a complex or new product or service without a human advisor.
- Does the institution have infrastructure in place to manage any new challenges or risks that may arise from digitalization? Digitalization can lead to a unique new set of challenges and risks; for example, the challenge of secure storage and transmission of customer information and the risk of an online platform being hacked. Institutions which have historically operated only in the analog world may at this stage come across regulatory requirements that appear entirely foreign to them. Another pertinent risk is the cross-border spread of a product or service. In the digital world, a platform may be accessible from anywhere. This may have unforeseen consequences (e.g., licensing risks) and an institution may need to implement geographical controls as a result.
- Is the regulator comfortable with the proposed digitalization? While a financial regulator would, typically, be more concerned with the launch of a wholly new

product, service, or business line, digitalization might still cause regulatory scrutiny and licensed institutions would need to consider whether it would be necessary or advisable to engage with regulators. Concerns of the regulator may run along similar lines to those explored above—is the consumer adequately protected against the potential lack of clarity around features of the product or service? Does the institution have the technical infrastructure in place to safely and securely operate the digitalized business? How fundamental is the digitalization to the business of the institution?

Crucially, none of the due diligence considerations above are significantly different from the due diligence that would need to be carried out on a new financial product or service in the analog world. Accordingly, the first step on the "digital customer journey" simply reapplies knowledge and skills from analog due diligence to assess some new, but ultimately familiar, risks.

Marketing and Design Considerations

Marketing through digital channels gives rise to a new and unique portfolio of risks and challenges that financial institutions are required to navigate. Ultimately, it is important that business teams engage with legal and compliance colleagues at the product design stage to ensure that any new product or service is designed with regulatory compliance in mind.

Information Availability and the Use of Disclaimers

Information on a website is available for 24/7 access and from anywhere on the globe, which means customers and potential customers may access the information anytime and from anywhere. In turn, this can give customers the perception that:

- The information being conveyed is accurate and complete at all times, giving rise to a liability risk in the event that a person (who may or may not be a customer of the financial institution) makes an investment or purchases a financial product or service on the basis of the information.
- The information is available for use in making specific investment decisions, giving rise to a risk that the financial institution is seen as giving financial advice to the whole world.
- The investment products or services being offered can be accessed from any location, which, among others, gives rise to regulatory and licensing risks for the institution in any country in the world from which people can access the website.

While these risks also exist in the analog world, they become more acute with a digital marketing platform where access is less easily controlled. Nevertheless, the risks can be mitigated using robust disclaimers and notices, much like the disclaimers that are typically used in analog documentation. Such disclaimers would seek to manage liability by making clear that:

- The information *may not* be accurate and complete at the time of consumption.
- The information should not be used for any investment decision without first obtaining independent financial advice.
- The investment products or services are limited to certain specific countries or locations (e.g., in federal jurisdictions such as the USA, institutions may want to specifically limit their offering to certain states where they have appropriate authorization).

Key new elements to consider with digital marketing are:

- Institutions need to make disclaimers sufficiently prominent. Examples of how to practically achieve this are commonly seen when surfing the internet: Pop-ups are often used which may or may not request an active acceptance or acknowledgement. Particularly with attempts to effect jurisdiction-specific restrictions, pop-ups may appear before a customer can access a website, and access may be denied to persons in certain jurisdictions.
- Whether a disclaimer, on its own, is sufficient to mitigate the regulatory risks. Since it is possible for consumers to click through disclaimers without necessarily taking in the content, should financial institutions be implementing other forms of control, such as geo-blocking technology, to outright prevent consumers in certain jurisdictions from accessing their products? What is considered acceptable and sufficient in practice will often depend on the regulator's view in the jurisdiction in question.

The need for disclaimers and the managing of legal and regulatory risk needs to be balanced with the requirement to have a user-friendly and appealing platform— whether desktop or mobile-app based.

Use of APIs

Digital marketing may also extend into the world of application programming interfaces (APIs). Engaging the services of a third party to advertise may trigger regulatory issues for the third party. Using someone else's API (e.g., an API embedded into a social media platform) may give rise to regulatory risk for the social media platform operator. Points to be considered here are very similar to those in the analog world, and include:

- Whether the third party is remunerated on a per-product-purchased basis or on a flat-fee basis

–   How specific the advertisement is (i.e., is it targeted at a specific person with a specific recommendation of an investment product or service, or is it a generic advertisement of the services offered by a financial institution?)

Chatbots and Comparison Tools

A commonly used digital marketing tool is the "chatbot" or its less-advanced cousin, the comparison tool. These tools allow customers to compare different available products or services and find out further (usually rudimentary) information about such products or services.

A key question in this space is: Does the use of a chatbot or a comparison tool amount to the provision of financial advice? This question is key because, if it is answered in the affirmative in Singapore, it will lead to a range of regulatory consequences such as licensing and obligations to ensure that the advice provided is suitable for the customer.

The precise parameters of a regulated financial advisory activity may differ between jurisdictions, but irrespective of jurisdiction, it will always be important to have sufficient control over the tool or the bot, and to be sufficiently comfortable in the capabilities and limitations of the tool or the bot (for example, by back-testing the tool or the bot to ensure that it does not give erroneous results). While the fundamental risk associated with a customer interacting with a bot is similar to the analog interaction with a human (i.e., that the bot, or the human advisor, makes an incorrect statement or recommendation), this is another risk that becomes more acute in the digital world. While a human advisor may have a bad day and, perhaps, make inadvertently inaccurate statements to one or two customers, a systemic and unchecked fault in a tool or a bot could lead to unintended consequences for hundreds, if not thousands, of customers.

The primary mitigation for these fundamental risks is control; however, financial institutions may find that while control over human advisors can be implemented through written policies and procedures (together with an element of training and monitoring), control over a tool or a bot will require the introduction of more technical (and technological) expertise.

IP Management

Any digital platform will undoubtedly have some intellectual property in it—whether it is the copyright in a new software platform, the design of the user experience on the platform, or a new brand or logo for the digital offering. Intellectual property can sometimes be one of the key ingredients that drives the value of a digital business and is therefore a critical intangible asset that must be managed properly.

Key considerations around intellectual property management will differ depending on who is developing that intellectual property. If that intellectual property is developed by an in-house development team, then the focus might be on how that content is developed and the "ingredients" that go into it to ensure that the organization is able to freely use (and perhaps exploit) that technology going forward. For example, this will involve ensuring that there are internal processes in place to mitigate against the risk of potential third-party infringement claims made against an organization's future use and exploitation of that intellectual property, and that no open source software which will have a "viral" effect on the platform (i.e., open source license terms that may put the entire platform into open source as well) is used to develop that platform.

If instead, the intellectual property is developed by an external developer, the conversation is slightly shifted. The risks raised above in the context of in-house development can be dealt with via contractual assurances from the developer (e.g., warranties and indemnities). Instead, the key issues to be concerned about here might be the platform development model adopted (e.g., "waterfall" or agile, objective-based approach), ensuring that the correct specifications for the platform are agreed upon and that the platform does what it is meant to do, and agreeing what after-sales support (e.g., maintenance, bug fixing, updates) will be provided by the developer. While all of this sounds like common sense, it can be problematic if specifications are not agreed to upfront!

Perhaps most importantly, however, is agreeing where *ownership* of that intellectual property lies. This can sometimes be a very emotional discussion between the developer and its customer because the platform may have elements that are proprietary to the developer and which it cannot be given away to any customer. There is no one-size-fits-all answer to this, but in certain cases, an expansively scoped intellectual property license may give the customer what is needed to achieve the commercial objectives for the platform.

Data Protection

Privacy has become a hot topic recently. With the Facebook/Cambridge Analytica scandal, the General Data Protection Regulation (GDPR) causing a massive shake up to data management globally, and several large-scale data breaches affecting millions of individuals globally, it is imperative that organizations scrutinize their privacy compliance requirements closely to ensure that they remain on the right side of the line.

Rolling out a brand new digital offering gives an organization a unique opportunity to take a "privacy-by-design" approach—meaning, designing the platform with privacy compliance requirements in mind—to the development of its new platform. The obvious concerns would be to ensure that the platform has comprehensive terms of use and privacy terms to ensure that the organization has complied with requirements (e.g., obtaining appropriate consents from users) to use personal data in the way it intends, and to have in place robust technological and operational measures to keep any data that it holds secure.

What may be less obvious, but equally important, is employing some creativity in finding a balance between achieving compliance while simultaneously enhancing user experience on the platform. Legal and regulatory requirements do not always come with a negative or oppressive impact on the customer experience! Virtually anything is now possible on a digital platform, and there is an opportunity for organizations to design creative ways to find this balance.

Pricing/Quoting

The use of a digital platform gives institutions a unique opportunity to dynamically price products or services on a never-before-seen scale. This is most relevant in industries where risk forms a key element of a price or quote—a prime example being the insurance market. However, the use of data and algorithms to dynamically price products or services gives rise to new risks.

Use of Data Analytics

Data is often referred to as the new, and most valuable, natural resource of the digital world. "Data analytics" simply refers to the process of analyzing (often large) datasets to discover useful information to improve operational efficiencies and find new solutions to existing problems. Financial institutions are extremely data-rich, and the opportunities to use that information to make good pricing decisions are endless.

However, in order to leverage that data, organizations must overcome several legal and operational hurdles. In most countries, there is often a patchwork of laws that regulate an organization's ability to use data, such as personal data, banking secrecy, and cybersecurity regulations. As mentioned in the earlier section on data protection, a key regulatory consideration is to ensure that the appropriate consents are obtained from users before their data is used for these purposes. Another key consideration might be cross-border transfer requirements that may apply to an organization's sharing of personal data with third parties (whether group entities or not) located offshore who assist with data analytics activities. On the operational side of things, many organizations have issues with getting the data into a compatible format to allow the analysis to be run, and so some effort may be required to get such data in good enough shape to realize the benefits of these data analytics activities.

Pricing Algorithms

While the use of a pricing algorithm can ensure a more objective price is obtained for the customer, institutions should always be conscious of overarching requirements to treat customers fairly and act in the best interests of their customers. It is important to remember that, with algorithms, a flaw, if undetected, can adversely impact a material number of clients in a short space of time.

Accordingly, institutions should be sure to mitigate the risks associated with the use of algorithms—for example, by conducting sufficient back-testing, implementing robust monitoring measures and having back-up strategies (e.g., human involvement) in the event of a serious or systemic fault.

Advisory Services

Not all financial institutions provide advisory services, but those who do owe a particular duty to their clients. Across many jurisdictions, advisors are required to ensure that their recommendations are suitable for their clients and consider a broad range of information, such as the customers' investment experience, financial objectives, and financial situation. Can a robot ever do this as thoroughly or thoughtfully as a human advisor and in compliance with applicable regulatory obligations?

Suitability

Suitability obligations are a prime example of regulations designed with the purpose of protecting the consumer against the risk of receiving inaccurate or misleading advice. The requirements in this area can (depending on the scenario) result in document-heavy processes being implemented which can be difficult to digitalize. Taking Singapore as an example, an institution providing investment advice to retail customers may be required to undertake enhanced know-your-client measures, conduct needs-analyses of customers, and meet prescriptive record-keeping and documentation requirements.

However, there is no reason that these processes cannot be fully or partially digitalized with the use of online forms and digital uploads of supporting documentation. Particularly in Singapore, regulations are generally "technology-neutral" in order to provide institutions with flexibility in how they comply and record or demonstrate such compliance, and regulations governing suitability are no different in this respect.

Robo-Advisors

What is a robo-advisor? To the layperson this might connote a robot that can provide individual, tailored financial advice. In fact, while this can be an accurate representation of a robo-advisor, robo-advisory services are typically seen as a phenomenon that has taken hold in the wealth management industry as a tool which is able to construct and rebalance client portfolios. It remains at a relatively nascent stage and represents, at this time, only a tiny proportion of assets under management in the wealth management industry; but it generates significant excitement for the future. There are multiple start-ups that offer the service with notably low fees (e.g., certain robo-advisory firms) while the more established industry players (e.g., private banks) are developing and deploying their own tools in response.

This is yet another application of algorithms—this time, to select a suitable portfolio based on a set of defined parameters, and then to manage the portfolio for a duration of time. The same issues considered earlier will again become relevant: Is the algorithm sufficiently back-tested and robustly monitored? Again, the risk of mistake or error is fundamentally the same as with a human investment manager, but the risk of widespread customer impact is increased.

Another point to consider is: Who is liable? When dealing with a traditional wealth manager, blame is easy to pin on the client manager providing the advisory service (although it is still possible to criticize the systems and controls governing their human behavior). In the robo-advisory space, the immediate fall-guy is removed. Should regulatory liability attach to the board of directors, or to the senior manager who is designated as responsible for running the algorithm instead? Or should blame be attached to the engineers, if any fault is technical in nature? The question of liability will be a key one for regulators to consider as robo-advisory services increase in pace and scale.

Purchasing the Product or Service

The point of purchase: Where the potential customer becomes the actual customer. At this stage of the Digital Customer Journey, there are a number of important considerations to be explored.

Onboarding: KYC and AML

Know-your-client (KYC) and anti-money laundering (AML) measures are notoriously well-known as two of the most significant pain-points in the financial services industry, with the processes at many financial institutions associated with tedious procedures and box-ticking. The standards are generally agreed across all major jurisdictions, given the standard-setting undertaken by the Financial Action Task Force. KYC/AML measures need to be conducted, except in exceptional circumstances, *before* the client is onboarded (which typically, including in Singapore, means that the measures need to be completed before financial advice is provided to the client).

In Singapore, like in most other major jurisdictions, the requirements that apply to regulated financial institutions are granular and prescriptive, such as in regard to information that needs to be obtained from any potential customer. This might give the impression that it is not possible to digitalize the KYC/AML process.

However, in recent times this impression has been proven to be inaccurate. For instance, it is now possible to open an investment account using only a mobile phone and for institutions to utilize biometric technology to verify the identity of an individual for KYC purposes. There is further potential in the future for blockchain and distributed-ledger technology to solve some of the key procedural issues with KYC. Given the often-touted immutability, efficiency, and real-time accuracy of the blockchain, it has been suggested that blockchain will herald significant cost savings for institutions, an enhanced customer experience, and significant benefits for regulators themselves, given the access and transparency of customer onboarding information.[2]

A key challenge in the future, particularly for financial institutions (e.g., private banks) dealing with sophisticated or complex clientele, will be how to use technology to obtain, beyond the basics such as name and domicile, the more challenging pieces of necessary KYC information such as source of wealth and funds. While there is no doubt that new technologies such as blockchain could, eventually, assist with such processes, a degree of trust in such technologies will need to be established first.

E-signing

The ability to contract, and sign, customer-facing documents electronically is becoming an area of increasing interest to financial institutions. Customers are starting to expect much more convenience and much less physical paperwork when they procure products and services in the digital world.

In a large number of countries, including Singapore, electronic contracting is permitted in the banking industry and contracts entered into electronically are generally recognized as equivalent to physical, written contracts.

However, there are three main risks that arise from contracting electronically.
- Identity risk: Organizations cannot always be sure that the other party entering into a contract is in fact the actual person. There is a chance that another person has, in fact, accessed the device in an unauthorized fashion and entered into a contract posing as someone else.
- Integrity risk: The very nature of going digital invites the potential for compromise in the security and integrity of electronic communications (e.g., through cyberattacks or network failures).
- Authority risk: This arises especially in the case of corporate counterparties, where there may be concerns about whether an individual entering into a contract on behalf of a corporate counterparty has the necessary authority to bind that party.

Accordingly, organizations looking to implement electronic contracting into their digital platforms should consider ways to mitigate the risks mentioned above. For example, two-factor authentications and biometric authentications are common ways of mitigating against identity risks. Additionally, organizations must have in place operational and technological measures to ensure that all electronic communications are kept secure and their integrity is preserved.

Another key point to note is that it is common for particular types of documents to be prohibited from being signed electronically. These include contracts documenting real estate transactions, powers of attorney, contracts that require notarization or certification, security agreements, articles of association, wills, negotiable instruments, and guarantees, and so on. Organizations should therefore consider what types of contracts will be signed on the digital platform, and whether applicable local laws allow for this.

Data Storage

Cybersecurity

With a number of high profile, large scale cybersecurity incidents happening recently, there has been an increased global focus on cybersecurity and data protection regulation. Singapore is no exception. The Cybersecurity Bill was passed in the Parliament on 5 February 2018, and is an omnibus cybersecurity law that applies equally to public and private sectors. The intention of this enhanced cybersecurity protection regime is to ensure that all sectors in Singapore subscribe to and implement a coordinated, consistent cybersecurity framework and that the regulator, the Cyber Security Agency, may address cybersecurity threats across all (and not just more critical and highly regulated) sectors. This in turn facilitates a proactive approach to cybersecurity, requiring measures to enhance the cybersecurity of computer systems before cybersecurity threats and incidents occur.

In addition, heightened responsibilities will be placed on designated owners of "critical information infrastructure" in Singapore—computer systems that are necessary for the continuous delivery of an essential service (e.g., energy, communications, water, healthcare, banking and finance, security and emergency services, aviation, land transport, maritime, government, and media), where a loss or compromise of any of these computer systems will have a debilitating effect on the availability of essential services in Singapore.

The enhanced regulatory regime is expected to take effect in the near future, and organizations (especially those with digital offerings) should consider carefully what their compliance exposure will be in light of the bolstered regime.

Personal Data Protection

Like many jurisdictions, Singapore's national data protection laws impose a number of obligations which organizations must comply with if they undertake activities relating to the collection, use, or disclosure of personal data. While there are nine main obligations that will apply regardless of the scale of an organization's digital offering, the three key obligations that an organization looking to digitalize should consider are:

- Ensuring that personal data is kept secure by implementing reasonable security arrangements to prevent unauthorized access, collection, use, disclosure, copying, modification, disposal, or similar risks.
- Ceasing to retain personal data or removing the means by which personal data can be associated with particular individuals as soon as the purposes for which the data was collected is no longer served or retention is no longer necessary for legal or business purposes.
- Ensuring that certain prescriptive requirements are met before data is transferred from Singapore to another country.

Given how the above obligations will change the way organizations interact with their customers (e.g., needing to obtain the appropriate consents for their business needs), there is merit in employing a "privacy-by-design" approach discussed earlier in this chapter.

Banking Secrecy

In addition to data privacy laws, Singapore also has a standalone statutory banking secrecy regime, which requires that banks protect the secrecy of all customer information that they hold, subject to certain exceptions. Accordingly, any bank seeking to digitalize would need to consider the obligations discussed above through the lens of banking secrecy as well as personal data protection.

Cloud Services

Cloud services are increasingly popular as a solution for data storage. Apart from promising cost efficiencies, cloud services are generally viewed by the market (including regulated sectors such as financial services) to be secure enough such that organizations are comfortable with storing large amounts of data (even critical data) on the cloud. Cloud service providers are also more aware of their customers' regulatory obligations and are willing to help their customers comply with these obligations. The MAS itself encourages licensed financial institutions to adopt cloud technologies, subject to these institutions taking appropriate safeguards and complying with applicable regulations.

Cloud storage solutions are typically deemed as an outsourcing arrangement. Where customer information is involved, however, cloud storage arrangements are considered "material" outsourcing arrangements under the MAS regulations, and attract suitably heightened regulatory expectations. Designation of the arrangement as a "material outsourcing arrangement" would also have an impact on contractual negotiations with the cloud service provider.

The MAS also expects institutions to develop comprehensive data loss prevention strategies. In particular, financial institutions must pay attention to the cloud service provider's ability to isolate and clearly identify customer data and must include in its contract with the cloud service provider the ability to properly remove or destroy data stored at the cloud service provider's systems and backups. Unsecure internet services (e.g., social media sites, cloud-based internet storage sites) should not be used to store or communicate confidential information of the financial institutions.

Customer Complaints

Complaints are an unpleasant but ultimately unavoidable step along any customer journey. Financial institutions must always be ready to receive complaints and to deal with them fairly, professionally, and promptly. At this time, this is not an area which is subjected to a significant amount of prescriptive regulation in Singapore, and should therefore be relatively simple to innovate and digitalize.

A complaint-handling procedure should be built in to any app implemented by a financial institution. The app functionality could allow customers to submit their complaints and, if relevant, easily attach photographs. An app could also function to direct, file, and organize customer complaints into distinct categories, saving human time in transferring a customer from department to department over the phone. Not only would such functionality save time and money for the financial institution, customers would be served with higher efficiency, thereby improving the customer experience.

To go a step further, chat-bots and algorithms could be utilized throughout complaint-handling procedures. A chat-bot may be able to handle basic queries or pass the customer on to the relevant department/person without the customer ever knowing that they are typing messages to a robot. An algorithm could have no direct customer interface, but could itself sort, file, and organize complaints and even propose written responses for human responders to vet.

Ongoing Customer Relationship

The final stage of the Digital Customer Journey is to examine the impact of technology on the business-as-usual ongoing customer relationship. Delivering services through a digital channel presents a plethora of opportunities for institutions to analyze the behavior of the client, and such analysis can lead to opportunities to better service their clients or to cross-sell alternative products or services.

Ultimately, the considerations to bear in mind throughout the ongoing customer relationship are broadly the same as those already discussed in this chapter: The use of data analytics, how customer data can be used and stored, how marketing should be conducted and when an institution will be deemed to be giving "advice," and how algorithms should be used and monitored.

Smart Nations: Collaboration and Competition Between Jurisdictions

A hallmark of many emerging technologies is that they are country-agnostic. Indeed, their very purpose may be to allow consumers to access services (e.g., via a banking app) anywhere in the world. Taking a customer-centric view, individuals and businesses alike are now accustomed to accessing a global market of commerce and finance, typically using a smartphone or other mobile device. Businesses frequently cooperate on a cross-border basis; for example, banks in different countries may connect their APIs to gather information from several sources and generate holistic solutions for customers.

The globalization of fintech is giving rise to regulatory challenges that are not new, but which are becoming increasingly complex to surmount. Singapore and other financial centers are keen to ensure they understand emerging technologies and can respond to these appropriately, to protect consumers and market participants from new risks but also to harness new benefits and incentivize market entrants. In doing so, a regulator like the MAS will scrutinize its local rules through a global lens. Compared with frameworks elsewhere, are the rules in Singapore likely to stimulate fintech growth and maintain Singapore's worldwide competitiveness? How are new fintech solutions regulated in other jurisdictions, and would it be appropriate for Singapore to take a similar regulatory approach in the interest of harmonization? Leveraging off its position as a center of fintech research and development, are there areas where Singapore can afford to act as a first mover or outlier when regulating a particular aspect of fintech?

Collaboration

Acknowledging these international synergies, the MAS has entered into multiple fintech cooperation arrangements with overseas authorities, both in Asia (e.g., Hong Kong, Malaysia, Thailand, the Philippines, and India) and further afield (e.g., France, Denmark, Lithuania, and Poland). The purpose of these arrangements is typically for the parties to facilitate referrals of innovative businesses, share information, and exchange expertise in the fintech arena. Some of these agreements may also focus on specific solutions or projects. For example:
- The MAS and the Hong Kong Monetary Authority have committed to developing the Global Trade Connectivity Network, a project to build cross-border trade-finance infrastructure that will use distributed ledger technology.
- The MAS and the Bank of Thailand have agreed to work together to link PayNow and PromptPay, which operate as payment systems in Singapore and Thailand, respectively.

- The MAS is collaborating on cross-border payments with the Bank of Canada, using blockchain technology.
- The MAS and the World Bank's International Finance Corporation have established the ASEAN Financial Innovation Network, which is developing a cloud-based industry platform that will connect banks and fintech firms across ASEAN (Association of Southeast Asian Nations) and provide a sandbox for the testing of cross-border solutions.

It is hardly contradictory that national regulators should assist their foreign counterparts in building a sound foundation for fintech regulation: International cooperation in this area admits a realization that fintech is a cross-border phenomenon and that no single financial center can "go at it alone" in this space.

Competition

Given the importance of international cooperation as an element of the regulatory policymaking process, it is unsurprising that the MAS attributes significant importance to Singapore's position relative to other jurisdictions when formulating its policy approach. This is particularly apparent in the following areas of fintech regulation:
- **Sandbox**: The MAS regulatory sandbox is aimed at encouraging innovation by allowing businesses to test their fintech offerings in a safe environment and subject to minimal regulatory requirements with a view to the businesses scaling up their operations and potentially becoming more extensively regulated once they exit the sandbox. Similar initiatives have been, or are in the process of being, rolled out in other jurisdictions, such as the UK, Australia, and Thailand, and the MAS specifically considered whether to adopt aspects of these in launching the Singapore sandbox.[3] The UK's Financial Conduct Authority has also considered the launch of a global regulatory sandbox, which would potentially allow financial institutions to conduct tests in different jurisdictions at the same time and allow regulators to work together to identify and solve common cross-border regulatory problems.[4]
- **Digital advisory services**: The MAS is also consulting on proposals to facilitate the provision of digital advisory services (commonly termed robo-advisory services) through the introduction of specific requirements in this area, such as rules around the use of algorithms. Part of the MAS rationale for these proposals is the global take-up of digital advisory services, particularly for client-facing tools.[5]
- **Payment services**: A further area in which the MAS is proposing changes is in payment services, where it intends to streamline existing rules and introduce a new activity-based regulatory framework. In calibrating the activities that will be subject to this framework, the MAS has specifically taken into account international practices in the payments space.[6]

- **Digital tokens**: Following the recent emergence of digital tokens such as bitcoin and ether both as virtual currencies and as a key component of business and fundraising structures, regulators around the world have responded divergently. Regulatory stances cover a broad spectrum, from a highly restrictive approach at one end (e.g., China has banned initial coin offerings, a form of fundraising, and prohibited the operation of cryptocurrency exchanges) to a more permissive position at the other end (e.g., Gibraltar will facilitate the orderly conduct of initial coin offerings by introducing specific rules on their sale and distribution). The MAS, for its part, has been careful not to unduly restrict the use of digital tokens while emphasizing that certain activities involving digital tokens are regulated. While the MAS does not regulate virtual currencies as such, it subject activities involving virtual currencies to AML requirements, and its securities laws apply where a digital token is structured like a security.[7]
- **Anti-commingling**: Under the MAS anti-commingling framework, banks in Singapore are prohibited from carrying on businesses other than banking and financial businesses and businesses prescribed or approved by the MAS. The MAS is currently consulting on changes to this framework to allow banks to operate digital platforms for consumer goods and services, and to sell such goods and services online. As other commentators have observed, these changes will allow Singapore banks to compete more effectively against financial institutions in locations such as China, which are already involved in running eCommerce marketplaces.[8]
- **Market operators**: The MAS is also consulting on proposals whereby different types of market operators in Singapore would be regulated differently, to better reflect the specific risks they pose. Part of the stated rationale for the proposals is to provide a more suitable framework for new business models in trading platforms, including trading facilities that make use of blockchain technology, and platforms that allow peer-to-peer trading. The additional flexibility is also intended to prompt operators to choose Singapore as their place of operation.[9]

While the MAS statements in these areas reflect a desire to maintain Singapore's international competitiveness in the fintech space, they also illustrate that Singapore will not seek to attract business at any cost. The objective is to create regulatory incentives for service providers to establish operations in Singapore, yet also to introduce or maintain requirements that mitigate or migrate relevant risks. These requirements may be particularly prescriptive in areas which the MAS perceives as high-risk, such as AML/KYC and other customer-facing activities.

Future Developments

The future outlook of law and regulation in the fintech space cannot be predicted with accuracy. However, there are presently some identifiable regulatory trends, and in the near team at least, it seems likely that regulators will continue along the trajectories they have recently set in response to fintech developments.

The MAS, for its part, will continue to pursue its objective of transforming Singapore into a Smart Nation (and within it, a Smart Financial Centre), an ambition which has fintech at its heart. To achieve this, the MAS will continue to foster an environment in which market participants ranging from start-ups to incumbent financial institutions can collaborate and innovate, encourage the use of technologies such as APIs to create a more interconnected ecosystem, use schemes and initiatives such as its sandbox and the Financial Sector Technology and Innovation scheme to support the development of new products and solutions within controlled parameters, and will seek to build a talent pool of suitably qualified individuals who can deploy their abilities to help achieve these aims.

Unsurprisingly, the promotion of fintech forms an integral part of the Industry Transformation Roadmap (ITR), published in October 2017, which the MAS has drawn up in consultation with industry participants along with unions, employers, and the government. While the ITR focuses on developing specific offerings and service propositions in Singapore such as (among others) wealth management, asset management, and foreign exchange trading, it envisages fintech as an overarching tool to achieve growth across the financial sector.

Notwithstanding this emphasis on fintech, for the foreseeable future it seems likely that the MAS will continue to exercise its powers in accordance with its stated "Tenets of Effective Regulation,"[10] which apply as much to the regulation of fintech as they do to the regulation of more traditional delivery methods for financial services. In particular, the MAS will likely continue to deploy a combination of outcomes-based, risk-based, and other approaches with a view to achieving a stable financial system; safety, transparency, fairness, and soundness of intermediaries and service providers; safety and efficiency of infrastructure; fair, efficient, and transparent markets; and well-informed and empowered consumers.

In plotting its course, the MAS will continue to collaborate with other authorities around the world to maximize the mutual efficiencies that arise from such cooperation. To some extent, the MAS will no doubt also adapt its approach to developments in the fintech sector as they emerge. While it will take precautions to ensure that its regulatory approach is not merely reactive and can pre-empt new developments where necessary, the adage that regulation must not front-run innovation will surely remain as one of the MAS' key guiding principles.

Conclusions

In this new age, the continued digitalization of the customer journey and more broadly, of the financial services industry, is inevitable. As this chapter has demonstrated, from product/service due diligence to customer complaints, digitalization of each stage of the customer journey gives rise to a new and unique set of risks and challenges that financial institutions and regulators must face. Yet, the conundrum faced by all parties at each stage of the customer journey is the same—there is a fine line that financial institutions and regulators alike must walk between facilitating innovation within the sector and meeting people's desire for efficiency and convenience, and jeopardizing the stability of the financial industry and individuals' privacy and information security.

While the solution to this problem continues to be a work in progress, it is clear that regulators around the world are slowly, but surely, charting a course. In doing so, the MAS has thus far remained relatively open to, or at least tolerant of, developments within the fintech space while simultaneously taking action to monitor and regulate those areas (such as KYC/AML) which it considers high-risk. Whether and how successfully the desired balance between innovation and creativity, and security and stability will be achieved both globally, and in Singapore, remains to be seen.

Endnotes

1 "Singapore's fintech Journey—Where We Are, What Is Next," Ravi Menon, MAS Managing Director (16 November 2016).
2 KPMG, "Could blockchain be the foundation of a viable KYC utility?" March 2018.
3 See, for example, paragraphs 2.4 and 2.5 of the MAS *Response to feedback received—fintech Regulatory Sandbox Guidelines,* dated 16 November 2016.
4 See https://www.fca.org.uk/firms/regulatory-sandbox/global-sandbox
5 Paragraph 1.2 of the MAS consultation paper *Provision of Digital Advisory Services,* dated 7 June 2017.
6 Paragraph 5.12 of the MAS consultation paper *Proposed Payment Services Bill,* dated 21 November 2017.
7 For an overview of the MAS position on digital tokens, please see the speech of Ravi Menon (Managing Director of the MAS) titled *Singapore fintech Journey 2.0,* delivered at the Singapore fintech Festival on 14 November 2017 (available on the MAS website) and the MAS *Guide to Digital Token Offerings,* dated 14 November 2017.
8 *Banks, experts welcome loosening of rules for banks to invest in non-financial businesses,* Channel News Asia, 29 June 2017.
9 Paragraphs 1.2, 2.3, and 4.2 of the MAS consultation paper *Review of the Recognised Market Operators Regime,* dated 22 May 2018.
10 As set out in a monograph available on the MAS website, last updated in September 2015.

Linklaters is a leading global law firm with a track record of advising the world's most prominent corporations, financial institutions, and governments on their most challenging transactions and assignments.

Peiying Chua leads the Linklaters Singapore financial regulation group. Peiying is an active participant in the industry discussion on fintech and in lobbying authorities on regulatory reform, including representing the Singapore fintech Association on various submissions to the MAS. She has advised on various innovative fintech initiatives, such as Asia-based digital securities offerings and partnership arrangements between banks and fintech firms.

Adrian Fisher is a senior technology and data privacy lawyer who supports clients in Singapore and across the Asia Pacific region on issues they face when procuring, building, and implementing new technologies.

Hagen Rooke is a senior member of the Linklaters Singapore financial regulation group. He has extensive experience working with financial institutions and fintech firms in London and Singapore. His areas of focus include financial services licensing and conduct requirements, digital token offerings, regulation of payment services, and other fintech matters.

Joel Cheang is a senior member of the Linklaters Singapore technology and privacy group. He started his career as an intellectual property litigator, specializing in trademark and patent litigation. He joined Linklaters in 2014, and now advises clients regionally on a range of matters including data protection, intellectual property exploitation, and technology management.

Peter Fairman is a member of the Linklaters Singapore financial regulation group. After completing his legal training in London and Singapore, he obtained extensive experience advising on a range of issues connected to the regulation of fintech institutions and initiatives, such as e-wallets and their providers, token generation events, and cryptocurrency fund management.

Chung Yee Gui is a member of the Linklaters Singapore technology and privacy group. He has extensive experience on intellectual property and technology related matters.

Chapter 26
Talent Development and HR Implications for Fintech

In the Global Fintech Revolution[1] forum held during the 2017 World Economic Forum Annual Meeting in Davos-Klosters, Switzerland, it was estimated that half of the global investment in fintech development is in Asia. KMPG estimates that global fintech investment is valued at US$8.7 billion in Q4 2017, up from US$8.2 billion in Q3 2017.[2] For Asia, fintech investment inflow amounted to US$748 million, with Singapore accounting for US$229.1 million, or around 31% of Asia-bound investments.

To study the adoption of fintech solutions, Ernst & Young launched the first EY Fintech Adoption Index[3] in 2015. In the 2017 report, the top five countries that ranked highest for fintech adoption were China, India, the United Kingdom, Brazil, and Australia. By general comparison, it is interesting to note that out of the top five global financial centers listed by Z/Yen, a commercial think-tank, consultancy, and venture firm headquartered in London, Singapore lagged behind in terms of fintech adoption. In the March 2018 release of the Global Financial Centres Index (GFCI)[4] published by the firm, only London has a higher rate of fintech adoption. The other four centers: New York, Hong Kong, Singapore, and Tokyo ranked lower in fintech adoption (see Table 26.1).

Table 26.1: Top ten Global Financial Centres Index fintech adoption ranking

Rank	Centers	Country	EY Fintech Adoption Rank
1	London	United Kingdom	3rd
2	New York	United States of America	10th
3	Hong Kong	Hong Kong SAR of China	11th
4	Singapore	Singapore	17th
5	Tokyo	Japan	19th
6	Shanghai	China	1st
7	Toronto	Canada	18th
8	San Francisco	United States of America	10th
9	Sydney	Australia	5th
10	Boston	United States of America	10th

Although the Ernst & Young report findings are based on survey responses collected over five pre-defined categories (money transfer and payments, financial planning, savings and investments, borrowing, and insurance), the results show that Singapore, Tokyo and to a slightly lesser extent, the US cities show a the gap between fintech users' adoption rate and the country's status as a top global financial center. In the US, non-governmental efforts drive fintech investment and a lack of public awareness impact the rankings and so they are not surprising. Given the investment in these

DOI 10.1515/9781547400904- 026

technologies in Singapore in particular, this report may broadly suggest that there is room for improvement in the space of talent development to achieve Singapore's vision to become a global fintech hub. The remainder of this chapter will look at some of the unique efforts to create an environment so that Singapore can take a leading role in this most important arena. In doing so, you will see how a country is able to get behind and drive an economic initiative that will serve to improve their standing in the world economic community.

Talent Development Infrastructure and Pipeline in Singapore

Developing Fintech Capabilities

To encourage and support the fintech movement, a fintech office was jointly set up by the Monetary Authority of Singapore (MAS) and the National Research Foundation (NRF) in May 2016 to serve as a one-stop virtual entity for all fintech matters and to promote Singapore as a fintech hub.[5] The Smart Financial Centre[6] was also set up to promote fintech development and adoption. Some of the schemes and initiatives introduced include a fintech regulatory sandbox to encourage fintech products and solutions experimentation, the Financial Sector Technology and Innovation (FSTI) Proof of Concept (POC) scheme, Global Fintech Hackcelerator and Fintech Awards Singapore. Other projects include Project Ubin which explores the use of distributed ledger technology (DLT) for clearing and settlement of payments and securities, the Financial Industry API Register, and an ASEAN KYC blockchain initiative spearheaded by Singapore's Infocomm Media Development Authority (IMDA). These initiatives serve to develop, promote, and regulate the adoption of fintech solutions in safe and convenient ways. Together with the Industry Transformation Map (ITM) for the Singapore financial sector launched in October 2017, they illustrate how Singapore is set to achieve transformative growth in this area.

Workforce Demand and Supply Gap

It is estimated that 4,000 net jobs would be created annually in Singapore through 2020, with three-quarters of these new jobs added in the areas of wealth management, insurance, and IT.[7] To meet the demand for new jobs creation, Singapore has had to step up efforts to develop a ready and sizable supply of fintech professionals to support this rapidly growing sector.[8] As of 2018, Singapore produces approximately 400 graduates from its universities and polytechnics equipped with the skillsets required for various fintech roles. This figure falls below the estimated supply of 1000 fintech professionals required per year domestically. Official data in Singapore puts the total demand for technology jobs in the financial sector to be more than 26,200 in 2016.[9] A survey conducted by the Singapore Fintech Association has also revealed that 47% of the association's members felt that there are insufficient professionals in Singapore with the required skills to fill jobs. It is clear that in order for Singapore to meet the talent crunch needed to establish itself as a global fintech hub, the country has to turn to attracting international fintech talent to the country and explore other creative means to re-skill and re-deploy its domestic workforce to fill the urgent gap.

International Talent Attraction Targeting Fintech Start-ups and Experts

In recent years, every country has maintained a cautious approach toward its foreign talents policy. By tightening employment permits, governments have been advocating a hire-local first policy amid a slowing down of job growth. With official statistics in many countries showing that local employment has improved significantly, the climate could be conducive to adopt a more accommodating approach for the hiring of fintech professionals.

Talent Development in Institutions of Higher Learning

In addition to increasing the talent pool of fintech professionals through international talent attraction, Singapore has also created a few avenues to develop domestic talents with the required fintech skills.

In October 2016, the MAS and the five local polytechnics in Singapore inked a memorandum of understanding to review and develop curriculum to develop a young talent pipeline for emerging fintech roles.[10] Polytechnic students will benefit from on-the-job learning from internships and participate in joint projects sponsored by industry. These final-year projects which involve mentorship from industry experts will cover agile software development, mobile applications development, user interface/user experience, cloud application development, data analytics, application programming interface development, and cybersecurity—domains that are core to fintech. In all, 2500 students are expected to benefit from this initiative known as PolyFintech100.[11]

Another program, the TechSkills Accelerator (TeSA) Fintech Collective, was launched in November 2016 by the Infocomm Media Development Authority (IMDA), Monetary Authority of Singapore (MAS), and SkillsFuture Singapore.[12] In addition to having all six local universities as partners, TeSA is also supported by five industry associations: General Insurance Association of Singapore (GIA), Investment Management Association of Singapore (IMAS), Life Insurance Association of Singapore (LIA), Singapore Fintech Association (SFA), and Association of Banks in Singapore (ABS). Similar to PolyFintech100, the scope of collaboration includes curricula development and training, experiential learning, internships, and industry project opportunities.

TeSA would also be extended beyond pre-employment education to include professional education and continuous education training.[13]

At Singapore Management University (SMU), for example, new fintech tracks have been incorporated into its degree programs such as the Bachelor of Science (Information Systems) and Masters of IT in Business. A range of continuing education training in fintech topics targeted at working professionals is also offered by SMU Academy, SMU's professional training arm. Depending on their existing levels of skill and comprehension, existing and aspiring fintech professionals may select from courses that range from introductory and intermediate to expert levels, and enhance their skills and knowledge through certification and modular programs.

Talent Development through Trade Associations, Organizations, and Government Agencies

Complementing talent development efforts at institutions of higher learning, continuing professional development (CPD) and outreach are also supported by the Singapore Fintech Association (SFA) and the Institute of Banking and Finance (IBF).

SFA, in collaboration with NTUC (National Trades Union Congress) U-Associates and Singapore Polytechnic (SP), offers a three-month Fintech Talent Program targeted at working professionals and managers to equip them with skills in areas such as design thinking, big data, digital currencies, blockchain, RegTech, cybersecurity, cloud computing, and application program interface (API).

Government agencies such as SkillsFuture Singapore[14] and the Employment and Employability Institute (e2i) support and encourage lifelong learning by providing generous grants to working professionals and companies to subsidize CET training courses—as much as 90% of the qualifying course fees based on eligibility criteria. A SkillsFuture for Digital Workplace (SFDW) series, launched to create awareness of digitalization changes, serve as a form of readiness gauge for the general population. On top of this, other support ranging from credits, study awards to fellowship awards are provided for working adults to further advance their professional development.

Understanding Fintech Roles, Skills, Sentiments, and Priorities of the Banking and Financial Community

Traditional Technology and Operations Roles versus Emerging Fintech Roles

What is interesting to note is that the majority of Fintech job titles are almost identical with job titles used by their non-fintech counterparts. In most job portals specializing in executive recruitment for banking and financial professionals, the key distinctions lie in the addition of the word "fintech" mentioned in the job title and details provided in job descriptions. The Adecco Salary Guide 2017/2018,[15] for example, provides a list of fintech titles that are commonly found across non-fintech roles, suggesting that there are in fact not a high number of new job types that are being created for fintech, but an increase in vacancies filled to achieve fintech deliverables (see Table 26.2).

Table 26.2: Fintech positions listed in Adecco Salary Guide 2017/2018

Fintech Positions
Business Development Manager
Cloud Platform Engineer
Data Engineer/Data Scientist
Enterprise Architect/Solutions Architect
Lead Java Developer
Mobile Developer (Payments)
SaaS Production Operations
Security Architect
Software Engineer/Full-Start/Front-End
Technical Support Officer
UI/UX Designer
Web Services Developer

Source: Adecco Salary Guide 2017/2018

Contextual Application and Disruptive Innovation Impact: Differential Factors for Fintech Skills in Demand

In September 2017, SMU Academy conducted an analysis of fifty-six job descriptions tied to DevOps and Machine Learning jobs advertised by the major banks in Singapore as part of their research for a Recognition of Prior Learning (RPL) project. It was observed that in most cases, the technical skills required are similar to those required for roles advertised by companies outside of banking and finance.

Two key differential factors, however, were derived from the analysis. First, a fintech skill often involves the application of a bank or financial institution context and its operational environment to the technology, systems, or design. Second, the expected outcomes are efficacy, value creation, and a competitive advantage for the industry.

Some of the attendant benefits include:
– Expanding products and services
– Increasing customer base
– Responding to competition faster

- Reducing cost headcount
- Decreasing IT infrastructure costs
- Leveraging existing data and analytics
- Differentiating from competitors
- Improving retention of customers

With such broad criteria, it is debatable which skills are fintech skills and which are not. This ambiguity also makes it a challenge for management and HR departments to identify which areas of training and skills development they need to focus on in order to advance their fintech goals (see Figure 26.1).

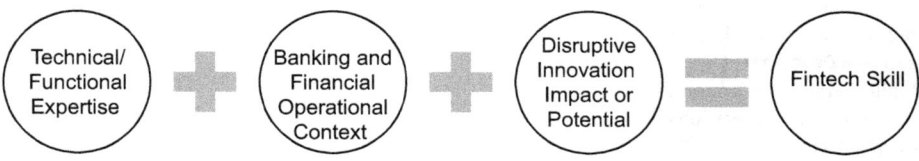

Figure 26.1: Development of fintech skills

Institute of Banking and Finance (IBF) Future-Enabled Skills

To focus on the important fintech skills that will help Singapore in its effort to become a global fintech hub, IBF has drawn up, in consultation with the banking and financial community in Singapore, a roadmap comprising six pillars, namely Digital Awareness, Data Driven Decision Making, Human Centred Design, Agile/Entrepreneurial Thinking, Future Communication, and Risk & Governance in the Digital World.

To raise awareness of these essential skills, IBF has launched a Learn@IBF app to encourage professionals in the banking and financial sector to keep abreast of trends in the fintech era. Almost every major bank in Singapore has a channel on this mobile app to track and upskill their staff competencies.

Industry Sentiments and Priorities

When fintech first gained attention in 2008,[16] the trend was largely met with skepticism among financial professionals. Financial institutions monitored the developments cautiously and continually defended their market position. Employees feared that they would be made redundant and lose their jobs to automation and the new competition. Ten years later, sentiments have changed. Contrary to the early years, banks have realized that they stand to gain more if they proactively leverage disruptive innovation to generate new revenue, having seen how earlier generations of fintech solutions have made a positive business impact. Employees have also become aware of the fact that skills upgrading can help them increase their employability and employment opportunities beyond just banks. In a turnaround, stakeholders are now eager to collaborate.

In the Global Fintech Report 2017 published by PwC,[17] a global survey of 1,308 financial services and fintech executives revealed insights that reflect eager willingness to cooperate and explore collaboration. The following sentiments were noted in PwC's survey (Table 26.3):

Table 26.3: Key sentiments from PwC Global FinTech Survey 2017

88%	are concerned they are losing revenue to innovators
77%	of Financial Institutions will increase internal efforts to innovate
82%	expect to increase fintech partnerships in the next three to five years
30%	of large Financial Institutions are investing in artificial intelligence (AI)
77%	expect to adopt blockchain as part of an in-production system or process by 2020
54%	of incumbents see data storage, privacy, and protection as the main regulatory barrier to innovation
20%	expected annual ROI on fintech related projects

Source: PwC Global FinTech Survey 2017

The fintech priorities among different members of the fintech community also revealed convergence or similarities.[18] Some of the hottest fintech-related training areas are in data analytics, application programming interfaces (API), mobile applications, digital wallet and payments, artificial intelligence and machine learning, cybersecurity, anti-money laundering (AML) and Know-Your-Customer (KYC), robotics process automation, biometrics and identity management, distributed ledger and smart contracts technologies, and cloud infrastructure. These are the technologies that are essential for secure and efficient digital transactions, risk management and governance, and pre-condition assurance. They are skills needed for any fintech service or solution.

As speed to market is important, organizations and professionals alike are beginning to compete to be the first to introduce new tech products and services to disrupt and capture market share. Accordingly, learning and skills acquisition will need to take place quickly.

An Integrated and Multimodal Approach for Effective Fintech Skills Development

Recognizing and Redefining the Components of a Fintech Skill

The multifaceted nature of fintech presents various challenges to training and development. The liberal labelling of fintech has resulted in the loose definition of many skills as a fintech skill, leading to challenges when organizations need to hire and develop talent to fill genuine fintech gaps.

For the purposes of this chapter, to help business leaders and human resources professionals identify what fintech skills are, we would like to describe a fintech skill as the composite of two primary competencies (C) and two smaller competencies (E) serving as enabling skills (see Figure 26.2).

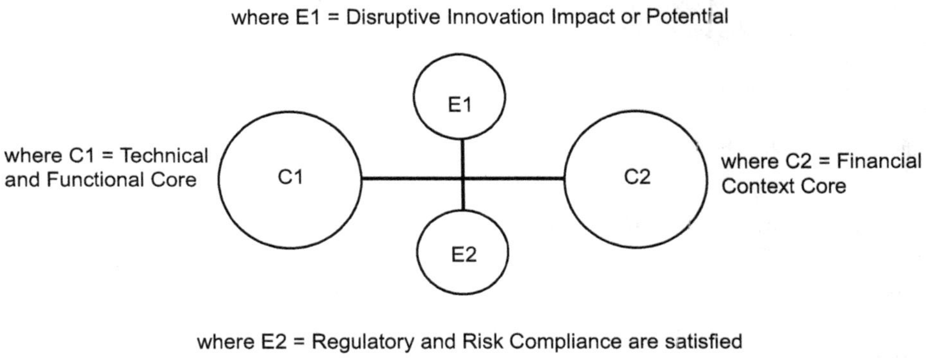

where E1 = Disruptive Innovation Impact or Potential

where C1 = Technical and Functional Core   C1   E1   C2   where C2 = Financial Context Core

E2

where E2 = Regulatory and Risk Compliance are satisfied

Figure 26.2: Components of a fintech skill

The first component (C1) is the *Technical and Functional* core which is a prerequisite that enables a fintech professional to understand, analyse, and create new or alternative digital or technical solutions. For example, moving documentation from manual to digital will require a team of software engineers and programmers capable of implementing a distributed ledger and smart contracts solution for digital letters of credit to be used by exporters, importers, shippers, insurers, and their intermediary banks.

The second component (C2) is the *Financial Context*. A good working knowledge, understanding, and experience of the business, and insights into the business functions and operations is essential to allow a digital solution provider to apply, integrate, and enhance financial value-chains. The rise and popularity of digital wallets and peer-to-peer lending, for example, has threatened banks' traditional business lending with innovations that match and deliver consumers' wants in revolutionary ways.

The two components together can lead to digital solutions to replace traditional banking and financial operations. However, the common expectation of a fintech solution is also that it should have a "wow" factor, be able to delight users with a better product, and simplify work processes. This is where the enabling skill (E1) *Disruptive Innovation*[19] is needed for differentiation. Innovation itself is a broad and expansive term. With the word "disruptive" attached to it, what is expected is that creativity must come with the use of technology to achieve more than marginal improvements.

A fintech solution would also need to address governing industry regulations and comply with risk and governance policies before it can be implemented. To this effect, *Regulatory and Risk Compliance* knowledge of the banking and financial industry is the other enabling and differentiating (E2) factor. Some of the international regulations that guide operations in financial institutions include Basel III, Dodd-Frank, Comprehensive Capital Analysis and Review (CCAR), General Data Protection Regulation (GDPR), Markets in Financial Instruments Directive (MiFID), and Revised Payment Service Directive (PSD2). Commercial and in-house fintech solutions would need to meet numerous regulatory requirements and stress tests before they can be implemented.

Developing Fintech Skills

The identification of the four components that make up a fintech skill can aid the design of appropriate training programs. Customized approaches can be designed with unique and effective instructional strategies and approaches to deliver and achieve specific results.

Technical and Functional Training

Technical and functional training for most professionals in Singapore begins as pre-employment training (PET) in the form of specialized education provided by academic and vocational institutions. Upon entering the workforce, professionals have access to continuing education training (CET) opportunities, often via part-time advanced diplomas or postgraduate qualifications. Traditional PET design often includes general and foundational topics that are important educational objectives for young adults without work experience. Often academic and extensive in coverage, the lead time can be long and costly for working adults and their employers who prefer more targeted and focused training. The rapid pace of technological advancements also means that companies have to carefully consider factors such as speed-to-market when developing programs, conducting training, or tracking the return on investment (ROI) for training.

A better alternative for fintech-related technical and functional training would be to break down and organize topics into micro-modules. Bite-size content facilitates quick and targeted learning at lower cost. It also allows for greater access and offers convenience for working professionals. Human resources professionals may consider CET programs that are designed using rapid-prototyping[20] as the instructional design for course development. These programs are especially useful where the learning objectives are tied to a technology used by the financial institution. In addition to providing hands-on practice or demo opportunities, the focused content delivers what-you-get-is-what-you-need solutions. Training efficiency tends to also improve as engagement levels are raised along with learning retention. In circumstances where financial institutions have in-house experts or consultants available, rapid-prototyping training interventions can be developed and implemented quickly.

Financial Context

An understanding of the business operations of financial institutions is usually gained with time spent in the business. The knowledge of work flows, processes, and insights which allows fintech products and services to address intended outcomes, is best achieved through talent development programs that are designed using models such as Kolb's experiential learning theory.[21] For existing PET programs, the PolyFintech100 and TeSA pipelines include company visits, internships, mentorships, and industry projects. For working professionals, options such as participating in professional conversion programs aimed at developing fintech professionals, in-house talent rotation, and job shadowing schemes may be considered. Other approaches include recruiting mid-career IT professionals who are interested in switching industries to join the banking and finance sector, or developing an in-house apprenticeship program helmed by in-house fintech experts acting as mentors.

A key process of experiential learning involves the internalizing and processing of observation, knowledge, and experience. As such, instructional materials such as observation checklists, standard operating procedures manuals, guided learning journals and assignments designed to extract learning, for instance, through demonstrated ability to apply knowledge and understanding business processes can be used. With a mentorship component added, this combination can serve as a useful training intervention or talent development program to be implemented at the workplace.

Disruptive Innovation

Programs to develop disruptive innovation skills often need to address four learning objectives. These objectives are *disruptive opportunity, creativity and the innovation process, solutions design,* and *commercially feasible implementation.*

Existing training within PET programs consists of courses such as creative thinking, design thinking, and innovation. These workshops often address the first three elements in generalized settings or non-business-specific scenarios, but stop short of discussing commercially feasible concerns associated with implementation.

To develop this skills component in fintech professionals, human resources personnel may consider engaging training providers or developing in-house programs that strive to disrupt and identify new opportunities. The learning objectives can be, for instance, structured into games, simulation and role-play settings, or scenario-planning workshops so that fintech professionals can work alongside their peers in operations and other functions to create fresh solutions capable of delivering new value and impact.

Regulatory and Risk Compliance

Regulatory and risk compliance knowledge is already a common focus of training for professionals working in the banking and financial sector. In diploma and undergraduate training, sections of regulations are covered within selective modules. For the working community, regulatory training tends to be organized by the human resources department as specialized workshops focused on a particular regulation or piece of legislation. In terms of training design and delivery, the seminar or workshop format remains a good option. To facilitate greater ease and access to this knowledge, human resources personnel can consider e-learning or mobile learning solutions as a more agile and flexible avenue for training access.

Based on the fintech skill model, the approach to developing fintech professionals who are already competent in the technology domains would be the easier path. It is also possible for those in business operations roles to develop the full range of competencies by picking up technical knowledge in a reverse approach, although this process can take longer before the level of IT is adequate.

Human Resources Trends for Fintech Talent in the Near Future

With the scarcity of fintech talent, the mobility rate of consultants and experts between traditional financial institutions, fintech start-ups, regulatory agencies, ICT and large tech companies, and other institutions, is expected to be high. This transnational talent migration is expected to correlate with the amount of Fintech investment flowing into the global fintech hubs. As such, business leaders and human resources professionals alike will need to review their human capital policies and practices to attract the best talent and retain them.

In a report, Millennial Careers: 2020 Vision (Singapore)[22] published by ManpowerGroup, a global firm specializing in innovative workforce solutions, it is estimated that millennials will replace and make up one-third of the global workforce by the year 2020. With the millennials poised to make up a significant demographic of current and future fintech talent, human resources experts should take note of the following findings:

a. Millennials want to be valued in their companies.
b. Millennials look for attractive raises and bonuses.
c. Millennials look for jobs with opportunities for skills and career development.

d.   Millennials prefer organizations that provide good work-life balance, alternative work modes such as flexi-working arrangements, telecommuting, and portfolio-style jobs.

Considering the talent scarcity and technological disruptions faced by all, fintech professionals and their global counterparts are more likely to be found working in different global financial centres and time zones, but connected and working closely with one another using technology-enabled solutions such as conference calls or secured digital systems and devices. This new norm of working will not only improve existing transnational organization structures,[23] which are already happening in most global banks and financial institutions, but also facilitate extended collaboration with external organizations such as clients, consultants, technology providers, or users more readily in the broader fintech ecosystem.

Conclusion

Fintech professionals will change how products and solutions are presently generated, replacing the need for project teams from different departments to come together and working on tasks from the outside. The future of fintech innovation will see specialized experts blending and integrating business processes and creating from within. A large diversity can be expected from international fintech talent as they hail from different professional backgrounds, functions, countries, and industries. This phenomenon will challenge certain conventional human resources practice such as recruitment, performance management, and talent management. The question and degree of organizational acceptance of job-fit and candidate-organization alignment may be an area where human resources policies will see change as management will need to consider whether they can accept fintech talent with the desired skillset but who may not be in sync with the organization's dominant work culture.

Performance management and goals setting will be another area where change will be expected. Innovation will be accompanied with failure as well as success. Business leaders and human resources professionals may need to consider a broader range of performance indicators beyond "hard" deliverables such as a fixed number of successful products.

The policies set by a country play a significant role in determining whether a financial centre will survive and thrive over time as a global fintech hub. The success of Singapore in this respect is dependent on many factors: Access to international talent, continuous flow of fintech investment, the quality of infrastructure, the sector's rate of growth, and market scale and scalability. Singapore has put in place business-friendly policies, a regulatory sandbox and talent development pipelines to transform its current standing as a leading financial centre to also lead in the area of Fintech. This journey will be a challenging one, given our population size and the fact that we have not previously put in place a strong pipeline of PET programs to train technology specialists.

Endnotes

1 The Global Fintech Revolution https://www.weforum.org/events/world-economic-forum-annual-meeting-2017/sessions/the-global-fintech-revolution

2 The Pulse of Fintech—Q4 2017 https://assets.kpmg.com/content/dam/kpmg/xx/pdf/2018/02/pulse_of_fintech_q4_2017.pdf

3 Ernst & Young FinTech Adoption Index 2017—Key Findings https://www.ey.com/Publication/vwLUAssets/ey-fintech-key-findings-2017/$FILE/ey-fintech-key-findings-2017.pdf

4 Global Financial Centres Index (GFCI) March 2018 Report http://www.longfinance.net/Publications/GFCI23.pdf

5 New FinTech Office: A One-Stop Platform to Promote Singapore as a FinTech Hub http://www.mas.gov.sg/news-and-publications/media-releases/2016/New-FinTech-Office.aspx

6 Smart Financial Centre http://www.mas.gov.sg/Singapore-Financial-Centre/Smart-Financial-Centre.aspx

7 4,000 jobs to be created in financial services and fintech under MAS blueprint https://www.todayonline.com/singapore/4000-jobs-be-created-financial-services-and-fintech-under-mas-blueprint

8 Singapore Has Fintech Dreams, But It's Short on Tech Talent https://www.bloomberg.com/news/articles/2018-05-29/singapore-s-fintech-ambitions-bump-up-against-immigration-curbs

9 Singapore's Schemes to Promote Finance and Treasury Activities https://www.edb.gov.sg/en/how-we-help/incentives-and-schemes.html

10 MAS and Local Polytechnics Sign Memorandum of Understanding to Promote Skills Development in Financial Technology ttp://www.mas.gov.sg/News-and-Publications/Media-Releases/2016/MAS-and-Local-Polytechnics-Sign-Memorandum-of-Understanding-to-Promote-Skills-Development-in-FinTech.aspx

11 PolyFintech 100 http://www.polyfintech100.sg/fintech/Pages/default.aspx

12 IMDA, MAS to push career development of Fintech professionals https://www.straitstimes.com/business/banking/imda-mas-to-push-career-development-of-fintech-professionals

13 TechSkills Accelerator (TeSA) Factsheet www.skillsfuture.sg/-/media/Files/Newsroom/TeSA-release_Annex-A.pdf

14 SkillsFuture Singapore http://www.skillsfuture.sg

15 Adecco Salary Guide 2017/2018 https://www.adecco.com.sg/media/adecco-singapore/client/2017%20Salary%20Guide%20-%20Updated/Adecco%20Salary%20Guide%201718.pdf

16 Fintech: Where did it start? http://www.theiyerreport.com/2017/fintech-where-did-it-start

17 Redrawing the lines: FinTech's growing influence on Financial Services https://www.pwc.com/jg/en/publications/pwc-global-fintech-report-17.3.17-final.pdf

18 2017 Fintech Disruptors Report—ACI Worldwide https://www.aciworldwide.com/-/media/files/collateral/trends/2017-fintech-disruptors-report.pdf

19 Disruptive Innovation http://www.claytonchristensen.com/key-concepts

20 Nixon, Elizabeth Krick, & Lee, Doris (2001). Rapid Prototyping in the Instructional Design Process. *Performance Improvement Quarterly*, 14(3), 95–116.

21 Kolb, D. A. (2015). *Experiential learning: Experience as the source of learning and development*. Upper Saddle River (New Jersey): Pearson Education.

22 Millennial Careers: 2020 Vision (Singapore) https://www.manpowergroup.com.sg/wps/wcm/connect/754983e5-6060-451e-8237-ec0c5f6d1475/Millennial+Careers+2020+Vision+%28Singapore%29.pdf?MOD=AJPERES

23 Daft, R. (1998). Organisation Theory and Design, Chicago, Chap. 7.

References

Ministry of Manpower Statement on Labour Market Developments—15 March 2018 http://www.mom.
    gov.sg/newsroom/mom-statements/2018/0315-statement-on-labour-market-developments
Institute of Banking and Finance Future-Enabled Skills https://www.ibf.org.sg/programmes/Pages/
    IBF-Future-Enabled-Skills.aspx

Goh Wee Kwong was a senior manager with SMU Academy. An experienced learning and talent development professional, he is always on a quest to explore new collaboration opportunities on talent pipelines, L&D initiatives and platforms, and customized learning programs design. Connect with him on LinkedIn at https://www.linkedin.com/in/wee-kwong-g-a08a8165/

Lim Lai Cheng is Executive Director of SMU Academy, the professional training arm of Singapore Management University (SMU) and Fellow, School of Social Sciences. She oversees SMU's SkillsFuture agenda, continuing education, and technology-related innovation in teaching and learning. She has extensive experience in the Singapore Education System and held key roles in corporate communications, curriculum planning, and policy development at the Education Ministry's headquarters.

Index

DOI 10.1515/9781547400904-027

Printed in the USA
CPSIA information can be obtained
at www.ICGtesting.com
LVHW021230010823
754026LV00004B/164